ATTLEE

—— AND ——

CHURCHILL

By the same author

Fit to Govern
Turning the Tide
Boycs
Jack and Bobby
Rosebery
Sir Alf
Spitfire
Lancaster
Hurricane
Jack Hobbs
Operation Sealion

ATTLEE

— AND —

CHURCHILL

Allies in War,
Adversaries in Peace

LEO MCKINSTRY

Atlantic Books
London

First published in Great Britain in 2019 by Atlantic Books,
an imprint of Atlantic Books Ltd.

123456789

A CIP catalogue record for this book is available
from the British Library.

Hardback ISBN: 978-1-84887-660-6
E-book ISBN: 978-1-78649-574-7
Paperback ISBN: 978-1-84887-661-3

Printed in Great Britain by Bell and Bain Ltd, Glasgow
Atlantic Books
An Imprint of Atlantic Books Ltd
Ormond House
26–27 Boswell Street
London
WC1N 3JZ

www.atlantic-books.co.uk

*This book is dedicated to
my dear brother Simon
and my sister-in-law Pauline*

Churchill   My Career Fife

CONTENTS

Part Three: Competitors

ILLUSTRATIONS

Section one

Churchill with his mother and brother, 1889 (*General Photographic Agency/ Getty Images*)

Churchill as a cadet, 1893 (*Print Collector/Getty Images*)

Attlee at University College, Oxford, c. 1902 (*Gillman & Co/Picture Post/ Hulton Archive/Getty Images*)

Attlee pictured with boys at the Boys' Club, Limehouse, c. 1910 (*Popperfoto/ Getty Images*)

Churchill at the Sidney Street siege, January 1911 (*Popperfoto/Getty Images*)

Churchill at Armentières, 11 February 1916 (*Keystone/Getty Images*)

Attlee in uniform, c. 1917 (© *Illustrated London News Ltd/Mary Evans*)

Churchill with his daughter Diana on Budget Day, 1928 (*Central Press/ Hulton Archive/Getty Images*)

Attlee speaking at a rally, 24 July 1938 (*Daily Herald Archive/SSPL/Getty Images*)

Attlee tries out a Bren gun, December 1939 (*Popperfoto/Getty Images*)

Churchill visits bombed buildings in London's East End, 8 September 1940 (*Mr Puttnam/Imperial War Museums via Getty Images*)

Atlantic Conference between Churchill and President Franklin D. Roosevelt on HMS *Prince of Wales*, 10 August 1941 (*Lt. L.C. Priest/Imperial War Museums via Getty Images*)

Members of the War Cabinet and ministers in the garden at No. 10 Downing Street, 16 October 1941 (*Express/Getty Images*)

Cartoon illustrating support of Churchill by David Low, *Evening Standard*, 14 May 1940 (*Hulton Archive/Getty Images*)

King George VI with Attlee, Churchill and other ministers in the grounds of Buckingham Palace, 4 August 1944 (*Popperfoto/Getty Images*)

Churchill waves to the crowd on VE Day, 8 May 1945 (*akg-images/Interfoto*)

Attlee speaking at the UN Conference, 1945 (*Ralph Crane/The LIFE Images Collection via Getty Images/Getty Images*)

Stalin, Harry Truman and Churchill during the Potsdam Conference, July 1945 (*Everett Collection/Mary Evans*)

Section two

Churchill campaigning at Walthamstow Stadium, 26 June 1945 (*Keystone/ Hulton Archive/Getty Images*)

Attlee at his Limehouse constituency, 5 July 1945 (*Popperfoto/Getty Images*)

Attlee and colleagues celebrate victory in the 1945 General Election, 26 July 1945 (*Daily Herald Archive/SSPL/Getty Images*)

Churchill delivering his 'Iron Curtain' speech at Fulton, Missouri, USA, March 1946 (*Popperfoto/Getty Images*)

Attlee gardening at his home in Stanmore, 1945 (*Popperfoto/Getty Images*)

Attlee leaves Downing Street with his wife, Violet, 8 February 1950 (*Monty Fresco/Topical Press Agency/Hulton Archive/Getty Images*)

Churchill painting at Chartwell, 7 January 1946 (*Fremantle/Alamy Stock Photo*)

Churchill arrives to register his vote in the General Election, 25 October 1951 (*Edward G. Malindine/Topical Press Agency/Getty Images*)

The new Queen arrives back in Britain from Nairobi following the death of George VI, February 1952 (© *Hulton-Deutsch Collection/Corbis via Getty Images*)

Attlee and Violet travel to the Labour Party Conference in Morecambe by bus, 30 September 1952 (*ANL/Shutterstock*)

Churchill makes a speech at the Conservative Party Conference in Margate, 1953 (© *Hulton-Deutsch Collection/Corbis via Getty Images*)

Churchill addresses Parliament, 30 November 1954 (*Bettman/Getty Images*)

Churchill and Attlee in conversation, 23 June 1959 (*Keystone/Hulton Archive/ Getty Images*)

Attlee at Churchill's funeral, 30 January 1965 (*Heritage Images/Keystone Archives/akg-images*)

Statue of Churchill in Woodford, January 1965 (*Jean Tesseyre/Paris Match via Getty Images*)

The unveiling of the Attlee's statue in the House of Commons, 12 November 1979 (*Dennis Oulds/Central Press/Getty Images*)

ACKNOWLEDGEMENTS

THIS BOOK, my twelfth, has been a major undertaking and there are a large number of people to whom I am indebted for backing me on the journey to publication.

First, I would like to thank James Nightingale, my heroic editor at Atlantic, who never lost faith in the project. He always gave me wise advice, ensured that the bulky original manuscript was turned into a manageable draft, and presided over the whole process with efficiency, humour and generosity. He also had an excellent team at Atlantic, including Kate Straker on publicity and Monica Hope, who was a superb copy-editor. In addition, my excellent agent Bill Hamilton, whose agency A.M. Heath marks its centenary this year, was a constant source of encouragement, even in the darkest hours.

I am grateful to those distinguished authors and historians who kindly read the manuscript, particularly Joshua Levine, Professor Andrew Roberts, Tom Bower, Sinclair McKay, Professor Tim Blanning, Professor David Wilson, and Professor Derek Beales. A special thanks to my friend Professor Simon Heffer, whose historical wisdom and output are a constant source of inspiration.

Much of the research took place in archives and I am grateful to the staff of many institutions for their unfailing courtesy and helpfulness. These include the British Library, the Bodleian in Oxford, the Working Class Movement Library in Salford, the National Library of Wales, the London School of Economics, the University of Iowa, the Liddell Hart Archives at King's College, London, the Imperial War Museum, the People's History Museum in Manchester and the National Archives at Kew. Anna Towlson, the Special Collections Manager at the LSE guided me through some of the papers of the long-serving Labour MP John Parker, while Jane Davies and Dominic Butler of the Lancashire

Infantry Museum enabled me to have full access to Attlee's unpublished First World War memoir. Darren Treadwell of the People's History Museum highlighted some of Churchill's early contacts with the trade unions, as well as the records of Labour's National Executive. But the biggest research debt I owe is to the Churchill Archives Centre at Cambridge, where the director Allen Packwood and his team were always diligent and insightful.

As regards quotations from material I am grateful to the following: Niall Harman at Curtis Brown and the Churchill family for permission to quote from the Churchill papers; Earl Attlee for permission to quote from his grandfather's papers; Rupert Colville and Harriet Bowes Lyon for permission to quote from their father's papers and diaries; and Leo Amery to quote from his grandfather's papers. I was also assisted in arranging permissions by: Madelin Evans of the Churchill Archives Centre; Sam Sales of the Bodleian Library; and Zoe Stansell of the British Library.

For direct assistance with my research I am grateful to: Mark Bonthrone for studying the East End press during Attlee's early career; the genealogist Alexander Poole for tracking down information about the background of the governess Caroline Hutchinson; to Caroline Hogan for her work on the Janet Shipton papers; and Mike Bryncoch for examining the Clement Davies papers.

Finally, and most importantly, I want to express my deepest gratitude to my dear wife Elizabeth, who not only supported me with her usual patience and devotion throughout the long hours of this project, but also carried out invaluable archival research in Oxford and Cambridge. Next year, we will have been married a quarter of a century, an even longer span than Attlee's leadership of the Labour party. Anything I have achieved as a writer I owe to her.

Leo McKinstry
Westgate-on-Sea
July 2019

ATTLEE

—— AND ——

CHURCHILL

INTRODUCTION

WESTMINSTER HALL

THE CEREMONY WAS unique in British history, reflecting both the extraordinary longevity of the Prime Minister and his continuing domination of the political landscape. On 30 November 1954 almost the entire membership of the Commons and the Lords, as well as several officers of state and other distinguished visitors, gathered in Parliament to mark the eightieth birthday of Sir Winston Churchill, the first premier since William Gladstone to have reached that milestone. The setting was the eleventh-century Westminster Hall, whose magnificent high-vaulted timber ceiling and mighty stone walls exuded an austere medieval grandeur. Out of respect for Churchill's venerable age, special electric heating pads had been discreetly installed in his designated chair on the dais facing the audience.

Political strife had largely been forgotten for the day. The partisanship that usually animated Westminster was temporarily replaced by a mood of restrained pride. A hush descended on the guests as the beating drums of the Royal Household's military band signalled the opening of the event. Just as the drum roll was completed, Churchill appeared at the top of the stone steps in his black frock coat, his distinctive, stocky frame silhouetted against the light flooding in from the window by the main entrance. With a broad smile, he turned to the audience and started to walk slowly down towards his chair, the Guards band now playing Elgar's 'Pomp and Circumstance'. His sometimes over-solicitous doctor Lord Moran described the scene. 'As he began to descend the stairs his right leg shot out in the air before it came down on the step; he was not very steady. I held my breath but nothing happened. He took his seat sitting bolt upright, his hands laid flat on his knees, while wide-eyed he searched all around him.'[1]

As the audience settled, the wiry, slightly diffident, figure of Opposition Leader Clement Attlee moved towards the lectern at the centre of the dais. Expectations were not high, for Attlee was never the most captivating of speakers. But this time he rose to the occasion. Drawing on his personal admiration for Churchill, with whom he had shared so many momentous experiences over the previous decades, he delivered a fulsome tribute. In warm-hearted language, he highlighted some of the key landmarks in Churchill's long career, especially his resolute leadership and inspirational speeches during the war. Having described Churchill as 'the daring pilot in extremity', he said that 'we who had the privilege of serving under you during those long days of war know well what the country owes to you'. Attlee also praised Churchill's record of liberalism in the Edwardian age and his imaginative military thinking during the First World War, inspired by his experience as a soldier in Queen Victory's army. Nor did he ignore Churchill's talent for confrontation, which was clearly manifested during the years of Tory Opposition after Labour's landslide victory in the 1945 General Election. 'We of the Government endeavoured to sustain your attacks with equanimity, whether they were delivered with the gravity of the elder statesman or, as sometimes happened, with the impetuosity of the cavalry subaltern of long ago,' he said. Attlee concluded that 'I should be in breach of my duty as Leader of the Opposition were I to wish you long continuance in your present office, but I hope that you will live to see the beginnings of an era of peace in the world after the storms which has been your lot to encounter.'[2] In the view of Labour MP Dick Crossman, normally one of Attlee's backbench critics, the speech was 'pleasant, dry and witty'.[3]

But Attlee's duties were not complete. He also had to present Churchill with two birthday gifts from his fellow parliamentarians. The first was an illuminated book containing the signatures of all but

26 of the 625 MPs; the tiny number of MPs who refused to sign largely comprised Celtic nationalists or diehard socialists. Far more controversially, Attlee had to ask Churchill to accept an official portrait, commissioned by Parliament, paid for by subscriptions from the two Houses and painted by the artist Graham Sutherland. A former official war artist, Sutherland was chosen by a Westminster committee because of his impressive record as a portrait painter; Somerset Maugham and Lord Beaverbrook were among his previous subjects. Unfortunately for Churchill, he was also renowned for his raw, unflattering depictions of his sitters. Sutherland created the final work from charcoal sketches that he made during visits in August 1954 to Chartwell, Churchill's country home in Kent. At first Churchill had been impressed. 'No one has seen the beginnings of the portrait except Papa and he is much struck by the power of his drawing,' wrote Churchill's wife, Clementine, to their daughter Mary.[4] But when he saw the finished product, shortly before his birthday, he was dismayed. He felt that, far from showing him as a dignified national leader, it represented him as a decrepit, seedy old man – 'like a down-and-out drunk who has been picked up out of the gutter in the Strand', he told one of his aides.[5] 'It makes me look as though I was straining at the stool,' was another of his private comments.[6] In fact, Churchill was so furious that he initially stated that the ceremony would have to go ahead without the portrait. Only the intervention of Clementine and the Conservative MP Charles Doughty, who told him that rejection would cause deep offence to the donors, prevented this drastic eventuality.

On the day itself, Churchill managed to handle the problem with a tactful euphemism. 'The portrait is a remarkable example of modern art. It certainly combines force with candour,' he said, prompting an outburst of laughter in the hall.[7] Yet Churchill never saw the humorous side of Sutherland's painting. He refused permission for it to be hung at Westminster, as originally planned, and instead had it hidden in a cellar at Chartwell. 'It's a horrible portrait – a horror and vile in colour,' he said in 1955.[8] Attlee shared this antipathy to Sutherland's effort. 'I tell people that it's lucky he did not depict the Old Man in plus fours with loud checks with one foot in the grave. That's his usual style,' he wrote to his brother Tom.[9] After her husband's death, Clementine arranged with one of his former secretaries for the portrait to be cut up and burned on a huge bonfire. She too had grown to hate it, believing that it revealed 'nothing of the warmth and humanity of his nature'.[10]

That quality of warmth shone through Churchill's response to Attlee's address. 'This is to me the most memorable public occasion of my life,' he began, adding that the celebration was an indicator of the health of the British parliamentary system and 'the underlying unity of our national life'. He thanked Attlee for the 'magnanimous appraisement he has given of my variegated career. I must confess that this ceremony, with all its charm and splendour, may well be found to have seriously affected my controversial value as a party politician.' Referring to Attlee's own long political career, Churchill pointed out that the two of them had been the only occupants of Downing Street since 1940. Indeed, 'there are no other Prime Ministers alive', he said with a triumphant if morbid flourish. But their alternating grip on power was another indicator, he claimed, of British democracy's strength. 'Mr Attlee's and my monopoly of the most powerful and disputatious office under the Crown is surely a fact which the outside world must recognise as a symbol of the inherent stability of the British way of life. It is not, however, intended to make it a permanent feature of the Constitution.' Churchill said he was grateful for Attlee's praise of his wartime speeches; but, in a passage that justly became famous, he told the audience that he had only expressed the 'remorseless' and 'unconquerable' will of the British people. 'It was the nation and the race dwelling all around the globe that had the lion's heart. I had the luck to be called upon to give the roar.'[11] When he resumed his seat, the applause was prolonged. On departing the Hall, Churchill, who was always inclined to lachrymosity, gave way to his feelings. 'He had done his part manfully – he had promised he would not let his emotions get on top – but now, as he stumbled through the North door into the winter day, he could no longer keep back his tears,' noted Lord Moran.[12]

In a poignant final part of his speech, Churchill had confessed of his premiership, 'I am now nearing the end of my journey.'[13] His prediction was soon to be realised. In April 1955, with a great deal of reluctance, he finally left Downing Street. A few months later Attlee gave up the Labour leadership after more than two decades at the helm. It was perhaps appropriate that these two titans should retire in the same year, for their public lives had long been interwoven. Sometimes turbulent, often fruitful, theirs was a relationship unprecedented in the annals of British politics. There have been long-running rivalries between party Leaders before and since. The 1870s were dominated by the feud between Gladstone and Disraeli, their political antipathy fuelled by personal dislike. The late 1960s and early 1970s saw Wilson and Heath fight four General Elections against each other, while the most prominent figures of the inter-war years were Stanley Baldwin and Ramsay MacDonald, who started as opponents and ended up as joint Leaders of the National Government, united mainly by their enthusiasm for procrastination.

But there has never been a connection like that between Churchill and Attlee. Brought together in the perilous hour of 1940, they forged a partnership that transcended party lines for five years. So important was Attlee to the wartime Coalition that Churchill created a new constitutional position for him as Britain's first-ever Deputy Prime Minister. In the last years of the war, Attlee became an increasingly powerful figure at the heart of Government, particularly in overseeing plans for national reconstruction. Once victory in Europe had been achieved, the two partners were opponents again, fighting a surprisingly acrimonious campaign in 1945, from which Attlee emerged as the overwhelming victor.

The man so often dismissed as a mediocrity turned out to be the architect of one of Britain's most successful reforming administrations. Under his unobtrusive leadership, the Labour Government embarked on a wide-ranging programme of change, from the creation of the National Health Service to the award of independence for India. It is a measure of Attlee's achievement that when Churchill regained power, in October 1951, he reversed little of Labour's post-war settlement despite his frequent denunciations of socialism.

A five-year partnership between two Leaders, followed by a decade of political strife, is unparalleled and unlikely ever to be repeated. Attlee and Churchill led their respective parties for a combined total of thirty-five years, an aggregate unmatched by any other pair of opponents in the history of British democracy. What adds to the peerless quality of their long rule is the breadth of their success. Other dualities, like that of Bonar Law and Lloyd George in the First World War and its immediate aftermath, were mired in gloomy controversy and failure. But the premierships of Churchill and Attlee were among the most romantic, uplifting episodes in Britain's story, when the nation clung on to its independence against overwhelming odds and then, having emerged undefeated from the exhausting struggle, embarked on the epic task of building a better society. If Churchill was the giant of the war, Attlee was the hero of the peace. In a sense, the two men represented different sides of the best of the English character. Churchill, quivering with martial spirit, showed that same courageous determination which had led to the victories like Agincourt and Waterloo; Attlee, on the other hand, embodied those quintessentially English qualities of decency, stoicism, fair play and dislike of ostentation.

It is a reflection of the lasting impact of these two Leaders that, more than sixty years after they retired, they both continue to exert a grip on the public imagination. Churchill is universally regarded as Britain's greatest wartime Leader, his name revered throughout the world. Attlee is at the head of the pantheon of Labour giants, eclipsing other Leaders like Harold Wilson and Tony Blair. In a public poll conducted by the BBC in 2002, Churchill was voted the greatest Briton in history. Two years later, in a survey of historians and political scientists, Attlee was voted the greatest Prime Minister of the twentieth century.

Their relationship might appear incongruous, given that Churchill was such a vivid personality and Attlee so apparently prosaic. Yet there were striking similarities between the two men. Both were patriots whose fine military records demonstrated their love of their country. In fact, as an officer in the South Lancashire regiment, Attlee took part in the notorious Gallipoli campaign of 1915, for which Churchill had been the leading advocate in Cabinet. It was an experience that led Attlee, in contrast to the attitude of most politicians, to defend Churchill's policy. 'I have always held that the strategic conception was sound. The trouble was that it was never adequately supported,' he later wrote.[14] Both men also served on the Western Front in the First World War – Churchill after his post-Gallipoli resignation; Attlee after his recovery from wounds received at the Battle of Hanna in Iraq. Before the conflict, they had both been protagonists for social reform: Churchill as Liberal Cabinet minister operating in league with Lloyd George; Attlee as a welfare worker and Labour activist in the poverty-stricken East End of London. It was one of Attlee's tasks in the East End to implement some of the social legislation that Churchill had helped to pioneer, such as the introduction of labour exchanges and National Insurance. In a sense, the establishment of the modern welfare state under Attlee's 1945 Government was a continuation of Churchill's Edwardian programme.

From his youth, Churchill never concealed his ferocious ambition to reach the top of politics; his sense of destiny fuelled his imperviousness to danger, his phenomenal work ethnic and his frustration at obstacles in his path. 'Curse ruthless time! Curse our mortality! How cruelly short is the allotted span for all we must pour into it,' he said at a dinner party in 1906, when he was just thirty-two and still a young MP.[15] But beneath his veneer of self-effacement, Attlee too had a strong desire for personal advancement. 'Life in the army was only worthwhile if one was in command,' he once told his brother, while his daughter-in-law Anne, Countess Attlee, said that he 'certainly had ambition. But it wasn't the kind of ambition that makes you go round, telling lies about people.'[16] Both men were at ease with power and enjoyed its exercise. 'I long for those boxes. I crave those boxes,' Churchill told his son Randolph after his defeat in 1945.[17] In the same vein, Attlee revelled in his position as post-war Prime Minister. 'He had great self-confidence and a strong streak of ruthlessness, and although he was an administrator of ideas rather than a creative thinker, he knew exactly what he wanted to do,'

recalled Francis Williams, his Downing Street Press Secretary.[18] For all
their ultimate success, both men were regularly written off as potential
contenders for the highest office. 'Attlee is a man I should say of very
limited intelligence and no personality. If one heard he was getting
£6 a week in the service of the East Ham Corporation, one would be
surprised that he was earning so much,' noted the newspaper proprietor
Cecil King soon after Attlee had entered the wartime Cabinet.[19] It was
an opinion shared by his Conservative colleague Harry Crookshank,
who recorded in June 1940 that 'Winston was to make a statement but
he has gone to France so Attlee did – poor still. He will never be Prime
Minister.'[20] The same dismissiveness was often applied to Churchill,
despite his more obvious talents and charisma. 'With all his genius
Churchill has got no judgement and that is why he will never get to the
first place, unless he mends his ways,' wrote Neville Chamberlain to his
sister as early as 1920.[21] When Churchill was marginalised within the
Tory Party in the late 1930s because of his opposition to appeasement,
his chances of ever holding office again looked bleak. The renowned
Hollywood actor Douglas Fairbanks Junior, who ran into Winston
and Clemmie at a London hotel in late 1938, said of their encounter, 'I
thought to myself what a shame that this brilliant old guy had missed
the bus with every chance he'd had. I now agreed that he seemed too
old and politically done for with hardly any useful future in sight.'[22]

The two men had other characteristics in common. Neither of
them was a natural orator. Attlee was inhibited not only by his innate
shyness but also his distrust of flamboyance. 'There was nothing which
his voice and delivery could not make uninspiring,' said the politician
and academic Lord Salter.[23] Churchill's case was more unusual. Part
of his magnetism was built on his compelling performances at the
Commons Dispatch Box and on the platform, yet these orations never
came easily. They took hours of laborious preparation, redrafting and
rehearsal, with Churchill usually sticking closely to his typed notes
when it came to the actual delivery. 'He strictly rationed his powers of
improvisation and hardly ever set sail upon unchartered seas,' recalled
his Conservative colleague Oliver Lyttelton, later Lord Chandos.[24]

On Churchill's 'note-bound' approach, Clementine was once in conversation with Sir Walter Citrine, the trade-union leader, who expressed surprise that 'with his quick brain and knowledge of language it didn't seem necessary for him to write out practically everything he said'. Clementine told Sir Walter that it was because 'he liked to have every sentence ready', though this meant that, in advance of a speech, 'the whole household is in turmoil for days before. It is like having our baby.'[25]

In private, Churchill rarely had any trouble about the flow of his words, although he had a tendency towards indulging in monologues. But this articulacy did not make always him an easy conversationalist, partly because of his habit of self-absorption. 'I am either sunk in sullen silence or else I am shouting the table down,' he once admitted to Lyttelton.[26] In his diaries, Lord Moran went so far as to describe Churchill as 'the poorest hand imaginable at small talk or even being polite to people who did not interest him'.[27] With his ingrained reticence, Attlee could be even more difficult. His favourite type of word was the monosyllable; his favourite subject was the sport of cricket. Beyond that limited range, silence was likely to ensue. 'He just couldn't mix,' recalled the Labour MP Ian Mikardo.[28] But Hugh Gaitskell, Attlee's successor as Labour Leader, thought that this lack of sociability was the secret of his strength. Referring to a conversation in 1949 with a senior Cabinet minister who had revealed 'the interesting and curious fact that he had never had a private meal with the Prime Minister since the Government was formed', Gaitskell wrote, 'of course the Prime Minister retains his authority partly because he stands above everything'.[29]

Another key source of security for Attlee was the happiness of his marriage. In this, he was again similar to Churchill. Both men were devoted husbands who were renowned for their fidelity. Attlee's romantic spirit was far more concealed than Churchill's, but nevertheless it was a strong part of his character, demonstrated in his fascination with the Italian Renaissance and his fondness for the poetry of Shelley. In their respective wives, both men found loving companions who gave them unflinching support throughout their political careers. Intriguingly, it seems likely that neither of them had much physical experience with women before they married. Attlee's own daughter Janet suggested in an interview that his first and only attachment was with her mother, Violet. 'I don't think he had never loved before. It is quite interesting; the one woman in his life, he loved and married.'[30] According to Clementine's latest biographer, she and Winston were 'both certainly virgins' when they spent their wedding night at Blenheim Palace, the Churchill family's ancestral home, although Winston had enjoyed a number of intense, if chaste, liaisons before this union.[31] The personalities of Violet and Clementine were not that different; both were fiercely loyal to their husbands, but were often exhausted by the strain of public life. Each suffered bouts of ill-health during their husbands' leaderships, Clementine from neuritis, Violet from the legacy of sleeping sickness that she contracted in the 1920s. Neither of them instinctively shared their husbands' political allegiances. Clementine was a lifelong Liberal, while Violet once confessed that she only joined the Labour Party five years after Clem became Leader. Family life was vital in both marriages, and, coincidentally, each couple raised three daughters and one son, though the Churchills lost another child, Marigold, in her infancy.

Yet all these similarities cannot disguise the far wider contrast between the two politicians. In several respects Churchill was almost the antithesis of Attlee. From his earliest years, Churchill had been hailed as a genius and an inevitable future Prime Minister. No one ever discerned such a prospect for Attlee when he entered politics. The surprise with Churchill was that he did not reach the top more quickly. The surprise with Attlee was that he reached the top at all. Where Churchill was bold and imaginative, Attlee was cautious and limited. Churchill's mind was highly original, Attlee's deeply conventional. Where Churchill embodied the spirit of the buccaneer eager for some new daring task, Attlee was like a headmaster bent on the strict enforcement of the rules. A prolific author, historian and journalist, renowned for his gifts of narrative and style, Churchill won the Nobel

Prize for Literature in 1953. The following year saw the publication of Attlee's autobiography, *As It Happened*, which was described by the left-leaning *New Statesman* as 'lamely written, clumsily constructed, much of it as boring as the minutes of a municipal gas undertaking. Mr Attlee is not Alcibiades or Churchill – not even a Pepys or a Trollope – and seldom has the absence of emotion been recollected in greater aridity.'[32] For all his egocentricity, Churchill emanated generosity, humanity and humour, one reason he inspired such loyalty in his own circle. 'We of his personal staff were completely devoted to him, even though he was inclined to be impatient. He was somebody who drew our deep respect and affection,' recalled one of his secretaries, Elizabeth Layton.[33] But the clipped, dry manner that Attlee universally adopted outside his immediate family made it difficult to establish any intimacy with him. One of his Labour colleagues, James Griffiths, said that he could be 'aloof and brutal'. Similarly, the veteran *New Statesman* editor Kingsley Martin found him 'cold and icy, with a sharp tongue'.[34]

The differences between them were also highlighted in their working habits. By the time of his wartime premiership, Churchill had developed his own eccentric routine, in which intensive activity existed alongside mornings in bed, siestas in the afternoon and discussions into the early hours. The approach suited him, but it often left his colleagues exhausted and exasperated. Nor was it conducive to the swift dispatch of paperwork. Attlee, on the other hand, was renowned for his orderly, systematic transaction of business. 'He has a voracious appetite for papers and telegrams. He consumes them like a boa constrictor,' recalled his wartime personal assistant Evan Durbin.[35] If Churchill was an erratic hand at the wheel of the Government machine, Attlee was the safe, reliable driver. Just after the 1945 General Election, Alan Brooke, who had been Chief of the Imperial General Staff under Churchill, wrote to one of his relatives about his relief at dealing with the new Prime Minister, 'Things have changed and I am no longer pulled out after dinner to see Winston. Work goes much quicker and I am no longer bombarded by a series of futile minutes. Life is much more peaceful from that point of view.'[36] Born into the aristocracy, used to being surrounded by servants, Churchill never had any anxiety about ensuring that his own demands were fulfilled; whereas Attlee, who combined a middle-class upbringing with an ingrained modesty, was far more hesitant about imposing himself.

Abstemiousness was central to Attlee's character but anathema to Churchill's. The Labour Prime Minister did not drink much beyond the occasional glass of port or claret; for Churchill alcohol was an essential lubricating fluid. Throughout most of his life he averaged half of bottle of champagne a day in addition to a regular intake of whisky – although, contrary to the rumour-mongering by his enemies, he was rarely drunk. His enthusiasm for drinking was part of his expensive, luxurious lifestyle, which featured the best in food, cigars, houses, travel and clothes. 'He was over-addicted to the good things in life,' recalled his aide Jock Colville.[37] But Attlee had neither the inclination nor the money for that sort of existence. Outside politics, his domestic routine was based on his family in his suburban home. Holidays for Churchill were often taken in Monte Carlo or the Riviera. For the Attlees, Frinton and North Wales sufficed. Churchill loved to sit up with friends late at night talking over the finest brandies. The highlight of Attlee's evening was making the bedtime cocoa with Violet. Interestingly both men suffered such severe financial problems in the 1930s that they were forced to contemplate leaving politics. But the roots of their difficulties were very different: Attlee's were the result of his reliance on the small salary then paid to MPs, whereas Churchill's were caused by his extravagance, including ill-judged ventures in the stock market.

For all his embrace of socialism, Attlee on a personal level was far more of a conformist than Churchill. As the Australian statesman Sir Robert Menzies recalled, 'Churchill, the Conservative, always looked and sounded like a crusader. Attlee, the Socialist, looked and sounded like a company director.'[38] One of Attlee's hallmarks was his fondness for almost every institution with which he had been connected, whether it be Haileybury School, the South Lancashire Regiment, the Labour Party or even Churchill's wartime Government. It was one reason he was a good administrator, because he was comfortable in dealing with established methods. Yet, as an avowed reformer, his devotion to Britain's traditional hierarchies, including the public schools, was surprising. Colville noted that in 1945, as the new Prime Minister, Attlee had chosen his new parliamentary private secretary Geoffrey de Freitas partly on the grounds that the young MP had gone to Haileybury. 'I concluded that the old school tie counted even more in Labour than Conservative circles.'[39] Churchill, in contrast, had always been rebellious since his youth. There was little of the social conservative about him. Unlike Attlee, he was always pushing at boundaries, challenging conventional wisdom. The senior civil servant Sir David Hunt, who served both men, once gave this insight into their differing attitudes:

> When you approached Mr Attlee with a matter – not of the first importance, say a Lord Lieutenancy of a county – the argument you would use was, 'Well, Prime Minister, this is the way we have always done it in the past.'
>
> 'Very good,' he would reply.
>
> But you would never dare say that to Mr Churchill because he would instantly say, 'That is a very good reason for doing it differently this time.' He loved change for the sake of change.[40]

This spirit of rebelliousness led Churchill to change parties several times in his career – in direct contrast to Attlee, who remained steadfast to the Labour cause for six decades. Attlee always professed himself to be the servant of his party, whereas Churchill was never happy with the constraints of party structures. A central theme of his political life was his yearning for coalitions and new combinations, something that both his premierships achieved; it is often forgotten that his last Government was an alliance between the Tories and the National Liberals, the centrist group that broke away from the main Liberal Party in the 1930s. Attlee's political consistency reinforced his image of iron integrity, which was a central factor in his long political success. As the Labour politician Douglas Jay argued, 'It was this respect and trust, which strengthened steadily over time, that enabled Attlee to hold together, as nobody else could have done, the prima donnas in his Cabinet.'[41] But, Churchill's inconstancy and defiance of his party's whip helped to fuel suspicion right up until the Second World War. His drinking, finances, perceived lack of judgement, vaulting ambition and partiality to dubious figures like the volatile press tycoon Lord Beaverbrook only added to the fires of hostility. In 1922, at the downfall of Lloyd George's post-war Coalition, the Tory MP Arthur Samuel described Churchill as 'rogue' and 'an unprincipled and arrogant gambler with the national counters in the interests of his own fortunes'.[42] Such views continued to be aired even after Churchill assumed the premiership in 1940.

In the context of Churchill's ardour for coalition government, there are a number of paradoxes. One is that a key element in his long-standing call for unity between the Tories and the Liberals was his desire to keep the Labour Party from office, since he regarded socialism as a menace to the country. Yet it was the Labour Party in 1940 that ensured he came to power. In turn, his premiership served as a vehicle for bringing Attlee and his fellow socialists right into the heart of government, with unprecedented control over the economy, the workforce and society. Indeed, with its sweeping controls over everything from the railways to food supplies, Churchill's administration was the most socialistic Britain had yet experienced. That is precisely how it helped to pave the way for Attlee's landslide of 1945. By making widespread state intervention acceptable, Churchill inadvertently stoked demand for change and acted as a catalyst for the implementation of Attlee's socialist programme. Moreover, by handing Attlee so much authority in war, he helped to give his rival the necessary credibility to win in peace.

It is these contradictions which make their relationship so interesting. Theirs was a long association of alternating conflict and co-operation, of high drama and low politics. The link stretched right back, indirectly, to their childhoods, but only came to real fruition in the 1920s when they faced other each in Parliament for the first time. It was a far deeper, more intensive relationship than is often supposed, and its nature is set out in the papers of the two men, as well as the voluminous public archives of their premierships and a wealth of contemporary commentaries. These records shed new light on so many of crucial episodes of British history, like the abdication, the downfall of Neville Chamberlain and the creation of Britain's own atom bomb, but they also cover less well-known incidents in the story of Churchill and Attlee, like the explosive Abbey by-election of 1924 or the row over a move to give them the joint Freedom of Leeds in 1949.

The two men could never be described as friends; their characters were too different for such closeness. When Jock Colville once suggested that Attlee should be put up for membership of The Other Club, an exclusive dining society, Churchill replied that 'he is an admirable character, but not a man with whom it is agreeable to dine'.[43] Churchill could also be sarcastic about Attlee's reserve; at the height of a Labour crisis in 1953, when the party was riven by a major split and had lost some of its biggest figures, Churchill impishly said that Attlee 'has had to fall back on resources of his own exuberant personality'.[44] At other times, Churchill could be dismissive; he once privately told an ally that Attlee had been 'feeble and incompetent' over the handling of post-war nuclear negotiations with the USA.[45] For his part, Attlee occasionally adopted his schoolmasterly tone with Churchill. 'Winston was an awful nuisance because he started all sorts of hares,' Attlee once said of the wartime Coalition.[46] In a separate verdict on Churchill's leadership, Attlee said he had 'courage, imagination, a great knowledge of things, but he always wanted someone by him at a certain point to say, "Now don't be a bloody fool."'[47] Towards the end of the war, Attlee grew so frustrated by Churchill's behaviour that he sent him a lengthy memorandum, typed by himself, full of complaints about Churchill's failure to read his papers or to chair the Cabinet efficiently.

But beyond such sniping, there was a sincere admiration that ran through their relationship. The two men who shaped Britain in the mid-twentieth century shared a deep respect for each other, built on long experience through years of turmoil. Sir John Rogers, the Conservative MP for Sevenoaks, recalled how he was once at Chartwell after the war when he referred to the Labour Leader as 'silly old Attlee'. According to Sir John's account, Churchill asked him to repeat the remark. Thinking he had not heard it properly, Sir John did so, only for Churchill to deliver a thunderous response: 'Mr Attlee was Deputy Prime Minister during the war and played a great part in winning the war. Mr Attlee is a great patriot. Don't you dare call him "silly old Attlee" at Chartwell or you won't be invited again.'[48] In 1946 Lord Birkenhead, son of the late Lord Chancellor F. E. Smith, asked Churchill which of his former Labour Cabinet colleagues he most admired, anticipating that the reply would be Ernie Bevin. 'He unhesitatingly said Attlee,' recorded Birkenhead.[49] Attlee's feelings towards Churchill were even stronger. He described Churchill as 'the greatest leader in war this country has ever known', who stood 'like a beacon for his country's will to win' and had 'the capacity for being a symbol, a figure that meant something to the fighting man'.[50]

This is the story of how their relationship was forged.

Part One

CONTENDERS

ONE

◆

BLENHEIM AND PUTNEY

THE BELL FROM the nursery rang in the servants' quarters. Immediately a maid went to the room to find out what was wanted. On her arrival, she encountered a scene of tension between the governess, Miss Hutchinson, and her young charge, Winston Churchill. The maid asked Miss Hutchinson if she had rung the bell, only for Winston to say peremptorily, 'I rang. Take away Miss Hutchinson. She is very cross.'[1]

Unable to tolerate Winston's recalcitrant behaviour, Miss Hutchinson left not only the nursery but also the household. She had been employed by Winston's father, Lord Randolph, to improve his education, but had found the job impossible. Soon afterwards, she took up a more amenable post as a governess with another family. By a remarkable coincidence, this was the Attlee household in Putney, southwest London, where Miss Hutchinson, it seems, did not actually teach the future Prime Minister but rather his older sisters. Clement, however, always enjoyed the strange fortuity of his childhood link through Miss Hutchinson to Churchill, as he wrote in his autobiography, 'She could never have thought that the two little boys were destined in turn to be Prime Minister.'[2] In a separate tribute to Churchill in 1965, he cited the role of Miss Hutchinson as evidence that 'my own fate has been closely bound up with his'.[3]

Miss Hutchinson herself appears to have left no record of her thoughts about Clem, though she was reported to have described Winston as 'an extremely strong-willed child'.⁴ Apart from that statement, there is little trace of her and indeed she does not even appear directly by name in the extensive Churchill archive or the more limited Attlee papers. Most histories of Churchill suggest that she must be the 'sinister figure' whom he described when recounting his experience of growing up in Dublin in the 1870s, where Lord Randolph temporarily served in the viceregal administration. With his family based in the official residence of Little Lodge in Phoenix Park, Winston claimed to be enjoying his Irish stay until his parents warned him of the impending arrival of his first governess. Such was his anxiety that, on her first day, he ran from the house and hid in the shrubbery that surrounded the Little Lodge.

Yet it is doubtful that the governess at Little Lodge was the Miss Hutchinson who later worked with the Attlee sisters. In the Churchill papers there are two letters, both sent in 1927, from a woman called Jane Graham, then living in the village of Tyrrells in County Westmeath. In them, she states explicitly that she was Winston's only tutor in Ireland. 'I lived in Dublin with your mother as nursery governess to you as a small boy and taught you your first lessons at the Private Secretary's lodge in Phoenix Park,' she wrote, expressing pride in Winston's progress in politics.⁵ In the next, she declared that, 'I was the only Resident Governess you had. You were very fond of history.' Relations between them cannot have been as fractious as Churchill remembered, since Jane Graham also reminded him how, one night in the nursery, they had both blacked-up and put on fancy-dress costumes. 'Lady Randolph said that we were like wild Indians.'⁶

It seems far more probable that Miss Hutchinson was recruited after the Churchills moved back to London in 1880, when Winston was still five years old. She may have tutored him not just in the family home but also on holiday. One of Winston's letters to his mother, written at the age of ten from Cromer in Norfolk, reveals exactly the same kind of antipathy that led to his dismissal of Miss Hutchinson from his nursery. 'The governess is very unkind and strict and stiff. I can't enjoy myself at all. I am counting the days till Saturday and then I shall be able to tell you all my troubles,' he wrote.[7]

The timing of Miss Hutchinson's move to the Attlee family in the mid-1880s makes it likely that she was based in London. Indeed, research through the census records and street directories, as well as the reports of the School Mistresses and Governesses Benevolent Institution, points to the probability that the woman in question was Miss Caroline Hutchinson, who was born in Jarrow, County Durham, in 1857, the daughter of a mechanical engineer called Ralph Hutchinson. In the early 1860s the family moved from the northeast to Putney; and, on reaching adulthood, Caroline began to work as a governess there. Like Attlee himself, she was from a large family as one of eight children; her sister also worked as a governess. In later life, while still living in Putney, Caroline worked for Burke's Peerage.

Whatever the truth about Miss Hutchinson, it is fascinating that Winston and Clem should have this juvenile connection. The coincidence is all the more arresting because the social backgrounds of the two men were so different. Whereas Clement hailed from the respectable middle class, Winston belonged to the patrician elite. The aristocratic nature of Churchill's upbringing was illustrated by the fact that he was born, on 30 November 1874, in Blenheim Palace, one of the architectural wonders of England and the family's ancestral home, built by the first Duke of Marlborough in the early eighteenth century to celebrate his victory over France in the Spanish Wars of Succession. Winston's father, Lord Randolph, the third son of the seventh Duke of Marlborough, was a brilliant but wayward Tory politician whose charisma was undermined by his rampant opportunism and lack of judgement, two vices of which Winston was often accused. His erratic ascent, which saw him reach the Cabinet in 1885, was helped by his American wife, Jennie, the captivatingly beautiful daughter of the New York financier Leonard Jerome.

These riches and transatlantic exoticism were far removed from the world into which Clement Attlee was born on 3 January 1883. The family home was a nineteenth-century villa in Putney, which was then a much more rural London suburb than it is today. Attlee's father, Henry, could hardly have been a more different character to Lord Randolph. A devout Christian in the High Victorian tradition, he worked as a solicitor in the City law firm of Druce & Attlee, where he rose to be a senior partner. Again in contrast to the eloquent Tory maverick Lord Randolph, he was an ardent Gladstonian Liberal who once considered standing for Parliament but was deterred by his 'ponderous' style of public speaking.[8]

Henry Attlee had to work hard at law in order to provide for the large family that he fathered. Whereas Winston had just one sibling – his younger brother, Jack, who was born in 1880 – Clem had no fewer than three sisters and four brothers, the eight children separated by a uniform two years' interval. Clem was the second-youngest of the brood. Robert, the eldest, was born in 1871 – almost a year after Henry had married Ellen Watson, the daughter of the secretary of the London Art Union, a commercial organisation that distributed high-quality reproductions and prints to its subscribing members. A warm, gentle mother with a strong Christian faith, she ensured that Attlee's early life was characterised by security, a quality absent from Churchill's. Even by the cold standards of Victorian aristocracy, Winston's parents were unusually neglectful. Randolph was too wrapped up in his politics, Jennie in her role as a great hostess and uninhibited socialite; among her many lovers were the Polish Count Charles Kinsky and the Prince of Wales. Of his mother's remoteness, Churchill once wrote poignantly, 'I loved her dearly, but at a distance.'[9]

The characters of the two boys were as different as their upbringings. Winston was such a boisterous, energetic boy that he regularly had to be chastised for his poor behaviour. 'A most difficult child to manage' was Jennie's description of him,[10] though his sense of adventure and wild vitality appealed to other young children. 'We thought he was wonderful because he was always leading us into danger,' said Shane Leslie, recalling how Winston led bird-nesting expeditions or attacks on makeshift garden forts.[11] Attlee was the opposite. Painfully shy, he never ended up in scrapes, never caused trouble. Even his one vice, a quick temper, he learned to control with the aid of his mother. As Clem's sister Mary remembered, 'She was so successful that, if he saw her coming, he would bury his head in a chair. This was known as "Clem penting", or in ordinary language, "Clem repenting".'[12]

Their contrasting natures were also reflected in their schooldays. At the age of seven, Churchill was sent to St George's School in Ascot, a bleak institution whose boasts of high standards in the classics hid a culture of sexual perversion generated by the sinister headmaster, the Reverend H. W. Sneyd-Kynnersley, who was such a sadist that he would beat pupils until they bled or lost control of their bowels. Winston's regular misconduct made him a prime target for Sneyd-Kynnersley's brutal ministrations. 'How I hated this school and what a life of anxiety I lived there for more than two years,' he recalled.[13] This tale of cruelty was later contradicted, however, by one of Attlee's post-war ministers, Douglas Jay, whose father was a contemporary of Churchill's at St George's. 'My father recorded quite different memories, put most of the blame on the mutinous young Winston and remained an admirer of the headmaster. The clearest memory which my father had of young Winston was his vivid language, reputedly picked up from the stable boys at Blenheim.'[14]

After a spell in a much less severe preparatory school in Brighton, he went at the age of thirteen to Harrow, as preparation for entry to the Royal Military Academy at Sandhurst. Contrary to historical myth-making, he was not a failure there. With his natural talent for language and powers of concentration, he excelled at English, and history, even winning a school prize for the tremendous feat of reciting 1,200 lines from Macaulay's *Lays of Ancient Rome*. He was also a fine swimmer and a good enough fencer to win the Public Schools Championship, while he revelled in every aspect of the School Rifle Corps, from the smart grey uniform to the mock battles. Despite his pleasure at such activities, Churchill did not enjoy his days at Harrow. His reluctance to submit to authority, combined with his unruliness, meant he was in regular conflict with teachers and fellow pupils. His housemaster Henry Davidson once felt compelled to ask Jennie to reproach her son. 'His forgetfulness, carelessness, unpunctuality and irregularity in every way have really been so serious that I write to ask you, when he is at home, to speak very gravely to him on the subject.'[15] Nor did Winston inspire respect among the older Harrow boys. 'He was a snotty little bugger, uppity but damn near useless,' recalled Archie MacLaren, the future England cricket captain, for whom Winston acted as a fag.[16] His troubles at Harrow were worsened by his parents' continuing remoteness and indifference. Jennie still put her energetic social life before her son's needs, while Lord Randolph did not even write to Winston until he had been there for three years.

Attlee had a much less oppressive experience. Until the age of nine, he had been taught at home by his mother, partly because he was a shy child with a delicate physique, and partly because Ellen Attlee was an excellent tutor: bright, widely read and knowledgeable in several subjects. But his sheltered life could not last. In the summer of 1892, just as Churchill started on his penultimate term at Harrow, Attlee was enrolled at the preparatory school of Northaw Place in Potters Bar, Hertfordshire. Housed in a seventeenth-century mansion set in extensive parkland, the school was run by the clergyman the Reverend F. J. Hall, whose two main interests were the Bible and cricket. In contrast to the reported sadism of St George's, Northaw was gentle and nurturing. The matron was kindly, the food excellent, the healthcare attentive. 'I certainly had a very happy time there,' Attlee wrote in his autobiography.[17]

In the spring of 1896, he left for Haileybury, the Hertfordshire public school with which his family had strong connections. It was a spartan place, with primitive facilities and mediocre teaching. Attlee excelled at neither his studies nor sports, though he showed an embryonic gift for leadership as a lance corporal in the school cadet force, one contemporary recalling that he 'ran things with unobtrusive efficiency'.[18] His greater self-confidence in his final period at Haileybury also resulted in his appointment as a prefect. 'I believe him a sound character and think he will do well in life. His chief fault is that he is very opinionated, so much so that he gives very scant consideration to the views of other people,' read his final housemaster's report.[19] Again unlike Churchill, Attlee was rarely in trouble with the authorities. The only time he received a thrashing was when he and most other pupils, defying the orders of the liberal-minded headmaster Edward Lyttelton, held a patriotic demonstration to celebrate the relief of Ladysmith in February 1900 during the Boer War. Unable to cane the entire school for this act of insubordination, Lyttelton picked out seventy-two boys from the upper school, Attlee among them, to expatiate for the sins of the rest. Fortunately for Attlee, the headmaster 'was tiring when he got to me'.[20]

On leaving their respective schools, Attlee and Churchill followed very different paths. The thrusting, restless intent that so consumed the latter was entirely absent from the former. In that passive manner that characterised much of his early life, Attlee simply accepted without question that he should try for a place at Oxford, largely because his elder brothers had been there. Therefore, after passing the entrance exam, Attlee went up to University College in October 1901 to read history. Just as at Haileybury, he was an average student who made no great mark on the institution, his chronic self-consciousness inhibiting his participation in many student activities. He joined no political party or club, rarely discussed politics with his university friends, and displayed no political ambition. Although he became a member of the Oxford Union, the breeding ground for so many future politicians, he was too shy ever to speak there. His detachment, however, did not extend to his work for his degree. 'He is a level-headed, industrious, dependable man with no brilliance of style or literary gifts but with excellent sound judgement,' wrote one of his tutors, a verdict that could have come from his fellow ministers decades later.[21] In his final year he worked so intently that another of his tutors felt he might gain a first. Had he done so, the history of twentieth-century British politics might have been very different, for in such circumstances, Attlee would probably have followed an academic career.

Given his mixed academic record, there had never been any question of Churchill trying for university after he left Harrow in 1892. Instead, he went to the Royal Military Academy Sandhurst as a cavalry cadet. Far from congratulating him on his acceptance, his father launched into a cruel tirade: 'If you cannot prevent yourself from leading the idle, useless, unprofitable life, you will become a mere social wastrel, one of the hundreds of public school failures, and you will degenerate into a shabby, unhappy and futile existence.'[22] But his father's predictions about his studies were wrong. Sandhurst gave Churchill liberation. No longer trapped in the drudgery of subjects he hated, he savoured most aspects of his training, including horsemanship, musketry, fortifications, trench-digging, drill and military tactics. In the two years he was at the academy, he proved an able student, graduating in twentieth place out of his class of 130.

When Attlee left Oxford, he reluctantly followed the obvious course of going into his father's profession, though as a barrister rather than a solicitor. He admitted to his sister Mary that he 'was not greatly attracted to the law, but he was going to read for it'.[23] His diligence and application meant that he passed his Bar exams without difficulty in the summer of 1905. Impressed with his son's progress, his father then took him into Druce & Attlee. But Attlee soon became bored with the dreariness of his office and his duties, which largely consisted of taking notes during partners' meetings with clients. The experience fed his concerns as to whether he was cut out for legal work at all.

Infused with an elevated sense of his own destiny, Churchill had never been assailed by such lack of confidence or doubts about his personal mission. While Attlee maintained his tranquil existence at Haileybury and Oxford, Churchill embarked on a life of adventure after Sandhurst. His determination to make a name for himself was given further impetus by the death of his father after a long physical and political decline. Lord Randolph had reached the zenith of his career in 1886 when he was appointed Chancellor of the Exchequer, but his quixotic resignation a few months later over military estimates had precipitated his slide into the shadows, made all the worse by a mysterious illness that may actually have been caused by an inoperable brain tumour, though syphilis was widely suspected. As the years went by, the symptoms of his malady grew worse. Always ill-tempered, he suffered from severe fatigue, acute high blood pressure and bouts of black despondency.

On 24 January 1895, Lord Randolph fell into coma and died, with Jennie, Winston and Jack at his bedside. His premature death at the age of forty-five was a seminal event for Churchill. Out of filial loyalty, he dedicated himself to vindicating his father's life. His study of Lord Randolph, published to acclaim in 1906 and later described by Attlee 'one of the finest biographies ever written',[24] was part of that process of rehabilitation, as was his determination to follow his father into public life. 'I took my politics unquestioningly from him. He seemed to possess the key to oratory and political life,' he wrote.[25]

Yet his father's death also brought freedom for Churchill. No longer subject to continual paternal reprimand, he could now chart his own course. Furthermore, the fact that his father had died so young infused Churchill with a deep sense of urgency, fearing that he too might not have long to fulfil his ambitions. This new mix of independence and haste was soon demonstrated in his decision to join, not the 60th Rifles as his father intended, but the 4th Queen's Own Hussars cavalry regiment. Churchill, though, never one to be bound by convention, did not contemplate a normal officer's career with regular promotions up the regimental hierarchy. What he wanted from his time in the army, apart from the excitement of action, was fame and money so that he could launch the political career he now planned. He therefore came up with the ambitious scheme of combining his military service with work as a war correspondent and author. This dual role took him across the world to scenes of conflict as disparate as Cuba, the North-West Frontier in India, and the Sudan, where, with a temporary commission in the 21st Lancers, he participated in the triumphant climax of the campaign at the Battle of Omdurman when the British under Horatio Kitchener overwhelmed the brave but ill-equipped local Dervish tribesmen.

In these early imperial adventures, Churchill displayed not only his incredible courage but also his instinct for lucrative writing. As well as reporting for the press, he produced two well-received books that won him praise for his 'unhesitating candour'[26] and 'abundantly keen powers of soldierly observation'.[27] Churchill's literary talent had been honed during his time with the Hussars, where he filled his hours away from his limited duties with intensive study, particularly of literature, history and politics. In this impressive programme of self-education, he devoured masses of books sent to him from England by his mother. Having performed inconsistently in his schooldays, Churchill was in a sense a highly accomplished autodidact. But, because his reading was not directed by any tutor, there were odd gaps in his knowledge and he did not always grasp what weight to attach to different evidence. Writing about Churchill as a historian, Attlee himself said that, while he 'admired his prose', he feared that 'somebody would get a curious idea of what has been going on in this country for the last 2,000 years if they had to get it all from Winston. He leaves too much of the important stuff out.'[28]

When the Boer War began in October 1899, Churchill seized the chance to add further lustre to his name, securing both a well-paid contract with the *Morning Post*, at £250 per month, and a commission in the Lancashire Hussars. His exploits in South Africa saw him rise to new levels of fame, particularly after his daring escape as a prisoner-of-war on the Natal front. The ingredients of that dramatic enterprise included his breakout from a Boer jail, an exhausting struggle through the veldt without a map or food, his concealment in a mine shaft, and a sixty-four-hour journey on a goods trains to neutral Mozambique, all against the backdrop of a manhunt that featured the reward of £25 for his recapture 'dead or alive'. Churchill's saga made headline news in Britain, serving as a tonic for the country amid the litany of military setbacks at the start of the South African campaign. But Churchill was never one to relax. On 24 December 1899, the very day after his return to British territory, he enlisted in the South African Light Horse. For the next six months, he fought in the war as a cavalry officer and covered it as a journalist, producing two more books based on his reports. As always, his instinct for adventure saw him in the heat of several of the fiercest clashes, including the relief of Ladysmith, the event that had led to Attlee's only caning at Haileybury. Attlee later recalled how 'in my last year at school' hearing 'of this remarkable young man who had already seen five campaigns and had written books about them'.[29]

TWO

❖

LANCASHIRE
AND STEPNEY

Bᴏᴛʜ Cʜᴜʀᴄʜɪʟʟ ᴀɴᴅ Attlee first rose to ministerial office as
progressive politicians, yet each of them was a Tory when they
were young. Unlike his Liberal father, Attlee was an ardent believer
in the British Empire and the established social order. At times, there
was a self-satisfied priggishness about his juvenile political stance.
His first published poem, which appeared in the Haileybury school
magazine in 1899, amounted to a sneer at striking London cabmen.
As an Oxford student, he was shocked when his father subscribed
to a fund for locked-out strikers at a Welsh quarry. He described the
Liberals as 'waffling, unrealistic have-nots' and condemned 'those
damned radicals'.[1] Recalling his school and Oxford days later, he said
he had been 'a good old-fashioned imperialist conservative'[2] with an
inclination towards 'ultra Tory opinions'.[3]

In contrast to Attlee, Churchill followed the political allegiance
of his father, the leading advocate of the populist new creed of 'Tory
democracy', which held that the Conservatives should embrace
reform rather than oppose it. Winston's first proper platform speech
was delivered in July 1897 at a fete near Bath held by the Primrose
League, the Tory organisation founded by his father and several allies
in 1883 in honour of the late Conservative Leader Benjamin Disraeli,
whose favourite flower was the primrose. Galvanised by its maxim

'Empire and Freedom', the Primrose League had grown into the biggest political movement in the country by the late 1890s, with more than 1 million members helping to cement the Tories' hold on power. In keeping with the approach Churchill adopted for the rest of his life, his speech was written out verbatim and carefully rehearsed, but on the day itself he delivered it with a vitality that betrayed neither nerves nor inexperience. Even at this point, he presaged many of the themes that were to dominate his early political career, like his belief in 'the splendour of the Empire' and the virtues of free trade, as well as his fear of a deepening clash 'between Capital and Labour', which would only be ended by enabling workers to embrace the fruits of prosperity.[4]

Churchill's youthful commitment to the Tory cause deepened in July 1899 when he was selected as one of the party's candidates in Oldham, a two-member constituency where a double by-election was imminent after the death of one of the sitting Conservative MPs and the retirement of the other on grounds of serious ill-health. His late father's popularity in Tory Lancashire, where his brand of patriotic radicalism had a particular appeal to the large nonconformist electorate, was a crucial factor in this decision. More unconventional was the choice of the other Tory candidate, James Mawdsley, who served as general secretary of the local Cotton Spinners' Union and was therefore thought to have a special connection to the working-class voters in Oldham. It was an incongruous alliance that led the press to nickname the pair 'the Scion and the Socialist'.

With typical panache, Churchill threw himself into the battle, campaigning hard even in hostile wards. He ran proudly as a Tory Democrat who emphasised the link between the strength of the British Empire and the need for domestic progress. 'We must have an imperial stock. That is why we are in favour of social reform. The Radicals would have no empire at all. We would have one, and let all share in the glory,' he argued on the trail.[5] But his message failed to win over the voters. Both Churchill and Mawdsley were defeated by around 1,300 votes. Churchill's brief nineteenth-century partnership with a representative of the labour movement had proved much less effective than his later, much longer twentieth-century association with Attlee.

Churchill was more successful, however, in his second attempt to win the Oldham seat, at the General Election in September 1900, helped by his Boer War gallantry. His large personal following meant that he split the Liberal duo, finishing in second place with over 400 votes more than his Tory running mate. At the age of just twenty-five he had become an MP. 'He simply radiates self-confidence. From what I have seen, he will never be content to be a backbencher,' wrote the American journalist R. D. Blumenfeld.[6] Watching Churchill's Oldham triumph from distant Haileybury was Clement Attlee, still just seventeen. 'I recall his election to Parliament when I, then a young Conservative, hailed him as the rising hope of our party,' wrote Attlee later.[7]

But during the Edwardian age, both Churchill and Attlee grew profoundly disillusioned with Toryism. Even before he entered Parliament in 1900, Churchill had been drawn to liberal ideas, including universal education, payment of MPs, a progressive income tax, and the extension of the franchise to all adult males. In a revealing letter to his mother, from India in 1897, he wrote, 'I am a Liberal in all but name. My views excite the pious horror of the Mess.'[8] Once he became an MP, his move towards Liberalism became more pronounced. He deepened his interest in social questions and the need for greater welfare, heavily influenced by Seebohm Rowntree's groundbreaking 1899 study of poverty in York. 'I see little glory in an Empire which can rule the waves and is unable to flush its sewers,' he said after reading Rowntree's book.[9] At the same time, he developed an enthusiasm for the idea of a Liberal-Tory coalition. 'I confess that the idea of a central party, fresher, freer, more efficient and above all loyal and patriotic, is very pleasing to my heart,' he wrote to Samuel Smethurst, a Lancashire Tory businessman. This aspiration was partly driven by his concern about the growing influence of socialism, as he told Smethurst: 'Sooner or later the best of the Liberals will have to fight with us against the great cosmopolitan labour movement, anti-national and perhaps communistic.'[10]

In a letter to his late father's friend, the ex-premier Lord Rosebery, in the summer of 1902, Churchill spoke of his disenchantment with Tory rule: 'I cannot work up the least enthusiasm on the Government's behalf.'[11] But the real breach with his party came the following year, when the Colonial Secretary Joseph Chamberlain embarked on his crusade for tariff reform, based on the theory that duties on imports from outside the British Empire would boost manufacturing and promote imperial unity. Protectionism appalled Churchill, who supported free trade in principle, believing that it lowered food prices and encouraged enterprise. As the Chamberlain creed grew in influence over the Tory Party, Churchill soon recognised that, if he were to have any future in politics, he would have to transfer his allegiance. He therefore made the journey to the Opposition benches, formally sitting as a Liberal from 31 May 1904. The switch was cemented when he accepted an offer to fight Manchester North West at the General Election as a Free Trade candidate with Liberal support. In his grandiloquent adoption speech, Churchill denounced Tory policy as 'the greedy gospel of material expediency' that would lead to 'extravagance at home and aggression abroad', whereas the Liberals would advance through 'well-tried English methods towards ancient and lofty ideals of citizenship'.[12]

With the Conservative Government of Arthur Balfour in deep crisis throughout 1905, Churchill sensed that political change was coming. 'We are on the eve of a gigantic political landslide,' he told the Duke of Devonshire, the elder statesman of Liberal Unionism.[13] For Attlee, too, change was on the horizon. In October that year, still a disgruntled lawyer without a sense of purpose, he made a visit that was to transform his life and put him on the road to supporting the very doctrine that Churchill despised. His destination was the Haileybury House Boys' Club in the East End borough of Stepney, which was supported by his old school and acted as the D Company of the 1st Cadet Battalion of the Queen's Regiment. Catering for working boys aged fourteen to eighteen and open five nights a week, the popular, well-run club offered a range of activities, from swimming to gymnastics.

Attlee had few expectations of his visit as he journeyed by train from Fenchurch Street Station to the East End. He had gone only because his brother Laurence had asked him to accompany him, playing on the family sense of duty that saw many of Attlee's relatives involved in philanthropy; two of his other brothers helped at London boys' clubs and his mother was a district visitor for the Church of England. Furthermore, with his spirit of institutional loyalty, Attlee always struggled to resist anything that had a connection to Haileybury. Besides, he was dissatisfied with his pupillage for the Bar, despite his undemanding, comfortable lifestyle in Putney and the City. He wanted some kind of distraction. To his surprise, he found it at the club. Immediately, he was taken with the earnestness and camaraderie of the boys. Amid all the privations of the East End, here was an oasis of fellowship. He decided to return. 'I became interested in the work and began making the journey from Putney to the club one evening a week,' he recalled.[14] So deep was his interest that he soon took a commission as a second lieutenant in the club's battalion, showing the same fondness for military routine that he had demonstrated in his membership of the cadet force during his schooldays. 'I think the key to him was that he was a conventional military man,' the Labour MP Barbara Castle once said in trying to explain Attlee's character.[15]

Even more importantly, in terms of his political future, the experience of Haileybury House forced him to learn about social conditions outside the middle class. For the first time, he was directly confronted with the problems of poverty, unemployment and inadequate housing. Some of his preconceived ideas, formulated in his prosperous, Anglican upbringing, no longer seemed relevant. He learned that middle-class charity could be condescending, that competition could translate into sweated labour, that the East End working class were more inclined towards generosity than thrift, that the slums were full not of the dregs of society but of decent people who had been denied fair opportunities. 'From there it was only a small step to examining the whole basis of our social and economic system,' he said.[16] The seeds of his socialism had been sown.

Nominally, he was still meant to be heading for a career as a barrister. His progression appeared steady. In March 1906 he was called to the Bar, a step that was followed by a spell in the chambers of Sir Henry Dickens, the son of the great novelist. But Attlee soon found that there was not much demand for a reserved, inexperienced barrister with only a half-hearted interest in the law. Nor was he under pressure to make money. Living at home with his parents in Putney, he still received the same £200-a-year allowance from his father that he had been granted at Oxford, generous enough for him to enjoy an easy bachelor existence. His sister Mary recalled that, after his graduation, he 'became something of a man about town. He was passably good-looking, paid attention to clothes, and enjoyed theatres and town life.'[17] But an alternative world was drawing him in another direction. As his visits to Haileybury House grew more frequent, he increasingly discovered a sense of fulfilment there. In the spring of 1907 the club, impressed by Attlee's commitment, asked him to take over as manager. After an initial hesitation, Attlee agreed, even though the salary was just £50 per year and he would have to live on the premises during the week. He soon proved he was a natural organiser, overseeing the club with the brisk efficiency that became the hallmark of his politics.

As a resident in Stepney, he now saw even more deprivation at first hand. With ever greater urgency, he pondered why the poor had to live this way. Attlee's own daughter Janet later said that the move to Haileybury House had been crucial for his political development:

It is what really inspired his involvement in the Labour Party. He disliked charity and its judgemental attitude about the deserving poor. My father was very influenced by a case of an unmarried couple who had a little baby. They were told that they were not eligible for support because their child was illegitimate. 'But these are like the people of Jesus Christ's family,' he said. He did not like that method of giving charity. He felt that people had a right to the basics of life.[18]

At much the same time, Churchill went through a similar epiphany. He had been triumphantly returned as the MP for North West Manchester in the General Election of January 1906, called after Balfour's decaying Government had finally resigned and the new Liberal Prime Minister, the imperturbable Sir Henry Campbell-Bannerman, asked King Edward VII for the dissolution of Parliament soon after forming office. It was a short but raucous campaign, during which Churchill, on his most combative form, evangelised for free trade and Liberalism at a series of packed meetings. The *Daily Mail*, observing him in action, reported, 'He glories in the crowds and the cheering and the frank, unaffected beaming manifestation of his delight in it all redoubles the interest and exuberance of the crowd.'[19] That enthusiasm was the precursor to his victory. In what had been a Conservative stronghold, Churchill beat his Tory opponent, William Joynson-Hicks (a future Home Secretary), by 5,639 to 4,398 votes. His win was part of a phenomenal Liberal landslide that saw Henry Campbell-Bannerman's party gain a majority of more than 240 over the discredited Tories. 'What a collapse of the Tory Party. This is the grand irretrievable disaster against which my father always wished to protect them. They have lost their democratic foundations,' Churchill wrote to the radical MP Sir Charles Dilke.[20]

During the campaign, Churchill had stayed in the magnificent Midland Hotel in Manchester with his loyal secretary Eddie Marsh. Just before they left the city at the end of the election, they took a long walk and, by accident, ended up in a slum area. Like Attlee in Stepney, Churchill was disturbed by what he saw as he wandered through the shabby buildings and darkened alleyways. 'Fancy living in one of these streets – never seeing anything beautiful – never eating anything savoury – never saying anything clever,' he said to Marsh. When that remark was published years later by Marsh, it was taken as evidence of Churchill's arrogance and condescension. But it was nothing of the sort. As Marsh himself stated, it was an indicator of how Churchill's social conscience had been pricked. 'Winston looked about him, and his sympathetic imagination was stirred.'[21]

Initially Churchill had little responsibility for domestic affairs, since his first post in the new Liberal Government was as the junior minister at the Colonial Office. The position came with a modest salary of £1,500 per year, but this sum was augmented by his earnings from his books. He had been paid an enormous advance for his biography of his father; with the addition of his other royalties, he was able to lease a Mayfair townhouse in Bolton Street, having previously had a bachelor flat in Mount Street nearby. Yet Churchill, who inherited the trait of extravagance from his mother, was never a man to live within his means. In 1906 his annual expenditure reached £1,700, which meant that, even with his literary revenues, he required a bank overdraft. As his friend F. E. Smith once famously remarked, 'Winston is easily satisfied with the best.'[22]

Yet, as with Attlee, his private affluence did not preclude a deepening belief in the need for social reform. After he became a Colonial minister, he occasionally spoke out on the need for greater action to combat poverty and neglect. In a speech in Glasgow on 11 October 1906, which heralded his growing radicalism, he declared that 'the cause of the Liberal Party is the cause of the left-out millions'.[23] He called for a number of progressive measures, such as the expansion of municipal enterprise, a new land tax, and the use of the state as a reserve employer. One of Churchill's aims, through such proposals, was to buttress the Liberal-Labour alliance that had played an important role in swelling the anti-Tory landslide at the last General Election. Under the terms of an agreement reached in 1903, the two progressive parties had agreed not stand against each other in thirty marginal seats. This deal had seen twenty-nine Labour MPs returned in January 1906, making the party, which had been founded only six years earlier, a significant parliamentary force for the first time. Churchill did not see Labour as much of a threat to Liberalism then, as he told his American friend and Democrat politician Bourke Cockran in June 1906: 'I am bound to say that I find their demands in nearly every case very moderate and reasonable. They are a stable force in the House of Commons and add a great deal of sincerity and reality to our debates.'[24]

Despite his acceptance of the politically pragmatic need to work with Labour, Churchill continued to express his hostility to socialism and anything that 'impaired the vigour of competition'. Even so, he was now willing to consider positively the ideas of collectivism, state intervention and a national minimum standard, the last a policy keenly advocated by the progressive campaigners Beatrice Webb and her husband, Sidney, through the Fabian Society. 'We want to draw a line below which we will not allow persons to live and labour,' he had said in his Glasgow speech. Churchill's openness to left-wing theories was further illustrated in the autumn of 1907 when, as part of his duties at the Colonial Office, he left for a lengthy tour of Africa, taking with him a number of books on socialism 'to see what the case really is'.[25]

In Stepney, Attlee was also reflecting on the state of England. But his analysis pushed him much further to the left. He too read political texts intensively, often guided by Tom Attlee, the elder brother to whom he was closest. The bonds between them were strong, for not only had Tom also been to Haileybury and Oxford, but, like Clement, he was working at a boys' club in the East End. On long walks through London or when home in Putney at the weekend, they spent hours talking about politics. 'We both came to the conclusion that the economic and ethical basis of society was wrong. We became socialists,' Attlee wrote.[26] Mere discussion was not enough for them. In October 1907, they applied to join the Fabian Society, the intellectual powerhouse behind the advance of the Labour Party. Among the leading Fabian members was the writer H. G. Wells, who also had an influence on Churchill's politics in the middle of the Edwardian decade. Several of the passages in Churchill's Glasgow speech – such as that concerning the need for the state to act as a reserve employer and to provide welfare assistance to citizens – were presaged by Wells in his book *A Modern Utopia*. 'I owe you a great debt,' Churchill wrote to Wells two days before that oration.[27]

Wells was present at the very first Fabian meeting that Tom and Clem attended after they were accepted into the society. He was one of a number of luminaries on the platform; others included George Bernard Shaw and Sidney Webb. What initially struck Attlee was the hirsute nature of both the speakers and the audience. 'Have we got to grow a beard to join this show?' he jokingly asked his brother.[28] He did not warm to Wells: 'Speaking with a little piping voice, he was very unimpressive.'[29] His aversion to the novelist was matched by his lack of rapport with the Fabians, many of whom he found patronising and self-satisfied, more interested in exchanging theories than in engaging with the poor.

Fortunately for Attlee, the Fabians were not the only route into socialist activism. The society was one arm of Labour's early diffuse structure; other elements included the trade-union movement and the Independent Labour Party (ILP), which had been founded in 1893 directly to advance the interests of the working class. Kier Hardie, the eloquent former Scottish miner, was the ILP's most prominent figure and his brand of practical but passionate socialism attracted Attlee more than the dry ruminations of the Fabians did. When Attlee joined the Stepney branch of the ILP, he was gratified to find that the small band of the other members welcomed him enthusiastically despite the class differences and his reserve. Soon Attlee's innate shyness was put to the test when he had to take his turn as an outdoor speaker for the ILP. Churchill's oratorical debut had been at a Primrose League fete in parkland at a country house near Bath; Attlee's was under a gas lamp in Barnes Street on a windy night in March 1908. The background noise from the gas, wheezing in the gusty air, almost drowned him out, but he managed to get through his speech in front of a dozen people. By now, in the absence of legal briefs, his life revolved around the East End. He continued to work at Haileybury House, sometimes extending his hours into the weekend to referee Saturday football matches. His ILP activities grew when he was elected Stepney Branch chair, whose duties included visiting local workplaces to boost recruitment among trade unionists.

From early 1908 Churchill was playing a much bigger role in the Liberal Government's domestic policy. When H. H. Asquith succeeded the dying Henry Campbell-Bannerman as Prime Minister in April, he elevated Churchill to the Cabinet by making him President of the

Board of Trade, the post previously held by Lloyd George, who had been promoted to Chancellor of the Exchequer. As soon as Churchill accepted, he encountered a serious obstacle. According to parliamentary rules that stood until 1926, any newly appointed Cabinet minister had to seek re-election before he could take office. During a bitter campaign in Manchester North West, he was attacked not just by the Tory and Independent Socialist candidates but also by an array of protestors, including suffragettes and Irish Catholics disgruntled at the concessions made by the Liberal Government to the nonconformist education lobby. Despite the presence of the socialist candidate, H. G. Wells lent Churchill his public support. 'We recognise in his active and still rapidly developing and broadening mind, in his fair and statesmanlike utterances, and in particular in his recent assertion of the need for a national minimum, a spirit entirely in accordance with the spirit of our time,' said Wells in an open letter to the Manchester electors.[30] The intervention of the Fabian novelist was to no avail. On a swing of 8 per cent to the Conservatives, Churchill lost by almost 500 votes.

He was not out of Parliament for long. Within minutes of the declaration, he received a telegram from the Liberals in Dundee, whose MP had just been made a peer. This was a stroke of luck. A largely working-class constituency dominated by jute-weaving and shipbuilding, Dundee was much more favourable Liberal territory than middle-class, suburban Manchester, especially now that that the tariff-reform issue had been temporarily stilled. Churchill fought with his usual vigour, finding an eager reception for his message of radicalism. But, as always, he was keen to draw a sharp distinction between his progressive Liberal outlook and the doctrine of socialism. In his most powerful speech in the election he declared, 'Socialism seeks to pull down wealth; Liberalism seeks to raise up poverty. Socialism would destroy private interests; Liberalism would preserve private interests in the only way in which they can safely and justly be preserved.' Another section of the speech warned of the authoritarian, bureaucratic impulse of socialism, in words that foretold Churchill's attack on Attlee's Labour Party during the 1945 General Election. 'Socialist society is a set of disagreeable individuals who obtained a majority for their caucus at some recent elections, and whose officials now look upon humanity through innumerable grilles and pigeon holes and over innumerable counters and say to them, "tickets please".'[31] Assisted by his rhetoric, he won the by-election convincingly by over 2,700 votes against the Tory in second place.

Churchill was still only thirty-three when he first became a Cabinet minister, but he had a clear vision of what he wanted to achieve at the Board of Trade, centred on a heavily interventionist social agenda. 'He is full of the poor whom he has just discovered. He thinks he is called by Providence to do something for them,' said the Liberal MP Charles Masterman.[32]

THREE

⬥

SIDNEY STREET

Churchill's potent ambition had brought him Cabinet status and literary fame, but it had left him little time for romance. The remorseless quest for glory had been his focus since his youth, to the exclusion of much else. An illustration of his priorities was provided by Christine Lewis, who was a passenger alongside Churchill on board a ship bound for England from India in 1899. 'Every day he sat beside us on the deck, working intensely on his book. He paid no attention to the gay chatter of young people on the adjoining chair as he wrote and re-wrote in that peculiar hand.'[1] Churchill's own daughter Mary said that her father in his youth 'neglected those charming but trivial small attentions which so often pave the way to gallant relationships'.[2]

But Churchill's personal life was not a barren wasteland. Before his arrival in the Cabinet, he had a number of intense liaisons. The first of them began when he was out in India, where he fell in love with Pamela Plowden, the daughter of the British resident at Hyderbad. He described her to Burke Cockran as 'the most beautiful girl I have ever seen'[3] but the affair ended when he discovered that she had become close to several other admirers. Later, according to his daughter Mary, he considered marrying Muriel Wilson, the heiress to a Hull shipping fortune, but she rejected him, as did the American actress Ethel Barrymore, who admitted that she was drawn to Churchill but felt 'she would not be able to cope with the great work of politics'.[4] Violet Asquith, the daughter of the Liberal Prime Minister, was another possible wife and Churchill appeared to give her encouraging signals. The problem was that, by 1908, his real romantic interest was elsewhere.

Churchill first met Clementine Hozier at a ball in 1904. 'He never uttered a word and was very gauche. He never asked me for a dance, he never asked me to have supper with him – he just stood and stared,' she recalled.[5] But four years later, when they met at a dinner party given by Lady St Helier, he was far more gracious and her response was very different. 'Winston paid her such marked and exclusive attention that everyone was talking about it,' noted another guest at the dinner.[6] Clementine was a Liberal-minded, artistic and clever aristocratic beauty but she brought neither money nor political connections to a potential match. Her father, Henry Hozier, a former Guards officer, had died in 1907. Her mother, Blanche, daughter of the Earl of Airlie, was a spendthrift, free-spirited woman whose infidelity had led to the break-up of their marriage in 1891. Indeed, there was some doubt as to whether Clementine was Henry's child at all, given the lengthy catalogue of Blanche's lovers. In the wake of her parents' divorce, Clementine had an unconventional upbringing, with spells in Paris and Dieppe as well as four years at Berkhamsted School, though her mother refused to allow her to go to university. In its paternal neglect, maternal vivacity and financial insecurity, it was a background not dissimilar to Churchill's, which was part of the mutual attraction. He proposed to her, in a slightly clumsy fashion, at Blenheim Palace and she accepted. The engagement was announced in August and the wedding ceremony took place on 12 September at St Margaret's Westminster, with 1,300 guests in attendance. 'Not for many years has a marriage excited such widespread interest,' said the *Scotsman*. After a few days at Blenheim, Winston and Clementine took their honeymoon in Italy, from where he wrote happily to his mother-in-law that being with her daughter was 'a serious and delightful occupation', while to his own mother, Jennie, he said that he had 'loved and loitered'.[7] Within a month, Clementine was pregnant with their first child, their daughter Diana.

In March 1909 the Churchills, in need of more space, sold their house in Bolton Street and bought the lease on 33 Eccleston Square,

Pimlico, where their eldest two children were born. By one of those odd coincidences that crop up throughout the Churchill-Attlee saga, the family sold this home for £2,350 in May 1918 to none other than the Labour Party, which used it as its headquarters before moving nearby to Smith Square in 1928. Attlee, as a Labour MP for most of the 1920s, would have known the place well.

The Churchill wedding was the start of a successful union that was to last almost six decades, buttressed by Clementine's loyalty and wisdom through all the vicissitudes of her husband's career. Lord Rosebery – sunk as so often in Caledonian pessimism – forecast that the marriage would fail because 'Winston is not the marrying kind'.[8] He could not have been more wrong. As Attlee himself said in a 1963 tribute to Clementine, Churchill's 'greatest good fortune was when he won the hand and heart of the beautiful and highly intelligent Miss Clementine Hozier'. She was, Attlee continued, 'a very exceptional woman who overcame all difficulties', 'managed him with infinite tact' and 'showed great skill in giving her husband a background of great material comfort. His habits with regard to eating and taking rest are highly individual but she contrived to run a household on orderly lines without attempts to change his habits.'[9]

At the time of his marriage, Churchill was deeply engaged in social reform. In December 1908 he sent Asquith a long memorandum, outlining the case for a radical programme, led by labour exchanges, unemployment insurance and a modernised poor law. 'The need is urgent and the moment ripe,' he told the Prime Minister.[10] Asquith welcomed his energy and encouraged him to bring forward his plans to Cabinet. His first scheme was designed to combat low pay in certain 'sweated' industries by establishing Trade Boards, made up of employers, independents and union representatives, to set minimum wages. It was a modest initiative, covering only 200,000 employees, but it cemented the principle, so strongly advocated by the Webbs, of a minimum standard in the labour market. Moreover, its scope soon expanded to take in more trades. Intriguingly, the Trade Boards Act of 1909 marked Attlee's first, albeit minor, input into Churchill's political career, for the new law partly owed its inspiration to the campaign run by the National Anti-Sweating League, whose secretary was Dr Jimmy Mallon. Attlee was a friend of Mallon, who later became the warden of Toynbee Hall. 'A very great citizen, a great East Londoner and a most lovable man,' was Attlee's verdict.[11] Some of the evidence for the Anti-Sweating League's campaign had been gathered by Attlee, who carried out investigations into the dreadful conditions for workers, most of them women, in the tailoring industry. 'I remember seeing two women who worked at trouser finishing. They were paid a penny farthing a pair, out of which they had to buy their own thread. Their weekly wage amounted to about five shillings,' he recalled.[12]

Churchill's next step was to create a national network of labour exchanges that would improve workforce mobility and help the unemployed find jobs by advertising vacancies. The Bill was introduced in May 1909 and successfully passed Parliament that session. 'You're doing very well, Mr Churchill,' said Beatrice Webb, always keen to exercise her judgemental faculties.[13] His third important measure, also aimed at assisting the jobless, was unemployment insurance, which would provide a time-limited benefit in return for contributions from the worker, the employer and the state. But the actual implementation had to be delayed, as unemployment insurance was subsumed within a wider scheme of social insurance developed by Lloyd George, who by now was engaged in the titanic struggle to drive through his tax-raising, wealth-redistributing 'People's Budget' against the ferocious opposition of the Tories, the Lords and much of the press. It was not until 1911 – more than a year after Churchill had left the Board of Trade – that the National Insurance Act came into effect. Nevertheless, his work at the department had greatly enhanced his political stature. 'One day, and that not far hence, he will attain the Premiership,' was the view of the *Daily Mirror*.[14]

As the Trade Boards Act demonstrated, Churchill had a new bearing on Attlee's life, which went through its own change in the autumn of 1908. Little more than a month after Winston had the joy of marrying, Attlee had the sadness of mourning, following the death of his father Henry on 11 October at the comparatively young age of sixty-six. Always a relentlessly hard worker, he had succumbed to a heart attack at his desk. For a tightly knit, loving family it was a heavy blow. His father, wrote Attlee in his dry but affectionate way, 'was a very able man and also an extremely generous one'.[15] Yet paradoxically, just as Churchill had been liberated by the death of Lord Randolph, so, to a lesser extent, was Attlee freed by the death of Henry. The awkward fact was that Henry regretted his son's estrangement from the law and his deepening involvement with socialist politics. When he heard the news that Clement had joined the ILP, he told Laurence, the younger brother, 'I wish I were a younger man. I'd argue it out with him and knock all that nonsense out of his head.'[16] By mid-1908, Clement was approaching a crisis in his relationship Henry. Always a dutiful son, he did not want to hurt his father's feelings; but he no longer wished to remain in his profession. He wanted a job of his own, one connected to his socialist beliefs. Henry's death enabled him to follow that course without any confrontation. There was also the advantage that, from Henry's estate, worth £70,000, Attlee now enjoyed an increase in his annual income to £400. Having irretrievably abandoned the law, he could therefore continue to live at Haileybury House while looking for a 'more congenial occupation'.[17]

The first arrived through Beatrice Webb. One of the milestones in the debate on Edwardian social reform was the publication in early 1909 of two contrasting reports about the future of the Poor Law, arising from the work of a long-standing Royal Commission on the issue. The Majority Report to the Commission proposed reforms to the management of workhouses and greater responsibilities for local authorities. But a very different approach was advocated in the Minority Report to the Commission, which was largely drawn up by Beatrice Webb and the future Labour Leader George Lansbury, then a socialist politician in the East London borough of Poplar. Described by Attlee as 'a remarkable document challenging the whole conceptions of public relief and distress',[18] the Minority Report called for the existing Poor Laws to be replaced by a welfare system overseen by central Government. It was an unashamedly socialist blueprint, foreshadowing the kind of structure that Attlee would introduce after the Second World War. With her usual indefatigability, Beatrice wanted to popularise her report through propaganda, so in June 1909 she hired Attlee to act as her campaign secretary. This gave him valuable political experience, but his diffidence was still apparent, as Mrs Webb told him when she wrote to thank him for his work. 'What I think you need to make you a first rate organiser is rather more of the quality of "Push" and the habit of a rapid transaction of business.'[19]

The post with Beatrice Webb was only temporary, but in August 1909 a vacancy arose as secretary at Toynbee Hall in Whitechapel, the best-known of the University Settlements. With his record of social work and connections in the East End, he was the obvious candidate for the post and was duly appointed. But he soon regretted the move. Missing the security of his circle in Stepney, which he had come to regard as his real home, he never settled in Whitechapel. More importantly, he grew uneasy with the ethos of Toynbee Hall, whose well-intentioned philanthropy he regarded as inadequate for the social problems of the East End. It was through his job as secretary, however, that Attlee wrote his first published comment about one of Churchill's policies. In the *Toynbee Record* for June 1910 Attlee had an article that analysed 'the Labour Exchange in relation to boy and girl labour'. It was a rather bland review of a book on the subject, but Attlee praised Churchill's measure as 'the first big step forward in organising the labour market'.[20] In another article for the *Record*, about citizenship education, Attlee reflected on the changing nature of political debate. 'Today the questions of moment are social rather than political and something more definite than the abstract love of liberty is necessary.'[21] This was very similar to the view held by Churchill, who had told J. A. Spender, the editor of the Liberal *Westminster Gazette*, in 1907, 'No legislation at present interests the democracy. All their minds are turning more and more to the social and economic issue. The revolution is irresistible.'[22]

The turmoil in politics had intensified by the time Attlee was working at Toynbee Hall, as the furore over Lloyd George's Budget turned into a full-blown constitutional crisis. On 1 December 1909, the Tory-dominated House of Lords threw out the People's Budget, an extreme move that contravened the parliamentary tradition that the peers did not interfere with Finance Bills. The Liberals now had to assert their authority. Their chosen method was an appeal to the country, by which they hoped to win a fresh mandate for the Budget. The General Election was held in January 1910 and Churchill was easily returned for Dundee, more than 6,000 votes ahead of his nearest Unionist rival. But, across the nation, the Liberals fared much worse, losing more than 100 seats and their overall majority, a poor result that heralded a bleak long-term future. Asquith's Government was now dependent for survival on the support of the Irish Nationalists, the price of which would be another Home Rule Bill, something that the Unionists would resist even more fiercely than they had the People's Budget.

As usual Churchill was to be at the heart of the battle. His success at the Board of Trade made him a prime candidate for promotion and in the post-election reshuffle Asquith elevated him to the Home Office, one of the great offices of state. Aged only thirty-five, he was the youngest Home Secretary since the appointment of Sir Robert Peel in 1822. But it was a role that badly damaged his progressive credentials. No longer the agent of social reform, he came to be seen as a politician of reckless impetuosity and poor judgement. It was an image that soured his relations with Labour for decades, even to the extent of undermining the chance of a united, anti-appeasement front in the 1930s. Meanwhile the claims of his unreliability made him an ever bigger target for fury from the Tories, already embittered by his supposed betrayal of his party and his class. All this obloquy was worsened by Churchill's handling of a number of crises that arose in the incendiary political atmosphere of pre-First World War England. The first occurred in November 1910 when rioting broke out in the town of Tonypandy during a major strike in the coalfields of South Wales. Fearing that he was about to lose control of the situation, the Glamorgan Constabulary Chief Constable Lionel Lindsay called for military reinforcements from southern England to quell the disorder. As

soon as he received this request, Churchill quashed the idea of sending
the troops immediately into Tonypandy, which he thought would only
inflame the conflict. Instead he dispatched 850 Metropolitan Police
officers to the area, then ordered the military to be held in Cardiff as
a reserve. Churchill's restraint worked. The rioting was largely quelled
by the police before the troops were finally sent in, though one striker
lost his life to a blow from a truncheon. As Churchill explained to the
Commons, 'The policy I have pursued in this matter had been to avoid,
at considerable risk, the danger of collision between the military and
an excited mob.'[23]

In some quarters, the charge against Churchill was that he had
been too lenient with the rioters and strikers. 'The vacillation shown
by those who are responsible for the absence of troops in the present
crisis cannot easily be excused,' argued *The Times* at the height of
the disorder.[24] But Labour and the trade unions took the opposite
view, painting Churchill as a dangerous class warrior bent on violent
repression. In the emotive words of ILP's Kier Hardie, 'Troops are let
loose upon the people to shoot down if need be while they are fighting
for their legitimate rights.'[25] The accusation was untrue, yet it grew into
part of Labour mythology about Churchill. John Parker, a long-serving
Labour backbencher, later wrote there was a feeling of 'distrust' in his
party towards Churchill 'dating back to the Tonypandy episode'.[26] It
was even asserted that in May 1940 Attlee was reluctant to consider
Churchill as the Prime Minister because of Tonypandy. Churchill's
closest ally, Brendan Bracken, claimed that, at this time, he dined with
Attlee to discuss the political scene. According to Bracken's account,
Attlee said 'his people would never forgive Churchill for Tonypandy'.[27]
Attlee subsequently dismissed Bracken's claim, saying that he had
never dined with him in his life, but the episode showed how large
Tonypandy loomed in the British left's anti-Churchill narrative.

Only a few months later, Churchill was involved in another controversy that allegedly displayed his impulsive enthusiasm for military
intervention. On the morning of 3 January 1911, Churchill was lying
in his bath at his family home in Eccleston Square when he received

an urgent message from the Home Office that an armed siege was under way in Stepney. This was no ordinary stand-off, but the latest in a series of shocking events that had left a trail of death across east London. In early December, a gang of armed Latvian revolutionaries, led by an anti-tsarist called George Gardstein, had been caught by the police in the middle of an attempt to tunnel into a jeweller's shop in Houndsditch. During the ensuing gunfight, three officers were killed, the worst multiple murder ever experienced by the English police in peacetime. Gardstein was also shot and, though helped by his fellow gangsters from the crime scene, later died from his wounds. A huge police hunt, headed by ninety detectives, now began for the other Latvians across London.

The brutal crime had, understandably, caused alarm and outrage in the public. Those feelings were expressed in remarkable scenes when the memorial service, attended by Churchill, was held for the three dead police officers on 22 December at St Paul's. No fewer than 750,000 people lined the routes of the cortege from the cathedral to the cemeteries, while the London Stock Exchange ceased trading for half an hour as a mark of respect. The reverberations were all the greater because the background of the criminals fed into public concerns about immigration at this time, fuelled by a rise in the number of Jews fleeing Russian pogroms and a growing incidence of anarchist terrorism in Europe. When Churchill received the news that two of the gang members were holed up in the top floor of a house in Sidney Street with an arsenal of weaponry, he knew he had a major incident on his hands.

Since midnight, when the report of the Latvians' location had arrived via an informer, the police had deployed over 200 officers to Sidney Street. But an attempt to raid the top floor was prevented by a hail of gunfire, which left one detective badly wounded. The police now decided they needed military reinforcements, and the request was put through to Churchill. In contrast to Tonypandy, he immediately gave permission because this was an unprecedented but contained situation where army experience was appropriate. The first troops, a unit of the Scots Guards from the Tower of London, arrived at 10.15 in the morning, backed up by artillery and machine guns. But Churchill was not content to just sit behind his desk in Whitehall and wait for the siege to unfold. He made his way to Sidney Street by car, wearing a silk top hat, a dark coat with an astrakhan collar and an expression 'of deep seriousness', according to the *Daily Mirror*'s reporter.

It has often been claimed that Churchill did not interfere with the operations, an assertion that he later made himself. 'It was no part of my duty to take personal control or give executive decisions,' he wrote.[28] But this does not match the eyewitness testimony by the press. *The Times* reported that, on his arrival, Churchill was 'full of resourceful suggestions',[29] while, according to the Liberal-backing *Daily Chronicle*, Churchill regularly issued detailed instructions; on one occasion he 'took four or five guards forward a few yards nearer the house and directed their fire'.[30] As word of the excitement spread, huge crowds also gathered in the vicinity. Among the spectators was Clement Attlee, in whose neighbourhood lay Sidney Street. Characteristically, at the moment of the siege, he happened to be strengthening his Haileybury connection by having the current headmaster, Dr Wynne Wilson, to stay as a guest, as he recalled: 'I was taking him for a walk to show him something of the district when I met one of our club boys who said, "I can't get to work. They're shooting like anything down the street." I said, "Let's go and see," and we went and viewed the scene.'[31] It was the first time that Attlee and Churchill were in physical proximity. In another account, Attlee remembered: 'I saw the Home Secretary watching the battle. Already at that time his political future was bright, but as far as I was concerned he was the other side – both the other sides. There he was, in the middle of the drama. He always had this feeling for the dramatic and he used it. He had this flair for presenting himself.'[32]

More than an hour after Churchill's arrival, the siege reached its climax. As the shooting continued, smoke was suddenly seen coming from the top floor. Whether by accident or design, the revolution-aries had set fire to the building. According to the *Mirror*, Churchill 'suggested that the firemen should throw a jet of water into the house, and thus bring the murderers to submission. It was not thought advisable, however, to act on this suggestion.'[33] This version is contradicted by Churchill's own account, in which he claimed to have told the chief fire officer, 'on my authority as Home Secretary' that the house 'was to be allowed to burn down and that he was to stand by in readiness to prevent the conflagration spreading'.[34] Whoever gave the decision, the fire raged until any survival inside was impossible. The firemen then doused the flames and, accompanied by the police, entered the burned-out building, where they found the two charred corpses of the revolutionaries. Tragically, during the search, one fireman was killed by falling debris to add to a roll-call of injuries in the emergency services, most of them from bullet wounds. Churchill inspected the premises then left, shortly after three o'clock.

The handling of the siege might have been seen as a success, especially when the police soon captured most of the Latvian gang, though one of its more notorious members, a mysterious character known to the public as 'Peter the Painter'* remained at large. Yet Churchill came in for sustained criticism for his presence in Sidney Street, which was perceived to have escalated the confrontation. 'I understand what the photographer was doing, but what was the Right Honourable gentleman doing?' asked Balfour, causing a wave of laughter through the Commons. Churchill himself was a little sheepish when he returned to Westminster; he told the Liberal MP Charles Masterman, 'Don't be cross, it was such fun.'[35] Amid the growing uproar, Lloyd George privately urged that Churchill should make it clear that 'he had nothing to do with directing operations', given that the affair had been so 'disastrously muddled by the police'.[36] Churchill gave just such an exculpatory public statement, protesting that 'From the beginning

---

* He could have been Peter Piaktov or Piaktoff. An alternative suggestion is that he was a Latvian artist and Bolshevik called Gerderts Eliass. Some historians have questioned whether this figure existed at all. But his name came to symbolise the terror that the gang inflicted on east London, culminating in the siege.

the police had an absolutely free hand.'[37] Such a claim was, at the very least, misleading.

Shortly before the siege occurred, the deadlock in Parliament over Lords' reform had prompted a second General Election at the end of 1910 with almost exactly the same result. Churchill retained his Dundee seat with another decisive majority and the Liberals were able to hold on to power with Irish and Labour support. After further months of constitutional wrangling and talk of defiance, the Lords finally gave way in August 1911 and passed the Parliament Act, which severely curtailed their powers. By then, Asquith was beginning to think that Churchill's bellicosity might be better utilised in a service department rather than at the Home Office, particularly as Germany was undertaking a massive programme of naval rearmament. In October 1911 the Prime Minister asked Churchill to exchange offices with Reginald McKenna, the First Lord of the Admiralty, who now transferred to the Home Office. Churchill was thrilled to take command of the Royal Navy at a crucial juncture when the international scene was full of tension and new technology was advancing rapidly. Always at ease with responsibility, he was now in charge of more than 500 ships and 130,000 men. Comparing his new position with his former one at the Home Office, he told Violet Asquith, 'Look at the people I have had to deal with so far – judges and convicts. This is a big thing.'[38]

There was nothing big in Attlee's life at this moment. In contrast to Churchill, he remained a bachelor but not out of choice. Beneath his reserved exterior, he had an unrequited yearning for love. 'My life is passing like a lonely stream', ran the opening line of a sonnet he wrote at this time.[39] In other ways, he was struggling to make any real advance. In 1909 he stood as an ILP candidate for Stepney Borough Council but, with the franchise still restricted in pre-war Britain, he received only sixty-nine votes. Afterwards an ILP colleague tried to raise his spirits by urging defiance for the sake of the wider struggle. 'Are we downhearted?' he asked Attlee rhetorically. 'Of course we are,' replied Attlee.[40] Nor did he succeed in two attempts to win election to the Limehouse Board of Guardians, despite a strenuous programme of public meetings and canvassing. In August 1910 he gave up the job he disliked at Toynbee Hall and moved with his brother Tom into a flat at a London County Council block by the river in Limehouse. There followed lengthy bouts of unemployment, interspersed with the occasional temporary post. For a time he was an 'official explainer' for the 1911 National Insurance Act, whose introduction owed much to Churchill's period at the Board of Trade. At one point he had to address a meeting in Woodford, Essex, which within fifteen years would be Churchill's constituency. To Attlee's anger, he encountered some abuse from the audience, as he recalled:

> A number of young Conservatives sat in front and booed loudly whilst I talked. I told them I was only an 'official explainer' but they continued to boo.
>
> I then said, 'You don't like Lloyd George.'
>
> 'No,' they yelled.
>
> 'You don't like Churchill.'
>
> 'No,' again.
>
> 'Then when next you see a sailor, you'd better hit him, because Churchill is First Lord of the Admiralty.' That quietened them.[41]

Attlee finally found more permanent work in 1912, when he was taken on as a lecturer in the newly established Social Work Department of the London School of Economics, which was founded by the Webbs in the 1890s. His job not only brought in an income sufficient for his modest needs but also allowed him time for political activities. He regularly took part in Labour and trade-union demonstrations, marches and conferences, becoming an increasingly well-connected figure in left-wing politics in the capital. 'In the Socialist movement one soon got to know all the more active spirits in the London area. The position of being a small fighting minority gave one a certain sense of exaltation,' he wrote.[42]

Churchill was operating on a much larger stage. His performance at the Admiralty displayed his characteristic zeal, heightened by the recognition that storm clouds of war were gathering. In another of his reformist blazes, he introduced fast submarines, created the Royal Naval Air Service, improved the pay for sailors, increased the calibre of ships' guns to fifteen inches, established the Royal Naval Division of reservists for joint operations, expanded naval expenditure from £39 million to £50 million, built up a naval staff at the Admiralty to oversee planning and switched vessels from coal to oil, thereby increasing their speed. His dynamism could grate with some of his colleagues. 'Churchill is ill-mannered, boastful, unprincipled, without any redeeming qualities except his amazing ability and industry,' wrote fellow Cabinet member Charles Hobhouse.[43] Others were impressed by the First Lord's relish in the challenge of his responsibilities, as the Liberal MP Cecil Harmsworth noted in March 1914 when he came across Churchill 'singing blithely to himself in the lavatory behind the Speaker's Chair. I thank him for his reassuring cheerfulness and he tells me that it is his habit to confront difficult situations with an outward serenity of aspect.'[44] However, that buoyancy was about to face its greatest test.

FOUR

❖

GALLIPOLI

IN A MOMENT of frank self-awareness on the eve of the First World War, Churchill wrote to Clementine, 'Everything tends towards catastrophe and collapse. I am interested, geared up and happy. Is it not horrible to be built like that?'[1] His martial spirit had been central to his character since childhood. From his early games with toy soldiers to his place at the front of the Omdurman cavalry charge, he had always been stirred by the clash of battle. Now, following Britain's declaration of war on 4 August 1914, he had the ultimate stage on which to express himself.

Some feared that his military enthusiasm could potentially be a national danger. The Labour Leader Ramsay MacDonald, who resigned his position in 1914 because of his opposition to the war, declared that 'Mr Churchill is a very dangerous person to put at the head of our fighting services. He treats them as hobbies.'[2] But there were many who felt that Churchill's outlook was exactly what Britain needed, particularly in a Liberal Government that had been so badly divided over entry into the war and was headed by a Prime Minister, H. H. Asquith, who had a limited interest in military strategy. Colonel Maurice Hankey, the Secretary of the Committee of Imperial Defence, believed that Churchill 'brought an element of youth, energy, vitality and confidence that was a tower of strength to Asquith's Cabinet in those difficult early days'.[3]

Attlee was also actively involved in the war from the start, in his case as a serving officer. Given the pacifist and anti-imperialist instincts of the ILP, such a commitment may have seemed incongruous. But Attlee had always enjoyed military life and, since joining Haileybury House in 1905, had continuously held a commission as a second lieutenant in the 1st Cadet Battalion of the Queen's Regiment. Moreover, his regimental membership matched much of the public's mood in his east London neighbourhood. 'We were brought up to be very patriotic and on Empire Day, we marched round the school playground, saluting the Union Jack,' recalled Stepney resident Henrietta Burkin.[4] When war was declared, Attlee was on holiday in Devon with his brother Tom, a conscientious objector, who was firmly against enlistment on principle. Clem was far more torn, later writing in his unpublished war memoirs of his conflicted feelings:

> On one hand my whole instincts as a socialist were against war and I had no illusions; nor was I convinced of Germany's sole guilt. On the other hand it appeared wrong to me to let others make a sacrifice while I stood by, especially as I was unmarried and had no obligations.[5]

He therefore decided to join up, becoming a lieutenant in the 6th Battalion of the South Lancashire Regiment, a newly established unit in Lord Kitchener's expanding volunteer army.

For the next nine months, Attlee was based in southern England, mainly undertaking guard duties and training in preparation for deployment overseas. There were early signs of that crisp, efficient leadership for which he later became well known, reflected in his promotions to the rank of captain in February 1915, then to a full company command in April. By then it seemed certain that his battalion was about to be sent to the France, where a blood-soaked stalemate now hung over the mud of the Western Front. 'In the first week of June we were given our maps of France.' But the following week the orders changed. 'We realised we were for the East and guessed Gallipoli.'[6]

The very name Gallipoli has become synonymous with the greatest setback of Churchill's career, cementing for decades afterwards his reputation for reckless impatience and poor judgement. In the sands of that Turkish peninsula, his critics found an almost inexhaustible supply of ammunition to blacken his name. What he had presented at the start of 1915 as a daring scheme to break the deadlock in the west had descended by the year's end into a catastrophe. Even before Gallipoli, there were growing doubts about Churchill's management at the Admiralty. After a number of blows to the Royal Navy, among them the sinking of three cruisers off the Dutch coast, the senior commander David Beatty wrote to his wife: 'It is inconceivable the mistakes and blunders we have made and are making.'[7] Those concerns were crystallised by Churchill's decision, extraordinary in a Cabinet minister, to take temporary personal charge of the defence of Antwerp in October, when the Belgian port was about to fall into German hands. Such was his excitement in this role that he even telegraphed Asquith asking to be relieved of his post as First Lord so he could be appointed a full commander with the necessary military rank. The Prime Minister found the whole idea absurd and told Churchill he could not be spared.

After a professional soldier, Sir Henry Rawlinson, had been given the Antwerp command, Churchill returned to London. The city did not hold out for long after his departure. It capitulated on 10 October, the Germans taking 2,500 men prisoner. Nevertheless, Churchill's mission may have delayed the fall by five days, a vital period that could have helped to shore up the British position further west. Yet Churchill came to regret his actions, feeling that he had been too embroiled in the tactical struggle while missing the strategic picture. 'Those who are charged with direction of supreme affairs must sit on the mountain-tops of control; they must never descend into the valleys of direct physical and personal action,' he wrote in 1932.[8] At the time, several contemporaries were far more scathing. The Tory Leader Andrew Bonar Law called it 'an utterly stupid business', while King George V's private secretary Lord Stamfordham declared Churchill to be 'quite off his head'.[9]

Churchill stored up more trouble for himself when he persuaded the seventy-four-year-old Lord Fisher to come out of retirement and reassume the role of First Sea Lord. Often seen, not least by himself, as the greatest sailor since Nelson, Jacky Fisher had been the driving force behind the wholesale modernisation of the Royal Navy in the first decade of the twentieth century, the centrepiece of which was the introduction of the mighty Dreadnaught class of battleship. In the years since he had formally left his post in January 1911, his name continued to be revered in naval circles. Churchill, an admirer of his energy, regularly sought his advice. Yet Fisher had always been an argumentative, mercurial leader, and those traits had only worsened in old age as he grew more erratic. His reappointment was the equivalent of a ticking bomb at the heart of Admiralty.

By November 1914, Churchill was ready to go on the offensive, using Britain's maritime power as an instrument to break the deadlock on the Western Front, where, in the course of an average day, 2,533 men on both sides were killed in action. 'Are there not alternatives other than sending our armies to chew barbed wire in Flanders? Further, cannot the power of the Navy be brought to bear upon the enemy?' he wrote to Asquith.[10] One scheme, which Fisher strongly favoured, was to launch a major operation in the North Sea by the seizure of the German island of Borkum off the Dutch coast, followed by an attack on Schleswig-Holstein to threaten the Kiel Canal and open the Baltic Sea. But Churchill was attracted to a grander initiative in a very different theatre. He contemplated a naval attack through the Dardanelles Straits lying between the Aegean and the Marmara Sea. In his view, a number of gains might flow from such a strike if it were successful: support would be given to Russia, now struggling on the Eastern Front; Turkey would be driven out of the war; Bulgaria, Romania and Greece would come in on the Allies side; and Germany would be left increasingly isolated. Fisher, still focused on the North Sea, was lukewarm and emphasised that attack should be a combined operation, not purely a naval one. Much of the Cabinet was more negative. 'Winston's volatile mind is at present set on Turkey and Bulgaria and he wants to organise a heroic adventure against Gallipoli and the Dardanelles, to which I am altogether opposed,' wrote Asquith to his young aristocratic mistress Venetia Stanley.[11]

But the situation was transformed at the start of 1915 when the Russians issued an appeal to the Allies for assistance against Turkey, whose forces had embarked on an offensive in the Caucasus. The time was ripe for Churchill to renew his Dardanelles plan, despite the continuing lack of ground support. At a meeting of the War Council on 13 January, he outlined his proposal to aid Russia and hit Turkey with a naval expedition to seize the Straits. As Council Secretary Maurice Hankey recorded, the politicians and military chiefs, frustrated by lengthy discussions about the Western Front, were now much more receptive: 'The idea caught on at once. The whole atmosphere changed. Fatigue was forgotten. The War Council turned eagerly from the dreary vista of a "slogging match" on the Western Front to brighter prospects, as they seemed, in the Mediterranean.'[12] In a mood of optimism, approval was given for detailed preparations to be made for the venture. But Fisher remained unconvinced, believing that a naval operation alone was inadequate. At the War Council on 28 January 1915, when it was agreed to proceed with naval assault, Fisher appeared to be on the verge of leaving the room in protest, but was persuaded by Kitchener to resume his seat – although, according to Asquith, 'he maintained an obstinate and ominous silence'.[13] In contrast, Churchill was buoyed up by thoughts of victory over Turkey, his cheerfulness made all the greater when Kitchener decided in mid-February, shortly before the operation began, that he could supply a military force to land on the Gallipoli peninsula, once the Turkish defences along the Straits had been crushed by Royal Naval bombardment. 'You get through. I will find them men,' Kitchener told Churchill.[14]

Churchill's hopes for an easy triumph were quickly dashed. The Royal Navy squadron, led by Admiral Sackville Carden, began its bombardment on 19 February but, after taking out the first few Turkish forts, soon encountered stronger resistance and worse weather than expected. Long delays and further ineffectual shelling followed, leaving Churchill dismayed and Carden demoralised. 'Winston is very jumpy about the Dardanelles. He says we will be ruined if the attack fails,' recorded Viscount Esher, the artful

Whitehall adviser and intriguer.[15] In the face of Churchill's demands for more urgency, Carden descended into a nervous breakdown and had to be replaced by Admiral of the Fleet John de Robeck. Yet he fared even more dismally. On 18 March a further attempt to take out the Turkish onshore batteries resulted only in heavy losses, with three Allied battleships sunk by mines. The Turks were jubilant, the Allies humiliated. Having ordered a general recall to save the remainder of his force, de Robeck warned the Admiralty that the army would now have to be landed on Gallipoli to destroy the Turkish guns and clear a safe passage through the Straits for the navy. But, because the operation had originally been envisaged solely as a naval one, the preparations for landings were insufficiently advanced, much to Churchill's fury. He felt that in any case another immediate attempt should be made by de Robeck to force the Straits, especially given Admiralty intelligence which claimed that the Turks were running short of ammunition. The longer the delay, he argued, the more time the Turks had to bring up reinforcements and replenish their supplies.

But vacillation now prevailed within the Government. The failures had sapped all decisiveness. Fisher, more distant than ever from Churchill, wanted little more to do with the affair. 'Damn the Dardanelles! They will be our grave,' he angrily told Churchill on 5 April.[16] Meanwhile Kitchener, an increasingly dominant figure in the planning of the campaign, insisted that the military landings could not take place until near the end of the month. Hankey the War Council Secretary feared that, even with greater preparations, the proposed landings were 'fraught with possibility of an appalling military disaster'.[17] Yet Churchill maintained his faith in the necessity and likely victory of the Allies over the Turks, telling Balfour on 8 April: 'You must not be unduly apprehensive of the military operation. The soldiers can do it.' The alternative of withdrawal, he wrote, should not be considered. 'No other operation in this part of the world could ever cloak the defeat of abandoning the effort against the Dardanelles. I think there is nothing for it but to go through with this business.'[18]

The pessimists were right; Churchill was wrong. The assault on Gallipoli, carried out by 52,000 British, French and Australasian troops of the Mediterranean Expeditionary Force under the command of Sir Ian Hamilton, a friend of Churchill's from their days together on the Indian North-West Frontier, made a promising start but ran into formidable opposition from the entrenched Turks, whose well-equipped forces now numbered 80,000 men. As the Allies' casualties mounted and their advance was halted, a bloody stalemate developed. The Dardanelles campaign had been conceived as an alternative to the Western Front yet now, in a bitter irony, the same hell was being replicated on the Gallipoli Peninsula. The shaken British Government was too committed to evacuate immediately, so the only options were to provide more reinforcements for Hamilton and aim for another, more effective naval bombardment by de Robeck. But while such steps were considered, Asquith's administration became engulfed in a full-scale political crisis, prompted by the angry, much threatened resignation of Fisher on 15 May.

Unfortunately for the Liberal Government, Fisher's departure came just at the moment when the news from the Western Front was at its blackest after further heavy losses in Flanders. Accusations of ministerial incompetence and lethargy were compounded by sensational reports in *The Times* of chronic shell shortages. In both Parliament and the press there was now intense pressure on Asquith for a wholesale reconstruction of the Government through the creation of a coalition with the Conservatives. Asquith, a traditional Liberal, found the idea of working with the Tories distasteful but the concept of a bipartisan coalition had long appealed to Churchill, who was never a strong party loyalist. As recently as February 1915, Asquith had noted that his First Lord was 'always hankering after coalitions and odd groupings'.[19] The paradox was that Asquith's reluctant acceptance of power-sharing with the Conservatives in 1915 spelled the downfall of Churchill. During protracted negotiations in May, the Tory Leader Andrew Bonar Law, a tough-minded Protestant whose family hailed from Ulster, made it clear that his party would insist on Churchill's removal from the

Admiralty. This was not just because of the mess at Gallipoli, but also because of his past switch of parties and his support for Irish Home Rule. His position was all the more vulnerable because he had few allies among the senior Liberals. 'Churchill will have to go. He will be a ruined man,' Lloyd George told his mistress and secretary Frances Stevenson without much sympathy.[20] 'It seems strange that Churchill should have been in politics all these years and yet not have won the confidence of a single party in the country or a single colleague in the Cabinet,' she noted her diary.[21]

In a series of five letters, Churchill pleaded with Asquith to be allowed to see through the operation in Turkey. 'Let me stand or fall by the Dardanelles, but do not take it from my hands,' he urged.[22] Asquith was unmoved. He firmly told Churchill on 22 May that 'you must take it as settled that you are not to remain at the Admiralty'.[23] Instead, he offered Churchill the Chancellorship of the Duchy of Lancaster, an archaic sinecure post that carried few responsibilities and represented the lowest rank in the Cabinet. 'I gather you have been flung a bone on which there is little meat,' sympathised his cousin the Duke of Marlborough.[24] The only consolation was that Churchill would remain a member of the War Council, now renamed the Dardanelles Committee.

It was a dramatic fall, one that brought to a juddering halt his rise towards the political summit. 'I am finished! Finished in respect of all I care for – the waging of war, the defeat of the Germans,' he said.[25] In his place as First Lord of the Admiralty, Asquith appointed Balfour, who resumed his long career in high office. He did not finally retire until 1929 and his total of twenty-eight years in the Cabinet is a record exceeded only by Churchill himself. But in 1915, like most other figures in politics, Balfour believed that Churchill was fatally flawed, as he told Violet Asquith's sister-in-law Cynthia when they met soon after his succession to the Admiralty. 'He spoke very nicely of Winston – enumerated all his wonderful gifts – but said that he thought he was "predestined" to failure.'[26]

One of Balfour's first decisions at the Admiralty was that the Dardanelles campaign must continue. Kitchener, anxious about the loss of prestige from withdrawal, backed him fully, as did Churchill from his lowly new perch as the Duchy Chancellor. To that end, the Dardanelles Committee resolved that five new divisions should be send to Gallipoli, among them the men of the South Lancashire Regiment. On 13 June Attlee and the rest of the 6th Battalion left their base at Frimley in Surrey and travelled overnight by train to Avonmouth Docks in Bristol, where they boarded the requisitioned liner SS *Ausonia* for the journey to the eastern Mediterranean. Exactly a fortnight later, the *Ausonia* arrived at Moudros harbour on the North Aegean island of Lemnos, the Royal Navy's base for the campaign. After staying on the island for two nights in unseasonably damp weather, Attlee's battalion was then transported to Cape Helles, the southernmost tip of the Gallipoli peninsula. The war now really began for Attlee. Almost a year since he had signed up, he had his initial taste of action as the Turks, who held possession of the hills overlooking the headland, opened up with machine-gun fire. But he and his company emerged unscathed as they made their way to Gully Ravine, where the Allies had managed to construct a primitive network of trenches close to the Turkish positions. Again replicating the deadlock of the Western Front, the Gully had already been the scene of two bouts of fierce but inconclusive fighting over the previous months and another bruising struggle was under way when Attlee's unit arrived.

His company had landed on Helles in preparation for the next big Allied push on the Peninsula, planned for early August. For almost a month they were on the defensive, moving from one trench to another and regularly under attack. On his first evening in the Gully, he was sitting in a trench, talking to a fellow officer, 'when two bullets struck the side just above our heads', he recalled.[27] Attlee's company also spent time in reserve behind the front lines, responsible for tasks like trench-digging and delivering rations. His biggest complaints about Helles were not directed at the enemy but at the boredom of night watch and the living conditions. The only way he found to relieve the former was through lengthy discussions with his NCOs about socialism, but he could do little about the latter. 'Flies swarmed everywhere. The sides of the dugout were black with them. At meals one's cup was filled with them while the jam pot was overcrowded. They were a real torment. The trenches too were not too sweet, owing to some Turks being embedded in them, while no man's land stank vilely,' he wrote later.[28] Unsurprisingly, like so many in his battalion, Attlee succumbed to a severe attack of dysentery. With his usual stoicism, he tried manfully to carry on despite the illness but, after several collapses, he was taken from the beach unconscious and transferred to a hospital ship, the SS *Devanha*. On board, doctors offered him the choice of going back to England or stopping for treatment in Malta. Keen to rejoin his unit as soon as possible, he chose Malta; so when the *Devanha* docked at Valetta harbour, Attlee was 'swung out of the ship on a stretcher by a derrick. It is an unpleasant sensation to twiddle round in mid-air,' he wrote.[29] He was moved by motor ambulance to the 'very comfortable' military hospital at Hamrun,[30] which was run by Jean, Lady Hamilton, the wife of the Gallipoli commander Sir Ian. Attlee was frustrated at 'hanging about in Malta'[31] yet, in terms of his own survival, he had been fortunate in the timing of his illness. Soon after he had been evacuated to Malta, the Allies began their renewed offensive to smash the Turks through further landings at the Anzac bridgehead, Sulva Bay and Helles. But the attacks descended into another savage failure, with Attlee's own division suffering a casualty rate of no less than 60 per cent. It is a tribute to Attlee's fortitude that, having learned in Malta of the deaths of so many comrades, he was determined to go back to Gallipoli.

Churchill had also been lobbying to go there. In the absence of a heavy workload at the Duchy office, he had conceived a plan in July to undertake a mission to confer with General Hamilton and Admiral de Robeck. The aim was both to provide a first-hand report of the situation and to stiffen the commanders' resolution. Having received strong backing from Asquith, Balfour and Kitchener for his idea, Churchill began his travel preparations, which included medical inoculations and the purchase of tropical clothes. He was due to start on 25 July but was thwarted at the very last moment when the Conservative aristocrat and Lord Privy Seal Earl Curzon got wind of the scheme. In a further indicator of Churchill's crushing unpopularity in Tory ranks, Curzon was able to stir up his colleagues against him. For the second time in two months, Asquith was forced to abandon Churchill because of a Tory veto. Instead, Maurice Hankey, the Dardanelles Committee Secretary, led the mission, which achieved little. Churchill's indignation at his ostracism now deepened, reinforcing his sense that he should quit politics.

While Churchill remained in London reluctantly, Attlee was preparing for combat. Fully recovered, he left Malta at the end of September, stopping in Alexandria before he reached Moudros. By now, following the heavy losses and lack of any breakthrough, the punch had gone out of the campaign. Britain's position had been made all the weaker by Bulgaria's entry into the war, on the side of the Central powers, which both opened up a direct route between Germany and Turkey and meant that Allied troop reinforcements had to be diverted to the Balkans. By October, evacuation was openly under discussion. Hamilton refused to countenance such a move, demanded ever larger reinforcements, and was sacked. But the Dardanelles Committee could not decide how to proceed. Curzon and Churchill were in favour of stepping up the fight; Lloyd George and Bonar Law wanted immediate withdrawal. Asquith, predictably, prevaricated. Hamilton's replacement, Lieutenant General Charles Munro, was therefore forced to adopt an attritional holding strategy as small numbers of troops continued to arrive.

After a violently stormy crossing of the Aegean, Attlee's company landed at Sulva Bay on 16 November and made its way to the divisional headquarters. Attlee was pleased to be back among his fellow South Lancashire officers and even enjoyed some attention at the HQ because of his political views, as he recalled: 'The Commanding Officer would say, "let's have a good strafe, send for Attlee" and after dinner we would discuss some proposition such as "All socialists are scoundrels".'[32] But the reality of war always intruded on regimental life. Whether in the trenches or the reserve, his company was under constant fire from artillery, machine guns and snipers, whose bullets 'some nights seemed to follow one about'.[33] A vivid description of front-line service at Sulva in November was left by Lieutenant H. Lechler, who served alongside Attlee. Writing of a spell on duty with a wiring party, which repaired Allied barbed-wire defences while trying to sabotage those of the Turks, he recorded how, when his group came under attack, 'we had no hole to get into, so we could only lie where we were and trust to luck. As the firing worked towards us, one voluntarily tightened every muscle and clenched one's teeth expecting to be hit. The experience was awful, hearing the firing coming nearer and knowing that it was impossible to get away and being without any cover.'[34]

The hazards of enemy action were compounded, at the beginning of December, by an appalling turn in the weather. Dugouts were flooded by torrential rain, which then turned to snow, leaving the men in Attlee's company soaked and shivering. Once more, in these miserable conditions, Attlee showed his leadership qualities. He got fires going in improvised braziers, organised makeshift shelters, carried out foot inspections, issued rations of rum and made the men who could stand run about so they would warm up. After three days the tempest relented. Attlee's battalion emerged from the ordeal as the only one in the Allied forces on the Peninsula without any deaths from the freezing damp. For the politicians and military commanders, however, the arrival of winter finally extinguished all lingering hopes of success. With the influence of Churchill and Kitchener so badly diminished because of the botched campaign, the evacuation lobby in Government, led by the assured new Chief of the Imperial General Staff, Sir William Robertson, was in the ascendant. Robertson – who strongly believed that Allied power had to be concentrated in France – ordered that the Sulva and Anzac sectors be evacuated by 20 December, and Helles by 8 January 1916.

There were widespread fears that the withdrawal would result in brutal losses. In fact, this turned out to be the most successful part of the campaign. With his customary efficiency, Attlee was instrumental in the operation at Sulva. His instructions from his commanding officer, Lieutenant General Frederick Maude, were to hold the perimeter line around the cove of Lala Baba, protecting thousands of Allied troops who were to embark from that point. For this task, he had 250 men and six machine guns, as well as a telephone to communicate with GHQ. Most of his men were placed on guard duty in trenches facing the enemy; a smaller detachment held the road to the sea. As soon as darkness fell, the retreating parties of Allied troops began to march through the gaps in the barbed-wire fences and down to the shore. So smoothly was the evacuation organised that it did not even arouse the suspicions of the Turks. 'Everything was very peaceful though there were occasional shots to be heard from Anzac,' wrote Attlee.[35] Eventually, at 3.30 a.m. on 20 December, Attlee received the message that the last of the parties had been taken from the beach. As he recorded in his own account:

> Then we got the order to move. The men hustled up the trench, machine guns going first. I brought up the rear and found a few military police, Maude and a few of the Staff. We went on board lighters which seemed to go round and round. Flames shot up from the dumps of abandoned stores. We were transferred to the *Princess Ida** and being very tired, I fell asleep on the saloon floor.[36]

'Thank God they got off Helles all right,' Churchill told Clementine when he heard the news.[37] Attlee's Gallipoli campaign was over. He had been the second-last man out of Sulva, followed by Maude. Within his regiment, his reputation had been enhanced by his cool-headed gallantry. Some of his men thought he might be mentioned in dispatches. That did not happen, but his personal success stood in contrast to Churchill's eclipse. Yet Attlee was always a stout defender of Churchill over Gallipoli. He never shared the conventional wisdom that it was an ill-conceived strategy. On the contrary, he thought that the scheme was

---

* In his unpublished War Memoirs, Attlee referred to this vessel as the *Princess Ida* but that is the title of a Gilbert and Sullivan opera. He obviously meant the SS *Princess Ena*, a passenger vessel built in Churchill's Dundee constituency and requisitioned by the Admiralty in April 1915.

perhaps the most imaginative of the war, one that could have ended the slaughter in the west. As he put it in his autobiography, 'Often I have thought how near we came to victory and I have tried to work out what the consequences would have been in that event. Unfortunately, the military authorities were Western-Front-minded. Reinforcements were always sent too late.'[38] In an article in the *Spectator* in April 1956, Attlee wrote that Churchill 'was for years pursued by the calumny that he had wantonly thrown away valuable lives in an adventure doomed to failure'. But this was unfair, thought Attlee: 'The Gallipoli show was the only imaginative strategic conception as an alternative to the wholesale butchery in which the Westerners believed. Its success may have shortened the war, saved innumerable lives and had incalculable effects on the world.'[39] At a northeastern dinner of the Gallipoli Association a year later Attlee was just as generous: 'I always take my hat off to Sir Winston Churchill. He had one strategic idea in the war. He did not believe in throwing away masses of people to be massacred. If we had had Sir Winston instead of Asquith and Lloyd George in the 1914–18 war, he would have saved a million lives.'[40]

Churchill himself could take little comfort in any theoretical justification of his strategy. 'When he left the Admiralty, he thought he was finished. I thought he would never get over the Dardanelles. I thought he would die of grief,' Clementine said.[41] But soon after his resignation from the Government, J. L. Garvin, one of his few Conservative supporters in the press, wrote in the *Observer* that it was unlikely his career was over: 'He is young. He has lion-hearted courage. No number of enemies can fight down his ability and force. His hour of triumph will come.'[42]

FIVE

‐◇‐

PLUGSTREET
AND KUT

For Churchill, the primary attraction of the Dardanelles theatre had been the potential to avoid the continuing brutal slog of trench warfare on the Western Front. By the end of 1915, he was a soldier in those trenches. Among the motivations for his highly unorthodox move from the Cabinet to the infantry were a patriotic desire for action and a growing frustration at political inactivity. In early November, Asquith had reconstituted the unwieldy Dardanelles Committee as a much smaller War Committee with just seven members. Churchill was not among them. He took this as his cue to depart from the Government, telling Asquith that he could not 'accept a position of general responsibility for war policy without any effective share in its guidance and control'.[1] Churchill's initial step after his resignation was to ask that he be appointed Governor-General of British East Africa, complete with command of the forces there, but that proposal was instantly rejected by the Cabinet.

The alternative to Africa was Flanders. Churchill was sent to the 2nd Battalion of the Grenadier Guards, which was moving into position at Merville near Dunkirk to replace the Indian Corps, now needed in the increasingly intensive Mesopotamian campaign. After a frosty reception, Churchill soon won over the men in the battalion with his toughness, knowledge of army life and stoicism in the face of the enemy. His plunge into the physical realities of war also brought him relief from the trials of politics, as he explained to Clementine: 'I am very happy here. I did not know what release from care meant. It is a blessed peace.'[2] His disillusion with politics was further reflected in a letter to C. P. Scott. 'I am determined not to return unless with proper executive power in war matters; and as this is not a likely condition to arise, I intend to devote myself to my old profession and absorb myself in it.'[3] Soon after his arrival in the front line, he wrote to Clementine requesting 'two bottles of my old brandy and a bottle of peach brandy. This consignment might be repeated at intervals of ten days.'[4] The consoling effects of drink helped to alleviate the relentless damp and lethal dangers the battalion had to endure. On one occasion a dugout he had just vacated took a direct hit from a German shell.

Having familiarised himself with trench warfare, Churchill was due to take command of a brigade in mid-December, as instructed by Sir John French, the outgoing head of the British Army. But then politics interfered again. When reports of the impending appointment reached London, another storm began to brew, driven once more by Tory animosity towards Churchill. The promotion was seen as far too rapid and reeking of favouritism. 'It is stated on excellent authority from a man at GHQ that Winston has been promised a brigade. It is an outrage if true,' wrote the Tory whip William Bridgeman in his diary, reflecting the mood in his party.[5] Conservative pressure was heightened by the opinion of the incoming new British Expeditionary Force (BEF) Commander-in-Chief, Douglas Haig, who argued that Churchill should not be made a brigadier until 'he has shown that he could bear responsibility in action as CO of a battalion'.[6] Already vulnerable because of the perceived weakness of his leadership, Asquith felt unable to stand up for Churchill. The offer of a brigade was withdrawn. Churchill had to make do with a lesser appointment to the command of 6th Battalion of the Royal Scots Fusiliers, a regiment made up largely of Lowland volunteers.

Promoted to the rank of Lieutenant Colonel, Churchill took charge on 5 January 1916, when the battalion was in reserve at Meteren in

France, about ten miles behind the front line. While Churchill was engaged in Western Europe, Attlee was fighting in the Middle East. After a restful Christmas on the Aegean island of Lemnos, his company moved in January to Port Said, the northern terminus of the Suez Canal in Egypt, to spend four weeks training and refitting. Attlee's clipped manner in conducting these exercises did not appeal to all his men, as Lieutenant H. Lechler noted in his diary. 'We did an attack against a skeleton army. Of course Attlee found any amount of things wrong with it, when, in his unpleasant way, he criticised everyone, officers included, in front of the company.'[7]

In February 1916, General Maude received instructions to take his division to Mesopotamia, the vast region that roughly corresponds to modern Iraq and Kuwait. The British Empire was on the defensive, seeking to protect the Persian oilfields and the lands to the east of the Suez Canal from the advancing Turks of the Ottoman Empire. After a journey lasting almost a fortnight, Attlee's battalion arrived in late February 1916 at its new base of Orahat, just east of Kut, where the Anglo-Indian garrison had been under siege from the Ottomans since December 1915. The aim of the expedition, in which Maude's division formed part of a 30,000-strong force, was to relieve the siege. Yet again, as had happened on Lemnos and Gallipoli, the division was hit by unusually poor weather, with heavy rains causing the Tigris to burst its banks. 'I found war in the Middle East surprisingly wet,' commented Attlee laconically.[8]

By the time of Attlee's service in the Mesopotamian theatre, Churchill's spell in the trenches of Flanders was coming to a close. At the end of January 1916, his battalion had been sent to the desolate village of Ploegsteert, inevitably nicknamed 'Plugstreet' by the BEF, just inside Belgium's border with France. His duty was not to go on the offensive but to hold the place, which was under regular German bombardment. To do so, Churchill had to raise the morale and effect-iveness of his unit. It was a task he performed triumphantly. He improved training, smartened up the drill, organised communal events and football matches, located extra equipment and showed concern for the welfare of his men. John McGuire, a Fusilier who served with him there, later said that 'he was a new type of commander who took an interest in everything'.[9] What particularly struck his battalion was his utter fearlessness. During his time in Ploegsteert, he made a reported thirty-six forays across no-man's-land towards enemy lines. Edmund Hakewill-Smith, a lieutenant in the Fusiliers, recalled that Churchill 'never fell when a shell went off; he never ducked when a bullet went past with its loud crack. He used to say, after watching me duck, "It's no damn use ducking: the bullet has gone a long way past you by now."'[10]

But not everyone who encountered Churchill was impressed by him, as a previously unpublished story from Barney Downes reveals. A soldier with Cameron Highlanders, Downes was ordered, alongside his corporal, to carry out tests in no-man's-land of an experimental new weapon, the 'Bangalore Land Torpedo', which could in theory rip through the enemy's barbed wire. Amid his other duties, Churchill – always drawn to military improvisations – took an interest in the device, much to Downes's regret:

> We were out in no man's land one night realigning the barbed wire for easier access when Churchill lumbered out of the darkness. He watched us for some time, proffering advice which we ignored. Then, getting bored, he teed up an empty Ticker's jam tin and gave it a terrific whack with his trench stick, which an alert sentry heard immediately, firing in the direction of the noise. By an amazing mischance the bullet hit the iron stake my corporal and I were screwing into the ground. The bullet disintegrated a small piece, lacerating the fleshy part of my arm and a larger piece slicing the Corporal's throat, the spouting blood indicating a very serious wound.

Meanwhile, according to Downes, Churchill was 'scuttling back' to safety 'leaving us to cope with rough and ready first aid while under spasmodic fire from the sentry post'. Eventually the two men were able to return to the front line 'where we were completely shocked and dismayed' to find that Churchill had not reported the incident. 'This dereliction of duty left us dazed,' Downes concluded.[11]

Churchill also caused damage to his reputation on a far more public scale with an ill-judged parliamentary intervention during a period of leave from the front. In contradiction of what he had told his wife and C. P. Scott the previous December, he yearned to return to the Westminster scene, not least so that he could try to clear his name over the Dardanelles fiasco. Freed briefly from his military burden, he intervened on 7 March in the Commons with an attack on Asquith's maritime policy. But his performance undermined his own standing far more than it did the Government. At the climax of his contribution, he made the incomprehensible suggestion that his own nemesis Jacky Fisher, with whom he had re-established relations, should be brought back as First Sea Lord. This was forgiveness carried to self-destructive eccentricity. Churchill's supporters were crestfallen, most politicians dismissive. Asquith said that the speech had been 'the grossest effrontery' and 'a piece of impudent humbug',[12] while his wife, Margot, described Churchill as 'a dangerous maniac, so poor in character and judgement, so insolent and childish'.[13]

Bruised by his experience, Churchill returned to Flanders at the end of his leave, though only after he extracted from Asquith an agreement that he could permanently return to London if 'a sense of public duty' made it necessary.[14] As that pledge showed, his humiliation in the Commons had only compounded his determination to get back to politics. He did not have long to wait. In April the BEF decided to merge 6th and 7th Battalions of the Royal Scots Fusiliers because of the shortage of manpower in the former. As the more junior of the two colonels, Churchill was passed over for the command of the newly merged unit. He therefore took the opportunity to leave the regiment and go back to England to see if he could revive his political career. On 7 May, the day after a munificent farewell lunch given by his fellow officers, he crossed the Channel once more. His friend Hugh Tudor of the Royal Horse Artillery, who had served with him in India in the

1890s and seen him frequently in Ploegsteert, confided in his diary that Churchill had taken the correct course:

> He is right to go back to a more important duty than that of Battalion Commander. At the time I heard the opinion expressed by a senior officer that Winston was finished in politics. I did not agree. I remembered how, wherever he is, he makes his personality felt. Even as a young subaltern in Bangalore, his influence in the station and his own regiment was evident. An officer of another unit once asked a major in the 4th Hussars, Churchill's own regiment, 'Why don't you sit on that young Churchill.' The major replied, 'My dear fellow, the whole British nation could not sit on the father so how do you expect a mere cavalry regiment to sit on the son?'[15]

The decision on the Fusiliers' merger came in the month that Attlee went through one of his toughest ordeals. As dawn broke on the morning of 5 April near Kut, he scrambled out of his trench to join a charge on the Ottoman positions. Moving forward at the centre of the line, he carried a large red flag whose purpose was to prevent friendly fire on the advancing troops by the British artillery at the rear. There was some shooting from the Turks, but far less resistance than expected. It was obvious that most of them had cleared out from their trenches. The real danger came from the British shelling, which grew ever closer as the line proceeded. A drastic step had to be taken to give the artillery a clearer signal that the barrage should be lifted from the forward area. By yelling orders to his subalterns, Attlee ensured that the line slowed down. Then, with a cool indifference to his own safety, he ran forward to the next Turkish trench. 'Just as I got there and was sticking my flag in the ground, a shrapnel got me from behind, lifting me up like a big kick,' he recalled.[16] Hit in both the left thigh and the right buttock, he was unable to move and was carried to the stretcher bearers by a member of his company. From the battlefield, he was taken to a dressing station, where he was bandaged up before a long drive to a field hospital at Orah by the Tigris. There his wounds were redressed – 'my legs being pretty painful'[17] – and he began the long voyage aboard a hospital ship, the SS *Valera*, to Bombay in India. During his recuperation at the Coloba hospital he wrote to his brother Tom: 'My wounds are going on nicely but will I expect give me some trouble in the heat.' In the context of their mutual socialism, he added, 'By the way it may interest comrades to know that I was hit while carrying the red flag to victory. I had a large artillery flag of that hue and was just planting it on the parapet when strafed.'[18] His comment about victory was unrealised. The British-Indian attack was repulsed by the Turks; the siege continued and, at the end of April, the Kut garrison surrendered.

Churchill wrote in *The Gathering Storm* that Attlee had 'a fine war record'.[19] Attlee himself was invariably more modest. In 1947, he even wrote to Roy Jenkins, then a young Labour MP working on the first biography of Attlee, 'I doubt whether the chapter on my 1914 to 1918 experiences is worth mentioning as my service was very ordinary.'[20] But Churchill was correct: Attlee's bravery, like his own, was outstanding. Even when Attlee had the chance to opt out, as he did after Mesopotamia in 1916 because of his lameness, he insisted on military service. After more convalescence in England, he was sent to Dorset to join what was called the Heavy Branch of the Machine Gun Corps, an awkward title that concealed the fact that this was the beginning of the Tank Corps, as the unit was officially renamed in July 1917. When Attlee arrived, the Heavy Branch had men but not yet any tanks. Most of the recruits, as Attlee's fellow officer Captain J. K. Wilson noted, were from the coalfields, as it was 'thought at the time that they would be most suitable for working in the cramped space of a tank'.[21]

The new weapon was still in its early stages of deployment, yet its existence owed much to Churchill, who had been the political driving force behind its creation. Soon after the conflict began he wrote to Asquith to suggest that a 'caterpillar system', using armoured 'steam tractors', would 'enable trenches to be crossed quite easily and the weight of the machine would destroy all wire entanglements'.[22] So convinced was Churchill of the possibilities of this development that in February 1915 he not only set up the Landships Committee of the Admiralty but also authorised the expenditure of £70,000 on eighteen prototype machines. One of these prototypes, known as 'Big Willie', was completed by December that year and went into production on a significant scale soon afterwards.

Attlee himself wrote in his autobiography that he 'had an interesting year with the Tanks, going to France twice on instructional tours'.[23] But that was hardly the whole story. In contrast to his usual ease of integration, Attlee had managed to alienate his commanding officer, Major W. S. Poe, and was consequently left behind when the unit embarked on its first full campaign on the Western Front, in March 1917. According to Captain Wilson's account:

> We were all very pleased when Major Poe told us that we had been selected to go to France as a unit, telling us how proud he was to command such a company. 'But there is one officer I shall have to get rid of: that damn fool Attlee.' I protested vigorously against this not only because Attlee and I had become good friends but also because he was a very efficient and experienced officer and well-liked by the men. But my protests were to no avail and Attlee was duly jettisoned.[24]

Attlee's compensation for his exclusion was his promotion to the rank of major but, as he admitted to his brother Tom, he found the decision 'absolutely sickening', believing it was based on prejudice against him because he was an 'Eastern Front' man and not a professional soldier. 'I fancy he wanted a regular,' he wrote.[25] His brother Tom experienced his own harsh treatment. In January 1917, he was jailed as a conscientious objector following the introduction of conscription, a measure that Clement strongly opposed.

Although they did not represent the tank campaign that Attlee wanted, the two instructional tours of France and Belgium in 1917 gave him an insight into Western Front warfare that Churchill had experienced the year before. In an episode similar to Churchill's, Attlee had a lucky escape on the first tour when a dugout he had recently left, at a trench near Loos, took a direct hit. On his return to England after the second tour, he was offered an army-staff job, but, still hoping for action, he transferred back to the infantry and ended up in December at a training camp on the 'windswept' island of Walney near Barrow.[26]

By this stage Churchill was much more content, back at the heart of power. At first his gamble on returning to politics in May 1916 looked like a failure, as he was forced to remain on the backbenches. Even when his old ally Lloyd George took the premiership from Asquith in a daring coup at the end of 1916, Churchill was excluded from the Government because of Tory objections. But his fortunes began to change in 1917, partly through effective performances in the Commons from the Opposition benches. A further crucial factor in the process of rehabilitation was the work of the Dardanelles Commission, an inquiry set up by Asquith in June 1916 to examine the disastrous campaign. Through a wealth of written evidence, Churchill was able to show that he had full political backing for the operation, including that of Asquith. 'I am slowly triumphing in this Dardanelles Commission and bit by bit carrying the whole case,' he told his friend and British Army liaison officer Edward Spears.[27] The shift in the political mood was also helped by divisions in the Tory Party under Bonar Law's inflexible leadership. By July 1917 Lloyd George felt strong enough to bring him back as Minister for Munitions, a vital position in view of the colossal needs of the British armed forces. Churchill proved a highly creative administrator. Haig himself, who in mid-1916 had maliciously suspected that 'poor Winston's head is gone from taking drugs', was impressed by his performance at the Ministry. 'Churchill is doing good work in co-ordinating the work of its numerous branches,' noted Haig in August 1917.[28]

By the last months of the war, Churchill's stock was far higher than would have seemed possible after his resignation three years earlier. From May 1918, Attlee served on the Western Front, the BEF having at last acceded to his wish for a return to action. He joined the 55th Division, based in the Artois region, and once more faced German shelling and sniping. Despite the risks, Attlee found the experience preferable to Mesopotamia and Gallipoli. 'Food was good and plentiful and one got letters and newspapers regularly. One also returned to rest in comfortable beds and could get baths.'[29] His division had expected a massive German offensive against its lines but by August it was clear that the enemy was 'cracking up', to use Attlee's phrase. It was the 55th Division that now began to move forward towards the retreating Germans around Lille. Then, with bathos rather than drama, Attlee's war came to an end. On 24 August, he had just led his men on to a captured German position when he 'got a heavy bump on the back from some timber that was dislodged by a shell'. The blow, serious enough in itself, exacerbated other ailments. 'I had been a long time in the line and was due for leave. My back was painful and I had bad piles and other troubles.' He was seen by a doctor, who operated on his back and ordered that he be sent to recover in England. Taken to the Third London General Hospital in Wandsworth, just across the road from the jail where his brother was incarcerated, Attlee underwent further treatment and suffered an attack of 'huge boils'. His miserable condition was alleviated only by the declaration of Armistice on 11 November, 'which we celebrated in the ward with champagne fetched by some Canadian officers'.[30]

At the eleventh hour that day, Churchill stood at the window of his Ministry, listening to the chimes of Big Ben and watching as enthusiastic crowds filled Whitehall. 'It was with feelings which do not lend themselves to words that I heard the cheers of the brave people who had borne so much and given all, who had never wavered, who had never lost faith in their country,' he wrote in *The World Crisis*.[31] Languishing in a Wandsworth hospital, Clement Attlee had been one of those brave people. The memory of the conflict never left him, as his daughter Janet recalled in a later interview: 'The effect of the First World War on my father was very, very deep but it was shut up inside him. He did not talk much about it. The pain was hidden deep inside him. This was one of the reasons he was so hard to get to know.'[32]

SIX

◆

LIMEHOUSE
AND DUNDEE

T HE END OF the First World War brought a transformation in the British political landscape. In the drive towards full democracy, the franchise had been extended in 1918 to all men over twenty-one and women over thirty. As a result, the size of the electorate had expanded enormously, from 7.6 million to 21.4 million voters. At the same time, the traditional two-party system, which had existed since the mid-Victorian age, was collapsing. The Liberal Party was hopelessly split between the supporters of Lloyd George's Coalition, like Churchill, and the loyalists to the ousted Leader H. H. Asquith. Meanwhile Labour was beginning to mount a real challenge as the authentic voice of the left.

The threat to the Liberals' future could be clearly seen in the General Election of December 1918, which Lloyd George called to give himself a post-war mandate. The Prime Minister reached an agreement with the Conservatives whereby most of his pro-Coalition Liberal candidates would be given a free run in their own constituencies, an arrangement that Asquith dismissively called the 'Coupon'. But there was no such alliance on the progressive side. For the first time the Labour Party decided to fight a General Election as an independent force, having abandoned its long-standing pact with the Liberals. The non-Coupon

Asquithians were reduced to a rump of twenty-six MPs.* After winning fifty-seven seats and 2.2 million votes, 850,000 more than the independent Liberals, Labour were now the largest Opposition party in the Commons.

As a Liberal recipient of the Coupon, Churchill retained his Dundee seat with a strong majority, though ominously a temperance campaigner, Edwin Scrymgeour, also performed well. Churchill's indispensability to the new Government was demonstrated in January 1919 when Lloyd George gave him two posts: one in charge of the War Office; the other at the recently created Air Ministry. As War Secretary one of his main preoccupations, apart from overseeing demobilisation, was the challenge of Soviet rule. Typical of his pugnacious spirit, he wanted to provide British military support to the counter-revolutionary White Russians fighting Lenin's regime, which he regarded as a deadly threat to Western civilisation. But the Cabinet was aghast at this belli-cosity, which awakened memories of the Dardanelles. 'An expensive war of aggression against Russia is a way to strengthen Bolshevism in Russia and create it at home,' Lloyd George warned him.[1] Churchill had to back down, having only strengthened his reputation on the left for reactionary aggression. Attlee himself later wrote that Churchill's policy was 'in disregard of all the lessons of history. Extreme pressure always consolidates a revolutionary regime by evoking patriotism.'[2]

Despite the hostility he provoked, Churchill understood more than most Liberals how British politics was changing. Beyond his Cabinet and departmental work there lurked a profound concern about the impact of Labour. The left-wing *Daily Herald* was right when it said that 'the nearer socialism comes, the more frantic gets Mr Churchill'.[3] He feared that the continuing advance of Labour would mean not only the destruction of the Liberals but also the introduction of a doctrinaire ideology into Britain. 'Winston said that he was all out to fight Labour.

* This figure is from A. J. P. Taylor's *English History*. Others put the independent-Liberal total slightly higher, at thirty-nine, but at this time of flux party labels were not always clearly defined. A small group of Coalition Labour MPs were also returned with Coupon support.

It was his one object in politics,' recorded the diplomat Duff Cooper after dinner with Churchill in January 1920, adding that this goal was making him 'splendidly reactionary'.[4] Others also sensed that, in the face of Labour's threat, he was returning to conservatism. 'Winston's tendency is all to the right and his principles are more Tory,' recorded the maverick peer Lord Beaverbrook in March 1922, by which time Churchill had become Colonial Secretary.[5]

In practical terms, Churchill had a three-pronged strategy for combating Labour. The first was to step up the ferocity of his rhetoric, as shown in an explosive speech in January 1920 when he described Labour as 'quite unfitted for the responsibility of Government' because of their attachment to class conflict and the break-up of the Empire.[6] His second theme, in direct contrast to such inflammatory language, was to urge the introduction of social measures to lessen working-class discontent. So, in an echo of his radicalism at the Board of Trade, he called for better social housing, rail nationalisation, a capital levy to crack down on war profiteering and a programme to alleviate unemployment. The third strand was his renewal of his long-held desire to form a powerful centrist group – a concept also endorsed by his close friend Lord Birkenhead, formerly F. E. Smith, the formidable but distrusted Conservative Lord Chancellor whose brilliance was dimmed by his alcoholism. Churchill and Smith had been dreaming of such an alliance since the Edwardian age, and the mix of the ruling Coalition and the danger of Labour rule gave an ideal opportunity to press this case. Effectively, both men wanted the Liberal-Conservative Coalition to become a solid front in the fight against socialism. At Loughborough in early 1922 Churchill set out his demand for a 'strong, united, permanent national party, Liberal, Progressive and Pacific in its outlook' that would give Britain 'five years of public thrift and trade recovery'.[7]

Attlee, in his own quiet way, manoeuvred in exactly the opposite direction, working for the triumph of socialism in Britain. Demobilised in January 1919, he had settled back into his job as lecturer as the London School of Economics, while throwing himself once more into local

Labour politics. In March 1919 he ran in Limehouse for the London County Council (LCC), emphasising his war service as 'Major Attlee' and his long commitment to the district. Although he lost narrowly to a popular Liberal baker, his campaign had sufficiently impressed for him to be nominated as Labour's parliamentary candidate in the Limehouse constituency at the next General Election. Despite his innate modesty, Attlee was delighted – especially because Labour were widely predicted to win the Limehouse seat. With his political prospects looking bright, he now needed a more permanent home in the area. Here again the inheritance from his father proved useful, for he was able to take a lease on a large dilapidated property called Norway House on the Commercial Road in Limehouse. Attlee renovated it, then rented out the top two floors, took the first floor as a flat for himself and handed over the ground floor to the Limehouse Labour Party for use as a club room and meeting place. To complete the domestic arrangements, Attlee employed a male housekeeper, Charlie 'Griff' Griffiths, an ex-serviceman who had been through Haileybury House. As Griffiths noted, Attlee's work inspired widespread respect in the area. 'They all knew about him. You could be in a Limehouse pub and run down the Tories, you could run down the Labour Party, but if you ran down the Major, somebody might come up and give you the old one-two.'[8]

Attlee's stature was further enhanced by the Stepney Borough Council elections in November 1919. As a local parliamentary candidate, Attlee was dissuaded from standing, but he was the architect of a local Labour campaign that saw the party win forty-three out of sixty seats to form Stepney's first socialist administration. In a further tribute to Attlee's growing local influence, the councillors unanimously co-opted him to be the Mayor of Stepney. From this position at the top of the municipality, he immediately began to implement some of the socialist policies he had propounded since moving to the East End, such as the introduction of free milk for children and the recruitment of health visitors. For all his diffidence, Attlee managed to exude a natural authority as Stepney mayor. The spare, headmasterly style of chairmanship, which future ministers came to know so well at Cabinet, was already in evidence in the council chamber. A profile in the *East London Observer* said that he spoke in 'intensely concentrated, firm – almost curt – precise and unmistakable sentences'.[9] Attlee was also making his mark beyond Limehouse. He was a regular speaker at ILP and Labour gatherings, his unflappable manner masking his shyness. What struck Manny Shinwell, later one of Attlee's more unreliable ministers, at the ILP Conference in 1920 was the contrast between his voice and his geographical affiliation: 'He spoke with such a polite accent. I could hardly believe that he represented a dockland and working-class area.'[10]

For all the heaviness of his political schedule and the camaraderie of Norway House, Attlee felt as lonely as he had done before the war. This feeling was compounded in 1920 when he lost both his sister Dorothy and his mother, Ellen, whose death entailed the sale of the family home in Putney. But, in the summer of the following year, his life underwent an unexpected transformation when he took a holiday to Italy with Cedric Millar, a friend of his brother Tom. Eric asked if he could bring his youngest sister, Violet, along – a request to which Attlee readily agreed without knowing the profound impact that his decision would have. From almost the first moment he saw the attractive twenty-five-year-old, he fell in love, his ardour increasing as they travelled through the romantic settings of Tuscany and Umbria. The daughter of an export merchant, Violet Millar had been born in Hampstead, one of eleven children. Like Clement, she was shy, a trait that was reinforced by her feeling of living in the shadow of her twin sister, Olive, who was more outgoing and academically gifted. While Olive graduated from Cambridge, Violet did not go to university and instead after leaving school stayed at home with her widowed mother. By 1921, companionship had turned to care as her mother became ill. It was a filial duty for which she was well equipped, having been a nurse in a convalescent hospital during the First World War. But that summer she was looking for release from her routine, and Attlee was the man to provide it. As he waxed about northern Italy's Renaissance marvels, which he had studied with such relish at Oxford, she reciprocated his love.

He proposed soon after their return to England. Her acceptance made Attlee, in his own words, 'as mad as a March hare with joy'.[11] They were married on 10 January 1922 at Christ Church, Hampstead, with their two ordained elder brothers jointly presiding over the ceremony. On their return to London after a honeymoon of golf and walking in Dorset, they started the search for a new home, since Attlee understandably felt that the bachelor flat he shared with Charlie Griffiths at Norway House was unsuitable for married life. They quickly found one, a semi-detached property in the Essex suburb of Woodford, where they soon began a family. 'Clem and I didn't have any sex problems. Everything was marvellous from the start,' Violet told one of her daughters.[12] They went on to have four children, a boy and three girls. Like the Churchills', the Attlee marriage was a generally happy one despite all the pressures of public life. Indeed, reflecting their devotion to their respective spouses, both Winston and Clement appear to have remained faithful during their marriages. Similarly, both Clementine, highly intelligent, and Violet, highly spirited, were both full of pride for their husbands. There was, however, a crucial difference. Clementine, a strong Liberal, shared her husband's politics when they married, whereas Violet cared little for socialism. She joined the Labour Party after Attlee became Leader; but this was out of marital loyalty rather than ideological conversion, as her daughter Janet recalled: 'He would explain to her his views and she would listen, but she was basically still a conservative person in her thoughts. She did not really understand his politics, though she supported him in what he did.'[13]

As Attlee was leaving Norway House to start his married life in Woodford, Churchill was going through his own domestic upheaval. The second year of the decade had been an emotionally shattering one for him and Clementine. On 29 June Winston's mother, Jennie, died in agonising circumstances, aged only sixty-seven. She had slipped downstairs and broken her ankle; gangrene had developed in her wound, resulting in the amputation of her leg. Soon after the operation, she succumbed to a fatal haemorrhage. 'These last weeks have been cruel and in spite of her courage, which was amazing. Their weight wore her down. We had reason and authority for hoping that the immediate dangers were warded off and surmounted. But the expected end was mercifully swift,' Churchill told the press tycoon Lord Northcliffe.[14] There was an even more painful descent into grief shortly afterwards when Churchill's youngest child, Marigold – known as 'Duckalilly' in the family – caught a bad chill during a seaside holiday in Broadstairs. Tragically, the illness turned into septicaemia and she died on 23 August. Having rushed to her bedside, both parents were there at the end. Winston wept copiously. Clemmie, according to her husband's secretary, 'screamed like an animal undergoing torture'.[15] The infant was buried in Kensal Green Cemetery three days later.

Yet in 1922 the clouds began to lift. In September, Clementine gave birth to another girl, Mary, who turned out to be the most balanced and contented of the four Churchill children; for the other three, Diana, Randolph and Sarah, all born before the war, had chequered lives beset by alcoholism, mental breakdowns and tempestuous marriages. That year also saw Churchill's home life became more physically anchored with the purchase of Chartwell, the part-Elizabethan manor house in Kent that he infused with the idiosyncratic grandeur of his personality as he turned it into the base of his literary and political endeavours. Before Chartwell, he and Clemmie had been leading a somewhat nomadic existence since his time at the Admiralty. After leaving 33 Eccleston Square, they had lived at an array of London addresses, some rented, some purchased, but nothing had been satisfactory. The couple had not been helped by Churchill's habitual money problems – worsened by his lack of journalism after 1917 because of ministerial office, for which the salaries were inadequate compensation. By 1921, his loans and overdraft stood at £28,000. But then his fortunes were dramatically improved by two bequests: one from his late mother's estate; the other from his relative Lord Herbert Vane-Tempest. 'It is like floating on a bath of cream,' he told Clemmie after the news of the second legacy.[16] The money enabled Churchill to pay off his debts, move financially into surplus for the first time in twenty years and buy

Chartwell for £5000. The prosperity did not last long, partly because the capital works on refashioning the house came to almost £30,000 and partly because of its heavy running costs. 'It's a charming place with a wonderful view and Winston is ruining himself over it – so at least Clemmie says. She is really quite sad about it,' wrote Duff Cooper after a visit there in 1924.[17]

The acquisition of Chartwell and the arrival of Mary may have thrilled Churchill, but his political fortunes suffered a catastrophic downturn in the autumn of 1922 when Lloyd George's Coalition fell. The immediate cause was widespread opposition to the Prime Minister's plan, backed by Churchill, to embark on military action against Turkish forces under the nationalist leader General Ataturk. Most Conservative MPs, long alienated by working with Lloyd George and Churchill, wanted to restore the independence of their party. The Turkish crisis gave them their opportunity for a break, which they seized at a meeting in the Carlton Club on 19 October, voting decisively to end the Coalition. Lloyd George had no alternative but to resign and call a General Election. For the first time, Attlee and Churchill were candidates in the same contest. At Limehouse, Attlee was up against the sitting pro-Lloyd George Liberal Sir William Pearce, a chemical manufacturer who had held the seat since 1906 and, despite the Carlton Club vote, had the support of the Conservative Party. Buttressed by a strong Labour machine and his own local popularity, Attlee ran on an unashamedly radical platform. 'Instead of the exploitation of the mass of people in the interests of a small rich class, I demand the organisation of the country in the interests of all as a co-operative commonwealth,' he declared in his election address.[18] In a newsletter to constituents his agent John Beckett, who later became a Labour MP before joining the fascist movement, extolled the virtues of Attlee's character: 'In his private life, it is difficult to express in cold type the essential loveableness of the man. Extremely shy, he masks his nervousness beneath a somewhat reserved exterior. Only on more close acquaintance is it possible to realise to the full the great love for his fellow human beings and the flame of service with which this man is lit.'[19]

North of the border in Dundee, Churchill faced a much more embittered fight. In this two-member constituency, he was up against not only Scrymgeour the Prohibitionist but also three others: an independent Asquithian Liberal; the charismatic communist Willie Gallacher; and an official Labour candidate, the distinguished writer and anti-war campaigner Edmund Morel. Churchill's hold on the seat was already precarious because of the Coalition's unpopularity as a result of the post-war depression. He was also physically constrained from full participation in the campaign because on 18 October he was struck down with acute appendicitis. After the operation to remove his appendix, he spent most of the period up to polling in bed at his London flat, only travelling to Scotland for the last four days. When he finally arrived in Dundee, looking pale and exhausted, he was unable to stand for the first set of hustings and thus spoke seated from a specially constructed chair. Most of his speech focused on his view of the contrast between socialism and liberalism. 'Socialism would destroy private interests; Liberalism would preserve private interests by reconciling them with the public right,' ran one passage.[20] In his next appearance, he was subjected to such rowdy heckling that he had to abandon his address after only a few paragraphs. 'As I was carried through the yelling crowd of socialists to the platform, I was struck by the looks of passionate hatred on the faces of some of the younger men and women. Indeed but for my helpless condition, I am sure they would have attacked me,' he wrote.[21]

The raw hostility presaged a heavy defeat. Scrymgeour, who topped the poll,* and Morel, the runner-up, were both elected. Churchill was pushed into a fourth place, with almost 12,000 fewer votes than Morel. It was a humiliation that reflected his own poor campaign and the continuing decline of Liberalism in post-war Britain. Even after the Carlton Club vote, the two wings of the Liberal Party were not reconciled and consequently badly weakened. The Asquithians won just sixty-two seats; Lloyd George's followers fifty-three. Lloyd George

---

* He was the only Prohibitionist ever elected in British politics.

was the only one of the senior Coalition Liberal Cabinet ministers in 1922 who kept his seat.

Labour gained eighty-five seats, taking their number of MPs to 142 – significantly more than the combined Liberal total – and became the Official Opposition to the triumphant new Tory Government. Attlee's own contest in Limehouse was emblematic of the shift; he won by 1,899 votes, a substantial majority in a constituency with a small electorate. For the first time, Attlee had overtaken Churchill in the political stakes. The pipe-smoking municipal activist was in Parliament, the mighty former Cabinet minister in the wilderness. Churchill now found himself, as he later wittily put it, 'without an office, without a seat, without a party and without an appendix'.[22] He sought consolation in his family, in holidaying in the south of France and in continuing his epic, multi-volume work on the war, *The World Crisis*, the first part of which was published in April 1923 to enormous acclaim and phenomenal sales. The subsequent volumes appeared over the next eight years, building up into what is widely considered Churchill's greatest literary work. He also found solace in painting, the pursuit he had first taken up after his Gallipoli downfall in 1915. Despite a lack of formal tutoring, he certainly had a talent for the art, with an impressive ability to convey light and atmosphere on canvas. When asked in November 1922 his opinion of Churchill's pictures, the great painter Augustus John said, 'I consider them to be very promising. Of course he requires more practice and if he contemplates being a serious artist, he will have to give up everything else and devote himself entirely to art.'[23] Churchill had no intention of abandoning politics. He wanted to be back where Attlee now was: in the Commons.

After Attlee retired, in the 1950s, Violet told his biographer, 'Clem was never really a socialist.'[24] That was a serious misreading of her husband's political history. Throughout his life he had been a principled adherent of socialism, though his beliefs were always tempered by pragmatism and tolerance. But it was probably in the 1920s that, flushed by electoral success, he was at his most radical. That spirit shone through his maiden speech, which called for greater government action to combat joblessness. 'Why was it that in the war,' he asked his fellow MPs, 'we were able to find employment for everyone?'[25] Despite his status as a parliamentary novice, Attlee had already built something of a name in Labour circles through his work in the East End. 'I've heard good accounts of a fellow named Attlee,' said Ramsay MacDonald, when he made him one of his Parliamentary Private Secretaries in his official capacity as Leader of the Opposition.[26] Attlee's political advancement was not matched by comfort on the domestic front, however; after the birth of their first child, Janet, in February 1923, Violet became ill and depressed, requiring treatment at a Hertfordshire clinic to deal with over-anxiety.

The strain she felt at the turbulence of political life was about to be repeated. Only six months after he had led the Conservatives to victory, Andrew Bonar Law was forced to resign as Prime Minister after he was diagnosed with terminal throat cancer. Law's successor was the Chancellor of the Exchequer Stanley Baldwin, whose manufactured image of the bluff Worcestershire squire hid a complex mix of shrewdness, fear, lethargy and subtlety. Not long into his premiership, he dramatically revived the dormant but incendiary issue of protection by appealing to the country for an electoral mandate to introduce tariffs. Apart from his genuine wish to protect British manufacturing, his twofold political aims were to unite the Tory Party and, more cynically, to revive the Liberals by bringing them together under the free-trade banner, thereby taking progressive support away from Labour. At a meeting in Chequers with the Canadian Prime Minister Mackenzie King, Baldwin explained that he 'felt that one effect of the campaign would be to restore the old political parties and prevent Labour, as a class, from attaining power'.[27] The attempt to cement the fractured Liberal Party temporarily succeeded in Churchill's case. Since his defeat at Dundee, he had been sliding back towards the Tories, seeing little future for Liberalism or his dreams of a coalition. Over lunch with the former Chancellor Sir Robert Horne, Churchill reportedly said, 'I am what I have always been – a Tory Democrat. Force of circumstance has compelled me to serve with another party, but my views have never changed, and I would be glad to give effect to them but rejoining the Conservatives.'[28]

But now his opposition to protection quashed the idea of his return to the Tories. On 11 November 1923, he told the press that free trade was 'vital to the British people and indispensable to the recovery of their prosperity'.[29] Little more than a week later, with the General Election looming, he accepted an invitation to stand in Leicester West for the reunited Liberal Party under Asquith. Fully recovered from his illness, Churchill fought a more spirited campaign than he had done in Dundee, but to no avail. At the poll on 6 December he trailed badly behind the Labour candidate, Frederick Pethick-Lawrence, later to be the India Secretary in Attlee's first Government. The wider result in the country was momentous. Baldwin's scheme to galvanise his own party at Labour's expense backfired. The Tories lost eighty-eight seats and Labour gained forty-nine to take their representation to 191 MPs – among them Attlee, who more than trebled his majority at Limehouse.

Asquith, with his combined Liberal force of 158 seats, held the balance of power. In theory, he could have propped up the Conservatives or even tried to revive the Coalition. But in practice he felt that the Tories had to go after the electorate's rejection of their manifesto. He was therefore willing to put Labour in, privately assuming that they would soon collapse and he would emerge from the wreckage as the Prime Minister. But the prospect of MacDonald's party in office appalled Churchill. He felt everything possible must be done to avoid such an eventuality. His two recent defeats at Labour's hands had made him despise socialism more than ever, reinforcing his belief in the need for a unified anti-Labour front. His friend Duff Cooper noted in his diary on 15 January 1924 how vexed Churchill had become: 'I had some heated arguments with Winston. He is very anxious to prevent at all costs a Labour Government from coming into power.'[30] Three days later Churchill went public with his misgivings by writing a letter to *The Times* in which he conjured the vision of a dark future for Britain if Labour were not kept from power. 'The enthronement in office of a

Socialist Government will be a serious national misfortune such as has usually befallen great states only on the morrow of defeat in war.'[31]

His bleak warnings were fruitless. Asquith felt Labour were too weak to be a real national danger, while the Liberals would be badly damaged by any renewed alliance with the Conservatives. His stance was decisive. On the evening of 21 January Baldwin's Government was defeated in the Commons. The next morning the King sent for Ramsay MacDonald to form the first Labour administration. There had been some debate in the Labour movement as to whether MacDonald should accept office, given that his party's lack of a parliamentary majority would make it difficult to push through socialist policies. But MacDonald believed that the experience of office would enhance Labour's credibility as the alternative to the Tories, a view that was shared by Attlee. 'The British elector is very sceptical of anything he has not seen,' he once wrote.[32] Little more than a year after entering Parliament, Attlee was given his first ministerial job, as MacDonald appointed him Under-Secretary at the War Office. It was a move welcomed even by the robustly conservative *Morning Post*, which stated that 'Major Attlee has the recommendation of excellent war service'.[33] The position was an awkward one for a socialist in the circumstances of the early 1920s, for within the Labour movement, especially the ILP, there was little enthusiasm for either the armed forces or military expenditure when there were so many other demands on the public purse. Indeed, soon after taking office, Attlee had to preside over cuts in the defence estimates of £7 million.

But his brisk efficiency and war experience also meant he was able to establish a rapport with the army. Alongside him was his friend the former coalminer Jack Lawson, the Financial Secretary at the War Office, who later recalled that Attlee 'was a master of detail, which means much in a department. Patient, then caustic, he fitted the Department.'[34] Attlee's competence was part of a pattern. The dark forebodings about a national catastrophe were left unfulfilled by the advent of Labour. To allay fears about socialism, MacDonald was keen on respectability, even urging his ministers to wear official court uniform for their appointments at the Palace. Few radical measures were attempted, apart from a Housing Act that required local authorities to build more homes to rent.

For Churchill, the first Labour Government was a turning point in his own political fortunes. He felt that Asquith had effectively signed the Liberals' death warrant. His shift towards conservatism now resumed – a move that accelerated when Stanley Baldwin announced in February 1924 that protection would be dropped from the party's programme. The last obstacle appeared to have been removed from Churchill's path back to the Tory fold. When Churchill openly expressed his support for the Conservative candidate in the Burnley by-election that month against Labour, the *Glasgow Herald* commented that Churchill was 'undoubtedly preparing the way of return to the party he left many years ago'.[35] But many Tories were reluctant to welcome the apparently reformed apostate.

SEVEN

◆

TREASURY

Throughout his public life, Churchill had a gift for bringing commotion and controversy to almost everything he touched. That was never truer than at the Abbey by-election in March 1924, when his unorthodox candidature sparked weeks of excitement and strife in a four-way contest. The by-election was caused by the death of the sitting Tory MP Brigadier John Nicholson, who had held the Abbey division of Westminster since 1921. As soon as he heard of the vacancy, Churchill sensed an opportunity to return to the Commons and step up his fight against socialism. Having spent almost twenty years as a Liberal, he was not yet ready to embrace fully the Conservative label, but he hoped to run as an independent anti-socialist with the support of the local Abbey Tory association.

At first the signs of Tory backing seemed good. Conservative Central Office, he wrote, was 'working tooth and nail to secure me the support of the official Unionist Association, though I made it clear I intended to stand as an Independent candidate with Liberal as well as Conservative supporters'.[1] Much of the Tory high command was on his side, he believed, because if he were returned to Parliament he could then give a lead to the band of about thirty Liberals who opposed Asquith's collusion with Labour and might become allies of the Conservatives. As he told his wife in a letter of 24 February, such an anti-socialist front was more badly needed than ever because 'MacDonald is making a great impression on the country and there is no doubt that he is bringing numerous adherents'. An independent position, he concluded, was the best way to counter this trend. 'Of course if I stood as a Conservative it would almost certainly be a walk over. But I cannot do this, and it is far better for all the interests we are safeguarding that I should carry with me moderate Liberals.'[2]

Speculation about the forthcoming by-election gripped the press. The *Morning Post*, referring to the idea of a united anti-socialist alliance, said that 'there is no difference of principle which separates Liberals and Conservatives',[3] though the *People* struck a far more negative tone: 'Mr Churchill has few worshippers in England, where his erratic conduct for years past has excited suspicion and created hostility.'[4] The majority in the local Conservative association felt some of the same antipathy. Despite pressure from Central Office, the Abbey Tories decided to put up their own candidate under the official party banner. Their choice was Otho Nicholson, the nephew of the deceased member. Unperturbed, Churchill announced on 4 March that he would stand as an independent anti-socialist, under the title 'Constitutionalist'.

The Abbey campaign began two days later. It was 'incomparably the most exciting, stirring, sensational election I ever fought', Churchill later wrote.[5] The elements of this sensation included Churchill's own vibrant personality, the volatile nature of party politics and the glamorous nature of the constituency, which featured the West End at its heart. 'Dukes, jockeys, prize fighters, courtiers, actors and businessmen all developed a keen partisanship. The chorus girls of Daly's Theatre sat up all night addressing the envelopes and dispatching the election address,' he recalled.[6] As well as the Conservative Nicholson, Churchill also faced a Liberal candidate, Scott Duckers, and Labour's Fenner Brockway, both of whom had been conscientious objectors in the First World War. But Brockway's pacifism was no bar to an energetic Labour campaign that made Churchill its prime target. Churchill's meetings were regularly interrupted by hecklers; his past record, particularly the Dardanelles campaign and his anti-Bolshevik agitation, was vociferously condemned. 'Nobody in British politics inspired more dislike in Labour circles than Winston Churchill,' recalled Manny Shinwell.[7]

Yet in the face of all this aggressive electioneering, there was one Labour voice that indirectly came to Churchill's defence: that of the Under-Secretary for War Clement Attlee. As a sign of his growing authority, Attlee was asked to speak on Brockway's behalf on 11 March and he did so in a manner that mixed mockery with a degree of admiration. 'I was in some of Mr Churchill's shows,' he told his audience. 'I was in Sidney Street as a spectator and I believe it was the escape of Peter the Painter that sent Winston off on his anti-Russian mood. I was in Gallipoli but I will give the devil his due. I think that Mr Churchill was right about Gallipoli.'[8] Attlee then concluded that he 'did not deny Mr Churchill a certain idealism but it was an idealism that was most unfortunate for the rank and file of the country'.[9]

Attlee's remark about Gallipoli drew him, for the first time, to the attention of Churchill, who had to campaign against a barrage of invective from Labour supporters. The virulence of the Opposition reached its climax at a meeting on 15 March at Pepys Hall on Rochester Row, where a crowd of 300 people gathered. According to the *Observer*'s account:

> The Socialists began to hurl epithets. 'Murderer', 'traitor', 'dog', they shouted. Mr Churchill was stung to protest against the Socialist habit of using 'abusive, foul, lying parrot cries' and mentioned in the street outside that he had heard shouts of Gallipoli. As a counter to that particular parrot cry, he quoted Major Attlee, the Labour Minister, who a few days ago generously, if in terms not conspicuous for good taste, had said, 'to give the devil his due, he was right about Gallipoli'.

But the reference to Attlee made no difference. Churchill had to sit down 'on the cover of a piano keyboard' while the hecklers set up a chant of 'We don't want you'. He rose to his feet again but the abuse became only louder, forcing him to abandon his speech. As he did so he complained that 'half a dozen men had prevented our enjoyment of the greatest possession of the British race – the exercise of free speech. It is a crime against democracy.'[10]

The opposition to Churchill from the official Tory side, while lacking such venom, was still powerful and may have swayed the hard-fought contest. After a re-count, Nicholson was elected with 8,187 votes, just 43 ahead of Churchill, whose demeanour was captured by the *Daily Express*'s correspondent at the scene. 'Mr Churchill was white and his smile hardened into a fierce, gripped mouth. The cigar he chewed was sodden, with dead ashes at the end. He looked at no man, not even Mrs Churchill, who was crying silently.'[11] In the immediate aftermath of his third successive parliamentary defeat, Churchill found little comfort in the closeness of the result. One of those standing near him at the declaration was Francis Williams, then working as a journalist for the trade union NALGO* and later to be Attlee's press officer in Downing Street. Despite his left-wing outlook, Williams had been beguiled by the campaign of Churchill, who 'made his opponents look like mediocre sheep. All the fire and glamour were with him.' At the re-count, recalled Williams, 'I saw that he was in tears. He made no attempt to hide them. His face crumpled like a baby's as his wife patted his arm. Absurdly, I felt tears coming into my own eyes in sympathy.' At this outpouring, Churchill tried to console Williams. 'Don't worry, young man, we will fight and win another day.' Williams then had to explain to Churchill that he was not one of his supporters. 'In that event, your emotion does you all the more credit.'[12]

For all his lachrymosity, Churchill's performance had been both creditable and significant. He had revealed not only the need for more vigour in the fight against Labour but also that he was too valuable a resource to be ignored by the Tories, especially now that the independent Liberal Party appeared to be an irrelevance, its vote having collapsed in the by-election. In May 1924, two months after the Abbey contest, Churchill addressed a large Conservative rally in Liverpool, the first

---

* National Association of Local Government Officers. While keeping the same acronym, the union changed its name in 1952 to the National and Local Government Officers' Association.

time since the early Edwardian age that he had taken to the platform at an exclusively Tory event. In his speech, he fulminated against every aspect of Labour policy, from the economy to empire, arguing that only the Conservatives commanded enough popular support 'for the successful defeat of socialism'.[13] After the meeting, having received prolonged applause, Churchill told his hosts that 'it's just like coming home'.[14] The die had been cast. There was now enough momentum behind Churchill to sustain his re-emergence as a Conservative-backed candidate. With the backing of the Tory chairman Sir Stanley Jackson and a number of City financiers, he was adopted by the local association in the safe Essex constituency of Epping in September. He did not have to wait long for the chance to prove his renewed Tory credentials. By the autumn of 1924 the minority Labour Government was beset by crises over unemployment, industrial disputes, the League of Nations (LoN) and diplomatic recognition of the Soviet Union. The downfall came on 6 October 1924, when Labour lost a confidence motion over accusations of political interference in the judicial process.

The General Election that followed was the third in two years. Labour lost forty seats, though their vote share actually increased by almost 1 million. Amid a further drastic decline in the Liberal vote, the Tories enjoyed a majority of over 200, the biggest Conservative victory since the advent of democracy in Britain. The lack of any effective Liberal challenge meant that both Churchill and Attlee won easily, Attlee in Limehouse by a majority of over 6,000 against his Tory opponent and Churchill in Epping by over 10,000. They were now both sitting in Parliament at the same time, at the start of an association that was to last for the next forty years. By another of those coincidental links, Attlee, whose family home was in Monkham's Avenue, Woodford, had also become one of Churchill's constituents. Indeed, soon after the General Election, Attlee suggested to the Parliamentary Labour Party (PLP) that each MP should, for campaign purposes, 'adopt' a Tory constituency as well as his or her own. 'I have offered to adopt a number of constituencies, including the Epping Division represented by Mr Churchill,' he said, but the idea attracted little enthusiasm.[15]

Churchill's rehabilitation into the Conservative cause was trium-phantly confirmed when Stanley Baldwin appointed him Chancellor of the Exchequer, partly on the grounds that the Treasury would act as a constraint on his exuberance and taste for confrontation. 'He said he'd give Winston the Exchequer where he wouldn't be able to talk about Labour, nothing but finance,' recorded Baldwin's friend Kathleen Hilton Young.[16] When Baldwin summoned him to make him the offer, Churchill was astounded, but he kept his feelings to himself. According to his account of their meeting, the Prime Minister asked, '"Will you go to the Treasury?" I should have liked to have answered, "Will the bloody duck swim?" but as it was a formal and important conversation, I replied, "This fulfils my ambition. I still have my father's robe as Chancellor. I shall be proud to serve you in this splendid office."'[17]

Churchill had little direct experience of economics, and was a hopeless manager of his own finances. Once, when referring to senior Treasury and Bank of England officials, he said, 'I wish they were admirals or generals. I can sink them if necessary. But when I am talking to bankers and economists after a while they begin to talk Persian and sink me.'[18] Attlee later claimed that Churchill 'was completely out of his depth with finance'.[19] This was an exaggeration. Churchill was always a supremely self-confident politician, brimming with ideas in every sphere. On the economy, he still adhered to the principles that had guided him since the Victorian age, based on his belief in free markets, fiscal responsibility and social reform. His most far-reaching decision was his reluctant acceptance in the spring of 1925 of Britain's return to the Gold Standard at the exchange rate that had prevailed before the First World War. He had been deeply sceptical about this step, fearing that, as he wrote in a memorandum to the Treasury civil servant Sir Otto Niemeyer, the Gold Standard could end up 'like a millstone round the neck of industry and on the public revenue until they become demoralised'.[20] But Churchill was unable to resist the weight of the ruling orthodoxy. After months of internal debate, he bowed to expert opinion. The decision later came to be seen as a disastrous one, with exactly the consequences of job losses and weakened manufacturing that Churchill had predicted. He himself confessed that it was 'the biggest blunder of my life',[21] while Attlee pithily called it 'unwise'.[22] But much of this condemnation was made with the benefit of hindsight. At the time, there was far less controversy. Even the Labour front bench was muted in its opposition. Only a few voices – like those of the economist John Maynard Keynes and the Liberal industrialist Sir Alfred Mond – raised strong protests.

The return to the Gold Standard was the centrepiece of Churchill's 1925 Budget, which balanced increases in pensions and death duties with reductions in both supertax and the standard rate of income tax. The Financial Statement was generally well received; 'a great triumph', said Chamberlain, who felt that Labour were 'thoroughly frightened'.[23] But Attlee showed hostility rather anxiety when he had the chance to challenge Churchill's policy. Now in his third year as an MP, he had so far spoken infrequently in the House and, when he had, he had made little impression with his dry, utilitarian style. 'Just an ordinary person, nothing spectacular, hardly going far,' was Manny Shinwell's verdict.[24] But in June 1925, the Finance Bill led him to give the chamber a muscular socialist analysis of the failings of the British economy and the Conservatives' plans for tax cuts. His language was sufficiently provocative to incite his first parliamentary clash with Churchill. 'Unionist members confound capital with private ownership of capital. I suggest that the use of available money by the Chancellor of the Exchequer as an investment for the nation would be better than its investment in the names of a few capitalists. We have not nearly enough capital in public hands.' At this point Churchill interrupted sarcastically, 'As in Russia.' To which Attlee replied that his own knowledge of Russia was not as great as Churchill's. 'My knowledge of Gallipoli comes from taking part in a campaign there, and his knowledge of Russia comes from the campaign he waged against her.' Attlee then returned to the socialist thrust of his speech: 'The trouble in this country is the existence of an enormous rentier class who draw money without working for it and deflect industry to the production of luxuries. The Chancellor of the Exchequer is deliberately putting

money into pockets of that class.' Churchill immediately responded
with a classic defence of the private sector. Attlee's speech, he said,

> was a spirited argument for the abolition of the capitalist
> system. No doubt that argument has done duty on many
> occasions and has received and will again receive its measure
> of popular applause. [Laughter.] The Member for Limehouse
> is in favour of a much greater development of state trading and
> he points out how much more fertile the national assets are in
> the hands of the nation. But the Government view is that the
> development of our national resources is more fruitful and rapid
> under private enterprise.[25]

In April 1926, Attlee launched another, much more personal attack on
Churchill's tax cuts, which he said had hurt state revenues and forced the
Government to take £1.1 million from the Insurance Fund for armed-
forces personnel. Soldiers, sailors and airmen had not contributed to
the fund, he told the House, so that the money would 'go to relieve the
needs of the Chancellor of the Exchequer who finds himself in difficulties owing to his over-generosity to his wealthy income taxpayers
and super tax payers last year'. Warming to his theme, Attlee then
questioned the morality of Churchill's action. 'It is an extraordinary
thing because the Chancellor of the Exchequer, who actually served
in the War, collects moneys which became due in respect of those who
died in the War and puts them to the benefit for the most part of people
who did not take part in the War, but did well out of it.' He concluded
that 'this is the meanest dodge that even the present Chancellor of the
Exchequer has produced'.[26]

Only weeks after this verbal assault, Attlee and Churchill were on
opposite sides during the greatest crisis to hit the second Baldwin
Government, when the TUC called a General Strike at the beginning of
May. The mass walkout, unique in British history, was the culmination
of a long-running dispute in the coal industry, in which the colliery
owners were pressing for pay reductions and longer hours from the

miners. Within the Cabinet, there were divisions about the required toughness of the official response. Baldwin, a natural conciliator, was in favour of a calm, measured approach. In contrast, Churchill was the leader of the ministerial militants who felt that the strike had to be crushed or the stability of the civic order might collapse. 'I am quite ready for a fight this time with the Coal Miners,' he wrote just before the strike began.[27] In the absence of most newspapers, Churchill was given the job of producing the Government's own daily bulletin, called the *British Gazette*, a publication that mirrored his own uncompromising approach to the strike. John Davidson, the Tory minister who worked alongside him at the *Gazette*, saw the best and worst of Churchill during those fraught days. 'He thinks he is Napoleon,' wrote Davidson, describing how Churchill distracted staff, caused problems with distribution and pushed people beyond their capacity. But Davidson also admitted that he was 'a most remarkable creature' whose drive made the *British Gazette* possible. 'He is the sort of man whom, if I wanted a mountain to be moved, I should send for at once.'[28] Attlee later said that the Tory talk of politicised unrest was both duplicitous and overdone. The Government's economic policy was to blame, he argued, for creating the climate in which industrial discontent flourished. Yet despite his position as a Labour frontbencher and friend of the miners' union, Attlee played no national part in the strike. His involvement was confined entirely to Stepney, where, as an alderman and chairman of the municipal Electricity Committee, he conducted negotiations with the TUC representatives over the maintenance of supplies to essential public services.

For all the conflict it engendered, the strike did not last long. After just nine days, it was called off by the TUC with few concessions having been made by the Government, though the miners' embittered dispute continued. During the remainder of his spell as Chancellor, Churchill's biggest project was the comprehensive reform of local-government finance through the abolition of the rates in agriculture, and their extensive reduction in industry and on the railways, with the shortfall in municipal revenues made up by central block grants paid for by new taxes. His proposal was largely implemented, though the drawn-out process of negotiation in Cabinet drained Chamberlain, who compared Churchill to 'a brilliant wayward child who compels admiration but who wears out his guardians with the constant strain he puts on them'.[29] Fellow Cabinet minister William Bridgeman was more forgiving. Having called Churchill 'the most indescribable and amazing character of all my colleagues', Bridgeman wrote in his diary that 'with all his peculiarities and irritating methods, one cannot help liking him, and his ability and vitality are marvellous'.[30]

Attlee made little impact in the Commons during the later 1920s, but he could not be blamed entirely for his parliamentary anonymity, for in 1927 he was nominated by MacDonald to serve on the Indian Statutory Commission, a body set up under the Liberal peer Sir John Simon to look at the possibilities of progress towards a form of self-government in the subcontinent. Attlee, having the responsibility of a young family, was reluctant to accept but the Labour Leader insisted. Membership of the Simon Commission, as it was known, entailed a couple of lengthy trips to India in 1928: the first with just his colleagues in the spring; the second with Vi in the autumn. But this work brought Attlee one great political benefit in that it gave him a deep understanding of the Indian question – something that was to be invaluable over the next two decades, especially when he came to power after 1945. Despite his conservative background at Haileybury and Oxford, he had never had the kind of disdain for Indian culture and nationalism that had characterised Churchill's viewpoint since he had first been there as a soldier more than thirty years earlier. 'I am looking forward to seeing civilisation again after the barbarous squalor of this country,' Churchill wrote to Jennie in 1897.[31] Distance and time had not modified Churchill's opinions. When he dined with Duff Cooper in 1920, Churchill declared that 'Gandhi ought to be lain, bound hand and foot, at the gates of Delhi and then trampled on by an enormous elephant with the new Viceroy seated on its back'.[32] In contrast, Attlee was instinctively sympathetic to the cause of Indian freedom and felt that the Empire could not last. As he told his brother Tom during his travels, 'The truth is that over there they have been trying to put an Anglo-Saxon façade on a Mogul building and the two pieces of architecture are not structurally connected.'[33] Yet his commitment should not be overplayed. While pondering different forms of government for India during his research with the commission, he came to the conclusion that its people were not yet ready for full autonomy. Dominion status of the kind enjoyed by Canada or Australia, he believed, was 'an impossibility'.[34]

Violet returned home in January 1929, while Attlee stayed behind with the six other commissioners. They did not embark for England until 13 April, by which time Baldwin had announced the start of the General Election. As the campaign got under way in Limehouse, Attlee found that his absences in India had become the focus for vilification by the Communists, who accused him of embarking on a lengthy 'joyride' while neglecting his constituency.[35] For the first time, they put up a candidate against him to exploit what they saw as local discontent against the compromising Labour establishment. But Attlee, with almost a quarter of a century's politics in the East End behind him, was dismissive of the threat. At a meeting in Limehouse Town Hall, he brought resounding cheers from his supporters with his denunciation of Communism, a creed that was the route to 'dictatorship' and 'the way to slavery'.[36]

Attlee was helped in his fight by the weaknesses of the Conservatives, who were handicapped by the recession that had descended on the economy, keeping unemployment and the fiscal deficit high. The Tories were further undermined by the lacklustre, cautious nature of their campaign, epitomised by the slogan 'Safety First'. With his usual ebullience, Churchill tried to liven up the Conservative effort. He wrote the economic section in the manifesto and gave by far the most persuasive of the election broadcasts on the radio. The *Daily Express* reported on 1 May that Mr Churchill 'knocked the six preceding broadcasts into a cocked hat. As an exhibition of polemical oratory it was superb. His voice was edged alternatively with sarcasm and warning.'[37] But he could not halt the swing against his party. In his own Epping constituency, his majority was halved by the Liberal candidate

Granville Sharp, and across the country the Conservatives lost 152 seats. Labour were the biggest winners, gaining 136 seats to become, for the first time, the largest party in Parliament. Attlee was among the comfortable victors, with a majority of over 7,200 against the second-placed candidate, the Conservative Evan Morgan.

The national result inevitably meant the return of a second Labour Government under MacDonald, much to Churchill vexation. Because his Epping count was the following morning, Churchill joined Baldwin in Downing Street on election night to view the early reports from the constituencies come through on the news tape machine. Tom Jones, the Deputy Cabinet Secretary, witnessed his combustible mood. 'As Labour gain after Labour gain was announced, Winston became more and more flushed with anger, left his seat and confronted the machine in the passage; with his shoulders hunched, he glared at the figures, tore the sheets and behaved as though if any more Labour gains came along he would smash the whole apparatus.'[38] Churchill was about to be out of power again and in the wilderness. Surprisingly, Attlee was to join him there.

EIGHT

◇

INDIA

THE INDIAN QUESTION spelled trouble for both Churchill and Attlee after the 1929 General Election, with the result that both men grew detached from their respective party Leaders. In Attlee's case, his membership of the Simon Commission was used as an excuse by MacDonald to keep him out of the new Labour Government. The episode reinforced Attlee's sense of disillusion with the Prime Minister, whom he felt was not only drifting away from the values of the Labour movement but was also excessively concerned with the approval of London Society. 'Despite his many fine qualities, he was an awful snob. He was frightfully vain and I am afraid he fell for the worship of the rich people. He spoke of the banker with bated breath,' wrote Attlee.[1]

What deepened Attlee's aggravation in 1929 was the emptiness of the pretext about India, for it soon became clear that MacDonald had little interest in the Simon Commission's work. During the rest of the year, Attlee helped to write the commission's report, which was published in May 1930, advocating strengthened representative government in the provinces, a federal assembly and the retention of the Viceroy's powers. Attlee described these as 'realistic recommendations'[2] but they found no favour among the Indian nationalists, who wanted far greater autonomy. That was precisely the direction in which the British Government in both London and Delhi was now moving. In October 1929, long before the report was published, the commission had been consigned to irrelevancy by the declaration from Viceroy

Lord Irwin that Britain's ultimate aim was to grant dominion status to India, which echoed MacDonald's own opinion. Indeed, much to Attlee's annoyance, MacDonald took complete charge of Indian policy without any involvement by Simon or commissioners.

Attlee was not the only one to be disgruntled at how the commission had been superseded. A large number of Tories, including Churchill, were also dismayed that Baldwin had pledged his backing for the dominion policy. In a *Daily Mail* article, Churchill argued: 'Dominion Status can certainly not be attained while India is a prey to fierce racial and religious dissensions. It cannot be attained while the political classes of India represent only an insignificant fraction of the 350 millions for whose welfare we are responsible.'[3] Although Churchill was willing to accept a degree of provincial self-government, he clung with ever greater fervour to the belief that British control of India must be maintained. This stemmed largely from his romantic attachment to the Empire, whose greatness, he felt, depended on India; nationalism therefore had to be challenged rather than accommodated. At times, this outlook descended into a form of bigotry. 'I hate Indians. They are a beastly people with a beastly religion,' he once declared.[4]

Churchill's disaffection over India was part of a wider disen-chantment with politics after the 1929 General Election. The diplomat and writer Harold Nicolson found in January 1930 that 'his spirits have also declined and he sighs that he has lost his old fighting power'.[5] Churchill still had no secure base in the Conservative Party, which was now moving once more towards a stronger stance on tariff reform in contradiction of his free-trade instincts. An early attempt by Churchill to woo Lloyd George into joining forces with the Conservatives to undermine the minority Labour Government had floundered on the protection issue. Churchill was now worried that a progressive alliance of Labour backed by the Liberals could lock the Tories out of power for years. Nor did there seem much chance that he, now in mid-fifties, would fulfil his ambition to reach the summit of politics. 'It is curious how out of things he is and how badly he has played his cards. No one ever mentions him as Conservative Leader,' wrote the Tory backbencher Victor Cazalet.[6] As they had been so often before, and despite the inheritances he'd received eight years previously, Churchill's personal finances were in a dire state. When he left the Treasury in 1929 his overdraft alone was above £8,000, and most of Chartwell had to be shut up to reduce its running costs. Thoughts about retirement from politics began to loom. On a voyage to America in 1929, Churchill frankly confessed to fellow passenger Leo Amery that he was thinking of starting a new life in Canada. 'He felt he had had a good innings and there was little hope of his ever becoming Prime Minister,' recorded Amery.[7] But, far from reinforcing any plans for a new start across the Atlantic, his US journey sank him further into debt, as he experienced severe losses in the Wall Street crash after heavy speculation in American stocks.

The only way to avoid bankruptcy was drastically to step up his literary output, which he did with remarkable success. In fact the early 1930s were some of his most productive years. Away from ministerial office, he was able once more to earn income from journalism and wrote for an array of publications, including the *Daily Mail*, the *Daily Telegraph* and the *Pall Mall Gazette* in England and the *Saturday Evening Post* in America. He was just as prolific in book production. As well as the final volume of his epic history of the First World War, he began his magisterial if hagiographic four-volume biography of his ancestor the Duke of Marlborough, the first part of which appeared in 1933. His most popular book, however, was his autobiographical *My Early Life*, published in 1930, which recounted his memories of his schooldays and imperial adventures. Attlee was so taken with it that, in a Commons debate in July 1932, he said that he had read it 'with a very great deal of pleasure', not least because of its 'breezy style which we all enjoy so much'.[8]

Although Churchill was now generating a healthy income, he remained badly in debt because of his gambling, stock-market losses and extravagant, champagne-lubricated lifestyle. Moreover, Churchill's literary work meant that, despite his continuing membership of the Tory front bench immediately after the 1929 election, he was unable

to give his full attention to the Westminster scene just as politics was
becoming more turbulent. Economic storm clouds now gathered over
the Labour Government, epitomised by soaring unemployment, which
reached almost 2 million in the spring of 1930. The Labour leadership
seemed paralysed, unable to break free of Treasury orthodoxies. So
infuriated by this timidity was Sir Oswald Mosley, the impatient
Chancellor of the Duchy of Lancaster, that he resigned from the
Government to begin his journey towards fascism. Mosley's place in
charge of the duchy was taken by Attlee.

When he turned to politics, Churchill's concentration focused on
India rather than the British economy. He was enraged at the prospect
of Indian self-government and made clear the depths of his hostility
to official policy when he spoke in London on 12 December 1930 to
the inaugural meeting of the Indian Empire Society, a pressure group
largely composed of Tory diehards. Calling for greater resolution in
the face of nationalism, he said: 'The truth is that Gandhi-ism and all
it stands for will, sooner or later, have to be grappled with and finally
crushed. It is no use trying to satisfy a tiger by feeding him with cat's
meat.'[9] Such remarks further widened the detachment of Churchill
from the Conservative leadership. A breach was now inevitable. It came
on 27 January 1931, the day after a Commons debate in which Churchill
had condemned the erosion of 'British rights and interests in India' and
Baldwin had replied by unreservedly defending the advance towards
a new constitution.[10] Having clashed so publicly with his Leader,
Churchill felt that his position as a frontbencher was untenable. He
therefore resigned from the Conservatives' Business Committee, effectively the Shadow Cabinet.

Some were only too glad to see him go. 'I am profoundly grateful
that we are rid of Winston,' wrote Neville Chamberlain.[11] From the
Labour side, Attlee attacked him on the floor of the House for his
'easy dogmatism'.[12] But now that he was free from any notions of
collective responsibility, Churchill intensified his India campaign,
winning new support from the public and the right wing of the Tory
Party. He addressed two packed gatherings in Lancashire, followed

by a well-attended constituency meeting and a mass rally at the Albert Hall. It was at the constituency event that he made the most notorious of all his utterances about Gandhi, who had recently entered talks with Lord Irwin about ending his campaign of civil disobedience against British rule: 'It is alarming and nauseating to see Mr Gandhi, a seditious Middle Temple lawyer, now posing as a fakir of a type well-known in the East, striding half naked up the steps of the Vice-regal palace.'[13] Such language may have repelled the moderates and the left, but Churchill's campaign represented another formidable challenge to Baldwin, who was already under savage attack for his perceived ineffectiveness. As internal dissent mounted against him in the Tory Party, the Beaverbrook and Rothermere press assailed him for not embracing their policy of Empire Free Trade, a reheated version of Joseph Chamberlain's protectionist concept of Imperial Preference. So weakened was Baldwin that Rothermere suggested to Churchill that, as a result of his India crusade, the Tory crown could soon be his. 'If you go unswervingly forward, nothing can stand in your way. The country is sick to death of the duds that surround their dud Conservative leader.'[14]

In March 1931, buffeted by the tempest raging against him, Baldwin considered resignation but ultimately decided to fight back against his critics. First, he directly took on Churchill and the India diehards in an impassioned speech in the Commons, claiming that the 'niggling, grudging spirit' towards any reform would ultimately 'cause a revolutionary spirit' in the subcontinent.[15] Churchill's response, in which he tried to defend himself against charges of extremism, was subjected to constant interruptions and cries of disbelief from all sides of the House. Baldwin then completed his revival with a damning assault on the Beaverbrook and Rothermere press during the rumbustious Westminster St George's by-election, which resulted in a Tory victory. Suddenly he was secure, while Churchill was left defensive and isolated.

Within the Labour Government, MacDonald was facing his own crisis as the economy deteriorated rapidly. His Chancellor, Philip Snowden, a classic Gladstonian liberal with a streak of puritanism, struggled to balance the budget in the face of dwindling revenues and rising unemployment. Angry at austerity and MacDonald's leadership, Sir Charles Trevelyan, the President of the Education Board, resigned in protest. His departure was a blow for the Government but good news for Attlee; the subsequent reshuffle saw him promoted to the position of Postmaster-General, his first ministerial job at the head of a department. The backdrop to his elevation may have been bleak, but this was exactly the sort of job that suited Attlee's gift for administrative efficiency and interest in structural change. He was now in charge of the Post Office, then rapidly expanding because of the growth of the telephone network.

But Attlee's elevation could not halt Labour's slide from power. Facing financial meltdown, MacDonald in desperation took up the idea of an emergency coalition under his continuing premiership. Talks were held with the King and the main Opposition leaders, though MacDonald failed to consult most of his colleagues or the wider Labour Party, a course that Attlee, far more sensitive to the movement's democratic instincts, wisely refused to follow in May 1940. On 24 August 1931, MacDonald presented his Cabinet with the plan for the new National Government, in which he would be Prime Minister, flanked by Baldwin and Herbert Samuel, temporarily Liberal Leader in the absence of Lloyd George, who was seriously ill at the time. Most of the Labour ministers were outraged at this collusion with the Tories. Only four of his colleagues, led by Snowden, agreed to serve. The anger towards MacDonald was shared by Attlee, who later wrote that the Prime Minister and Chancellor had perpetrated 'the greatest betrayal in the political history of this country'.[16] For his part, MacDonald thought his internal opponents were wallowing in socialist purity without facing up to economic realities. 'They choose the easy path of irresponsibility and leave the burdens to others,' he noted in his diary.[17]

Churchill, indifferent to party labels, had always been an advocate of coalition politics. Yet his marginalisation within the Tory Party meant that he played no role in this one's creation. His lack of political influence was graphically illustrated by the fact that, at the height of political crisis, he was not consulted by any of the protagonists, was never considered for office and was not even in the country, having decided to continue a painting holiday in the south of France. When he returned, he fiercely argued that the 'Tories should take no responsibility whatsoever for the Government plans'.[18] But his opinion was an irrelevance.

Snowden's Emergency Budget did nothing to stop the continuing run on the pound; nor did punitive rises in interest rates. On 21 September the Government was finally compelled to abandon the Gold Standard, more than six years after its fateful introduction by Churchill. The impact was immediate. Exports rose as the exchange rate fell by 25 per cent and economic recovery began. Having weathered the worst of the economic emergency, MacDonald had no intention of breaking up the Coalition. On the contrary, he decided to put his Government on a more secure, long-term foundation by calling a General Election in October. Although the Coalition partners published their own separate manifestos, they stood as a united force under MacDonald in seeking a 'Doctor's Mandate' to cure the country's economic ills. Against them were the demoralised, discredited Labour Party, under the temporary Leader Arthur Henderson, and a rump of independent Liberals under Lloyd George.

It turned out to be the most lopsided General Election in British history, one that appeared to have shattered the traditional two-party system. National candidates were elected in 554 seats, 470 of which were taken by the Conservatives – an extraordinary turnaround in Baldwin's fortunes. The official Labour Party was utterly routed and left with just 46 MPs. At Epping, Churchill had one of the biggest wins of his entire career, gaining a majority of over 20,000. Attlee had a much tougher fight in Limehouse, where he was opposed by a dashing young Conservative, Richard Girouard, the son of the Canadian-born engineer and colonial governor Sir Percy, who had been greatly admired by Churchill for his 'comprehensive' planning of the project to build the Sudan Military Railroad in the 1890s.[19] Despite his comparative youth, Richard Girouard's connections enabled him to bring several high-profile supporters on to the campaign trail; among them was

Lord Beaverbrook, who was eager to propound his gospel of Empire Free Trade.

Given the spirited campaign run by Girouard and the huge national swing against Labour, Attlee feared the worst as the counting began in Limehouse. 'I was very doubtful as to the result,' he admitted.[20] But, unlike most of his parliamentary colleagues, he managed to scrape home. His majority was just 551, compared to the 7,000-plus he'd had in 1929. The decisive factor in his narrow victory was the respect in which he was held by many Limehouse voters, based on decades of unstinting work in the constituency. The full scale of the landslide became apparent when the bedraggled remnants of Labour's beaten army returned to Westminster. Of the forty-six MPs, the majority were trade-union-sponsored timeservers, bereft of parliamentary talent or experience. As the *Manchester Guardian* put it, the Official Opposition was 'less gifted in the arts of Government than any group of men who could readily have been chosen'.[21]

Yet in the crater of Labour's humiliation lay the seeds of Attlee's unexpected rise. The 1931 General Election was perhaps the greatest piece of luck he enjoyed in his career. At a stroke, he was suddenly transformed from a middle-ranking politician into one of the most senior figures in the Labour Party. Almost all his future rivals for the leadership, such as Hugh Dalton and Herbert Morrison, had been ejected from the Commons. His new status was highlighted at the first meeting of the PLP when he was elected Deputy Leader unopposed, serving under George Lansbury, the seventy-two-year-old MP, veteran pacifist and Christian socialist who was renowned for his integrity if not his political realism. There were no other nominations, and Attlee took office without vote. It soon became clear that much of the real burden of leading the Parliamentary Party would fall on him, since, as Attlee put it, 'Lansbury always tended towards individual action and was somewhat of a freelance.'[22] Attlee's lack of charisma was seen by some as an asset after the turmoil of recent months. 'We had enough rhetoric with MacDonald. Now we wanted quiet men we could trust,' wrote the Labour-supporting journalist Francis Williams.[23]

Attlee's first major contribution in the new Parliament arose on 11 November, when he responded to the King's Speech. In a letter afterwards to his brother Tom, Attlee reflected on his own dramatic ascent due to Labour's wipeout, 'It is a funny position, being one of the seniors in the House just now.' More surprising, as he told Tom, was Churchill's frank confession of anxiety to Attlee before his own speech. 'It is at present a difficult house to address, the benches full of unknown quantities. Winston said he was seldom so nervous.'[24] The two men had been in the House together for almost a decade but had never before exchanged any intimacy. Churchill's habitual method of dealing with his nerves before any speech was to write it out verbatim; he once told his fellow Tory minister Oliver Lyttelton that it took him six to eight hours to prepare a contribution of just forty minutes. Apart from copious notes, Churchill occasionally also used a more biological stimulus to improve his performance. Before some of his big speeches, he inhaled pure oxygen to give him a lift; in fact a couple of oxygen cylinders were often part of his travelling equipment on the campaign trail. Attlee never employed this kind of measure; nor did he resort to meticulous preparation. But his more extempore approach, compared to Churchill's rigidity, could not bridge the chasm between them as speakers. For all their carefully rehearsed nature, the best of Churchill's speeches were magnificent, sweeping orations. Attlee could never rise to such heights, as the *Manchester Guardian* once commented: 'He does not coin a striking phrase. He has none of Winston Churchill's power of self-dramatization.'[25]

What Attlee lacked in drama, he tried to make up for in diligence in his new role. Few MPs in the 1931 Parliament worked harder. According to the record that he kept in his own private papers, as Deputy Leader during the 1931–32 session he made no fewer than 125 speeches in the Commons, totalling 352.5 columns in Hansard, the daily parliamentary record, while the following session he filled another 229 columns.[26] Churchill featured in several of Attlee's contributions, often in a gently mocking way. In a debate in December 1931 about the balance between parties in the allocation of radio broadcasts, he referred to the 'difficult

question' created by a figure such as Churchill, 'who is a semi-detached
Member of the Conservative Party and is, so to speak, on the transfer
list'.[27] During a debate on the economy in April 1932, he made another
reference to Churchill's supposed status as a political freelancer. 'We are
like the poor infantry under fire and we are anxious because the Right
Honourable Gentleman the Member for Epping may go cruising
about, like a tank, in No-Man's land ready to fire on either side and at
any convenient target.'[28]

Privately, Attlee felt that Churchill's detachment from the
mainstream Tory Party could be the precursor to a bid for the nation's
leadership in league with his old Liberal ally Lloyd George. In July
1932 he wrote to Tom: 'Lloyd George and Winston are I think in
collusion although the one professed to be "left" and the other "right".
I think they anticipate that as we get deeper into the mire, a change
of leadership of the Coalition will be called for and they will come
in.'[29] But Attlee had misread the political situation. Churchill's icono-
clasm had left him further from power than ever. The cause that he so
determinedly backed in the early 1930s, that of resistance to Indian
self-government, was greeted largely by indifference from the public
and hostility from Parliament beyond the Conservative Party's right
wing, whose numbers amounted to only about eighty MPs. Far from
strengthening his position as an alternative Leader, Churchill's fixation
with India caused severe damage to his reputation.

The flames of Churchill's antagonism towards Indian reform reached
a new intensity from early 1933, as a result of the National Government's
White Paper proposing an elected federation for the subcontinent. A
Joint Committee of both Houses of Parliament was to be established
to examine this scheme before any legislation would be enacted. Attlee,
as Labour's India expert, was inevitably nominated for membership of
the committee. But to Churchill the plan was another act of treachery
towards the Empire, as he made clear in a controversial intervention
during a debate on India in March. He was derided by MPs from all
sides for his obstinacy and came in for particular criticism when he was
unable to substantiate his incendiary claim that officials in the Indian

civil service owed their advancement to their willingness to promote Government policy. Sir Austen Chamberlain, the former Foreign Secretary, noted in his diary how 'Winston stammered and blundered and for the rest of a very long speech had a steadily dwindling and offended audience. The fact of the matter is that on this subject he has become hysterical. It is impossible to discuss it with him.'[30]

Attlee was equally unimpressed, as he told his brother Tom: 'Winston was a complete failure. He really persuaded himself that he is right about the imminent dissolution of the Empire and the loss of India. I had some talk with him on the subject. He also realised that he was beaten. He was serious, long and laboured. In the middle he made a great mistake by attacking the Indian Civil Service.'[31] Attlee now recognised how much Churchill's prospects had been undermined by his diehard stance. 'If the Tories had a leader, they would like to oust MacDonald, but there is no one at present, Churchill having cut his throat.'[32] But, for all his egotism, Churchill was not a calculating politician who would finesse his views for opportunistic ends. Because he so deeply believed in the cause of Britain's Indian empire, he was determined to plough on with his fight against dominion status, no matter what the cost to his career. 'Trouble with Winston: he nails his trousers to the mast and can't climb down,' Attlee once said of him, words that exemplified his Indian campaign.[33] Despite the parliamentary setback, Churchill intensified his activity with every political weapon he could wield. He spoke at further rallies in London and Lancashire and helped to establish a new anti-reform pressure group, the India Defence League (IDL), which soon attracted the support of fifty-seven Conservative MPs. The diehard stance, however, remained a minority position in the wider party. At a meeting in June 1933 of the National Union, the Conservatives' governing body, a resolution in support of the White Paper was given an overwhelming majority after Baldwin had delivered an effective reply to Churchill at the meeting. Nor did his rallies attract any surge in public support. Sir Raymond Streat, a leading figure in the Lancashire cotton trade, saw him in action at Manchester's Free Trade Hall for the new IDL but was left unmoved: 'He got a good reception when he stood up but a poor one when he sat down. He certainly did not grip the audience.'[34]

Churchill's vulnerability was further exposed in October when he gave evidence to the Joint Select Committee, clashing with Attlee over the question of provincial finances. Attlee asked him if his demand for the exercise of greater fiscal responsibility at the centre was based on the argument that the British administration in Delhi had earned the right to intervene through its provision of subsidies to the provinces. Churchill agreed with this construction, to which Attlee reminded him that there had been a period when the central Government was subsidised by the provinces. Did this mean, Attlee asked innocently, that in such circumstances the provinces should control the centre? Churchill protested at what he called 'a ridiculous interpretation' of his case. 'I wanted to see whether it was really financial rectitude that impelled you to make the suggestion,' replied Attlee, satisfied that his interrogatory tactic had revealed Churchill's weak grasp of the intricacies of the India question.[35]

But Churchill was not done. In the spring of 1934 he detonated his most incendiary row yet on India, using as his explosive charge the claim that the Manchester Chamber of Commerce had manipulated its evidence to the Joint Select Committee. This may have sounded like an obscure technical point, but Churchill knew that the prosperity of the Lancashire textile industry was central to the debate about the future link with India. Churchill had hoped that Manchester's business leaders would denounce Indian autonomy as a threat to their trade, but the Chamber's statement to the Joint Select Committee turned out to be a balanced one. Sensing a Government plot, Churchill discovered that the Chamber had changed its evidence after its senior members had attended a dinner hosted by Lord Derby, the Lancashire Tory magnate, at which Sir Samuel Hoare, the India Secretary, was also present. On 16 April 1934, in a scene described by the *Daily Express* as 'more tense and dramatic than any witnessed in the House of Commons for many years', Churchill condemned the action of Hoare and Derby as 'grossly irregular and highly objectionable'. Their pressure on the Manchester Chamber, he said, meant that 'the new statement was only a ghost of the original, a poor shrunken emasculated thing'.[36] The Speaker, impressed by Churchill's argument, immediately referred the case to the Committee of Privileges to see if there had been a breach of parliamentary rules. The Committee of Privileges was no minor disciplinary body. On the contrary, it contained several of the country's most senior politicians, including MacDonald, Baldwin and Sir Austen Chamberlain as well as Attlee. Its importance was reflected by not only its membership but also the precedence it took over work of the Joint Select Committee on India, whose proceedings were now reaching their conclusion.

The Committee of Privileges sat for six weeks from late April, dealing with a wealth of written and oral testimony from Churchill and other witnesses. Hindered from carrying out their other duties, the members were frustrated by the burden of this investigation, a feeling that only deepened the hostility towards Churchill. In exasperation, Attlee told his brother, 'Winston's stunt was a great nuisance to me as I had to spend hours which I could ill afford on the Committee. My Indian Committee was boiling up at the same time and I had a mass of other work.'[37] Indeed, while Churchill was alienating his parliamentary colleagues, Attlee was quietly winning them over with his effectiveness. Sir Austen Chamberlain, who also served on both the Privileges and Joint India committees, wrote a diary entry in October 1933 after a meeting of the latter: 'Attlee has impressed me and his help would be very useful as he is the principal or at least the most distinguished Labour member.'[38]

Annoyance with Churchill meant that the Committee of Privileges was not inclined to support him, especially when his case against Lord Derby and Sam Hoare turned out to be weak. Its report, agreed unanimously by the members, concluded that there had been no breach of privilege because the Joint Select Committee was not a judicial body; therefore any pressure on the Manchester Chamber of Commerce was acceptable as part of the normal political process. But even now Churchill continued to show his defiance. When the report was debated in the House on 13 June, he rejected its findings, claiming that its authors were not only guilty of 'a complete misrepresentation of the facts' but had also 'cast a slur' on the liberties of Parliament by their dismissal of any judicial status for the committee.[39] His arguments carried little weight in the House, and he was subjected to a wave of ridicule during a response by Leo Amery, who said Churchill's policy amounted to the belief that 'if I can trip up Sam, the Government is bust'.[40] Less sarcastic but just as damaging was Attlee's contribution. In his concise manner, he explained that 'no other finding was possible' because the Joint Select Committee 'could not be regarded in any way as judicial'. Referring directly to Churchill, he said that 'if the right honourable Gentleman had thought of his own evidence before the Joint Select Committee, it was a valuable opinion of an experienced statesman on a great problem. There was no evidence of facts.'[41]

The Committee of Privileges' report was accepted without a division by the House, a further sign of Churchill's isolation. Yet even after this humiliating reversal he did not desist over India. His new focus was the legislation to grant a greater measure of Indian self-rule, which emerged from the lengthy deliberations of the Joint Select Committee. After more than 170 sittings, the committee published its proposals for constitutional reform in November 1934, advocating the creation of an All-India federation, with a two-tier representative assembly and eleven self-governing provinces. Attlee, who had become increasing radical over India since his first cautious days as a member of the Simon Commission in the late 1920s, felt this scheme was too limited in its scope and rightly believed that it would not satisfy the growing Indian nationalist movement. In a sign of his burgeoning confidence, he voted against the official report; then, with the support of his three Labour colleagues on the committee, he produced his own minority version, which soon became known as the 'Attlee Draft'. Based on the conviction that the Indians should be trusted to govern themselves, this bolder plan urged a reduction in powers for the Viceroy and Indian princes, a clear timetable for dominion status, a wider electoral franchise, and Indian control over foreign policy. Even though it had no chance of implementation in the mid-1930s, the Attlee Draft gave Labour a coherent policy on India and paved the way for the drive towards independence after the war.

Attlee may have disputed the Joint Select Committee report but he and his party lent their full support to the massive Government of India Bill, which implemented the report's recommendations, pursuing the twin themes of provincial autonomy and the establishment of a federation. In contrast, Churchill remained as hostile as ever. On the Bill's introduction to the Commons, the *Daily Express* described how 'looking much as Napoleon might have looked in the Elba of banishment, he sat glumly resting his chin in his hand'.[42] During the passage of the Bill through Parliament in 1935, Churchill was one of the few senior MPs to speak out against it, prompting Attlee on one occasion to attack him not just for his intransigence but also his attempt to obstruct the discussion of certain clauses through the use of unsubstantiated press comment. On 5 March, having been absent from the House with a minor illness, Attlee condemned Churchill for quoting at length from a *Morning Post* article that purported to provide a verbatim account of a secret meeting of the Indian princes in Bombay to discuss federation. In the kind of language that might have been adopted by a schoolmaster in dealing with a wayward pupil, Attlee said: 'I think we have had quite enough already about discussions in party meetings and party newspapers. I think it is an abuse of the practice of the House for the right honourable gentleman to get up and again make, as I understand he has done several times already, a speech on a particular point.'[43] This provoked an indignant response from Churchill. 'The honourable Member for Limehouse has been indisposed for the last 10 days. I am sorry if one of the symptoms of what we now see is a happy convalescence should be a bad temper.' With a note of scorn, he told the House that Attlee should be aware of 'how admirably his colleagues have filled his place in his absence'. Had Attlee been present, continued Churchill, 'he would not have gone out of his way, on no information and not having been in touch with the Committee and its work, to deliver such a very striking and dictatorial lecture to me'.[44]

The Government of India Bill completed its passage through Parliament at the end of July 1935. As Attlee had warned, it turned out to be an ineffectual measure because the growing strength of nationalism could not now be assuaged by limited constitutional reform. Churchill too, was correct in his prediction that federation would prove unworkable. But by time the Bill became law, his standing with his fellow Tories had plummeted. Baldwin's ally John Davidson recalled: 'He cut very little ice with the Conservative Party. In fact, the diehard Tories who opposed us over India never regarded him as a Conservative at all but as a renegade Liberal who had crossed the floor. He was regarded as unstable politically.'[45] Now aged sixty, Churchill's prospects as a national politician looked bleak. 'He seems to have reconciled himself to the part of farewell tour of politics,' wrote Beaverbrook.[46] But Churchill had already embarked on another crusade, on a question much closer to home than India.

NINE

❖

GERMANY

A**FTER THE START** of the Second World War, the left cultivated the myth that the supine, Conservative-dominated National Government was entirely to blame for Britain's military ill-preparedness in the run-up to the conflict with Germany. It was a charge set out in the bestselling book *The Guilty Men*, co-authored by Michael Foot and published in July 1940. Figures like Neville Chamberlain, Sir John Simon and Stanley Baldwin were condemned with 'unrelenting crudity', to use Foot's own phrase,[1] while Labour politicians escaped any responsibility. Yet during much of the 1930s, Labour was a strident ideological opponent of any form of rearmament. Even with the arrival of the dictators on the European stage, the party placed a credulous faith in the efficacy of peace talks, while attacking any increases in defence expenditure. Labour later denounced the Conservatives for failing to protect the country, when its own policy in the early and mid-1930s had long made a virtue of impotence.

The party took its cue from its Leader, George Lansbury, whose pacifist political principles were inspired by his version of Christianity. At the Labour Annual Conference in October 1933 he told delegates, 'I would close every recruiting station, disband the army and dismiss the RAF. I would abolish the whole dreadful equipment of war and say to the world, "Do your worst."'[2] With his heroic war record and reputation for patriotism, Attlee as Deputy Leader might have been expected to challenge Lansbury's stance. Yet at this time Attlee was no pragmatic centrist. Instead, like Lansbury and other socialists, Attlee subscribed to the theory that war, military spending and dictatorships were the products of a voracious capitalist system. In the long-term, therefore, the overthrow of the system would bring about a lasting peace; in the immediate term, it was useless to rely for self-defence on resurgent military programmes that only heightened the potential for tension and conflict. The real answer lay in pressure for international co-operation to promote collective security and achieve disarmament. Burgeoning defence estimates, he argued, were 'nationalist and imperialist delusions, far more wild than any of the idealist dreams of the future we hold. We are on the side of total disarmament because we are realists.'[3]

The vision of collective security through the LoN became a central theme of Attlee's in the early 1930s. He put his faith in global government at the expense of national autonomy. 'Nothing short of a world state will be really effective in preventing war. I want us to come out boldly for a real long-range policy which will envisage the abolition of the conception of the individual sovereign state,' he told his brother Tom just days before Hitler came to power in 1933.[4]

Attlee was slower than many politicians to recognise the unique nature of Nazi tyranny. More than a year after Hitler's takeover, he complacently told the House that 'there is a decline in the movement towards dictatorship owing to the failure of the dictators'.[5] His attitude contrasted dramatically with Churchill's, who perceived the dangers of Nazism before Hitler had even become Chancellor. His gift of political prescience told him that the mood in Germany had become a menace to European civilisation, which could only be maintained by resolution. Eddie Marsh, his former secretary, recorded Churchill telling his guests at a lunch in Salzburg in the summer of 1932 how the Germans 'would do anything to avenge the fatherland [...] It begins by a sort of humming and seething, like a pot before it boils, and then it all comes out at once.' Marsh further noted that Churchill 'spoke of the young men of Germany marching by torchlight through the woods'. At this his guests laughed a little, and one or two of them said, 'Oh Winston, you're always talking about another war.'[6] On 23 March 1933 – on the very day that the German Reichstag passed the Enabling Bill that gave Hitler full dictatorial powers – Churchill warned of the risks of war and the dangers of disarmament. Ramsay MacDonald's period as Prime Minister, he told the House, had 'made us weaker, poorer and more defenceless', while the current international Disarmament Conference at Geneva was 'a solemn and prolonged farce'.[7]

Just as he felt the push for disarmament was a disastrous folly, so he had little time for the sympathetic portrayal of Germany as the victim of brutal Allied post-war policies. It was an outlook that he powerfully challenged during a parliamentary debate on foreign affairs called by the Opposition on 13 April 1933. Opening for Labour in this debate, Attlee declared that Germany 'as she today is the creation of the Versailles Treaty' and 'we in this House, and indeed, the country as a whole, I think, fully recognise Germany's claim for justice'. He argued that economic problems had further fuelled German extremism, claiming that 'the Nazi revolution is very largely a demand for bread'. In response, Churchill said that the criticism of Versailles had been overdone: 'Germany got off lightly after the Great War. I know that is not always a fashionable opinion, but the facts repudiate the idea that a Carthaginian peace* was in fact imposed upon Germany […] I do not think we need break our hearts in deploring the treatment that Germany is receiving now.' On the contrary, Germany was now in the hands of a 'most grim dictatorship', driven by 'militarism and appeals to every form of fighting spirit'.[8]

In the following months, alongside his campaign on India, Churchill kept up his barrage of warnings about Nazism and the need for stronger national defence. On St George's Day 1933, at the annual meeting of the Royal Society of St George, he attacked the 'unwarrantable self-abasement' of too many intellectuals and politicians. 'What have they to offer but a vague internationalism, a squalid materialism and the promise of impossible utopias?' he asked.[9] But even after the

---

* The phrase was coined by the economist J. M. Keynes.

mounting evidence of Hitler's tyranny and Germany's withdrawal from the LoN in October, Attlee still refused to accept the need for British rearmament, instead clinging to the notion of international governance. The widening chasm between the two men was apparent in a debate about disarmament on 7 November 1933. In his speech, Churchill again dismissed the idea of German victimhood, arguing that 'the philosophy of blood lust is being inculcated into their youth in a manner unparalleled since the days of barbarism'. He advocated collective security with other European powers to hold Germany in check, but that required Britain to expand her military strength. As it was, Britain had been disarmed 'to the verge of risk – nay, well into the gulf of risk'.[10]

Attlee took a completely different line, extolling just the kind of internationalist doctrine that Churchill had denounced in his St George's Day speech: 'We have to realise that the whole conception of nationalism is out of date, that we need internationalism,' he said, adding that the 'failure since 1919' had been down to the refusal to move 'beyond the individual states' and develop 'some super government of the world'. Attlee even downplayed the need to confront Nazism. Referring to the claim that Hitler had 'united' Germany, he described this as 'the same silly assumption that the Prime Minister makes when he speaks about the National Government and no more return to party strife'. At this Churchill interrupted in defence of MacDonald: 'He does not use the same methods.' In reply Attlee tried to justify his remark: 'I agree, but at the back of it all, although we get a different method, we get the same kind of idea, this is an inflated nationalist idea and the conception of the nation.' This passage led Attlee to make an early use of the term 'neo-Conservative', long before it gained currency in 1970s American politics. The belief in the nationalist state, he maintained, 'is put forward most of all by your neo-Conservative, whether he wears a black shirt or a brown shirt or any of those various shirts that seem to be the popular wear in politics nowadays'. It was pointless, said Attlee, to denounce nations because 'you have considered they were oppressed by some small gang. The same old thing […] was said by the Right Honourable Gentleman the Member for Epping against the makers of the Russian revolution; and I do not believe that it is very much use in this House to indulge in strong language against the Nazi regime.'[11]

Attlee's views on European policy gained a new importance at the end of the year, when he became Labour's acting Leader after Lansbury badly broke his hip in a fall. But his enhanced status brought no change in Labour's foreign and defence policy. If anything he was even more uncompromising in his opposition to rearmament, an approach that reinforced his vast divergence from Churchill. One particular aspect of the debate over defence that had become urgent in 1934 was air power, where rapidly advancing technology had the potential to transform the nature of warfare. Moreover, there was mounting evidence that Hitler's regime had embarked on the creation of a powerful air force, in direct contravention of the Versailles Treaty, which permitted only civil aviation in post-war Germany. In the face of this development, Churchill was concerned about the reluctance of the National Government to bolster the RAF, as he stated in BBC radio broadcast on 16 January: 'the least we ought now to do is to have an air force as strong as that of the nearest power that can get to us'.[12] In the Commons soon afterwards, Attlee attacked Churchill's position, which he said undermined the spirit of mutual obligations under the LoN: 'We have never concealed our belief that you have to go for security and total disarmament.'[13]

Even a modest increase by the National Government in the air estimates was too much for Attlee, who told MPs that Labour would vote against the plan: 'There is no effective defence against air attack.' Then, calling for an end to separate national air forces, Attlee cited the fourth volume of Churchill's history of the First World War, entitled *Aftermath*, in support of his case: 'The right honourable gentleman is one of those brilliant erratic geniuses who, when he sees clearly, sees very, very clearly.' A keen reader of Churchill's works, Attlee noted that *Aftermath* contained a scene at the Versailles Conference, illuminated by the author's 'brilliant imagination', in which the world statesmen discussed the possibility of giving control of military air power to the LoN. The idea was not pursued in 1919, but that is what Attlee now advocated on an even bigger scale to encompass all aviation, including the civil sphere. 'I believe that the Government should have worked for the entire internationalisation of aviation and for the creation of an international air force.'[14] Unmoved by Attlee's compliment, Churchill adopted the opposite line, arguing that the Nazi threat required a determined national response. 'Germany is arming fast and no one is going to stop her,' he warned. 'I dread the day when the means of threatening the heart of the British Empire should pass into the hands of the present rulers of Germany,' he said before adding that 'there is still time to take the necessary measures'.[15]

The clash over air policy soon resumed with even greater ferocity. Attlee was as firm as ever in his rejection of more funding for the RAF and even claimed the Nazi menace was exaggerated. On 13 July, he denied Hitler's warlike intentions and claimed his regime was 'falling down'.[16] Churchill knew very differently because he had his own private sources of information about Britain's preparations compared to Germany's. One was Ralph Wigram, a young British diplomat who leaked classified material to Churchill as a matter of patriotic duty. Another was Desmond Morton, a civil servant and head of the Government's Industrial Intelligence Centre. A former artillery officer, Morton had become a friend of Churchill's during the First World War, in which he fought heroically, even returning to action after he had been shot in the heart during the Battle of Arras. Through these clandestine advisers, Churchill gained a wealth of detailed figures about air force expansion in Germany in defiance of Versailles. According to one of Morton's estimates, the German air force would be growing at the rate of 1,000 aircraft a year from the end of 1935. Statistics like that were effectively deployed by Churchill in an air debate on 30 July, when the Opposition, still led by Attlee, moved a vote of censure against the National Government for its extremely limited increase in air expenditure, which would raise the number of home squadrons from 52 to 75 over the next five years. In an opening speech of conviction if not realism, Attlee denounced the very concept of self-protection: 'You have to go forward to an ordered world system. We believe you have got to have the abolition of national fighting forces.'[17]

Attlee's approach led to a verbal onslaught from Churchill, who found it absurd that the Opposition refused to accept even the 'very minute and modest' proposal for enhanced air defences, particularly when Germany 'has already, in violation of the Treaty, created a military air force which is now nearly two-thirds as strong as our present home defence force'. The Labour front bench had 'the same sort of look of pain and shocked surprise and disgust which came over the face of Mr Bumble when Oliver Twist held out his little bowl and asked for more'.[18] The Labour vote of censure was defeated by 404 votes to just 60.

But Attlee still did not alter his stance. At Labour's Conference in Southport in early October 1934, he set out an even more extreme rejection of national self-defence than anything he had expounded on the floor of the Commons. In one extraordinary section he declared,

> We have absolutely abandoned every idea of nationalist loyalty. We are deliberately putting a world order before our loyalty towards our own country. We will be called very disloyal because we owe allegiance here to a world order rather than to what is called patriotism. We say we want to see put on the statute book something which will make our people citizens of the world before they are citizens of this country.[19]

Churchill himself was so struck by this language that he kept a note of the passage in his papers, and, after the war, sometimes taunted Attlee with it during defence debates.

That same autumn Attlee returned to his previous job as Deputy Leader as George Lansbury, fully recovered from his broken hip, again took the helm of Labour. By then the party's anti-rearmament position, even when cloaked in rhetoric about the LoN, was becoming unsustainable. As Hitler, Mussolini and Spanish chaos threatened European peace, the political mood at Westminster began to shift towards greater firmness in defence. Although still ostracised over India, Churchill found that his warnings about air policy had more resonance than

before, as was shown on 28 November 1934 when, in league with
several other Tory backbenchers, he put down an amendment to the
Address, deploring the inadequacy of Britain's national defences. In
an impressive Commons speech he provided both a detailed analysis
of the potential German threat and a cogent argument for a strong
RAF with a powerful strategic bombing capability. Allowing mastery
of the air to the enemy would lead to 'absolute subjugation', he warned,
with 'no opportunity of recovery'.[20] Churchill's exposition of the Nazi
plans for the German air force again owed much to Desmond Morton
but the research for the scientific side of the speech, covering technical
matters like the impact of incendiary bombs, was carried out by
another supporter, Frederick Lindemann, a professor of Experimental
Philosophy at Oxford, whose Jewishness fed an implacable hatred of
Hitler's regime. Churchill's appeal struck a chord with the majority of
the House. He forced Baldwin to give a pledge to the House that the
Government would not accept 'any position of inferiority with regard
to what air force may be raised in Germany in the future'.[21] In response
to Baldwin's conciliatory attitude, Churchill withdrew his amendment.
Instead, he joined his colleagues in inflicting an overwhelming defeat,
by 276 to 55, on Labour's amendment, which had expressed regret at the
Government's drive for increased armaments.

Attlee maintained his insistent opposition to national defence into
1935, even as events at home and abroad rendered Labour's policy danger-
ously utopian. In early March the Government launched a Defence
White Paper promising an extra £10 million that year, marking a major
change in state policy after the long, failed negotiations at Geneva over
disarmament. Still infused with his belief in world government, Attlee
told the House on 11 March: 'We loathe and detest the military spirit,
the tyrannical spirit which has shown itself all over the world. You will
never beat this by attack. You will only beat it by putting something far
bigger in its place.'[22] Attlee's criticisms of the White Paper provoked
fury from the Tory benches, even from a normally non-partisan figure
like Sir Austen Chamberlain. 'If war breaks out, do you think he will
hold the language he has held today? If he does, he will be one of the

first victims of the war, for he will be strung by an angry – and justi-
fiably angry – populace from the nearest lamppost,' said Sir Austen, to
resounding cheers from his own side.[23]

Soon after the launch of the White Paper, Hitler announced that the
German air force, in defiance of Versailles, had already reached parity
with the RAF. The Führer's boast was an exaggeration, but it showed
the Reich's intentions and sent a wave of apprehension through the
Government. On 5 April Churchill wrote to Clementine, who was on a
cruise, that Hitler's announcement 'completely stultifies everything that
Baldwin has said and incidentally vindicates all the assertions that I have
made'.[24] Yet Attlee rebuked Churchill in early May for his forebodings
about German's bellicosity. 'I think it is a very dangerous thing to start
a panic [...] You can carry that a great deal too far,' he said in the
Commons.[25] Hugh Dalton, fiercely anti-German, was unimpressed by
Attlee's performance for Labour on foreign policy. 'Little man, little
head, little speech, little essay,' he wrote after one appearance in May.[26]

At the beginning of June 1935, Baldwin replaced MacDonald, who
had become hopelessly enfeebled and indecisive, living up to Churchill's
description of him as the 'boneless wonder'.[27] Although he was no
admirer of Baldwin, Churchill had harboured some private hope that
the change in the premiership might lead to his own return to Cabinet
office. But the doubts about his temperament and reliability that had
dogged his entire career once more held him back. Those perceived
failings were also highlighted by Attlee during a post-Budget speech
in April 1935, comparing Churchill to Neville Chamberlain. 'We all
know the great qualities of the right honourable Member for Epping
but he never quite gives the same impression of solid respectability
as does the Chancellor. Whatever the right honourable Member for
Epping is doing has always a little touch of the buccaneer and perhaps
of the condottiere* about it.'[28] Yet Baldwin did not freeze out Churchill
completely. On the advice of the dynamic new Air Secretary Sir Philip
Cunliffe-Lister, the Prime Minister offered Churchill a place on the

---

* An Italian mercenary of the fourteenth and fifteenth centuries.

official Air Defence Research Committee, which had been established a few months earlier. Churchill provisionally accepted, provided that he could 'remain free to debate all the general issues of Air strength, Air Policy'.[29] Baldwin quickly reassured him: 'My invitation was not intended as a muzzle but as a gesture of friendliness to an old colleague.'[30]

The sense of darkening crisis in Europe in mid-1935 was exacerbated by Mussolini's aggression towards Ethiopia, then widely known as Abyssinia, which bordered the colonial territory of Italian Somaliland. The belligerence of the Fascist regime dominated the proceedings of the LoN, desperate to avert a conflict, but Churchill and Attlee once more took divergent views. Churchill had never seen Mussolini's Italy as anything like the menace to the British Empire that Hitler's Germany represented. Indeed, he had in the past praised Il Duce both for acting as a bulwark against Communism and for reviving Italian self-confidence. 'Your movement has abroad rendered a service to the whole world [...] It provides the necessary antidote to the Russian virus,' he told Mussolini after they met in 1927.[31] The National Government, particularly Baldwin's new Foreign Secretary Samuel Hoare, shared his reluctance to bracket Italy with Germany, and also feared that too vigorous a condemnation of Mussolini might push him into an alliance with Hitler. But Attlee, more concerned with his ideal of collective security, adopted a far harsher line on Italy, whose hostile attitude towards Abyssinia he regarded as a crucial test of the LoN. In the Commons on 7 June, Attlee said that a failure to stand up to Mussolini risked bringing the 'whole system of the League' into disrepute. Britain, he urged, was 'bound to act against the aggressor'.[32]

Attlee may have wanted more resolve from the National Government in confronting Mussolini, but the Abyssinian saga exposed the hole at the centre of Labour's policy; for without the military power, the collective will of the LoN could not be enforced against the Italian dictator. It was Churchill who highlighted this weakness during a Commons debate about Italy on 11 July, when Attlee launched another of his fusillades against the Government for failing to stand by Abyssinia. In response, Churchill criticised Attlee for the emptiness of his moral invective. The speech by Labour's Deputy Leader, he said, was 'entirely devoid of any kind of constructive suggestion'.[33] Anthony Eden, the League of Nations Minister and increasingly an ally of Churchill's, joined in the condemnation of Attlee: 'It is surely the height of folly to say that you must play your part, and a full part, in collective action in a fully armed world and yet not have the means to do it.'[34]

The contradictions in Labour's approach came to a head in October 1935 when, after months of rising tension on the Abyssinian border, Mussolini mounted a full-scale invasion. As the Italian leader had foreseen, the Western democracies refused to act in concert against him; even the few economic sanctions imposed on him were limited in their scope. Churchill, with his focus still on Hitler, was not opposed to this muted reaction. He believed Abyssinia was ungovernable and war there 'a very small matter' that paled beside the 'one great fear' of 'the power and might of the re-armed strength of Germany'.[35] But Attlee's devotion to the LoN meant that he wanted a far tougher response, even involving, if necessary, the use of force. That put him on a collision course with Lansbury, the radical MP Stafford Cripps and the pacifist wing of the Labour Party, who still put all their faith in absolutist non-resistance. The conflict over policy exploded at Labour's Annual Conference in Brighton, when the trade-union leader Ernie Bevin launched a withering assault on the pacifism of Lansbury, whom he accused of 'hawking your conscience around from body to body'.[36] In a decisive break with his Leader, Attlee sided with Bevin in his own speech: 'We are against the use of force for imperialist and capitalist ends, but we are in favour of the proper use of force for ensuring the use of law.'[37] The Conference subsequently rejected Lansbury's call for non-resistance, rendering his position as Leader untenable. A noble anachronism in this age of discord, Lansbury resigned on 8 October.

Immediately speculation turned to his successor, with Attlee the prime candidate. His stature had been enhanced not only by the deputy leadership, but also by flaws in his potential rivals. The austere Stafford Cripps, despite his support among activists, was ruled out by his adherence to the same non-resistance policy as Lansbury's. Neither

Dalton nor Morrison had managed to return to Parliament, while Arthur Greenwood, the genial MP for Wakefield, was gripped by alcoholism. Even so, there was little excitement in the party or the press about the prospect of Attlee taking over once again. The *Daily Mail* felt that at best he could be only a temporary replacement until the bigger figure of Morrison came back to the Commons; the *Manchester Guardian* argued that Greenwood had 'a more positive and interesting personality'.[38]

On the day of Lansbury's resignation, the PLP met at Transport House to vote for its new Leader. But the decision was postponed, both to avoid more turmoil after the divisive Conference and because a General Election seemed likely soon, which would mean that the party would have a greater choice of candidates in the new Parliament, based on the presumption that Labour would make up some of its losses from the disaster of 1931. Attlee was therefore once more asked to act as caretaker. 'I've got a hard job in difficult times,' he confessed.[39]

Labour's supposition about the imminence of the General Election was correct. On 25 October Parliament was dissolved after Baldwin went to the Palace, eager to exploit Labour's vulnerability and inexperienced leadership. The National candidates, most of them Conservatives, fought on a platform of limited rearmament and continuing economic growth. Labour proclaimed its belief in socialism, disarmament and peace. 'A vote for the Tories is a vote for war,' was one of the party's slogans.[40] On the campaign trail Attlee was no match for Baldwin, who was in his fifth General Election as Leader and exuded an avuncular solidity. Attlee, for all his composure and diligence, struggled to captivate his audiences. The *Daily Telegraph* noted that he 'lacks colour, nor has he coined a single memorable phrase'.[41] In an election speech supporting his son Randolph, who was standing for the Conservatives in Liverpool West Toxteth, Churchill poked fun at Attlee's transient status: 'Almost all their experienced leaders are gone. Some are turned out, some have resigned; in fact there are just as many late leaders of Labour as there are would-be leaders. You have a double queue – one at the exit and one at the entrance. [Laughter.] They are unable to choose a leader. They have to have a *locum tenens* for the Election.'[42]

The inevitable outcome of the election was a further landslide for the Conservatives, who won 387 seats – part of a National parliamentary force of 429 MPs. Churchill had another crushing victory in Epping, marginally increasing his majority to 20,419 over Granville Sharp, the Liberal barrister who, with optimistic indefatigability, had stood in every election in the constituency since 1922. After the calamity of 1931 Labour saw some improvement. Attlee's party gained 3 million votes and over 100 seats to reach a total of 154 seats. Attlee's own vote was the second-highest he ever had in Limehouse. But there was a widespread perception that Labour's performance was a disappointment, given the National Government's chequered record. Herbert Morrison, who had taken over the leadership of the London County Council in 1934 and had now been returned for Hackney South, implied that Attlee was to blame: 'We have not yet evolved a clear leadership. Most of us had hoped to win more seats. We ought to have done better,' he wrote.[43] The Whitehall grandee Tom Jones also felt that Attlee's limited appeal was a central reason for Labour's heavy defeat, while he believed that Baldwin's moderate image was boosted by his distance from Churchill. Three days after the election, Jones wrote that the Prime Minister had 'kept clear of Winston's enthusiasm for ships and guns' but had also been 'much helped by the division in the Labour ranks and their lack of leadership. Attlee is an unknown.'[44]

Attlee's time in charge, which had lasted only a few weeks, looked likely to end once a proper leadership contest was held when the PLP reconvened at Westminster. He was certain to face a strong challenge from Greenwood, who was popular among MPs despite his weakness for alcohol, and a formidable one from Morrison, whose ambition was matched by his gift for public speaking and his organisational skills. The scars of his personal life, bred of a cold, sexless marriage, damaged eyesight and an unhappy childhood as the son of a bullying policeman, had driven Morrison to pour his considerable energy into his political career. As the first round of voting approached on 26 November 1935, he looked like the favourite to win against the self-effacing incumbent. But his bid started to unravel. His pushiness and air of intrigue grated with some MPs. Others, especially on the left, were suspicious of his closeness to business. There were also fears that he was too divisive, too devoted to the capital's affairs as leader of the LCC. Attlee was not nearly as charismatic, but he had proved himself a loyal, hard-working servant of the party. In the first ballot, Attlee came out marginally ahead of Morrison, by fifty-eight to forty-four, with Greenwood further behind on thirty-three. As the lowest-placed candidate, Greenwood was eliminated. Subsequently, all but four of his initial supporters transferred to Attlee, who emerged victorious from the second round with eighty-eight votes to Morrison's forty-eight.

Attlee's was a triumph against the odds. He had won because he was more trusted than Morrison and had far more parliamentary experience. Attlee also had a much bigger union following than Morrison, as shown by the confidence he inspired in Ernie Bevin, leader of the Transport Workers. During a meeting at Transport House in mid-1935, Bevin complained vociferously about Lansbury's leadership. 'Yes, but what's the alternative?' asked one of those present. Bevin replied, 'You see that little man, sitting over there who smokes a pipe and says nothing. I don't know him very well, but he'll do.'[45]

But others thought the PLP had taken a wrong step. Douglas Jay, then a centre-left journalist, said he was 'filled with deep gloom'; while the *New Statesman* argued that Attlee 'lacks the spectacular gifts required for national leadership. He is a natural adjutant, not a general.'[46] Dalton went even further, writing in his diary that it was 'a wretched and disheartening result. And a little mouse shall lead them.'[47] Morrison was so crushed by the outcome that, according to his wife, 'he faced the wall for a week'.[48] Beatrice Webb tried to comfort him with the observation that Attlee was only a stop-gap, but he was having none of it. He told her 'that the members of the Parliamentary Labour Party were sentimental and, having once made a man leader, would stick to him'.[49]

TEN

◇

FORT BELVEDERE

DESPITE HIS NEW status as the elected Labour Leader, Attlee failed initially to make much of an impact on the political landscape. He exuded neither authority nor power. 'Attlee looks like a black snail and is equally ineffective,' noted the gossipy Tory MP Sir Henry 'Chips' Channon after a foreign-affairs debate in December 1935.[1] Apart from the limitations of his unobtrusive personality, the central reason that he struggled lay in the weakness of Labour's defence policy, which was still detached from the realities of a European Continent engulfed by crisis and conflict.

His stance could hardly have been in greater contrast to that of Churchill, the foremost advocate of British rearmament and vigilance against Nazism. The differences between the two men were highlighted in March 1936, when they argued about the role of the LoN, whose credibility had been severely eroded by the Italian conquest of Abyssinia. Churchill, as usual, was little concerned by the events in Africa and called for an end to ineffectual economic sanctions against Italy. In Europe, however, he believed in the LoN as a potential guardian of collective security, a view that was sharpened after Hitler's remilitarisation of the Rhineland in contravention of the Versailles Treaty. But he saw the LoN as an extension of strong national self-defence, not as an alternative. In the Commons, Churchill urged that 'we should endeavour now to establish collective security' through the 'encirclement' of aggressors and by linking up 'the forces at the disposal of the League for defence'.[2] In response, Attlee expressed surprise that Churchill had taken up the cause of the LoN. 'As I listened to the right honourable gentleman the Member for Epping, I thought what a pity it was that the convictions which he now holds so strongly had not been with him during the past five years.' Churchill rose to deny Attlee's charge, claiming that he had been long been using the same language about the LoN. Attlee welcomed his support, though he added: 'I always had the impression that he was not particularly strong on the League of Nations until comparatively recently.' Attlee further argued that Churchill's profession of enthusiasm was undermined by his wish 'to withdraw sanctions' against Italy. 'Are you going to sacrifice Abyssinia entirely? I would say that the duty of this country regarding the vindication of the League in the case of Italy is quite as vital as in the case of Germany.'[3]

Churchill and Attlee remained far apart on the question of defence. Under Attlee's leadership, Labour MPs continued to uphold their tradition of voting against the estimates for the armed forces, a stance that Dalton found absurd in view of the party's demand for collective security. 'Our leadership is small and uninspiring,' he wrote.[4] Churchill shared Dalton's view. At a meeting in Horsham on 23 July, he complained that the Labour front bench still mocked 'the most modest and reasonable precautions'.[5] He was further aggrieved by Labour in late July, when Baldwin reluctantly agreed to receive a deputation of senior politicians to discuss Britain's defences. Churchill felt that this could be a moment to galvanise the National Government into stepping up its rearmament programme, especially if the deputation could be put on an all-party basis. To his disappointment, Attlee refused an invitation to join, without providing any explanation. 'I have considered the matter with my friends and I do not think it would be desirable for His Majesty's Opposition to follow this procedure at this juncture,' he wrote to Churchill.[6] The deputation met Baldwin for two days at the end of the month. Armed with more figures from Morton on German production, Churchill again set out the case for greater urgency, but Baldwin refused to be persuaded.

Labour was even more complacent than the Prime Minster. Attempts in the autumn of 1936 by moderates like Bevin and Dalton to reverse the party's anti-rearmament policy failed, partly because of Attlee's hostility to the current Tory-led administration. 'There is a good deal of scare feeling over Hitler which is not without justification but makes some people want to support the Government policy on armaments which is stupid,' he told his brother.[7] At its Annual Conference in Edinburgh, the party incoherently declared that it would accept rearmament under the auspices of the LoN but not the Government, after Attlee told delegates that he would not give Baldwin 'a blank cheque'.[8] After Conference, the Labour peer Lord Ponsonby wrote that the gathering had been beset by 'utter confusion' because Attlee was 'without a spark of talent for leadership'.[9]

In contrast, Churchill's reputation underwent a revival in 1936 now that his campaign on India was over, since defence of the British nation had a much wider appeal as a cause than the defence of the Raj had had. Churchill had begun the year still hoping for a post in the Government but that ambition had finally been dashed in March, when Baldwin had appointed the rotund lawyer Sir Thomas Inskip to the newly created post of Minister for Defence Co-ordination. This was a position for which Churchill seemed perfectly suited, both by experience and interest, whereas Inskip had devoted his political career almost exclusively to legal questions. Yet Churchill's exclusion did not impede his fight for rearmament and against Nazism, which gathered pace during the remaining months of 1936. In addition to parliamentary speeches and radio broadcasts, his campaign was carried on through a number of pressure groups, the most influential of which was the Focus in Defence of Freedom and Peace, more commonly known as Focus. By emphasising the central importance of the LoN in challenging Nazi Germany, Focus had a reach far beyond the Conservative Party. Asquith's daughter Violet – now a Bonham Carter – was a stalwart member, as were Hugh Dalton and the highly respected General Secretary of the TUC Sir Walter Citrine, who became an ally of Churchill's in the 1930s through their joint awareness of the Nazi threat.

After years of being branded an anachronistic extremist, Churchill began to find that, as foremost champion of anti-Nazism, he was increasingly seen as an elder statesman and even a possible Prime Minister. 'All the left-wing intelligentsia are coming to look to me for protection of their ideas and I will give it wholeheartedly, in return for their aid in the rearmament of Britain,' he told his son Randolph.[10] Even Attlee, who was now softening his opposition to strengthened British defences, started to see Churchill as a possible bulwark to uphold the LoN and democracy. At the end of November, Churchill's cousin Freddie Guest, a senior Conservative MP and the former Chief Whip in Lloyd George's Coalition, approached the Labour Leader to explore the possibility of greater co-operation. The result seemed positive. 'Attlee will support you on any rearmament programme. He admires and likes you. The door is open if you want to talk to him,' Guest told Churchill on 25 November 1936.[11] 'I hope to get in touch with Attlee later,' replied Churchill.[12]

But the initial collaboration, centred on the LoN, was not straight-forward. Keen to cast the anti-Nazi net as widely as possible, Churchill contacted Lord Cecil of Chelwood, a former Tory minister who was now a key executive member of the League of Nations Union (LNU), an important association that campaigned for collective security. For some Tories, the LNU smacked too much of pacifism and naïve idealism. Churchill himself had once written of its members: 'What impresses me most is their long suffering and inexhaustible gullibility.'[13] But in the autumn of 1936 he wanted all the support he could find across civic life in Britain to build up pressure for a steadfast response against Hitler. He therefore wrote to Cecil to explain that the anti-Nazi groups were planning joint action to create 'the strongest possible force that will resist unprovoked aggression and tyranny'.[14] Cecil responded by asking Churchill to sign an international declaration in support of the LoN against the dictatorships, telling him that among the signatories were Dalton, Citrine, and Archie Sinclair, the Leader of the Liberal Party. In a further letter, Cecil explained that Attlee had agreed to sign the declaration 'subject to one alteration. He wants some reference to the peaceful settlement of international disputes.'[15] Churchill was not taken with Attlee's proposal. 'I do not think there is much value in the additions […] They do not improve the swing.'[16] Indeed, Churchill became disillusioned with the entire plan and the calibre of the signatories. 'I must confess I do not see the advantage of your manifesto at this stage. The list of names you have sent me is not at all impressive. In fact, it is nothing but the League of Nations Union notabilities,' he said to Cecil on 2 December.[17] Cecil was dismayed, telling Churchill that his stance 'fills me with consternation' and adding that Attlee, among others, had 'nothing to do with the League of Nations Union'.[18]

Yet Cecil's scheme was a sideshow compared to a much more immediate, higher-profile initiative that preoccupied Churchill. His Focus group, backed up by the other anti-Nazi organisations, had decided to hold a major rally at the Albert Hall, London, on 3 December to galvanise public opinion in favour of rearmament and collective security. Using the theme of 'Arms and the Covenant', the organisers stressed the inclusive, non-partisan nature of the gathering. Citrine, graceful and assured, was in the chair, while twenty MPs from all parties sat on the platform. The arena was packed as Churchill, never a good timekeeper, arrived just minutes before the scheduled start. But his speech did not disappoint the expectations of the huge audience. 'Was it not time that the free nations, great or small, here or across the Atlantic, should take the measures to place themselves in a state of security and in a state of adequate defence, not only for their own safety but also that they might hold aloft the beacon lights of freedom?' he asked, to prolonged applause.[19]

The rehabilitation of Churchill seemed to be continuing. Citrine called his speech 'masterly'.[20] Both the *Spectator* and the *New Statesman* predicted that a popular new coalition would soon emerge with Churchill at its head. Yet in the immediate aftermath of this success, Churchill was suddenly embroiled in a constitutional crisis which revived all the old doubts about his judgement, party loyalty and reliability, as well as widening the chasm with Attlee's Labour Party. The cause of the crisis could be discerned at the end of his Albert Hall event, when the 5,000-strong crowd sang the national anthem with extra passion. For at the very moment of the rally, the public was in the grip of fevered speculation about the future of King Edward VIII, whose affair with Mrs Wallis Simpson had only just been revealed by the British press. The news was so explosive because Mrs Simpson's status as a twice-divorced woman made it impossible for Baldwin's Government to accept the King's plan to make her his Queen. If the King was really determined to marry her, either he would have to give up the throne or Baldwin would have to be replaced by a new Prime Minister more sympathetic to the royal cause.

Both Churchill and Attlee were crucial in this saga, and once more they ended up on different sides. Throughout the crisis, Churchill was by far the most powerful advocate of the King's position. He had not only been a personal friend of Edward VIII since 1910, but was also a fervent monarchist who felt it was his absolute duty to serve the Crown. 'Winston is the last man who actually believes in the Divine Right of Kings,' his wife once said, only half-jokingly.[21] Attlee was also a strong monarchist but much less of a romantic cavalier than Churchill. In line with his respectable Victorian upbringing in Putney, he regarded Mrs Simpson as a wholly unsuitable consort.

The Labour front bench might have been expected to give more support to the King, given his reputation for concern about deprivation, as shown in his well-received tours of economic black spots such as the South Wales coalfields. Indeed, Attlee later said that, on meeting the King a couple of times during his short reign, he was 'struck by his genuine solicitude for the unemployed'.[22] But Edward VIII's supposed progressivism was shallow, little more than another aspect of his self-conscious rebellion against the Court. 'Don't believe the nonsense you hear that he's a socialist. He is no more a socialist than J. D. Rockefeller or any other rich man who had pricklings of conscience,' the left-wing academic Harold Laski told an American friend.[23] Furthermore, doubts about Edward VIII's character were confirmed after his succession, as he displayed his disdain for official duties and the traditions of his position. Following the accession meeting of the

Privy Council, Baldwin told Attlee of his fear 'as to whether the new King would stay the course'.[24] Labour MP John Parker, later a minister in Attlee's post-war Government, recalled that when Edward VIII opened Parliament in November 1936 'he read the King's speech in such a way as to make nonsense of it. Nobody mentioned that in *The Times*. He read it with an American accent! He was obviously spoiling for a fight.'[25]

Having hoped for an easy journey into his long-anticipated retirement, Baldwin was forced to grapple with an unprecedented crisis. His predicament deepened on 16 November, when the King confirmed that he wanted to marry Mrs Simpson following the start of divorce proceedings from her second husband. One possible way out of the impasse was the unconventional idea, dreamed up by Churchill, of a morganatic marriage, which would have prevented royal rank and prestige from passing to Mrs Simpson. Baldwin felt it unlikely that the Commons would accept such a measure, but he had to ascertain the views of other politicians – especially Attlee, as Leader of the Opposition.

On 25 November, he summoned Attlee, along with Churchill and Archie Sinclair, to Downing Street. In Baldwin's account of his talk with the Labour Leader, Attlee was explicit about the morganatic proposal.

> His first impression was that Labour would not touch it with a bargepole, but had promised to make discreet enquiries. The Prime Minister had then asked him what would be the reaction of Labour to abdication. Mr Attlee had replied that he thought on the whole they would be sympathetic to the King and would say that he had done the right thing and there would be a sigh of relief.[26]

But the most important question put to Attlee was how he would respond if the National Government were forced to resign in the event of the King refusing to abdicate while insisting on marriage to Mrs

Simpson. Attlee simply pledged his constitutional loyalty to Baldwin and said the Labour Party would refuse to form an alternative admin-istration. It was a vital answer that gave Baldwin enormous leverage in his negotiations with the King, secure in the knowledge that he would have the support of the official Opposition.

Some on the left, like the fiery ex-miner Nye Bevan, later felt that Attlee had been overly cautious and should have exploited the crisis to bring down the Government, or at least split the Tories. 'The Labour Party has too much reverence,' wrote Bevan in *Tribune* magazine.[27] Such a claim ignored the reality, as Attlee intuited, of working-class opinion wedded to respectability. Popular backing for the King was limited. Francis Williams, editor of the mass-circulation *Herald*, which in the mid-1930s had daily sales of 2 million, wrote: 'It was clear that the great mass of middle- and working-class readers of the *Herald* were deeply upset by the suggestion that a woman who had twice been through the divorce courts might become Queen.'[28] Or, as trade-union leader Ernie Bevin put it, 'Our people won't have it.'[29]

Asked the same question about the possibility of the Government's resignation, Archie Sinclair gave the same answer as Attlee, saying he would refuse to take office. But Churchill was more circumspect. He told Baldwin that 'though his attitude was a little different, he would certainly support the Government'.[30] Neither Baldwin nor the Chancellor, Neville Chamberlain, who was also present at the meeting, sensed that Churchill was being straightforward. They suspected that behind his words lurked an ambition to use the crisis as a vehicle to seize the premiership as his own, aided by Lord Beaverbrook. It was an indicator of the profound mistrust that Churchill continued to provoke that he could be regarded as a ruthless intriguer against the Government. As the crisis intensified, wild rumours circulated that he and Beaverbrook were ready to form 'a King's Party' to smash the Government. Ramsay MacDonald, ageing fast but still a senior Cabinet minister as Lord President of the Council, noted in his diary a story he had heard that 'Churchill, at private lunch, made no bones about his determination to drive Baldwin from office and destroy the National

Government'.[31] This concern was mirrored on the Conservative back benches. Tory MP Cuthbert Headlam wrote at the height of the crisis that 'neither Winston nor Beaverbrook are men who would stop at anything to secure their own ends, but it only shows (if they intervene in this business) how little they know of public opinion. The country is not behind His Majesty and the sooner he realises it the better it will be.'[32]

Yet this frenzied speculation about Churchill's motives was unfair. He was never a plotter. For all his ambition, he was too transparent, too expressive of his feelings to be one. His aim throughout this affair was to protect the King, not advance himself. His strategy, to which he clung tenaciously despite widespread opprobrium, was to push for a delay in any decision, so that over time either Edward VIII might be persuaded to give up his relationship with Mrs Simpson or she would abandon the idea of marriage. He did not see why, with such grave constitutional questions at stake, precipitate action needed to be taken. Baldwin took the opposite view, believing that the crisis had to be resolved urgently to prevent lasting damage to the Crown and Parliament. On 2 December the Prime Minister confirmed to the Cabinet that the morganatic marriage proposal was simply unfeasible, not least because it had been comprehensively rejected by the Dominion Prime Ministers and by Attlee. 'He had again seen the Leader of the Labour Opposition, who had told him that not a single member of the Labour Party would vote for such a Bill,' reported Baldwin.[33] The next day, Thursday 3 December, the national papers, which had shown remarkable restraint until that moment, finally covered the burgeoning crisis. In an atmosphere of mounting ferment, the question was openly raised for the first time in the Commons, with Attlee asking the Prime Minister if 'he has any statement to make'. Baldwin replied that 'the situation is of such a nature as to make it inexpedient I should be questioned about it at this stage'. Attlee pressed his case for a statement 'in view of the anxiety which reports are causing in the minds of the people'. In the quiet, measured voice he used throughout the crisis, Baldwin said, 'I have to assure the Leader of the Opposition that I have all that he says very much in mind.' Churchill then rose. In line with his pressure for a delay, he urged Baldwin to 'give us an assurance that no irrevocable step will be taken before a formal statement has been made to Parliament'. His question provoked some grumbles on the Conservative benches, but Baldwin stonewalled: 'I have nothing to add.'[34]

Away from Westminster, there was a continual flurry of activity that day. Attlee saw Baldwin again, reiterating that the 'whole of the Labour Party would vote against the proposal' for a morganatic marriage. His stance was endorsed later in the day at a meeting of the PLP executive. Churchill met Beaverbrook at the *Express* owner's London residence of Stornoway House, along with the King's solicitor, George Allen. The three men agreed that Edward VIII should be given the right to make a radio broadcast to the British public, setting out his case to be allowed to marry Mrs Simpson. But Baldwin, during another audience with the King, said that such a broadcast would be 'thoroughly unconstitutional' because it would 'go over the heads of your Ministers'.[35] Baldwin then told the King that a decision would have to be made swiftly on his marriage, if possible by the weekend. 'You will not have to wait much longer,' replied the King. At the conclusion of this painful audience, the King asked if he could see Churchill, 'an old friend with whom he could talk freely'.[36] Baldwin reluctantly agreed.

That evening, as Baldwin talked to the King, Churchill attended his 'Arms and the Covenant' rally at the Albert Hall. Although he did not know about the decision on the broadcast, it was clear that his concern for the King weighed heavily on his mind. As he rushed into the venue, he told the chairman, Walter Citrine, that he would have to insert a reference to the King into his speech. Citrine strongly objected, emphasising that the meeting was to demonstrate unity against the Nazis. 'We haven't come to talk about the King or anything else,' said the TUC chief.[37] Churchill backed down and did not mention the crisis in his address. Citrine's tough line showed that the unions largely shared Labour's unsympathetic view of Mrs Simpson. In fact, as he had told Churchill over lunch earlier in the week, Citrine had already informed Baldwin that he had 'no doubt the trade union movement would back the Government even if it came to the King's abdicating'.[38]

The climax was now approaching. Confronted by a near-unanimous establishment, Edward VIII sensed that the crown was starting to slip away. But Churchill, with the indefatigability that was his hallmark, continued to press for a delay. On the night of Friday 4 December, as urgently arranged with the Palace, he went to Fort Belvedere, the King's residence at Windsor. The conversation was intimate but troubled, with the King at times losing the thread of his argument because of the strain he felt. At one stage, he asked Churchill if the Government would resign unless he agreed to abdicate. In reply, Churchill again stressed that no hasty step should be taken, while he also bitterly complained about Baldwin's use of Attlee to put pressure on the King. In his account of the audience, Edward VIII wrote:

> Mr Churchill was particularly outraged by Mr Baldwin's action in securing from the leaders of the Opposition parties, namely Mr Clement Attlee of the Labour Party and Sir Archibald Sinclair of the Liberals, a promise not to participate in the formation of a new Government were he to resign and were I to ask them to form another in its place. The practical effect of this *modus vivendi* was to confront the Sovereign with an ultimatum.

At the end of the audience, Churchill once more urged the King not to rush into any decision. 'Sir, it is a time for reflection. You must allow time for the battalions to march,' said Churchill as left.[39]

The next morning, Saturday 5 December, Churchill sent Baldwin a record of his audience at Fort Belvedere, using the excuse of the King's health to push for a postponement in any decision. 'It would be a most cruel and wrong to extort a decision from him in his present state,' he told the Prime Minister.[40] In public Churchill kept up the pressure for a delay by issuing a lengthy statement to the press, which was published that Sunday morning, 6 December. Yet again, Churchill pleaded for 'time

and patience', not only for the King but also to allow 'a searching constitutional debate' in Parliament.[41] Displaying the same tone of indignation
that he had used at his Fort Belvedere audience, he also condemned the
part that the Government had forced Attlee to play in the crisis.

> If the King refuses to take the advice of his Ministers they are
> free to resign. They have no right whatever to put pressure upon
> him to accept their advice by soliciting beforehand assurances
> from the Leader of the Opposition that he will not form an
> alternative administration in the event of their resignation and
> thus confronting the King with an ultimatum.[42]

Without complete honesty, Attlee publicly replied that 'there was no
foundation whatever in saying that any assurance had been received
from him'.[43]

By now the mood across most of the political class had turned
against Churchill and his calls for a delay. Concerns about a 'King's
party grew', while pressure mounted for an urgent resolution of the
crisis rather than further prevarication. Even Edward VIII was on the
verge of giving up the struggle, as Beaverbrook told Churchill when
they met that Saturday. 'Our cock won't fight,' he warned.[44] The slide
towards capitulation dominated a crucial emergency meeting of the
Cabinet on Sunday, where Baldwin reported that he had again seen the
King, who was now prepared to abdicate. Yet Churchill still refused to
yield. Ensconced at Chartwell on Sunday afternoon with Sinclair and
the Tory MP Bob Boothby, he came up with a new, desperate scheme to
buy time and avoid abdication, whereby the King would issue a public
statement promising 'not to enter any contract of marriage contrary
to the advice of his Ministers'.[45] Churchill's thinking was that, since
Wallis Simpson's divorce would probably not be absolute until April
1937, a final decision could be postponed for at least four months. But
the King was unmoved when the formula was put to him by a friend of
Boothby's on Monday morning, 7 December. He had all but made up
his mind to choose Wallis rather than the throne.

Edward's rejection of the plan was the prelude to one of the darkest moments of Churchill's parliamentary career. In the House of Commons that Monday afternoon, in response to a question from Attlee, Baldwin made another holding statement in which he said, rather deceitfully, that 'it is the earnest desire of the Government to afford His Majesty the fullest opportunity of weighing a decision'. Alluding obliquely to Churchill's weekend press notice about the political pressures on the King, he said with even less candour: 'No advice has been tendered by the Government to His Majesty, with whom all conversations have been strictly personal and informal.'[46] Attlee and Baldwin, who prided himself on his image of emollient non-partisanship, then indulged in expressions of mutual respect and warmth. 'I agree with every word of what he says,' declared the Prime Minister soothingly, after the Labour Leader had spoken of his sympathy for the King and the need for the House to receive 'the fullest information as soon as possible'.[47] This cordial exchange, cheered by both sides, was in dramatic contrast to the scene that followed as Churchill rose to his feet. He had been presiding at the Anglo-French Luncheon Club, an engagement that prompted suspicions among MPs about his sobriety. The antagonism could be felt from the moment he began to speak. For the third time in four days, he asked that 'no irrevocable step will be taken before the House has received a full statement', but his words were almost drowned out by a barrage of abuse. 'No', 'Sit down', 'Twister' and 'Drop it', shouted MPs.[48] From the Tory benches, Lord Winterton said that 'it was the angriest manifestation I have ever heard against any man in the House of Commons'.[49] Churchill tried to continue, but that only further aggravated the members. The uproar reached its climax when the Speaker ruled Churchill out of order for trying to make a speech rather than put a question. Shaken and humiliated, he stormed out of the chamber with the words, 'You won't be satisfied until you've broken him, will you?'[50]

Churchill appeared to have sunk his own fortunes just as they were undergoing a revival. In his diary, Ramsay MacDonald wrote gleefully that night: 'He mishandled his piece in both tone and attitude and ended his canter in a ditch. Sulky and crestfallen, he walked into the Division Lobby having done the King no good but harm: an able, resourceful unlovely man whose opportunities have been legion but thrown away.'[51] Even Churchill's allies were dismayed at the damage he had inflicted not only on his own career but also on the cause of anti-Nazism. 'He has undone in five minutes the patient reconstruction work of two years,' wrote the National Labour MP Harold Nicolson in his diary.[52]

With Churchill's humiliation, the resistance was over. On the morning of Thursday 10 December the King signed the Deed of Abdication, which Baldwin then brought to the House of Commons that afternoon. Announcing the King's decision, Baldwin told MPs, 'I am convinced that where I failed no one could have succeeded. His mind was made up.'[53] After a brief adjournment, Attlee made his own contribution, in which he again showed his warmth towards Baldwin: 'we can all appreciate the strain which these events have placed on the Prime Minister, and he is entitled to our sympathy'.[54] When Attlee sat down, there was an outburst of cheering. Churchill followed and received a much warmer reception than he had on Monday. Much of the antipathy towards him had evaporated now that abdication had become a reality. Admiration for the King and personal friendship had motivated his actions, Churchill explained: 'I should have been ashamed if, in my independent and unofficial position, I had not cast about for every lawful means, even the most forlorn, to keep him on the throne.'[55] Such was his affection for the departed King that, long afterwards, he kept a photograph of the Duke of Windsor on a table in his bedroom at Chartwell, signed 'Edward R. I., the night before his abdication'.[56]

Attlee has proved a shrewder judge than Churchill of the political mood. When he gave a report about his handling of the crisis to Labour's National Executive Committee (NEC) on 7 December, there was no dissent. 'It would be best to leave the Parliamentary Labour Party to deal with the matter,' the NEC agreed.[57] For some, the fact that the Labour movement largely accepted Attlee's approach was a cause for regret. On holiday in the Caribbean, Lloyd George wrote to his daughter Megan on 9 December, 'If the King wants to marry his American friend – why not? […] Labour have as usual played a cowardly part.'[58] But Attlee's outlook was bound to prevail in a party that so valued respectability, a trait epitomised by the Leader himself. Baldwin's ally John Davidson, who praised Labour's decisive influence in the crisis, wrote: 'There was not the slightest doubt on the part of Attlee or Bevin that the only alternatives facing the King were renunciation of Mrs Simpson or abdication. No compromise was possible.' As evidence for his thesis, Davidson cited the case of a Labour official who tried to make his mistress the hostess of an official function at the Annual Conference.

> None of the leading members of the party would shake her hand. This small episode emphasised the strong Puritanism on such matters within the Labour Party. It was impossible to conceive of the Labour or trade union movement tolerating Mrs Simpson as the consort of the King. We were close friends of the Attlees and the Bevins and I never had doubt where they stood in the crisis.[59]

The affair enhanced Attlee's stature. Unlike Churchill, he was seen as having played straight and avoided unconstitutional meddling. Later he strongly denied a rumour that he had actually gone to Mrs Simpson to persuade her to abandon the idea of marriage. 'Never seen her in my life,' he said in a 1965 interview.[60] But there was one point on which Attlee and Churchill agreed. They both came to believe that George VI, aided by his determined wife, was better suited than his wayward elder brother to be sovereign. In his autobiography, Attlee wrote that the abdication turned out to be 'fortunate' because it 'enabled King George VI and Queen Elizabeth to raise' the monarchy 'to a greater height than ever before'.[61] After all his efforts to defend Edward VIII, Churchill confessed in 1940 that he 'had been mistaken' in his attempt to prevent the abdication, 'since that monarch and his wife would not have been such a popular rallying pair as the present King and Queen'.[62]

Churchill had certainly sustained a heavy, perhaps even terminal, blow to his reputation. 'I was so smitten in public opinion that it was the almost universal view that my political life was ended,' he later wrote.[63] 'To my mind, he seemed terribly blind to public opinion,' recalled Attlee.[64] But, despite his eclipse in the wake of the abdication, Churchill's warnings about Nazi Germany were more pertinent than ever. He was still the politician who grasped most clearly the threat that Britain faced. Even at the end of his regretful speech on 10 December, he concluded that 'Danger gathers upon our path. We cannot afford – we have no right – to look back.'[65] The wisdom of his analysis would grow over the remainder of the decade, and with it his ultimate indispensability. Soon after the abdication, Churchill visited Paris and, by coincidence, ran into Beaverbrook. He told the press baron of his fear that his political career might be over. Beaverbrook replied, 'What nonsense. A man in your position may be in the depths of despair one day and the next raised to the heights and appointed Prime Minister.'[66]

ELEVEN

◆

MUNICH

THE ABDICATION WAS the last major event of Baldwin's premiership. In May 1937 he retired from public life and was succeeded by his Chancellor, Neville Chamberlain, who now reached the office that had eluded both his father Joseph and his elder half-brother Austen. For both Churchill and Attlee, Chamberlain's elevation was a negative step. Prim, self-confident and guarded, the new Prime Minister warmed to neither of them. He did not even consider offering Churchill a post in his new administration. To the War Secretary Leslie Hore-Belisha, the Prime Minister explained, 'If I take him into the Cabinet he will dominate it. He won't give the others a chance of even talking.'[1] Nor did Chamberlain, in contrast to Baldwin, have any rapport with the Labour front bench. He once told his sister that 'intellectually, with a few exceptions, they are dirt'.[2] Attlee's opinion of Chamberlain was just as low: 'I thought he was absolutely useless for foreign affairs – ignorant and at the same time opinionated.'[3]

At the centre of Chamberlain's foreign policy was his belief in the appeasement of Nazi Germany, based on his vain delusion that Hitler was a rational leader with legitimate grievances that could be the settled by negotiation. This offended every instinct of Churchill, who regarded such as outlook as a form of cowardice and defeatism. As he famously put it, 'an appeaser is one who feeds a crocodile, hoping it will eat him last'.[4] Attlee was coming round to the same view. After years of maintaining Labour's anti-rearmament line, he began from late 1936 to recognise that the defence of the nation could not be contracted out to the LoN. One catalyst for his change of mind was his identification with the Republican side in the Spanish Civil War against Franco's Nationalist forces, which were strongly backed by Hitler and Mussolini. Idealism about the rule of international law was swept away by the Iberian conflict, with its modern weaponry, aerial bombing, civilian massacres and guerrilla fighting.

The strongest manifestation of Labour's more realistic approach came in July 1937, when the PLP finally abandoned its long-standing habit of voting against the annual defence estimates. It was a move orchestrated by Bevin and Dalton, but Attlee, who had long upheld this voting tradition, now saw that the previous stance was untenable. In the autumn of that year, his party's Annual Conference adopted a tougher line, stating that a future Labour Government 'should be strongly equipped to defend the country and play its full part in collective security'.[5] Attlee also understood that, in the new era of aerial warfare, the strength of the RAF was a crucial factor in national self-protection; consequently he began to develop a much deeper understanding of air strategy and technology.

During 1937, in a debate on unemployment, Attlee told the House that he had been re-reading Churchill's speech as Chancellor on his experiment in derating to boost industry. 'Whatever else he may be, he is a man of vision and able to put things in a vivid way,' Attlee said.[6] Despite such praise, Attlee tended to keep his political distance from Churchill, partly because he was still vulnerable as Labour Leader and was widely seen on the left as little more than a stop-gap in advance of a takeover by a bigger figure. In May 1937, Beatrice Webb wrote that 'Attlee is a nonentity' and Morrison 'is the only possible leader'.[7] From the radical socialists came growing attacks on his perceived failure to give more vocal support to the Soviet Union or build a united, anti-Conservative front of all groups on the left. Journals like *Tribune* and the *New Statesman* were persistent critics. Kingsley Martin, the editor of the latter, wrote that Attlee was like an ineffectual school-master 'in his study watching over the boys, some of them too big to handle when they are fresh'.[8]

Attlee's leadership may have been assailable, but in his domestic life he was enjoying a new security. Financially, his position was improved in 1937 by two developments. One was the successful publication of his book entitled *The Labour Party in Perspective*, which had sales of 60,000 and brought him a profit of £600, a small amount compared to Churchill's vast literary earnings but far more than he had expected. The other was Parliament's decision to grant the Leader of the Opposition an annual salary of £2,000, the first time that the position had been officially rewarded. The increase in his income eased the burden of running the family home, the Attlees having moved in 1931 from their house in Churchill's constituency to a much larger property called Heywood in Stanmore, Middlesex; though they were never well off and Violet was always anxious about money. That concern shone through an interview that Violet gave in April 1937 to the *Star*, the popular London paper, about her routine. 'We have breakfast early – quarter to eight – and as we haven't a cook – we can't afford one – I have to start very early. Then there's the clearing up, shopping and arranging the meals for the day. I have a little car, but my husband uses the tube. Quicker and cheaper!' Asked about her hobbies, she replied, 'We haven't any. We haven't time or money.'⁹ Even so, Violet's home was a contented one. Attlee was a devoted husband and a good father to his four children, despite his heavy duties. Heywood was a haven from politics, especially at the weekends, and Attlee loved to play with the children, potter in the garden or carry out household maintenance. His daughter Janet recalled, 'If things were broken, he fixed them. He recovered dining room chairs. He was not brilliant with his hands but he was creative. One night the police knocked on the door and said to Mother, "Ma'am, there is a man on the roof." She replied, "Yes, it's my husband, he's cleaning the gutters."' Janet also remembered her father's powerful moral influence. 'It was not directive, not preachy, but I learned from him that integrity was the most important thing you had.'¹⁰ One indicator of that integrity was how Attlee lived up to his political rhetoric about his abhorrence of Nazism. As anti-Semitism worsened in Germany, the family took in a Jewish refugee called Hans

Paul Willer, who came to Britain with the Kindertransport scheme and stayed with the Attlees until the start of the war, when he was evacuated to the countryside. 'Attlee was a modest man. He did not try and glorify himself in any way,' Willer remembered.[11]

Churchill's own domestic life at this time was less serene. His phenomenal workload and erratic routine were a constant source of tension, while he was still beset by financial problems because of his extravagance, stock-market losses and the upkeep of his two properties: his London flat at Morpeth Mansions and his country house at Chartwell. Drastic economies, including cutbacks in champagne and staff, did little to reduce his debts. By early 1937, he had borrowed £22,500 from his bank and insurance companies and another £12,000 from his family trusts. Even his production line of books and articles could not dig him out of his trouble, with the result that he had to put Chartwell on the market. No buyer came forward and by 1938, when his liabilities were compounded by a tax bill of £4,700, he was staring bankruptcy in the face. He was rescued only by the generosity of the Austrian-born banker and businessman Sir Henry Strakosch, who was a strong admirer of Churchill because of his stance against the evil of Nazism. A large loan from Sir Henry, negotiated by Churchill's loyal acolyte Brendan Bracken, allowed debts to be covered and Chartwell to be taken off the market. By the end of 1938, thanks to further large earnings from his pen, Churchill was in credit.

The course of his marriage was not entirely smooth either at this time. Although she adored Winston, Clementine was sometimes exhausted by his egocentric personality and the strain of his endlessly controversial public life. Her respite lay in lengthy holidays abroad. On one such trip, a cruise to the South Pacific in early 1935 organised by the Guinness heir Lord Moyne, she developed an infatuation towards another guest, the dashing unmarried art dealer Terence Philip. Although the relationship may have been unconsummated, there is no doubt that she had romantic feelings towards Philip as they travelled across the balmy, exotic seas. 'She tasted the always heady elixir of admiration and knew the pleasures of companionship,' wrote her own daughter

Mary.[12] Captivated by Philip, she stayed on the voyage for four months, to the exasperation of her children and Winston. 'Papa is miserable and frightfully naughty without you,' said Sarah, then aged twenty and just at the start of her acting career.[13] Clementine finally returned in April 1935 and saw Philip only a couple of times again. But Churchill did not modify his behaviour, as Clementine revealed to the TUC chief Walter Citrine when they both went on an official trip to the Caribbean in 1938. With surprising openness, she told Citrine that 'all her life she had been arguing with Winston. He always won by simply beating down her arguments.' There were other insights into their relationship. 'She had spent most of her married life tidying Winston up! "He never says so, but I do my best."' On his time-keeping, Clementine told Citrine, 'Winston is the most unpunctual man in the world.'[14]

Space for domestic life became even more limited for Churchill and Attlee as the political pressures on the two men escalated because of the worsening European crisis. In February 1938 the Yorkshire peer Lord Halifax became Foreign Secretary after the resignation of Anthony Eden in protest at Chamberlain's attempts to appease Italy. Attlee voiced his opposition to the appointment, not on personal grounds but because he believed that at a time of such international danger the Foreign Secretary should be answerable to the Commons. 'This is no time for foreign affairs to be taken away from the purview of this House,' he said.[15] In response, Churchill made what the *Daily Express* called 'a boisterous, rollicking speech'[16] that managed to both counter Attlee's argument and heap ironic praise on Chamberlain. After pointing out that a host of Foreign Secretaries had sat in the Lords without any constitutional problem, he denied that there was anything 'derogatory' to the Commons about such an arrangement, given the dominant role of Chamberlain. 'When you have a Prime Minister, what is the good of worrying about the Foreign Secretary? What is the point of crying out for the moon when you have the sun, and you have that bright orb of day from whose effulgent beams the lesser luminaries derive their radiance?'[17] Attlee's motion of objection was rejected by 226 votes to 99.

Almost immediately on taking office, Halifax met the brutish reality of German bellicosity. On 12 March the Nazi regime annexed neigh-bouring Austria, eliminating all internal opposition through mass executions and deportations to concentration camps. The ruthless absorption of Hitler's native land into the Reich, a process known as the Anschluss, precipitated a mood of alarm and outrage in London. In the House, both Attlee and Churchill argued that Chamberlain's weak policy had facilitated the Nazi takeover. The Prime Minister 'yields to force all the time', said Attlee, now firmly aligned with anti-appeasers.[18] In his own speech, Churchill warned that Europe was 'confronted with a programme of aggression, nicely calculated and timed, unfolding stage by stage'. With his habitual prescience, he predicted that Czechoslovakia would be next to face Germany's intimidation.[19]

The rhetoric of condemnation was accompanied by talk of new alliances and a restructured Government. In the mood of anxiety, some glimpsed the prospect of a major realignment in party groupings and there was even speculation that Churchill, apparently supported by Labour and other anti-Chamberlain forces, might be propelled into the highest position. Hugh Dalton, who relished intrigue, recorded in his diary after a lunch with *New Statesman* editor Kingsley Martin: 'The idea of a new Coalition Government was very much in the air. Churchill was to be the Prime Minister and Eden the Foreign Secretary. The Labour Party and Liberal Party would both be strongly represented in the Cabinet.' Martin then explained to Dalton that he had been acting as a go-between to push the scheme. 'He had seen Attlee, who, at the beginning had not been favourable to the idea. Later he had changed his mind. Greenwood had been much interested, Herbert Morrison even more so.'[20] But Martin's Cabinet-making had little grounding in practical politics. His proposal never gathered any momentum, justi-fying Attlee's lukewarm response. The Labour Leader had correctly recognised that the scale of the potential anti-Chamberlain rebellion in the Conservative ranks had been greatly exaggerated. In fact, the Prime Minister's stranglehold on his party was tighter than ever, as the Tory MP Ronald Cartland told Dalton: 'It was astonishing how the bulk of the party followed him blindly.'[21]

The same embellishment could be found when, immediately after the Anschluss, Chamberlain and Halifax had a talk with the Opposition leaders to discuss the implications for Britain's foreign policy and security. This discussion, during which Halifax found Attlee 'intelligent and sensible',[22] was little more than a briefing of the sort that Governments routinely give; but, in the excitable atmosphere of the moment, it was elevated into a potential precursor for a refashioned approach. Churchill picked up on these whispers and allowed himself to think that a real change could be coming, as confided to Harold Nicolson MP over dinner on 16 March: 'He said that he will wait a day or two in the hope that the negotiations which are now going on between Chamberlain, Attlee and Sinclair for a formula of policy that will command the assent of the whole House, have either failed or come to fruition. But if no clear statement is issued between now and Wednesday next, he will refuse the whip and take some 50 people with him.'[23] This was all fantasy. There was no army of Tory rebels, nor did the meeting have much significance. As Nicolson himself recorded, 'Attlee later denied that any such conversations had taken place.'[24] In fact, Attlee was so angry at the inference that he was in negotiations with Chamberlain that he verbally abused Citrine when the subject was raised. 'Attlee had sworn at him in front of several others [...] because Citrine had pressed for information on Attlee's conversations with Chamberlain and Halifax,' noted Dalton.[25]

The only change that the Anschluss brought was a magnification in the official policy of appeasing the dictators while rearming Britain. Churchill soon recognised that, as long as Chamberlain was in Downing Street, there would be no Cabinet reconstruction or any drive to enforce collective security. When the Liberal MP Richard Acland wrote to him urging the construction of an all-party group with Attlee, Sinclair and Eden, Churchill dismissed his suggestion as pointless. 'The Government have a solid majority, and Chamberlain will certainly not wish to work with me.'[26] Far from fostering a new unity after the Anschluss, Attlee and Churchill maintained their distance. The gap between them could be seen in a letter that Churchill sent Attlee on 17 March about Lord

Cecil's plan to set up a new committee that would sponsor 'a Campaign for the Covenant of the League' if the Government proved irresolute. Presaging Attlee's non-involvement, Churchill wrote: 'For myself I think that if we do decide to have a Committee, it would be better to confine it to unofficial members of our party, otherwise it would look as if there was a significance quite beyond anything which our educative campaign implies.'[27] In his reply to Churchill, Attlee agreed with this position. 'Exactly the same reasons as you state seemed to me cogent.'[28]

With the drumbeat of war echoing in the background, Germany built up its menacing pressure on Czechoslovakia. 'I think we shall have to choose in the next few weeks between war and shame, and I have very little doubt what the decision will be,' Churchill wrote to Lloyd George in August 1938.[29] The Czech crisis reached its climax in September as Hitler aggressively cultivated the grievances of the German-speaking Sudeten region to push for the dismemberment of the republic. In response to Hitler's intimidation, the Governments of Britain and France, who had promised to defend the territorial integrity of Czechoslovakia, now clung ever more tightly to the policy of appeasement. After the years of anti-rearmament, the Labour Party – with the exception of a few pacifists on the far left – was now firm for resistance. That tougher mood was reflected when the National Council of Labour, the joint body of the party and the trade unions, agreed at its meeting in Blackpool on 8 September to issue a declaration condemning Hitler's coercion of Czechoslovakia and called on the Government to unite with France and the Soviet Union in confronting Germany: 'Whatever the risks, Britain must make its stand against aggression.'[30] This was exactly Churchill's line. On 10 September, appalled at signs that Chamberlain's Government was pressing the Czechs to concede to the most extreme Nazi demands over the Sudetenland, he demanded that Downing Street send an immediate ultimatum to Hitler. The following day, Churchill saw Halifax and proposed that 'we should tell Germany that if she set foot in Czechoslovakia, we should at once be at war with her'.[31] But Chamberlain and Halifax were not persuaded to move in that direction. They had no attachment to Czechoslovakia, felt that Britain was ill-equipped for war, and abhorred the idea of a pact with the Soviets, regarding Communism as an equally dark threat as Nazism.

Chamberlain planned to take a very different route – one that was to become the lasting symbol of his appeasement policy. On 13 September he offered to fly to Germany to meet the Führer, to whom he would put the idea of a plebiscite in Sudetenland. Hitler accepted, proposing that the summit be held at his residence in Berchtesgaden on 15 September. Shortly before Chamberlain left, he saw Attlee, who, according to his own account, told the Prime Minister that 'we mustn't give in to threats, we had a duty to the Czechs and principles which all parties in Britain now adhered to must not be compromised. I reminded him of the Blackpool Declaration. He had very little to say: nothing really.'[32] Churchill was disheartened at the news of the planned trip, viewing it as the precursor to capitulation. 'Winston says it is the stupidest thing that has ever been done,' reported the diplomat Oliver Harvey.[33]

Those fears were realised when Chamberlain explained on his return that he had effectively agreed to the separation of the Sudetenland from Czechoslovakia. Even some loyal ministers were shaken, as Sir Thomas Inskip noted after Chamberlain had reported to Cabinet: 'It was plain that Hitler had made all the running. He had in fact blackmailed the Prime Minister.' Inskip also recorded Chamberlain's self-delusion about Hitler's good faith: 'The Prime Minister had come to the conclusion that though Hitler was determined, his objectives were strictly limited.'[34] Perturbed at the reports of Chamberlain's submission, the National Council of Labour issued a press statement reaffirming their Blackpool Declaration. On the publication of this statement, there was a crucial moment in the relationship between Churchill and Attlee that might have opened a new period of co-operation. Churchill immediately rang the Labour Leader to say that he had 'done honour to the British people'. But all Attlee said in response was a typically blunt 'I am glad you think so' before putting the phone down.[35] Apart from his natural taciturnity, Attlee's reluctance to engage with Churchill was caused by two factors. One was his belief that there was still little mood for a large-scale, open rebellion on the Tory side against Chamberlain. The other was the fear that Churchill remained too much the renegade to win the support of Labour, a view that was shared by Dalton. 'It would not strengthen any appeal of ours if it were associated with Churchill or Eden or the Liberals, even if they would join,' he wrote.[36] But Dalton also heard that Churchill was disappointed by Attlee's conduct. 'Churchill intended it to be the overture for some form of concerted action and he was huffed that Attlee did not make a warmer response.'[37]

Chamberlain agreed to another meeting with Hitler, on 22 September, this time in Godesberg, where he would present Anglo-French plans for the cession of the Sudetenland. Once more before he left he had an interview with Attlee, who was more scathing than he'd been on the previous occasion. Attlee later reported to the National Council of Labour that he had told the Prime Minister, 'You have abandoned these people completely. You have made a complete and abject surrender. All Eastern Europe has fallen under Hitler's sway. We are full of the most profound disgust, and this is one of the biggest disasters in British history.'[38] Churchill used much the same language in public when he issued a press statement on the eve of Chamberlain's second German trip: 'The partition of Czechoslovakia under pressure from England and France amounts to the complete surrender of the Western Democracies to the Nazi threat of force. Such a collapse will bring peace and security to neither England nor France.'[39] While Chamberlain was parleying with Hitler in Godesberg, Churchill held a discussion at his Morpeth Mansions flat with some of his allies, including Sinclair, Bracken and Nicolson. They decided that if Chamberlain returned from Godesberg having either broken off the talks or achieved peace with honour, they would support him; but if he brought back peace with dishonour, they would 'go out against him'. The worst outcome of all, they felt, would be some kind of 'general agreement' in which a wholesale surrender was balanced by 'such quite valueless concessions as "a fifty year peace"'. During their conversation, they were interrupted by a call from Attlee, saying that 'the Opposition are prepared to come in with us if we like'. But now it was Churchill's turn to be unreceptive. According to

Nicolson, the offer was 'vague' so it was not pursued, another indicator of the lack of connection between the two potential leaders of the anti-Chamberlain movement.[40]

At Godesberg Hitler indulged in even more blackmail as he demanded the acceptance of the immediate military occupation of the entire Sudetenland. The only concession he made was to hold off his annexation until 1 October. Chamberlain returned without an agreement. War now seemed inevitable. Czechoslovakia, well armed and fortified, rejected Hitler's demands and ordered a full mobilisation of its forces. In Britain, trenches were dug in London parks, gas masks issued to the public and air-raid warning sirens tested. At Westminster, news of Hitler's intransigence led to an apparent stiffening of resolve in many quarters. Attlee was energetic in trying to bolster the Czech cause. He wrote a personal letter to Chamberlain, again setting out the terms of the Blackpool Declaration, and followed this up with another visit to Downing Street, accompanied by Arthur Greenwood. On 26 September he addressed a huge rally at Earl's Court in London, along with other Labour and trade-union figures, to call on the Government to 'stand by the Czechs'.[41] Churchill was just as active. He spoke to contacts in Russia and the United States in the quest for a collective defence of Czechoslovakia. Once more, he met his circle of allies at Morpeth Mansions, where, according to Nicolson's diary, it was agreed that 'if Chamberlain rats again, we shall form a united block'. Alternatively, if the Prime Minister did not back down and conflict began, 'we shall press for a Coalition Government and the immediate application of war measures'.[42] In fact there was now widespread speculation that a coalition would soon be formed, as the *Daily Mirror* reported on 24 September: 'Opposition leaders – Mr C. R. Attlee, Sir Archibald Sinclair [...] and possibly Mr Winston Churchill and Mr Eden – will probably be taken into Government if the Czech crisis takes a more serious turn at the weekend. An all-party Council of State may be formed.'[43] Like Attlee, Churchill visited Downing Street, where, on 26 September, he urged Chamberlain and Halifax to declare their solidarity with France and Russia in defence of Czechoslovakia.

'Lord Halifax and I were at one, and I certainly thought the Prime Minister was in full agreement,' he wrote later.[44] That resolve seemed to infuse the Foreign Office communiqué sent that night, which stated that if 'a German attack is made on Czechoslovakia' France would 'be bound to come to her assistance and Great Britain and Russia will certainly stand by France'.[45] In another step that smacked of a new firmness, the British fleet was mobilised on 28 September.

But even now Chamberlain was planning a further retreat. By the time of the Royal Navy's mobilisation, he had already asked Mussolini for his intervention to start a new round of negotiations over Czechoslovakia. The answer came on the afternoon of 28 September in a dramatic scene in the Commons, when Chamberlain was speaking on the crisis. The feeling in the chamber was apprehensive, tense and sombre. War seemed only a matter of hours away, Hitler having brought forward his ultimatum to the Czechs. Suddenly a message was brought in for the Prime Minister. Barely able to conceal his smile as he read it, he then revealed to the House that Hitler had invited him to a four-power conference, with Italy and France, at Munich. At this news, loud cheering echoed along the Tory benches. Only a few backbenchers, Churchill among them, remained seated. The reaction from Labour was recorded by the Admiralty Secretary Duff Cooper: 'The Government supporters were rising and cheering while the Opposition sat glum and silent. And then, when Attlee gave the plan his blessing, our side all rose again and cheered him – cheers with which the Opposition had to join, though looking a little foolish.'[46]

The following day, as Chamberlain arrived in Munich, Churchill lunched at the Savoy with some friends, among them Violet Bonham Carter, Nicolson and Sinclair. There they conceived the idea of sending Chamberlain a telegram to warn him that he would face a fight in the House if his Government betrayed the Czechs. The plan was to heighten the pressure on the Prime Minister by persuading a range of major political figures, including Eden and Attlee, to sign the telegram. Attempts were made during the afternoon to contact the potential signatories, with the task of reaching Attlee entrusted to the respected

Labour MP Philip Noel-Baker, who was a strong supporter of the LoN.* The same party met at the Savoy Hotel in the evening to hear progress on collecting the signatures. But soon it was clear that the plan was stillborn, as Violet Bonham Carter recorded in a later interview:

> Then the trouble began. Attlee, in spite of Noel-Baker's telephonic entreaties to him to do so, which we heard one side of, said that though he was in complete sympathy with our object, he couldn't do so without the approval of his party. As for Anthony, he proved a terrible disappointment to us. He said that he agreed with us but if he signed it would be taken as a sign of hostility to Chamberlain. We didn't feel the remaining signatures were representative enough to count and all our friends went out, one by one, defeated. Winston remained, sitting in his chair immobile, like a man of stone, with tears in his eyes […] At last he said, 'What are they made of? The day will come when it won't be signatures we'll have to give but lives, the lives of millions.'[47]

Later that night Churchill's sorrow turned to anger, and he went to the Other Club in a towering rage. Once inside, he lashed out at those around him, provoking a serious of ferocious rows over the failure of others to support him against Chamberlain's 'squalid, sub-human and suicidal' policy.[48] 'Winston ended by saying at the next General Election he would speak on every socialist platform in the country,' recalled Duff Cooper.[49]

For all Churchill's fury, it is doubtful if the telegram would have achieved anything. No intervention from a group of British politicians, particularly not one headed by Churchill and Attlee, would have deterred Chamberlain from reaching a deal at Munich with Hitler and Mussolini. The terms of the agreement represented a complete

---

* Noel-Baker, a superb middle-distance runner in his youth, is the only man to have won an Olympic medal and a Nobel Prize. He was awarded the Peace Prize in 1959 for his work on global disarmament.

surrender to the dictators, allowing the immediate German takeover of the Sudetenland. Yet, far from being humiliated, Chamberlain was hailed by many as a national hero on his return to Britain. The sense of relief that war had been averted led to a public outpouring of gratitude, reflected in the crowds that gathered in central London to cheer him when he appeared on the balcony of Buckingham Palace alongside the King and Queen. This widespread elation enabled Chamberlain to emerge unscathed when the Munich Agreement was debated in Parliament, despite fierce criticism from anti-appeasers on all sides. In one of his more compelling performances, Attlee denounced the deal as a 'victory for brute force' and 'a terrible defeat' for democracy that had left the Czechs 'betrayed'.[50] This was a theme taken up by Churchill in a magnificent but mournful speech in which he predicted that soon Czechoslovakia 'will be engulfed by the Nazi regime'. Churchill's conclusion, with its dark foreboding about the inevitability of the struggle to come, rightly became famous: 'This is only the first sip, the first foretaste of a bitter cup which will be proffered to us year by year unless by a supreme recovery of moral health and martial vigour, we arise again and take our stand for freedom as in the olden time.'[51] But his words could not break Chamberlain's grip on his party. Despite thirty Tory abstentions, the Government's motion in support of Munich was passed easily, while the only resignation from the Cabinet was that of Duff Cooper.

The build-up to Munich exposed the weakness of the anti-appeasement forces. Despite growing doubts about his policy, Chamberlain was put under little pressure because of the lack of unity among his opponents, fostered by a climate of suspicion on both the Labour and Conservative sides. Naturally cautious, Attlee played it safe in the face of hostility within the Labour movement towards Churchill as a result of his image as an uncompromising right-winger. Branding Churchill an enemy of the unions, Ernie Bevin asked in late 1938, 'Is it any wonder he makes no appeal to us?' This view was mirrored by Robert Fraser, the editor of the *Daily Herald*. He wrote to Dalton just after Munich to warn against any collusion with Churchill, who would 'settle down with his lousy and reactionary friends to organise the nation on fascist principles for a war to settle scores with Hitler'.[52] On the other hand, Attlee complained that insufficient Conservative MPs were willing to split with Chamberlain and join Churchill. 'That was the root of the trouble. You could never get the revolting Tories up to scratch,' he recalled.[53] Nevertheless, in the immediate aftermath of Munich there was another attempt to establish some kind of anti-Chamberlain pact in the Commons. With Attlee's support, Dalton had talks with Harold Macmillan, then a leading dissident and Tory radical, who suggested formal co-operation on guarantees to the Czechs, rearmament and a more vigorous foreign policy. But, once more, this proposal failed because neither Duff Cooper nor Eden was willing to move towards Labour, and other Tories followed their lead.

Only Churchill was ready to stand with Labour, but that just emphasised how badly isolated he still was from the Tory political mainstream. He might have been admired by a large section of the public but at Westminster he was a marginalised figure. The young Conservative lawyer John Boyd Carpenter, later one of Churchill's post-war ministers, reflected at the time on 'the tragedy of this man with such a distinguished past but with no present or future and seemingly nothing else to do except sit drinking before lunch in the hall of the Carlton Club'.[54]

TWELVE

◈

ADMIRALTY

IN THE FEBRILE atmosphere of post-Munich politics, both Attlee and Churchill came under threat, the former from the left of his party, the latter from elements within his Essex constituency. The driving force behind the Labour rebellion was Stafford Cripps, the radical socialist who now devoted his energies towards the creation of a unified multi-party movement to strengthen collective security against Nazism. Known as the Popular Front, the alliance he advocated would embrace all anti-appeasement forces, from the Tory dissidents on the right to the Communists on the left. For him, one key advantage of the formation of such a front would be the replacement of Attlee by a more charismatic figure, preferably Herbert Morrison. 'A whispering campaign is being carried on inside the Labour Party Parliamentary ranks against Mr Attlee,' reported the *Sunday Chronicle* in December 1938.

Aware of the danger to his leadership, Attlee fought back against Cripps. He first ensured that the Labour's NEC rejected the Popular Front proposal. He then launched a personal attack in an article in the *Labour Herald*, arguing that the 'demand for an alliance with capitalists' meant that there could be 'little trust in Cripps's judgement'.[1] The tide turned against Cripps. Neither Morrison nor Dalton was willing to back him. Bevin and the unions were opposed to any action that under-mined the solidarity of the Labour movement. Left isolated, Cripps and his allies, who included Nye Bevan, faced expulsion from the party unless they abandoned their advocacy of the Popular Front. This they refused to do and by May 1939 both Cripps and Bevan had been kicked out of Labour, a remarkable development given their subsequent stature in the party's history. It was a victory for Attlee, but one that further destabilised the chances of any co-operation with Churchill. Nor did Attlee gain much credit. In March, at the height of the battle for Cripps's expulsion, the Labour stalwart Susan Lawrence claimed that the 'NEC was a hopeless body of which Dalton was the devil, Greenwood a confirmed drunkard and Attlee of no account'.[2]

During these post-Munich months, Churchill's position was no stronger. His fight seemed to have deserted him; at the age of sixty-four, his faculties appeared to be in decline. After a stumbling performance by Churchill in a debate on the army in December 1938, the Liberal National MP Bill Mebane turned to Harold Nicolson and said, 'He is becoming an old man.'[3] But the greatest immediate menace to Churchill came from within his own Conservative Association in Epping, where many local members were irritated by his regular attacks on the Government's foreign policy. This fractious mood was eagerly stoked by Colin Thornton-Kemsley, a young Essex estate agent who backed appeasement and had his own political ambitions. Behind the scenes Conservative Central Office, which was now wholly committed to the Prime Minister's cause, discreetly encouraged the internal opposition to Churchill. 'It was clear to me that the growing revolt in the Epping division was welcomed in high places,' Thornton-Kemsley admitted.[4] Disquiet at Churchill spread through several Epping branches, among them Buckhurst Hill, which agreed a motion that read: 'We feel increasingly uneasy at Mr Churchill's growing hostility to the Government and to the Prime Minister in particular.'[5] Despite securing a resolution of support at the Epping Conservative Central Council on 4 November, by 100 votes to 44, Churchill continued to face discontent in early 1939.

But in March the nascent rebellion suddenly lost its momentum, leaving Churchill secure and the pro-Chamberlain lobby in retreat. Apart from a fightback by his own network of loyalists, the prime reason for this regained ascendancy was Hitler's invasion of Prague, which made a mockery of the Munich Agreement. At a stroke, all Churchill's grim warnings about the so-called peace deal were proved right. His often lonely crusade against Nazism had been vindicated. Alternatively, the German occupation of Czechoslovakia now made Chamberlain a diminished Leader, broken by his own credulity.

Following the Czech occupation, the Central Council of the Epping Division agreed to a motion of confidence in its Member of Parliament. But, in the transformed political climate, there was now a growing clamour for Churchill to assume a much bigger national role at the heart of reconstructed Government. 'I think you should go to 10 Downing Street and offer your services, in whatever the PM wishes to place you,' Margot Asquith wrote to him on 18 March.[6] The day before, the *Daily Mirror* had predicted that Chamberlain would imminently be forced to create 'an All-Party Council of State to advise on foreign affairs', the members to include Churchill, Attlee and Lloyd George.[7] Towards the end of the month, more than thirty Conservative MPs, with Churchill, Eden and Duff Cooper at their head, put down a parliamentary motion calling on the Prime Minister to establish a genuinely national coalition in response to the crisis.

But Chamberlain had no intention of bringing in Churchill or any Opposition politicians. His reaction was not a major reconstruction but rather to dish out guarantees to Poland and Romania, now under greater than ever threat from Hitler, as well as Greece, menaced by Mussolini after the Italian occupation of Albania in early April. In an apparent display of new firmness, Chamberlain pledged that Britain would come to their aid if they were attacked by the dictators. Churchill agreed with the policy, but felt that such promises would have been far more effective if adopted when Czechoslovakia was still able to resist. Furthermore, he believed, as did Attlee, that the real deterrent to further German aggression in Eastern Europe would be an alliance with the Soviet Union, something that Chamberlain was reluctant to embrace. The only change the Prime Minister made in the Government was the creation of a new Department of Supply, which was to be headed by the nondescript Liberal National MP and former Transport Minister Leslie Burgin. Churchill had long advocated just such a step to improve the delivery of equipment to the army and RAF,* though he did not covet the position for himself. 'He said he would not like the job if it were offered him, but added puckishly "Don't tell the PM I said so,"' recorded Leslie Hore-Belisha during a visit to Chartwell on 11 April, where he found that Churchill had 'a real and realistic grip of the situation' and was 'the only man out of office who retains his power and influence'.[8]

Even after Prague, when Churchill tried for a spell to adopt a constructive approach to the Prime Minister, Chamberlain remained deeply suspicious of him, as was illustrated in the parliamentary debate immediately after Mussolini's invasion of Albania, which had prompted the British guarantee to Greece. In Churchill's contribution, said Chamberlain, 'there was an acid undertone which brought many cheers from the Labour benches and again I felt depressed when he sat down'.[9] Chamberlain's antipathy to Attlee was far more visceral. 'Attlee behaved like the cowardly cur he is. I had seen him several times during the week and he appeared (and I believe he was) completely satisfied.' Chamberlain therefore confessed that he was 'dumbfounded' when Attlee later attacked him in the House over his foreign policy. 'I have done with confidences in the Labour Party. They have shown themselves implacably partisan.'[10] Yet the Nazis' destruction of Czechoslovakia had not dented Chamberlain's self-confidence or his dismissiveness of his opponents. After a dinner with some Birmingham journalists in late April, he wrote that the country was 'solidly' behind him, so 'I believe I can snap my fingers at Churchill and Attlee and Sinclair'.[11]

Yet such disdain was completely misplaced in the case of Churchill, whose star rose dramatically after Prague. With each passing week, the demand for his return to Government strengthened. An opinion poll in the *News Chronicle* showed that 56 per cent of the public wanted Churchill in the Cabinet. With the exception of the pro-appeasement

---

* The Admiralty remained in charge of naval supply.

Times and *Daily Express*, the national papers across the political spectrum were unanimous in the view that Churchill was badly needed in this hour of looming peril. 'That one who has so firm a grasp of the realities of European politics should not be included in the Government must be as bewildering to foreigners as it is regrettable to most of his countrymen,' said the *Observer*.[12]

His appeal now extended to the left, as his resolve against Nazism diluted anger over his past stances on India and the General Strike. When Churchill sent Attlee his latest book, a collection of some speeches and articles on foreign policy under the title *Step by Step*, Attlee replied in warmer terms than usual: 'It must be a melancholy satisfaction to you to see how right you were [...] Let's hope it is not too late.'[13] Even Stafford Cripps now wrote personally to Churchill to press for his return. 'Could you not make a public statement, stating your preparedness to give your services to the country?'[14] But Churchill judged that this would only heighten Chamberlain's stubbornness. 'I am quite sure that any such demarche would weaken me with the gentleman in question,' Churchill replied.[15] He was right. The louder the campaign for Churchill grew, the more fixed Chamberlain became in his determination to keep him out. When the *Telegraph* owner Lord Camrose had a meeting with the Prime Minister to advocate a post for Churchill, Chamberlain explained that, on past experience, he did not feel 'that Churchill's inclusion in the Cabinet would make his task any easier'.[16]

While Churchill soared in popularity after Prague, Attlee went through the opposite process. Rising international tension led to further criticisms of his suitability to lead the official Opposition. Where commentators wanted to know why Churchill was out of office, Attlee's growing army of critics asked why he was still in it. There was particular anger among anti-appeasers when the Government introduced conscription soon after the German invasion of Czechoslovakia and Labour opposed the measure, reviving memories of the party's anti-rearmament stance of the early 1930s. In the House, Attlee tried to justify his policy by claiming that compulsory national service would 'weaken this country and divide it at a time when it should be strong and united'.[17] For once able to give his backing to Chamberlain, Churchill appealed to the Labour and Liberal parties not to undermine the fight against Nazism: 'If the Opposition won and they established the principle of no compulsory National Service, I say – make no mistake about it – the whole resistance of Europe to Nazi domination would collapse. All countries, great and small alike, would make the best terms they could with the Nazi power.'[18] Other observers were just as scathing about Labour. Chips Channon said that while Churchill's speech was 'a magnificent effort', Attlee's was 'a lot of terse rot'.[19] The *Daily Mirror* columnist William Connor, who wrote under the name Cassandra, was cruel in his assessment: 'It grieves me to see Clement Attlee feverishly grabbing a spade and digging a grave for the Labour Party. Their attitude to the latest political crisis shows how desperately they are out of touch with national sentiment.'[20]

Attlee's difficulties were compounded by a serious illness that was to plague him for months, brought on by an infection to his prostate. In late May, after travelling to Southport for Labour's Annual Conference, he felt so unwell that he was largely confined to his hotel room and managed to make only a brief speech from the platform. On his return to London he was taken to hospital, where he underwent two operations before embarking on an extensive period of recovery. His lengthy absence not only provided more scope for sniping about the inadequacies of his leadership but also stimulated internal discussions about possible alternatives. 'I hear the view is now taken by Citrine and Bevin that a change in leadership must be made,' noted Dalton at the end of the Southport Conference.[21]

The danger to Attlee's position was worsened by the surprising effectiveness of Greenwood as his temporary replacement. At first Greenwood was daunted by the responsibility of leading Labour at a fraught moment in Britain's history, but soon he began to win praise. After hosting Chamberlain for a weekend in July, Victor Cazalet noted in his diary, 'Neville rather likes Greenwood who, since Attlee's illness, has led the Opposition and does it well. If only he were a little more temperate he might be quite a big figure.'[22] The following month, Dalton wrote that Greenwood 'is going pretty well – better than poor little Rabbit* – seeing the Prime Minister and Halifax frequently, taking notes of his talks, reporting frequently to his colleagues'.[23]

Those talks with the Government became all the more serious as Germany fixed its predatory attention on Poland. Given London's guarantee to Warsaw and the widespread revulsion at the thought of another Munich, war now looked inevitable. More than any other British statesman, Churchill had long known that the conflict was coming. 'It is too late for any appeasement. The deed is signed and Hitler is going to make war,' he said in late July to the senior army officer Edmund Ironside, who was soon to be the Chief of the Imperial General Staff.[24] What infuriated Churchill was the lack of urgency from the Government even as invasion of Poland drew near. In early August, he clashed bitterly with Chamberlain over the Government decision to allow Parliament to go into recess until October, just when, as Churchill put it, 'all along the Polish frontier from Danzig to Cracow there are heavy massings of troops and every preparation is being made for a speedy advance'. He went on: 'it would be shameful for the House to write itself off as an effective and potent factor in the situation',[25] a view to which Chamberlain expressed his ferocious objection. As the Prime Minister reported to his sister, 'I did turn on him savagely then and barked out that I totally and utterly disagreed with him. He was in a state of red fury.'[26]

Churchill was at the centre of the political action in those fateful weeks of August 1939. Attlee was far from it. After a spell in a nursing home following his second prostate operation, he decided to continue his convalescence by travelling with his family to a farmhouse near the coastal town of Nefyn in North Wales. In this beautiful but remote spot, communication with London was limited. He could pick up the news on a portable radio, but had to rely on a coin-operated telephone kiosk to make calls to London. It was while listening to the radio on

---

*   Dalton's nickname for Attlee.

the beach on 23 August that he heard the ominous report from the BBC about Hitler's pact with Stalin, which left the Germans free to invade Poland. Even then, as Parliament was recalled the following day to discuss the crisis, Attlee was too unwell to travel to London. He was still in Wales a week later when the news broke on Friday 1 September that the Reich's forces had crossed the Polish frontier, unleashing the terrifying new brutality of Blitzkrieg on the defender.

Back at Westminster, the political atmosphere was turbulent. As the British Army was mobilised, Chamberlain held a series of meetings in Downing Street to refashion his Government. Among those summoned to discuss the new administration was Churchill, who travelled up from Chartwell to meet the Prime Minister in the early afternoon. During their meeting, the two men agreed that the War Cabinet should comprise just six members, with the three Service Ministers excluded so they could concentrate on their departments. Chamberlain told Churchill that he planned to invite him to join the new Cabinet as a Minister without Portfolio. After eleven long, often painful years on the backbenches, Churchill now seemed certain to return to power. But there was to be no place for any Labour politician. As Chamberlain explained to Churchill, the party had sent a message to Downing Street declining to take part in a coalition. This decision had been taken by the PLP executive that morning, after the Prime Minister had asked Greenwood if Labour would be prepared to co-operate. Greenwood had managed to refer this request down the phone line to Nefyn, where Attlee had been vehement in his opposition to the idea. 'In the ranks of Labour there was no confidence in Chamberlain and his immediate associates,' wrote Attlee later in justifying this decision.[27]

Attlee's dark opinion of the Prime Minister was upheld by his Government's vacillating response to the invasion of Poland. Instead of standing by their Polish guarantee, regularly confirmed over previous months, Chamberlain and Halifax seemed eager to renege on it. Dismayed by the prevarication and having had nothing confirmed about any Cabinet job, Churchill wrote to Chamberlain from Morpeth Mansions in the early hours of 2 September. After emphasising that

Poland had been 'under heavy attack for 30 hours', he expressed his trust that Chamberlain would be able to make a declaration of war 'when the House meets this afternoon'.[28] Churchill's hope was not fulfilled as the Prime Minister continued to stonewall. It was only after severe pressure from both the Cabinet and the Commons that he finally abandoned his resistance, agreeing that an ultimatum should be sent to Germany at 9 a.m. the following day, 3 September. No response came from Berlin. At 11.15 a.m., in tones of self-pity rather than inspiration, the Prime Minister broadcast to the public that Britain was at war with Germany. Just after he had finished, an air-raid warning sounded. Winston and Clementine, 'armed with a bottle of brandy and other appropriate medical comforts',[29] went to their local shelter, though the stay was a brief one as the all-clear sounded within ten minutes. Churchill then made his way to the Commons, where he listened to Chamberlain make a pedestrian speech before he made his own typically lyrical contribution. 'We are fighting to save the whole world from the pestilence of Nazi tyranny,' he declared.[30] The contrast between his offensive spirit and Chamberlain's downbeat address struck Leo Amery. 'I think I see Winston emerging as Prime Minister out of it all by the end of the year,' he noted in his diary.[31]

This was the last major speech Churchill ever gave as a backbencher. When the House adjourned, Chamberlain invited Churchill to his room at the Commons, where he explained that he had changed his mind about the exclusion of the three Service Ministers and would now have them in his nine-strong Cabinet. Churchill, much to his relief, was therefore offered his old position of First Lord of the Admiralty. 'I naturally preferred a definite task to that exalted brooding over the work done by others that may well be the lot of a Minister, however influential, who has no Department.'[32] Soon afterwards, the Board of Admiralty flashed the signal 'Winston is Back', a tribute to the hopes invested in him.[33] His impact was immediate, as his volcanic energy ran like an electric charge through his new department. His dynamism made a mockery of the prediction by Lord Stanhope, his immediate predecessor, who said that Churchill would not 'stay the course of administrative work after years of soft living'.[34] At the Admiralty, Churchill moved into a private apartment and his phenomenal work rate could be seen in the long hours he toiled, in the energetic visits he made to naval bases and in the barrage of minutes he fired about an extraordinary range of subjects, from ammunition supplies to the unloading of ships. 'I fell under the spell of this man: totally concentrated, supremely courageous,' said Frank Mottershead, his private secretary at the Admiralty.[35] Churchill's diligence was also noted to Albert Sylvester, Lloyd George's aide, who reported to his chief in mid-September that 'Winston has been to Chatham. He has been to the North Sea fleet base. He is in his office at 8.30am. He works hard all day, rests from six till eight, then has a dinner and a staff conference, and is busily writing his orders until the early hours of the morning.'[36]

Attlee too was impressed by Churchill's performance. By late September he had recovered sufficiently from his operations to return to London from North Wales. One of his first tasks was to take part on 26 September in a debate on the war situation, in which Churchill gave a wide-ranging, confident statement about the performance of the Royal Navy. In his response, Attlee praised Churchill's 'robust, vigorous statement' that exuded a 'cautious optimism' and provided 'a reassuring account of the position of this country at sea'. But Attlee also expressed concern that the Cabinet had insufficient experience to handle the economic side of the war. 'There is only one member of it who has ever had any dealings with trade questions intimately, and that is the protean member for Epping, who 30 years ago was at the Board of Trade.'[37] This was a serious weakness that could be addressed only by giving a War Cabinet minister responsibility for economic planning, he claimed.

Other MPs were just as taken with Churchill's speech. That night, Harold Nicolson wrote in his diary, 'One could feel the spirit of the House rising with every word.'[38] Churchill's position was made all the stronger because his pugnacity was so different to the sense of drift from the Government, reflecting the outlook of Chamberlain, who still behaved like a peacetime Prime Minister. 'The war goes on placidly and some people say that the public are bewildered,' noted Sir Thomas Inskip.[39] The reluctance of Chamberlain to go on the offensive increasingly undermined his leadership and fed gossip at Westminster about the choice of his possible successor. At the end of the September, James Grigg, the Permanent Secretary at the War Office, wrote to his father, 'I am told Winston's stock is going up and that people are expecting him to be Prime Minister before long.'[40] Less than a fortnight later, Sylvester told Lloyd George that 'if there were a change of premier now, the successor would be Halifax. But Halifax says that he does not want the responsibility and it is known that he would nominate Winston.'[41] But, for all the swing of opinion in his favour, there were also suspicions in some quarters that Churchill, now aged almost sixty-five, was too old for the highest position. Jock Colville, one of Chamberlain's own private secretaries, recorded in his diary on 28 September, 'It would probably be a good thing if Chamberlain resigned soon and left the conduct of the war to a younger, forceful successor. Unfortunately I can see no Lloyd George figure on the horizon at present; Winston is a national figure, but is rather too old.'[42] That was, interestingly, also the view that Attlee held, as he told some Oxford students during a visit early in the war to Jesus College. Among them was Harold Wilson, the future Labour premier, who recalled that Attlee was asked about Churchill's chances of succeeding Chamberlain. 'No, not Winston. 65. Too old for a Churchill.'[43]

Ironically, the only open challenge that took place against a party leader in the autumn of 1939 was focused not on Chamberlain but on Attlee, whose return to Westminster only prompted more whispers about his failings. Discontent over the Government's conduct of the war mixed with frustration at Attlee's ineffectiveness. At a meeting of the PLP in early November, the disgruntled backbencher Alfred Edwards, who later joined Churchill's Conservatives out of his disillusion at Attlee's post-war policy of nationalisation, nominated Dalton, Greenwood and Morrison as alternatives for the leadership. In a contemporary account, Dalton recorded:

There was a queer, desultory discussion, full of expressions of goodwill (the Labour Party is apt to be dangerously good at this sort of thing). Attlee, asked directly by Edwards, said that he would never resent or regard as 'disloyal' the nomination of any colleague for the leadership. We were a democratic party. And then Greenwood rose and declined the nomination. He gave very poor reasons, his chief point being that it would encourage Hitler if we now had a contest for the leadership.

Morrison and Dalton also refused to be nominated, thereby ensuring Attlee's survival. In private, Dalton admitted that the 'the whole thing is pretty feeble' and to Morrison he complained about Labour's habitual vacillation and sentimentality about incumbents: 'the way of the earth shifters is hard in this political allotment'.[44]

Despite the evaporation of the challenge, Attlee's position was no stronger. The same problems remained: Attlee was seen as unable either to galvanise the war effort or provide a realistic alternative to the Chamberlain Government. Nor did Attlee convey a sense of fighting determination in a major speech of early November setting out Labour's war aims, which was immediately circulated as a pamphlet. He repeated his favourite themes of upholding 'the rule of international law' and the need to establish new forms of global government through a revamped LoN and a European Federation. 'Europe must federate or perish,' he declared in words that would later haunt him during the early post-war debates about European unity. He also urged restraint towards Germany. 'We have no desire to humiliate, to crush or to divide the German nation.'[45] Tellingly *The Times*, the organ of the Chamberlainites, welcomed the speech, stating that 'in no essential particular is there any divergence of opinion' between Attlee and 'the declarations of Lord Halifax'.[46] Attlee's lack of bellicosity shone through a profile by *Daily Mail* journalist Emrys Jones in early December: 'Nobody looks less like a typical major than the Leader of the Opposition. Instead of being stocky and fierce, he is slim and gentle. As he talks, he clasps his hands, intertwines his fingers so hard that the knuckles show white, even when he is saying something that doesn't touch the emotions.' The article further noted that Attlee was 'a very strong family man' who regularly read aloud to his children as they gathered round the fire. 'My guess is that some of the Attlee family have heard Churchill's speeches read to them, for Attlee is an admirer of Churchill the writer. He has just finished re-reading *Marlborough*.'[47]

In the spirit of his ancestor, Churchill was carrying on the fight for Britain. He was the most militarily engaged of all Cabinet ministers. There was no Phoney War at the Admiralty. Two of the Government's most vital policies – the maintenance of the economic blockade against Germany and the protection of shipping supplies from the U-boat menace – depended on the resilience of the Royal Navy. Churchill had his heavy setbacks, such as the sinking of the battleship the *Royal Oak* at the Home Fleet base of Scapa Flow in October, with the loss of 833 lives; but there were also triumphs, like the daring operation in December by three cruisers in the South Atlantic that forced the commander of the mighty *Graf Spee* to scuttle her off the coast of Montevideo. Equally audacious was the raid into Norwegian waters in February 1940 by the destroyer *Cossack* to release 299 Allied prisoners carried aboard the German supply ship *Altmark*. It was a step that was to have strategic significance far beyond the liberation of the prisoners, for the incident strengthened Hitler's suspicions that the Allies were planning a campaign in Norway, something he was determined to pre-empt.

Churchill's perceived success at the Admiralty reinforced his leadership credentials, despite some concerns about his suitability for the highest office. 'Halifax is still the favourite for the next Prime Minister – if only ad interim – though many are doubtful if he could hold it. Winston is a good second but everyone is nervous of his instability,' wrote the well-connected Oliver Harvey at the end of 1939.[48] An insight into Churchill's outlook in early 1940 came from the pen of Cecil King, the advertising director and later chairman of the *Daily Mirror*, who had lunch with him on 8 February. During their discussion, King reported that a recent study by the public-opinion research group

Winston Churchill as a child, with his brother Jack and his mother, the glamorous American heiress Jennie Jerome. 'I loved her dearly, but at a distance,' he wrote.

Churchill as a Sandhurst cadet in 1893. His success at the military academy confounded his father's low expectations of him.

Clement Attlee as a student at University College, Oxford, in 1902. 'He is a level-headed, industrious, dependable man with no brilliance of style or literary gifts but with excellent sound judgement,' wrote one of his tutors.

Above: Attlee at the Haileybury House Boys' Club in the East End of London. His work there inspired his lifelong attachment to socialism.

Left: Dodging anarchists' bullets, Churchill as Home Secretary takes command at the siege of Sidney Street, January 1911. As an East End resident, Attlee witnessed Churchill's central role in the drama. It was the first time the two men were in physical proximity.

Having been forced out of the Cabinet by the Dardanelles disaster, Churchill volunteered for service on the Western Front and was appointed a lieutenant colonel in the Royal Scots Fusiliers. Alongside him is Archibald Sinclair, his loyal friend and future Liberal leader.

During the First World War, Attlee saw action in Gallipoli, Mesopotamia, and the Western Front. Churchill later wrote that Attlee had 'a fine war record'.

Churchill as Chancellor of the Exchequer, flanked by his daughter Diana, on Budget Day, 1928. Attlee once said that Churchill 'was completely out of his depth with finance'.

Attlee addresses a political rally in the summer of 1938 as the storm clouds of war began to gather.

Attlee, still in opposition, tries out a Bren gun in December 1939. He had been less enthusiastic about self-defence in the early 1930s. 'We believe you have got to have the abolition of national fighting forces,' he told the Commons.

Churchill surveys the devastation in the East End of London after the first night of the Blitz, 8 September 1940.

Churchill with Franklin D. Roosevelt aboard the HMS *Prince of Wales* during the Atlantic Conference, August 1941. The event sparked a new warmth in his relationships with both the US President and Attlee.

The war-winning Coalition Government in 1941, with Churchill and Attlee at
its heart. Among the other ministers here are Anthony Eden (*sitting third left*),
Herbert Morrison (*standing in the middle*), Ernie Bevin (*sitting first left*) and
Lord Beaverbrook (*sitting second left*), whom Attlee described as 'the only evil
man I ever met'.

ALL BEHIND YOU, WINSTON

David Low's famous cartoon in the *Evening Standard* captured the nation's
defiant mood after the formation of Churchill's Government in 1940. Attlee's
wife Violet liked the picture so much that she bought the original to hang in
their family home.

King George VI with Churchill, Attlee and other ministers at Buckingham Palace, August 1944. The King had initially been hostile to the idea of Churchill as Prime Minister, but soon grew to admire his qualities.

Churchill waves to the ecstatic crowd in Whitehall on VE Day, 8 May 1945. According to one witness, 'an ear-splitting roar went up' when Churchill appeared on the balcony.

Attlee, as Deputy Prime Minister, speaking in May 1945 at the San Francisco Conference, which gave birth to the United Nations.

In his last days as wartime Prime Minister, Churchill, alongside Marshal Stalin and President Truman, at the Potsdam Conference, July 1945.

Mass Observation had found that Churchill was 'the popular choice to be Prime Minister, with Eden in second place'. Churchill's response was that the premiership was 'not much of a catch these days and he would only take it if offered to him by common consent'. Moreover, he 'would rather have Chamberlain than Eden by 8 to 1'. The talk then turned to Labour:

> the Labour Party presses the Government very hard, and fatuously seemed to think it could at a pinch turn the Government out. I asked him why the Government submitted to such pressure – after all, Attlee had no support in the country and the Government could just defy the present Labour leadership. Churchill took a poor view of the Labour leaders and said that they wanted to win the war and then give away our colonies. What weakness! What folly![49]

Churchill's poor view of Attlee was common in the first months of 1940. Beatrice Webb went to hear him give a talk on Labour's war aims at the London School of Economics and was trenchant about his performance. 'He looked and spoke like an insignificant elderly clerk, without distinction in the voice, manner or substance in his discourse', which was nothing more than 'a string of vague assertions about an international authority'.[50] Ever the conspirator, Dalton briefed *Sunday Express* journalist Peter Howard for an article in late February 1940 forecasting the demise of Attlee. 'Mr Attlee is ailing. The Leader of the Opposition has not made a full recovery from the operation he endured last year. He still suffers some pain and a great deal of discomfort. On that account many members of the party believe that Attlee may before long retire from public life altogether.' The piece discounted the possibility of Greenwood or Morrison as Attlee's successor, and instead talked up Dalton's claims: 'Most Socialist MPs take the view that sooner or later they are bound to form a Coalition with the existing Government. Dr Dalton is their boy for this proposition.' But, according to the *Sunday Express*, they were unlikely to work with Chamberlain because 'he is regarded with deep suspicion and grave mistrust in Socialist circles'. Instead, claimed the paper, the Cabinet minister they were 'most ready to serve under' was Samuel Hoare, the Lord Privy Seal and Chamberlain loyalist.[51] The *Express*'s claims were without a shred of foundation. Most Labour MPs despised Hoare as much as they did Chamberlain and the other arch appeaser Sir John Simon. In fact, the reliable A. V. Alexander told Albert Sylvester that he and his party were so 'disgusted with the present regime that they would not enter a Government which contained Chamberlain, Hoare or Simon'. Philip Noel-Baker went so far as to say that the Government would 'never do any good until Chamberlain, Hoare and Simon were taken out in a destroyer and dropped in the sea'.[52] The *Express*'s eagerness to talk up Hoare was driven by Beaverbrook, the paper's owner, who at this stage of the war was highly ambivalent about Churchill, as the Soviet Ambassador found when he met the press tycoon. Beaverbrook told him that Chamberlain would soon retire for reasons of ill-health and that 'Hoare or Halifax will succeed him. Churchill, apparently, has no chance at all.'[53]

Part Two

COMRADES

THIRTEEN

◆

NORWAY

CHURCHILL HAD BEEN forced out of his position at the Admiralty in the First World War by the calamitous Dardanelles adventure. Yet, despite the lasting damage to his reputation, he retained on his return as First Lord that same streak of creative originality towards naval operations.

One of the schemes that emerged from his fertile mind was to place a barrier of the mines along part of the Norwegian coast with the aim of hindering the supply of iron-ore exports through the northerly port of Narvik to Germany, where this raw material was used in the steel industry. Predictably, Churchill encountered strong opposition to the proposal, not least because it would involve the violation of Norwegian neutrality. On 15 January 1940, he complained of the Cabinet's 'immense walls of prevention, all built and building' against his eagerness to go on the offensive.[1] But, with the same indefatigability he had shown over the Dardanelles, he persisted with this idea, which was soon expanded to involve a major military operation at Narvik. The plan was to organise landings there of Allied troops, who would then make their way across Scandinavia to provide support to the embattled Finns, currently putting up a heroic defence against the invading forces of the Soviet Union, still in its temporary alliance with Nazi Germany. There was some backing for this in Cabinet but a final decision was delayed for weeks, partly because of political negativity at home and abroad. The French, permanently on the defensive, were against the plan, as was King Haakon VII of Norway, who told George VI that he hoped the Allies would not contravene his country's neutrality. Further objections came from Attlee and Greenwood, who were briefed about the scheme by the Foreign Secretary in mid-February. Halifax subsequently told the Cabinet that Attlee and Greenwood 'had shown considerable anxiety lest, through giving active aid to the Finns, we might ourselves become involved in war with the USSR, a contingency which they regarded as most undesirable'.[2] In addition, they said that mining Norwegian waters could 'expose that country to attacks by Germany'.[3]

The hesitations over Norway highlighted the continuing absence of any forceful purpose at the heart of the Government. Chamberlain's strategy was to hold back, take no risks and wait for the Reich somehow to self-destruct. But the Prime Minister also recognised that his Government was too narrowly based to command public appeal. Consequently in March he made a discreet approach to Labour to see if some form of co-operation could be established through the promise of several posts in his administration. The civil servant Charles Peake, head of the Foreign Office News Department, told his fellow diplomat Oliver Harvey that Labour had been offered positions at the Admiralty, in Supply and Economic Co-ordination. 'Attlee would not come in but Alexander, Greenwood and Morrison were seriously considering it.' Harvey and Peake agreed that 'if they should refuse, they would take a big risk of being labelled unpatriotic'; on the other hand, 'for Labour to go in without undertakings as to the conduct of the war would be fatal to them'.[4] Chamberlain's move was also noted by Albert Sylvester, who reported to Lloyd George, 'This is very hush hush. I gather the Labour people are not disposed to go in with the Government. They are inclined to keep out. They argue that they can get better terms when something big is likely to happen.'[5] Sylvester also saw one of Greenwood's advisers, who told him that 'he and his friends were wholly dissatisfied with the present Government but he could not see a possible National Leader as Prime Minister in his own party. There were only two people and one was Lloyd George and the other was Winston and he said that the Labour Party would not serve under Winston's premiership.'[6]

After his fruitless bid for Labour support, Chamberlain tried the alternative tactic of tinkering with the structure of his Government. At the beginning of April, he made Sam Hoare Secretary of State for Air and abolished the post of Defence Co-ordination Minister, then held by Lord Chatfield. This minor change entailed an increase in Churchill's duties, for he took over the chairmanship of the War Cabinet's Military Co-ordination Committee, which had previously been under Chatfield. But his ally Brendan Bracken was doubtful if the arrangement would work. 'This office, if one can use such a word, adds to his responsibilities, but gives him no real powers,' he said.[7] Attlee also felt that Churchill had been overburdened. In an article for the *Daily Herald* about the machinery of government, he wrote that 'in the recent rearrangement of the Cabinet, the co-ordination of defence, including supply, was given to the First Lord of the Admiralty. But surely, if he is to devote himself to the higher strategy of the war, he ought to be free from the obsessions of a particular department.'[8] The forebodings of Bracken and Attlee proved correct. Within a fortnight, exasperated by his lack of any authority to direct other Service Ministers or departments, Churchill handed over the chairmanship of the committee to Chamberlain, who was only too pleased to take the reins and prove his administrative superiority to his First Lord. 'It was getting into a sad mess, quarrelling and sulking,' he told his sister Ida on 20 April, adding that since he had taken the chair the result had been 'magical. We were always unanimous.'[9]

Not so magical was Britain's war effort. By the time Chamberlain took charge of the committee his Government was embroiled in its first major campaign of the war, after Hitler launched a full-scale invasion of Denmark and Norway on the night of 8 April. Soon the Nazi forces had occupied all of Denmark and every significant Norwegian port from Oslo to Narvik, as well as a string of airfields. In response to Norway's appeal for aid, the Allies sent an expeditionary force, while the Royal Navy went into action against the Kriegsmarine, suffering some heavy losses but also inflicting severe damage, especially on the German destroyer fleet. Yet, from the start, the Allied mission was doomed. The troop numbers were inadequate, the plans confused.

As the most prominent Service Minister and the architect of Norwegian naval operations, Churchill inevitably came in for his share of criticism. His detractors drew parallels with Gallipoli, another combined operation crippled by delay and confusion. Labour MP Manny Shinwell later recalled the denigration against Churchill when the Norwegian disaster was unfolding. 'It was said that he drank too much; he was prematurely aged; he was the real culprit of the Norwegian catastrophe, which was a repetition of his ill-started Gallipoli campaign; he could not be trusted.'[10] One of the more surprising and indignant critics was Sir Roger Keyes, the MP for Portsmouth North and a former Admiral of the Fleet, who told Churchill that 'you won't have to wait for the verdict of history for the scathing denunciations you have merited'.[11]

It was not just the Norwegian campaign that was imperilled; the very existence of Chamberlain's Government hung in the balance. Public speculation about the succession was now rife. An opinion poll in April asked, 'If Mr Chamberlain was to retire, who would you like to succeed him as Prime Minister?' More respondents chose Eden than did Churchill; they received 28 per cent and 25 per cent of the vote respectively. Attlee was far behind, on just 6 per cent.[12] Faced with military failure, the Prime Minister resorted to another bout of administrative restructuring. He decided at the start of May that Churchill should be Deputy Chairman of the Military Co-ordination Committee but with enhanced powers. In this new, wider role, which made him a quasi Minister of Defence, he could give directions to the Chiefs of Staff, attend their committee meetings and summon them for consultation, though Major General Sir Edward Spears, the MP for Carlisle, a vigorous anti-appeaser and Churchill confidant, thought the scheme was 'ludicrous' because it was 'a means of increasing confusion behind a cardboard pretence of leadership'.[13] More importantly for the long-term, Churchill was provided with his own 'Senior Staff Officer',

Major General Hastings Ismay, who quickly became one of his most trusted associates.

Despite enhancing Churchill's nominal responsibilities, the Prime Minister remained suspicious of him – a feeling exacerbated by the rumours swirling around Westminster of manoeuvres to overthrow the Government, as Chips Channon, a diehard Chamberlain loyalist, recorded on 25 April: 'Winston, it seems, has had secret conversations with Sinclair, Alexander and Attlee and they are drawing up an alternative Government, with the idea of succeeding at the first favourable moment.'[14] Although the bulk of the Conservative Party at Westminster still supported Chamberlain, there were two increasingly powerful, internal dissident groups ready to challenge him. One was the network of around twenty MPs that had built up around Anthony Eden since his resignation as Foreign Secretary in February 1938. After Eden's acceptance of office in 1939 as Dominions Secretary, this group was led by Leo Amery and usually held its meetings over dinner in a private room at the Carlton Hotel on Pall Mall. The other main group was the Watching Committee, created in April 1940 by the 4th Marquess of Salisbury and his eldest son, Viscount Cranborne, known as 'Bobbety'. The principal aims of the Watching Committee were a more vigorous military policy and the formation of a truly national War Cabinet. At first, the committee members did not make explicit their wish to see Chamberlain replaced but this was undoubtedly a motivating factor, as Secretary Paul Emrys-Evans later remembered: 'They wanted Winston's hand to be strengthened and in the back of their minds the majority would have liked to see him succeed Chamberlain.'[15] Churchill himself had since his entry into the Government been fastidiously loyal to Chamberlain and had no involvement with either dissident group. Indeed, when he met Salisbury on 19 April he denounced any intrigue on his behalf. 'He was resolutely opposed to any change which would deprive him of this great position of authority and usefulness in order to be mere chairman without power,' reported Salisbury.[16]

Beyond the Conservative Party, another parliamentary body played a vital role in the growing opposition to Chamberlain. This was the

All-Party Action Group, also known as the Vigilantes, which was headed by the erratic Welsh Liberal Clem Davies, who, like Arthur Greenwood, suffered from alcoholism but who could in his more sober moments be an effective political operator. Bob Boothby, the hedonistic, instinctively rebellious Tory backbencher and Churchill ally, was another key member, while Davies was also close to Attlee and Greenwood, whom he met regularly at the Reform Club. The attitude of the Labour leadership was certain to be pivotal as the political crisis unfolded, for no new National Government could be formed without their support. With a sufficient number of Tory dissidents, Attlee would not only have the power to break Chamberlain but would also have a veto over the choice of his successor.

Amid talk of rebellion, plotting intensified. On 2 May Dalton had discussion about 'alternative Prime Ministers' with the dependable Sheffield Hillsborough MP A.V. Alexander. Dalton said he was 'inclined to favour Halifax' and mentioned that there was now a suggestion of Attlee as Leader of the Commons. 'He and I both shrugged our shoulders comprehendingly at Attlee in that role. None the less, I do not dismiss the possibility. Alexander, I think, would rather like Winston to be Prime Minister.'[17] From the National Labour side, aspiring rebel Harold Nicolson wrote on 4 May: 'People are so distressed by the whole thing that they are talking of Lloyd George as a possible Prime Minister. Eden is out of it. Churchill is undermined by the Conservative caucus. Halifax is believed (with justice) to be a tired man.'[18] The independent Stafford Cripps, still ostracised from the Labour Party, felt that Chamberlain would have to step down, but that 'Winston could not be Prime Minister and it would have to be Halifax'.[19] On 6 May, using the anonymous but not modest title of 'a leading member of the House of Commons', Cripps had a letter published in the *Daily Mail* in which he urged the creation of a new Government under Halifax, with Churchill, Eden and Morrison as Ministers without Portfolio and Attlee as Chancellor of the Exchequer. The stir caused by the letter was sufficient for the *Daily Telegraph* to go to the effort of unmasking Cripps as the author. 'There is no man in

public life with as little title to undertake the role of Cabinet maker,'
declared the paper.[20]

The crisis now focused on the imminent adjournment debate about
the Norway campaign. Many felt that Chamberlain, though wounded,
would survive the ordeal. Beaverbrook told the Soviet Ambassador
Ivan Maisky just before the debate that 'no serious consequences would
follow. Chamberlain's position is secure.'[21] Some on the Watching
Committee felt that Attlee was partly to blame for this. 'I am afraid
that the weakness of the Opposition will leave Chamberlain at the
head of affairs,' said Churchill supporter Lord Lloyd. Chamberlain
himself professed to be confident, as he told his sister Ida, 'It is a vile
world, but I don't think my enemies will get me down this time.'[22] But
he did not help himself when he opened what became known as the
Norway Debate on Tuesday 7 May with a complacent, weary speech.
Attlee followed in his characteristic waspish, clipped style, attacking
the entire conduct of the war. He could have disparaged Churchill over
the naval campaign in Norway but, in a telling indicator of his respect
for the Admiralty chief, his tone was one of sympathy, especially over
his extra responsibilities:

> It is against all good rules of organisation that a man who
> is in charge of major strategy should also be in command
> of a particular unit. It is like having a man commanding an
> army in the field and also commanding a division. He has a
> divided interest between the wider questions of strategy and
> the problems affecting his own immediate command. The First
> Lord of the Admiralty has great abilities, but it is not fair to
> him that he should be put into an impossible position like that.

Attlee concluded with a frank demand for a rebellion in the Tory Party.
'To win the war, we want different people at the helm from those who
have led us into it.'[23]

Despite the strong language, Attlee had not shattered Chamberlain's
carapace. Sir John Reith, the former head of the BBC and now a Liberal

National MP, felt it did 'no great damage' to the Government.[24] The real injury was inflicted by two attacks that followed from the Conservative side. One came from Sir Roger Keyes, wearing his gold-braided, medal-encrusted uniform as the former Admiral of the Fleet, who came to Churchill's defence as he turned his guns on Chamberlain: 'I have great admiration and appreciation of the First Lord of the Admiralty. I am longing to see proper use made of his great abilities.'[25] Even more devastating was the philippic from Leo Amery, who quoted the famous injunction of Cromwell to the Long Parliament: 'You have sat too long here for any good you have been doing. Depart, I say, and let us have done with you. In the name of God, go.'[26]

After Amery's speech, even the most fervent Chamberlain supporters knew that his Government was in severe trouble. That night, the Prime Minister saw King George VI, who offered to intervene with Attlee and ask Labour to join a coalition under Chamberlain's leadership. 'Would it help if I spoke to Mr Attlee about the national standpoint of the Labour Party and say I hope they realise they must pull their weight and join a National Government?' asked the King.[27] Chamberlain advised him to delay any such step until Labour had held its Annual Conference, due to begin at the end of the week in Bournemouth. On the constitutional position, Harold Nicolson had met Clem Davies, who made the extraordinary but correct observation that, in the event of Chamberlain's downfall, 'if there is not to be a Coalition, the King would have to send for Attlee'.[28] Attlee had no intention of thrusting himself forward in the crisis. His aim was to effect a change in Government, and he was by no means determined that Churchill must take over. Towards the end of his life, he recalled: 'I was convinced that, whatever happened, the war had to be won first, that Winston was the man to handle the war, and that the leaders of the Labour Party could handle Winston.'[29] Attlee was later also dismissive about the idea of a Halifax premiership, arguing that the Yorkshire peer was 'quite unsuited for the job'.[30]

But that was written with the benefit of hindsight. Throughout the political crisis of early 1940, Attlee appeared willing for Labour to serve under Halifax in a national coalition. Clement Davies, who felt that Churchill was the only possible Prime Minister, had been urging Attlee in the build-up to the debate 'not to agree to serve in a Halifax-led Coalition' but as late as 7 May 'Attlee had said he would'.[31] Similarly, Brendan Bracken, Churchill's staunchest follower, claimed that on the first evening of the Norway Debate he dined with Attlee, who told him that if there was a new administration 'his people would expect a Coalition Government to be headed by Halifax, with Churchill as Minister of Defence'. In the account that Bracken subsequently gave to Leo Amery, he, 'entirely on his own responsibility, had insisted that Churchill would not and could not serve under Halifax […] and had persuaded Attlee at any rate not to refuse to serve under Churchill if the occasion arose'.[32] To his biographer Kenneth Harris, Attlee later denied that he had ever dined with Bracken or had any such conversation with him.[33] Attlee's memory was not infallible, not least because he never kept a diary, but Bracken may have indulged in some creativity to boost Churchill's cause. In Amery's narrative, Bracken then briefed Churchill that, if negotiations began over the formation of a new Government, 'he could ignore the argument that he would have major difficulties with Labour'.[34]

What can be said with certainty is that the first day of the Norway Debate changed Labour's view about a confidence motion. The interventions by Amery and Keyes convinced the bulk of the party's MPs that the best way to the exploit the growing mood of rebellion on the Conservative benches would be to demand a vote of censure against Chamberlain's Government. But even here, there is a historical dispute over which senior Labour figure took the initiative. The confidence issue, which was to be crucial in deciding the Prime Minister's fate, was raised at the Administrative Committee of the PLP on the morning of Wednesday 8 May. Never overburdened by modesty, Herbert Morrison later claimed that he was the one who first pushed for a censure vote. In his version of events, when the meeting came to discuss the second day of the debate 'neither Attlee or almost any member of the Labour Front Bench Committee had considered what to do on this important occasion'. His argument to colleagues, he said, was that 'Labour must seek' Chamberlain's defeat and 'be ready to take our share of responsibility as part of a different Government'.[35] Morrison's account was backed up by Welsh stalwart Jim Griffiths, the MP for Llanelli, who wrote that 'Herbert was the actual leader and saw the chance to destroy the Government'.[36] But this was strongly contested by Attlee, who always had a deep personal antagonism towards Morrison. 'I presided at the Party meeting and I not Morrison proposed that we should call the vote against the Government. Morrison agreed reluctantly,' Attlee told the historian Laurence Thompson.[37] Some voices were raised against the move to push for a confidence vote – most notably that of Dalton, who feared that a heavy defeat for the Opposition motion might 'consolidate' Chamberlain[38] – but the majority of opinion at the Administrative Committee was strongly in favour of the challenge. The decision was later endorsed by the wider PLP, with only Nye Bevan and George Strauss opposed.

Labour's robustness meant that the die had been cast against Chamberlain. Once the party's decision became known in the early afternoon, an increasing number of Conservative MPs, particularly those in the services, made up their minds to vote against Chamberlain. Attlee was informally told by a rebel that '20 Government MPs, perhaps as many as 50, would vote with the Opposition'.[39] Sensing the tide turning against him, Chamberlain dispatched his parliamentary private secretary Lord Dunglass (later Sir Alec Douglas-Home) to tell Emrys-Evans, Secretary of the Watching Committee, that the Prime Minister 'was prepared to carry out a drastic reconstruction of the Government'. In response, Emrys-Evans said 'that the Government should have been reconstructed at the beginning of the war or even as late as Christmas but that time had now passed'.[40] The hostility towards Chamberlain was clear once the second day of the Norway Debate began at four o'clock. Morrison opened for the Opposition in typically powerful fashion, highlighting a detailed catalogue of military errors by the Government and announcing Labour's decision to press for a vote of censure. Immediately, the Prime Minister leapt from his seat, 'showing his teeth like a rat in the corner', to use Dalton's memorable description,[41] and declared that he 'welcomed the challenge' because 'I have friends in the House'.[42] It was a note of partisanship and divisiveness that only further alienated his critics.

Throughout the afternoon and evening, the rhetorical bombardment continued, headed by a devastating assault from Lloyd George, who not only praised Churchill for his past wisdom about the Nazi threat but also largely absolved him from blame for the Norway fiasco. 'I take complete responsibility for everything that has been done by the Admiralty and I take my full share of the burden,' Churchill intervened. At this, Lloyd George reiterated his determination to rescue the First Lord from the failure that enveloped the rest of the Government: 'The Right Honourable Gentleman must not allow himself to be converted into an air-raid shelter to keep the splinters from hitting his colleagues.'[43] After Lloyd George had sat down, Churchill whispered to fellow frontbencher Kingsley Wood, 'This is all making it damned difficult for me tonight.'[44]

Churchill was due to wind up for the Government after ten o'clock, but an hour before he spoke there was a crucial meeting of the Amery Group, its attendance boosted by members of the Watching Committee and Vigilantes as well as a host of usually loyal Tories who had been disillusioned by Chamberlain's poor performance in the debate. Bob Boothby was among those present: 'It was an enormously attended meeting. The feeling was passionate and I felt at that time that a great many Conservative members were prepared not only to abstain but even to vote against the Government. I came away from that meeting with feelings of great tension.'[45] Another dissident, Duff Cooper, told the MPs to guard 'against being too much affected by Churchill's brilliant oratory. "He will be defending," I said, "with his eloquence those who have long refused to listen to his counsel, who have treated his warnings with contempt and refused to take him into their confidence. Those who had so often trembled before his sword will be only too glad to shrink behind his buckler."'[46] Churchill undoubtedly had a daunting task. He had to justify a disastrous campaign and a failing Prime Minister, while not undermining his own chances of the succession. Before he went into the Chamber, he had a brief word in the Smoking Room with the anti-Chamberlain MP Harold Macmillan, who later recalled: 'I wished him luck but added that that I hoped his speech would not be too convincing. "Why not?" he asked. "Because," I replied, "we must have a new Prime Minister and it must be you." He answered gruffly that he had signed on for the voyage and would stick to the ship.'[47]

At the Dispatch Box, Churchill immediately went on the attack with what Attlee later described as 'very loyal effort to turn the tide'.[48] Churchill frankly admitted that the results of the campaign in central Norway had been 'very disappointing', but ended with an uplifting call for national unity. 'Let party interest be ignored, let all our energies be harnessed, let the whole ability and forces of the nation be hurled into the struggle.'[49] His speech, however, could not prevent a major rebellion, as 41 Government supporters marched through the Opposition lobby and another 60 deliberately abstained. In the face of this revolt, Chamberlain's nominal majority shrunk by more than half, down from 213 to just 81. Amid a 'terrific buzz' outside the chamber after the division, Dalton told listening MPs that Chamberlain 'must go along to the Palace' and resign.[50] The Tory MP Harry Crookshank agreed, noting in his diary that night: 'Winston was very good but all to no purpose as the tide was very strong. I think it means the end of Neville.'[51]

True to his spirit of loyalty in this crisis, Churchill tried to rally Chamberlain that evening, telling him to 'strengthen your Government from every quarter and let us go on until our majority deserts us'.[52] But the Prime Minister knew his chances of survival were negligible, especially given that Labour appeared hostile to entering any government under his leadership. The recognition that Chamberlain was probably doomed gave rise to fevered confabulations at Westminster the next morning. Amery's name was mentioned as a possible national saviour, while Lloyd George put forward the theory that Chamberlain should advise the King to send for Attlee. When Attlee related this, Dalton 'told him that I thought that he could not possibly be Prime Minister in this situation. He quite agreed. The PM must be a Ministerialist.'[53]

Beyond the realms of fantasy, the political reality boiled down to a few key points: the attitude of Halifax to the premiership; the ambitions of Churchill; and the wishes of the Labour leadership about Chamberlain's successor and their own acceptance of office. In some respects, Halifax should have been the obvious choice. Urbane, and respected on all sides, he had none of the baggage that accompanied Churchill, the 'greatest adventurer of modern politics', to quote the notorious description by Halifax's Deputy Foreign Minister Rab Butler.[54] Halifax's judgement was seen as sounder than Churchill's, his political outlook less erratic. He also had the support of the majority of Tory MPs. But he was undermined by several factors. One was that he sat in the Lords, while Government business was focused on the House of Commons. Unlike Churchill, he had no military experience and had never studied military strategy. When Lord Salisbury and his Watching Committee met him at the start of the Norway Debate, they were dismayed at his 'depressing' and 'tired' outlook.[55] Moreover, Halifax was tainted by his long support for the discredited policy of appeasement. 'He is not the stuff of which a Prime Minister is made in such a crisis,' wrote Cadogan, who knew him better than most, on 9 May.[56] Halifax's greatest drawback was his own doubt as to whether he wanted the job or could even do it. As early as December 1938, over an intimate dinner at the Dorchester, he told his confidante and lover Lady Alexandra 'Baba' Metcalfe, the glamorous daughter of Lord Curzon, that he 'would not take on the premiership if offered, his reason being that not being in the Commons makes the position too difficult'.[57]

In fact, as the possibility of his accession to Downing Street drew near, he began to feel psychosomatic discomfort in the form of a pain in his stomach. His hesitations came out during an interview with Chamberlain at 10.15 that morning. According to Halifax's account, the Prime Minister said that, if there were to be a coalition, 'it was clearly Winston or myself, and appeared to suggest that if it were myself he might continue to serve in Government'. Halifax admitted that 'the conversation and the evident drift of his mind left me with a bad stomach ache. I told him again, as I had told him the day before, that if the Labour people said they would only serve under me I should tell them I was not prepared to do it, and see whether a definite attitude would make them budge.'[58]

On that Thursday morning, Churchill had at first remained dismissive of Labour's role. The Chancellor of the Exchequer, Sir John Simon, noted in his diary: 'Winston had apparently originally taken the view that the Labour people had nothing to contribute and that the way to broaden the Government was to bring in a selection of last night's rebels instead, together of course with Archie Sinclair, with whom Winston has long been in close relations.'[59] But reports soon filtered back to him that Clement Davies's Vigilantes, which had now amalgamated with the Amery Group, had insisted that there had to be 'a truly national Government'.[60] The same stance was adopted by Salisbury's Watching Committee, which decided that 'Neville should now resign and either Halifax or Winston form a real War Cabinet on national lines'.[61] Churchill now accepted that Labour would have to be involved, a requirement that he felt made Chamberlain's continuation in office impossible. This he told Anthony Eden, who visited the Admiralty that morning: 'Winston rang up to see me as soon as possible. He thought that Neville would not be able to bring in Labour and that a National Government must be formed.'[62] The widespread recognition of the need for a coalition gave Labour tremendous leverage, but the crucial question remained whether the party's leadership would favour Halifax or Churchill. The pressure to provide an answer was made all the greater because of two other factors. One was military, for British intelligence was warning that Germany was about to order a major offensive in Western Europe. The other was political, with delegates at Labour's imminent Annual Conference bound to want an end to the uncertainty.

Labour was torn, with opinion divided throughout the party. Churchill might be the warrior against Nazism, but he was also seen as a reactionary and imperialist. Halifax might be more reliable and collegiate, but he lacked Churchill's determination to fight. Dalton believed that Halifax should be Prime Minister because Winston 'would be better occupied in winning the war'.[63] That was also the view of Morrison, who felt that 'Labour would welcome the Foreign Secretary in that capacity' because the party 'feared the prospect of the First Lord succeeding as Prime Minister'.[64] The fiery Manny Shinwell, on the other hand, viewed Halifax as 'a namby-pamby Foreign Secretary who could deal with the diplomatic stuff but was not particularly capable. There was no one else other than Winston Churchill.'[65] That opinion was echoed by John Parker, who believed that 'Halifax was not acceptable to the Labour Party'.[66] The differences ran right up to the party's leadership. Arthur Greenwood was strongly in favour of Churchill, telling Emrys-Evans that 'we should go for the right man straight away'.[67] But Attlee was still much more ambivalent. In fact, Dalton came away from his talk with Attlee on the morning of 9 May under the impression that, 'he agrees with my preference for Halifax over Winston but we both think that either would be tolerable'.[68]

Against the backdrop of a potential German attack in the West, the machinations over the Government's future were approaching a decisive point. Chamberlain was due to hold discussions with Halifax, Churchill and the Labour leadership on the afternoon of Thursday 9 May at Downing Street. Before those talks took place, however, both Churchill and Attlee were showered with advice about the courses they should adopt. The mercurial Beaverbrook, now firmly in the anti-Halifax camp, called with the faithful Bracken on Churchill at the Admiralty to encourage him in pressing his own case. According to a note left by Beaverbrook,

I asked – do you intend to serve under Halifax? He answered, 'I will serve under any Minister capable of prosecuting the war.' It was a disappointment for I had hoped that Churchill would lead us. Indeed, I believe it necessary to the safety of the Kingdom and the country wanted him. Any other choice would be a shock. The choice of Halifax would simply mean the continuance of the present administration. Brendan Bracken intervened. He asked Churchill to remain silent and after much argument Churchill agreed.[69]

Another account, written by Churchill's doctor Lord Moran after the war on the basis of a conversation with Bracken, placed this intervention late the night before, with Bracken acting alone. In Lord Moran's version, Bracken got wind of a rumour that Churchill had agreed to serve under Halifax and was determined to change his mind. 'At one o'clock in the morning, he found him. "You cannot agree to this," Brendan spluttered, but Winston was obdurate; he would not go back on his word. "Well," Brendan persisted, "at least you must promise you will not speak first when you get to No.10. Promise?" At last Winston said he would promise.'[70]

The suggestion that the normally loquacious Churchill should be silent in his forthcoming Downing Street interview, if asked about his willingness to be subordinate to Halifax, was to prove crucial. Yet, although Beaverbrook and Moran attributed the idea to Bracken, another, more incongruous figure may have also had some responsibility. That Thursday, Churchill had lunch with Eden and Kingsley Wood, the Lord Privy Seal, who had been one of Chamberlain's most loyal lieutenants but now viewed Churchill as the only possible Prime Minister. In Eden's account of the lunch, it was Wood who took the initiative in urging silence on Churchill. 'The future was discussed. Kingsley thought that Winston should succeed, and urged that he make plain his willingness.' Eden then related how Wood warned Churchill that Chamberlain would ask him if he agreed to serve under Halifax. '"Don't agree," Kingsley Wood insisted, "and don't say anything." I was shocked that Wood should talk in this way, for he had been so much Chamberlain's man, but it was good counsel and I seconded it.'[71]

In a different part of central London, another significant lunch took place when Attlee and Greenwood met Clement Davies at the Reform Club. Davies later said that he was disturbed to find Attlee in a hesitant mood, vacillating even over whether Chamberlain should be driven from the premiership in view of the precarious situation on the Western Front. 'Attlee was platitudinous and indecisive, arguing that the rapidly unfolding events in Europe meant a change of leader should be postponed. Davies turned to Arthur Greenwood to seek his help in stiffening Attlee's resolve,' wrote Davies's biographer.[72] Reportedly, after two hours of argument, Attlee was persuaded to back Chamberlain's ejection in favour of Churchill. This may have been a distorted version of the lunch, aimed at boosting Davies's own influence. 'Clem Davies has a lot to say about comings and goings, but I fancy he embroiders a bit, exaggerating his own part,' wrote Attlee in 1960.[73] Nevertheless, there is no dispute that Davies was energetic in pushing Churchill's cause. After seeing the Labour leaders he told Bob Boothby at the House that 'Attlee and Greenwood are unable to distinguish between the Prime Minister and Halifax and are *not* prepared to serve under the latter'.[74]

Primed with the advice on self-restraint, Churchill went to his Downing Street discussion with Chamberlain in the late afternoon. Halifax was already present when he arrived. The Prime Minister told the two men that 'the main thing' was national unity, which meant that Labour had to come into office. If Attlee's party refused to serve under him, then he was 'quite ready to resign'.[75] Chamberlain expressed a willingness to serve under either man and did not offer a preference. Soon afterwards, Attlee and Greenwood turned up, looking 'pale and evidently in a state of some tension', according to the *Daily Telegraph* proprietor Lord Camrose, who was in Downing Street at the time.[76] The two Labour leaders sat down on one side of the table, with the Government trio facing them. According to the account Attlee gave in 1961 of the forty-five-minute meeting, Chamberlain 'appeared calm. He was hardly worried and still seemed to think that he could carry on' – a remark that illustrates how successfully the Prime Minister concealed his emotions. To continue with Attlee's version, Chamberlain

> told us he believed there was now a paramount need for a National Government and asked if we would join it and serve under him. Then Winston joined in and urged us to come under Chamberlain. Halifax did not speak, he said nothing all through, so far as I remember. I could understand Winston's loyalty but I thought it best to be frank. It is not pleasant to

have to tell a Prime Minister to his face that he must go, but I thought it was the only thing to do. I said, 'Mr Prime Minister, the fact is that our party won't come in under you. Our party won't have you and I think I am right in saying that the country won't have you either.'[77]

Greenwood's own account, which he passed on to Clem Davies, gave himself a starring role in a more vivid drama. Having said that Attlee was 'completely flabbergasted' by Chamberlain's invitation 'to join *his* government', Greenwood claimed to have taken 'up the running and explained that the Prime Minister was entirely mistaken and that there was not the slightest prospect of the Opposition joining a Government under him'. When Churchill came to Chamberlain's defence with an 'eloquent eulogy' about his efficiency and personal charm, Greenwood apparently cut him short. 'This is no time for oratory. The truth of the matter is that there is not one on our side who trusts the Prime Minister.'[78] In contrast to this tale of open confrontation, Churchill's memory was that 'the conversation was most polite',[79] while Halifax recorded that the Labour leaders 'were a bit evasive'.[80] All accounts agreed, however, that Attlee and Greenwood emphasised how they could not definitively commit their party without consulting their senior colleagues, who were then beginning to gather in Bournemouth in advance of Conference. It was therefore agreed that they should travel to the town and urgently put two questions to Labour's NEC, due to meet on Friday 10 May: would the party be prepared to join a Government a) under Chamberlain; or b) under a different Prime Minister? Attlee promised to give Downing Street the answers the following afternoon. With that, the two Labour leaders rose and left the Cabinet Room.

The three ministers remained behind and were soon joined by the Chief Whip, David Margesson. Echoing Chamberlain's earlier line, Margesson stressed that unity was essential, but, given Labour's stance, it would be almost impossible to achieve this if the Prime Minister stayed in office. He was not yet prepared, however, to name which candidate the Conservative backbenchers preferred. The task of questioning Halifax and Churchill about their assessment of the succession now fell to Chamberlain. Chilly and inscrutable, the Prime Minister turned his gaze first on Churchill, asking the First Lord if there was any reason why a peer should not be Prime Minister. The enquiry appeared designed to ensnare Churchill: a positive answer would reek of divisive, self-serving ambition; a negative one would open the way for Halifax. But, forewarned by Bracken and Wood, Churchill said nothing. 'As I remained silent, a very long pause ensued. It certainly seemed longer than the two minutes which one observes in the commemorations of Armistice Day. Then at length Halifax spoke.'[81] Throughout the afternoon, Halifax had been plagued by his stomach ache, an ailment that only worsened as Churchill adopted his unchar-acteristic Trappist reticence. Driven by his inner turmoil, Halifax felt compelled to be frank about his reluctance to take the premiership. 'I said it would be a hopeless position. If I was not in charge of the war and if I didn't lead the House, I should be a cipher. I thought that Winston was the better choice.' Churchill had shown unimpeachable loyalty to Chamberlain since the declaration of war, but as the prize of the premiership came within his grasp, he now felt no such obligation to Halifax. Of Churchill's response to his own self-abnegation, Halifax wrote that 'Winston, with suitable positions of regard and humility, said that he could not but feel the force of what I had said, and the PM reluctantly, and Winston evidently with much less reluctance, finished by accepting my view.'[82] Churchill, in his own narrative, also recorded how Halifax listed the hurdles he would face, especially his position in the Lords: 'He spoke for some minutes in this sense, and by the time he had finished it was clear that the duty would fall upon me – had in fact fallen upon me.'[83]

Chamberlain's own testimony largely endorsed this narrative. A few months later, in October 1940, he gave a pithy summary to the US Ambassador Joe Kennedy, in which he admitted that 'he wanted to make Halifax Prime Minister' but that at the crucial meeting 'Edward, as is his way, started saying, "Perhaps I can't handle it being in the

House of Lords." Finally Winston said, "I don't think you could." And he wouldn't come and that settled it.'[84] A similar version came from the pen of Lord Camrose, whom Chamberlain briefed after his interview with Halifax and Churchill. Camrose's own record noted that Halifax 'had said that he would prefer not to be sent for as he felt the position would be too difficult and troublesome for him. He (Neville) would therefore advise the King to send for Winston.'[85] Later, Halifax also gave another, slightly different tale to his private secretary Charles Peake, who noted it in a diary entry for June 1941. In this, the silence was broken not by Churchill, but by Margesson, who said that, 'much as he admired Edward, he rather thought at the moment Winston was more the man they were looking for' – a point with which Halifax ostentatiously agreed by claiming that 'no other choice was possible' because of Churchill's 'talents, his character, his long experience and his genius'. In Peake's diary record, Chamberlain at the outset was unequivocally in favour of Halifax, stating that 'he had come to the conclusion that the man to succeed him was Edward'.[86]

Yet the Prime Minister may not have been as antipathetic to Churchill as he sometimes appeared. There was no constitutional requirement for him to consult Churchill; he was perfectly within his rights to simply urge the King to send for Halifax, something that would have been welcomed by George VI, who not only had harboured a deep distrust of Churchill since the abdication crisis but was also close to Halifax. According to the courtier Alan 'Tommy' Lascelles, George VI's private secretary, Sir Alec Hardinge 'knew that Winston was the man, but he had a hard job of selling him to the King who was very anti-Winston'.[87] Churchill himself recognised that Chamberlain had been fair to him, telling the *Manchester Guardian* journalist W. P. Crozier soon after he began his premiership that 'I owe something to Chamberlain, you know. When he resigned, he could have advised the King to send for Halifax and he didn't.'[88]

By the early evening of 9 May, everything appeared to be moving in Churchill's direction. At the close of the Downing Street meeting, Margesson reported that opinion among Tory MPs was 'veering towards' Churchill.[89] Similar welcome news came from Bob Boothby, who wrote to Churchill after canvassing opinion all day at the House. 'Opinion is hardening against Halifax as Prime Minister. I am doing my best to foster this but I cannot feel he is, in any circumstances, the right man.'[90] That evening Churchill spoke over the telephone to his son Randolph, then billeted with the army in Northamptonshire. 'I think tomorrow I shall be Prime Minister,' he said.[91] This outcome was also predicted in the press. Reporting on the Downing Street conference between Labour and the Conservative ministers, the *Daily Mirror* stated:

> The Socialist leaders informed Mr Chamberlain that they would not serve in any Government of which he was premier. They did announce that they would be prepared to serve in a Cabinet headed by Mr Churchill. That talk determined Mr Chamberlain's fate […] When he does go to the Palace formally to tender his resignation he will recommend Mr Churchill as the new Premier.[92]

But, early in the morning of 10 May, there was a sudden new twist in the saga as the Germans began their long-awaited invasion of Western Europe, beginning with air raids on Belgium and Holland. In Chamberlain's view, the Nazi offensive transformed not only the military situation on the Continent but also the political landscape at home, justifying his retention of office. As he told the Air Secretary Sam Hoare early that morning, his 'first inclination was to withhold his resignation until the French battle was finished'.[93] Many key players were angered by his stance, however, perceiving that the German attack only strengthened the case for reconstruction. Churchill held that opinion and so did Kingsley Wood, who told Chamberlain to his face that the German invasion 'made it all the more necessary to have a National Government, which alone could confront it'.[94] Meanwhile, Emrys-Evans phoned Lord Salisbury to ensure that the Watching Committee would not allow Chamberlain's escape. 'We must maintain our point of view that Winston should be made Prime Minister during the course of the day.'[95]

Nonetheless, the Conservatives alone would have struggled to force Chamberlain out if he was determined to hang on. Only Labour could make him depart, by refusing to take office under his leadership. That was why Chamberlain tried on the morning of 10 May to persuade Attlee to accept his retention of the premiership. Attlee and Greenwood were due to travel from London Waterloo to Bournemouth on the 11.34 train; but before they left, Chamberlain rang Attlee to suggest 'that the German attack had changed the whole situation, presuming that he would continue in office for the time being. Attlee replied, "Not at all," and that he had better made way as quickly as possible.'[96] In the version of events given by Hugh Dalton, who met Attlee and Greenwood at the Commons before their trip, Chamberlain had asked them to issue a statement 'saying that the Labour Party supported the Government at this grave crisis of the war'. It was a demand that prompted Dalton to write in his diary that 'this old man is incorrigibly limpet and always trying new tricks to keep himself on the rock'.[97] The subsequent press release, of which Dalton claimed authorship, heightened the pressure for change rather than backing the Prime Minister. 'The Labour Party, in view of the latest series of abominable aggressions by Hitler, while firmly convinced that a drastic reconstruction of the Government is vital and urgent to win the war, reaffirms its determination to do its utmost to achieve victory.'[98] When the news of this text was relayed to Downing Street via the ticker-tape machine, Chamberlain was furious. As Sir Antony Eden recalled, the Prime Minister, who was at the time chairing the Cabinet, explained to his colleagues that 'he had asked Attlee to put out a notice which would include support of the Government pro tem, but when announced on the tape it did not say more than support for the war effort'. Eden noted, though, that round the Cabinet table Labour's statement 'impressed many present with the difficulties of prolonged delay, especially as the conditions for change might become more rather than less difficult'.[99]

Chamberlain's tumultuous spell as Prime Minister now had only a few hours to run. Attlee was the agent of its end. In Bournemouth, he and Greenwood met the party's NEC in mid-afternoon at the Highcliffe Hotel. The NEC agreed unanimously that Labour were 'prepared to take our share of responsibility in a new Government which, under a new Prime Minister, would command the confidence of the nation'.[100] The NEC did not specify its preference for the new Prime Minister, but nor did it impose any veto. Soon after the meeting Attlee phoned Downing Street to answer the two questions Chamberlain had asked the previous evening about Labour's willingness to serve either under him or a different premier. With his usual briskness, Attlee came straight to the point. 'The answer to the first question is No. To the second, Yes.'[101] Determined to banish any doubts about Labour's stance, Attlee then read out the NEC's resolution and insisted that this be conveyed immediately to Chamberlain.

The Prime Minister was in yet another Cabinet meeting when his private secretary delivered Attlee's definitive response. Chamberlain looked at the note without betraying any emotion, then revealed its contents to the Cabinet. 'In the light of this answer,' he announced, 'I have reached the conclusion that I should at once tender my resignation to the King.' In dry prose, the official minutes recorded that 'the War Cabinet agreed to the course suggested'.[102] By the time that Attlee and Greenwood boarded their train at Bournemouth for the return journey to London, Chamberlain was already on his way to the Palace, where George VI received him with sympathy. As they discussed his successor, the King pressed the case for Halifax. He said the Foreign Secretary was 'the obvious man' but Chamberlain explained that this was impossible since Halifax had indicated that he was 'not enthusiastic'.[103] Reluctantly, George VI had to accept that Churchill was the only figure who could form a government.

It is possible that some of Halifax's reluctance stemmed from his affair with Lady Baba Metcalfe, to whom he unburdened a wealth of state secrets. After closing his townhouse in Eaton Square, he resided at the Dorchester Hotel, with Baba conveniently installed on the floor above. Such behaviour not only undermined his much-vaunted moral authority and reputation for integrity, but also exposed him as danger-ously indiscreet. The affair may have been behind the rumour that Albert Sylvester later reported to Lloyd George about Halifax's spell as Foreign Secretary in 1940. 'Halifax was notoriously careless with his papers. Instead of locking them up carefully in his safe each night, he left them lying about his suite.' Consequently one secret report was sent 'to Switzerland – and there is little doubt that no time was lost in sending it to Germany'. Sylvester admitted that the 'the story is a very libellous one' but he was 'sure that at the time a report was sent to Attlee and it has never been denied'.[104]

Halifax had faded from the scene by the afternoon of 10 May. Just after 6.30 p.m., Churchill arrived for his audience with the King. In his own account that Churchill wrote: 'I told the King that I would immediately send for the leaders of the Labour and Liberal parties and that I hoped to let him have at least five names before midnight.'[105] At the age of sixty-five and after almost forty years in Parliament, Churchill had finally made it to Downing Street. The grand ambition that had fired him since his days as a cavalry officer in Queen Victoria's army had been fulfilled. Yet his inheritance could have hardly been bleaker, with the Reich's war machine in the ascendant across Europe. 'I hope it is not too late. I am very much afraid it is. We can only do our best,' he told his bodyguard Detective Walter Thompson as he left Buckingham Palace.[106] But, despite Britain's grim prospects, he was liberated rather than daunted by the responsibility he had assumed. For the first time in his career, he had the real power to guide the nation's fortunes. He wrote in his wartime memoirs of his feelings on retiring to bed that night. 'I was conscious of a profound sense of relief. At last I had the authority to give directions over the whole scene. I felt as if I were walking with destiny and that all my past life had been but a preparation for this hour and this trial.'[107]

Some in the political establishment were appalled at Churchill's rise, given his image as an egotistical, heavy-drinking maverick long past his prime. The former Tory Party chairman Lord Davidson, who had a large streak of Scottish puritanism, felt that 'the crooks are on top as they were in the last war'; while Nancy Dugdale, the wife of Conservative MP Sir Thomas Dugdale, regarded Churchill's arrival in Downing Street as 'a greater disaster than the invasion of the Low Lands'.[108] A more balanced, though still critical, assessment came from the backbencher Sir Cuthbert Headlam, who wrote in his diary after the news of Chamberlain's downfall: 'I have never believed in him. I only hope that my judgement of the man will be proved wrong. He certainly possesses imagination, courage and drive.'[109] Others were more positive, including several newspapers. The *Guardian* believed that Churchill 'has the confidence of the nation even more than Mr Lloyd George had when he became Prime Minister in 1916', while the *Daily Mirror* felt that the highest office was reward for his foresight: 'He is one of those who have never been deceived by the character and purpose of our treacherous enemies.'[110] The *Mirror* director Cecil King, however, regretted that, alongside Churchill, 'we must be burdened with many of the duds of the Attlee-Greenwood type'.[111]

Attlee and Greenwood were unaware of the latest development until they arrived back at Waterloo from Bournemouth. There they were met by a naval officer with a message that Churchill was now the Prime Minister and wanted to see them as soon as possible. The Labour leaders were then driven to the Admiralty to begin the process of negotiating the membership of the new Government. Attlee may not have seen Churchill as the only possible choice for the premiership, but – given Halifax's reluctance – the inexorable logic of his rejection of Chamberlain was Churchill's advance to that position. Attlee himself told the *News Chronicle* after the war that 'Churchill was made Prime Minister by the Labour Party, one of the ironies of history'.[112] Although he exaggerated, he was not entirely wrong. Labour could have blocked Churchill; and indeed many of the party's MPs had grave reservations about him because of his long crusade against socialism. But Attlee never had any doubts about accepting him if he emerged as the prime candidate. 'I have sometimes been asked whether, when asked to join a Government under him in 1940, I had any misgivings about serving under the man "who sent the troops to Tonypandy". I did not [...] I never believed that Winston had been hostile to the working-classes.'[113] Attlee's was absolutely the right decision. His assent ensured that Britain was now to be governed by the ideal wartime Prime Minister. As Attlee, who rated him 'the greatest leader in war this country has ever known',[114] put it, 'What once earned him the reputation of being a reactionary and a warmonger was the same quality that enabled him to save civilisation from the greatest dangers it has ever faced.'[115]

———◇———

FOURTEEN

DUNKIRK

CHURCHILL'S RELATIONSHIP WITH Attlee was transformed by his appointment as Prime Minister. Until 10 May 1940, they had been parliamentary opponents for almost two decades, respectful towards each other but never warm. Across the floor of the House, they generally exchanged barbs rather than pleasantries. The chasm between them was based not just on party and policy, but also on their respective political statures. Long dominant in the Westminster landscape, Churchill was an endlessly controversial figure who had regularly been in ministerial office and attracted national headlines since his youth. In contrast, Attlee had never even served in Cabinet and was overshadowed by several of his fellow frontbenchers.

But now, through the turning wheel of history, they had ended up as partners in Government. The two unlikely colleagues had the challenge of leading the nation in its moment of greatest peril. Rarely can a pair have seemed less well matched for such a heavy responsibility: one egocentric, voluble, powerful and maverick; the other diffident, prosaic, taciturn and conventional. 'Temperamentally Churchill remained a radical just as Attlee by temperament was a conservative,' said Jock Colville, who worked for them both.[1] Everything from their working methods to their drinking habits was different. Yet they were united by the one simple goal of winning the war. Through this patriotic sense of purpose, they forged a bond that was to last until the achievement of victory in Europe. That their union survived all the vicissitudes of war at home and abroad was partly a reflection of Churchill's greatness and partly of Attlee's patience. They were the only two men who served in the War Cabinet from the French campaign until VE Day. Churchill understood he could trust Attlee because throughout the war the Labour Leader was never after his position. 'He knew Clem wouldn't do a coup or anything,' said Attlee's grandson John.[2] Meanwhile Attlee, a deep admirer of the new Prime Minister's dynamism and strategic vision, felt that one of his primary duties was to focus Churchill's creativity on a practical course. As Attlee wrote later:

> He was always throwing out ideas. Some of them were not very good, and some of them were downright dangerous. But they kept coming and they kept one going and a lot of them were excellent. My relations with him in Cabinet always seemed to me to be very good. He talked to me extremely frankly, more frankly, I suspect than he talked to some of his Conservative colleagues.[3]

The feeling was reciprocated. In his own war memoirs, Churchill said that Attlee's 'long experience in Opposition was of great value', adding, with a degree of generous exaggeration, that 'we worked together with perfect ease and confidence during the whole period of the government'.[4] Churchill and Attlee demonstrated their surprising compatibility on the first evening of the new premiership, as they began negotiations at the Admiralty over the formation of the Coalition. Churchill, who described the talks as 'pleasant',[5] was keen that his Government should be as broad-based as possible; he therefore sought to be generous to Labour. Of the smoothness of the discussions, Churchill later commented, 'It is probably easier to form a Cabinet, especially a Coalition Cabinet, in the heat of the battle than in quiet times. The sense of duty dominates all else and personal claims recede.'[6] For his part Attlee did not want to paralyse the working of the new administration with partisan bargaining. 'I was very conscious that in the First World War, there had been a lot of haggling over places.

It seemed to me that this was the reason for some of the failures of the military show then and I determined that we would not haggle this time.'7 Both Attlee and Greenwood were given places in the new five-strong War Cabinet, the former as Lord Privy Seal and the latter as Minister without Portfolio. Outside the Cabinet, Alexander took up Churchill's former position as First Lord of the Admiralty, Sinclair was given charge of the Air Ministry and Eden became War Secretary.

The other two members of the War Cabinet were Halifax, who remained Foreign Secretary, and Chamberlain, whose position was the only source of friction during the negotiations. Churchill felt indebted to Chamberlain for his advice to the King, and he also knew that the former Prime Minister, still party Leader, had a large store of political capital among Conservatives. Soon after leaving the Palace, Churchill had decided to offer Chamberlain the posts of Chancellor of the Exchequer, Leader of the House and Lord President of the Council. But Attlee strongly objected when Churchill put this proposition to him. 'I was absolutely opposed to that. I didn't think the House would stand it and our people certainly wouldn't.'8 In a letter to his sister Ida, Chamberlain reflected on Churchill's generosity and Attlee's hostility:

> I must say that Winston has been most handsome in his appre-
> ciation of my willingness to help and my ability to do so […]
> He would have given me the Exchequer if I had been willing
> to take it but I saw it was impossible. With Labour's set at me,
> I should have seemed an obstacle to all they wanted and they
> would have quickly made my position untenable.9

Having dropped the proposal of the Chancellorship, Churchill then offered a compromise whereby he himself would be Leader of the House and Chamberlain his Deputy, in addition to serving as Lord President. But even this was too much for Attlee, who insisted that the importance of the Commons meant that Labour should have the Deputyship. A few days later, Chamberlain wrote to Hilda:

I have agreed to let Attlee be Deputy Leader of the House. Although Winston's first idea was that I should do this, the Labour Party made trouble about it and I saw that it would involve me in much tedious sitting in the House and very likely lead to ill-temper and bad manners. So I gave it up without a sigh. I am to retain the Leadership of the Party which I think essential if Winston is to have whole-hearted support.[10]

On the afternoon of Saturday 11 May, after the War Cabinet was settled, Attlee telephoned Dalton, who was still in Bournemouth with Labour's NEC in advance of the Annual Conference. He asked for the NEC's endorsement of the decisions that he had provisionally agreed with Churchill. Attlee strongly urged acceptance, stressing that excluding Chamberlain from the Cabinet was impossible because to do so would stir up such bitterness on the Tory benches as to make the life of the new Government 'brutish and short'.[11] Dalton duly relayed the message to the NEC. According to his diary, they 'boggled a bit at some of this, and Morrison was rather awkward, saying that this didn't sound like a government that would stand up any better than the last one'. But, after a debate, Dalton was authorised to phone Attlee back and tell him to accept 'so that Winston can publish the five in the War Cabinet plus the three Defence Ministers tonight. Attlee says to me, "We are getting several more important offices and you are well in the picture."'[12] Indeed, Labour did well from the further distribution of offices that Churchill carried out over the next two days, with a third of the posts going to the party. The Ministry of Economic Warfare went to Dalton, Supply to Morrison, and Labour to the heavyweight trade-union boss Ernie Bevin. The new Pensions Minister was the left-winger Ellen Wilkinson, who showed more admiration for Churchill than she ever had towards Attlee. After the new Prime Minister had interviewed her, she said, 'I felt I had been in the presence of a very great man and a very great leader.'[13] Her acceptance pleased Churchill, enabling him to boast to Harold

Macmillan that 'my Government is the most broad-based that Britain has ever known. It extends from Lord Lloyd of Dolobran* to Miss Ellen Wilkinson.'[14] Ironically, there was no place in the Coalition for Stafford Cripps, whose Popular Front movement in the late 1930s had been the foremost advocate of multi-party unity. But at this time his expulsion from the Labour Party still remained in force, while neither Churchill nor Attlee personally warmed to him.

As the process of reconstruction reached the more minor posts, Churchill's attention began to wander and he itched to return to military conduct of war. According to the testimony of Brendan Bracken, who helped Churchill with the process alongside Chief Whip David Margesson, they 'sat up till three going through lists. Winston was not the least interested once the major posts had been filled and kept on trying to interrupt them by discussing the nature of war and the changing rules of strategy'.[15] The outcome of these deliberations was not greeted with anything like universal acclaim. Violet Bonham Carter wrote in her diary that 'the War Cabinet is deplorable and seems to have been entirely dictated by Party – Winston, Halifax, Attlee, Greenwood, Ombrello†: all symbolic sexagenarians‡. Not an executive instrument or even a good shop window. Winston will of course run it, but the others do not even present a surface on which the mind could strike.'[16] For Ivan Maisky, the weakness was not just the old guard but also the Labour elements: 'Chamberlain and Halifax are simply poisonous and Attlee and Greenwood are nonentities. What do these men bring to the Cabinet? How can they help Winston?'[17] But Dalton, usually a critic of Attlee's, felt his party Leader had negotiated effectively with Churchill. 'I think he has made his selections and omissions well [...] He has got a lot of our people in.'[18]

---

* The former Governor of Bengal and Churchill's ally in the diehard fight against Indian Home Rule, Lord Lloyd became Colonial Secretary.

† Her nickname for Chamberlain, whose ubiquitous rolled black umbrella was a much-caricatured symbol of failing leadership.

‡ Lady Bonham Carter had exaggerated Attlee's age; he was actually fifty-seven.

On the evening of Sunday 12 May, as Churchill continued to construct his Government, Attlee and Greenwood travelled back to Bournemouth to prepare for the beginning of Labour's Annual Conference. That night they gave a full report in person to the NEC, leaving opinionated socialist Harold Laski unimpressed: 'I felt as though the cook and the kitchen maid were telling us how they had sacked the butler.'[19] Morrison was another grumbler. 'These aren't the right people to represent the party,' he complained.[20] But the next morning Attlee was on stronger form as he appealed to his party to back Churchill's Government for the sake of the struggle against Nazism. For once abandoning his usual dry style, he captivated the delegates with his powerful justification for joining the Coalition. He said that he had told Churchill: 'If Labour representatives in the House of Commons are to come into the Government, they can come in only if they have the support of their movement. We come in as partners, not as hostages.'[21] He then warned against a refusal to compromise. 'What trade unionist has ever got exactly what he wanted? There must be included in the Government some people we do not like. Yes, but there are some of us they do not like.' His peroration, which brought the Conference to its feet, was a frank appeal to humanity in the fight against Nazism. 'Life without liberty is not worth living. Let us go forward and win that liberty.'[22] For more than four years, Attlee had never looked comfortable in his role as Leader. But suddenly his elevation to the War Cabinet gave him a new standing as a national politician. Zita Crossman, the wife of the campaigner, academic and future Labour MP Dick Crossman, noticed the change: 'His voice seemed to have taken on a new power and authority, lacking at former conferences.'[23] Before the Conference vote was taken, Attlee and Greenwood had to return to London for parliamentary and Cabinet business. But the delegates overwhelmingly endorsed Attlee's approach by 2,450,000 votes to 170,000.

Churchill had also appointed himself to his newly fashioned post of Minister of Defence, giving him oversight of the service departments, command of strategy and direct access to the Chiefs of Staff. Some felt that he was taking on too much, particularly given his additional role as Leader of the Commons. Leo Amery wrote in his diary: 'How Winston thinks he can be Prime Minister, co-ordinator of defence and leader of the House all in one is puzzling [...] Certainly, no one can co-ordinate defence properly who is not prepared to be active head of the three Chiefs of Staff.'[24] Yet that is precisely the kind of leadership that Churchill was planning to provide. He wanted to avoid the sort of experience he had endured under Asquith in the First World War, when little civilian control was exerted over the military. 'I am determined that the power shall be in no other hands than mine. There will be no more Kitcheners, Fishers or Haigs.'[25] Churchill was able to establish his ascendancy not only through his compelling personality but also because of his own profound grasp of military affairs. In Attlee's view, Churchill's swift establishment of his authority over the service chiefs was his greatest achievement:

> I rate him supreme as Britain's leader in war because he was able to solve the problem that democratic countries in total war find crucial and may find fatal: relations between the civil and military leaders. Lloyd George had an instinct that told him when the generals were wrong but he did not have the military knowledge to tell the generals what was right. Churchill did. He did not overrule the generals. But he always had chapter and verse with which to meet their protests and to lead them to a positive course of his own.[26]

On the afternoon of 13 May, Churchill spoke to the Commons for the first time as Prime Minister. Entering the chamber, he received a far warmer reception from the Labour and Liberal benches than he did from the majority of Conservative MPs, who reserved their acclamation for Neville Chamberlain – an indicator of the suspicion with which Churchill was still viewed by much of the Tory establishment. 'The claque was busy and Neville got the greater cheer,' wrote Harry Crookshank, Financial Secretary to the Treasury.[27] In a symbol of the Government's political unity, Attlee took his place beside him, prompting Chips Channon to write acidly in his diary, 'that little gadfly looked smaller and more insignificant than ever on the Government front bench, dwarfed by Winston'.[28] Thoroughly prepared as ever, Churchill proceeded with his compelling 'blood, toil, tears and sweat' statement, the first of the great speeches he made in the early summer of 1940 that collectively served as a clarion call to national self-defence. 'You ask, what is our aim? I can answer in one word: It is victory, victory at all costs, victory in spite of all terror, victory however long and hard the road may be, for without victory there is no survival,' he told MPs.[29] Later, the House passed a vote of confidence in the new Government without a single voice of dissent.

Following his Commons statement, Churchill held a further meeting of the War Cabinet at 6.30 p.m., the first to be attended by Attlee and Greenwood. Discussion revolved around the RAF, focusing largely on the bombing of industrial plants in the Ruhr. In a balanced opening, Churchill argued that such bomber raids had 'ample justification', given the 'many atrocities the enemy had already committed', and that Germans would not yet 'have secured depth to their air defences'. On the other hand, he said, it 'might be better to concentrate the whole resources of our Air Force in an effort to defeat the German armies' in the Western land battle. Attlee, in his first-ever Cabinet contribution, said that, 'while an immediate attack on the Ruhr might upset German plans and would probably have a considerable psychological effect, it would have no immediate effect on the land battle'.[30] The Cabinet eventually agreed to put off any bombing raid for a few days, until the position in France became clearer. The decision to proceed was taken on 15 May, with Attlee at the forefront of the pressure for action, contradicting the post-war myth that he was opposed to strategic bombing. 'The Lord Privy Seal considered that the moment had arrived when it was essential that we should counter-attack. The proposed attack on German railways and oil refineries seemed to provide the best way of doing this,' noted the Cabinet minutes. Churchill fully agreed with Attlee. 'He considered that the proposed operations could cut Germany at its tap root, and was hopeful that they might even provide an immediate contribution to the land battle.'³¹ The first large-scale bombing raid of the war was duly enacted by the RAF on the night of 15–16 May, though only twenty-four of the ninety-six dispatched bombers actually found the Ruhr at all.

Impressed by the Labour ministers, Sir Edmund Ironside, the Chief of the Imperial General Staff, noted in his diary that 'Attlee, Greenwood and Alexander are definitely better than the men we had before'.³² Halifax, filled with growing doubts about the military campaign, felt the opposite about Labour's senior trio: 'Certainly we have not gained in intellect.'³³ The wider immediate perception was that the Coalition had brought a new sense of purpose after the years of appeasement and division. It was a view perfectly captured the next day by the publication in the *Evening Standard* of a cartoon by the New Zealander David Low, who portrayed the ministers with their sleeves rolled up and fists clenched, marching forward behind Churchill, Attlee at his side. 'All behind you, Winston', read the uplifting motto below the image. The cartoon was a favourite of Attlee's, reflecting his pride in persuading Labour to join Churchill's Government. Years later, Violet contacted Low to buy the original and displayed it prominently in their home.

Churchill's impact on Whitehall was immediate. The mood of vacillation disappeared, replaced by a new sense of vigour driven by the Prime Minister's phenomenal work rate and restless energy. 'Within a few days of his becoming Prime Minister, the whole machinery of Government was working at a pace and an intensity of purpose quite unlike anything which had gone before,' wrote the Cabinet Secretary Sir Edward Bridges.³⁴ Churchill's slogan, 'Action This Day', was attached to a ceaseless flood of instructions that emanated from his office. He dictated minutes everywhere, from the back of his official car to his bathtub. 'It was clear that the days of co-ordination were over for good and all. We were going to get direction, leadership and action – with a snap in it,' recalled General Leslie Hollis, who served as deputy to Pug Ismay.³⁵ Marion Holmes, a Downing Street secretary who had previously worked for Chamberlain, remembered, 'It was as if a superhuman current of electricity had gone through 10 Downing Street. Time off and leave vanished. We worked incredibly long hours. Respected civil servants were seen running down corridors.'[36]

The pace had to intensify because the Western Front was buckling under the pressure from the Germans' Blitzkrieg. Early on the morning of 15 May, Churchill received a panicky call from Paul Reynaud, who wailed that 'the road to Paris was open and the battle was lost'.[37] Just five days into his premiership, Churchill was confronted with the brutal reality that France could soon collapse, leaving the Reich utterly dominant in Europe and able to turn all its firepower on Britain. But the goal of helping to prevent France's downfall presented him with a dilemma. He could urge his Chiefs of Staff to pour as many resources as they could into the Battle of France, especially aerial support. Yet, if France's will had already been broken, such a policy would achieve nothing except the diminution of Britain's own military capability, weakening the RAF and leaving the nation ill-defended. Churchill's solution was to use his own personal influence in an attempt to strengthen France's resoluteness. Over the next month, he made six visits there to meet French politicians and military leaders as he tried to galvanise the resistance against the Germans. But, for all Churchill's powers of persuasion and warrior spirit, Britain was in a weak position to lecture France. The British Expeditionary Force, with just ten divisions, was not only small compared to the Republic's 103 divisions but was also retreating in the face of the Wehrmacht onslaught. Moreover, the RAF and the Air Ministry were deeply opposed to sending any more fighters across the Channel. During his second visit, on 16–17 May, Churchill submitted to London a request from the French for six squadrons, to which the War Cabinet reluctantly agreed a compromise whereby the requisite planes would be assigned to the battle but would still be based in southern England. Despite the bravery of the pilots, they could do little to halt the German advance. By 25 May it was clear that the Allies were facing catastrophe. The head of the British Expeditionary Force, General John Gort, decided that his only hope of survival was to retreat to the northernmost ports of Calais and Dunkirk.

The War Cabinet were not just concerned with military setbacks in France. The astonishing success of the Germans in the West and Scandinavia also prompted anxious thoughts about Britain's preparedness for a possible Nazi invasion. One of the Government's first steps was to set up a new voluntary force called the Local Defence Volunteers, though on the insistence of Churchill the name was soon changed to the Home Guard. The Cabinet also decided to shift Ironside from the Imperial General Staff to the Command of Home Forces, in which role he embarked on a massive programme of the construction of coastal and roadside defences. Fears about a Nazi Fifth Column operating in Britain led to a new Treachery Act, as well as the mass internment of right-wing extremists and German and Austrian nationals. In addition, ministers introduced Emergency Powers legislation that gave the Government almost unlimited authority over citizens and their property. With Churchill absent on another of his French visits, the task of piloting this far-reaching measure through the Commons on 22 May fell to Attlee, who enthusiastically supported the Bill because it represented a move towards the kind of state influence and central planning that he had long advocated as part of his socialist vision. He later praised the egalitarian ethos of the legislation. 'It gave us complete control over persons and property; not just some persons but all persons, rich and poor alike, not just some property but all property.'[38] But, despite its incendiary nature, the Bill did not cause much of a stir in the Commons, because of the prosaic manner in which Attlee introduced it. The American journalist Vincent Sheean described his visit to Parliament that day:

> When I went into the diplomatic gallery, I found only a small attendance as word had been passed round that Mr Churchill would not speak. Instead we were offered the sight and sound of Major Attlee, the head of the Labour Party and second in command of the new Government, presenting a law which sounded like a social revolution. It was and remains the most comprehensive assumption of powers ever made by a modern

democratic Government. Mr Attlee read it out in a colourless voice.[39]

In his first radio broadcast to the nation that night, Attlee told listeners that 'our ancient liberties are placed in pawn for victory; nothing less than the destruction of Hitlerism will redeem them'.[40]

But the task of guiding the Emergency Powers Act through Parliament paled beside the enormous responsibility that was about to be placed on the collective shoulders of the War Cabinet members. Effectively, they had to decide whether Britain should continue the fight against Germany or sue for peace. It is no exaggeration to say that the fate of Europe and the entire course of the war lay on their decision. Had they followed another path during their momentous deliberations, the history of the twentieth century would have been very different. Churchill's part in determining the Government's policy was inevitably supreme but he owed a huge debt to Attlee and Greenwood, without whose support he might well have been forced to abandon the struggle. Indeed, their steadfastness was probably the greatest service they rendered the Prime Minister throughout the war. Long into his retirement, Attlee was asked in an interview, 'Was there at any time the possibility of surrender or a separate peace considered by the Government?' Attlee replied, 'never', adding that such a scenario was not even 'talked about'.[41] But his memory was at fault. The idea of a separate peace was certainly discussed in depth by the Cabinet during a tortured series of nine meetings between 26 and 28 May 1940.

The urgency of the discussions was fuelled by an increasingly desperate military position. In France and the Low Countries the German advance seemed unstoppable, while the British Expeditionary Force was now at Dunkirk with little hope of salvation. When Paul Reynaud visited London on 26 May, he warned that his country's armed forces were hopelessly demoralised and that Marshal Petain, the First World War hero who had been brought in to bolster the French Government, was now openly defeatist. On that same day, in an atmosphere of mounting alarm at the disaster unfolding on the Continent, Lord

Halifax first put to the Cabinet a proposal to consider the opening of peace negotiations. Having never completely abandoned appeasement, he had seized on a suggestion from the Italian Embassy that Mussolini's regime might be willing to act as a broker with Hitler to achieve a new peace deal. On 25 May, Halifax met the Italian Ambassador Giuseppe Bastianini and revealed his inclination towards seeking Mussolini's aid. 'Matters which caused anxiety to Italy must certainly be discussed as part of a general European settlement,' he told Bastianini.[42] Halifax seemed to be preparing the ground for another Munich, using the mechanics of diplomacy to hide behind a further capitulation to Nazi force. In a report to the Cabinet on the morning of 26 May, Halifax explained that he had told Signor Bastianini how 'peace and security in Europe' were 'our main object, and we should naturally be prepared to consider any proposals which might lead to this, provided our liberty and independence were assured'.[43] Bristling at such language, Churchill responded that 'peace and security might be achieved under a German domination of Europe' but that Britain 'could never accept' such an outcome. He was 'opposed to any negotiations which might lead to a derogation of our rights and power'.[44]

However, Churchill had to tread carefully. His own lack of popularity among many Tory MPs, combined with the fraught war situation, meant that he could not be abruptly dismissive of the Foreign Secretary. Instead of adopting a posture of open confrontation, he had to play for time, wear down Halifax and forge alliances. Despite his reputation for egocentric bombast, Churchill could be a consummate political operator, as he demonstrated in holding the Coalition together throughout the war or in building the Anglo-American alliance with Roosevelt. Here too, in the crisis of late May 1940, he played his hand with an assured touch. At the third War Cabinet meeting on 26 May, when Halifax again pushed the idea of talks hosted by Italy, Churchill expressed his fear that an approach to Mussolini implied 'we were prepared' to make concessions to Germany 'to get us out of our present difficulties' when actually 'no such option was open to us'. Herr Hitler, Churchill continued, 'thought he had the whip hand. The only thing to do was to show him that he could not conquer this country. If, on Monsieur Reynaud's showing, France could not continue, we must part company.' On a more emollient note, Churchill said that 'he did not raise an objection to some approach being made to Signor Mussolini', though he now used a crucial delaying tactic to prevent Halifax acting immediately. The plight of the BEF at Dunkirk gave him the perfect excuse for a postponement, the Cabinet having agreed to start a major evacuation of the Allied forces there codenamed Operation Dynamo. The minutes recorded: 'The Prime Minister thought it was best to decide nothing until we saw how much of the Army we could re-embark from France. The operation might be a great failure. On the other hand, our troops might well fight magnificently and we might save a considerable portion of the force.' Attlee, who had largely been quiet during the discussions about Italian diplomacy, made two points about Dynamo: first to suggest that smokescreens be used during the re-embarkation; and second to warn that 'Germany might well attempt some diversion against this country while we were engaged in re-embarking the Force'.[45]

That night Reynaud returned to Paris convinced that Churchill and most of his Cabinet were being unrealistic. 'The only one who truly understands is Halifax. He is clearly worried about the future and realises that some European solution must be reached. Churchill is always hectoring,' he recorded.[46] Back in London, Churchill revealed the strain he was under, as General Ismay recalled: 'He was unusually silent during dinner that evening, and he ate and drank with evident distaste. As he rose from the table, he said, "I feel physically sick."'[47] The pressure continued relentlessly the next day, Monday 27 May, with another three Cabinet meetings. At the first in the morning there was a report from the Chiefs of Staff on the Dunkirk evacuation, which had started well. The discussion then shifted to the question of Britain's ability to resist a German invasion in the event of France's collapse. After Churchill had argued that the Chiefs of Staff had underestimated the strength of the RAF, Attlee emphasised that prospect of a full-blooded Nazi attack was very real. 'If Germany gained complete air superiority, we could not prevent German tanks and infantry from obtaining a firm footing on our shores,' he said. But he did not believe there was any cause for despair; on the contrary, 'we should have numerous highly mobile units, ready to act quickly on their own initiative. Spain and Finland had provided examples of what could be done against tanks by brave and determined men and he saw no reason whatever for accepting it as a foregone conclusion that German tanks were invincible.'[48] Dalton, who saw Attlee at 2.30 that afternoon, was struck by his resolve, which was very similar to Churchill's. 'He says I need have no fear [...] We shall fight it out and are confident that with the resources behind us, we shall win. Attlee is in very good form.'[49]

Resistance was not on Halifax's mind when the War Cabinet met again at 4.30 that afternoon and he once more put forward his proposal for an Anglo-French approach to Italy for Mussolini to act as a potential peace mediator. He met a frosty response. His old ally Chamberlain was ambivalent, torn between his belief that the approach 'would serve no useful purpose' and his reluctance to alienate France in its darkest hour. The Air Secretary Sir Archibald Sinclair, whom Churchill had exceptionally invited to the meeting in order to bolster the anti-appeasement cause, said that 'any weakness on our part would encourage the Germans and Italians and would tend to undermine morale both in this country and in the Dominions'. Attlee was just as tough, arguing that an 'approach would be of no practical effect and would be very damaging to us'. Emboldened by his Labour and Liberal ministers, Churchill then made a formidably defiant contribution, as the Cabinet minutes recorded:

> The approach would ruin the integrity of our fighting position in the country [...] At the moment, our prestige in Europe was very low. The only way we could get it back was by showing the world that Germany had not beaten us. If, after two or three months, we could show that we were still unbeaten, our prestige would return. Even if we were beaten, we should be no worse off than we should be if we were now to abandon the struggle.

Let us therefore avoid being dragged down the slippery slope
with France. The whole of this manoeuvre was intended to get
us so deeply involved in negotiations that we should be unable
to turn back.[50]

Halifax was angry at how the Cabinet had turned against him, and
insinuated that he might now resign. The threat shook Churchill,
who could not let his Government be destabilised so soon into his
premiership. He therefore adopted a more conciliatory tone, and
allowed the Cabinet discussion to peter out before he took Halifax for
a walk in the Downing Street garden, where he repeated his assurances
of his respect for the Foreign Secretary. Halifax later left a diary note of
this fraught meeting and its aftermath:

> I thought Winston talked the most frightful rot, also
> Greenwood, and after bearing it for some time I said exactly
> what I thought of them, adding that if that really was their view
> and if it came to the point, our ways must separate. Winston,
> surprised and mellowed, and when I repeated the same thing
> in the garden, was full of apologies and affection. But it does
> drive one to despair when he works himself up into a passion of
> emotion when he ought to make his brain think and reason.[51]

News of the clash soon spread beyond the Cabinet room. Jock Colville,
increasingly drawn to Churchill, noted that 'the Cabinet are feverishly
considering our ability to carry on the war alone in such circumstances
and there are signs that Halifax is being defeatist'.[52] Alternatively Joe
Kennedy, the American Ambassador to London and an arch sceptic
about the Allied cause, sent a telegram to Washington on 27 May that
read:

> I suspect the Germans would be willing to make peace with
> both the French and the British now – of course on their own
> terms, but on terms that would be a great deal better than they

would be if the war continues. Churchill, Attlee and others will want to fight to the death but there will be other numbers who realise that the physical destruction of men and property in England will not be a proper offset to a lot of pride.[53]

For the pessimists, the sense of looming disaster was exacerbated by news that Belgium was on the verge of surrender, an eventuality that would further weaken the Allies on the Western Front and leave the British Expeditionary Force more exposed.

Halifax did not resign that night. His failure to do so greatly weakened his position, exposing his unwillingness to mount a serious challenge against Churchill. The next day, Tuesday 28 May, the Prime Minister rammed home his advantage, helped by reports that Operation Dynamo was proceeding more successfully than he had dared to hope, with a further 11,400 men evacuated overnight. After his first Cabinet meeting that day, the Prime Minister went to the Commons to give a short but typically robust statement. Whatever happened on the Continent, he told MPs, it would not 'destroy our confidence in our power to make our way, as on former occasions in our history, through disaster and through grief to the ultimate defeat of our enemies'.[54] His speech reinforced the mood of resolution at Westminster; this was the very opposite of Halifax's fatalism, which was on display when the War Cabinet reconvened at 4 p.m., this time in Churchill's room at the Commons. Halifax again tried to put the case for an Anglo-French approach to Italy, on the basis that the Government should be willing to make concessions provided 'our independence could be secured'. Galvanised by the favourable response he had received in the Chamber, Churchill now refused to concede any ground to his Foreign Secretary. If Britain ended up in talks with Herr Hitler, 'we should then find that the terms offered us touched our independence and integrity. When, at this point, we got up to leave the Conference table, we should find that all of the forces of resolution which were now at our disposal would have vanished.' In a further dismissal of any appeal for mediation, Churchill said that 'nations which went down fighting rose again, but those which surrendered tamely were finished'.[55]

Now on the defensive, Halifax protested that 'nothing in his suggestion could be described as ultimate capitulation'. But it was a measure of how the atmosphere had changed over the last two days that even Chamberlain now deserted his old ally Halifax and came in behind Churchill. 'Mediation at this stage,' he said, 'could only have the most unfortunate results.' Attlee added his voice to the chorus of condemnation, telling his colleagues that public opinion in Britain would have to be taken into account: 'There was a grave danger that, if we did what France wanted, we should find it impossible to rally the morale of the people.'[56] In the draft of his war memoirs, Churchill wrote with gratitude that 'I found Mr Chamberlain and Mr Attlee very stiff and tough.' The omission of the Foreign Secretary's name was telling; although in the final version he avoided any criticism of Halifax by changing this sentence to read, 'I found my colleagues very stiff and tough.'[57]

Churchill further undermined the Foreign Secretary with his next move. Soon after 6.15 p.m., the War Cabinet members left Churchill's room to be replaced by a much larger group of ministers outside the Cabinet. By now Churchill was exhausted after almost three days of fraught negotiations. But he knew this meeting was a unique chance to widen official support for his policy of resistance, and he brilliantly exploited it to the full. As ministers filled the room, Churchill found new reserves of energy and eloquence. One of those in attendance was Leo Amery, now Secretary for India, who wrote of the meeting: 'All of us were tremendously heartened by Winston's resolution and grip of things. He is a real war leader and one whom it is worthwhile serving under.'[58] Hugh Dalton recorded how Churchill finished with a highly personalised, dramatic passage, using lines that would reverberate throughout 1940. 'I am convinced that every man of you would rise up and tear me down from my place if I were for one moment to contemplate parley or surrender. If this long island story of ours is to end at last, let it end only when each one of us lies choking in his own blood upon the ground.'⁵⁹ At that closing remark, there was a thunderous cheer.

This meeting was the final, decisive blow against the Foreign Secretary, who had been comprehensively outmanoeuvred by Churchill. When the War Cabinet reconvened at 7 p.m., the extent of the Prime Minister's triumph became clear. He told his colleagues that the other ministers 'had expressed the greatest satisfaction when he told them that there was no chance of giving up the struggle. He did not remember having ever heard before a gathering of persons occupying high places in political life express themselves so emphatically.'⁶⁰ In an indicator of Halifax's humiliation, the only item of business was to discuss the draft of the telegram that Churchill would send that night to Reynaud, rejecting the idea of any Italian mediation. The agreed version, dispatched at 11.40 p.m., stated that this would 'not be the right moment' for an approach to Mussolini, partly because, echoing Attlee's earlier point, 'the effect on the morale of our people, which is now firm and resolute, would be extremely dangerous'. Churchill's telegram concluded, 'our success must depend first on unity, then on our courage and endurance'.⁶¹

Halifax's rout was complete. He was forced to abandon his Italian scheme. Although in later months he still hankered after peace feelers, he never dared again to bring any such proposal to the Cabinet. Just as importantly, Attlee had shown Churchill that he would be a far stauncher ally and prosecutor of the war than the vacillating Foreign Secretary. Churchill's growing respect for the Labour Leader was revealed when he asked Attlee to accompany him on his next visit to France on 31 May for another meeting of the Allied Supreme War Council, the body that was now staring at defeat. The only good news, from Britain's point of view, was the continuing success of Operation Dynamo at Dunkirk. By the time Churchill and Attlee flew to Paris, no fewer than 146,000 troops had been rescued from the beaches and the harbour. Reports of this achievement seemed to buoy Churchill's spirits, as his military envoy General Spears recalled of the two politicians' arrival at Villacoublay Air Base: 'Churchill was as fresh as a daisy, obviously in grand form. He might not have had a care in the world. This was perhaps due to the fact that he had had a rest in the plane but was more likely generated by the sense of danger inherent in such a journey. Danger, the evocation of battle, invariably acted as a tonic and a stimulant to Winston Churchill.' In contrast to Churchill, wrote Spears, Attlee was an 'unexuberant figure' on whose head 'was the black homburg, impervious as always to the personality of its owner'.[62]

At the meeting of the Council that afternoon, Churchill made a highly charged appeal for unity after the French military had complained about being 'left behind' in the exodus from Dunkirk. With tears in his eyes, he said, 'We are all companions in misfortune. There is nothing to be gained from recriminations over our common miseries.' At this, wrote Spears, 'a stillness fell over the room, something different from silence. It was like the hush that falls on men at the opening of a great national pageant.' Then, after a further discussion about evacuation and the German advance, Churchill urged that 'even if one of us is struck down, the other must not abandon the struggle'. Attlee followed and 'completely endorsed every word the Prime Minister said. He emphasised that he was speaking as a member of the Government and as a Leader of the Labour Party. "Every Englishman knows that the very basis of the civilisation common to France and England is at stake. The Germans kill not only men but ideas."' That night Spears dined at the British Embassy with Churchill, Attlee and a few others. 'The talk was desultory; it was an anti-climax to the afternoon's meeting.' Churchill's early optimism had also evaporated. 'He realised in his heart that the French were beaten, that they knew it and were resigned to defeat.'[63] Attlee, too, felt that the atmosphere in France had been one of 'utter hopelessness'. He later said that, at the Supreme War Council, 'Winston had put bit of heart' into the French politicians but 'then it wore off'.[64] But Attlee's performance in Paris made a deep impression on Pug Ismay, who had also been present. 'He was brave, wise, decisive, and completely loyal to Winston. His integrity was absolute and no thought of personal ambition seemed to enter his mind.'[65] Oliver Harvey's view after the visit was more mixed: 'Attlee strikes me as very determined but he is a man on a small scale. He has a good military mind, I should say.'[66]

During Churchill and Attlee's visit to France, Operation Dynamo had continued with remarkable effectiveness against the odds. Altogether, by the end of 1 June, 260,000 men had been evacuated. But the Battle of France was now drawing to its bloody close. At further meetings on 2 and 3 June, the War Cabinet discussed last desperate pleas from the French Government for more RAF fighter support; but these were rejected, with Attlee arguing strongly for refusal. 'We must not impair the essential fighter defences of this country,' he told colleagues.[67] Churchill still ached to do something for France, but the case for sending more planes was finally demolished at the Cabinet on 3 June by Sir Hugh Dowding, the head of Fighter Command, who warned that the Home Defence squadrons could not cope with 'the tremendous drain which would be involved in the dispatch of any large numbers of fighters to France'. Churchill finally accepted this argument. But he and Attlee agreed that long-range bombers should be used 'to exert pressure' on Germany.[68]

Sporadic bombing raids were futile. The German conquest of northern France continued through the first week of June, though the Reich's war machine failed to prevent the successful completion of Operation Dynamo. By 4 June, 338,000 Allied troops had been taken to England by the armada of vessels. That day, in one of his most celebrated wartime speeches, Churchill told the House of Commons that Dunkirk had been 'a miracle of deliverance'. But wars 'are not won by evacuations', he warned, and the nation now had to be prepared for an epic struggle in its defence. In a majestic closing passage that encapsulated his valiant spirit, he promised that Britain would fight in the streets, the hills, the beaches and the landing grounds. To cheers, he boldly declared that 'we will never surrender'.[69] Less than a month earlier, when he first became Prime Minister, Churchill had been given a cool reception by his own Conservative MPs. Now his growling courage had transformed attitudes towards him. Sir Alan Herbert, the independent MP for Oxford University, felt that Churchill's bravery was infectious: 'The greatness of that speech was that it filled in, with simple, vivid strokes, a picture of the impossible made possible. Every man saw himself in that picture somewhere, fighting "on the beaches, in the streets, in the hills"; and we all went out refreshed and resolute to do our best.'[70] The Prime Minister's fortitude was also conveyed to radio listeners. Although he did not broadcast the speech in full on the BBC that evening, as he did with many later addresses, extracts were read out in news bulletins. 'Even repeated by the announcer, it sent shivers (not of fear) down my spine. I think one of the reasons one is stirred by his Elizabethan phrases is that one feels the whole massive backing of power and resolve behind them, like a great fortress,' wrote the novelist Vita Sackville-West to her husband Harold Nicolson.[71] Nor was Churchill's rhetoric just bravado. Despite the disaster in France, he genuinely believed that Britain could ride out the storm, as he told Victor Cazalet over lunch on his return from Paris: 'He is very full of confidence. The period has now come when we can hit back. Invasion will fail. Our Air Force is growing every day. We shall soon have air superiority.'[72]

—◊—

FIFTEEN

EMPIRE AND COMMONWEALTH

HALIFAX MAY HAVE been vanquished by Churchill and Attlee at the end of May. But as the plight of France worsened and the threat of a German invasion grew, the British press became increasingly agitated about the continuing presence of the pre-war appeasers in the Government. Disparagingly known as the 'Men of Munich' or the 'Old Gang', Chamberlain and his allies were blamed both for the descent into war and for Britain's military weakness in the face of the Reich. So strident were the attacks that in early June Chamberlain offered his resignation to Churchill if it would help him 'out of certain difficulties'. But Churchill categorically refused to accept this, as Chamberlain told his sister Ida. 'Winston declared that he certainly wanted me to stop. I was giving him splendid help and he wasn't going to have the Government which had only just formed knocked about.'[1] Instead, Churchill promised that he would ask Attlee and Greenwood to persuade the Labour-supporting *Daily Herald* to ease up on its denigration of Chamberlain – which, following a brief discussion after Cabinet on 6 June, they agreed to do – while he himself would talk to the *Mirror*'s senior director Cecil King. On 7 June, Churchill gave an interview with King in which he warned that his Government might collapse if the paper kept up its anti-Chamberlain campaign. Showing his continued political vulnerability within the Conservative

Party, Churchill reminded King that only a year ago there had been a concerted attempt to 'hound him out of his constituency' in Epping. If he now 'trampled' on Chamberlain's supporters, they 'would set themselves against him and in such internecine strife lay the Germans' best hope of victory.'[2]

These pleas had an immediate effect, though the press vituperation was renewed again the following month on the publication of the bestselling book *The Guilty Men*. But any personal gratitude from Halifax at the temporary end of the heresy hunt in June was balanced by his anger at Labour's hypocrisy in their attacks on the appeasers: 'The truth is that Winston is about the only person who has an absolutely clean sheet. Both Labour and Liberals have to share with the Conservatives the responsibility of being late with rearmament.'[3] Attlee came in for criticism on other grounds at this moment, with his detractors unaware of his important role in the War Cabinet's rejection of peace talks. Reflecting on the Labour personalities in the Government, Beatrice Webb wrote in her diary on 9 June that Morrison and Bevin were 'admirable and impressive' whereas 'Attlee is neither gifted nor competent, simply a yes man to Churchill as he was to the Labour movement'.[4] Attlee's own Labour colleague Harold Laski was just as scathing. 'Nature meant him to be a second lieutenant,' wrote Laski, claiming that Attlee 'hasn't an ounce of leadership in him'.[5] From the opposite side of the political divide, Tory backbencher Cuthbert Headlam described Attlee's performances in the House as 'poor stuff – feeble, inaudible and ineffective'.[6] On the other hand, Churchill was beginning to emerge as the unrivalled national hero in the approaching hour of crisis. Having been so dismissive of Attlee, Headlam wrote in the same diary entry about his admiration for the Prime Minister's 'courage, his abilities, his quickness of uptake and his fervid patriotism. In many ways he is the right man for the present situation.'[7]

Churchill's immediate aim after Dunkirk was to keep France in the fight against Germany, but this was a doomed cause. Britain could offer little beyond supportive words, being unable to do much militarily to help after suffering her own disastrous setbacks and seeing her fighter force badly overstretched. It was a predicament made all the worse by Italy's entry into the war on 10 June, a move that required a sizeable portion of the Royal Navy to be tied up in the protection of the Mediterranean. That same day the Germans occupied Paris, forcing the French Government to flee westwards to the coast. Churchill again turned to diplomacy, making two more visits across the Channel to bolster morale, accompanied on the first by Eden and on the second by Halifax. There briefly seemed a glimmer of hope when, on 13 June, President Roosevelt sent Reynaud a message that his administration was doing 'everything in its power to make available to Allied Governments the material they so urgently require and our efforts to do more are still being doubled'.[8] With a note of wishful thinking, Churchill told the Cabinet that the President's words 'could only mean that the United States intended to enter the war on our side'. In the new mood sparked by the optimistic interpretation of Roosevelt's message, Attlee dropped his habitual restraint and 'urged that a statement in dramatic terms should be issued to hearten the people of France'.[9] Attlee's suggestion was taken up enthusiastically by the Cabinet. 'There was general agreement that an announcement in dramatic terms of solidarity of Britain and France should be issued.'[10] Late that night Churchill put the spirit of Attlee's proposal into a formal declaration to be sent to Reynaud: 'Great Britain will continue to give the utmost aid in her power. We take this opportunity of proclaiming the indissoluble union of our two peoples and of our two Empires [...] We are sure that the ordeal by fire will only fuse them together into one unconquerable whole.'[11]

A group of officials, including Desmond Morton, Sir Robert Vansittart and the Frenchman Jean Monnet,* put more practical flesh on the Declaration of Union between the two countries. But the hopes invested in this lofty initiative soon came crashing down to earth. Roosevelt made clear to the British Government that he had no intention of breaching the USA's neutrality laws by entering into

---

* The future architect of the European Economic Community.

the war; in addition he refused to allow publication of his message to Reynaud, even though Churchill felt that such a move might act as a deterrent to the Germans. Even worse, in the face of defeat, the French Government was plunged into crisis, with its Cabinet unable to give a unified response to the Declaration. In fact Petain, when its words were repeated to him by Reynaud, showed his disdain for Britain's war prospects by saying that it was 'like an invitation to marry a corpse'.[12] The hopelessness of the cause was physically brought home to the British Government in the evening of Sunday 16 June, when Churchill and Attlee, along with Sinclair and the Chiefs of Staff, were preparing to travel to Bordeaux for an emergency meeting with the French leaders to discuss the Declaration and the possibility of continued resistance. A special train was due to leave London at 9.30 p.m., taking the passengers to Southampton, from where a cruiser would depart for France. As Churchill recalled in his war memoirs, 'There was an odd delay in it starting. Evidently some hitch had occurred.'[13] The hitch, as the British Ambassador Sir Ronald Campbell urgently telegraphed to London, was that Reynaud had resigned and been succeeded by Petain, who now wanted an armistice with Germany. There would be no journey to Bordeaux. The Declaration was an irrelevance.

With France on the verge of surrender, Britain was now effectively alone in the fight against the Axis powers in Europe. Yet Churchill, far from being daunted, was invigorated by the struggle, as Edmund Ironside noted in his diary for 17 June: 'There is no doubt that Winston has any amount of courage and experience. Thrown with his back to the wall, he may lose some of his lack of balance. But he is quite undismayed by the state of affairs.'[14] Churchill gave a powerful illustration of his outlook the next day, when he reported to MPs on Britain's chances of survival following France's collapse. Attlee once wrote that 'if somebody asked me what exactly Winston did to win the war, I would say, "Talk about it."'[15] Churchill never spoke in more noble style than in the famous peroration to his speech that afternoon, in which he predicted that the forthcoming Battle of Britain would ultimately decide the fate of Europe and the world. 'Let us therefore brace ourselves to our duty and so conduct ourselves that if the British Empire and its Commonwealth should last for a thousand years, men will still say, "This was their finest hour."'[16] Yet, despite the power of his address, Churchill did not seem to come across so well when he used the same words in a radio broadcast to the nation. This was much to the dismay of Harold Nicolson: 'As delivered in the House of Commons, that speech was magnificent, especially the concluding sentences. But it sounded ghastly on the wireless. All the great vigour he put into it seemed to evaporate.'[17] Part of the problem was that Churchill, while schooled in the habits of Victorian and Edwardian oratory, never mastered the intimacy of the radio, something that was to cost him dearly in the 1945 General Election. The renowned BBC broadcaster Richard Dimbleby said of Churchill, 'He breaks every accepted rule of broadcasting. He drops his voice where he should raise it. He alters the recognisable system of pronunciation to suit himself (some of his scripts were virtually unintelligible to anyone else), he speaks much of the time with anything but clarity.'[18]

Within the political arena, even as Britain's independence hung in the balance, there were still pockets of antagonism towards Churchill, particularly in the Tory Party, which meant he could not feel entirely secure in his leadership. Hugh Dalton noted that Churchill's Finest Hour speech was cheered more loudly by Labour than the Conservatives and later commented on this to John Wilmot, the reliable Labour MP for Kennington. 'He said that many Tories now feel quite out of it. They think the Labour Party has much too large a share, both in offices and in the determination of Government policy.'[19] The fiercely anti-appeasement Liberal MP for North Cornwall Tom Harobin spoke to Cecil King about his own dissatisfaction with Churchill: 'He is all right as a speaker and a figurehead; but so many of our problems are administrative and Churchill is not a good administrator and is not interested in the subject. In any case he is now so much in the grip of the old bunch that people are calling him Neville Churchill.'[20] The discontent was more than just talk. In mid-June a group of Under-Secretaries, sympathetic to Churchill but frustrated with the running of the war, came together under Amery and Boothby to push for a radical restructuring of the Government. Their bold plan was that Parliament should be sidelined, the War Cabinet replaced with a Committee of Public Safety and ministers handed 'dictatorial powers'. Amery put their case to Churchill, who was infuriated by this meddling. He angrily told Amery that 'he was going to make no changes of any kind and would sooner resign than be forced to do so'.[21] The so-called 'Under-Secretaries Plot' had been crushed.

Yet Churchill was contemplating one important change to his Government. Ever since he had become Prime Minister in early May, he had hankered to bring his old Liberal ally Lloyd George, now aged seventy-seven, back into office. Adding the First World War victor to his administration would, he believed, broaden its appeal and provide some political protection. Lloyd George rejected all the overtures from his former Cabinet colleague. He made the presence of Chamberlain and Halifax, 'the architects of this catastrophe', the initial pretext for his refusal. But there were several other reasons, including his loss of faith in Britain's cause and his disdain for Attlee and Greenwood. He privately set out his objections over a lunch with the Whitehall grandee Tom Jones, who recorded in his diary:

> I found him adamant against going in. It was like calling in a specialist when the patient's case was nigh hopeless. Winston was at the political mercy of Neville with his party majority. 'If I went in what would I achieve with Attlee and Greenwood. Whatever I put up would be suspect and would be opposed. I should waste my time in endless meetings and agendas and secondary points,' he said.[22]

Lloyd George may have been overly influenced by the stream of anti-Churchill commentary from his aide Albert Sylvester. At the end of June, one of Sylvester's contacts described Churchill as 'the biggest washout he had ever seen', while little more than a week later Sylvester told his chief, 'There are those who feel that at this rate Winston cannot last. They point out that he was brilliant in opposition. Where is the brilliance now?'[23] Lloyd George never returned to Government in any capacity and indeed hardly spoke in Parliament again.

He and other critics were wrong about Churchill. The summer of 1940 was the moment when his unique political qualities gave Britain the leadership it so urgently needed. His rhetorical exhortations, which had sometimes in the past been overblown, now fitted exactly the national emergency and were combined with his military insight, his volcanic energy, his ruthless streak and his sense of historic destiny. 'Winston was the driving force, a great War Minister. No one could have done the job he did,' said Attlee.[24] In another tribute, Attlee described Churchill as 'brave, gifted, inexhaustible, and indomitable', adding that 'he was so suited to fill a particular need. The absence of anybody of his quality was so blatant that one cannot imagine what would have happened if he had not been there.'[25] Throughout his career, Churchill had the habit of concentrating on a single or couple of dominant objectives rather than spreading his attention across a range of subjects. 'When he had some major problem to resolve, he turned the searchlight of his mind on it, neglecting all else in favour of his concentration,' said his long-serving aide Jock Colville.[26] Sometimes this was a defect, as became apparent later in the war when, despite Attlee's promptings, he tended to ignore domestic politics and social reform. But, after the fall of France, simplicity of purpose was a virtue. The only question that mattered was the survival of Britain. Everything, from diplomacy with Roosevelt to the disposition of the Royal Navy, had to be geared towards that goal.

Following the Armistice on the Continent, which was formally concluded on 22 June, the most urgent issue was the future of the French sea power. Churchill was rightly worried that if a significant part of France's navy, the fourth-largest in world, fell into German hands, Britain's maritime supremacy would be instantly eroded. Drastic action was therefore needed. In Churchill's view, the most important part of the Gallic fleet, based at Oran in North Africa, had to surrender to the Royal Navy or retire to distant waters on the other side of the

Atlantic. His opinion was shared by most of his ministers. At Cabinet on 24 June, Attlee dismissed the Germans' pledge that 'they had no intention of using units of the French Fleet for their own purposes' as 'illusory' because 'the Armistice could be denounced at any time by the German Government'.²⁷ Churchill agreed, and further argued that little credence could be attached to private French promises that they would scuttle their ships in the event of an attempted German takeover.

The refusal to compromise was about to culminate in one of the most bloody episodes of the early war. At 5.30 p.m. on 3 July, the French Admiral Marcel-Bruno Gensoul confirmed his final rejection of the British ultimatum to either surrender or take his fleet to the West Indies. Less than half an hour later, the Royal Navy task force opened up with one of the most devastating broadsides in British maritime history. Amid the carnage, 1,297 French sailors were killed, one battleship was sunk and five other vessels were severely damaged. But the political impact was even greater. The British Government had given a practical demonstration of its determination to continue the war. Public morale at home was lifted, while in America there was widespread praise for Britain's belligerent spirit, a crucial factor given Britain's need for aid. Typical was the comment of Roger Ingersoll, editor of *PM* magazine, who wrote, 'I'm all for sending supplies to England as long as it's governed by a Churchill who will fight.'²⁸ This was not just empty talk. Over the coming months, as Roosevelt responded to Churchill's requests for military, the USA delivered vast amounts of materiel to Britain, including 615,000 M1917 Enfield rifles and 50 destroyers, the latter sent in return for the British military bases in North America. But it was Churchill's own position that was most radically affected by Oran. His unflinching decisiveness finally swept away the lingering doubts about him within parts of the Tory Party, bringing a new spirit of new unity to Westminster. As he addressed the Commons about Oran, Churchill was aware of the tangible change in atmosphere. He later described the scene at the conclusion of his speech: 'Everybody seemed to stand up all around, cheering, for what seemed a long time. Up till this moment the Conservative Party had treated me with some reserve, and it was from the Labour benches that I received the warmest welcome when I entered or rose on serious occasions. But now all joined in solemn stentorian accord.'[29]

One man less favourably moved by Oran was Adolf Hitler, who, after Dunkirk and the fall of France, had convinced himself that Britain would be ready to sue for peace. The destruction of the French fleet shattered his delusion, sinking his headquarters into 'general consternation and succeeding gloom', according to the Führer's naval adjutant.[30] In his rage, Hitler now began to contemplate a full-scale military invasion of England as he ordered his military staff to work up plans for a seaborne assault across the Channel. The full directive for the invasion, known as Unternehmen Seelöwe or Operation Sea Lion, was issued on 16 July, less than a fortnight after Oran. Three days later, in a much-hyped speech at the Reichstag that he described as his 'last appeal to reason', he adopted a pose of magnanimity and called on Britain to accept peace terms. The oration took over two hours but contained no concrete proposal. To his exasperation, the speech was treated with contempt by both the British Government and the British public. That night, Churchill told Jock Colville that he did not plan to make any personal reply 'to Herr Hitler, not being on speaking terms with him'.[31] When the War Cabinet discussed it the next morning, Churchill suggested that a motion of rejection be passed by both Houses of Parliament, but Attlee countered that such an approach would invest Hitler's Reichstag address with too much importance. It was agreed that Halifax, who was due to make a radio broadcast on the evening of 22 July, should announce the Government's dismissal of Hitler's overture.

As German planning for Operation Sea Lion proceeded, so the preparations of the British Government against an invasion intensified. Inevitably Churchill was at the centre of the defence planning. He pushed for the deployment of stronger naval forces around the southern and eastern coasts. He delighted in the development of improvised weaponry, from Molotov cocktails to roadside flame traps. He urged the creation of elite combat units by the army and a secret auxiliary force in the Home Guard. He kept up his barrage of requests to the White House for more aid. He made regular tours of inspection of the army front lines and gun emplacements. It was on one visit to Brighton in early July that he first met Bernard Montgomery, then commander of the 3rd Division in Sussex, who emphasised the need for greater mobility in the army's anti-invasion forces on the south coast, as opposed to reliance on Ironside's static defences. On 17 July, Churchill made another tour of the south, this time in the company of the stern Ulsterman Alan Brooke, the British Army's Southern Commander who shared Montgomery's preference for mobility over Ironside's rigidity. Soon afterwards, on 19 July, the War Cabinet's Defence Committee, on which Attlee sat alongside Churchill, decided that Brooke should replaced Ironside as Home Forces Commander. 'He is full of the most marvellous courage, considering the burden he is bearing,' wrote Brooke about the Prime Minister soon after his appointment.[32]

But even more important than the army's defences was the strength of RAF Fighter Command, for any German invasion would be dependent on the establishment of air superiority over the Channel. The Spitfire and Hurricane had already proved themselves a match for the Luftwaffe in combat, but losses had been heavy in the Battle of France and over Dunkirk. Fortunately, Beaverbrook had been in charge of aircraft production since mid-May, using all his creativity, bullying and manipulation to drive up fighter output. In the short-term, he achieved a phenomenal increase in production to almost 500 planes a month, though his mercurial style left a trail of fractured relation-ships in his wake. Churchill, focused on the war, cared only about results and described his minister as 'a genius'.[33] Beaverbrook's reward was elevation to the full War Cabinet on 2 August, while remaining in charge of aircraft production. By then the Luftwaffe had already spent several weeks making raids against coastal airfields, ports and Channel shipping. These attacks were the precursor to the main aerial assault that began on 13 August, known to the Germans as Adlertag or Eagle Day. The aim was to use massed waves of bombers, protected by fighters, to wipe out Fighter Command on the ground. But from the start, the Luftwaffe's strategy faltered badly as the RAF provided far stiffer resistance than German intelligence had estimated. The vulnerability of the Luftwaffe was illustrated on 15 August, just two days after Adlertag, when the RAF shot down seventy-six German planes in return for the loss of thirty-four aircraft. Inevitably the heroism of Fighter Command's pilots appealed to Churchill's sense of chivalry and that day he visited Bentley Priory, Dowding's headquarters at Stanmore, to see the action himself. He returned to Downing Street in an ecstatic mood, telling Colville that this was 'one of the greatest days in history'.[34] He was even more impressed the following day when he called on the Uxbridge Operations Room of No. 11 Group, which covered the southeast of England, the arena of the fiercest aerial combat. Having intently followed the action on the map table, Churchill then returned to his car with Ismay for the journey to Chequers. According to Ismay's account, 'Churchill's first words were, "Don't speak to me; I have never been so moved." After about five minutes, he leaned forward and said, "Never in the field of human conflict has so much been owed by so many to so few."'[35] The phrase became part of the lexicon of the British defiance in the summer of 1940, once Churchill had used it in his tribute to the RAF during a speech to the Commons on 20 August.

Throughout the summer months, Attlee was generally supportive of Churchill, bowing to his judgement on military strategy. He made some important interventions, such as his settlement of a dispute between Bevin and Lindemann, Churchill's scientific adviser, over the performance of the Ministry of Labour. He was on occasion willing to challenge Churchill, most notably when the Special Operations Executive (SOE) was established in July 1940 to co-ordinate espionage, covert campaigns and resistance movements in occupied Europe. Churchill wanted to place the SOE under the control of Earl Swinton, the dynamic head of the Security Executive, which handled internal state protection and clandestine counter-invasion preparations. But Attlee felt that the post should go to Dalton, already the Minister for Economic Warfare, partly because Dalton had a subtle grasp of European politics and partly because Swinton was already over-burdened, often working sixteen hours a day on national security. Churchill not only had his doubts about Dalton's capabilities, but also personally disliked him. 'Keep that man away from me. I can't stand his booming voice and shifty eyes,' he once said.[36] But Attlee refused to budge. 'If Attlee digs his feet in, he will win,' Desmond Morton told Dalton.[37] He was proved right. During the meeting to decide the SOE leadership, Churchill again expressed his preference for Swinton; but Attlee, with the rest of the Cabinet behind him, prevailed.

The SOE appointment was an unusual moment of dispute. As Morrison later wrote, 'I imagine Attlee had decided that Churchill should have his head and so rarely disagreed with him. His custom was to nod in approval while Churchill was still making his proposal, or to say, "Yes, yes!"'[38] Indeed, after playing his instrumental part in Churchill's rise to power and in the rejection of Halifax's peace manoeuvres, Attlee once more retreated into his habitual diffidence. At Cabinet and committee meetings, his voice was heard infrequently. His standing within Government was eclipsed by bigger Labour figures such as Bevin and Alexander. Beaverbrook, always erratically drawn to powerful men like Churchill and Lloyd George, was not taken with Attlee, claiming that at meetings of the Cabinet's Defence Committee 'he never made any contribution to the discussion'.[39] Almost from the first moment of his entry into the Cabinet, Beaverbrook was manoeuvring against Attlee, as Dalton noted in his diary for 29 August: 'The Beaver is constantly engaged in intrigue against all his colleagues in turn [...] His immediate object of intrigue is Greenwood, but he is reported to have said that he would soon get both Attlee and Greenwood out of the Cabinet.'[40] During a lunch with Attlee and Frederick Pile, the head of Anti-Aircraft Command, Beaverbrook gave a clear show of his disrespect for the Labour Leader. 'I was much impressed by Beaverbrook's forcefulness,' wrote Pile later; but Attlee, 'with his less flamboyant qualities, did not shine by comparison. Halfway through lunch he was taken badly to task by Beaverbrook because he had not taken a firm line in some matter which he (Attlee) knew was right. Beaverbrook kept saying, "Well, why did you not put it right? Why did you not do something?" To which bullying Attlee had nothing to reply.'[41]

Although never approaching anything like such hostility, Churchill at times gave glimpses of disappointment in Attlee's contribution. In late June, Chips Channon dined with Brendan Bracken and learned that 'all is far from well in Churchill's paradise and there are endless squabbles among the new ministers. Brendan attacked Attlee and Greenwood, thus reflecting Winston's mind.'[42] On 19 July Churchill said that only three men – himself, Eden and Beaverbrook – 'carried the Government'.[43] Despite such grumbles, the personal relationship between the two men was perfectly civil, if not warm. Attlee, who lived during the week at 11 Downing Street while his family remained at Stanmore, was a neighbour of Churchill's once the Prime Minister moved from the Admiralty to Number 10. One of Churchill's aides, John Martin, recalled Attlee attending a lunch in 10 Downing Street on 15 July, when Churchill was on 'very good form', attacking food rationing, joking with his family and 'playing with a little dog and making absurd remarks to it'.[44] Churchill also invited Attlee and his wife to stay at Chequers in early October, a visit that thrilled them. 'It is a wonderful place and I was very glad to see it. I slept in a magnificent Elizabethan four-poster,' Attlee wrote to his brother Tom.[45] Jock Colville in his diary recorded how the conversation between the two men had been lively, focusing on the creation of the National Government in 1931 and past election campaigns. 'The Prime Minister said that had learned one great lesson from his father: never to be afraid of British democracy.'[46] There was one unfortunate but comic consequence of the visit. Soon afterwards, Attlee's secretary A. M. R. Topham had to contact Colville to ask whether he knew 'who has got Mr Attlee's tin hat? Mr Attlee took his to Chequers last week and the one he brought back is several sizes too big.'[47] Colville replied: 'As far as I can discover Mr Attlee took Randolph Churchill's tin hat and Randolph, faute de mieux, went off with Mr Attlee's.'[48]

There were other moments of humour, such as one that occurred when Churchill and Attlee had an interview in August with Frank

Pick, the former head of London Transport, now the new director-general of the Ministry of Information. Pick had a strong character but also a streak of self-righteousness, a trait that Churchill loathed. As the Director-General proceeded to give the two men a priggish lecture on the importance of sticking to the truth in propaganda, Churchill grew exasperated, while Attlee became so bored that, beginning to descend into sleep, he slipped off the settee on which he was sitting. In response, Churchill barked, 'Rise up, Major Attlee. It is not every day you have an opportunity of shaking hands with a man who has never sinned.'[49] Churchill's link with Attlee also led to an instance of drollery down the telephone wires. The Prime Minister was in the habit of phoning the War Office late at night to find out if there was any news about operations. One evening a captain in the Dorset Regiment was on duty and, believing that all was quiet, nipped out for a breath of fresh air. Unfortunately, the very moment he left his post Churchill rang, so the telephone had to be answered by a lowly warrant officer. The next morning, one of Churchill's private secretaries rang the War Office to complain. 'The Prime Minister considered it unforgivable that no commissioned officer had been on duty,' he said. But the Gunner Major who took this call disagreed. 'After all, when the Prime Minister goes away, he leaves Mr Attlee in charge.' Unable to think of a reply, the Downing Street secretary rang off.[50]

By early September, Churchill's demands for information had a new urgency, for British intelligence and RAF reconnaissance showed that the German preparations for invasion were well advanced, with ever larger numbers of troop-carrying barges now moored in the occupied French and Belgian Channel ports. Furthermore, Fighter Command had started to show the strain of the repeated pounding it had taken over the previous weeks, especially in the loss of trained pilots. The politicians felt the pressure of the Battle of Britain as well. When Anthony Eden confessed at the end of 1940 that there had been times earlier in the year in which he experienced despair, Churchill replied. 'Yes normally I wake up buoyant to face the new day. Then I woke with dread in my heart.'[51] According to Eden's second wife Clarissa, who was Churchill's niece, both Anthony and Winston each kept a cyanide pill to be taken in the event of a German conquest. After the war, Attlee admitted that the country's lowest ebb was during 'the Battle of Britain. If we hadn't pulled that off we might not have made it.'[52] But the tide turned dramatically after that first week in September, when the Luftwaffe suspended their assault on the facilities of Fighter Command and instead embarked on the night-time Blitz against Britain's industrial centres, beginning with east London. The decision was in part driven by German's mistaken belief that British morale, already badly weakened, would crack completely under the bombs. The lull in daylight attacks gave Fighter Command the chance to regroup. By the time the Germans renewed their offensive on 15 September, Dowding's force was stronger than at any time since July and was able to inflict the heaviest losses on the Luftwaffe since the opening week of the Battle. The German attempt to gain the mastery of the skies over southern England had ended in failure. Two days later, on 17 September, Hitler ordered the indefinite postponement of Operation Sea Lion.

But the British Government was not aware of this decision. On the very day that Hitler postponed Sea Lion, Churchill told a secret session of the House of Commons that the Führer's 'assembly of his ships and barges is steadily proceeding and a major assault may be launched upon this island'.[53] Concern about an imminent invasion was compounded by the continuation of the Blitz, which in its first month left 5730 Londoners dead and over 9000 injured, yet resolve only appeared to be strengthened. With his instinctive empathy, Churchill made regular visits to the East End and found himself profoundly moved by the stoicism of the residents, as Ismay recalled of one trip to the badly damaged London docks were a crowd gathered to cheer him. '"Good old Winnie," they cried. "We thought you'd come down and see us. We can take it. Give it 'em back."'[54] Ismay also remembered one elderly woman showing her phlegmatic outlook in a more unusual fashion, as she came up to Churchill and told him, 'There's one thing about these 'ere air raids: they do take your mind off the bloody war.'[55] Attlee had an even deeper emotional connection to the ordeal of the

Blitz, for the borough of Stepney was repeatedly hit by the Luftwaffe. It was estimated that no fewer than 40,000 German bombs fell on the district. On the morning of 8 September, after the first night of the Blitz, he went to his Limehouse constituency, 'watching while the digging went on among the rubble and talking to a pathetic queue of people waiting for the news of their next of kin'.[56] Like Churchill, he was struck by the fortitude of the public under fire. During another visit after a heavy German raid, a man came up to him and said, 'Hullo, Major, old Hitler's bombed me out of Eastfield Street and has bombed me out of Maroon Street, but he's bloody well not going to bomb me out of old Stepney.'[57]

The Blitz went on until May 1941, causing the deaths of around 43,000 civilians. But from the end of September, evidence gathered that the threat of invasion had lifted as the Germans began to disperse their barges and loading facilities. Clear confirmation of Sea Lion's postponement came in the form of an intercepted Luftwaffe message, which was deciphered by the code-breakers at Bletchley Park. The decrypt was then presented to a joint meeting of the Cabinet and the Chiefs of Staff on the evening of 27 October in the reinforced underground War Rooms below Downing Street – just as yet another German bombing raid was under way. According to the recollection of Group Captain Frederick Winterbotham, the RAF intelligence offer, he told Churchill that the new information showed that 'Hitler had in fact given up on the idea of invasion'. Winterbotham's account continued:

> Everyone sat back in their seats. Churchill also sat back, pulled out a big cigar, lit it and said, 'Well, gentlemen, let's see what is happening upstairs.' There was a terrific blitz going on [...] Everyone tried to prevent him going up because there was so much metal flying about. Not a bit of it. I can see him today, with his hands on his stick, smoking his cigar, with the Chiefs of Staff and Ismay behind. And he said, 'My God, we'll get the buggers for this.'[58]

The British repulsion of the Reich's invasion dream, achieved against overwhelming odds, was the first real German setback of the war. Churchill himself put the triumph in context when he told MPs on 5 November of Sea Lion's abandonment.

> The plain fact that an invasion, planned on so vast a scale, has not been attempted in spite of the very great need of the enemy to destroy us in our citadel and that all these anxious months, when we stood alone and the whole world wondered, have passed safely away – that fact constitutes in itself one of the historic victories of the British Isles and is a monumental milestone in our onward march.[59]

It was also Churchill's greatest achievement, the one that left his country forever in his debt. 'He revived people's confidence, hope and optimism when everything seemed absolutely hopeless and the whole world thought we were defeated,' said the maverick Tory Bob Boothby.[60] A poll in September 1940 gave him an approval rating of 88 per cent. 'His popularity is astounding. Everywhere crowds rush up and cheer him wildly, encouraging him with shouts of "Stick it"', recorded Brooke about a visit to Kent.[61] When Churchill dined with J. M. Keynes, the great economist was amazed by the Prime Minister's calmness and lack of bombast. 'I found him in absolutely perfect condition, extremely well, serene, full of normal human feelings and completely uninflated. Perhaps this moment is the height of his power and glory, but I have never seen anyone less infected with dictatorial airs and hubris,' Keynes wrote to his mother.[62]

But the successful defence of Britain also worsened a domestic political problem for Churchill. When the air battle was at its peak, all that mattered was national survival. Yet the passing of the invasion threat heightened the pressure, particularly from the left, for a clear statement of war aims and promises of social reconstruction. Churchill had little time for such agitation. In his single-mindedness, he believed that victory over the Nazi regime was a sufficient goal in itself. Besides, he argued, a list of pledges would only store up trouble. 'Precise aims would be compromising, whereas vague principles would disappoint,' he declared.[63] Furthermore, he feared that continual debate on future progress could be a distraction from the hard job of actually fighting Germany: 'Too much concentration on post-war problems affords an opportunity for those who will not face up to war to salve their consciences by planning a new world.'[64] Attlee, however, took a very different line. Ever since the outbreak of war, he and his party had pushed for greater emphasis on the objectives behind the war beyond just victory. His conviction was that such an approach would promote national unity and raise morale, by giving all members of the public, especially the working class, a stake in the outcome. In addition, he was haunted by the legacy of MacDonald's 1931 Coalition, when National Labour was quickly subsumed by the Conservatives. He therefore wanted to show that his Labour Party could act as a force for social progress even under Churchill's leadership. His continuing attachment to socialism shone through his declaration in June 1940 that 'We are fighting a conservative war and our objects are purely negative. We must therefore put forward a positive and revolutionary aim admitting that the old order has collapsed and asking people to fight for the new order.'[65] He won the occasional concession for his cause, like the decision by the War Cabinet to approve a scheme to provide free subsidised milk to mothers and their children under the age of five. It was also on his initiative that Cripps was appointed as Britain's Ambassador to the Soviet Union, Attlee arguing that the political sensitivity of the role required 'an important figure in public life'.[66] Even after the Battle of Britain began, Attlee kept his demands for an official clarification of Britain's war aims. Finally, on 23 August, Churchill relented and agreed to establish a formal 'War Aims Committee' of the Cabinet, under the chairmanship of the Lord President of the Council Neville Chamberlain, 'to make suggestions in regard to a post-war European and world system'.[67] Yet, having won the argument, Attlee was frustrated that the new committee did not meet throughout late August and the whole of September.

There was, however, a poignant reason for this. Chamberlain had been diagnosed with cancer and was gravely ill, eventually resigning all his posts on 1 October. In his last days, Churchill was deeply solicitous towards him, but his sad departure was an opportunity for a major reconstruction of the Government. Had Attlee proved himself a more forceful minister in the preceding months, he would have been a contender to take over a big departmental position, perhaps even becoming a kind of political supremo on the Home Front. In fact there had been widespread speculation that Attlee would be given a more prominent position. 'Mr Churchill wants to make his War Cabinet more active, more capable of cutting red tape and getting things done quickly [...] Mr C. R. Attlee is to become Lord President of the Council in place of Mr Chamberlain,' predicted the *Daily Mirror* at the end of August.[68] But Attlee's self-restraint told against him. In the subsequent reshuffle, the austere former Home Secretary Sir John Anderson was made Lord President with a wide-ranging brief across domestic policy. His place at the Home Office was taken by Attlee's biggest rival Herbert Morrison, while Kingsley Wood and Ernie Bevin were both elevated to the enlarged War Cabinet, another sign that Churchill felt that the two current Labour incumbents were lacking in weight. Perhaps the most important change was Churchill's decision to take over the vacant Conservative leadership himself. In some respects it was a remarkable step, given Churchill's past fractious relationship with the party hierarchy, his instinct as an individualist and his reputation for political disloyalty. His wife, a natural Liberal, was appalled by the move. As their daughter Mary recounted, she told him that 'by accepting the Conservative leadership, he would affront a large body of opinion in the country. Clementine put her view with vehemence and all her latent hostility to the Tory Party boiled over; there were several ding-dong arguments between them.'[69] Clementine always felt her husband had made a mistake which turned him into a partisan figure and alienated the non-Conservative working class, ultimately paying the price in the 1945 General Election. But Churchill believed that the leadership consolidated his position within the Tory

Party, a view shared by George Harvie-Watt, the Assistant Tory Whip who later became his trusted parliamentary private secretary. The Prime Minister 'must have a majority and I was sure this majority could only come from the Conservative Party', he advised.[70]

In early November 1940, Neville Chamberlain died. Churchill, who had grown much closer to his predecessor during their year together in the War Cabinet after their decades of friction, wrote a generous letter of sympathy to his widow and gave a warm tribute in the Commons. 'Neville Chamberlain acted with perfect sincerity according to his lights and strove to the utmost of his capacity and authority, which were powerful, to save the world from the awful, devastating struggle in which we are now engaged,' he said.[71] The same essential decency infused Attlee's response to Chamberlain's passing, as Chips Channon found when he sat next to him at a Belgian Embassy lunch. 'I was pleasantly surprised by the courtesy of the little man. He is a gentleman, or nearly so, no revolutionary he. We discussed Mr Chamberlain, whom he once hated. Today he was kind about him.'[72] In fact Attlee was one of the four pallbearers at Chamberlain's funeral, along with Sinclair, Wood and Halifax. The following month, another death provided Churchill with a further opportunity to remove the last traces of appeasement from his War Cabinet. On 12 December Lord Lothian, the British Ambassador to the United States, succumbed to a fatal kidney infection, having refused all medical treatment because of his belief in Christian Science. There were rumours that Bevin, Greenwood, or the Tory Viscount Cranborne might fill the vacancy. Attlee's name was another one mentioned. Almost a year later, the distinguished journalist John Carvel informed Dalton that 'Attlee was told that he could have the Washington Embassy if he wanted it,' though Dalton rightly thought this 'a bit unlikely'.[73] It was also suggested to Churchill that Cripps could be transferred from Moscow to Washington. The Prime Minister did not favour the idea. 'He is a lunatic in a country of lunatics. It would be a shame to move him,' he told Colville.[74] Churchill's own initial choice was Lloyd George, and he even went so far as to win the approval of President Roosevelt. But there was dismay in British diplomatic and political circles at the proposal because of both Lloyd George's age and his reputation for defeatism. Attlee himself was strongly opposed and was relieved when Churchill told him that his interview with Lloyd George had gone badly. 'He gave the impression of a very old man' whose 'nose was as sharp as a pen and he babbled of pigs', Attlee relayed to Dalton.[75] On his doctor's advice, Lloyd George turned down the offer. Churchill then decided to opt for Halifax, who was deeply reluctant to take the post but was told that he had to do his civic duty. As he departed for Washington, his place as Foreign Secretary was taken by Anthony Eden, a figure who was much more congenial to both Churchill and Attlee, not least because of his strong anti-appeasement record.

Amid the autumn reshuffles, the only new duty given to Attlee was the chairmanship of the War Aims Committee, previously held by Chamberlain. Meanwhile Greenwood, still in the grip of alcoholism, was asked to chair a Post-War Reconstruction Committee in addition to presiding over a couple of economic policy committees. But Churchill was not remotely interested in the work of any of these bodies. When Attlee sent him a number of papers from the War Aims Committee, Churchill took little notice. Nor did Attlee inspire much confidence with another of his positions, chairing the Food Policy Committee, which was meant to act as a co-ordinator between the Ministries of Agriculture, overseeing supply, and Food, dealing with rationing. In late December the Food Minister Lord Woolton, a superb adminis- trator with long experience as a retailer, saw Churchill to complain that some of the Home Front machinery 'was not good enough for the job it had to do', he said. 'The Food Policy Committee, under Attlee, also came to no decisions and that the latter was so weary that he had great difficulty in keeping awake – and didn't always succeed.' Woolton found Churchill 'receptive and helpful to his problems'.[76] After subsequent meetings in Downing Street at the end of the year, Churchill decided to strengthen the management of the Home Front by creating two new bodies: an Import Executive and a Production Executive, both of them under Ernie Bevin. At the same time, Greenwood lost his economic role and was instructed to concentrate on reconstruction, while Attlee's War Aims Committee slid further into irrelevance.

The year ended with stock of the two Labour leaders at a low point. 'Frightfully inefficient', was the verdict of Tory MP Sir Herbert Williams on the pair.[77] 'Attlee and Greenwood have failed to grasp to the full the opportunity granted to them. Labour is the poorer for the fact that its two representatives in the War Cabinet have become mere ciphers,' argued the *Daily Mirror*. In contrast, Churchill's esteem had never been higher. 'I suppose the outstanding fact of this war is the courage and determination of Winston. We are indeed lucky to find him ready for anything,' wrote Ironside to a friend in Canada on the last day of 1940. But the hard slog of 1941 would begin to undermine his reputation – and change his relationship with Attlee.

SIXTEEN

◈

ATLANTIC

WITH CHARACTERISTIC PRESCIENCE, Churchill wrote to the South African statesman Jan Christian Smuts in June 1940: 'If Hitler fails to beat us here, he will probably recoil eastwards.'[1] Churchill's belief that the Germans were poised to attack Russia was accompanied by two further convictions about the unfolding war. One was the absolute necessity of securing greater American support. The other was the need to exploit the military weakness of Italy, whose failings would require Germany to tie up more resources in other theatres. In fact, the campaign against Mussolini's forces had brought some of Britain's brightest successes of the early war, such as the daring raid by the Royal Navy on Taranto in November 1940, which wiped half of the Italian fleet's capital ships in a single night. Much more important was the land campaign in North Africa. Even at the height of the Battle of Britain, Churchill had felt that the defence of Egypt was essential to the maintenance of the British Empire, so he had ordered heavy reinforcements of men, equipment and planes to the British force in the region under General Archibald Wavell. Rearmed and re-equipped, Wavell's force did far more than just defend Egypt. In a bold, improvised advance between December 1940 and February 1941, the British overwhelmed a numerically far superior Italian army in Cyrenaica, taking over 130,000 prisoners.

The march to victory against Italy in North Africa provided welcome news for Churchill at the moment he was intensively wooing the United

States, a task in which he had been helped by the re-election of Franklin Roosevelt in November 1940. Sympathetic to the British cause and close to Churchill personally, the President sent in January one of his most trusted advisers, Harry Hopkins, on a mission to assess the morale of Britain before deciding what aid America would provide. During his stay, Hopkins was profoundly struck by Churchill's strength of purpose, as he wrote to Roosevelt in mid-January: 'Churchill is the government in every sense of the word. He controls the grand strategy and often the details – Labour trusts him – the army, navy and air force are behind him to a man.' The favourable reports from his confidant helped to convince Roosevelt of the need to pass the Lend-Lease Act in March 1941, by which American supplies could be delivered to Britain without cash payment. Churchill later called Lend-Lease 'the most unselfish and unsordid financial act of any country in all known history'.[2]

Britain needed all the support it could get in the spring of 1941, for the military picture had become much darker after triumph in North Africa over Italy. As Hitler stepped up his preparations for his invasion of the Soviet Union, he threatened Yugoslavia and Greece, with the aim of securing his southern flank. As early as January, Churchill actually doubted Greece could be saved from Axis occupation, something that he admitted to Hopkins. Yet, for reasons of prestige, since Britain had guaranteed in 1939 to come to Greece's aid in the event of a German attack, the War Cabinet agreed at its meeting on 7 March to send 55,000 troops to the peninsula from North Africa. It was a fateful decision, pushed through by Churchill but fully supported by Attlee and reluctantly accepted by Wavell and the other services chiefs. John Kennedy, the Director of Military Operations, felt that this acquiescence by the chiefs was because they were 'overawed and enormously influenced by Winston's overpowering personality'.[3] The consequences were disastrous. When Germany invaded Yugoslavia and Greece in April, both countries collapsed quickly. The British Expeditionary Force made little difference to the Greek resistance and, at the end of the month, had to be evacuated. The majority of the British troops, 26,000 in all, were taken to Crete with the aim of ensuring that the island could be held against an imminent German attack; but the only result was another defeat and humiliating evacuation. Even worse followed in June, when the newly arrived German General Erwin Rommel broke through the badly weakened British lines at Cyrenaica and prompted a full retreat to Egypt. All the gains against Italy had been lost; 'a most bitter blow', as Churchill wrote.[4]

The Prime Minister was heavily criticised for weakening the British position in North Africa to prop up a losing cause in Greece. Later in the year, Churchill himself privately admitted to Colville that the Government had made an 'error' over Greece. 'We could and should have defended Crete and advised the Greek Government to make the best terms it could.'[5] The wide-ranging military setbacks abroad in early 1941 formed a backdrop to growing political turbulence at home. After the unity in the face of mortal peril in 1940, friction began to grow within Westminster and there were mutterings of revolt among the Prime Minister's detractors. 'One hears increasing criticism of Churchill. He is undergoing a slump in popularity and many of his enemies, long silenced by his personal popularity, are once more vocal. Crete has been a great personal blow to him,' wrote Chips Channon in early June.[6] Labour's Manny Shinwell, a supporter of Churchill's during the downfall of Chamberlain, had now turned against him, claiming that he had 'picked him up out of the gutter but now wished he had left him there'.[7] Inevitably, Lloyd George's secretary Albert Sylvester relished Churchill's troubles. After the evacuation from Greece, he wrote on 23 April: 'Members of Winston's own administration are saying that it cannot go on. They are likening it to Asquith's Coalition. They say secretly that it cannot win the war and there must be change.'[8] Sylvester further reported in May that some MPs were attaching blame to Attlee for Churchill's problems. 'It was pointed out today that the reason Winston is such a one man show is because he really has no one else upon whom he can rely. Attlee shows himself to be a weaker man every day.'[9]

Much of the press, especially the *Daily Mirror*, was increasingly critical of the Government. In fact, the previous autumn Churchill had once again been so aggravated by the *Mirror*'s hostile stance that he had asked Attlee to complain to Cecil King, the paper's senior director. But, at their subsequent meeting, held in an air-raid shelter near Downing Street, Attlee's manner only irritated King, who later wrote that he found the Labour Leader 'so vague and evasive as to be quite meaningless'. King 'got the impression that the fuss was really Churchill's and that Attlee had been turned on to do something he was not really interested in and had not bothered to read his brief'.[10] The attacks intensified in early 1941, prompting Churchill to write a vituperative letter to King, in which he said that his group's papers were motivated 'by a spirit of hatred and malice against the Government'. King was so shaken by this letter that he sought an interview with Churchill. But in person Churchill was no more restrained, launching into 'a great tirade' against King's papers for 'magnifying grievances'. In defence, King claimed that they still supported Churchill 'as much as ever but others thought him unworthy of high office and said so'. King was referring to Attlee, as soon became clear when Churchill asked if this meant 'we arrogate to ourselves the right of appointing Ministers of the Crown'. According to his own account, King replied, 'No, but surely loyalty to him as Prime Minister did not carry with it loyalty to Attlee as Lord Privy Seal? He conceded this point more or less.' After more than an hour, the discussion concluded. In King's vivid description, 'Throughout, Winston was very difficult to talk to, getting up and striding about, shooting remarks at me that often had nothing whatever to do with his last remark or anything I was saying, sitting down again, leaning on the fireguard or lighting his cigar.'[11]

As the *Mirror* saga demonstrated, Attlee was widely perceived as one of the weak points in Churchill's Government, yet his loyalty and integrity were never in question. In January 1941, Dalton noted a conversation with Anthony Eden, in which the new Foreign Secretary said of his Labour colleagues that he was 'agreeably surprised' to find 'how easy they all are to work with. Attlee, he says, the Prime Minister likens to a terrier who, when he gets hold of an idea will not let it go.'[12] Attlee's steadfastness was also demonstrated after the Greek debacle, when Churchill sought a vote of confidence in the House of Commons to reinforce his position. Opening for the Government, Attlee made a strong defence of the Prime Minister, denying that he had been complacent. 'He had never led the House or the country to believe that the situation was at any time other than difficult or dangerous.' But on a more reassuring note, Attlee said the gloom over the military situation was badly overdone: 'Our position in the summer and autumn was infinitely more threatening than it is today.'[13] He was certain that ultimately the British would prevail in North Africa. His contribution helped Churchill win the confidence vote easily by 477 to 3.

But the perennial problem of Attlee's inability to inspire led to continual sniping. Only a fortnight after his positive conversation with Eden, Dalton saw Noel Hall, the Director of Intelligence at the Ministry of Economic Warfare, who 'spoke ill to me of Attlee, obviously echoing Morton. He was said to be sick and small and to bore the Prime Minister.'[14] As Dalton wrote, this may have only reflected the thinking of Desmond Morton, who was often capricious, later turning his ire on Churchill himself. Still the comment reflected some of the attitudes towards Attlee within Downing Street. A further indicator of official exasperation at Attlee's ineffectiveness could be seen in a report of March 1941 to the Prime Minister by the Cabinet Secretary Sir Edward Bridges on the inadequacy of Attlee's Food Policy Committee: 'The Chairman finds it very difficult to adjudicate between the Ministers of Food and Agriculture in the larger differences.' This paralysis lent an air of 'unreality to the proceedings' and prompted 'a growing volume of opinion that the Food Policy Committee is rather a waste of time'.[15] The committee lingered for another year, but in practice food policy was essentially decided by Churchill, the Cabinet and Woolton. The Food Minister, who administered the rationing scheme so skilfully, was never entirely happy with Churchill's involvement. 'It isn't easy to work with him', wrote Woolton, not least because 'he is benevolently hostile to anything that involved people not being fed like fighting cocks'.[16]

There were other sources of discord within Government that Attlee had to handle. One of the most combustible was a row that blew up in February 1941 between Dalton and Bracken, then Churchill's parliamentary private secretary. Often insecure behind his domineering presence, Dalton was aggrieved to learn that Bracken was badmouthing him at semi-public functions, including a lunch at the grill room of the Carlton Hotel. Having secured written confirmation of Bracken's behaviour from several witnesses, Dalton presented his evidence to Attlee, who feared that this could be part of an 'anti-Labour intrigue' in collusion with Morton. Attlee felt the complaint was sufficiently serious to take directly to Churchill. The talk in Downing Street seemed to go well. Attlee reported back to Dalton that Churchill had been 'very angry, that these two had no business to talk like that and in particular they had no business to use his name, that what they had been saying did not represent his own view'.[17] Dalton was temporarily mollified by this report, but in reality Churchill was far less concerned than Attlee's version suggests. After Attlee's visit, he sent for Bracken and asked him if it was true that he had abused Dalton. 'What I said was that Dalton was the biggest, bloodiest shit I've ever met,' replied Bracken. Churchill's response was to laugh.[18]

Bracken was joined in his troublemaking by Beaverbrook. The two men were not only Churchill's closest allies but were also both colonial outsiders, the former an Irishman with links to republicanism, the latter a Canadian of Scottish Presbyterian stock. Like Beaverbrook on a lesser scale, Bracken had made his fortune in news publishing and lived in grand style in a Westminster townhouse. Clementine disapproved of the pair, finding them vulgar and brash, but she came to recognise their loyalty. Indeed, such was Bracken's devotion that he was rumoured to be Churchill's illegitimate son. It was a piece of gossip that Bracken did nothing to suppress, though there was no evidence for it. Like Bracken, Beaverbrook had little time for either the traditional establishment or the Labour Party. Referring to Churchill's dominance of the political scene, he wrote in May that 'the front bench is part of the sham. There Attlee and Greenwood, a sparrow and a jackdaw, are perched either side of this glittering bird of paradise.'[19] The feeling of contempt was more than reciprocated by Attlee. 'He was the only evil man I ever met.

I could not find anything good to say about him,' the Labour Leader once said.[20]

In early and mid-1941, Beaverbrook was in a restless mood, tired of his work at the Ministry of Aircraft Production but eager to enhance his role within Government. Having clashed repeatedly with Bevin over industrial policy, he was moved by Churchill in May to the role of Minister of State with a watching brief to support Downing Street. But the change did nothing to lessen his frustration or mischievousness. Having attended a lunch of industrial correspondents at Claridge's on 4 June, the journalist Haydn Davies, who was attached to the Ministry of Economic Warfare, reported that Beaverbrook had drunk heavily throughout the meal and then used his speech to attack his colleagues in Government. 'The Prime Minister was a grand fellow,' Beaverbrook allegedly said, 'but who had he got to help him?' Bevin and the rest were of 'very little use'. When asked what he did as the new Minister of State, Beaverbrook replied, 'I am not in charge of the home front. That is supposed to be Attlee's job.' Finally Beaverbrook indulged in a moan about his departure from the Ministry of Aircraft Production, before he left the lunch to drink more whisky in a side room.[21] When Dalton relayed Haydn Davies's account to Attlee that evening, the Labour Leader called Beaverbrook 'a frightful humbug', declared that 'this sort of thing must be stopped' and promised to speak to Churchill about it. When Attlee did so, Beaverbrook denied to Churchill that he had been disloyal towards his fellow Labour Party ministers. He even collected statements from other journalists who contradicted Davies's report. One such was the Russian V. Brodsky, who wrote: 'I cannot remember one remark which could be interpreted as criticism or disparagement about your colleagues, Labour or otherwise.' He added that, 'in reference to Mr Attlee, you said he "brought great wisdom to the counsels of the Cabinet"'.[22] Under further scrutiny, Davies then retreated from his earlier report, but Attlee was gratified that Beaverbrook had been forced on to the defensive. Within less than a year, he faced a much more incendiary challenge from Beaverbrook the outcome of which was to shape the Cabinet for the rest of the war.

Attlee's tribulations were compounded by the pressure from his own party. He continually had to perform a balancing act between his loyalty to Churchill and the demands from Labour, especially the left of the party, for recognition of progressive war aims and the need for social reconstruction. While sympathising with the call for socialism, Attlee was reluctant to do anything that would undermine the Coalition. In fact in January, he remonstrated with the perennially outspoken Laski, telling him that 'I am sufficiently experienced in warfare to know that a frontal attack with a flourish of trumpets, heartening as it is, is not the best way to secure a position.'[23] Laski was not the only voice on the left haranguing the leadership. Nye Bevan, who was close to Beaverbrook at this time, also felt that Attlee was far too submissive towards Churchill. 'The Labour leadership insists upon regarding itself as a junior partner in the Government when in fact it is alone the custodian of the inspirations and policies through which victory can be achieved,' complained Bevan.[24] In a riposte to his critics, Attlee persuaded the NEC in May to issue a glossy document entitled *Labour in Government: A Record of Social Legislation in War Time*. One passage, justifying the party's role in the Coalition, stated that 'Labour Ministers hold key offices and are taking a full share in the direction of the war effort. Clement Attlee, leader of the party, shares with the Prime Minister the great responsibility of leading the country to victory and a successful peace.'[25] But the document was long on rhetoric and short on substance. Attlee needed some concrete measures to reassure Labour supporters, yet the problem remained the opposition of Churchill, who was as doubtful as ever about war aims and social programmes. As Tory Leader, he was wary of betraying the party's convictions. 'We could not expect the Conservatives to swallow things that would be put forward by the socialists,' he wrote in March 1941.[26] When Greenwood urged that his Post-War Reconstruction Committee be given enhanced authority through the inclusion of a host of senior ministers and a high-profile programme, Churchill slapped him down. 'We must be very careful not to allow the remote post-war problems to absorb energy which is required, maybe for several years, for the prosecution.'[27]

Nevertheless, Attlee tried to achieve some reforms. One case for which he argued strongly was the repeal of the 1927 Trade Disputes Act, which was passed when Churchill was Chancellor in the wake of the General Strike. Bitterly opposed by Labour and the TUC, this had imposed restrictions on industrial action and trade unions' political funds. In a long letter to Churchill in April, Attlee argued that repeal would display the Coalition's unifying credentials. 'We ought not to shrink from necessary changes because they had been in the past bones of contention between parties. The continuance of an existing grievance may be as much the cause of division as its amendment.'[28] But Churchill did not concede any ground, knowing that the Conservative majority in the House would throw out any such legislation. The same was true of Labour's call to consider the nationalisation of the railways, which was rejected by the War Cabinet.

In similar vein, Attlee was thwarted in his desire to oust Horace Wilson, the Permanent Secretary to the Treasury, head of the Civil Service and influential backer of appeasement under Chamberlain. The dismissal of Sir Horace, Attlee told Churchill, was 'really necessary to overcome a peace-time hangover and to get the Cabinet's drive pushed home'.[29] Showing his habitual interest in the machinery of government, he also urged that the head of the Civil Service should be answerable to Downing Street rather than the Treasury. Churchill was sympathetic, and in a letter to the Chancellor Kingsley Wood argued there was 'much to be said' for Attlee's proposals. The present arrangement, Churchill wrote, had 'a very serious cramping effect upon our war preparations', while Sir Horace had 'a very bad record and is the object of widespread distrust'.[30] Wood refused to accept any of this. In an angry, six-page, handwritten letter to Churchill, the Chancellor said the sacking of Sir Horace would play into the hands of 'the Socialists' who 'like to see the position and prestige of the Treasury weakened as much as possible'. Denying that the Treasury had held back expenditure for the war effort, Wood told Churchill he could see 'no advantage but many disadvantages in Attlee's suggestions and especially in time of war considerable additions to the responsibility of the Prime Minister in the civil field would not be understood'.[31] As a result of Wood's defence, Sir Horace did not retire until 1942, when he reached the age of sixty. There was one small success for Attlee, however, when he dissuaded Churchill from moving the popular Welsh Labour MP and former coal miner Dai Grenfell from the Board of Trade, where he was in charge of coal mines, to fill an official vacancy in New Zealand. 'I do not think we can afford to put the miners off at the present juncture when so much depends on their increased efforts. Politically the miners are very strong in our party and form the most loyal and steadfast group in their support of the War,' he told Churchill, who accepted his case.[32]

The wider pressure on Attlee from the left for radicalism was not eased when Hitler launched Operation Barbarossa, his long-expected invasion of Russia, on Sunday 22 June. The defence of the Soviet Union against Nazi tyranny gave a new cause around which progressive opinion could unify, while public sympathy for Moscow provided the chance for the promotion of socialist ideals and criticism of the Tories. On the very day of the attack, Churchill decided – largely on his own initiative and without much consultation – that Britain would give Russia all the aid it could. That evening he justified the decision during a radio broadcast, in which he said that 'no one has been a more consistent opponent of communism than I have for the last 25 years' but now 'the Russian danger is our danger'.[33] The next morning at the War Cabinet, Churchill explained that 'it had been necessary to act very quickly following the German attack'. The minutes recorded that 'there was general agreement with the line that the Prime Minister had taken in his broadcast'. Yet, while Churchill saw tremendous military advantages in having Hitler engaged on the Eastern Front, he remained implacably hostile to Soviet ideology and urged his Labour colleagues to adopt the same stance. 'The Prime Minister thought it was important that the Labour members of the Cabinet, in any speeches which they might make, should continue to draw a line of demarcation between the tenets of the Labour Party and those of Communism.'[34] Attlee agreed strongly with this, as he pointed out to Education Minister Chuter Ede that 'our help must be governed by military possibilities and not political considerations'.[35]

But, militarily, British forces had stumbled in North Africa against Rommel. A major offensive in mid-June to clear the Germans out of Cyrenaica and raise the Siege of Tobruk, codenamed Operation Battleaxe, had failed miserably, with the loss of almost 1,000 men and 100 tanks. Now despairing of Wavell's leadership, Churchill decided that he should exchange places with Claude Auchinleck, the Commander-in-Chief in India, who exuded an aura of strong generalship. Ismay advised the new North African commander to show sensitivity in his role. 'The Prime Minister is a woman. You have to woo him,' he said.[36] But Auchinleck was never able to establish a rapport with Churchill, who grew increasingly suspicious that the general had an overly defensive outlook. To provide more political authority in the region, Churchill sent Oliver Lyttelton to Cairo as Minister of State for the Middle East; while to improve his Government's relations with the press at home he appointed Brendan Bracken his Minister for Information.

In contrast to the desert problems, Churchill had more success in his effort to win further support from America, all the more important now that war was extending across the globe. The Lend-Lease Act was accompanied by the arrival of a new US Ambassador, John Winant, who was much more supportive of the British cause than his pro-appeasement predecessor Joe Kennedy had been. Winant soon established a close relationship with Churchill and his family – so close that he ended up having an affair with Winston's daughter Sarah. In London in 1941 he was soon joined by the wealthy banking tycoon Averill Harriman, who came as Roosevelt's special envoy and co-ordinator of the Lend-Lease programme. Like Winant, the intensity of his backing for Churchill's fight spilled over into romance, as he fell in love with Pamela Digby, the wife of Randolph, who was currently serving in North Africa. On a political level, the deepening links were reinforced by another successful visit in July by Hopkins, who was now on terms of comfortable intimacy with Churchill. While Hopkins and Harriman were at Chequers on Saturday July, Clement and Violet Attlee came to stay, giving the Americans a chance to see the contrast between the Prime Minister and his loyal Labour colleague. In an amused account written by Jock Colville, 'After dinner, we had a deplorable American film *Citizen Kane*, based on the personality of William Randolph Hearst. The Prime Minister was so bored that he walked out before the end [...] After the film, we sat up till 3am while the PM talked about food supplies and imports.' The conversation became too much for some of the guests. 'Finally Attlee and Harriman were yawning so much that Hopkins insisted that the PM, in irrepressible spirits, should go to bed.' This only prompted Churchill to utter a series of dire threats on 'what he was going to do to the Nazi leaders after the war – and the Nazi cities during it', until Hopkins jocularly complained about 'the way you keep going on'. At that moment 'everybody started looking at their watches and the Prime Minister was forcibly taken to bed'.[37]

Despite his exhaustion with this nocturnal exuberance, Hopkins acted as one of the instigators of the first wartime summit between Churchill and Roosevelt, the beginning of a series of historic conferences that helped to decide the Allies' grand strategy throughout the rest of the war. The opening meeting was held in early August at Placentia Bay off the coast of Newfoundland, where the Americans were building a naval base. For the sake of secrecy, Roosevelt travelled part of the way on the presidential yacht under the guise of making a fishing trip before he transferred to the naval cruiser *Augusta*. Accompanied by Hopkins, two of his three Chiefs of Staff and Cadogan from the Foreign Office, Churchill sailed from Scapa Flow on 4 August aboard the new Royal Navy battleship HMS *Prince of Wales*, which a few months earlier had seen action against the *Bismarck*.

While at sea, Churchill worked through official papers, using the ship's Map Room to follow the fortunes of British forces around the globe and keep in touch with the War Cabinet by telegraph. In his absence from London, Attlee was effectively in charge of the Government. The Labour Leader had occasionally deputised for Churchill before, but this was the first time that he had been acting Prime Minister for a significant period. Always a strong monarchist, Churchill had asked the King formally to authorise this arrangement before he set sail. 'I should leave the Lord Privy Seal, should Your Majesty approve, with full powers to act for me. I hope Your Majesty will feel that all this is in accordance with the public interest,' he wrote.[38] The King agreed.

With Churchill away Jock Colville was struck by both the diminution in the Downing Street workload and Attlee's relish for administration. 'The PM's absence makes an astonishing difference: there is practically nothing to do, though Attlee – who is deputising in the PM's absence – keeps ringing up to know whether there are any papers for him to sign, like a child with a new toy it is longing to use.'[39] But one early scare for Attlee occurred when British intelligence reported to him that news of Churchill's voyage may have reached the Germans. Immediately Attlee telegraphed the ship to ask if any action should be taken. According to the account left by Sir Ian Jacob, one of Churchill's aides: 'The Prime Minister did not seem to worry in the least and is secretly hoping the *Tirpitz* will come out and have a dart at him.'[40]

The Atlantic trip was a crucial turning point in the story of Churchill and Attlee, because it heralded the beginning of much more fruitful, trusting relations between them. Until then, their wartime connection had been unbalanced, with Churchill both distant towards Attlee and rather dismissive of his work. During Churchill's time in Placentia Bay, however, he was impressed by the swiftness and judgement that Attlee brought to the conduct of business. As he grew in respect for Attlee, so Attlee grew in confidence. Until August 1941, he had been continually bracketed with Greenwood. Now, in chairing the Cabinet and liaising with Churchill, he began to outpace his deputy. For Attlee, there was another great gain from this summit, in that Churchill and Roosevelt moved towards the adoption of the sort of clear, progressive war aims that he had been advocating for more than a year.

The new warmth between the Prime Minister and his Deputy was evident before Churchill even left Scapa Flow, when he wrote to Attlee on 3 August about the possibility of a statement to the House the following day on the military situation: 'I leave the matter entirely to your judgement, as I am sure you would make a very excellent survey.'[41] Attlee decided to go ahead with a wide-ranging overview of the war. He warned against too much optimism, but told MPs that the Russians were putting up 'a magnificent fight against the massed forces of Germany'; that at home Britain's ground defences were 'immeasurably greater' than last year; that more support was arriving from the USA; and that the RAF had air superiority in the Middle East.[42] From the front bench, Chuter Ede found Attlee's 'phrasing excellent but his voice thin and unimpressive'.[43] Attlee himself told Churchill that 'the debate on the war situation went very well' and 'the House was in a good mood'. Reflecting the growing cordiality, he expressed the hope 'that you have had a good voyage and have some rest in the course of it'. And, with some sensitivity, he also told Churchill that his protégé Brendan Bracken 'has made a good start. I understand that Fleet Street is pleased with him.'[44] Privately, to his brother Tom, Attlee confessed that he had been rather anxious about opening the war debate. 'I had to take the place of the PM as the reviewer of the war situation, no easy thing to follow such an artist. I eschewed embroidery and stuck to plain statement. It is no use trying to stretch the bow of Ulysses.'[45]

HMS *Prince of Wales* arrived at Placentia Bay on the morning of Saturday 9 August, Churchill then taking a barge over to the *Augusta* to meet the President. They had actually encountered each other once before, in 1918, at a dinner in London when Roosevelt was on an official visit as US Assistant Naval Secretary. He had not been impressed with the bullish Munitions Minister, later describing Churchill as a 'stinker' who enjoyed 'lording it over us'.[46] But Churchill's heroic wartime leadership had transformed Roosevelt's attitude. It was a tribute to his admiration for Britain's Prime Minister that he was willing not only to undertake the sea crossing to Newfoundland but also to put himself through the physical ordeal of greeting Churchill on the upper deck in a standing position – for Roosevelt, having contracted polio in 1921, was paralysed from the waist down and could remain upright only with the support of metal leg braces, the arm of one of his sons and tremendous willpower. Churchill, too, honoured the President by the seriousness with which he approached their forthcoming conference, even rehearsing his planned dialogue. After the introductions aboard the *Augusta*, Churchill handed Roosevelt a personal letter from King George VI that read, 'This is just a note to bring you my best wishes and to say how glad I am that you have at last an opportunity of getting to know my Prime Minister. I am sure you will agree that he is very remarkable.'[47] Roosevelt was indeed taken with Churchill, having given him a tour of the ship and lunch. Harriman wrote to his daughter that 'the Prime Minister has been in his best form', while the President 'is intrigued and likes him enormously'.[48] Harry Hopkins later described Roosevelt and Churchill as 'the most fluent conversationalists of their age. Even when substance was lacking in their exchanges, there was no danger of silences. They had in common social background, intense literacy, love of all things naval, addiction to power and supreme gifts as communicators. Both were stars on the world stage.'[49]

That night over dinner, Roosevelt put forward the idea of a joint declaration of broad principles that, in Churchill's words, 'animate the US and Britain at this fateful time'.[50] Despite his dislike of any discussion about war aims, Churchill immediately saw the potential propaganda value of such a statement, particularly when set against the tyranny of Nazism. Early the next morning, Churchill went to work with Cadogan on a draft, which set out eight goals for the Anglo-American alliance, emphasising the two countries' embrace of freedom and democracy and rejection of territorial aggrandisement and the rule of force. Most of this was uncontentious and even deliberately bland, reflecting Churchill's wish to avoid specifics. But there were two points that were to cause trouble for the British, both of which touched on the maintenance of the Empire. One was the third clause on self-determination, establishing 'the right of all peoples to choose the form of Government under which they will live'.[51] As Churchill later found to his regret, those words could be interpreted as a rallying call for the anti-colonial movement. A more immediate problem involved the fourth clause, which dealt with trade, a sensitive subject for the British because of the system of imperial preference that had operated within most of the Empire since 1932. The Churchill-Cadogan draft on this point could hardly have been more nebulous, merely stating that the two nations, 'will strive to bring about a fair and equitable distribution of essential produce, not only within their territorial boundaries, but between the nations of the world'.[52]

Following a Sunday-morning religious service aboard the *Prince of Wales*, Churchill handed the document to Sumner Welles, the US Under-Secretary of State. Back on the *Augusta*, Welles and Roosevelt beefed up the fourth clause to encompass free trade on the basis of promoting 'the enjoyment by all people of access, without discrimination and on equal terms to the markets and to the raw materials of the world'.[53] At the next bilateral meeting, on Monday 11 August, Churchill objected to this new wording, which he said contravened Britain's current trade obligations to its dominions and colonies. He explained that he would have to refer the new draft to the Cabinet in London, but feared 'that it will be difficult if not impossible to gain acceptance of the text in its present form'.[54] The consultation, he warned, could last a week. It was at this point that Churchill began his liaison with Attlee, taking a course that would dramatically enhance the Labour Leader's standing. That afternoon, Churchill sent Attlee a telegram with the draft, highlighting both the difficulties over the trade clause and the need for urgency.

> You should summon the full War Cabinet, with any others you think necessary, to meet tonight and please let me have our views without the slightest delay [...] I fear the President will be very upset if no joint statement can be issued and grave and vital interests may be affected. I had proposed to leave on the afternoon of the 12th, but we now have both postponed departure.[55]

Churchill's telegram arrived in London after midnight and immediately Attlee swung into action. Despite the late hour, he was in his element. Drafting documents and negotiating clauses had been his political lifeblood since he had first joined the Labour Party. Furthermore he was shrewd enough to see an opportunity to further the left's progressive agenda. He called a Cabinet for 1.45 a.m. and another at 10 a.m. on Tuesday 12 August, allowing all the senior members of the Government to be consulted. During these discussions, two vital decisions were made. One was to agree an amendment, as suggested by Churchill, that the expansion of free trade must be subject to the two countries' 'existing obligations', a change that took account of imperial preference. The other, on the urging of Attlee and Bevin, was to expand the fifth clause so that it called for 'improved labour standards, economic advancement and social security' in the post-war world.[56] At a stroke, Attlee's brand of socialism had now become central to the aims of the Allied cause.

When the new draft from London reached the *Prince of Wales* in the middle of the night, it was picked up it by Leslie Hollis, Assistant Secretary to the War Cabinet, and taken to Churchill. According to one account, the Prime Minister was rather nervous as to what Attlee and his colleagues had agreed: "'Am I going to like it?' he asked, rather like a small boy about to take his medicine. However, all was well, and Hollis was able to assure him that he would like it.'[57] Cadogan was delighted that Attlee had acted so swiftly, as he recorded: 'Hollis brought me the telegram from London showing that they agree in general. Pretty quick work! Quite a satisfactory day.'[58] All went well at the next bilateral meeting, on 12 August, as Churchill and Roosevelt settled on a final version that included a few rhetorical flourishes. As the architect of the New Deal, the President was particularly enthusiastic about Attlee's insistence on the inclusion of social security. For all its elevated language, described by the *Daily Mirror* as 'a wave of wishful thinking',[59] the document was a vital one. Known as the Atlantic Charter, it went on to serve not only as the ethical foundation of the Allied war effort but also the inspiration for the United Nations. So smoothly was the business concluded that Churchill's ship was able to leave that afternoon, much earlier than expected. As he prepared to depart, he expressed his gratitude to Attlee and his hopes about the impact of the Placentia Conference. 'Please thank the Cabinet for amazingly swift reply,' he wrote, adding that 'I trust my colleagues will feel that my mission has been fruitful.

I am sure I have established warm and deep personal relations with our great friend.'[60]

As Churchill travelled back to Britain, Attlee had the duty of setting out the terms of the Atlantic Charter in a broadcast to the public on 14 August. The early news reports that Churchill and Roosevelt had agreed a joint declaration provoked widespread anticipation of a major new development in the war. Attlee's statement, delivered in his usual dry style, did not fulfil those expectations. Churchill's own parliamentary private secretary George Harvie-Watt wrote that 'this speech ought to have an electrifying effect on the nation and if Winston had been making it, it certainly would but Attlee was not an orator and he made the announcement seem rather dull and almost unimportant'.[61] Attlee himself sensed that he had given a rather bland recitation, as he told his brother. 'I addressed my largest audience to date in blowing the gaff on the Prime Minister's meeting with Roosevelt. I felt I was taking the place of Bruce Belfrage* rather than making any original contribution.'[62] Yet Attlee's Labour colleague Chuter Ede was sufficiently moved to write to him, 'Your announcement yesterday was very heartening. As an exposition of our general aims it could not be bettered.'[63] Nonetheless, Labour's interpretation of Britain's war aims soon came into conflict with that of Churchill and many of his fellow Conservatives who wanted to uphold the Empire. The arch imperialist Leo Amery felt there would be trouble over the third clause. 'We shall no doubt pay dearly in the end for all this fluffy flapdoodle,' he wrote after listening to Attlee's broadcast.[64] Amery's fears were soon realised when Attlee, in an address to the West African Students' Union in London, proclaimed that 'the Charter's principles would apply to all peoples of the world'.[65] In an attempt to reassure Amery, Churchill told him that he was 'sure' Attlee 'did not intend to suggest' that the 'the natives of Nigeria or of East Africa could by a majority vote choose the form of Government under which they live, or the Arabs by such a vote expel the Jews from Palestine. It is evident that prior obligations require to be considered.'[66]

---

*   An actor and unflappable wartime BBC newsreader.

Churchill then went even further. Having told the Cabinet on 4 September that the Charter was 'not intended to deal with the internal affairs of the British Empire', he then made an explicit statement to the Commons. With the third clause, he said, he had 'in mind, primarily, the restoration of sovereignty, self-government and national life of the states and nations now under the Nazi yoke' – an entirely separate problem from 'the progressive evolution of self-governing institutions in the regions and peoples that owe allegiance to the British Crown'.[67] As the historian Richard Toye pointed out, his speech only inflamed nationalist sentiment, as typified by the telegram to Downing Street from Nnamdi 'Zik' Azikiwe, editor of the *West African Pilot* newspaper, seeking clarification over the discrepancy between Churchill's statement in the Commons and Attlee's address to the Students' Union. Churchill replied blandly that the Government's policy on Empire was 'already entirely in harmony with the high conceptions of freedom and justice which inspired the joint declaration'.[68] Nevertheless, it was Attlee's pro-decolonisation that prevailed after the war, most famously in India and Burma.

Despite such problems, Churchill received an immediate boost from the declaration. Even one of his most nagging critics, Albert Sylvester, admitted to Lloyd George at the beginning of September that 'one thing is certain: the Atlantic Conference has been very timely for him. The immediate reaction has been to put up Winston's stock.'[69] A few weeks later, through gritted teeth, Sylvester told his chief that in the cinema, 'whenever Winston is flashed on the screen, he is received with terrific applause [...] He represents the indomitable spirit of the nation.'[70] In October 1941, Churchill's overall approval ratings still stood at 84 per cent. But fine words would not win the war. What truly counted was the defeat of the Axis powers. The Soviet Union's epic defence of its homeland was going better than expected – though Stafford Cripps, the British Ambassador in Moscow, much of the press and the left of the Labour Party complained persistently that Britain was providing insufficient aid. Partly to relieve the strain on the Russians, partly to protect the eastern part of the Empire and partly to transform the vast

Mediterranean theatre, Churchill knew that Britain needed its own victory against Rommel's forces in North Africa. For that reason, he kept up the pressure on Auchinleck to go on the offensive, showing no patience with the general's emphasis on the need to replenish his equipment and train more men before he could go on the attack. As Churchill pointed out, the British land force in the desert had far greater resources than Rommel possessed, but there was an ever lengthening tail; out of 750,000 men in the Middle East, only 100,000 were actually in the front line. 'The war could not be waged on the basis of waiting until everything was ready. He thought that it was a frightful prospect that nothing should be done for four and a half months,' he told Auchinleck at the beginning of August. Attlee agreed with the Prime Minister. At the Defence Committee, he asked how Egypt could be saved 'if we waited till the Germans had ample time to reinforce?'[71] Auchinleck, after more delays and badgering by the Cabinet, eventually accepted the date of 1 November for the start of his offensive against Rommel, to be codenamed Operation Crusader.

Then there was a further hesitation, as Auchinleck complained of difficulties in unloading tank reinforcements. This was too much for Churchill, who feared that Britain was handing the initiative in the Middle East to the Germans. But there was also a very specific reason for Churchill's indignation over the postponement of Crusader; and this related to Attlee. Churchill had agreed that his Lord Privy Seal should attend the extraordinary conference of the International Labour Organisation (ILO) to be held in late October in New York. The Prime Minister was not particularly interested in labour questions, but he saw the conference as another instrument for cementing his alliance with Roosevelt, particularly as the President was due to address the event. To this end, he planned to use Attlee as an envoy to bring a highly secret letter for Roosevelt, setting out Churchill's analysis of the Russian Front, the North African theatre and the possible risks of a German invasion of Britain. Because the letter contained sensitive military details, Churchill claimed that the timing of Attlee's departure had been related to the start of Operation Crusader. In a reproachful telegram to Auchinleck of Saturday 18 October, Churchill said that 'it is impossible to explain to Parliament and the nation how it is our Middle East Armies have had to stand for 4½ months without engaging the enemy while all the time Russia is being battered to pieces'. He then turned to Attlee's planned visit to New York.

> The Lord Privy Seal leaves Monday for United States carrying with him a personal letter to the President which I did not wish to entrust to the Cables or Cipher Department. In this letter, which would be handed to the President for his eyes alone and to be burned or returned thereafter, I was proposing to state that in the moonlight of early November you intended to attack [...] I fixed the date of the Lord Privy Seal's mission in relation to the date you had given us. Of course, if it is only a matter of two or three days, the fact could be endured. It is not, however, possible for me to concert the general movement of the war if important changes are made in plans agreed upon, without warning or reason.[72]

Even so, Churchill reluctantly had to accept Auchinleck's delay for another three weeks.

Just before Attlee left for America there was a dinner party at the Commons in his honour. In another indicator of the deepening bond between the two men, Churchill graced the event with his presence and paid a personal tribute to the Lord Privy Seal, as Dalton recorded: 'The PM is in very good form and in addition to making a short and cordially phrased speech about Attlee and His Majesty's Government in general, holds forth at great length on the war and kindred topics.'[73] Attlee's journey, undertaken by flying boat rather than battleship, was swifter than Churchill's of two months earlier. As well as participating in the ILO Conference in New York, he was invited by Roosevelt to join him on the presidential yacht for a cruise on the Potomac. 'He was a charming companion, a brilliant raconteur and full of ideas,' said Attlee, who was also struck at how close the USA now seemed to the final abandonment of neutrality. In one theatrical moment during their talks, Roosevelt took hold of a world atlas and pointed to Algiers: 'That is where I want to have American troops' – a wish that accorded exactly with the demands of British North African policy.[74] Giving a greater insight into the Government's thinking, Attlee handed him Churchill's much heralded secret letter about the war situation, the key points of which were the imminence of Auchinleck's attack and the probability of a German assault on Britain in the spring if the Soviet Union weakened. 'We must expect that as soon as Hitler stabilises the Russian front, he will begin to gather perhaps 50 or 60 divisions in the west for the invasion of the British Isles,' wrote Churchill. But the Prime Minister was optimistic about North Africa: 'All my information goes to show that a victory in Cyrenaica of the British over the Germans will alter the whole shape of the war in the Mediterranean.' He concluded, 'Let me tell you how I envy the Lord Privy Seal in being able to fly over to the United States and have a good talk with you. My place is here.' Fortunately for posterity, Roosevelt did not fulfil Churchill's request to consign the letter 'to the flames'.[75]

Writing to his brother at the end of his American tour, Attlee made two shrewd observations about Churchill. The Prime Minister, he told Tom, had

> an extreme sensitiveness to suffering. I remember some years ago his eyes filling with tears when he talked of the suffering of the Jews in Germany while I recall the tones in which, looking at Blitzed houses, he said poor, poor little homes. It is a side of his character that is not always appreciated. Another is his intense realization of history. He sees all events taking their place in the procession of past events as seen by the historian of the future; the gallantry of Greece, the heroism of our people, the moral breakdown of the French, are always seen in perspective.[76]

More than ever, Attlee would now be alongside Churchill as further pages of wartime history were written.

SEVENTEEN

◈

WASHINGTON AND SINGAPORE

A TTLEE'S VISIT TO the USA gave him a brief respite from all the problems that the Government faced in the autumn of 1941. The war situation remained as grave as ever. Despite the heroic fight of the Russians, an ultimate German victory on the Eastern Front looked inevitable. In North Africa, Rommel's unbeaten forces represented a growing threat to Egypt, while losses to the U-boats in the North Atlantic continued to mount.

The political arena at home was just as troubling. The Coalition came under ever greater strain as the Labour left grew restive over the perceived lack of a distinct progressive agenda. From the opposite side, many Tory backbenchers felt that the socialists were too influential. There was also friction within the Government, some of it fuelled by the intrigues of Bracken and Beaverbrook, those two idiosyncratic allies of Churchill. Bracken, the powerful Minister for Information since July, had continued to torment Hugh Dalton, particularly over the issues of propaganda and access to Downing Street. On Attlee's return from America, Dalton unburdened himself, complaining about Bracken's interference and his habit of 'running round' to Churchill to give him 'an account of our affairs'. Attlee, having also read some of the vicious letters that Bracken sent Dalton, declared that 'this man is not fit to be a minister in the middle of a war'.[1] In early December, he spoke on Dalton's behalf to Churchill, who outwardly professed that he was 'very much shocked' by the 'impropriety of the behaviour of the offender'.[2] But in private, Churchill was irritated by Dalton's lamentations, describing him as 'an intolerable person'.[3]

The cohesion of the Government was also undermined by the continued manoeuvres of Beaverbrook, who was deeply antipathetic towards Attlee. Part of this hostility stemmed from Beaverbrook's disdain for Attlee as a political personality, but another factor was Russia. Since heading an official mission to Moscow in September 1941 for the purposes of organising Allied supplies, Beaverbrook had become a passionate advocate of the Soviet cause and an admirer of Stalin. This brought him into conflict with Attlee, who, like many Labour moderates, was suspicious of the Soviet Union because of his lifelong fight against communism, most clearly manifested in his ferocious opposition to the Popular Front in the late 1930s. Yet Beaverbrook had an ulterior motive for his devotion to the Soviets. He wanted to exploit the phenomenal enthusiasm of the British people towards Russia for his own political gain, enhancing his power and perhaps even ascending to the premiership. The Soviet struggle against Germany had certainly gripped the imagination of the public in the autumn of 1941. When a booklet of Stalin's collected speeches was published, it sold out in days. Equally successful was a Beaverbrook initiative entitled 'Tanks for Russia', under which all output of armour from British factories during a single week in September was sent to the Soviet Union. Stirred by all this adulation for Stalin's regime, Beaverbrook began to contemplate wholesale change at the top of British politics, using both his press and his official position for self-advancement. Cecil King recorded that 'intimates' of the press baron were saying that 'Beaverbrook is convinced we cannot win this war' and that he is 'the man to succeed Winston'.[4] One such intimate, the left-wing MP Aneurin Bevan, told guests at a private dinner hosted by the *Mirror* that Beaverbrook 'thinks a major political crisis is coming in the next few months', from which he will emerge 'either as Prime Minister or as an overwhelmingly powerful figure in a reconstituted Churchill Government'.[5] Inevitably

Albert Sylvester picked up on the rumour, as he told Lloyd George, 'Beaverbrook has got it into his head that he could lead the Labour Party!'[6] This led Beaverbrook to pursue the extraordinary idea of an alliance with Ernie Bevin, a prospect at which he deviously hinted in a letter of late November. 'Can we make a platform for you where I can stand by your side? I am sure you can do so if you determine to build it,' he wrote. But Beaverbrook, whose ambition was not matched by his judgement, had chosen the wrong target. Bevin's trade-union background meant he had no time for disloyalty, as he told Beaverbrook. 'I came into the Government not for any personal position but solely to contribute what I could to our common effort under the leadership of the Prime Minister.'[7] Attlee always felt a debt to Bevin for his unflagging fidelity. 'He would square up to anyone physically or morally with relish. He looked and indeed was the embodiment of common sense. Yet I never met a man in politics with as much imagination as he had, with the exception of Winston.'[8] But Bevin's dismissal of Beaverbrook only postponed by a few months a titanic confrontation between the press lord and Attlee, one that turned into perhaps the most serious ministerial crisis of Churchill's Government.

Arthur Greenwood had predicted such trouble, telling Churchill six months earlier that Beaverbrook was 'a very wicked and disturbing influence'.[9] But the machinations of Beaverbrook were indicative of wider political discontent, with some on the left now questioning whether Labour should remain so closely tied to Churchill. The question of peace aims was raised again at the TUC's annual meeting in the autumn of 1941, forcing Attlee to tell delegates that it was the primary duty of the Labour movement to see 'that the ship weathers the storm'.[10] The stress on the Coalition was also reflected in the growing antipathy towards the wartime truce by which the main parties agreed not to put up candidates against each other at by-elections. Some Labour left-wingers now felt reluctant to provide endorsement where the Government candidate was a Conservative. To keep the truce in operation, Attlee came up with a compromise, proposing that in future there should be a 'statement of support' for the official Coalition

candidate signed by each of the three party leaders.[11] This scheme
was narrowly backed by the NEC, much to the fury of radical figures
like Manny Shinwell. Attlee explained the dilemma and his planned
solution to Churchill:

> You will be aware of the difficulties which lie in the way of direct
> recommendation of the candidate of another party through
> the medium of a personal letter from myself, in view of the
> constitution and practice of the Labour Party. My colleagues
> and I thought the best way of meeting this would be by the
> issue of a general appeal at each by-election, asking the electors
> to support the Government candidate under the joint names of
> yourself, Sinclair and myself.[12]

Churchill, never much interested in party labels, accepted the plan.

Further rows blew up over allowances for the army and the lack of any
moves towards the nationalisation of the railways or the mines. At an
explosive meeting of the PLP in October, Manny Shinwell complained
that 'the Labour Ministers in the Cabinet had not advocated party
policy' – a remark that brought Attlee angrily to his feet. 'That's a
damned lie,' he said.[13] Aid to Russia was another flashpoint, as Shinwell
urged a full parliamentary debate on the issue. His call was rejected by
Attlee, who told his MPs that 'either people had faith in the willingness
of the Government to do what they could for Russia or they had not
[…] the Government could not make any statement without helping
the enemy.' The trade unionist Jack Lawson, Attlee's ally, was withering
about Shinwell's pronouncement on war strategy. 'Shinwell does not
know the difference between a platoon and a platinum blonde.'[14]

An even bigger altercation occurred in December over the National
Service Bill, which significantly widened the scope of conscription to
include all unmarried women under the age of thirty and men under
sixty. A large section of the Labour Party, still suspicious of military
compulsion, believed that the Bill could be a vehicle for greater radicalism
by expanding the concept of conscription to embrace public ownership

of all industries deemed vital for the war effort. The move, based on an amendment to the National Service legislation, provoked a major crisis at Westminster, and, for a moment, threatened Labour's participation in the Coalition. On the afternoon of 3 December, at an embittered meeting of the Administration Committee of the Parliamentary Party, the scale of the potential rebellion became apparent. In response to the disquiet, Attlee explained 'that if the test was the effective prosecution of the war, then the Government was willing to take all necessary steps but ideological considerations were ruled out'. As so often before, Attlee was let down by his poor oratory. 'He probably said the right things but said them so ineffectively that he worsened the position,' noted Chuter Ede, who was 'utterly pessimistic' about the immediate future. 'If the smash is to come, it had better come now. The worst thing would be, not a sudden climax, but a creeping paralysis of activity.' [15] At a full meeting of the PLP on 4 December, there was no sign of the rebels backing down. Nye Bevan, who revelled in his image as the keeper of the socialist flame, led the charge with his claim that there was overwhelming backing in the country for nationalisation. Such was the potential level of revolt that Attlee felt compelled to warn of his possible departure. 'He said that he was not prepared to stay in the Government unless he had the support of the Party for the policy the Government were pursuing,' recorded Ede.[16] But even that admonition had little impact. In the division on the amendment to nationalise coal and transport, a third of Labour MPs abstained and forty-two voted against the Government. Attlee, however, did not act on his threat.

Amid such disputes and the fraught war situation, dissatisfaction with the two leaders was mounting in the last months of 1941. Churchill was seen by his critics as too domineering and erratic, Attlee as too weak and submissive. Victor Cazalet, once an admirer, wrote in October that Churchill was now 'unapproachable and dictatorial. How long can it last? I am sure the war organisation is all wrong.'[17] Another Conservative MP, Sir Herbert Williams, told a public meeting in November that 'although Mr Churchill possesses the capacity for inspired speech, he is not so good as a manager of the war effort'.[18] Annoyance at Churchill's unorthodox methods was persistent. Beaverbrook had reportedly taken to describing the Prime Minister as 'Old Bottleneck' because of his reluctance to delegate, while two ministers, Robert Hudson at Agriculture and Lord Woolton at Food, complained that Churchill 'has Ministers out of bed at two in the morning and engages them in long talks about things that have nothing to do with their departments. He will not listen to any of their problems and some go so far as to call him an old fool at times.'[19] Others felt that the two Labour leaders bore much of the responsibility for the atmosphere of crisis. In December, a scathing article about the Labour pair appeared in the magazine *World Review*, published by the magazine proprietor Sir Edward Hulton, who was a strong advocate of greater industrial efficiency: 'This is the war of wars, the struggle of struggles. In the inner Cabinet of Ministers whom do we find? Attlee and Greenwood. It is enough to make one turn one's face to the wall and give up the ghost. Can you tell me that no better men can be found than these?'[20]

From the political left, Beatrice Webb described Attlee in September 1941 as an 'ultra political half-wit' while she eagerly noted gossip from Westminster that 'Winston is already wearing out and will not survive as Prime Minister when the war is over.'[21] The pressure that Churchill experienced at this time was reflected in a volcanic outburst of temper on 4 December at a meeting of the War Cabinet over the supply of fighter planes to the Soviet Union. His combustible display of anger was noted by General Alan Brooke, who had recently taken over from his fellow Ulsterman Sir John Dill as Chief of the Imperial General Staff, Churchill having decided that Dill was too unimaginative and cautious. According to Brooke, when the War Cabinet argued that the proposal to send ten squadrons to Russia was 'too definite', Churchill exploded. 'We were told that we did nothing but obstruct his intentions. We had no ideas of our own and whenever he produced idea we produced nothing but objections, etc. Attlee pacified him at once, but he broke out again, then Eden soothed him but to no avail. Finally, he looked at his papers for some five minutes, then slammed them together, closed the meeting and walked out of the room. It was pathetic and entirely unnecessary. We were only trying to save him from making definite promises which he might find hard to keep. It is all the result of overworking himself and keeping too late hours.'[22] The next morning Churchill agreed to the terms that had so exasperated him the night before.

There was a degree of relief for the Government when Auchinleck's much delayed Operation Crusader achieved some success in North Africa by mid-December, relieving the vital port of Tobruk, occupying Cyrenaica and forcing Rommel back to a new front line at Gazala. But more important, in global terms, was America's entry into the war after the Japanese attack on Pearl Harbor on 7 December, which meant not only that Roosevelt's great 'arsenal of democracy' was fully engaged on the Allied side but also that, as Churchill later commented, four-fifths of the world's population lived in countries opposed to the dictators. The dark days of Britain standing alone against the Reich's war machine in Europe were long over. Total war across the world now represented the route to Britain's salvation. 'So we won after all,' was one of his first and most joyful reactions to the news of Pearl Harbor. Another response was his determination to make another visit to Roosevelt in order to co-ordinate strategy and to ensure that, despite the Japanese attack, the American focus was on Europe rather than the Pacific, a task that had been made all the easier by the talks at Placentia Bay in August.

Roosevelt warmly agreed to an urgent conference. 'It would also be a very great pleasure to me to meet you again and the sooner the better,' he wrote.[23] Churchill wanted to depart for Washington almost immediately but Eden, who had left on a long-arranged mission to Moscow, was perturbed at the idea of the Prime Minister and the Foreign Secretary both being out of the country simultaneously. He therefore rang Attlee from onboard his ship and asked him to persuade Churchill to delay his American visit. In agreement with Eden, Attlee promised to raise the issue at the Cabinet. But Churchill refused to budge, saying that 'his plans were all made'.[24] Oliver Harvey was not impressed, writing that 'the Cabinet are a poor lot for stopping anything'.[25] But the outcome was that Attlee would be fully in charge of the Government in London once more, a prospect that caused anxiety in some quarters. 'Not everyone was wholly reassured by Attlee's presence at the helm,' wrote Cadogan.[26]

Churchill may have welcomed the dramatic widening of the war's scope after Pearl Harbor, but Japan's aggression was now a potent menace to Britain's position in the Pacific and her eastern Empire. Indeed, the War Cabinet ministers had been so concerned about Japan's potential bellicosity in this theatre that in October they had decided to deploy a force under Admiral Sir Tom Phillips as a deterrent, comprising the modern battleship *Prince of Wales*, the First World War battle cruiser *Repulse* and four other destroyers. Churchill was often blamed for this deployment against the advice of the naval staff, but Attlee had also argued strongly for it at the Defence Committee. When Philips said that a flotilla of older vessels should be 'a match for any forces the Japanese were likely to send against them', Attlee replied that 'it seemed sounder to send a modern ship' to the Far East, since Britain would find it very difficult 'to remain on the defensive'.[27] Churchill and the Defence Committee agreed and consequently the *Prince of Wales* was sent eastwards – but, tragically, without any effective air cover. The savage reality of the new campaign in the Pacific became clear on 10 December, just as Churchill was preparing to leave for the USA, when the Admiralty telephoned to give him the news that both the *Repulse* and the *Prince of Wales* had been sunk by Japanese aircraft, with Admiral Phillips among the casualties. 'I put the telephone down. I was thankful to be alone. In all the war I never received such a shock.'[28]

Yet the catastrophe in the Pacific made Churchill feel that it was all the more imperative for him to meet Roosevelt. He left London on the night of 12 December, travelling to America on the battleship *Duke of York* with a party of eighty, including the three service chiefs and Sir John Dill, Alan Brooke's predecessor, who had been appointed to head the British military mission in Washington. It was another measure of Roosevelt's respect and affection for Churchill that he put up the Prime Minister at the White House for three weeks over Christmas, though his wife, Eleanor – the radical, abstemious First Lady – approved of neither his politics nor his drinking. 'Mother would just fume,' recalled Roosevelt's son Elliott.[29] In contrast, Churchill felt at ease in his surroundings, as he made clear in a telegram to Attlee. 'We live here as a big family in the greatest intimacy and informality.'[30] That informality was highlighted on one occasion, when Roosevelt wheeled himself into Churchill's dressing room. Churchill had just had a bath and was not yet dressed, but with a complete absence of self-consciousness told Roosevelt, 'You see, Mr President, I have nothing to conceal from you.'[31] During their lengthy conversations about strategy, the President confirmed both that the European theatre would be America's priority and that, as he had told Attlee in the autumn, he wanted his first intervention to be joint landings in French North Africa. He also agreed that American troops could be stationed in Northern Ireland to allow British forces to be deployed elsewhere.

Churchill's stature in America was reinforced on Boxing Day 1941, when he was given the rare honour of addressing both Houses of Congress. As usual, Churchill had prepared his speech with painstaking thoroughness, and the effort ensured another rhetorical triumph. The reception among the US politicians was made all the greater by Churchill's poignant references to his American heritage from his mother's side. He ended on a note of confident optimism, expressing the belief that 'in the days to come the British and American peoples will for their own safety and for the good of all walk together side by side in majesty, in justice and in peace'.[32] Chuter Ede, listening on the wireless back in Britain, felt the address 'came over remarkably well. He had a tremendous ovation on rising. His voice was resonant, his phrasing superb and the flow of his words more easy than usual.'[33]

In the account left by Churchill's doctor Sir Charles Wilson, who had accompanied him to America on Clemmie's insistence, 'the Senators and Congressmen stood cheering and waving their papers till he went out'.[34] That night, back at the White House, Wilson had a more delicate task to perform than merely listening to Churchill's oratory. When trying to open a window in his bedroom, Churchill suddenly experienced shortness of breath and a dull pain in his chest.

Immediately he summoned Wilson, who discovered that Churchill had suffered a mild heart attack. However, to avoid alarming Churchill or the public, he decided not to reveal the truth. So he sat 'tight' and merely told Churchill not to overexert himself. In fact, Churchill's schedule was remarkably unaffected by the episode.[35] He carried on with his bilateral talks, then visited Canada to address the Parliament in Ottawa before returning to Washington where, on New Year's Day, he and Roosevelt issued a declaration, later signed by the Soviet Union and the other Allies, in which they agreed not to make a separate peace with the enemy. Churchill's only concession to his troubled health was a brief stay in Palm Beach, Florida, before he embarked on the return journey to England in mid-January, this time by flying boat.

While he had been away, Attlee headed the Government in his restrained style, which was beginning to impress a few of his colleagues. After a Defence Committee session on 15 December, Alan Brooke wrote in his diary that 'PM now away and the meeting was run by Attlee very efficiently and quickly'.[36] Major General Sir John Kennedy felt that 'Attlee's staccato, matter-of-fact approach' was 'very effective'.[37] But Attlee's efficiency could not hide the reality that the war in the Far East was going badly, with the sinking of the two capital ships compounded by Japanese attacks on RAF airfields in Malaya and Burma. Nor was the growing discontent among MPs alleviated by a statement by Attlee to the Commons on 20 December. His speech, as George Harvie-Watt told Churchill, left a 'very lively and critical feeling against the Government'.[38] Writing to Churchill the same day, Attlee admitted that the House had been 'fractious and difficult', adding: 'The Russian Front and Libya are bright spots in a rather gloomy landscape, but we none of us have been under any delusions as to what Japan's entry into the war meant.'[39] The position became even worse when the British colony of Hong Kong came under siege from the Japanese forces. The War Cabinet had to decide whether to give the Governor, Sir Mark Aitchison Young, permission to surrender or order the British troops to fight it out. Attlee contacted Churchill in America, who predictably said that 'the garrison should fight to the last'.[40] But resistance swiftly collapsed and, in another blow to British prestige, Hong Kong fell on Christmas Day.

The darkening war situation called for another debate in the House on 8 January, with Attlee again taking the lead for the Government. This time it was his duty to report swift Japanese advances in Malaya and an impending attack on Burma. The bad news, combined with Attlee's dry delivery, only deepened the anger of the Commons. 'It was a dull speech which did not at all impress the House. He added little to what was already known. It was really a "marking time" debate. Members felt that there was little use in raising points unless you yourself were present,' Harvie-Watt told Churchill.[41] Inevitably, Sylvester was thrilled to tell Lloyd George of Attlee's 'complete flop'. His speech, Sylvester wrote, 'was incredibly bad. He was asked a number of questions and he dealt with them in a very fumbling manner which cast no credit on his understanding.'[42] The *Daily Mirror's* 'Cassandra' column, written by William Connor, was damning about Attlee's performance in Churchill's absence: 'The Government, under the depressing leadership of Mr Attlee, has been trundling along like an old car with a flat tyre. While the Master's away, the mental mice of Westminster haven't even had the strength to play.'[43] So dire was the Government's position that many disgruntled MPs began to speak openly of the need for wholesale change. At a National Labour gathering in mid-January, the MP Frank Markham openly argued that 'we must get rid of Churchill who will never win the war'.[44] The complaints sometimes gave way to intrigues. Welsh Liberal Clem Davies, now disillusioned with Churchill, claimed that 'the crack is coming' and whispered of his liaison with dissident Tories and Labour MPs to achieve that end. In this conspiratorial atmosphere, Greenwood told Davies that he was 'terribly concerned and now realises that nothing will save Attlee, Alexander, Morrison and possibly himself'.[45]

This was the political landscape that greeted Churchill when he returned from the USA on 17 January, arriving from Plymouth at Paddington railway station, where he was met by Attlee and the rest of the War Cabinet. The military position was just as dismal. In North

Africa Rommel's force had been heavily reinforced and was advancing eastwards, taking back Benghazi before the end of the month. Even worse, the Japanese advance was now beginning to threaten Singapore, which was meant to be an island fortress but was in reality dangerously vulnerable. Churchill was appalled to learn that, contrary to all the assurances he had been given by the military, the defences were woefully inadequate, with most of the limited batteries designed to resist a seaborne frontal assault rather than landings from the north. Even so, he warned his chiefs that 'Singapore Island must be maintained by every means' and 'defended to the death'.[46] Just as he had in 1941, Churchill decided that he would have to strengthen his political authority by calling for a vote of confidence in the Commons. In advance of the debate, there were intense discussions within the PLP about the stance to adopt towards the Government, with some figures on the left calling for a rebellion. Nye Bevan, now emerging as Churchill's most bitter Commons opponent, pleaded for 'large-scale abstentions', but his proposal was overwhelmingly rejected at a PLP meeting by fifty-three votes to sixteen in favour of a motion to support the Government. One of the strongest voices in favour of the Coalition was that of Attlee's long-time ally Jack Lawson, the former Durham miners' leader, who warned about playing into the hands of the Tory appeasers, who were 'anti-Churchill. They would try to step in at some appropriate time and save Hitler's skin.'[47] With no revolt from Labour, the confidence debate went more smoothly than Churchill had expected, helped by his own powerful opening speech in which he justified Britain's weakness in the Far East by arguing that his Government had been forced to concentrate its resources on the two most vital campaigns: aid to Russia and the fight against Rommel. Attlee provided strong backing for Churchill with his own harshly realistic contribution, in which he condemned 'extravagant optimism' in the face of Germany's 'tremendous military machine'.[48] Conservative minister Harry Crookshank described it as 'his best speech ever'.[49] In the subsequent division, the Government won by 464 votes to 1, the ILP radical James Maxton as the sole dissenter. Chuter Ede described the scene: 'A great shout of triumph rose. Churchill surveyed the scene and the Members stood to cheer him as he walked out. His voice had shown traces of a heavy cold but he looked happy if somewhat pale. I walked down the corridor with Attlee who was naturally pleased with the result.'[50]

Yet this was something of a pyrrhic victory. Despite the overwhelming vote of confidence, Churchill's stock continued its decline as Britain's military fortunes worsened significantly in the first weeks February. The British press and public were bewildered when a Kriegsmarine squadron, comprising the two massive battleships the *Scharnhorst* and the *Gneisenau*, as well as the heavy cruiser *Prinz Eugen*, managed to break through a British blockade at the Reich-occupied port of Brest on the Atlantic, racing up the Channel and eventually reaching the safety of Germany despite repeated attacks by the RAF. A few days later, on 15 February, came the devastating but inevitable news that Singapore had surrendered to Japan. It was perhaps the worst British defeat of the Second World War, made all the more shameful by the fact that the Japanese forces were numerically inferior. This was no gallant last stand, no Dunkirk. Churchill, as he confessed to Violet Bonham Carter, was haunted by the fear that Britain's troops lacked the courageous spirit of previous generations: 'We had so many men in Singapore, so many men, we should have done better.'[51] Soon after the fall of Singapore, Churchill's slide to despondency was witnessed by Captain Richard Pim, who was in charge of the Downing Street Map Room: 'He said he was tired of it and he was very seriously thinking of handing over his responsibilities to other shoulders.'[52] Others close to Churchill saw how depressed he was. Averill Harriman told Roosevelt that 'unfortunately Singapore shook the Prime Minister to such an extent that he has not been able to stand up to the adversity with his old vigour. A number of astute people, both friends and opponents, feel it is only a question of a few months before his Government falls.'[53] Churchill's own wife, Clementine, wrote to her sister: 'These are, as you say, days of anguish for Winston, so full of strength and yet so impotent to stem this terrible tide in the Far East. We pray that the country will show patience and constancy.'[54]

But those two qualities were lacking as the military disasters unfolded. The crisis precipitated a torrent of antipathy against the Government. 'Everyone is in a rage against the Prime Minister,' wrote Chips Channon. 'This is not the post-Dunkirk feeling, but anger. The country is more upset about the escape of the battleships than over Singapore. The capital seethes with indignation.'[55] Having been a member of the Government for almost two years, Lord Woolton complained that the Prime Minister was 'not a good strategist' and had 'lost a little of his vitality under the strain'. Nor did Woolton believe that Churchill's oratory was nearly as important as it had been in 1940: 'The use of words won't win the war and I'm afraid the feet of clay are beginning to be discerned.'[56] The press was also turning against the Prime Minister. 'Have we not been hypnotised by Mr Churchill's personality into acquiescence in an inefficient war direction?' asked the *News Chronicle*. Meanwhile the *Daily Mail* warned ominously that 'no man is indispensable'. Several critics felt that Churchill's problems were exacerbated by the weakness of Cabinet and the strain of serving as Defence Minister as well as premier. 'The man takes too much upon himself – too great a burden and it is absurd he should go on doing so. His War Cabinet as at present constituted is a farce – no one except himself counts,' wrote the Tory backbencher Cuthbert Headlam.[57]

The alternative to Churchill's departure was a reconstruction of his Government, which was exactly the line he took in February 1942. The need to accommodate the wishes of all the main political parties made the reshuffle process difficult enough. But it was further complicated by the ambitions of those two powerful, independent-minded, rebellious personalities Lord Beaverbrook and Stafford Cripps, each of whom saw himself as a potential successor to Churchill. Restlessly oscillating between threats of resignation and demands for promotion, Beaverbrook had long pressed for the creation of a new production supremo, with command over the whole of British industry and manpower. Naturally, he saw himself in this overarching role and his idea was also supported by Churchill, who found Beaverbrook's company a necessary restorative even if this addiction sometimes left him exhausted. But Labour ministers and the trade unions were fiercely opposed, not just because of their suspicions about Beaverbrook but also because of their hostility to any reduction in the powers of Ernie Bevin's department. In fact, one of Labour's key conditions on joining Churchill's Coalition in May 1940 was that Bevin would have control over manpower. Attlee, when consulted by Churchill, made it clear that neither he nor Bevin would tolerate the emasculation of the Ministry of Labour. Bevin also made his feelings clear to Churchill. When the Prime Minister told him that Beaverbrook was 'a magician' in his effect on output, Bevin sourly replied, 'he's a magician all right; the principal job of a magician is to create illusions'.[58] Consequently Churchill had to implement a far less radical scheme, by which the new Minister of Production concentrated on the supply of materials and output while Bevin's empire remained intact. With deep reluctance, Beaverbrook accepted on 4 February, having been told by Churchill that, if he refused, 'you will judged harshly by history'.[59] From the moment of his appointment, however, Beaverbrook was unhappy, his sourness deepening as the military crisis worsened.

Cripps represented an even bigger problem for Churchill. Already acclaimed by the public for his somewhat exaggerated role in building Soviet resistance to German aggression, Cripps returned to Britain from Moscow on 23 January and was given a hero's welcome. In the troubled climate of the time, with Churchill's stock in decline, he was suddenly seen as the potential national saviour, the man whose radicalism and efficiency could win the war. His personal austerity and renowned asceticism, which was in part necessitated by his severe colitis, seemed to embody the spirit of wartime self-sacrifice. 'He lives on a pea and a lentil, with the occasional orgy of a carrot,' said Churchill sarcastically.[60] Cripps's image as a figure of non-partisan integrity was reinforced by his refusal to make any move towards rejoining the Labour Party following his expulsion in 1939. Amid mounting adulation, an air of excitement accompanied his public appearances and pronouncements. When he gave a speech on 7 February at the Hippodrome in Bristol, the city he represented in Parliament, more than 2,500 gathered inside and a further 2,000 outside. The following day, half the nation tuned in to a BBC radio broadcast he gave in which he openly espoused the need for more progressive war aims and social reform. An opinion poll soon afterwards found that 90 per cent of listeners agreed with him.

In response to this surge in popularity, Churchill had to tread a delicate path. On one hand, there was a risk that a top post in Government would enhance Cripps's credentials as the alternative national leader and a rival for the premiership. On the other, Cripps's exclusion at a time of crisis might cause public outrage, weaken the Coalition, and undermine his own authority as Prime Minister. Churchill therefore took a middle course by offering Cripps the position of Minister of Supply without a seat in the Cabinet. Cripps, never one to underestimate his own talents, rejected the offer on the grounds that he would be 'relegated to a secondary position' under Beaverbrook, the new production chief.[61] In reply, Churchill told him that it would be impossible to keep the War Cabinet small if the Minister of Supply were included, because then political heads of all the service departments would have to be members, as would the Minister of Aircraft production. Churchill concluded on a waspish note: 'I shall always be ready to receive your advice, though what I wanted was your active help.'[62] Privately, Churchill thought Cripps had been conceited and had exaggerated his credentials. 'Lots of people want to be in the War Cabinet. You could fill the Albert Hall with people who want to be in the War Cabinet,' he told his old friend Violet Bonham Carter, before adding, 'What has he ever done? What post has he ever held? He wasn't a success in Russia. Stalin didn't care about him.'[63]

But a renewed, more generous offer had to be made much sooner that Churchill anticipated, as military failure cranked up the pressure for political renewal and Beaverbrook made his dissatisfaction ever more apparent. An additional personal factor was the widespread doubt over Arthur Greenwood's capacity for office, given his continuing alcoholism. 'The poor chap couldn't even sign his name after midday,' said Dalton.[64] But Attlee, always respectful of Labour's constitution, was initially adamant that Greenwood should not be pushed out, particularly not to make space for Cripps. According to the diary of Graham Spry, Cripps's aide, Attlee 'said that he would resign if Arthur is dropped and this threat alarmed Winston'.[65] Over a convivial lunch on 8 February, Dalton also warned George Harvie-Watt that Labour would not tolerate any demotion of their leaders.

> We speak of possible reshuffles and he says that there are some who want Attlee, Greenwood, Eden and Wood all out of the War Cabinet. I say that as regards Attlee and Greenwood, this would lead to a riot in the Labour Party and they would no longer support the Government. Attlee and Greenwood, whatever others may think of them, happen to be the Leader and Deputy Leader of the Labour Party, from which Cripps was expelled three years ago.[66]

The political drama of the reconstruction reached its climax after Singapore and the Channel Dash. Both Churchill and Attlee confounded their stereotypes, the former proving a subtle political operator as he played a difficult hand with finesse, the latter displaying both ruthlessness and an instinct for self-preservation. The key to the reshuffle was Churchill's recognition that, in his desperate predicament, he now had no choice but to offer Cripps a major role at the heart of the War Cabinet. The position he suggested, the Leader of the Commons, was one of his own responsibilities; Cripps was only too happy to accept, in view of its prestige and involvement with the whole range of public policy. Eden, one of Churchill's confidants during the reshuffle, was annoyed at this, both because he feared that Cripps wanted 'to groom himself for Prime Minister' and because he coveted the job for himself – a fact about which Churchill was dismissive. 'You are a man of action and not talk. I can't think why you want it,' he told Eden.[67] To make room in the War Cabinet for Cripps, Churchill decided that Greenwood had to go. But this meant the risk of a damaging split with Attlee who not only saw himself as Greenwood's protector but also, like Eden, was unhappy with the idea of Cripps as Leader of the

Commons. As Beaverbrook shrewdly but cynically put it, 'Having excommunicated Cripps in the peace, Attlee is not going to make him assistant Pope in the war.'[68]

There were only one way that Churchill could win Attlee's agreement to both the exit of Greenwood and the elevation of Cripps: he would have to promote the Labour Leader. In an imaginative step, he therefore decided to appoint Attlee the Deputy Prime Minister, a position that had never previously existed in British politics – primarily because such an innovation could be perceived as limiting the Sovereign's choice of Prime Minister. Indeed, Churchill had to reassure both Eden, widely seen as his natural successor, and King George VI on this very point. According to Oliver Harvey's diary, when Churchill saw Eden on 17 February, 'he said that, although he would make Attlee Deputy Prime Minister, this did not mean that Attlee had any claim on the succession as the Prime Minister must be a Tory'. Harvey himself was not enamoured of the step. 'The real lightweight is Attlee himself in the smaller set-up but he must be included as head of the Labour Party.'[69]

Churchill proposed to enhance Attlee's status still further by giving him a major department to run as Dominions Secretary, taking over from Viscount Cranborne. With the conflict becoming more global, the Dominions Office was important for Britain's war effort, especially in liaising with the Governments of Australia, Canada and New Zealand. Mollified by this dual preferment, Attlee now accepted Greenwood's sacking and the rise of Cripps, who also became Lord Privy Seal as well as Commons Leader. But Lord Beaverbrook was appalled at the idea of Attlee as Deputy Prime Minister, adding the planned appointment to his catalogue of grievances against the Government. For almost two years, discord had been smouldering between the two men, fuelled by their mutual antipathy and Beaverbrook's fondness for intrigue. They also continued to disagree strongly over Russian policy, with Attlee remaining adamant that the Allies should not acquiesce in Stalin's demand for recognition of the Soviet Union's 1941 frontiers.

Now the reshuffle brought the friction to a new level as it culminated in an extraordinary personal confrontation in the fortified annexe of

10 Downing Street. During 18 February, Eden had talked to Attlee, who had 'been vehement in his denunciation of Max* and would not allow him any value in any post'.[70] That evening, Beaverbrook turned up for yet more discussions with Churchill about the reshuffle. The press baron was in an acrimonious mood, expressing his desire for retirement and his preference for Eden as Commons Leader. Then, with even greater bitterness, he poured his scorn on the Labour Leader. 'Attlee should not be Deputy Prime Minister. His abilities do not warrant that position. His contribution towards fighting the war has been nothing, save only as a leader of a party who is always seeking honours and place for his followers. There is no reason for him to hold high place. We want tougher fellows at a time like this, fighting men.' Churchill listened to all this without interruption, then stood up and ushered Beaverbrook into the main Cabinet room, where Attlee was sitting in conversation with Eden, Brendan Bracken and Chief Whip James Stuart. Churchill asked Beaverbrook if he would repeat to the group what he had said privately next door. Unabashed and still angry, Beaverbrook delivered a diatribe to Attlee's face, this time adding that the Labour Leader's recent poor speeches 'provided an additional reason why he should not be Deputy Prime Minister'. In response, Attlee asked him: 'What have I done to you that you treat me in this way?' Beaverbrook replied: 'Why should I not talk frankly? You criticise me and I make no objection.' Without complete truthfulness, Attlee said, 'I never did.' Beaverbrook then pointed to Attlee's attacks on him and Bracken over Dalton's performance as Minister of Economic Warfare.[71] It was now almost midnight and the highly charged meeting was about to break up. But before he left, Beaverbrook told Churchill that he would resign from the Government because of his objection to Attlee as Deputy Prime Minister and Cripps as Commons Leader, as well as the limitations on his powers as Minister of Production.

This time Churchill did not try to stop him leaving. 'The long and harassing discussion which took place in my presence between him

---

* Max Aitken, 1st Baron Beaverbrook.

and other principal Ministers convinced me that it was better not to press him further,' wrote Churchill in his war memoirs. [72] Part of this willingness to let Beaverbrook go was sheer exhaustion. As Churchill told him: 'My patience is at an end. I have lavished my time and strength during the last week to make arrangements which are satisfactory to you and the public interest.' The influence of Clementine, who disliked Beaverbrook on moral grounds, was also important. She admitted to her husband that Beaverbrook outside the Government might be hostile, but asked: 'Is not hostility without better than intrigue and treachery and rattledom within? Exorcise this bottle imp and see if the air is not clear and purer.' [73] But by far the most crucial factor was Attlee. In its final stage, the battle over the reshuffle came down to a choice between Attlee and Beaverbrook. Churchill sided with the socialist Leader against one of his oldest political allies simply because he could not afford Attlee's resignation, whereas Beaverbrook's would have had little political fall-out. Had Attlee gone, almost all the other Labour ministers would have followed, breaking up the Coalition and probably bringing an end to his premiership. That reality in itself was a tribute to the respect and loyalty that Attlee commanded in his own party, as Beaverbrook himself recognised. 'Attlee's resignation when in the wrong would have been more important than mine when in the right. For Attlee has a party, I have none. Attlee has political friends, I have none.' [74] But the political rumour mill held that Beaverbrook had not departed happily. 'I was told that Beaverbrook had slept in an "official dormitory" in Westminster that night and had spent the entire time groaning,' recorded Lord Woolton. [75]

Just as in 1935, when he had won the Labour leadership against apparently stronger opponents, Attlee had defied his critics by emerging triumphant from the reshuffle. In a private note written at the time, Beaverbrook described Attlee as 'a miserable little man who can't even control his own party' and whose appointment as Deputy Prime Minister was 'damaging to the administration'. [76] Yet Beaverbrook had been outmanoeuvred by this politician he professed to despise. The vacancy that Beaverbrook left as Minister of Production was filled by

Oliver Lyttelton, while Kingsley Wood was removed from the Cabinet, though he remained Chancellor. Another old guard Tory, David Margesson, was sacked as War Minister and, in a highly unorthodox procedure, replaced by his own Permanent Secretary at the War Office Sir James Grigg, who was subsequently elected for Cardiff East standing on a National ticket. Such was the controversy over Grigg's appointment, which to some smacked of Churchillian favouritism, that Attlee had to write to local Welsh Labour MPs, reminding them that 'it is the duty of our members to support the Government candidate' in the Cardiff by-election and urging them 'to speak on his behalf'.[77] But, during the wider reconstruction of the Government beyond the War Cabinet, Attlee also put up another fight on behalf of the Welsh Labour MP Dai Grenfell, the Minister for Mines, whom Churchill wanted to sack. 'Attlee says that he has put his foot down against the PM's wish,' recorded Dalton. 'He told the PM that he couldn't stand a second row about firing a Labour Minister just now after Greenwood.'[78] The departure of Greenwood, who was 'very bitter' about the way he had been treated,[79] meant that the Government needed a new minister for post-war reconstruction, a subject that Attlee told Churchill made 'a very definite contribution to the maintenance of the morale of the people, both service and civilian'.[80] At Attlee's suggestion, Churchill, who still cared little about the issue, appointed the Labour MP and former Solicitor General William Jowitt, 'a man with a very good brain and of judicial temper', as Attlee described him to Churchill.[81]

Like Churchill, Attlee was drained by the process of the reshuffle, with all its clashing personalities and party demands. 'I had a pretty damnable week fixing up changes in the Government. These questions are the very devil owing to inevitable conflicts of loyalty,' he wrote to his brother Tom.[82] Those conflicts were on display at a meeting of the PLP on 25 February, at which there complaints that Churchill 'had undermined the party by throwing out people without consultation'. In tones of weary defensiveness, Attlee explained that 'he had done his best. He would willingly give his job to anyone else. Agreeing to the dropping of Greenwood had been a sad necessity. We could not have a continuing political crisis at home while stupendous military dangers faced us throughout the world.'[83] Intriguingly, according to Woolton's diary, Churchill used similar tired language when he set out the first tranche of changes to his fellow ministers: 'Winston wasn't very cheerful and made a purely emotional speech. He said that he didn't want to be Minister of Defence; it was a rotten job and anybody could have it. It isn't true, of course. If there is one thing that Winston is at present determined not to give up it is the Defence Ministry.'[84]

The overall reception for the reshuffle was mixed. There was widespread approval of the reduction in the size of the War Cabinet from nine to seven members, while few were disappointed at Beaverbrook's departure. 'It is still not quite right but may do and anyhow gets rid of Beaverbrook, public danger number one,' wrote Treasury Minister Harry Crookshank in a balanced assessment.[85] But complaints came from Labour and Tory partisans who felt that their leaders had failed to uphold their own party interests. On the left, Harold Laski was fiercely critical of Attlee, openly calling him a failure and claiming that he had allowed the Coalition to be fatally compromised. At a meeting of the Society of Labour candidates in March, Laski went so far as to declare that 'the net result of Mr Attlee's leadership is to keep Labour united with its historic enemy. It is a betrayal of democracy.'[86] Some in the Tory Party were equally disgruntled. Rab Butler felt that, after the reshuffle, 'there was no orthodox Conservative in the War Cabinet: Winston was not orthodox; Eden was not liked; Anderson had never called himself a Tory; Lyttelton nobody knew and was regarded as a City shark.' Butler found it 'staggering' that 'a revolt of the right had brought about a War Cabinet more to the left'.[87]

Beyond narrow party irritation, there was a bigger problem. The primary aim of the reshuffle had been to restore the authority of Churchill and his Government, but it had largely failed in that goal. The sense of crisis remained. Concerns about the direction of the war were still profound. In their new posts, ministers immediately came under attack. 'The changes are not much good, and the general impression is one of confusion,' wrote Victor Cazalet.[88] In his Cassandra column in the *Daily Mirror* William Connor argued that the reconstructed Government was wholly inadequate for the challenge that Britain faced in trying to win the war. 'Mr Attlee, whose mediocrity shines like a piece of putty, long ago promised to conscript wealth. He has not done so. He could not do so anyway because he has not the depth of power and fanaticism to throw this country on to a real war footing. The people would follow Churchill if he led the way. But Churchill is pre-eminently a military leader.'[89] In the days after the reshuffle, there was little appreciation in Churchill's own political stock. In fact, just the opposite was true as gossip spread about his decline. 'We are all convinced that the Prime Minister cannot last much longer and the present is only a temporary arrangement which can at most go on for two or three months,' recorded Oliver Harvey on 27 February.[90] This chimed in with the experience of Ernie Bevin, who told Dalton on 5 March that he 'felt the present set-up could not last very long and that the PM in Cabinet now seemed to alternate between being "a beaten man", sitting collapsed in his chair and plaintively saying, "I suppose this is another of the concessions I must make for the sake of national unity", and a violently aggressive, resentful man. There was no doubt that he felt the loss of Beaverbrook badly.'[91]

As Churchill had feared, the reshuffle only accelerated talk of Cripps's succession. One of Chuter Ede's civil servants told him of a rumour in the City that 'Churchill would soon be replaced by Cripps on the demand of America and Russia', a tale that was even printed in the Labour-supporting *Daily Herald*. Now firmly in the anti-Churchill camp, Cecil King recorded on 5 March with relish that 'Winston has now no authority in his own party. The Tories are wondering what office he should hold in the Cripps Government.'[92] If he were to restore his fortunes, Churchill needed not more political initiatives but a military victory. Yet, in early 1942, the horizon showed precious little sign of one.

EIGHTEEN

RUSSIA AND EGYPT

I N EARLY 1942 the question of Indian self-rule had become another major problem for Churchill's Government. The flames of nationalism, fuelled by growing civil disobedience from followers of Gandhi, were burning ever more brightly. In addition, the growing threat of Japan in the East made it vital for the British Government to maintain order within the Indian Empire, a goal which some politicians felt could be achieved by pacifying the continent through a new promise of self-rule. Churchill, still clinging to his diehard views from the 1930s, was deeply reluctant to take any such step. He believed that toughness, not compromise, was the answer 'at a moment when the enemy is at the frontier'. Nor did he think that a new political initiative would help the defence of India militarily, as he told Attlee. 'The Indian troops are fighting splendidly but it must be remembered that their allegiance is to the King Emperor and that the rule of the Congress and the Hindoo Priesthood machine would never be tolerated by a fighting race.'[1] But Attlee, who was widely regarded as Labour's expert on India, strongly disagreed with Churchill and found him 'obstinate and ignorant' on the question.[2] Feeling that a new approach was needed, Attlee persuaded the Prime Minister to set up a Cabinet India Committee, under his own chairmanship, with a view to developing a draft plan for post-war self-government. At this stage, Attlee was no crusader for independence. He still believed that India should remain within the Empire and feared domination by 'a brown oligarchy'.[3] One Labour whip, the Anglo-Irish peer Lord Listowel, was surprised at Attlee's conservatism, which he felt bore traces of Churchill's. 'My youthful illusions were soon shattered when I found the representatives of the Labour Party on the India Committee were no more radical than their Conservative colleagues and that Attlee as Chairman was a muted echo of his master's voice.'[4]

Yet, for all his caution, Attlee came up with a two-pronged plan to conciliate India. First, his committee put forward a liberal scheme for a new post-war constitution, on the basis of dominion status and governance through an elected constituent assembly. Second, he urged that a 'figure of high standing' should be asked to go to India to negotiate a settlement.[5] The obvious politician for this task was Stafford Cripps, given his stature and his long friendship with the Congress leader Jawaharlal Nehru. Again Churchill, weakened by political crisis, felt he had no alternative but to sanction the Cripps mission, though privately he opposed its purpose since he feared it would strengthen the nationalist cause. As he wrote to the Canadian Prime Minister Mackenzie King, 'we have resigned ourselves to fighting our utmost to defend India in order, if successful, to be turned out'.[6] Cripps was keen to accept the role, not only because he genuinely believed in Indian self-rule but also because success would enhance his prestige and advance his claims on the premiership. 'If he brought this Indian settlement off, he would certainly replace Winston,' wrote one of his aides.[7] It was an indicator of Cripps's high political stock that when Churchill announced the mission in the Commons on 11 March there was, according to Harold Nicolson, 'a slight anti-climax' as the Prime Minister said that 'my Right Honourable friend the Lord Privy Seal has agreed to undertake the task'. In the Chamber, 'eyes turned to Attlee, but the mood of the House turned to delight as the word went round, "he means Cripps".'[8]

The mission turned out to be a failure, much to Cripps's frustration. Even though in his negotiations he went considerably further along the road to independence than Attlee's committee had envisaged, he was unable to secure the agreement of Gandhi or the Congress leaders, who wanted an immediate transfer of power, not a promise of one after the war. The offer of post-war dominion status was famously described by Gandhi as 'a post-dated cheque drawn on a crashing bank'.[9] Attlee, who had been 'greatly surprised' by Churchill's willingness to approve the venture, blamed the Indian leaders for their intransigence.[10] Privately, Churchill felt relief that Cripps had been damaged and the Indian Empire maintained. The Government could now resort to the more repressive, anti-nationalist policy that he had always wanted to adopt, particularly once Gandhi stepped up his protests with his Quit India movement.

In another part of the British Empire, a delicate personal problem arose through the frustrations of the Duke of Windsor, then in exile as the Governor of the Bahamas. By the spring 1942, the Duke had spent almost two years in the role and now wanted a more demanding position. 'I cannot contemplate remaining in the Bahamas as Governor for the duration of the war,' he told Churchill on 18 April. What he sought was some form of 'colonial administration' where 'my services could be more usefully employed in a wider sphere'.[11] Churchill considered that the Governorship of Southern Rhodesia might be a suitable post, but Attlee took a very different view. He feared not only that such an appointment might inflame republican opposition in neighbouring South Africa but also that the Duke's dubious record made him unsuitable. 'The Governor of Southern Rhodesia, unlike the governors-general in other Dominions, is specifically charged with responsibility to the Secretary of State for the welfare of the native population. This duty requires close attention and judgement. Would this be forthcoming?' asked Attlee.[12] It was an opinion reinforced by Smuts, the South African elder statesman, who warned Churchill that the Duke could be an embarrassment in the governorship. 'This is decisive,' noted Churchill.[13] The Duke remained in the Bahamas for the rest of the war.

None of this, however, immediately helped the fight in Europe or North Africa. The latter was a theatre where Auchinleck's apparent lack of aggressive leadership, despite regular reinforcements, was causing Churchill increasing concern. Still deeply perturbed by the Singapore debacle, Churchill wanted the British 8th Army in the desert to go on the attack, but Auchinleck was reluctant to do so, pleading insufficient training and equipment. His stance prompted a furious outburst from Churchill on 1 March. 'Armies are expected to fight, not stand about month after month waiting for a certainty which never occurs.' Having warned Auchinleck that further delays were weakening the Allies' position in the Mediterranean, he argued that Auchinleck's complaints about supplies were unjustified. 'You must outnumber the enemy in Africa by two to one. You have an enormous mass of artillery. You have for the present command of the Air.' Churchill concluded with a stark warning. 'No one is going to stand your remaining in deep peace while Malta is being starved out, while the Russians are fighting like mad and while we are suffering continued disasters in Burma and India at the hands of the Japanese. The whole system of command will have to be revolutionised.'[14]

Until this moment, Attlee had rarely intervened in military strategy; but with his new status as Deputy Prime Minister he felt emboldened to comment to Churchill, even daring to question the entire desert strategy. The picture drawn by Auchinleck, he told him, was 'one of indefinite stalemate at the best. Every increase of our forces seems likely to be met by a similar increase by the enemy.' Given Britain's 'limited forces' and 'commitments elsewhere', Attlee asked, 'can we afford to keep so large a concentration for the defence of Egypt's left-flank? If we cannot during our most critical period mount an affective attack, ought we not to consider what are the minimum forces required for defence in Libya and use the rest elsewhere?'[15] But Churchill had no time for such doubts. North Africa was central to his military thinking in 1942. It was the key to control of the Mediterranean, the Middle East and the vital British territories of Malta and Gibraltar. It was the only place that Britain was actually fighting the Reich, and victory there had the potential to pave the way for an Allied assault on Southern Europe. He therefore continued to insist that Auchinleck should go on the offensive.

The stalemate in North Africa was accompanied by the start of agitation within Britain, led by Beaverbrook and the political left, for the Allies to open up a second front in Western Europe and relieve the savage pressure on Russia. In March no fewer than 40,000 people gathered at Trafalgar Square for a demonstration in favour of a second front. 'There is an extraordinary and misguided enthusiasm for the Russians. Stalin is more of a hero than the King or even Winston,' wrote Sir John Kennedy, the Director of Military Operations.[16] Given the weakness of the British Army at home, the calls for a second front were militarily fanciful in early 1942; but politically they served as a stick with which to beat Churchill's Government. In April the Conservatives, despite Attlee's support, narrowly lost the Rugby by-election to the independent candidate William Brown, whose campaign espoused a second front. Yet there was an alternative to a doomed ground invasion across the Channel. At the time of the tortuous Cabinet reshuffle in February, the Government had made a vital change at the top of the RAF when the aggressive Rhodesian Sir Arthur Harris was appointed the head of Bomber Command. An uncompromising believer in the wholesale bombing of German cities, Harris felt that the Reich could be put on the defensive in its own territory. Churchill shared this vision, unencumbered by qualms over the loss of civilian life.

But Attlee, again showing his new willingness to intervene on military strategy, had his doubts about this approach – not on moral grounds but because of concerns about the diversion of resources from other theatres, especially North Africa and India. On 16 April he wrote to Churchill:

> I think that our air policy should be reviewed. There was great justification of intensive bombing of Germany when this was our only means of counter action against Germany for the relief of Russia. A certain amount of bombing is still desirable. In view of our latest decisions do we still hold that the intensive bombing of German is the road to victory? If not, should we not, in view of the paramount necessity of holding our positions in the Near East and India during the period which must elapse before a big offensive, reconsider the allocation of our air effort?[17]

In response, Churchill was dismissive of Attlee's argument:

> These views are certainly fashionable at the moment. Everybody would like to send Bomber Command to India and the Middle East. However it is not possible to make any decisive change [...] It is no use flying out squadrons which sit helpless and useless when they arrive. We have built up a great plant here for bombing Germany which is the only way in our power of helping Russia. From every side people want to break it up. One has to be sure that we do not ruin our punch here without getting any proportionate advantage elsewhere.[18]

The strategy was set. The RAF dramatically stepped up the aerial assault on Germany, beginning with a huge 1,000-bomber raid on Cologne at the end of May.

Concerns over military strategy were mirrored by friction over domestic politics in the spring of 1942. The Labour left wanted Attlee and his leading ministers to push for a much more explicitly socialist programme in government, headed by steps towards greater nationalisation and welfare support. As usual Harold Laski, one of Attlee's fiercest critics, was at the forefront of such moves. In a memorandum to the NEC, he argued that 'the immense support that the Labour movement has brought to Mr Churchill has not resulted in any measures for the future of the workers. Mr Churchill has conceded very little that he would not have been compelled to concede had we remained in opposition.' Laski concluded: 'I do not think we are entitled to go on with Mr Churchill.' Attlee was angered by this diatribe and took on Laski directly at a meeting of the NEC on 9 April. Having accused Laski of 'political naivety', he pointed out that the Tories vastly outnumbered Labour in Parliament so outright socialism was 'unfeasible'. If Labour broke up the Coalition, the party would both undermine the war effort and face an 'electoral rout'. It would be held, he said, 'that the party had slipped out of responsibility when things looked black'. After this unaccustomedly powerful speech, the NEC backed Attlee, agreeing that any step to leave Churchill's Government would be 'disastrous'.[19]

He then used that greater authority to cement Labour even further into the Coalition by demanding that the party give full and automatic support to the official Government candidate in every forthcoming by-election. His proposal followed a string of recent defeats for the Government, including that in Rugby, where large numbers of Labour activists had campaigned for the independent. But the NEC did not agree and refused to vote for Attlee's plan at its meeting on 22 May. The Deputy Prime Minister was not done. He brought the issue to Labour's Conference a few days later, arguing that it was an essential part of the electoral truce with the Conservatives. There was widespread opposition from left-wing politicians and the press. Welsh firebrand Nye Bevan told delegates that Attlee's policy was 'leading Labour to the political graveyard' and would eventually result in 'the complete fusion of the Labour and Conservative parties'. Herbert Morrison presented the case for the continuation of the truce and his intervention proved decisive, as the Conference voted by a margin of just 60,000 votes, out of a total of 2.5 million, in favour of Attlee's position. In private, Morrison expressed pride in his own performance and criticism of Attlee. 'Really, it was Attlee's job, not mine, but they put it to me. When there is a really nasty job like this, I have to do it,' he said, adding that Labour's divisions were caused by 'too much soft leadership in the past'.[20] A wider motion, effectively demanding an end to the Coalition, was overwhelmingly thrown out at the Conference, by 2.3 million votes to just 164, after Attlee delivered a lecture on the realities of wartime politics. 'There may be some who think we have turned the corner in this war and can afford to return to party strife and direct our minds from the objective of winning the war. They make a great mistake.'[21] But the verdict of the *People* newspaper was that 'Attlee did not shine at the Conference. Morrison did. Right or wrong, he is a brave man.' It was a view backed up by Churchill, who personally congratulated Morrison on 'the spirited manner in which you faced our critics at the Labour Conference and recalled the main body of the party to its duty.'[22]

Beyond the Labour Party, Attlee also demonstrated his loyalty to Churchill and the Coalition. In the Commons on 19 May, during a fractious debate about the war situation, he defended the Prime Minister against charges of autocracy and bullying. 'When matters come before the War Cabinet, it is not a body of people which sit around and listen to one man. It is a disservice to the Prime Minister to suggest he is a dictator.' Attlee further denied that the military chiefs were marginalised. 'The Chiefs of Staff give their opinions very freely. This attempt to suggest that all the time there is some frightful contest going on between the Government – the Prime Minister in particular – and his military advisers – is simply not true.' His concluding words showed the depths of his admiration for Churchill: 'We have in the Prime Minister a leader in war such as this country has rarely had in her long history.'[23] Attlee's sentiments about Churchill were genuine. The problem was, as it had so often been before, his lack of charisma and force. As Harvie-Watt wrote to Churchill: 'Members lost interest very quickly and by the time he ended there were comparatively few left in the chamber.'[24] Even more critical was the National Labour MP Harold Nicolson, who wrote that 'the only interesting thing about it was the fact that the Deputy Prime Minister, at such a crisis in our history, *could* make such a dull speech. But Attlee succeeded where lesser men would have failed.'[25]

Despite Attlee's words in the chamber, there were deep strains within the Coalition over domestic policy, most graphically symbolised in a major row over the future of the coal industry. Hugh Dalton, who had been made Trade Minister in the February reshuffle, came up with a scheme for coal rationing to limit demand, but Churchill, most Conservatives and the colliery owners were strongly opposed because they saw the scheme – with some justification – as a precursor to nationalisation. The battle dragged on for weeks, leaving Dalton increasingly disillusioned with Churchill. 'I never thought so ill of the Prime Minister nor been so vexed by him before. He talks more than half the time and has clearly not concentrated his mind on the details of the subject at all,' wrote Dalton after one meeting in which Churchill had argued that an appeal to economy would be better than coal rationing.[26] Dalton recorded that Attlee and Cripps were both 'very furious at the manner of the meeting'. As the controversy unfolded, Cripps became bullish about the need for nationalisation. 'It is essential to requisition the pits,' he told Dalton, even maintaining that it was an issue on which he was prepared to resign.[27] Dalton found Attlee less forthright and engaged. 'He gives me the impression of being rolled up very tight in a frightened little ball. He was rather afraid of his followers over coal.'[28] Eventually, a compromise was achieved through negotiations held by the Lord President Sir John Anderson, whereby Dalton's rationing scheme was dropped in return for dual control of the industry, with the state running operations and the owners in charge of finance – both under the overall control of a new Ministry of Fuel and Power.

Churchill was, according to Dalton, in a 'very expansive and agreeable mood' once the compromise was agreed, but disputes like this did nothing to improve his political stock. As he told Malcolm MacDonald, the British High Commissioner to Canada, he had no illusions about the decline in his popularity. 'I am like a bomber pilot. I go out night after night, and I know that one night I shall not return.'[29] His standing fell even further when, just as he had feared, Auchinleck presided over a disastrous setback in North Africa as the vital port of Tobruk, long under siege, fell into hands of Rommel's forces on 21 June. Over 30,000 British and Commonwealth troops were captured. Churchill received the news while he was on another visit to see Roosevelt at the White House, accompanied once more by his doctor Lord Moran. 'I am ashamed. I cannot understand why Tobruk gave in. More than 30,000 of our men put their hands up,' he told the doctor.[30] Instead of chastising Churchill for another military failure, Roosevelt was profoundly sympathetic and offered American logistical support in North Africa, particularly aircraft and tanks. As it turned out, the fall of Tobruk worked to Churchill's long-term military advantage, in that it convinced the Americans to co-operate with his North African strategy instead of concentrating on a premature invasion of northwest Europe.

In the immediate term, however, the defeat plunged Churchill's premiership into another draining crisis. The night of the catastrophe, as Eden related to Oliver Harvey, the Defence Committee met under Attlee's chairmanship and 'sat until 2 am, not very usefully. Attlee had asked all the War Cabinet to attend and much time was taken up by Bevin declaiming: "We must have a victory. What the British public wants is a victory!" As if all didn't want one.' The only concrete decision was the diversion to Suez of 120 tanks and 24 Hurricane fighters that had been intended for India. After the meeting, Eden spoke to Churchill in Washington and told him he ought to come back. 'The Prime Minister appeared peevish and reluctant and implied he was doing most important things there.'[31] But Churchill recognised that he had to return to face the political storm, which was made all the greater by the Government's loss of the Maldon by-election just four days after the fall of Tobruk. The victor, with more than 60 per cent of the vote, was the flamboyant journalist and radical left-winger Tom Driberg, whose erratic hidden life encompassed promiscuous homosexuality and espionage for the Soviet Union. 'This is Tobruk,' commented Churchill after learning of the defeat.[32] At Westminster, there was a growing sense in some quarters that Churchill's premiership and the Government might be doomed. 'There is a great deal of feeling about Winston and the muddle, interference and confusion at the top appears as bad as ever,' wrote the disgruntled Victor Cazalet.[33] The former War Secretary Leslie Hore-Belisha, previously an admirer of Churchill, declared that 'when your doctor is killing you, the first thing to do is get rid of him'.[34]

But Churchill's position was not as weak as his eager critics suggested. His approval ratings with the public were still just below 80 per cent. Furthermore the senior Labour ministers, having defeated the anti-Coalition forces at their Annual Conference, now threw their weight behind Churchill. Central to the Prime Minister's defence was Attlee. There was mounting pressure, led by Bevan, in the PLP for a motion to be put in the Commons calling for a full inquiry into the North Africa failure. But Attlee angrily rejected the proposal when it was put to the PLP, as Chuter Ede recorded: 'He spoke very strongly in the most forceful speech I have ever heard him make. He repudiated the idea that the Prime Minister could be separated from the Government. He and the War Cabinet took the major decisions and were collectively responsible.'[35] Attlee was particularly annoyed by Bevan, who was not only whipping up hostility to Churchill but also spreading scandalous gossip about him. Bevan alleged that the great filmmaker Alexander Korda had been promised a knighthood in return for the £2,000 fee that Churchill received for acting as a historical adviser on the movies *Lady Hamilton* and *Young Mr Pitt*. When he learned of this behaviour, Attlee said that 'Bevan was like a pet poodle gobbling filth in West End drawing rooms and then vomiting.'[36]

The fightback against the Coalition critics intensified when the right-wing Conservative backbencher Sir John Wardlaw-Milne put down a motion of confidence in the Government. There was soon speculation that this could be the Norway Debate all over again, with a vulnerable Prime Minister brought down by MPs on a confidence vote after a military disaster. The Tory MP Jim Thomas, in conversation with Oliver Harvey, expressed his fear that 'if the vote fell as much as Narvik, Winston would have to go. Jim didn't think, nor did I, that the King could send for anyone else but Eden. Attlee was out of the question.'[37] But Attlee himself shrewdly recognised that Wardlaw-Milne's censure motion, far from heralding Churchill's demise, could actually shore up the Government if it was taken on and crushed. For Churchill was no Chamberlain; nor was there any realistic alternative to his leadership. That was why Attlee insisted that the motion be put to the House after Wardlaw-Milne, seeing the turmoil he created, had suggested that it be withdrawn.

A tremendous air of expectancy descended on the Commons as the confidence debate began on 1 July. The chamber had not been so crowded since May 1940. Churchill was nervous as he took his place on the front bench beside Attlee. 'I have never seen him so troubled and anxious as he was then. People were talking quite freely about the fall of the Government,' recalled Bob Boothby.[38] Yet Attlee's instincts about the need to expose the Opposition to the full glare of parliamentary scrutiny soon proved correct. Opening the censure debate, Wardlaw-Milne quickly brought an air of farce to the proceedings with his demand that the Duke of Gloucester, a minor royal, be made Commander-in-Chief. At this 'fantastic suggestion', recalled Driberg, 'there was a roar of laughter and a howl of disappointment from some quarters. From then on, the debate never recovered its momentum.'[39] The relief felt by Churchill at this moment was almost tangible, as Chips Channon noted: 'I at once saw Winston's face light up, as if a lamp had been lit within him and he smiled genially. He knew he was now saved.'[40] The next day Bevan tried to stage a recovery for the anti-Coalition forces with a slashing personal attack on Churchill, whom he accused of losing 'battle after battle. The country is beginning to say that he fights debates like a war and the war like a debate.'[41] Churchill, assured of easily winning the vote, delivered a powerful response, admitting to the military problems but pointing to the Allies' advantages. 'The duty of the House of Commons is to sustain the Government – or change the Government. If it cannot change it, it should sustain it,' he said.[42] Eden thought this was 'one of his most effective speeches, beautifully judged to the temper of the House'.[43] In the subsequent division, the Government won by 425 to 25, with 119 Labour MPs, the vast majority of the PLP, backing the Coalition.

The immediate political danger had passed, yet Churchill knew that ultimately the Government's survival depended on military success. Retreat on the battlefield in North Africa and absence of a second front meant that the attacks continued. Typical was grumbling from the former minister Maurice Hankey, sacked from the Government in the February reshuffle, who could regularly be found in the Dorchester Hotel condemning Churchill's leadership. 'If you keep him, we shall not win the war, we shall lose it,' brooded Hankey.[44] The discontent inevitably fuelled the machinations of rivals for the crown. Soon after the confidence vote, Cripps complained of 'his dissatisfaction with Churchill', citing Attlee's promotion to the position of Deputy Prime Minister as an example of the Prime Minister's poor leadership. Cripps also poured out his criticisms to fellow minister Malcolm MacDonald, declaring that Churchill had become 'a liability instead of an asset and someone should replace him'. Macdonald, in his account of their conversation, wrote that 'what astonished me most of all was the name of the man whom he thought should succeed Winston – none other than Cripps himself'.[45] Another senior Government member who indulged in thoughts of Downing Street was Lord Woolton: 'The Conservative Party is becoming uneasy about the value and strength of Winston as PM,' he wrote in his diary, adding grandly that 'the party wouldn't mind having me if I would take it on'.[46]

On a personal level, part of the problem for Churchill in these months was that he missed the companionship of Beaverbrook, his mercurial ally. 'Winston took him as a kind of stimulant or drug,' Attlee once said.[47] The reticent Labour Leader was no substitute and there were signs that Churchill found his company awkward. In mid-July, Oliver Harvey recorded happily that Churchill was now turning more regularly to Eden for advice. 'I say how excellent this is. It enables him to guide the old gentleman a good deal. He hates bringing Attlee and all into his inmost counsels.'[48] In the same week, Sylvester gleefully told Lloyd George that Churchill 'is undoubtedly a very lonely man […] When the Beaver left, Winston felt a frightful gap. It is known that he thinks nothing of his senior colleagues such as Attlee and Cripps and in any case one cannot imagine his talking to them in the same way as he would talk to the Beaver.'[49] Churchill's dejection over the absence of Beaverbrook led to rumours, just months after the reshuffle, that he wanted to bring the press baron back into the Cabinet. Bevin and Cripps both threatened to resign if that happened, while Attlee spoke out 'in the strongest possible terms' against such an appointment.[50] Churchill was forced to reassure the Labour ministers that he had no intention of making any such recall.

Attlee may not have been the ideal companion for Churchill but he was an increasingly valuable and thoughtful colleague. On 12 July his unquestioning loyalty was again demonstrated when in a speech at Tunbridge Wells he said, 'whatever he has done, right or wrong, his colleagues stand by the Prime Minister' – though this was misreported in the *Daily Express* as 'nobody can buy the Prime Minister', an error for which Attlee demanded a correction.[51] Two days previously, on 10 July, there had been further sign of his self-assurance when he sent the Prime Minister a lengthy paper about Britain's military strategy. Pointing to the effectiveness of the German armed forces, which combined aerial support with hitting power, mobility on land and 'enterprising leadership', Attlee argued that the key unit of the British Army, the division, was 'cumbrous to a degree' and 'provided with an immense litter of ancillary services which almost swallow up the fighting men'. He also turned again to the theory that the war could ultimately be won by the RAF's heavy bombers.

> If this is right we should not have devoted our resources to building up land forces beyond the minimum needed to hold this island as a jumping off place for bombing Germany. We ought to have put all our energy into aircraft production. If it is wrong, if the bomber is not going to win the war on its own, if navies and armies are necessary, all evidence goes to show that they must be provided with air forces and that these air forces must be integral parts of the Army and Navy.

Attlee reaffirmed that he believed 'in the bombing of Germany but as a method of winning the war it must be viewed as only part of the necessary action'.[52]

Churchill, though somewhat irritated at 'the great many questions' and 'commonplace' criticisms in Attlee's paper, did his Deputy the courtesy of providing a full, eight-page reply. He denied that the RAF's support in the Libyan campaign had been any less effective than the Luftwaffe's, but explained that the overall shortage of air-transport machines was because aircraft production had rightly been concentrated on fighters and bombers. 'We only had just enough fighters to come through the Battle of Britain and we have too few bombers now to do justice to the targets presented in Germany.' He disputed Attlee's arguments about the divisional structure, though he agreed on the need to reduce the excess of logistical support. 'As you know I have persistently worked to comb the tail in order to sharpen the teeth.' The RAF, however, could not be used as a form of tactical support for the army and navy.

> The real test must be the maximum air action against the enemy, which certainly could not be achieved by keeping large masses of the Air Force idle. Continuous reflection leaves me with the conclusion that, upon the whole, our best chance of winning the war is with the big bombers. It will certainly be several years before British and American land forces will be capable of beating the Germans on even terms in the open field.

The end of strategic bombing, if the RAF were turned into 'a mere handmaid of the Army', would be 'a great relief to the enemy', he wrote.[53]

The change that Churchill now contemplated was one in the North African command, where his exasperation with Auchinleck had reached new heights. Churchill had now decided on the drastic step of flying out to Cairo himself to assess the problems and the morale of the desert force. Eden was against the idea, telling Churchill that he would 'not be able to help and would be in the way'. To this Churchill replied, 'You mean like a great blue bottle buzzing over a cow pat.' Eden said this was exactly what he meant.[54] But Churchill was not dissuaded. At the end of July, Auchinleck had sent a telegram stating that 'in present circum-stances, renewal of our efforts to break enemy front or turn his southern flank is not feasible'.[55] Churchill told the Cabinet on 1 August that this 'very depressing' message 'made him all the more convinced that it was necessary that the position should be considered on the spot. He hoped that, as a result of his visit, he might be able to make arrangements which would result in a more vigorous handling of matters.'[56] Change at the top was all the more imperative because a high-powered American military delegation to London, led by General George Marshall, had just agreed that the immediate focus of US military resources should be – not on the Pacific or Northern Europe but on landings in French North Africa at the end of the year, to be known as Operation Torch. But the success of Torch, like Churchill's own future, depended on a British victory over Rommel.

Churchill's trip was approved by Attlee and the rest of the War Cabinet. Its scope had widened to encompass not just Cairo, but also Moscow, after Stalin agreed to meet Churchill to discuss Allied-Soviet co-operation. Just as his first journey across the Atlantic in 1941 had established a new level of trust by Churchill in Attlee, so a year later this vital odyssey deepened their official relationship. Attlee was both in temporary charge of the Government and served as the chief conduit for Churchill's liaison with the Cabinet and the Chiefs of Staff. The visit, made in a converted, black-painted spartan B-24 Liberator because a flying boat was considered too dangerous, took place amid utmost secrecy and high security. Churchill travelled under the name 'Colonel Warden' and, at one stage, even considered donning a false beard, though that outlandish scheme was quietly dropped. He arrived with Alan Brooke and his doctor Charles Wilson* on 4 August in Cairo, where he was met by Smuts, one his most trusted advisers. Churchill quickly recognised that the Desert Army was badly demor-alised and in awe of Rommel. 'There is something wrong here. I am convinced there has been no leadership out here. What has happened is a disgrace,' he told Wilson.[57] After a day of prolonged consulta-tions with serving officers and discussions with Brooke and Smuts, Churchill sent Attlee a telegram on 6 August explaining that 'drastic and immediate change is needed'. His proposal, as set out to Attlee, was to split in two the British forces in the theatre. One was to be a new 'Near East Command'. covering Egypt, Palestine and Syria, and headed by General Harold Alexander, a favourite of Churchill's who had distinguished himself in France and Burma and was earmarked to head the British participation in Torch. The other was to be a 'Middle

---

* Later Lord Moran.

East Command', comprising Persia and Iraq, for which position he put forward Auchinleck. The new commander of the 8th Army was to be Lieutenant General William Gott, a senior officer with long experience of the desert. Interestingly, Churchill also proposed that Montgomery should take over Alexander's role in Torch. 'Montgomery, though a first-rate soldier, would not be suited to the varied duties of the Near East Command. He is, on the other hand, in every way qualified to succeed Alexander in Torch,' he told Attlee.[58]

The following morning, 7 August, Churchill's scheme was discussed by the War Cabinet under Attlee's chairmanship. There was only partial approval, as Attlee explained in a subsequent telegram to Churchill. 'They agree that General Auchinleck should be relieved of his present Command and they warmly approve the selection of General Alexander.' But then Attlee reported that War Cabinet liked neither the creation of the new Middle East Command nor the planned appointment of Auchinleck to the new post. 'The War Cabinet feel that the arrangement which you propose will convey the impression that the Command is being created for the purpose of letting down General Auchinleck lightly. Having been removed from his present High Command, he is unlikely, in a far reduced but still important position, either to have confidence in himself or to inspire confidence in his troops.'[59] Churchill replied the same day, maintaining that the split in Commands had been made 'entirely on merits' because of the lack of 'natural unity' between them, based on geographical separation and different supply routes.[60] On the receipt of this message, Attlee and the War Cabinet gave way. 'Your further telegram has not entirely removed our misgivings, either as to the division of command or as to Auchinleck's position. But as you, Smuts and the CIGS,* who are on the spot, are all in agreement, we are prepared to authorise the action proposed,' wrote Attlee.[61] As it turned out, Auchinleck rejected the appointment, deeming it a demotion, so instead the post went to General Maitland Wilson. More tragically, Gott was killed when the

---

*   Brooke, Chief of the Imperial General Staff.

plane flying him to Cairo, on the route that Churchill had just travelled, was shot down by enemy action. Montgomery took Gott's place at the head of the 8th Army, beginning the rise that was soon to make him Britain's most famous wartime general. By appointing him, Churchill showed shrewder judgement than Attlee, Eden and Lyttelton. In private talks immediately after the decision was made, the three said they were 'much worried about the outcome of the Prime Minister's action' for 'Montgomery was admittedly a fine soldier but had no desert experience', while he and Alexander were 'not likely to get on, for they were too much alike'.[62]

On 10 August, after settling the military structure, Churchill embarked on his long journey by air from Cairo via Tehran to Moscow for his discussions with Stalin. But it was not an easy task, given the capriciousness of the Soviet dictator. Churchill opened the first meeting, held on the evening of 12 August at the Kremlin, by explaining that there would be no second front in Europe during 1942. 'I thought it was best to get the worst over first,' he wrote in his report of the four-hour conference to Attlee. Churchill then tried to change the tone by pointing to the RAF's 'ruthless bombing of Germany, which gave general satisfaction'. To Churchill's relief, Stalin was even more pleased when he was told of the plans for Operation Torch, which he said would 'hit Rommel in the back', overawe Spain and 'expose Italy to the whole brunt of the war'. Churchill reinforced the strategic importance of Torch by drawing an image of the Axis as a crocodile, with the Allies striking at its soft underbelly through the Mediterranean rather than its snout through Northern Europe. Altogether, Churchill told Attlee, the meeting had gone well. 'We parted in an atmosphere of great goodwill.'[63] But at the next conference, the following evening, Stalin was ill-natured once more as he expressed his anger over the lack of a second front and questioned the fighting quality of the Allies. At an official banquet the next night, Stalin was offhand rather than aggressive as he wandered around the hall speaking to subordinates while leaving Churchill for long periods on his own. 'I got no opportunity of talking about serious things,' Churchill reported to Attlee.[64] Annoyed at this ill-mannered treatment, Churchill left the banquet at 1.30 a.m., an early hour for him, but Stalin, sensing the Prime Minister's irritation, hurried after him, and insisted on accompanying him through a maze of corridors to the front door to say goodnight. The belated gesture did little to ease Churchill's temper. Wilson, his doctor, was amazed at the 'depth of resentment he had worked up' during the car journey back to his guest villa on the edge of the city.[65] Yet, in their fourth and final meeting, cordiality was fully restored when Stalin invited Churchill up to his private Kremlin apartment to discuss Torch, Allied supplies to the Soviet Union and the bombing campaign in more depth. What started as just a drink turned into a lengthy dinner lasting nearly five hours, the culinary highlight of which was the arrival at 1.30 a.m. of a head of a suckling pig, which Stalin proceeded to devour alone. By now gripped by a splitting headache, Churchill managed to get away at 2.30 a.m., which gave him just enough time to debrief his colleagues, have a bath and make it to the airport for his 5.30 a.m. flight back to Tehran. The trip to Moscow, wrote Alan Brooke in his diary, had 'served a very useful purpose, that of creating the beginnings of a strange understanding between Winston and Stalin'.[66]

Churchill and his party arrived back in Cairo on 17 August. Immediately, he was struck by the improvement in morale brought about by Alexander and Montgomery, telling Attlee on 21 August: 'A complete change of atmosphere has taken place from what I could see myself of the troops and hear from their commanders [...] the highest alacrity and activity prevails.' He then concluded on a generous note to his Deputy and Cabinet colleagues: 'I thank you all most warmly for the support you have given me while engaged on these anxious and unpleasant tasks.'[67] After a round trip of no fewer than 14,000 miles, Churchill returned to England on 24 August, landing at RAF Lyneham near Swindon before catching a special train to Paddington, where he was met by Attlee, Cripps and several of the military chiefs.

Having endured military setbacks and political strife throughout the first half of 1942, Churchill had been invigorated by his adventure, despite its exhausting elements. He now had real hope for the North

African campaign, especially when the reorganised British desert forces under Montgomery easily repelled a renewed offensive by Rommel in September. When he gave a full report to the Cabinet of his trips to Cairo and Moscow, Lord Woolton was impressed by his renewed energy. 'I left feeling that there was the old Churchillian buoyancy and optimism.'[68] The next day Woolton dined with Churchill and found him in an expansive mood. 'He was most friendly; of course, his lively sense of humour the whole time makes him very attractive [...] He told me that if we could get victory it would make so much difference and he believed that we were going to get it in Egypt. He said he thought the Russians would hold out, that they were as determined as we were to have no more truck with Hitler.'[69]

Political prospects at home were also brighter, with the noisy anti-Coalition faction increasingly marginalised. In the early autumn Laski maintained his condemnation of Attlee over Labour's closeness to Churchill, in one article claiming that 'no-one can point to a serious effort by Mr Attlee to make the idea of a partnership with the people a conscious part of the Prime Minister's policy'. In another article, this time in *Reynold's News*, he argued that the party must demand reform from Churchill or leave the Government. So brazen was his criticism that he only narrowly avoided expulsion from the party. Just as hostile to the Coalition but equally isolated was Nye Bevan, who kept up his denunciations of Churchill, declaring his 'complete distrust' of the Prime Minister's more repressive policy towards Indian nationalism.[70] On 10 September, Churchill announced in the House that Gandhi and other anti-British protestors had been interned as a security measure, to which Bevan demanded to know if Attlee and Cripps had consented to his statement. To loud Tory cheers, Churchill told Bevan that the Labour pair had actually helped draft it. 'Then they ought to be ashamed of themselves,' complained Bevan. In the left-wing magazine *Tribune*, Bevan carried on his attack, accusing Attlee of selling out the party through his link to Churchill. 'In the name of Labour and socialism, he has underwritten one of the blackest documents that imperialist bigotry has yet devised – Mr Churchill's Indian effusion.'[71]

But Bevan's outbursts only further diminished his standing. The liberal *News Chronicle* called him a 'rather shallow-minded politician' and 'arch exhibitionist' whose attacks on Churchill were 'a nonsensical expression of his monomania' which 'belongs to the schoolroom'.

But the greatest political gain for Churchill, and to a lesser extent Attlee, was the decline in the prestige of Stafford Cripps. In February 1942, he had been Churchill's most potent rival, widely regarded as his likely successor. As late as July, he had still seen himself in this light. But during his time in the Cabinet he had failed to enhance his reputation. MPs did not like his condescending manner as Leader of the House; Churchill did not value his advice as a strategist. Dissatisfied with the conduct of the war, Cripps had pressed for a major change in military and production planning, based on the establishment of a new war directorate. But Churchill had no interest in such a proposal. He told Cripps it was 'unhelpful' and would do nothing but create 'a planners' playground'.[72] By September, Cripps recognised that his influence in the Cabinet was on the wane. He told the Labour policy-maker Patrick Gordon-Walker that he had come into the Government 'on the understanding that he and Winston were to run the war. And it went like this until he went to India. Since then he has dropped right out. He never sees Winston except at Cabinet meetings.' Cripps went on to say that 'all the Cabinet is worried about the way things are done, including Attlee [...] But in the last resort none of them will go to the point of leaving Winston.'[73] That was exactly the course that Cripps, thoroughly depressed, was now contemplating. On 1 October, he explained to Gordon-Walker that he wanted to resign. 'Churchill is now bad for the war. The greatest man with the greatest character, but he makes mistakes and makes the Cabinet system impossible.'[74] That same day, he saw Churchill and told him they had reached 'a parting of the ways' because of 'how badly the war was run'.[75] Churchill was infuriated, thinking this was all part of a Machiavellian plot by Cripps to bring him down and create a government of national salvation. He was also concerned that any controversy over Cripps's resignation might destabilise his Government on the eve of the Torch. He therefore instructed Eden and Attlee to see if Cripps could be dissuaded from this dramatic step. To Beaverbrook, Churchill was much more savage about Cripps, saying that he 'felt like having him arrested'.[76]

Set on their mission, Eden and Attlee tracked down the disillusioned Lord Privy Seal and, with a mixture of charm and realism, managed to halt his departure from the Government. Attlee warned him that he would 'never be forgiven if he left at this critical moment';[77] while Eden said, that 'if Torch failed, we were all sunk. If it succeeded, he was free to act as he wished.'[78] Cripps eventually agreed to stay in the Cabinet until Torch, after which he would consider taking a new, purely departmental, role as Minister of Aircraft Production. He told Eden, however, that 'we should all get on much better without Winston'. Later Eden phoned Churchill with the news. 'I think he was relieved, though he is certainly exasperated by Cripps. The hostility between them is bound to deepen.'[79]

Helped by Attlee and Eden, Churchill had comprehensively outmanoeuvred Cripps, who had proved both naïve and over-ambitious. As for Attlee, he had once again shown his usefulness and fidelity to the Prime Minister. In mid-October, Sylvester reported to Lloyd George: 'There is a rumour that Winston is trying to get rid of Attlee and that one method is that he should be appointed Governor-General of Canada.'[80] This piece of gossip was without any foundation. Attlee's position was stronger than ever, as was Churchill's when the triumphant news came through of the Montgomery's defeat of Rommel at El Alamein. The victory over the Germans that the Prime Minister had long craved had finally been achieved. It was soon followed by the successful landings for Operation Torch, which spelled the beginning of the end for the Axis powers in North Africa. The balance of the war in the West had dramatically shifted, and with it the domestic political landscape. Shortly before the offensive, Brendan Bracken said that 'the PM must win his battle in the desert or get out'.[81] Now he was safe. In a speech at the Mansion House on Tuesday 10 May, Churchill captured the jubilant mood of the nation: 'The bright gleam has caught the helmets of our soldiers and warmed and cheered all our hearts.'[82]

That evening there was a celebratory ministerial banquet in Downing Street, where, despite wartime rationing, the menu included soup, turkey, plum pudding and cheese. After the dinner, Attlee proposed a toast to the health of Churchill, who, 'when the outlook was blackest, never faltered'. In his reply, Churchill described Attlee as 'a staunch friend, a loyal colleague and a good fighting animal'.[83]

The following Sunday, on Churchill's orders, the church bells were rung out across the country for the first time since 1940, when they had been silenced so that they could be used solely to warn of a German invasion. Now it was the Reich that was on the defensive.

NINETEEN

DOWNING STREET

A TTLEE'S DAUGHTER JANET Shipton once spoke of the familial separation that his wartime workload imposed. 'To some extent I lost my father. He became a public person. Because he was so busy he was not involved in our lives. He had so much that he was doing that I felt I did not really exist for him in a sense.'[1] Throughout the week, Attlee usually stayed at 11 Downing Street, only returning to the family home in Stanmore at the weekend. He tended to rise early, take a walk in the park and then have breakfast at the Oxford and Cambridge club in Pall Mall. Good at compartmentalisation, he disliked any attempt to broach the subject of politics at the club. The Labour peer Lord Longford recalled that when one member approached him to ask about some aspect of Government business, Attlee snapped in his clipped, military manner, 'Don't talk shop in the mess.'[2] Having breakfasted, Attlee then returned to Downing Street before nine o'clock for a full day of business. Unless he was on an official engagement, he dined at the nearest Whitehall canteen to Downing Street. Finally, well after midnight, he retired to a small, single bedroom above his office.

Churchill's daily routine was far less conventional and often exasperated those who had to work with him. Driven by his voracious appetite for work, his unorthodox method was based on the theory that he could effectively cram two days into one by having a siesta, thereby allowing him to carry on far into the early hours. He generally awoke for the first time at eight o'clock in the morning, but did not get up.

Instead he worked on his red boxes until his first meeting of the day or lunch. In the late afternoon, almost without fail, he took his siesta followed by a bath which left him refreshed for the evening ahead. 'He had this wonderful ability to go into a deep sleep for an hour, sometimes with a black bandage over his face,' said one of his secretaries, Marion Holmes.[3] His late-night meetings, known as the 'Midnight Follies',[4] were vital to his output but were the bane of his political colleagues and military chiefs who were left yearning to retire. 'I usually did not get to bed until 2.30pm,' recalled his aide Sir Ian Jacob.[5]

One of the paradoxes of Churchill's style was that, despite his loquacity, he liked to conduct his business on paper rather than orally, partly because this approach helped to formulate his thoughts and partly because it left a detailed record that was, as cynics pointed out, invaluable for his own subsequent histories of the war. 'Let it be very clearly understood that all directions emanating from me are to be made in writing or should immediately afterwards be confirmed in writing,' he wrote to his Downing Street Secretariat in July 1940. According to the senior civil servant Norman Brook, this insistence on documentation 'played an important part in bringing his personal impact to bear on the administration [...] Ministers received direct and personal messages, usually compressed into a single sheet of quarto paper and showing beyond doubt that they were the actual words of the Prime Minister himself.'[6] Sir Ian Jacob found that Churchill 'spent very little time interviewing people. He did not see his staff to talk over the matters they were working on for him. They had to address him in writing, and his replies or instructions came back in writing.'[7] That was why there was a daily flood of material from Churchill, much of it carrying the label 'Action This Day' to propel a sense of urgency. 'Everything that he wanted had to be done at once; all demands, however exacting and unreasonable, had to be met,' said Jacob.[8] He had his eccentricities about his paperwork, like his preference for green tags and his dislike of paper clips. To maintain his deluge of minutes and memoranda Churchill needed a string of secretaries constantly at hand to take his stream of dictation. The words had to be taken either through shorthand or on a typewriter – a custom-build silent Remington because, in another of his quirks, he loathed the sound of keys striking paper. Nor was he keen on other forms of office technology. 'Winston could never use a Dictaphone. He had tried but he could not make the necessary corrections,' his wife once explained.[9] Recording his words could be a difficult task because of his idiosyncrasies, including a lisp that meant he struggled to pronounce the letter *s*. 'It was not always easy to hear Churchill because often he would have abandoned his dentures and he had a slight speech impediment. And he might at that moment be smoking a cigar,' said Marion Holmes.[10] As in so many other areas, Attlee's technique was very different. The shorthand typist or stenographer was not nearly so essential a part of his equipment. In fact, he did some of his own typing on a battered portable machine. 'The typing mayn't be first rate. I use three fingers, but at least I can say that I have never signed anything that I have not written myself or do not thoroughly understand and agree with,' he once said.[11]

A key strand of Churchill's dictation was for his speeches, which were always typed out verbatim and usually went through several drafts. In a sense Churchill was a great reciter rather than a great orator, since he spent hours on the preparation of every major address. 'To speak in public takes a great deal out of me. I never excelled as a platform speaker,' he admitted.[12] Another of his secretaries, Elizabeth Layton, later recalled the painstaking construction of a forthcoming speech one evening at Chequers in 1941.

He was wearing his red, green and gold dragon dressing gown, a favourite garment of his. He started walking up and down. Then the words started flowing out, slowly at first, and then as his thoughts came to him, the words poured out. Always when Mr Churchill dictated something or was preparing something about which he felt deeply, he would gesture, just as he would when he was finally giving his speech. It was quite like a little pantomime for his shorthand writer. It was very inspiring.[13]

Attlee had nothing like Churchill's charisma or gift for majestic language, yet he was far less reliant on set, rehearsed texts. Douglas Jay, who was for a time a personal assistant to Attlee, later becoming a Labour minister, remembered how hard it was to draft speeches for him. Jay was pleased with one highly literate effort he produced for Attlee on welfare reform, only to find 'it was a failure. "Notes, not a lecture", he said.'[14] Even when Attlee did write a full script, he often physically did so himself; this fact was observed by Percy Cudlipp, editor of the *Daily Herald*, in drawing a contrast with Churchill, who

> treated the preparation for his speeches like the build-up to a play, apostrophising his secretary and delivering great sulphurous phrases. Attlee dislikes – the word despises is too strong – any such finery. Whenever a personal speech must be made he takes himself off to the study [...] sits down at an ancient portable typewriter and taps out the first draft of his speech with two fingers – and possibly a thumb. Half the character of the man is concentrated in the scene, sitting alone before a typewriter, making phrases of his own in preference to the polished periods he could so easily command.[15]

Another key difference in the working routines of the two men was that Attlee, extraordinarily in a politician, had little interest in the press and barely glanced at the newspapers, apart from the *Daily Herald* which was effectively the Labour house journal, though he also gave some brief attention to *The Times* mainly for its crossword and cricket reports. 'He was allergic to the press. He took no interest in what was written about him and never sought the company of journalists,' wrote his public-relations officer Francis Williams.[16] Churchill was the opposite. He had all the first editions sent to him at Downing Street by special courier late at night so he could go through them in detail. 'I get far more out of them than official muck,' he once said.[17] Ministers were often surprised to receive a minute from him the next morning about some item in the papers that related to their jobs.

Greater extravagance was another feature of Churchill's wartime lifestyle compared to Attlee's. Austerity suited Attlee's lean frame and spartan character. For Churchill, rules on restraint were there to be stretched. As Prime Minister, he could circumvent the rationing system by steps such as the acquisition of extra coupons for official entertaining or the acceptance of special gifts, like pheasants from the Sandringham Estate and caviar from the Soviet Embassy. Nor was his renowned consumption of alcohol reduced during the war. He was still able to indulge in his favourite drinks of whisky, vintage champagne and fine old brandy, which he once described as 'something to be treasured'.[18] By any normal standards, Churchill's alcoholic consumption was consistently high, yet his staff denied that it had much effect on him or that it was as excessive as rumours indicated. Jock Colville, who worked alongside him for so long, claimed that the glass of whisky that Churchill habitually kept on his desk throughout the day was little more than 'a mouthwash' because it was so watered down.[19] Marion Holmes agreed that the gossip was exaggerated: 'I never ever saw him the worse for drink. It was one of those myths. He would sometimes drink quite a lot of brandy but after a huge meal. He was a regular drinker but never drank until he was the worse for wear.'[20] It is little surprise, given his consumption, that throughout much of his career he suffered from indigestion and acid reflux, ailments that he found could be alleviated by massage.

No one ever levelled the charge of either nutritional or alcoholic overindulgence against Attlee. 'Though we were well-to-do middle class, our life was kind of spare. There were no extras,' said Janet Shipton.[21] Generally abstemious, Attlee tended to confine himself to a glass of claret with dinner and a glass of brandy only 'in extremis'.[22] Once, when the journalist Leslie Hunter was going to lunch with Attlee, Dalton advised him: 'Give him a glass of red burgundy. One glass, not two. He'll be annoyed if you press him and he'll only dry up again if he has it.'[23] The gap between Attlee and Churchill extended to their wardrobes. Whereas Attlee dressed conventionally, Churchill displayed more creativity; he devised his own all-in-one garment, known as his 'siren suit', for work at home and had a penchant for footwear with zippers instead of laces. He also showed a degree of disdain for household economy, as Clemmie related during a visit to an anti-invasion committee in Shoeburyness, Essex:

> My husband is a terror. He puts a shirt on in the morning. A couple of hours later he will take it off and put another one on. That's how it goes on. I said to our housekeeper, 'Now look, these shirts are not dirty and we cannot keep washing them. Just iron them and put them back. He won't know.' But he did notice. He said to me, 'I thought I would do anything for King and Country, but I won't wear hotted up shirts.'[24]

Intriguingly, at the height of the war Violet Attlee also felt she had cause to complain about her husband's treatment of his wardrobe, especially because of severe shortages and lack of domestic help. 'His habit of shrugging his shoulders when he sits down gives a suit no chance,' she said in 1941, adding that she also despaired of the way he casually 'throws his clothes on'.[25]

Besides shirts and drink, another of Churchill's indulgences was his cigars, of which he smoked about fifteen a day. Even at the peak of the war he managed to maintain his supply, thanks to the generosity of the Cuban Embassy whose support helped him evade customs regulations on the import of tobacco. To prevent his cigars becoming too soggy as he smoked and chewed, he invented his own tool, called the belly-bando, a thin strip of brown paper that could be glued around the end. In contrast, Attlee was the quintessence of the respectable England gentleman in his enthusiasm for his pipe, which he puffed throughout the day. 'Mr Attlee chain smokes pipes, not cigarettes. He has three carefully laid out on his desk and as one fails he takes up another,' noted Percy Cudlipp.[26]

Churchill once said to Attlee, 'Of course I am an egotist. Where do you get if you're not?'[27] His egotism was not a form of selfishness but rather a ruthless focus on his own work and its demands. As the wartime Conservative Chief Whip James Stuart put it, 'Concentration was one of the keys to his character. It was not always obvious, but he never really thought of anything but the job in hand. He was not a fast worker, especially dealing with paper, but he was essentially a non-stop worker. His power of application at any time of day or night was phenomenal.'[28] So intense was Churchill's concentration that on one occasion, while he was giving dictation in bed, he did not even notice that some fallen hot ash from his cigar had started to smoulder in the bedclothes. A secretary rushed for help and found a Downing Street aide, who quickly put out the incipient fire. Yet immediately after this incendiary commotion had been stilled, Churchill resumed his dictation as if nothing had happened. The same obliviousness sometimes applied to his staff, whose own needs were frequently disregarded. 'He was incredibly inconsiderate as regards hours. Without being a selfish man, because he was very generous, he was enormously egocentric and it never occurred to him that what suited him might be extremely inconvenient for other people, whether they were his colleagues in the Cabinet or his staff,' said Colville.[29] As his Deputy, Attlee felt Churchill's 'greatest weakness was his impatience. He never understood that a certain time was bound to elapse between when you ask for something to be done and when it can be affected. He worked people terribly hard and was inconsiderate.'[30] James Stuart shared that view. 'He was not an easy man to serve, far from it. He was argumentative. He wanted his own way and was a bit of a bully.'[31] Another member of the government, John Moore-Brabazon, who served at the ministries of both Transport and Aircraft Production, wrote bitterly in his autobiography that wartime meetings were 'the most unpleasant' he ever attended because Churchill 'behaved as if he were a bullying schoolmaster. Everyone, in his opinion, was a halfwit; and if anyone said anything he was jumped on and snubbed.'[32] Even Churchill's wife had to reprimand him for his selfish conduct early in his premiership. 'There is a danger of your being generally disliked by your colleagues and subordinates because of your rough, sarcastic and overbearing manner,' she wrote in June 1940.[33] Again there was a graphic contrast with

Attlee, whose inherent diffidence meant that he was reluctant to thrust forward his own demands. There was a clear instance of that modesty when Attlee was in a meeting in the Commons with the senior civil servant Leslie Rowan. Attlee was asked if he would like a cup of tea, to which he replied that he would get it himself from the Commons tea room. 'No need, I'll send for a messenger.' Attlee insisted, maintaining that the messenger was 'probably busy'. According to Douglas Jay, who was also present, 'Attlee tripped off down the passage. Rowan, who had spent many months with Churchill, was left speechless.'[34] On another occasion, there was some embarrassment in Attlee's office because, in a press release of a statement to the Commons about industrial policy, the typist accidently left out a crucial passage. But Attlee, apparently, 'did not mind a bit. He said he would put it right in Hansard and say it was inadvertence on his part.'[35]

Yet many of Churchill's staff forgave him for his self-centredness, because of both the mammoth responsibility he faced and his essentially warm-hearted nature. Moreover, he was aware that he could be exacting. Marion Holmes recalled that he told her, soon after she had been recruited, 'Miss Holmes, you must never be frightened of me when I snap. I am not thinking of you, I am thinking of the work.'[36] Elizabeth Layton, too, felt his inner circle was forgiving. 'The negative side was only on the surface and underneath he was a very caring person.'[37] But even those closest to him could find Churchill trying. In a revealing description of their friendship, Brendan Bracken once said that Churchill was

> utterly impossible. I don't know why any of us put up with him. Being friendly with him is like being in love with a beautiful woman who drives you mad with her demands until you can bear it not a minute longer and fling out of the house swearing never to see her again. But the next day she smiles at you knowing there is nothing you wouldn't do for her and she crooks her little finger and you come running.[38]

Others, more jaundiced, felt that his self-centredness could amount to disloyalty, believing that Churchill exploited their friendship for his own political gain. That was certainly the feeling of his former aide Desmond Morton who found himself increasingly marginalised, then ignored, in the years from 1940. It was an experience that later led him to pour out his vitriol against Churchill:

> Winston as a boy, youth and young man must have been a howling cad, but never in matters of sex and religion, only in selfishness and disregard for anyone's feelings but his own [...] The full truth, I believe, is that Winston's friends must be persons who were of use to him. The idea of having a friend who was of no practical use to him, but a friend because he liked him, had no place.[39]

That was also the view of the colourful Bob Boothby, who had been close to Churchill in the pre-war fight against appeasement and served as a junior Food Minister until 1941, when he was forced to resign in a scandal over the distribution of seized Czechoslovakian assets. 'He used men when he had a particular job to do. When they'd done the job, he dropped them. He was pretty ruthless in his dealings with individuals.'[40]

Attlee never provoked such emotive reactions, partly because his reserved, self-contained personality meant that he neither developed intense friendships, nor abandoned his reticence with subordinates. 'He was an odd man, whom few, even of his closest colleagues, really understood,' said the veteran Labour politician Denis Healey.[41] Anthony Eden, who served alongside him throughout Churchill's wartime premiership, felt that he was 'a man with whom it is easy to be friendly but difficult to be intimate'.[42] Unlike most senior politicians, Attlee never tried to build his own court or team of followers. His military mind, with its belief in hierarchies and sound administration, meant that he saw loyalty as something owed to his position, not his own personality. That was why he never felt compelled to bring in his own people when he took up a new post; he instinctively trusted the officials that the civil service provided. 'His integrity was matched by a remarkable self-sufficiency. He had no time for intimates or sycophants. His own nature inclined him in any event to a solitary role,' wrote Francis Williams.[43] Again there was a graphic contrast with Churchill, who found comfort in surrounding himself with familiar faces. 'He preferred people he knew and felt he could trust, so he could concentrate on his work,' said Elizabeth Layton.[44] This need for the reassurance of accustomed figures could be a weakness, thought Jock Colville: 'The call of Auld Lang Syne was very strong with him and he did make some appalling appointments.' The desire for the recognisable could be carried to extremes, as Colville found when he returned to Downing Street sporting a moustache after a spell on military leave. At once, Churchill ordered him to shave it off. 'The face had to be familiar, literally so,' said Colville.[45]

Amid his deluge of post-war criticism, Desmond Morton argued that Churchill had an 'overweening desire to dominate'.[46] That point was echoed by the senior RAF commander Arthur Tedder, who played a crucial role in the planning of D-Day. 'Eisenhower made the people around him bigger, but Churchill made them smaller,' he said.[47] In truth, however, Churchill dominated not out of insecurity but through the grandeur of his towering personality. 'His face, projected forward by hunched shoulders, could be grim and forbidding. In the mood he could make one feel as small as a pebble. But when the light came, it was a glorious awakening,' recalled the Australian Premier Sir Robert Menzies.[48] Churchill's ability to shape events by his will, magnetism, wisdom and eloquence made him a leader of epic proportions, a statesman whose courage was equalled by his imagination. The rich spirit of history was never far from his deeds and words. The philosopher Sir Isaiah Berlin once wrote that Churchill envisaged 'life as a great Renaissance pageant', likening him to 'a dramatist who sees persons and situations as timeless symbols and embodiments of eternal, shining principles'.[49] During the war, that sense of drama conveyed itself to those around him. 'He had this extraordinary power. He made you feel you were a great actor in great events,' said Oliver Lyttelton, contradicting the view of Tedder and Morton.[50] Marion Holmes described him as a 'multi-talented colossus' who 'made us believe that we were unconquerable. He was indomitable. He once asked me when we were in the Downing Street annexe being bombed and there was a terrific racket going on, "Miss Holmes, are you frightened? Are you sure you're not frightened?" I said no. How could one be frightened in the presence of that man? One never was. He exuded this feeling that we would win, despite all the odds.'[51]

No one could have called Attlee a colossus, despite his qualities of sincerity, judgement, loyalty and competence. While Churchill seemed a natural Prime Minister, Attlee was seen by many as an incongruous Deputy. His position in the front rank was often a source of puzzlement, as the Labour MP Raymond Blackburn recorded after meeting him for the first time. 'I felt astonished that such a man should be the leader of a party containing men of such outstanding ability as Bevin, Cripps, Bevan and Morrison.'[52] George Harvie-Watt once shared a train with Attlee on a wartime visit north. 'A nice man but not very stimulating. It was incredible to think that he was the Deputy Prime Minister.' Harvie-Watt also dined with Clementine one evening in August 1942 when her husband was in Egypt and Attlee was charge of the Government. 'Clemmie was most indiscreet and was scathing in her criticisms of some of the ministers. Mr Attlee she thought a funny little mouse.'[53] Yet Churchill's doctor Charles Wilson, who had been unimpressed when he first met Attlee, detected hidden depths on coming to know him. After a conversation in August 1944, Wilson wrote: 'Most of these politicians are cool customers, who have spent their lives dealing with human nature, but Attlee does not seem to have any self-confidence. He answered my questions in a quick, nervous manner, though he told me he never got worried about anything, he did his best. I have a feeling that there is good deal more to him than this. Winston, I am pretty sure, underrates him.'[54] The same sense of authority behind the shy exterior was captured in an *Observer* profile of Attlee in 1944, which opened:

At Cabinet meetings the Deputy Prime Minister always sits on the edge of his chair. The trick is typical of the man. It is the sign of a diffidence, a lack of confidence, perhaps better, a modesty, that must be almost unique in high politics. Yet this is the man who, on merit, is wartime Number 2 to Mr Churchill of all people. The debt owed to loyal Clem Attlee by the Prime Minister, the country and the Labour Party is big.

The paper went on to outline his value to Churchill:

In Downing Street there is a Leader. Mr Churchill needs a Chairman for the humdrum, essential work of government [...] The Deputy Prime Minister is, in these offices, the first-class captain of a first-class cricket side who is not himself a headliner. He is a political catalyst. The historians will give Clem Attlee his due, even under the shadow of Churchill, for he too is an English worthy, though not a Great One.[55]

Indeed, Attlee gained a wartime reputation within officialdom for his swift, unsentimental conduct of business, perceived by many to be more efficient than Churchill's style, which regularly featured his own lengthy discourses and inconsequential diversions. In fact, Attlee once challenged him on this approach at a Cabinet meeting where Churchill, after his own long intervention, declared, 'Well, gentlemen, I think we can all agree on this course.' Before anyone else could speak, Attlee interjected: 'You know, Prime Minister, a monologue by you does not necessarily spell agreement.'[56] It was Douglas Jay who coined the phrase that Attlee would 'rarely use one syllable where none would do',[57] but his laconic manner frequently came as a relief to ministers who found their Cabinet and committee meetings significantly shortened when Attlee was in charge. Interviewed during one of Churchill's wartime visits to the White House, the Home Office Minister Ellen Wilkinson said:

When the Prime Minister is away, Mr Attlee presides. We meet at the appointed time and go through the whole agenda and make all the necessary decisions. We go home at night knowing we have done a good day's work. When Winston is in charge, we have no agenda, make no decisions at all and go home after midnight conscious that we have been present at a historic occasion.[58]

Wilkinson's Labour colleague Hugh Dalton accepted that Churchill had 'a tremendous power of leadership' but when he was away, 'both his Cabinet colleagues and the Chiefs of Staff felt a great sense of relief' because 'then Attlee took the chair and there was brief and business-like discussion ending in clear and definite decisions'.[59] An example of Attlee in action was noted by the Chief of the Imperial General Staff Alan Brooke after a Cabinet meeting in September 1943, with admiration for the Deputy Prime Minister's briskness tempered by concern about his lack of charisma. 'A Cabinet under Attlee. How different to those under Winston! In many ways more efficient and more to the point, but in others a Cabinet without a head.'[60]

Oliver Lyttelton thought that Churchill's discursive technique was partly a deliberate tactic rather than a form of verbal self-indulgence. 'His method was to extract and test a man's opinions by reacting violently and provocatively. Heat, he believed, refines the metal.' But Lyttelton recognised the benefits of Attlee's style. 'We got through a great deal more day-to-day business than we did under Churchill. Winston regarded committee as opportunities for ventilating his own views, or even for his speeches a trial run. He was frequently irrelevant and often impatient. Attlee was a chairman and Winston was a leader.'[61] Others were less impressed with Attlee as a prime-ministerial understudy. 'While Winston is ill, rat-faced, rat-hearted little Attlee calls a cabinet to settle all the most trivial questions,' wrote the diplomat Valentine Lawford in his diary for late February 1943.[62]

Attlee's own verdict on Churchill's wartime Cabinets was that 'were not good for business but they were great fun'.[63] Those words showed the amused affection and warmth that Attlee had for Churchill. According to historical mythology, Churchill did not reciprocate that feeling. Legend has it that he found Attlee an over-promoted bore, too hesitant for the cut-and-thrust of high politics. 'I think he found him a somewhat colourless personality,' recalled Churchill's valet Norman McGowan, a former sailor who worked for him from 1949.[64] One of Churchill's most famous alleged lines about Attlee was his description of him as 'a sheep in sheep's clothing', an insult recorded in August 1945 in the diary of the Tory backbencher Cuthbert Headlam: 'Told yesterday by someone (forget who) that Winston describes Attlee as a "sheep in sheep's clothing" which I think is too clever a description of our new PM to be forgotten.'[65] Yet it seems unlikely that Churchill ever actually said this of Attlee. The Downing Street aide John Peck was certain that Brendan Bracken, not Churchill, made the quip, while the Scottish historian D. W. Brogan believed that the line was about Ramsay MacDonald rather than Attlee. 'Sir Winston Churchill never said of Clement Attlee that he was a sheep in sheep's clothing. I have this on the excellent authority of Sir Winston himself. The phrase was totally inapplicable to Mr Attlee. It was applicable, and applied to, Ramsay MacDonald, a very different kind of Labour leader.'[66] Even more doubt must be cast on another famous remark that Churchill is often alleged to have said of Attlee, namely that 'an empty taxi drew up to No.10 and Mr Attlee got out'. As the historian John Bew pointed out in his biography of Attlee, this quotation was taken from the popular short story *The Wrong Set*, written by Angus Wilson in 1949.[67] Wilson's joke went round Westminster at the time but, as Jock Colville recalled, Churchill was infuriated when it was attributed to him. After Colville repeated it in his presence, there was 'an awful pause'; then Churchill said, 'Mr Attlee is an honourable and gallant gentleman who served his country well at the time of her greatest need. I should be obliged if you would make clear whenever an occasion arises that I would never make such a remark about him and that I strongly disapprove of anybody who does.'[68]

In a post-war interview Colville remembered how, just like F. E. Smith's son Freddie Birkenhead, he had once asked Churchill, sometime after the 1945 election, which of his Labour colleagues he liked and admired most during the war. I expected him to say Bevin because I knew he was very fond of Bevin and thought very well of him. Rather to my surprise, he said Attlee. I do not think they were really attuned to each other. They did not have the same sense of humour but they both respected and admired each other.[69]

Despite the lack of easy congeniality between the two men, Churchill occasionally extended hospitality to Attlee and his family. In early 1943, Attlee's own younger children surprised their father by asking if they could meet Churchill. Having happily agreed to this request from his Deputy, Churchill welcomed them to the Downing Street annexe where he planned the war. 'Winston was there in his boiler suit. He gave us some orange juice and showed us round, showed us all the maps,' remembered Felicity, Attlee's second daughter.[70] During the war, having completed her training, she worked as a nursery-school teacher in both London and, with evacuees, in the country. The two younger children, Alison and Martin, were sent to boarding school in Salisbury, while the eldest, Janet, suspended her studies in psychology to serve in the Auxiliary Territorial Service (ATS). Interestingly Janet struck up a distant friendship with Churchill's youngest daughter, Mary, who, after spells in the Red Cross and the Women's Voluntary Service, joined the ATS in 1942. Mary was the most responsible and well balanced of Churchill's four children, with something of her father's authority, and became an anti-aircraft battery commander. Her relish for military life shone through one letter she wrote to Janet Attlee in June 1942. 'Life is pretty hectic one way and another on our gun site – but it's great fun and we are outdoors nearly all the time, which I love.'[71] Churchill's other two daughters also went on active service: Diana Sandys with the Women's Royal Naval Service; and Sarah, unhappily married to the film star Vic Oliver, with the Women's Auxiliary Air Force, in which organisation she worked as a map interpreter for the North African campaign in 1942. Randolph, the only son, had a varied, sometimes heroic, wartime career as a journalist and soldier, seeing action in the Western Desert and Yugoslavia. He was also elected the Conservative MP for Preston at a by-election in September 1940, though his subsequent appearances in the Commons were limited by his active service and his erratic, alcohol-marinated nature. The long-term political career that he craved, in order to emulate his father, always eluded him. In 1945 he lost his seat, following which his slide into disillusion and heavy drinking accelerated.

Both Violet Attlee and Clementine Churchill were prominent in the war effort. As a Red Cross Commandant, Violet established a number of refuges for bombed-out Londoners, in addition to giving lectures to first-aid volunteers. Clementine, too, was involved in the Red Cross, but in a more political role as the highly successful Chairman of its Aid to Russia fund, for which the Soviet Union awarded her the Order of the Red Banner of Labour. But wartime service was not accompanied by any sense of financial security. For Violet, running the family house at Stanmore was a difficult task in those years, as Janet recalled.

> She had to manage everything with the children on her own. There was not any help and she had to go down every day to the shops. There were no privileges at all for the Deputy Prime Minister's family. On the contrary, mother was mad because father knew they were going to have clothes rationing and he did not tell her. We had old linen sheets from grandmother. We were a very economical family but we were left struggling.[72]

Extravagance rather than limited means continued to be Churchill's problem. During the war he continued to be plagued by financial troubles, especially in the opening years, despite his accommodation at Downing Street and Chequers plus his extra rationing allowances. But holding office meant that his income from journalism and books was once more drastically reduced. So severe was his plight that on the eve of the Battle of Britain he again faced bankruptcy because of the interest payments on his loans as well as unpaid bills from merchants.

Again Brendan Bracken organised an emergency rescue by Sir Henry Strakosch, the Austrian-born businessman and banker. On condition of anonymity, Sir Henry wrote out a cheque for £5,000 – an act of generosity that saw Churchill through his financial crisis to remain in power as he plotted victory over Germany.

TWENTY

CONFERENCE
AND CABINET

THE PARADOX OF El Alamein was that it simultaneously secured Churchill's premiership in the short-term and undermined his party in the long-term. Until November 1942, the nation had concentrated on grim survival against the ascendant Reich. But after Rommel's defeat, combined with Russia's heroic offensive at Stalingrad, the British public could finally look forward to the prospect of peace, freed from the threat of Nazi tyranny. With the shackles of fear removed, a sense of optimism and hope began to spread across the country. To many, the fight was no longer for national salvation but for a better, fairer Britain.

The problem for Churchill was his reluctance to embrace this progressive mood, not least because the Axis had not yet been beaten and a long struggle still lay ahead. 'The most painful experience would lie before us, if we fell to quarrelling about what we should do with victory before that victory had been won,' he told the Cabinet soon after El Alamein.[1] Just as importantly, the fires of his belief in social reform had long been dimmed by an instinctive hostility towards socialism. With much of the country yearning for a new approach, his stance appeared reactionary and anachronistic. After dining with Churchill in November, Jan Christian Smuts wrote: 'There is a world of change taking place, big fundamental change. Winston lives in the 18th century and does not see what is happening.'[2]

For Labour, this changing atmosphere presented a new opportunity to press for more radicalism. With the pressure for a military
victory now released, sections of the left felt that, rather than allow
Churchill to set the domestic agenda, the party's ministers could now
embark on a programme of reconstruction. Inevitably Nye Bevan was
at the forefront of this demand for more socialism as he condemned
Attlee for becoming too close to Churchill in the first years of the
Coalition. In the left-wing magazine *Tribune* he wrote that 'Mr Attlee
is no longer the spokesman of the movement which carried him from
obscurity to the second position in the land. He remains loyal but only
to Mr Churchill.'[3] The accusation of slavish loyalty to Churchill was
also levelled against Attlee by John Parker, the backbench Labour MP
for Romford. At a meeting of Labour MPs, Parker made 'a bitter attack
on Attlee' for his alleged failure to stand up to Churchill, saying that he
should sometimes 'tell the Prime Minister to go to hell'. In the account
left by Chuter Ede, Attlee's laconic reply was that 'on occasions, he told
the Prime Minister where he should go'.[4]

Yet the critics had misread Attlee. The Deputy Prime Minister
remained true to his socialist principles. He had loyally supported
Churchill so far because of the urgent demands of the war, but he was
now willing to put more weight behind reform. The perfect vehicle
for that approach arose at the end of November 1942 with the arrival
of the much-anticipated report by the liberal-minded civil servant Sir
William Beveridge into the future of social security, which had been
commissioned by Arthur Greenwood in 1941. Both Churchill and Attlee
had known Beveridge since their Edwardian involvement in fighting
poverty. Indeed, Beveridge had been a sub-warden at Toynbee Hall
from 1903 to 1905, where Attlee later worked, and he also administered
the implementation of Churchill's Labour Exchanges Act of 1909. But
neither politician warmed to him. Attlee found Beveridge self-satisfied
and prickly, while Churchill thought he was 'an awful windbag and a
dreamer'.[5] Nevertheless, they recognised that the Beveridge plan would
have tremendous implications for the Government, the welfare system
and the public finances. Aimed at tackling the 'five giants of Want,

Disease, Ignorance, Squalor and Idleness', his scheme pledged to create a national health service, achieve full employment, introduce family allowances without means testing and establish comprehensive social insurance, based on weekly contributions.[6]

But the Chancellor Kingsley Wood warned Churchill that Beveridge's plan would not only require 'an impracticable financial commitment' but would also squander money on people who did not need it.[7] Some of those doubts surfaced at the Cabinet on 26 November, when Wood revealed that the plan could cost £100 million. Churchill, though he said he liked the report, urged his colleagues to think of 'the impact on finance and rates of taxation'. What particularly worried him was the potential response in the USA. 'If we promise this largesse, far ahead of US standards they may say, "We are being asked to pay for this."' To this comment Attlee replied, 'The US reaction may be good. They may be impressed with our boldness.'[8] Eventually, despite the reservations of Churchill and Wood, the Cabinet agreed that the report should be published on 2 December, with a debate in Parliament fixed for mid-February 1943. When it came out, it created a sensation, reflecting the public's thirst for social change. Within a few weeks all 635,000 printed copies had been sold.

Against a backdrop of overwhelming support for Beveridge, the Cabinet had to formulate a response before the February debate. As Deputy Prime Minister, Attlee was in charge of the discussions during January, because Churchill was at the Casablanca Conference with Roosevelt deciding the Western Allied strategy for 1943. But just before he left for Morocco, Churchill sent the Cabinet a memorandum outlining some of the benefits of the Beveridge plan, but also warned against 'false hopes and airy visions of Utopia and El Dorado'.[9] His view illustrated the Conservative approach, which saw the Beveridge plan merely as a guide for future post-war reform, whereas Labour wanted to have preparations made for its full implementation. At the Cabinet on 14 January, over which Attlee presided in Churchill's absence, ministers felt that that the scheme was too complex for a swift decision to be made. In typical Attlee style, therefore, the Cabinet agreed to set up a committee under the Lord President Sir John Anderson to examine the report in detail.

But a split between Churchill and Labour could not long be postponed. Attlee once wrote that 'whenever we got on to the subject of planning for post-war Britain, Winston was ill at ease. He always groused about my being a socialist. Whenever a Cabinet committee put up a paper to him on anything not military or naval, he was inclined to suspect a socialist plot.'[10] The friction came to a head on the Prime Minister's return from Casablanca, Churchill having concluded that the report could not be implemented in the current Parliament. His negativity was worsened by a bout of poor health when he contracted mild pneumonia that brought on a fever. Even from his sickbed, he was able to dictate another memorandum to his Cabinet colleagues, in which he said that Beveridge's scheme would be 'an essential part of any post-war scheme of national betterment' but that a General Election would have to be held before implementation, since the 1935 Parliament had no mandate for such a change.[11] Belying Bevan's claims of submissiveness, Attlee hit back at Churchill with his own lengthy response. He told the Prime Minister that he was 'disturbed' by the argument about the 1935 Parliament, since this contradicted the deal under which the Coalition was formed in 1940. 'I understood and have repeatedly stated that while the Government was necessarily precluded from carrying out a party programme, it would be prepared to legislate on matters on which agreement had been reached.' Attlee then questioned whether Churchill grasped how the war had changed domestic politics. 'I doubt whether in your inevitable and proper preoccupation with military problems you are fully cognisant of the extent to which decisions must be taken and implemented in the field of post-war reconstruction before the end of the war.' Attlee told Churchill that there was 'a remarkable consensus' in public opinion of the need for a strong social policy. 'I do not think the people of this country, especially the fighting men, would forgive us if we failed to take decisions and implement them because of some constitutional inhibition.'[12] The row spilled over into the Cabinet meeting of 15 February on the eve of the Commons debate, with Churchill back in the Chair. Once again, Churchill stuck to his case that reconstruction plans could be prepared but not implemented; to this Attlee said that 'if the Prime Minister's line is taken, it will provoke a demand for a General Election'. There followed a sharp exchange between Churchill and his Deputy.

Churchill: 'No promises, no commitments, every conceivable preparation.'

Attlee: 'Preparations all involve decisions of policy.'

Churchill: 'I would agree to legislation by the Parliament to prepare for post war, but not to legislation taking decisions binding on the future.' At this point Herbert Morrison interjected in support of Attlee, maintaining that if 'we can have no enabling legislation for post-war problems, then we shall be in an indefensible position'.[13] Churchill relented to a degree and the Cabinet agreed to an awkward compromise, whereby 'the Government should not be committed to introducing legislation for the reform of social services during the war, but equally there should be no negative commitment debarring the Government from introducing such legislation during the lifetime of the present Parliament'.[14]

But this unconvincing line could not easily be held in the Commons against the fervour of Labour MPs who had eagerly rallied to the Beveridge cause. On 16 February, there was uproar at a meeting the PLP's Administration Committee. In its truculent mood, Labour decided to put down an amendment for the second day of the debate, throwing out the compromise and urging 'the early implementation' of the Beveridge plan.[15] At the Cabinet the next day, Churchill, still plagued by a heavy cold and a sore throat, was told by Attlee that the Coalition would have to give more ground if it were not to sink into more trouble. 'The mandate of the Government is not limited to "blood, tears and sweat". The Government must either govern or get through a General Election a Government that will,' said Attlee. His remark was the cue for another clash between the two leaders. Churchill called the Beveridge plan 'a peril to financial security' leading to 'irresponsible commitments'. Attlee was indignant at this charge. 'The Labour

Party are not irresponsible about this,' he replied. Churchill fired back: 'Everyone wants it, but how can you pay for it? You can't pass the bill until you know where you are.'[16] Once again, Morrison came to Attlee's aid, as he informed Churchill: 'if we said no legislation until after the war, the House of Commons would not have it. This is a political crisis.'[17] Confronted with the ferocity of Labour's united opposition, Churchill had to retreat, saying that he would not object to the introduction of legislation for the Beveridge Report, as long as the timing for implementation was left open.

This was enough for the Labour Cabinet ministers, but not for most of the party's MPs. As the debate reached its climax, Morrison made a rousing defence of the Cabinet's position of support for the Beveridge plan without a definitive timetable. But this could not prevent a huge rebellion, with ninety-seven Labour MPs voting against the Government, one of the biggest parliamentary revolts of the war. Attlee was disappointed in his own party. 'The Beveridge debate was not a good show though Morrison was first-class. On these questions so many of our fellows – good men, not mischief makers, tend to use their hearts to the exclusion of their heads,' he told his brother Tom.[18]

The discord within Labour spread beyond Parliament. Labour's NEC urged that 'the necessary legislation' to implement the Beveridge Report should be introduced 'at an early date';[19] this was much to the annoyance of Attlee, who pointed out that Labour was in a national government not a party government, so 'it could not be expected that the full Labour policy would be acceptable in its entirety to the parties'.[20] But so deep were the divisions that the NEC refused even to pass a formal vote of confidence in the Labour ministers, a fact that reflected the committee's anger at 'a series of blunders' from the parliamentary front bench.[21] In this atmosphere of crisis, the left-inclined *Observer* warned that the Government's very existence was under threat: 'This Coalition has always been fragile and its fragility increases as the dangers which drew men together recede.'[22]

To reunite his Government, Churchill decided that he would have to compromise further on the question of domestic policy. He did so through the dramatic vehicle of a BBC broadcast to the nation from Chequers on 21 March 1943. The tone of this address, which was written with the help of Attlee and Bevin, was very different to the martial speeches he had made in 1940. Displaying an apparent relish for change that he had not shown in recent Cabinet meetings, Churchill announced that once victory over Germany and Italy had been achieved, his Government would embark on a four-year programme of recon-struction, including the establishment of a national health service, an extension of state education and a social security scheme in line with the Beveridge Report. 'The time is ripe for another great advance. You must rank me and my colleagues as strong partisans of national compulsory insurance for all classes for all purposes from the cradle to the grave,' he told listeners.[23] Through its progressive idealism, Churchill's broadcast made a powerful impact. Indeed, even A. J. Sylvester, normally so critical of Churchill, reported to Lloyd George that 'a very shrewd observer' had described it as 'one of the great speeches in history and certainly the greatest Winston has ever made'.[24] Joining in this chorus of approval was the Labour economist Evan Durbin, who told Attlee that Churchill's 'magnificent' broadcast was 'a most encouraging sign of his willingness to mobilise our resources of imagination and courage to win the campaigns of peace'.[25] Within the PLP, there was some shock in left-wing quarters that Attlee had been involved with the broadcast and even approved its contents. Concern was also expressed that Churchill's four-year plan implied the creation of a post-war National Government in which Labour would not have the freedom to pursue its own socialist agenda. But, addressing the PLP, Attlee strongly denied that Labour would remain tied to the Conservatives after victory, while he also defended his co-operation with Churchill on the grounds that the broadcast 'put political problems into perspective and would clarify the mind of the nation'.[26]

Churchill had adroitly managed to still the storm over Beveridge, but the lull was only temporary. Labour's desire for real change could not be permanently assuaged by warm words, especially since the public appetite for reform was so strong. Yet the Prime Minister also had a vast military strategy to oversee in concert with his Allies; and from January 1943, he embarked on an ever greater number of visits overseas. This frenetic, often heroic, shuttle diplomacy further enhanced the Labour Leader's authority, both because it left Attlee in charge of the Cabinet for long periods and because it enabled him to develop a deeper relationship with the Foreign Secretary Eden. Indeed, the bond between the two men became crucial to the conduct of the war, often serving as a counterweight to Churchill.

The Prime Minister's first trip of the year was to meet Roosevelt at the Casablanca summit in French-held Morocco, a conference from which Stalin absented himself because of the military pressures of the Eastern Front. Apart from representing Roosevelt's first wartime trip to the Western theatre, Casablanca was significant for a couple of major decisions. The first was to continue the drive to push the Axis out of North Africa, already successfully begun at El Alamein and the Torch landings. The second was that, after victory in North Africa, the two Western Allies would concentrate on control of the Mediterranean in the remainder of 1943, rather than launch a cross-Channel invasion of Northern Europe, the option for which General George Marshall, the US Chief of Staff, had been pressing. But the Americans had to accept the priorities of Churchill, who rightly believed that the Allies were not yet nearly prepared for such a colossal undertaking and would do better to exploit the opportunities offered by an attack on Italy. 'I am satisfied that the President is strongly in favour of the Mediterranean being given prime place,' wrote Churchill to Attlee. [27]

After the satisfactory conclusion of Casablanca, Churchill now drew up plans to travel to the Cairo headquarters of the Desert Army before journeying to Turkey, where he hoped to persuade President Inonu to join the Allies' side, echoing his pre-Gallipoli belief that Germany was vulnerable on its Balkan flank. Attlee and the Cabinet were opposed to this dual visit, which they felt would serve no purpose, as the Labour Leader wrote in a stiff message to Churchill: 'We should frankly feel much happier if you could forgo your visit to Cairo. Parliament and the public will wish to welcome you back and to hear from you as soon as possible.' Attlee was even more vehement about the Turkish journey, which he feared might 'alarm' Inonu's regime and was likely to end in 'a failure'.[28] But Churchill rejected such concerns in his reply to Attlee. 'Even if the Turks should say no it will do no harm. I have no false pride in these matters. The capture of Tripoli and the increasing Russian victories and the fact that I speak for the great allies creates a most favourable occasion.'[29] After further discussions, Attlee and the War Cabinet relented, and approved the visit. 'I am most grateful to you for allowing me to try my plan. We may only get a snub in which case it will be my fault, but I do not think it will do to wait,' Churchill replied.[30] As he left for the first leg of his trip across North Africa, he sent Attlee a telegram to express, rather unconvincingly, his regret at not returning to London to be with his Cabinet colleagues. 'We are just off over the Atlas Mountains which are gleaming with their sunlit snows. You can imagine how much I wish I was going to be with you on the Bench but duty calls.'[31] According to the account he gave Attlee, his meeting with the Turkish President went well. 'He was most warm and cordial in all his attitude and he and his ministers reiterated again and again that they longed for the victory of England.'[32] But, as Attlee and the Cabinet had predicted, the visit achieved nothing tangible beyond an agreement for some supplies of military equipment. Turkey remained neutral until the last few months of the war.

After further military discussions in Tripoli and Algiers, Churchill finally arrived at RAF Lyneham on the morning of 7 February, having been out of England for almost four weeks. Despite his punishing schedule, he insisted on presiding at the War Cabinet that night, giving his colleagues an optimistic report on Casablanca, Turkey, and the military position in North Arica. A few days later, on 11 February, Churchill made an equally vigorous statement to the House of Commons about the Allies' prospects, which had been further enhanced by the victory of the Russians at Stalingrad. 'Winston made a fine speech today, in his best style. The man's vitality and self-confidence are superb,' wrote the backbencher Cuthbert Headlam.[33]

The impending victory in Tunisia, which became inevitable once Montgomery's 8th Army had crossed the Mareth Line on 28 March, meant that Churchill felt the need for another strategic conference with Roosevelt. The scale of the Axis powers' collapse in both Russia and North Africa had revived pressure for a second front in Northern Europe, while there were also crucial decisions to be reached on relations with the Free France movement, the focus of the proposed Allied attack on Italy and the Atlantic campaign. The Prime Minister and his entourage arrived in Washington on 11 May. It was Churchill's third wartime visit to the capital, but the equality that had once characterised his relationship with Roosevelt was beginning to dissipate. This was partly because the might of US military and industrial power was growing rapidly, meaning that Britain's influence counted for less, and partly because the Soviet regime commanded a new presence on the global stage after Stalingrad. Nevertheless the Washington Conference opened in auspicious circumstances, as the news came through of the final surrender of the Axis forces in Tunisia, with the capture of at least 230,000 German and Italian prisoners. In the flush of triumph, Churchill wrote to Attlee: 'I feel very strongly that the bells should be rung for Victory in the Gulf of Tunis as we did after Alamein. Surely it would be appropriate to have a Thanksgiving Service next Sunday.'[34] Both his instructions were followed, and when Attlee and Violet attended the service in St Paul's Cathedral, they were accompanied by Clementine Churchill. The Tunisian victory required another task from Attlee, one that he performed less satis-factorily. With Churchill absent in Washington, it fell to him to give the statement to the House of Commons on the Axis surrender, but, as so often before, his oratorical weakness let him down. George Harvie-Watt reported to the Prime Minister that 'Attlee was most uninspiring and everybody said what a pity it was that you could not have made the announcement yourself and received the personal congratulations you deserved.'[35] Following the statement, the National Labour MP Harold Nicolson wrote to his wife, 'Attlee stood there like a little snipe pecking at a wooden cage.'[36]

Nevertheless, Attlee conducted the business of the Cabinet with his usual efficiency, acting as a conduit for Churchill and co-ordinating the views of his colleagues. In fact Churchill openly expressed his gratitude to Attlee in one message soon after his arrival in Washington. 'You and your friends have been a great help to me in all the work we have done together. We all have much to be thankful for.'[37] The Washington Conference, codenamed Trident, proceeded smoothly enough. Crucially, Roosevelt rejected the proposal of General Marshall that America abandon its 'Germany first' strategy and instead concentrate on the Pacific theatre, the President arguing that such an approach would be of no help to the Soviet Union. However, in the context of Europe, Roosevelt agreed with Churchill that there was 'no possibility' of a cross-Channel crossing in 1943, even to secure a single bridgehead, but that there should be a full-scale invasion in the spring of 1944. Churchill warned, however, that British and American troops could not be left 'idle' for months while Russia was engaged in a titanic struggle on the Eastern Front.[38] As a result, the Americans agreed to an invasion of Sicily, beginning in July, though they were reluctant to approve any wider assault on Italy until that operation had proved successful. Even so, Churchill was pleased with the outcome, as he told Attlee: 'We have a free hand in the Mediterranean until November,' after which the Allies would focus on the preparations for the northern invasion into zones of occupation.[39]

Other strategic issues involved Attlee and Eden more directly. One was the friction in the Free France movement between General Henri Giraud and the notoriously prickly de Gaulle. The Americans were so exasperated by de Gaulle that they felt he should be 'eliminated as political force', a proposal that Churchill urged the War Cabinet to consider. But, with Attlee and Eden at the helm, the Cabinet was strongly against such a break, which ministers feared would cause divisions in the Free France movement, give the appearance of submissiveness to the USA and undermine Britain's relations with Allied governments from other Nazi-occupied powers. Attlee and Eden subsequently sent Churchill a telegram objecting to the American policy in the strongest possible terms, since 'there is no likelihood of the French National Committee continuing to function if de Gaulle were removed <u>by us.</u> The same is probable of the Free French fighting forces.'[40] In response, Churchill decided that the question would have to be settled by personal intervention by himself and Eden in bringing the two Frenchmen together once more in North Africa. Much to Churchill's pleasure, given his growing taste for wartime travel, this would require him to make another trip to Algiers. Some felt that Churchill's restlessness meant that he was neglecting his duties back in Britain. 'It is high time that the old man came home. The American atmosphere, the dictatorial powers of the President and the adulation which surrounds him there, have gone to his head [...] Eden and even Attlee are fed up at this lecturing and hectoring across the Atlantic,' noted Oliver Harvey.[41]

But Churchill continued his travelling, and undertook the arduous journey by flying boat from the USA to Algiers. There he once more set out his plans to the Americans for a full attack of the Italian mainland following July's invasion of Sicily. This, he argued, would bring down Mussolini and change the whole dynamic of the war, though Eisenhower and the other US generals remained uncommitted until they saw how the Sicilian operation unfolded. There were other, more productive, features of the visit. One was the achievement of a new spirit of co-operation between Giraud and de Gaulle, lubricated by the charm of Eden, who, on Churchill's insistence, had flown out to North Africa for this mission. 'He is much better fitted than I am to be best man at the Giraud-de Gaulle wedding,' Churchill told Attlee.[42] The Prime Minister also undertook further reviews of victorious British troops, as well as indulging in some bathing in the warm waters of the Mediterranean. 'I need some rest in this sunshine after the hustle of Washington,' he confessed to Attlee.[43]

On his return to England, he had to face some domestic political discontent. His March broadcast had temporarily lessened the pressure for social reform, but by June impatience was growing once more. Labour's desire for change was bolstered by a new self-confidence on the left and by two opinion polls that gave the party a lead over the Conservatives of between 7 and 11 per cent. At their Annual Conference in London in mid-June, Labour voted overwhelmingly to stay in the wartime Coalition but emphatically rejected the idea of maintaining any pact once victory was achieved. There was also some criticism of the Labour leadership in showing too much inhibition towards Churchill while allowing him to seize the reform agenda with his BBC broadcast. Barbara Betts,* a passionate young delegate from St Pancras, told the Conference, 'Churchill has pinched the reforming pants of our leaders while they have been bathing in the pool of national unity.'[44] The *News Chronicle* directed its fire at Attlee personally, describing him as 'the most platitudinous and non-committal of all Government Ministers'.[45]

Apart from the great questions of military strategy and domestic reform, Attlee also had to liaise regularly with Churchill in his capacity as Dominions Secretary over a wide range of subjects, such as the role of the Australian forces in Burma, military supplies for the Eire Government and submarine activity off the southern African coast. As always, Attlee was fascinated with the machinery of government; consequently Churchill received lengthy missives from him about the Dominions' relations with the proposed United Nations Council, their role in the post-war peace conferences and the possible creation – suggested by the Australian Prime Minister John Curtin – of an Imperial Consultative Council, an idea that found little support in London. By far the biggest imperial issue remained India, which was made so combustible by the mix of nationalism and the Japanese threat. Attlee had no direct responsibility for the region, since its oversight was in the hands of Leo Amery, the Secretary of State, but from late 1942 Attlee's name became central to its future governance. At that time, the Viceroyalty of the 2nd Marquess of Linlithgow was drawing to a close. Although an experienced Scottish Unionist politician, Linlithgow was regarded as insufficiently adroit at handling the nationalist agitation engulfing India. A higher-calibre leader was needed. As he told Churchill in a letter of 13 November 1942, Amery felt that Attlee was the

---

* Later the controversial Labour Cabinet minister Barbara Castle.

man for the task, in preference to the widely touted Sir John Anderson. 'Attlee knows the Indian problem and has no sentimental illusions as to any dramatic short cut to its solution. He also has a shrewd understanding of military matters and at this time the Viceroy has to be the prime mover in the war effort as well as the political head.'[46] Churchill showed little enthusiasm for this proposal, and Amery came up with other names, including Rab Butler and Archie Sinclair. Attlee himself did not want the post and pushed for Butler, never a favourite of Churchill's. With no decision reached, Amery returned in April 1943 to the idea of Attlee. 'If he lacks personality, he has at any rate ability and shrewd judgement and would, I think, handle his Council effectively.'[47] But Churchill still was not interested. His mind had turned towards Eden, the one man he felt who had 'the sole chance of lifting the whole India problem out of its present disastrous rut', as he put it to George VI.[48] To his gratification and surprise, Eden was willing to consider the position. But the King was strongly opposed to Eden's departure, because of both his command of Foreign Affairs and his closeness to Churchill, while Attlee was 'hot against it' when informed of the idea.[49] In the end, Churchill decided that he could not spare any front-rank politician from London, so he came up with the solution of elevating Archibald Wavell to the Viceroyalty, with Auchinleck taking over from Wavell as Commander of the Indian Army.

Despite political disagreements, Attlee remained on good terms with Churchill. At the end of June he and Violet were invited by the Corporation of London to the ceremony at which Churchill was presented with the Freedom of the City. In his speech, Churchill had struck a bullish note about the progress of the war, a sense of optimism that was fully justified by the success in July of the Allies' Sicilian invasion. 'It is a tremendous feat to leap on shore with nearly 200,000 men,' he telegraphed to Eisenhower on 10 July.[50] The swift triumph of the Sicilian venture prompted Churchill to urge a full-scale attack on the Italian mainland, with the objective of swiftly taking Naples and Rome and refashioning the course of the war in Central Europe. Although the Americans were willing to accept an assault on Italy, Churchill's concern was that they would attach insufficient priority to this theatre, given not only their focus on the cross-Channel invasion of France planned for 1944 but also the demands of the Pacific campaign against Japan. Another bilateral conference was therefore held to define the military strategy, this time in Quebec in mid-August. Churchill travelled to Canada aboard the *Queen Mary* once more, accompanied by a 200-strong party that included Clementine and his daughter Sarah. Again, just two months after his last spell in charge, Attlee was acting Prime Minister in London as he performed his usual role of receiving Churchill's views and co-ordinating the Cabinet.

The Quebec Conference resolved a number of questions, not all to Churchill's satisfaction. Roosevelt and the American chiefs insisted on the primacy of the French invasion over Italy, reflected in their instruction that seven Allied divisions be shifted from the Mediterranean to England in preparation for the cross-Channel crossing, now codenamed Overlord. American dominance was further highlighted in the fact that Roosevelt decided that General Marshall had to be the Overlord Commander, even though Churchill had promised the post to Alan Brooke. Churchill went along with this on the grounds that US troops would make up the majority of the Overlord force. He told Attlee of his admiration for the US leader. 'I have the greatest confidence in General Marshall both as a man and as a soldier. I am sure that established in our midst he would work most harmoniously with us all.'[51] Brooke, however, was hurt that Churchill had given way so easily. 'He offered no sympathy, no regrets at having to change his mind, and dealt with the matter as if it was of minor importance.'[52] More positively for the British, it was agreed that Alexander should be in charge of the Mediterranean, while the relatively junior Lord Louis Mountbatten was made Supreme Commander in Southeast Asia. 'He is a master of combined operations and his appointment would, I think, command public interest and approval and show that youth is no bar to merit,' Churchill wrote to Attlee, who strongly agreed with the promotion.[53] The Allies also agreed to invite Stalin to a tripartite conference, the location of which, after much aggravated negotiation with Russia, was fixed for Tehran in late November.

But in the context of the long-term relationship between Churchill and Attlee, perhaps the most important feature of Quebec was the decision reached over nuclear weapons. In August 1941, Churchill had approved the development of an atomic bomb, largely in response to fears that the Germans were conducting their own research in this field. This highly secret project was codenamed Tube Alloys and overseen by Sir John Anderson, who had been a brilliant scientist before he entered Government service. 'Although personally I am quite content with existing explosives, I feel we must not stand in the way of improvement,' said Churchill.[54] But from October 1941 the Americans were working on their own atomic bomb, through the Manhattan Project run by the US Army, exploiting their vastly greater resources and lack of enemy threat to their territory. Recognising that Britain would struggle to bring Tube Alloys to fruition, Churchill suggested the Allies pool their expertise – a proposal to which the Americans consented. By the spring of 1943, however, Churchill was concerned that Britain was being shut out from co-operation despite sharing its atomic knowledge. At Quebec, he therefore sought to put the collaboration on a more formal basis. Roosevelt concurred and on 19 August the two men signed the Quebec Agreement, whose key clauses stipulated that neither power would use the bomb without the other's consent and that information about Tube Alloys would not be passed on to any third parties 'except by mutual consent'.[55] Churchill was delighted with the deal, but there were a number of problems. First, since the agreement had been arranged privately between Churchill and Roosevelt, it was largely kept secret from the British and American military, thereby limiting its impact. Second, its wording was vague and easily open to misinterpretation. Third, it revealed that the USA was clearly the senior partner in the atomic race, with Britain in a far more supplicant position. This dominance meant that the Americans could abandon the agreement whenever they wanted, with huge implications for Britain's defence policy.

Churchill was back in England on 20 September. Militarily, the war in the Mediterranean was not progressing as swiftly as the Allies had hoped, despite the fall of Mussolini and the Italian surrender in late July. The Germans offered stiff resistance in both Italy and the Dodecanese islands in the Aegean Sea, which Churchill, in one of those peripheral operations he so cherished, had planned to seize in order to provide air bases for an attack on the Nazi-controlled Balkans and persuade Turkey to join the war. There was more trouble on the Home Front. The very day after Churchill arrived back in Downing Street, the Chancellor of the Exchequer Sir Kingsley Wood suddenly dropped dead from a heart attack. In the subsequent reshuffle, the vacancy as Chancellor was filled by Sir John Anderson, whose own place as Lord President of the Council, effectively the domestic-policy chief, was taken by Attlee. There was a degree of cynicism about Attlee's elevation to a more enhanced role at the heart of Government. 'I am not sure whether Attlee's succession as Lord President will be a very popular one,' wrote Sylvester to his chief, Lloyd George.[56] Cecil King felt that Churchill used Attlee to give the illusion of consultation and thereby cover up his own supposed autocratic style of governance. 'The Prime Minister is careful to inform Attlee of almost everything. Attlee can be relied on to have no views of his own and his connivance rather spikes the guns of other Labour ministers if they get restive.'[57] Nor did Churchill himself seem to have much faith in his reshuffled Cabinet, as he told Eden: 'Except for you and me, this is the worst Government England ever had.'[58]

But, as so often before, Attlee had been underrated. Strengthened by his new status as the Lord President, he went on the attack against Churchill over the Government's continuing lack of progress on domestic reform. A policy document that he had written with Bevin and Morrison in the early summer, entitled *The Need for Decisions*, was used as the basis to crank up the pressure for reconstruction, especially on housing and social services. At a Cabinet meeting on 14 October, Attlee made the renewed case for action. 'There were many subjects on which the formulation of policy could not await the end of the war;

if decisions had not been taken and preparatory action put in hand, the end of the war would find us unprepared,' he told his colleagues.[59] Churchill was unfavourable to these arguments, as the Cabinet minutes recorded: 'He recalled the dangers of the campaigns on which we should be required to embark in 1944. We were approaching the grimmest climax of the war.' As a result he found 'the greatest difficulty in giving close attention' to 'the discussion of social policy'.[60] Backed up by the other Labour ministers, Attlee continued to press for more Government urgency until Churchill had to call the meeting to a halt because he had a dinner engagement with the King. Later he complained, half-jokingly, that he had been 'jostled and beaten up by the Deputy Prime Minister'.[61]

Without the buttress of Kingsley Wood's fiscal conservatism, Churchill was now in a weaker position. His resistance to Attlee soon crumbled. At the next Cabinet discussion about social policy, during a meeting on 21 October, he adopted a much more conciliatory tone. Far from blocking reform, he now took steps to embrace it. He proposed a transition period from war to peace, defined to cover either two years from the defeat of Germany or four years from January 1944, whichever ended sooner. 'The supreme objectives must be to assure food and employment in the transitional period,' he declared; but a 'number of other matters', such as education, social insurance and the rebuilding of bombed cities, 'must be brought to a high degree of preparation during the war'.[62] According to Dalton's account of the meeting, Churchill's poetic imagination was fired by the literary possibilities of the new progressive approach.

> He then elaborates, with great dramatic details, how we should prepare a great book, the Book of Transition, like the War Book, running to perhaps a thousand closely printed pages or taking the form of a number of Reports and precise plans contained in drawers, one above another, so that if any amateurish critic says, 'You have no plan for this or that', it will be easy to pull out a drawer, bring out a paper, and say, 'Here it all is.'[63]

Dalton felt that that 'very great credit is due to Attlee, and, in a lesser degree, to Morrison for having brought about this remarkable change in the PM's attitude. They have both been having a great go on him, and tonight the PM, who is in very good temper and great spirits, says that he has been led to see this question quite differently.' Later, after the Cabinet meeting, Dalton saw Attlee to offer his personal congratulations. 'He said there had been a frightful row last week, and loud explosions from the PM. But now the smoke had cleared away, the PM [...] had led his Tory troops through the breach which we had made in their defences.'[64]

Yet this was not the end of Attlee's conflict with Churchill that autumn over reform. To give more impetus to the new transition policy, Attlee wanted to add a Labour peer to the Government's Reconstruction Committee, but Churchill strongly objected, feeling that the socialists were already well represented. There was further discord when Churchill decided to appoint a new, more powerful Minister of Reconstruction to replace the present, ineffectual incumbent, Labour's William Jowitt.

To fill the post, Churchill at first considered Beaverbrook, whom he had brought back to the Government as Lord Privy Seal in September. Attlee had been furious at the return of his bitter enemy but at least, as Lord Privy Seal, Beaverbrook was not in the War Cabinet. He would be, however, if Churchill made him Minister of Reconstruction. Attlee was alarmed at the idea and directly confronted Churchill about the proposed appointment. 'Attlee says that he saw the PM last night and they had "quite a row, as we usually do" but the result is that Beaverbrook is to have nothing to do with post-war,' recorded Dalton.[65] In place of Beaverbrook, Churchill chose Lord Woolton for Reconstruction, a move that Attlee welcomed, not least because Woolton, like himself, had been a social worker before the First World War.

The quarrels over reconstruction revealed that authority was beginning to drain from Churchill. Now aged almost sixty-nine, he was no longer the commanding warrior he had been in 1940. When Lord Woolton arrived for lunch at Downing Street to discuss the minis-terial offer, he found Churchill 'grumpy' and 'obviously not looking well', though 'he wakened up a bit after his second whiskey'.[66] As the balance of power shifted in the Cabinet, Churchill gradually diminished while Attlee grew in stature. The balance was also moving on the global stage, with America and Russia dominant and Britain increasingly reduced to a supporting role. Setbacks in British-led initiatives accelerated the process. Bomber Command's vast strategic offensive had not broken the Reich, while the assault on mainland Italy against Germany, which began on 3 September, was proving tough. Even worse, the Dodecanese campaign ended in disaster as the Germans seized the islands in November, with 4,600 British casualties. In a telegram to Attlee, Churchill tried to justify his pet venture by claiming that 'great prizes were offered. It was our duty to try to seize them with the forces available [...] If we are only to work on certainties we must prepare for a very long war.'[67] But, given that the Americans had been strongly opposed to this operation, its failure only further weakened Churchill's influence. 'I can control him no more,' wrote Brooke bitterly, adding that the Prime Minister had 'worked himself into a frenzy of excitement' over the attack so that he 'can no longer see anything else', even at 'the expense of endangering his relations with the President and the Americans'.[68]

The sense of ebbing power made Churchill all the more determined to ensure that the Tehran Conference with Roosevelt and Stalin in November was a success. The discussions, dominated by the questions of Overlord and the campaign in Eastern Europe, went reasonably, though Churchill was often on the defensive against Stalin. At one point, the Soviet leader asked him if he really believed in the northern invasion. The Prime Minister replied, 'It is our stern duty to hurl across the Channel every sinew of our strength.'[69] Stalin agreed to launch a major offensive to tie down German troops in the east and the date of Overlord was confirmed for May 1944. 'We have had a grand day here and relations between Britain, the United States and the USSR have never been so cordial and intimate. All war plans are agreed and concerted,' Churchill told Attlee on 1 December.[70] Churchill and Stalin also discussed British domestic politics, the Prime Minister admitting that the public had become keener on progressive ideas. 'It might now be said to have gone so far as to be termed pink,' he told the Russian leader, who replied that 'this is a sign of improved health'.[71]

Later at the conference, Churchill and Roosevelt provisionally settled most of the Anglo-American military commands for the escalating conflict, the key one of which was leadership of Overlord. Having decided that he needed Marshall to stay in Washington, Roosevelt proposed the appointment of Eisenhower as Supreme Commander, a step that Churchill accepted. 'Marshall, it appears, cannot leave the United States for political reasons, as he is a pillar of the Administration,' Churchill explained to Attlee.[72] A large number of other appointments followed from this change, including the RAF senior officer Arthur Tedder as Eisenhower's Deputy. Churchill set these out in a telegram to Attlee of 14 December for the Cabinet's approval; but, illustrating that he still did not have complete confidence in Attlee, he also contacted Eden. 'Please see my long telegram to Attlee about the Commands. I rely upon you to help me get this all settled without derangement.'[73]

Churchill's doubt was understandable, for during the Tehran Summit a domestic row blew up in London that badly undermined his faith in Labour. The storm was caused by the decision of the Home Secretary Herbert Morrison to release the BUF Leader Sir Oswald Mosley from detention at Holloway prison on the grounds of ill-health, for Mosley was suffering from phlebitis. In the House on 23 November, Morrison announced the move, which initially provoked little hostility among MPs. 'Home Secretary made an admirable statement on the Mosley release. Majority of members in all parties satisfied,' Attlee telegraphed to Churchill that day.[74] An instinctive liberal on penal policy, Churchill welcomed Morrison's decision and felt that the Government should go even further by moving to dispense altogether with the Defence Regulation 18B introduced in May 1940, under which suspects could be held indefinitely without trial. Writing jointly to Attlee and Morrison, he said: 'On no account should we lend any countenance to the totalitarian idea of the right of the executive to lock up its political opponents or unpopular people. The door should be kept open for the full restoration of the fundamental British rights of habeas corpus and trial by jury.'[75] Morrison had no intention of repealing Regulation 18B, as he told Churchill on 26 November: 'In the present situation it would be tactically bad that it should go. Things are pretty hot, though, I think, cooling.'[76] But Morrison was wrong. The mood in both the Labour Party and the public was far from cooling and was in fact becoming more inflamed, as Clementine informed her husband two days later: 'Public opinion of Mosley's release is surprisingly unanimous, though most bitter and violent from the left because of the suspicion that class and money gave him preferential treatment.'[77]

The discord now spread to the top of the Government. Reflecting the views of the National Council of Labour, which had voted to dissociate itself from the Mosley decision, Bevin launched a fusillade against Morrison at the Cabinet on 29 November, warning that, if there was a vote in the Commons on the release, 'his only course might be to resign from the Government'.[78] That night Attlee, alarmed by this development, wrote to Churchill to warn of Bevin's potential departure and a rebellion in the Commons: 'It is likely that a number of Labour MPs will vote for the amendment and if there is not a greater number in the Government lobby, the position of Morrison and myself will be very difficult.'[79] On receiving this telegram, Churchill was incensed, not only by the equivocation over the principle of liberty but also the elevation of this issue into a major political controversy just as the fate of global war was being debated at Tehran. 'I am perplexed at what seems to be a loss of proportion in some of our colleagues. Of course, we shall have to address ourselves to any situation that may arise as the war will certainly have to be carried on,' he told Attlee.[80] Still in a fury, Churchill now drafted two further telegrams in which he poured out his ire against Labour. One was to Ernie Bevin, previously regarded by Churchill as the epitome of solid loyalty: 'You are the last man whom I thought would stab me in the back like this at a time when I am absent on public duty.'[81] The second draft was to Attlee, effectively accusing him of political irresponsibility. 'If Labour Ministers choose to leave the Government on what I can only regard as a frivolous pretext of this kind and I am entrusted by the King with the duty of carrying on the war, I shall certainly not flinch from it.' Having again expressed his approval of Morrison's decision, he warned Attlee, 'If you force a political crisis I will immediately come home by air to the detriment of much important business and will address myself to the public, both in Parliament and by broadcasting.' He concluded, 'Please realise that if the Labour Party force this issue, the war will still have to be carried on, and I am sure that both Parliament and the Nation will support those who faithfully bear the burden.'[82]

Having vented his feelings on paper, and being wary of deepening the political crisis, Churchill decided not to send these two telegrams. But in the privacy of his quarters at Tehran he became embroiled in a rare political argument with his doctor Charles Wilson, to whom he raged about 'Labour's folly and stupidity'. Wilson, according to the account in his diaries, told Churchill that 'he could not govern England without Labour. It would impair unity and interfere with production. At this he shouted that he could get on quite well without them. He would not get rid of them but they could go if they wanted.'[83]

In reality, however, Churchill knew that he could not preside over the break-up of his Coalition. In place of confrontation, he decided to try conciliation. His faithful disciple Brendan Bracken, a skilful backstairs operator, was therefore instructed to pull Bevin back from the brink. Bracken did so with an artfully composed letter to Bevin that stressed both the damage that would be caused by his resignation and the increased burden Churchill would have to endure. Contrary to the public view that Churchill was 'a man of limitless strength', wrote Bracken, he actually needed 'all the encouragement which he can get from his colleagues and the more worries that can be kept from him, the better for his health'.[84] The letter succeeded in its objective; Bevin withdrew his threat of resignation. With that, the crisis passed. The PLP decided, by a narrow margin, to support Morrison in the Commons vote on Mosley's release. In the subsequent division, sixty-eight Labour MPs voted for the Government and fifty-one against – a revolt too large for Attlee's liking but nevertheless still a minority.

Much of the saga had been driven by Ernie Bevin's personal antipathy to Morrison, yet it was the Home Secretary who emerged with his political reputation enhanced. 'He stands head and shoulders above the other Labour leaders,' argued the *Daily Express*. In contrast, Attlee's hesitant performance did not bring him much credit, justifying some of the concerns that Eden had felt before he travelled out to join Churchill. 'His chief anxiety was leaving the House of Commons to be handled by Attlee during the next fortnight,' recorded the King's private secretary Tommy Lascelles after a conversation with Eden, who was so wound up by prospect that he acted 'like a caged beast'.[85]

The political crisis in London may have been resolved, but, still out of the country in December 1943, Churchill now faced another, much more personal one.

TWENTY-ONE

NORMANDY
AND ITALY

A s ATTLEE LEANED forward at the Dispatch Box, a hush descended on the House of Commons. It was 16 December 1943 and Churchill was absent in Tunisia, where he was staying at Eisenhower's villa in Carthage, following the conclusion of the Tehran Conference. But Attlee was not about to give a report on the Allies' military strategy. Instead, to audible gasps around the chamber, he told MPs that the Prime Minister was seriously ill with pneumonia. His announcement sent a wave of consternation through Parliament and the press, the *Spectator* recording that there was 'universal alarm' at the development.[1]

The Prime Minister had picked up his infection as he travelled from Cairo when he already suffering from a heavy cold. Unfortunately his plane, bound for Carthage, had gone to the wrong airfield and had to wait for clearance to reach its correct destination. Churchill's navigator Air Commodore John Mitchell later recalled,

> The incident might have been funny had the Prime Minister not decided to leave the aircraft and sit glumly on a packing case in the cold, whilst contact was established. There were angry words and some confusion. The sudden change from a warm cockpit to a cold winter's morning meant that the damage was quickly

done. Although we were in the air again within half an hour, the PM's cold was already turning to pneumonia.[2]

When Churchill's condition deteriorated rapidly on his arrival in Carthage, his doctor Charles Wilson came under pressure from the Cabinet to take drastic action, with the result that several specialists were sent to the scene. Also travelling to Carthage was Clementine, though the plan for the trip was kept secret from Churchill because, in her view, 'details of the journey may cause him anxiety'.[3] Churchill's daughter Sarah, who served as a map reader in North Africa, was already at the Eisenhower villa in Carthage, and on the worst night of the medical crisis was at her father's bedside, watching him sleep. 'Once he opened his eyes, and must have caught my troubled look before I had time to mask it. He looked at me without speaking for a moment, then said, "Don't worry, it doesn't matter now. The plans for victory have been laid and it is only a matter of time", and fell into a deep sleep once more.'[4]

Fortunately, by the time Clementine arrived on 17 December, Churchill had improved and was no longer in danger. The recovery continued over Christmas in Carthage, after which Churchill flew with Clementine to Marrakesh, where his spirits were further raised by the presence of Lord Beaverbrook, as well as Allied successes like advances in Burma, and the sinking of the German battle cruiser *Scharnhorst* at the Battle of the North Cape. While he was in Marrakesh he also discussed with generals Alexander and Montgomery his daring plan to land two British divisions on the beach at Anzio on the central-western coast of Italy, bypassing the Germans who were successfully defending the Gustav Line further south. If it were successful, the seizure of the Anzio beachhead could break the stalemate in Italy and open the way to the swift capture of Rome. Having fixed the details of the plan, codenamed Operation Shingle, with his military chiefs, Churchill then wrote to Attlee on 8 January 1944. 'The battle is one of the highest consequence and by no means free of hazard, mainly through weather. I am convinced that it should be launched as planned and that it is in the most confident and resolute hands.'⁵ The War Cabinet agreed, with the Anzio landings set for 21 January.

By this point of the war, Attlee was an experienced and confident Deputy Prime Minister. His new authority was demonstrated when, in place of Churchill, he delivered the Government's New Year broadcast to the nation. He opened with a generous reference to Churchill: 'As the year drew to a close we were relieved of our anxiety for the Prime Minister's health. We are able to celebrate with the knowledge that he was convalescent.' Attlee then turned to the two themes that were to dominate the final period of the Coalition. One was the ultimate defeat of the Germans. 'The hour of reckoning has come for them and they know that 1944 will mean for them only heavier attacks.' The other was the need to prepare immediately for post-war reconstruction, including 'a national health service and a system of social services and the provision of full employment'.⁶ Rarely celebrated for his gifts as a communicator, Attlee was on this occasion showered with congratulations from all sides. Labour minister Ellen Wilkinson wrote to say that his broadcast 'gave a lead, instead of the usual museum collection of platitudes that we have had to endure'. Even George Harvie-Watt was fulsome: 'I had the pleasure of listening to your broadcast and I thought it was so good that I must drop you a note of congratulation. It was just what the nation wanted at this time.'⁷

Churchill arrived back in London on 18 January and was met by the full Cabinet at Paddington station. Given that the Tehran Conference had begun in November, he had been away from England no fewer than sixty-seven days. Immediately, he plunged back into official business. Chairing the War Cabinet at 12.15 p.m., he outlined the progress of the Allied plans: 'Recent secret intelligence showed that Hitler's position was still very strong. If Operation Overlord did not achieve considerable success, many people would no doubt start objecting to the demand for unconditional surrender,' he warned his colleagues, the call for such a surrender having been agreed at the Allied summits in 1943. After an audience with the King at Buckingham Palace, he went to the Commons, where he was greeted by a remarkable outpouring of affection from MPs in the chamber, as described by Harold Nicolson. 'He was flushed with pleasure and emotion, and hardly had he sat down when two large tears began to trickle down his cheeks.'[8]

For all such adulation, however, there were signs of the Prime Minister's mental and physical degeneration from the beginning of 1944. Dalton noted how, after one Cabinet meeting in March which Attlee chaired while Churchill was again away, several ministers said 'how much quicker things go when he is absent'.[9] Dalton's ministerial colleague Leo Amery, who as India Secretary had come to despise Churchill's reactionary attitude towards governmental reform in the subcontinent, said of one Cabinet that 'a complete outsider coming to that meeting and knowing nothing of his reputation would have thought him a rather amusing but quite gaga old gentleman who could not understand what people were talking about'.[10] The reality was that Churchill, after bearing for years the mammoth responsibility of the fight against Nazi tyranny, had endured a heavy physical blow. Many lesser men would have been finished by his recent illness, but even his renowned powers of recuperation had their limits. Indeed Charles Wilson later wrote that, after the episode in Carthage, Churchill 'never seemed to me the same man again'.[11] His decline could also be seen as a metaphor for the political situation. The Conservatives, portrayed as anachronistic and blinkered, were sinking in the mire of unpopularity; while Labour were full of plans for rebuilding post-war Britain. Churchill and the Tories represented a heroic past, Attlee and Labour a brighter future.

Yet Labour's position was complex, driven by the internal conflict between apprehension and hope. Many in the higher echelons of the party were anxious that the magnetism of Churchill would ultimately ensure Labour's defeat at the next election. Still a titanic figure on the global stage, he had, they feared, the potential to repeat the example of Lloyd George's landslide of 1918, when the Liberal Leader exploited the public euphoria at the end of the war. That was why in early 1944 most of Labour's senior politicians favoured a long gap of at least six months between the defeat of Germany and the date of an election, so that Churchill's prestige might dissipate. The idea of lengthening the life of the Coalition appealed to Churchill himself, with his romantic, nostalgic attachment to cross-party Government, as he said to the War Cabinet on 1 February. 'When Hitler was defeated, it might be that the parties would feel that the time had come when they should part honourably and amicably and have an election. On the other hand, they might well feel that they ought to hold together for, say, another couple of years.'[12] In addition there were concerns on the left that Attlee, for all his growth in stature during the war, did not have the weight to take on Churchill in a contest. Cecil King, whose *Daily Mirror* strongly backed Labour, asked Morrison if the party 'really meant business' by refusing to change the leadership. 'It is about to go to the country appealing for votes for Attlee as our next Prime Minister. Such a choice was irresponsible. I would not employ him as a lift attendant.'[13]

Despite such reservations, Attlee's party was gaining ground; one poll in the spring of 1944 gave Labour a fifteen-point lead over the Tories. 'There is undoubtedly a leftward swing, especially in regard to post-war problems,' wrote Attlee to Bevin in March.[14] Nor was Churchill as universally popular as Labour feared. A survey in February 1944 found that 62 per cent of the British public were against Churchill becoming the post-war Prime Minister.[15] During a visit to south London in February, Harold Nicolson saw on a lavatory wall at Blackheath station the scrawled slogan, 'Winston Churchill is a bastard'. Nicolson pointed this out to the Wing Commander who was with him. 'Yes, the tide has turned,' replied the airman.[16] That changing tide was most graphically seen in a series of by-election defeats suffered by the Conservatives, most notably in February at West Derbyshire, where the seat, long a fiefdom of the Unionist Cavendish family, was taken by the independent Labour candidate after an acrimonious campaign in which Labour activists openly breached the electoral truce by canvassing against the Coalition. The result, wrote Jock Colville, 'caused a pall of blackest gloom to fall on the Prime Minister'.[17] After West Derbyshire, some in the Labour Party felt that the truce should be diluted or even abandoned. Churchill wanted to go in the opposite direction, urging that ministers should campaign vigorously for Coalition candidates at future by-elections, though Attlee felt this approach was impractical, as he told Bevin: 'the Prime Minister has tried to meet the by-election difficulty by urging all parties in the Coalition to greater activity on behalf of Government candidates and has intervened vigorously himself. All the evidence goes to show that this has had the contrary effect. The general demand is for loosening, not tightening, the conditions of the truce.'[18] But Attlee was equally opposed to ditching the compact, despite the impatience of many Labour members. In late February, under his guidance, the NEC issued a statement that read: 'Back us in supporting Mr Churchill to victory. We are working out our own reconstruction plans for after the war on the assumption that the next General Election will find us in the field as an independent party.'[19] Apart from the need for national unity against the enemy, Attlee felt that too many socialist critics were now inclined to exaggerate the negative side of the Coalition. He pointed out that Labour had since 1940 achieved considerable progress in the field of welfare, including more free school milk and meals, a rise in unemployment assistance and the introduction of supplementary pensions. More importantly, he claimed that they had gained immeasurably from the experience of accepting responsibility under Churchill. In a speech to the Midlands Regional Council of the Labour Party in May, he referred to the nationwide 'swing to the left' and asked: 'Would it have occurred if we had stood out, if we had not taken responsibility or if we had adopted the attitude of mere criticism of others? I say to you no. This swing has been due very largely to the fact that Labour men like Morrison, Bevin, Alexander and Dalton have taken on difficult jobs.'[20]

But the maintenance of the Coalition could be difficult, particularly as Attlee continued to endure the charge of failing to stand up to Churchill. That accusation was made by Bevin in late March over Churchill's plans for a minor reshuffle of the second tier of his Government, including the move of Bracken to the Dominions and Gwilym Lloyd George to the Ministry of Information. According to the account he gave Dalton, Bevin listened to the proposed changes outlined by Attlee, then asked,

'Have you agreed to all this?' Attlee replied that he had talked about it to Churchill. 'Did you raise no objection?' demanded Bevin. Attlee admitted he had not. 'You ought to be ashamed of yourself, letting all these jobs go to Tories.' Bevin was even more infuriated when Attlee explained that Churchill wanted Manny Shinwell, the arch Labour rebel, at the Ministry of Fuel and Power. 'If that bugger is brought in, I shall go out and you can tell that to the PM. I won't stand for it.'[21] As it happened, there was no need for such a scene since Churchill did not proceed with the reshuffle. At Attlee's request, however, Churchill agreed to appoint Viscount Stansgate, the father of the Labour radical Tony Benn, as Deputy Leader of the House of Lords, though he refused on financial grounds to offer him the additional sinecure of Captain of the Gentleman-at-Arms. 'It is true that the emoluments of this post are only £700-a-year, but I understand that Stansgate has a substantial private income* – enough at any rate to come within the range of destructive taxation. His status is fixed by his position as Deputy Leader of the House,' Churchill wrote to Attlee on 27 May.[22]

By far the bitterest dispute in Parliament arose in late March during the passage of Rab Butler's Education Bill, which refashioned and expanded secondary education in Britain. The Conservative MP Thelma Cazalet-Keir, sister of the late Victor Cazalet, who had been killed in action in 1943, put down an amendment to introduce equal pay for women teachers. Despite a three-line whip, her change passed by a single vote, the only time the Coalition was defeated during the war. Attlee was indignant, calling the rebellion 'the culmination of a course of irresponsible conduct'.[23] Churchill was even angrier and decided that the equal-pay amendment should be overturned in the House on a vote of confidence. When told by one Tory MP that he was making too big a deal of a minor issue, Churchill replied, 'I am not going to tumble round my cage like a wounded canary. You knocked me off my perch. You have to put me back on my perch, otherwise I won't sing.'[24]

---

* Much of it derived from the Stansgate Abbey Farm near the Blackwater Estuary in Essex, which remains in the Benn family.

To Rab Butler, Churchill drew on a different analogy from nature. 'The amendment advocates a perfectly good principle which is not suitable for insertion in this clause. It is quite easy to have a perfectly good thing in the wrong place. This amendment is like a potato in a gooseberry pie.'[25]

Determined to uphold the Coalition, Attlee was just as keen for the vote of confidence to succeed. According to Chuter Ede's account, at a meeting of senior Labour ministers on the night of 20 March, 'Attlee said that unless he received strong support from the rank and file of the party, he was not willing to continue. We agreed that he should say this to the party tomorrow.'[26] Attlee did so the following morning at the meeting of the PLP, where Bevin also made a powerful appeal for Government unity. The pressure worked. By 425 votes to 23, the amendment was overwhelmingly thrown out. Soon afterwards, Attlee told a party rally in Yorkshire that the right course had been followed. 'A great party like ours, aspiring to power to make great changes, cannot tread the path of the Independents.' A doctrine that any defeat on domestic policy could just be accepted 'would be fatal to the working of responsible government', he warned.[27] The huge vote of confidence put Churchill in a jovial mood, but, unlike Attlee, he paid a heavy long-term price that only strengthened the Tories' image as reactionaries. Quentin Hogg, a young, progressive backbencher, felt that Churchill's 'extraordinary behaviour' demonstrated that he had 'no understanding of the national mood for social justice'.[28] A less jaundiced view came from Hugh Dalton, who wrote of the atmosphere inside the Government at the height of the controversy, 'We are all showing various signs of disorder and strain, while waiting for the invasion.'[29]

Dalton was right. The build-up to the start of Overlord, now fixed for 5 June, was a time of high tension, for the fate of the war in Western Europe depended on the success of the landings. The difficulties inherent in a vast amphibious operation were highlighted, on a much smaller scale, by the failure of the Anzio assault to break the stalemate on the Italian front, even though the bridgehead was successfully secured. 'I had hoped that we were hurling a wild cat on to the shore, but all we got was a stranded whale,' Churchill wrote later.[30] Attlee, effectively the supremo on the Home Front by 1944, rarely intervened in military strategy but the Anzio experience prompted him to write to Churchill a series of notes about the potential lessons for Overlord. The danger, he said, was that Normandy landings might also develop into a static, fortified bridgehead, surrounded by heavy German forces. The alternative was to plan for a much wider base for offensive action through 'the capture of considerable territory to give space to bring over land and air forces'. Such a strategy, Attlee said, 'involves taking very vigorous action and accepting great risks'. Referring to Attlee's notes, Churchill told the Chiefs of Staff on 11 March: 'I am in sympathy with their general tenor.'[31] But Attlee's advice was redundant. A massive invasion across a wide front was exactly what Eisenhower, Tedder and the other strategists were planning. Indeed, Overlord was to be by far the largest seaborne military operation in history.

At times, as D-Day approached, Churchill seemed despondent. Scarred by memories of Gallipoli, he was concerned about the potential Allied casualties, as well as the diversion of military resources from his cherished Italian campaign, especially when the Americans decided to follow up Overlord with an invasion of southern France, an operation codenamed Dragoon. He thought the Riviera assault 'a complete waste of time for Allied troops', recalled Jock Colville, for in Churchill's view it not only stalled the thrust through Italy but also destroyed the chance to attack the Germans in the rear through Austria and Hungary.[32] He was also dispirited by the prospect of Soviet totalitarian dominance in post-war Eastern Europe, as well as the USA's marginalisation of Britain in favour of Stalin's regime. Another factor was his sense of exhaustion, all too apparent at certain moments before D-Day. At a Conference of Dominion Prime Ministers in London on 1 May, Churchill spoke for one and a half hours, but Brooke was scathing about his performance. 'Dull, lifeless and missing the main points. He looked very old and tired and in my opinion is failing fast.'[33] Three weeks later, he gave a stumbling speech in the House on foreign affairs. Part of the problem on this occasion may have been Churchill's habit of producing a verbatim script, as Dalton noted after seeing the Labour Leader. 'Attlee told me later that the PM had been sitting up till 3 a.m. preparing this speech. In any case, on the eve of great events, it must be a great effort to concoct this sort of oration and I really don't know why he thought it necessary, just at this moment, to do it all.'[34] Even when he turned to military affairs, usually the catalyst for a burst of energy, he could not shake off his fatigue. In mid-May he visited Montgomery's headquarters for a briefing with senior staff about Overlord. After Montgomery had delivered one of his precise lectures, Churchill mounted the platform. According to the Director of Military Operation Major General John Kennedy, he 'spoke without vigour. There was the usual wonderful flow of fine phrases, but no fire in the delivery.'[35]

Yet Churchill, whose soul had always responded to the trumpet blast of action in the past, felt sufficiently galvanised by the looming prospect of D-Day to come up with an eccentric plan whereby he would join the invasion fleet and take part in the early wave of landings at Normandy. Most of the top military chiefs were fiercely opposed, not just on grounds of safety but also because the Prime Minister needed to be contactable at the height of the battle. Eventually and with almost petulant reluctance, Churchill backed down when King George VI raised his objections. Like the rest of his Cabinet, he therefore had to wait in England to find out how the operation unfolded. The signs were ominous when Eisenhower was forced to postpone the attack a day because of poor weather and Churchill fretted to Clementine on the night of 5–6 June. 'Do you realise that by the time you wake up in the morning 20,000 men may have been killed?' he asked.[36] Attlee also had an anxious night, first sitting in the Admiralty during the early hours to follow the progress of the fleet, then returning to No. 11 Downing Street for a few hours' sleep, from which he was woken by the sound of 'the mighty wings continually beating overhead as the air force went in'.[37] But the fears and caution of the two leaders were misplaced. Despite meeting strong German resistance, the landings achieved their goal of seizing enemy territory across Normandy, with the loss of only 3,000 troops on the first day.

Now victory was within the Allies' grasp. There were still fierce struggles ahead, but it was the beginning of the end for the Nazis in Western Europe. In the wake of D-Day's success, Churchill and Attlee took the opportunity in the summer to visit the Continent and follow the Allies' progress. Churchill, inevitably, was the first to go to Normandy, travelling there on 12 June for one day then making a longer visit in late July. After his initial journey Churchill was so excited that, when he dined at the Palace on 14 June, he subjected the King and his guests to a long discourse about the invasion. As Tommy Lascelles recorded, 'This lasted until 2 am, Winston talking without a break for long periods while Smuts and Attlee, on either side of me, slept unashamedly.'[38] Attlee made his own trip to northern France in the first week of August. He was impressed by both the Allies' advance and the high spirits of the French, despite the widespread damage caused by artillery and aerial shelling. 'I was received with much kindness everywhere,' he wrote.[39]

Meanwhile, in the Far East theatre, the retreat of Japan opened up new strategic opportunities. As in the Dodecanese campaign, Churchill was keen on a peripheral attack through the British seizure of Sumatra and the Andaman islands in the Indian Ocean, but his plan found little support among the rest of the Cabinet, the Chiefs of Staff or the Americans. This opposition provoked Churchill into another of his towering rages, climaxing at a combustible meeting of the War Cabinet on 6 July, during which Attlee was the target for his venom. Churchill was 'in a maudlin, bad-tempered, drunken mood, ready to take offence at anything, suspicious of everybody', recorded Brooke. When he accused the British generals of being too cautious over his plans for the Indian Ocean, the rest of the meeting sided against him. 'This infuriated him more than ever and he became ruder and ruder. Fortunately he finished by falling out with Attlee and having a real good row with him concerning the future of India! We withdrew under cover of this smokescreen just on 2 am, having accomplished nothing beyond losing our tempers and valuable sleep.'[40] Churchill never won the argument over his Indian Ocean venture, but only succeeded in further spreading disillusion.

The Chief of the Imperial Staff was therefore relieved when Churchill left London in early August on an extended visit to Italy, for relaxation, troop inspections and military conferences, his trip made all the more appealing because the Allies had captured Rome two days before the Normandy invasion. 'I am extremely well and the constant movement and clatter is extremely restful,' he told Attlee by telegram.[41] Churchill even felt in sufficient good humour to watch, from a Royal Navy destroyer, the start of Riviera landings which he had so strongly opposed. His absence also put Brooke into a better mood. 'Cabinet at 5.30 pm run by Attlee and finished in half the time,' he recorded on 14 August. A day later, he noted that

> life has a quiet and peaceful atmosphere about it now that Winston has gone to Italy. Everything gets done twice as quickly, everybody is not on edge, one is not bombarded by a series of quite futile minutes and the whole machinery settles down to efficient, smooth running. I fear we have reached the stage that for the good of the nation and for the good of his own reputation it would be a godsend if he could disappear out of public life.[42]

The future of Churchill and the Coalition was also discussed intensively within the highest Labour circles. On 19 July, Attlee dined with Dalton, both men once more agreeing that 'there should be no election until six months after Germany surrenders'. Dalton then argued that 'it would be a good thing, both for the country and the Prime Minister's own reputation, if the latter were about then to retire to write the history of these days. Attlee says that he doesn't quite despair of the PM accepting this view.'[43] A month later the Labour Leader spelled out to the party's NEC his view on how Churchill would react politically after the German surrender:

> The moment will come when the PM will say to him that he hopes, having gone through the war in Europe together, we

can go on together through a General Election on an agreed programme. Attlee would then reply that he is afraid that this is impossible and that, when the General Election comes – and we should do nothing to hasten it – we must offer the country the choice between two alternative programmes. But we should aim at closing our association with the Conservatives without any bitterness or ill-feeling and with expressions of mutual respect. There might well be an exchange of letters between the PM and Attlee, which might be published, in the course of which Attlee would pay a very warm tribute to the PM as a war leader and in that case he is sure the PM will respond generously towards the Labour Party.[44]

Attlee had the chance to talk directly to Churchill afterwards when he flew, via Gibraltar and Algiers, to visit the Italian theatre. After their Cabinet rows in July, Churchill was in a much more genial temper as a result of sunshine, sea-bathing and the sense of being near the military action. It was the only time during the entire European war that Attlee and Churchill were out of the country at the same time, but the Prime Minister saw no problem. In his memoirs, Attlee recalled that when he first proposed his Italian visit, with its overlapping absences, Churchill had replied, 'That's all right, we can leave for a day or two to the automatic pilot – meaning that very experienced administrator Sir John Anderson.'[45] But Attlee's memory may have been faulty. In fact, it seems more likely that Eden was put in charge rather than Anderson, according to a telegram that Churchill sent Attlee on 17 August. 'There is no reason why you should not start before I get back […] I think it would be all right and Eden could carry on.'[46] Freed briefly from their responsibilities, Churchill and Attlee spent an enjoyable day in the Bay of Naples, at one point travelling out to visit the famous Blue Grotto at the island of Capri, where sunlight creates shimmering reflections of the water on the walls of a vast sea cave. While on their boat, they also came across a convoy of British troops heading for France; Churchill, who had just been bathing, stood on the stern and gave the men his renowned two-fingered victory salute. Aside from such pleasant distractions, Attlee had a serious political conversation with Churchill, as he reported to Dalton on his return from Italy:

> The PM quite understands that when the next election comes, the Labour Party will fight independently. He also thought, Attlee says, that although this is a very old Parliament and badly needs renewal, we ought not to have a General Election for about six months after the end of the European war, as there would be so much to be done in those first months. Attlee thinks it should be possible to make the break without any personal crisis or bitterness.[47]

There was soon friction, however, once politics resumed after the Italian break. Having been back in England for just six days, Churchill then travelled on the *Queen Mary* to Canada for a second Anglo-American Conference in Quebec, codenamed Octagon. The geniality of August had been replaced by disgruntlement, made all the worse by the humid, muggy weather in the Atlantic. Churchill spent much of his time in his cabin reading Anthony Trollope novels, but when he returned to official business, he soon found cause for annoyance at Attlee. The Deputy Prime Minister had sent a telegram informing him of a scheme to increase the pay of British servicemen in Japan. Churchill was 'livid', recorded Jock Colville, not only because he thought the proposals 'inadequate and ill-conceived' but also because of Attlee's announcement that the War Cabinet had decided to publish the scheme before his return from Quebec. 'He said Attlee was a rat and maintained that there was an intrigue afoot. He dictated a violent reply (which was never sent) full of dark threat,' noted Colville in his diary.[48] But he did dispatch a more measured telegram, addressed to both Attlee and Eden. This declared that it 'would be utterly impossible for me to commit myself to a scheme of this kind for the war against Japan which I have not even heard discussed and with which, so far as I have studied it, I am not in agreement'. Asking his colleagues 'to show some consideration to me when I am absent on public duty of the highest consequence', he told them that 'we can go into the whole matter together' when he was back in London in a fortnight.[49] In his anger at Attlee, he told Colville and Brooke over dinner on the *Queen Mary* that 'he would not regret the loss of any Labour colleague from the Government save Bevin, the only one whose character and capacity he esteemed'.[50]

More discord between the War Cabinet and Churchill arose when he arrived in Quebec for the conference, one of the key issues at which was settlement of post-war Germany. 'The Conference has opened in a blaze of friendship. The staffs are in almost complete agreement,' he wrote to Attlee on 15 September.[51] But senior ministers in London did not feel the same way when Churchill gave them the news that he and Roosevelt had approved a radical plan for the wholesale deindustrialisation of Germany. The blueprint, which essentially sought to return German society to an agrarian state so it could never wage war again, was devised by US Secretary to the Treasury Henry Morgenthau, a patrician Democrat, wealthy Jewish financier and believer in Teutonic guilt for the war. In Churchill's telegram to Attlee justifying his approval of the plan, he emphasised the advantages to Britain: 'The goods hitherto supplied from these German centres must to a large extent be provided by Great Britain. This may amount to 300 or 400 million pounds-a-year. I was at first taken aback at this but I consider that the disarmament argument is decisive and the beneficial consequences to us follow naturally.'[52] But the War Cabinet strongly disagreed. Consequently Attlee, who was also chairman of the Cabinet's Armistice and Post-War Committee, sent a message arguing that the Morgenthau plan was actually against British interests since it would make the task of post-war occupation more difficult and would deny any chance of a German economic contribution towards the rebuilding of Europe. The American State Department shared this view and the plan was effectively stillborn. After this episode, the Allies moved towards a less vengeful, more constructive settlement featuring federal governance, the international control of industry, comprehensive de-Nazification and the division of Germany in zones of occupation.

The Morgenthau row was indicative of an awkward, unproductive conference in which Churchill felt keenly the marginalisation of Britain as American dominance grew. In Europe, the US now had 3 million troops compared to Britain's 1 million, and the Americans were determined to use this might to smash Germany with a central thrust through the west, joining up with the Russians from the east as soon as possible. Churchill, in contrast, was deeply concerned about a Soviet takeover of Eastern Europe – which was one reason he was so keen on a breakthrough from Italy into Austria and Czechoslovakia in order to give the Anglo-American forces a strong presence in that theatre. He was equally worried about Britain's isolation in the Far East and therefore pushed for the full involvement of the Royal Navy in the fight against Japan once the European war was over. Although Roosevelt was happy to agree, others, like Admiral of the Fleet Ernest J. King, were more equivocal, believing that Churchill's principal aim was to shore up Britain's eastern Empire.

Just as militarily Churchill sensed the eclipse of Britain's global power by the Americans and the Russians, so, on the political front, he sensed his power draining away to Attlee and Labour. Victory threatened to bring about his demise. To Charles Wilson his doctor, he complained of his tiredness and said that he wished to go to the south of France: 'I have a very strong feeling that my work is done. I have no message. I had a message. Now I only say, "fight the damned socialists". I do not believe in this brave new world.'[53] Churchill was right to think that a brave new world was on the horizon, with Labour full of ideas on how to extend socialism. There was now no doubt that Attlee's party would fight the next election as an independent party; the only question was how soon the Coalition would end after a German surrender. Churchill still hankered after a few years of cross-party Government, but other Tories felt that the contest should be held quickly to capitalise on his leadership. Meanwhile Labour was torn between its desire to embark on its programme and its wish to avoid handing an early electoral triumph to Churchill. While Churchill was in Quebec, Attlee drafted a statement for his party, which argued for remaining in the Coalition until 'the cessation of hostilities', reaffirmed Labour's determination to fight the election independently and then stated that the actual moment of Labour's departure from Government would be decided by the NEC and the Annual Conference, just as the decision to join in May 1940 had been made by those two bodies.[54] Attlee's statement was approved without any changes by the NEC, which ordered its immediate publication. Not everyone in the party was happy. Ernie Bevin complained bitterly about Attlee's lack of consultation, claiming that 'all our Government colleagues' had been 'left entirely in the dark' about this 'amazing procedure', which was 'a strange way to maintain loyalty'.[55] But Attlee had successfully stamped his authority on his party by this tactic. It was another indicator of how he had gained in stature by serving as Deputy Prime Minister, especially during Churchill's many absences. Cecil King noted that the Labour Leader was 'rather pleased with his own record in the last year while Winston has been away so much'.[56]

Even Churchill complained that Labour, with its strong programme, now led the debate on social policy and reconstruction within the committee machinery of Whitehall. As he put it in a letter to Attlee, 'I feel very much the domination of these committees by the force and power of your representatives, when those members who come out of the Conservative quota are largely non-party or have little political experience or party views [...] Moreover, you have a theme, which is Socialism, on which everything is directed, whereas our people are merely considering matters on their merit from day-to-day.'[57] Part of the problem for the Conservatives was that Churchill was not a natural Tory and, in graphic contrast to Attlee, never immersed himself in his party's operations or administration. His fondness for coalition also inhibited him from acting decisively in the Conservative cause, as the backbencher Cuthbert Headlam perceptively remarked. 'He thinks that some kind of compromise can be made with Labour, and so he is disinclined to give his own party a lead. I think he is living in a fool's paradise,' wrote Headlam in late July. By October, Headlam was in despair. 'None of us has an inkling of what the PM has in mind – what his intentions are or when he is going to disclose them. Never was a party so leaderless as the Conservative Party today. It is, I think, drifting to its doom.'[58]

But another crucial factor in Churchill's party political detachment was his concentration on the war. Less than a week after Headlam made that diary entry, Churchill was on his travels again, this time to Moscow to see Stalin, with whom he wanted to reach an agreement about the future of Poland and the Balkan countries, including Greece. The reception from the Russians was lavish, including what Churchill described to George VI as a series of 'very lengthy feasts and very cordial toasts'.[59] In contrast to this munificence, the political discussions were brutally realistic. No deal was reached over Poland because of the chasm between Soviet ambitions and the national spirit of the Polish Government in exile, but with grinning cold-bloodedness, Stalin accepted a proposal from Churchill and the British negotiators, set out in the notorious 'naughty document', whereby responsibility for Balkan countries was to be ruthlessly apportioned between the powers. According to the document, 90 per cent of control in Romania and 75 per cent in Bulgaria went to the Soviet Union, while Britain retained 90 per cent of the influence over Greece. The other two affected countries, Yugoslavia and Hungary, were to be divided 50:50. Aware that this decision would appear ruthless, Churchill sought to justify it in a telegram to Attlee and the War Cabinet. 'The arrangements made about the Balkans are, I am sure, the best that are possible. Coupled with our successful military action, we should now be able to save Greece and I have no doubt that the agreement to pursue a 50:50 joint policy in Yugoslavia will be the best solution to our difficulties [...] The Russians are insistent on their ascendancy in Romania and Bulgaria as Black Sea countries.'[60] But Churchill's gloss could not disguise the onward march of Soviet totalitarianism, which was to become one of his central concerns in the last months of the war.

Having returned from Moscow, Churchill gave a report to the Commons on 27 October about his negotiations with Stalin. 'He did it with the utmost ingenuity, calm and skill. In fact, he was quite himself again. A few months ago he seemed ill and tired and he did not find his words as easily as usual. But today he was superb,' wrote Harold Nicolson.[61] Churchill gave another strong performance in the chamber four days later, when he announced that the Cabinet had decided to prolong Parliament into the following year. Explaining to MPs that the war was likely to last until the early summer of 1945, he said that Labour might well leave the Coalition as soon as organised resistance in Germany had ended, though there could be a delay in holding a General Election, for time would be needed to sort out the voting register and the ballot of services personnel.

When the new session of Parliament began at the end of November, Churchill, recognising that a unique era was drawing to a close, adopted an open, affectionate, even nostalgic tone. In the King's Speech, twelve bills were announced, including one to create a National Health Service, Churchill declaring that all parties were committed to 'this great mass of social legislation'.[62] He was in an even more expansive mood as the Government held a banquet for ministers that evening, as Chuter Ede recorded.

> The Prime Minister gave the toast of the King and then Attlee proposed the PM's health, alluding to him as a great leader and a great statesman. Attlee said that he did not know that we should be together another year, but until the defeat of Germany we should stay united. The Prime Minister, replying, said that he had been greatly eased of his burdens by the loyalty and determination of his friend Clement Attlee. He had been able to leave the country with the certain knowledge that any difficulty that might arise could be met with great wisdom and undaunted courage. The time for parting might come but he hoped the bitterness of party conflict would be assuaged by the knowledge we had gained of one another's zeal in the cause and in devotion to our country.

Basking in the warm, post-prandial glow on his journey home by train, Ede reflected that 'in his talk about the Government tonight, the Prime

Minister said that most Coalitions had stuck in the nostrils of the people of this country but this Coalition was held in high honour everywhere for its courage and its deeds. No member need ever recall other than with pride his association with this great administration.'[63] Yet darker times soon lay ahead for the Coalition, and for the relationship between the Prime Minister and his Deputy.

TWENTY-TWO

⸻◇⸻

BRITANNIA

T HE FINAL MONTHS of the war should have been a contented time
for Attlee. After the desperate struggles of 1940 and 1941, victory
in Europe was in sight. His alliance with Churchill had not only saved
Britain in its darkest hour but had raised the stature of the Labour
Party to unprecedented heights. One survey by Gallup in February 1945
put Labour on 42 per cent and the Conservatives on just 24 per cent.[1]
Yet this period was also a troubled one for Attlee. The release of military
pressures eroded the strength of the Coalition, while there were also
severe strains in his relationship with Churchill, not least because of his
exasperation with the Prime Minister's working methods and fading
powers. In addition, Attlee faced difficulties from within his own party
over a range of vexed questions. One was the timing of the General
Election, with many Labour figures still worried about Churchill's
potential appeal to the public in a snap campaign. Another was the
demand from the left, led by radicals like Nye Bevan and Harold Laski,
for more full-blooded socialism.

The umbrage of the left against Attlee was on display during the
crisis that arose in Greece in the wake of Allied advances on both
fronts at the end of 1944, heaping more tension on the Labour Leader
over his link with Churchill. As the Reich lost its dominance in the
Balkans and began to withdraw from Athens in October, Churchill
persuaded the War Cabinet to agree that a British force under General
Ronald Scobie should be dispatched to stabilise the capital. It was a

decision that Attlee accepted, though he expressed the hope that the operation would be largely a humanitarian one. That did not turn out to be the case. The two Greek Communist resistance groups EAM and ELAS began a guerrilla campaign to seize control of the country from the caretaker Government in Athens. But Churchill was determined to prevent a Communist takeover, telling Eden – in reference to the 'naughty document' he had signed with Stalin – that 'having paid the price we have to Russia for freedom of action in Greece, we should not hesitate to use British troops'.[2] Yet elements of the left interpreted Churchill's stand against communism as a willingness to thwart democratic populism. The elderly Fabian author H. G. Wells came out of his retirement to claim that Churchill 'seems to have lost his head completely'.[3] Within Labour's ranks, feelings ran high and Attlee was accused of collusion with Churchill in trying to uphold reactionary rule in Greece. At a highly charged meeting of the PLP on 7 December, John Parker the Romford MP claimed that Churchill was 'in favour of keeping the parties of the right armed and disarming the parties of the left'. In an angry response, Attlee pointed out that the incumbent Greek Prime Minister was a Social Democrat. Furthermore he reminded the meeting that in June 1941, 'without waiting to consult his Labour colleagues, Churchill declared his support for Russia when Hitler attacked'. The next day, 8 December, Churchill vigorously defended his Greek policy in a Commons debate, attacking the attempt to portray the Communist fighters as champions of pluralism. 'Democracy is no harlot to be picked up in the street by a man with a tommy gun.'[4] In what Ede described as his 'most truculent vein', Churchill used the threat of resignation to turn the issue into one of confidence. The manoeuvre worked. Churchill easily won the confidence vote by 279 to 30, with only 24 Labour MPs voting against him.

But the controversy was far from over. It grew more intense when the American newspaper the *Washington Post* acquired a leaked copy of a telegram that Churchill had sent to General Scobie on the night of 4–5 September, ordering him to open fire on the Communist guerrillas if necessary. 'Do not hesitate to act as if you were in a conquered city where a local rebellion is in progress,' was one of his incendiary phrases.[5] Liberal opinion on both sides of the Atlantic was outraged. By chance, when this revelation was printed in the US press, Labour's Annual Conference was under way in London, providing more scope for fulmination against the Coalition's Greek policy. As often before, Attlee failed to give a decisive lead in his own 'very dull' speech, which largely ignored the question of Greece.[6] It was left to that old trade-union warhorse, Ernie Bevin, to defend the Coalition, explaining that the Greek strategy had not solely been Churchill's but had been agreed by the whole War Cabinet. 'I don't know what Churchill or other people thought. I know what I thought,' he said.[7] With the help of Bevin's union supporters, Labour's Annual Conference passed a bland motion calling for an 'armistice without delay' and 'the establishment of a strong democratic system'.[8]

Yet the unanimity of the Coalition over Greece was fragile. It soon came under more strain as Churchill, an instinctive monarchist, expressed his support for a return to power of the Greek King George II of the Hellenes, currently in exile in London. Others, including Eden and Harold Macmillan – then Minister Resident in the Mediterranean – felt that a more secure arrangement would be a regency led by Archbishop Damaskinos, the head of the Greek Orthodox Church. But Churchill developed an intense antipathy towards the prelate, whom he regarded as a menace to Allied interests. At the War Cabinet on 21 December, Churchill again expressed his opposition to Damaskinos as Greece's regent. 'I won't install a dictator,' he said, a remark that provoked Attlee to reply, 'We have often heard you say that but you haven't provided any evidence to support your thesis.'[9] Isolated but determined to find a solution to the impasse, Churchill flew out on Christmas Day from RAF Northolt to Athens, accompanied by Eden, his doctor Charles Wilson, Jock Colville and two of his secretaries. Because of the conflict raging in the Greek capital, conditions were appalling. Concerns about safety meant that Churchill's party were transferred for a time to the Royal Navy cruiser HMS *Ajax* and when negotiations were held in the city after sunset they had to be conducted in freezing temperatures by the light of hurricane lamps because of electricity cuts. Nevertheless, the visit proved successful. The Greeks, impressed by Churchill's willingness to engage in diplomacy over Christmas at some personal sacrifice, approached the negotiations about their political future in a co-operative spirit. More importantly, Churchill changed his mind about Damaskinos. In person, the tall, bearded cleric impressed Churchill, who was intrigued to discover that he had been a champion wrestler before he entered the Orthodox Church. Eventually an agreement with all parties was reached, by which the Archbishop was to rule as regent until free elections were held.

Churchill's success in Greece was in contrast to the mounting concern about his efficiency as Prime Minister. Unsurprisingly, after more than five years of war, he often seemed exhausted. There were persistent complaints about his dilatoriness and his reliance on cronies, especially Bracken, Beaverbrook and Lord Cherwell. Worried about Churchill's fading powers, Colville wrote in early 1945 that 'the PM is now becoming an administrative bottleneck'.[10] As so often, Brooke as Chief of the Imperial General Staff was almost at the end of his tether. 'He is finished and gone, incapable of grasping any military situation and unable to give a decision,' wrote Brooke on 23 January.[11] But it was Attlee, so often derided for his timidity, who decided to remonstrate directly with Churchill over his working methods. With unaccustomed forthrightness, he penned a 2,000-word letter of censure to the Prime Minister in late January, attacking Churchill's style of running the Cabinet and his reluctance to engage with the machinery of Government. It was one of the most forceful rebukes sent to Churchill during the war. The very fact that Attlee was willing to put such a reproach on paper indicated the changing balance of their relationship, as well as the ebb of political power from the Conservatives to Labour. Attlee had been building up to this intervention for some weeks as he grew ever more exasperated by the Prime Minister. He had been particularly annoyed by one Cabinet meeting after Churchill's return from Athens, at which the Prime Minister launched into a thirty-minute diatribe against the BBC over its coverage of the Greek crisis while Attlee waited in frustration to present a paper on the warning system for London to counter Hitler's V-2 rockets. He was also aggrieved at the poor attendance by other ministers at his Lord President's Committee. 'The main purpose of the creation of the Committee was to provide for decisions to be taken on a high level, thus relieving the burden of the War Cabinet. This purpose is defeated if ministers with the power to take decisions are not present,' he wrote to colleagues on 17 January.[12] Attlee's complaint prompted those two mavericks, Beaverbrook and Bracken, to send Churchill a sneering letter that quoted from Samuel Taylor Coleridge's famous lines in *The Rime of the Ancient Mariner*:

> Our attention has been called to the lament of Mr Attlee that ministers do not attend his committee. We now offer to fill two of the vacant places. We are moved to make this offer by the sad plight of the Lord President,
>> 'Alone, alone, all, all alone.
>> Alone on the wide, wide sea.'[13]

But the mockery was misplaced. By the time the pair had sent their letter, Churchill had already received Attlee's own formidable catalogue of remonstrance. On Friday 19 January, Attlee had retired to his study at 11 Downing Street and hammered out the first draft of the missive on his own manual typewriter, performing the task himself because he wanted the contents to remain secret. 'I have for some time had it in mind to write to you on the method, or rather the lack of method, of dealing with Cabinet decisions,' he began, going on to say that 'I consider the present position inimical to the successful performance of the tasks imposed upon us as a Government and injurious to the war effort.' Attlee then warned that he would state his views 'bluntly'. He lived up to those words. Admitting that Churchill's preoccupation with the military conduct of the war limited the time he could give to civil affairs, Attlee argued that it was therefore vital that the Prime Minister put trust in his Cabinet colleagues and their committees. 'On the contrary you exhibit a very scanty respect for their views', which led to 'exasperation and a sense of frustration'. The committees, Attlee explained, tried 'to reach agreement and to subordinate party views to the general interest'. Their conclusions

> are brought to the Cabinet in memoranda which we try to keep as short as possible in an attempt to save members the trouble of reading long disquisitions. What happens then? Frequently, a long delay before they can be considered. When they do come before the Cabinet it is very exceptional for you to have read them. More and more often you have not even read the note prepared for your guidance. Often half an hour or more is wasted in explaining what could have been grasped by two or three minutes reading of the document. Not infrequently a phrase catches your eye which gives rise to a disquisition or an interesting point only slightly connected with the subject matter. The result is long delays and unnecessarily long Cabinets imposed on ministers who have already done a full day's work and who will have more to deal with before they get to bed.

Continuing his theme, Attlee said that the Government's work was further undermined by Churchill's practice of submitting proposals, already agreed by committee, to Beaverbrook and Bracken, 'two Ministers without Cabinet responsibility, neither of whom have given any serious attention to the subject'. Attlee said that he had written all this 'very frankly', not on his own account, but to express the concerns of colleagues from all parties. 'I would ask you to put yourself in the position of your colleagues and would ask yourself whether in the days, when you were a Minister, you would have been as patient as we have been.'[14]

Attlee pulled the final page of the draft from the typewriter and then re-read the entire letter to make some handwritten amendments. He toned down some of the more trenchant criticism, such as the references to ministers being kept from their beds and the need for Churchill to show more empathy. He also added a new final sentence: 'Please excuse rough typing as I have written this myself for your eye alone.'[15] But the overwhelming majority of the text remained the same. The letter was sent that night. The next day Attlee had to attend the wedding of Roy Jenkins, serving army officer, Labour candidate, and son of the Labour MP Arthur Jenkins, who was Attlee's parliamentary private secretary. 'In his typically laconic speech at the reception, it is hardly necessary to say that he made no reference to the delayed-action bomb which he had dispatched. Nor did he seem more tense than usual,' recalled Jenkins.[16]

But a combustible reaction there certainly was. That Saturday, with heavy snow falling in London, Churchill was not at Chequers, to where he usually retreated at the weekend, but at Downing Street. His mood, already low because of a heavy cold, was dramatically worsened when Attlee's letter arrived as he lay in his sick bed. At the end of his second paragraph, Attlee had written, 'I am sure you will not resent plain speaking',[17] but he had misjudged his recipient, as Jock Colville later recalled in a BBC interview. 'He was livid. And he sent for a typist and dictated a reply. I sat and listened patiently and it ran to something like six pages of the most beautiful purple prose, a really extremely rude letter and he was rather pleased with it.'[18] Colville had overestimated the reply's length; in fact the draft ran to only four pages. But he was right about the purple prose. Having expressed his belief in 'the importance of frankness and even bluntness in time of war', Churchill then slid into a passage of ironic self-deprecation.

> I am very ready to admit my own shortcomings in the matter of civil affairs. The great mass of war and foreign business, as well as the other tasks which fall to me, including heavy Parliamentary work, have made it difficult for me to follow the details of all the legislative and other proposals which your Committees bring to the Cabinet. I note what you say as to my laxity in these matters, and, heavy and exhausting as is my present burden, I will try my best to be better acquainted with these subjects in the future, so as not to take up your valuable time in explaining them to me in the Cabinet.

Then he turned to the question of political balance, pointing out Labour's influence in the machinery of Government. 'A solid mass of four socialist politicians of the highest quality and authority, three of whom are in the War Cabinet and on the Home Affairs Committee, exercises a dominating force of which you are yourself no doubt unconscious.' Given that 'there is a large independent majority of Conservatives' in the House of Commons, 'it seems to me indispensable that their counter case should be properly and even boldly stated'. That was why, wrote Churchill, he turned for advice to Bracken and Beaverbrook, 'two characteristic Conservatives of very long experience'. Churchill said that he was well aware of Labour's resentment. But he argued that 'both sides of Party opinion' had to be expressed. 'I could not accept the suggestion that once the Lord President's Committee had pronounced upon a subject, the Cabinet had no rights and the matter must be taken as settled.' In practice, Churchill wrote, Attlee had 'very little to complain of', especially since the Conservative side of the War Cabinet was much less cohesive than Labour's. 'I am very weak there on Party grounds, as I am by no means a typical Conservative myself.'[19] After his typist had handed him the draft, Churchill made a few amendments, dropping the references to his own Conservatism and augmenting the sarcastic self-criticism: 'I need scarcely say that I am deeply conscious of my own failings and that I will certainly try to live up to the standards you require.'[20]

Now happy with his response, Churchill decided to consult his closest colleagues. According to Colville's BBC interview, he

> rang up first of all Brendan Bracken and read over Attlee's letter and his reply. And there was a bit of a silence – I was listening on the extension I remember – then Brendan said, 'Well, I think it was very courageous of him to send that letter.' Churchill put down the telephone in fury and rang up Beaverbrook from whom, to his surprise and indeed mine, he got a rather similar reaction. So he felt he was being deserted by his friends. Just at that moment into the room came Mrs Churchill and he said

he had received an abominable letter from the Deputy Prime
Minister which he showed her. Then he showed her his reply.
And she said, exactly like Brendan, 'Well, I think that's very
brave of Mr Attlee and I'm sure he's representing the views
of the Cabinet as a whole, and indeed all your friends and
well-wishers.'[21]

By the evening, Churchill was fed up with the whole saga. To lift his
spirits after dinner, Churchill went with Colville to the nearby Air
Ministry for a film showing, which included a newsreel of a Luftwaffe
attack on Holland and the Hollywood movie *Dark Victory*, starring
Bette Davis and Ronald Reagan. As the pair left Downing Street for
the Ministry, Churchill turned to Colville and said, 'Let us think no
more about Attler or Hitlee.'[22] But he still had to reply formally. On
Monday morning he did so, in far pithier style than he had originally
planned: 'I have to thank you for your Private and Personal letter of
January 19. You may be sure I shall always endeavour to profit by your
counsels.'[23]

Amid all this epistolary drama, the grim business of war was
proceeding. On the day that Churchill sent his note to Attlee, the Red
Army reached the River Oder, heralding Soviet domination of Eastern
Europe. On hearing the news, Churchill told Colville, 'All the Balkans,
except Greece, are going to be bolshevised; and there is nothing I
can do to prevent it. There is nothing I can do for Poland either.'[24]
In fact, Britain and America were now planning to give further assistance to the Russian advance, largely through the strategic bombing
of eastern Germany to smash supply lines and hinder the dispatch
of the Wehrmacht's reinforcements. On 25 January Churchill asked
the Air Ministry whether, in the light of latest military intelligence:
'Berlin and no doubt other large cities in East Germany should not
now be considered especially attractive targets.'[25] In reply, the RAF
chief Sir Charles Portal told Churchill that the Air Staff were planning
attacks on Berlin, Dresden, Leipzig and other cities 'to cause confusion
in the evacuation from the East' and 'hamper the movement from

the West'.[26] Churchill was able personally to convey his support for Russia little more than a week later when he travelled to Yalta in the Crimea for his final wartime summit with Stalin and Roosevelt, by now an extremely sick man. Among the key decisions at Yalta were the post-war establishment a United Nations Security Council, a Soviet promise of involvement in the Pacific War, and the division of Germany into occupied zones, including one to be held by France. There was disagreement about Poland, both over its frontiers and the nature of its government, but, given the strength of Russian power in the East, there was little Churchill could do to block Stalin's wishes. Otherwise, the atmosphere at the conference was generally cordial, with Churchill's affability enhanced, wrote Cadogan, by 'drinking buckets of Caucasian champagne which would undermine the health of any ordinary man'.[27] At Yalta's conclusion, Churchill wrote to Attlee, 'Nothing was shirked and the most difficult things were taken first. I am profoundly impressed with the friendly attitude of Stalin and Molotov.'[28] The politics of totalitarianism, however, continued to intrude. Explaining how he would probably soon have to fight an election against Labour, Churchill told Stalin at one dinner, 'You know we have two parties in England,' to which the Soviet leader replied, 'One party is much better.'[29]

When Churchill arrived at Yalta on 4 February 1945, the first question that Stalin put to him was: 'Why haven't you bombed Dresden?'[30] His enquiry reflected the importance that the Soviet Union attached to an attack on the city, following intelligence reports that Germany was moving large numbers of troops towards the Breslau Front. Churchill was able to assure Stalin that just such an Allied attack was imminent. But in his absence at Yalta along with Portal, the formal decision to bomb Dresden was made by Attlee, in co-operation with Sir Douglas Evill, the Vice-Chief of the Air Staff. Attlee, who had been an advocate of mass bombing as far back as 1940, had few qualms about this decision, especially in view of the Soviet request for aerial support. His only doubts about the policy related to its effectiveness in breaking the enemy, not to its morality. 'The ultimate responsibility for bombing policy lay with the Cabinet and I don't seek to evade it, but I thought that concentration on strategic targets such as oil installations would have paid better,' he said in 1960.[31] Once Attlee had given his approval, four raids were undertaken between 13 and 15 February, during which 722 Allied planes dropped almost 4,000 tons of bombs on the city, devastating its centre and killing around 25,000. The Dresden attack was not the most deadly of the RAF's strategic bombing initiative against Germany; in July 1943, 43,000 people were killed in the port of Hamburg by Operation Gomorrah. However, Nazi propaganda exaggerating the death toll combined with the timing near the conflict's end led Dresden to become one of the most controversial episodes of the war. Churchill himself, on his return from Yalta, was sufficiently disturbed by the results to write to Portal, 'It seems to me that the moment has come when the question of bombing German cities simply for the sake of increasing the terror, though under other pretexts, should be reviewed.'[32] In response, Portal persuaded Churchill to tone down this minute, leaving out the word 'terror'. Nevertheless, as a result of Churchill's intervention, instructions were issued to Bomber Command that 'area bombing designed solely with the object of destroying industrial areas is to be discontinued'. Typically, Sir Arthur Harris – always a law to himself – largely ignored this order.[33]

By the time of Churchill's return from Yalta, the Allies were on the verge of victory in Europe. The impending defeat of Germany brought the problems of building a new post-war order to the forefront of global politics, one of the most pressing of which was the formal establishment of the United Nations and its permanent Security Council. To achieve this goal, a major international conference was to be held in San Francisco from the end of April, with invitations extended to fifty countries that had challenged Axis domination. For all the noble intentions of the San Francisco conference, the proposed make-up of the British delegation soon provoked another controversy over Churchill's relationship with Attlee. Much of the Labour Party was indignant when the Government announced that the British party would be headed by the Foreign Secretary Anthony Eden, with Attlee as his deputy. Given that the Labour Leader was officially the

Coalition's second-in-command, this looked like a calculated insult bred of Tory arrogance and Attlee's diffidence. *Tribune* magazine, then the voice of the left, argued that Attlee would 'affront his own followers and demean the status of the whole Labour movement by agreeing to serve as lieutenant to Anthony Eden', adding that 'he seems determined to make a trumpet sound like a tin whistle'.[34] The row extended to the House of Commons, where Churchill was forced to defend Attlee's role. When the Labour MP Moelwyn Hughes asked why Attlee was not leading the delegation, Churchill replied, rather disingenuously, that it was normal practice for the Foreign Secretary to lead a diplomatic mission; Attlee was going to San Francisco not as Deputy Prime Minister but as the Lord President of the Council. 'He agreed to it because he is not a self-serving man and always tried to play the game,' said Churchill. To this, Manny Shinwell replied that the Government's treatment of Attlee proved that the Tories 'are now going to get everything which is useful in their own hands'. Churchill strongly denied the charge. 'Any man would say that the socialists have had fair representation.'[35]

President Roosevelt, the driving force behind the creation of the United Nations, was meant to preside at the San Francisco Conference but he died from a stroke on 12 April. Despite the successful relationship he had built with the late President and his fondness for wartime travel, Churchill did not attend the obsequies in America, excusing himself on the grounds of pressing business. Soon after a memorial service for Roosevelt at St Paul's, Attlee led for the Government in a Commons debate on the forthcoming San Francisco Conference, but failed to inspire MPs with excitement. 'Attlee opened the debate in his usual dreary style, quoting every cliché on world affairs that has been made in the last 25 years,' Harvie-Watt reported to Churchill.[36]

Fuelled by the hopes of building a better world, the Conference went about its business energetically, agreeing the structure of the United Nations within two months. But Attlee's presence in San Francisco meant that he had to miss the epochal moment on 7 May when General Jodl, the German Chief of Staff, signed the unconditional surrender of the Reich to the Allies. In the weeks before victory, Churchill had once more been displaying signs of lassitude. Jock Colville had commented bitterly in his diary on 23 April that 'the Prime Minister's box is in a ghastly state. He does little work and talks far too much.'[37] In his own memoirs, Churchill admitted that at this time 'I was very tired and physically so feeble that I had to be carried upstairs in a chair by the Marines from Cabinet meetings under the Annexe.'[38] But, understandably, the triumph gave him a surge of new energy. That night, he sat up late until 3.45 a.m. preparing the text of his broadcast to the nation. The following day, 8 May, which officially marked Victory in Europe, he lunched with King George VI and then at 3 p.m. delivered his speech from Downing Street. It was relayed not just by radio to millions of homes and troops overseas but also by loudspeakers to a huge crowd gathered in Whitehall, and was full of the resounding Churchillian rhetoric that had made such a contribution to the defeat of Nazi tyranny. Having reminded his listeners that the war against Japan still had to be won, he concluded, with a justified choke in his voice, 'Advance Britannia! Long live the cause of freedom. God save the King.'[39] After this oration, Churchill travelled by open car from Downing Street to the Commons. Such was the size of the teeming throng that it took him more than half an hour to reach the chamber. There he repeated the statement he had just broadcast, before adding words of gratitude to the Commons for preserving 'all the title-deeds of democracy while waging war in the most stern and protracted form'.[40] He then led MPs to St Margaret's Church for a service of thanksgiving, returned to Parliament for an hour in the Smoking Room, and went with the War Cabinet and the Chiefs of Staff to Buckingham Palace for a congratulatory meeting with the King. For Evan Durbin, Attlee's adviser, there was a sense of regret at the Labour Leader's absence from the VE ceremonies. 'I am very sorry you have not been here to take your historical place by Churchill's side. You have helped and sustained him as no-one else could have and your loyalty to him will not be forgotten by the historian since it has been one of the main political foundations of our victory,' wrote Durbin.[41]

After dinner with his family in Downing, Churchill was persuaded to address the jubilant crowd that had swelled to enormous proportions in Parliament Street. At half-past ten, to deafening cheers, he appeared on the balcony of the Ministry of Health building, flanked by Bevin, Morrison and other members of the War Cabinet. 'An ear-splitting roar went up,' recalled the civil servant James Meade, who had perched on a temporary tower to catch a glimpse of the Prime Minister. 'The mood was so good-humoured, patient and happy; the floodlighting so striking after the blackout; the sense of relief from danger and tension so marked, and the evening itself so balmy that I climbed down from the tower with tears in my eyes.'[42] In another uplifting speech, Churchill lavished praise on the British people for achieving victory 'from the jaws of death, out of the mouth of hell'. Now the nation must 'begin the task of rebuilding our hearth and homes, doing our utmost to make this a land in which we all have a chance'.[43] When he had finished, the crowd responded with renditions of 'Land of Hope and Glory' and 'For He's a Jolly Good Fellow'. 'We all sang at the tops of our voices. He had terrific applause, doubled when he waved his hat and puffed on his cigar which he did deliberately at well-chosen moments throughout his speech. It was wonderful to have seen it,' wrote spectator Miss E. Tate to her mother.[44] Churchill's secretary Elizabeth Layton, who had transcribed his broadcast and speeches, remembered that for the next few days, Churchill 'could not move from the office without being mobbed in every street. He took to driving in an open car, so that he could sit in the back and wave his hat to the crowds, who appeared from nowhere wherever he was to be seen. Letters, telegrams and gifts poured into the office from all over the country. I think he enjoyed it. He knew he deserved it.'[45]

But the adulation for Churchill was by no means universal in the British public, as opinion polls had reflected. There was a widespread feeling that, whatever he had achieved on the war front, he was not the man to build the peace. Little more than a week before the German surrender, the Churchill Government had suffered a catastrophic defeat in the Chelmsford by-election, when a Tory majority of over 16,000 was replaced by a 6,000 majority for the independent left-wing Commonwealth Party. The result did not surprise perceptive Tory backbencher Cuthbert Headlam, who felt that 'Winston is not going to be so great an asset' as imagined, since 'once the war is over, his record will be forgotten and his misdeeds remembered'.[46] The author Vera Brittain mirrored the views of many on the left at the time of VE celebrations. After listening to his broadcast, she felt that he had 'introduced no phrase of constructive hope for a better society'.[47]

Public attitudes towards Churchill were now crucial, because the end of the war in Europe meant that a decision had to be made about the timing of the General Election. He had never had any doubts about his ambition to stay in office. When Clementine suggested he should 'retire rather than become one half of the nation against the other', he told her that he was 'not ready to be put on a pedestal'.[48] Nor was there any question of repeating the political experiment of 1918, when the war-winning Coalition had sought a mandate to continue in peacetime office. Labour had long made it clear that it would campaign as an independent force on its own programme of socialist reform. Furthermore, unlike in 1918, the Coalition had already reached the end of its natural life; now that Nazism had been conquered, there was nothing to bind the two main parties together. 'The Coalition is getting more and more threadbare,' wrote *The Economist* in March 1945, citing a host of unresolved domestic problems like the future of the coal industry, the implementation of the Beveridge plan, and the need for a major housing initiative.[49] Labour's suspicions about the Prime Minister's potential outlook in peacetime were articulated by Ernie Bevin, who told Dalton in late April that Churchill was 'all right as a National Leader, but when he turns into the Leader of the Tory Party, you can't trust him an inch. He just turns into a crook.'[50] With the Coalition doomed, the only question to resolve was when the General Election would be called. Churchill and some of the Tory high command were drawn to two very different alternatives: either an immediate contest, to capitalise on VE euphoria, or one delayed until after victory over Japan to maintain a unified national sense of purpose. Most senior Conservatives favoured the former option as the best route to an electoral win. 'The greater the delay, the more time they have to spread their poison in an effort to discredit you,' warned George Harvie-Watt. 'Demand an election at the earliest,' advocated Lord Woolton.[51]

Many of Labour's activists, eager to begin the fight for socialism, were also keen on a swift election but the party's chiefs were much more cautious, urging that October would be the best date. This was partly because of the fear that, despite the polls, Churchill's charisma would sway an early contest. The Labour candidate Raymond Blackburn later wrote that 'of all the Labour leaders I met at Transport House, in Parliament and at Labour Conferences, none but Aneurin Bevan regarded it as a possibility that Labour could attain a sweeping victory at the polls as long as Churchill fulfilled expectations and led the Conservatives at the General Election.'[52] But there were also two more practical, less partisan reasons for advocating a delay until the autumn. One was that a new electoral register would not be ready until October. The other was the difficulty of organising the votes of the services personnel overseas.

Churchill had still not made up his mind by VE Day, not least because he needed to consult Attlee and Eden before making a final decision. Attlee was planning to be back by 20 May for the beginning of Labour's Annual Conference at Blackpool, but Churchill wanted both men to return earlier. On 9 May, therefore, he wrote to Eden, 'You and Attlee really must come back. I have to take a very difficult decision in the next week in which you are both needed.'[53] Eden replied at once in a telegram that illustrated his view of Attlee's dispensability: 'We shall open ourselves to attack if it could be said that my departure from here had brought the Conference tumbling down. You must forgive my seeming conceit but there is a real danger of this [...] If you wanted Attlee back two days earlier than me, that would be acceptable to me.'[54] Apparently as co-operative as ever, Attlee expressed his willingness to accommodate Churchill's wishes, writing on Friday 11 May: 'If it would help you, I will return at once.'[55] The same day as Attlee sent that telegram from San Francisco, Churchill was occupied in London with further consideration of the election date. At 12.30 p.m. in Downing Street, he told Morrison, Bevin and the Tory Chief Whip James Stuart that he was 'under strong pressure' to hold 'a quick election', to which the Labour representatives put the case for an autumn contest, but said that their party was 'in good shape' for one in June.[56] After this meeting, Churchill wrote again to Eden, explaining that he had 'not finally settled between June and October', though a decision would have to be made in the next few days. 'There is a consensus of opinion on our side that June is better for our party; that October would prolong the present uneasy electioneering atmosphere in which many questions requiring settlement are looked at from Party angles and Government paralysed.' On the other hand, 'the Russian peril, which I regard as enormous, could be better faced if we remain united. I expect the Labour Party will offer to stay on till October, no doubt to their party advantage.'[57] In his reply the next day, Eden said that he now felt the balance of the argument now tilted towards June. Such a date 'would probably be better for our party than an October one', while continuing the Coalition until the autumn 'with the certainty of parting then will be an uncomfortable business'.[58]

But a new factor now entered the equation, when the new US President Harry Truman issued a stark warning to the Soviet Union and its allies against further aggressive expansionism in Europe. America would stand up to totalitarianism, he declared, backing this message with a pledge to keep his country's land and air forces on the Continent. Churchill called this 'one of the most far-sighted, sure-footed and resolute telegrams which it has ever been my fortune to read,' but on the purely domestic level of the British election, a firm stance with the USA implied a further continuation of the Coalition. He told Eden:

> We can hardly ask for the support, in so serious a venture, of
> our Labour colleagues and then immediately break up the

Government. If there is going to be trouble of this kind, the support of men like Attlee [...] is indispensable to the National presentation of the case. In that event, I should on no account agree to an election in October, but simply say that we must prolong our joint tenure.[59]

In a further telegram to Eden, sent on 14 May, Churchill wrote that 'every national argument points to a speedy election except the tremendous weight of unity in foreign affairs, and especially Russia'.[60]

The discussions over the end of the Coalition intensified once Attlee arrived back in London from San Francisco. On the evening of 16 May, he met Churchill at Downing Street, where the two men had an amicable conversation. According to his own recollection, Churchill pointed out 'the unfair position in which we should be put by a prolonged period of electioneering carried on inside the Cabinet'.[61] Attlee again pushed for a delay because of the need to update the register and organise the servicemen's vote. But both men agreed that Britain should maintain a united front on international affairs in view of the Soviet crisis and the Japanese war. Churchill concluded with a promise to send Attlee a letter which would set out his arguments for either an early election or the retention of the Coalition until victory in the Pacific. At 8.30 p.m. the following day, Thursday 17 May, Churchill dictated the first draft of this letter. In response to Labour's suggestion that the Coalition should continue until the autumn, he said that such a step would not be 'in the public interest' since fundamental differences over domestic policy between the parties meant that to 'prolong this lack of agreement for a mere three or four months would, in practice, prove detrimental both to our Ministerial and Parliamentary work'. But there was an alternative to this strife. 'It would give me great relief if you and your friends were found resolved to carry on until a decisive victory had been gained over Japan, and thus finish the job.' Then Churchill came up with a suggestion which even he admitted would be an 'extraordinary expedient'. To gain public approval for continuing the Coalition until Japan's surrender, Churchill said that a referendum could be held so that the decision rested with the 'whole electorate'. Though the device of a referendum had never previously been used in Britain's parliamentary system, Churchill argued that it could be justified on the grounds of the international stresses 'through which we are making our way'.[62] This draft was then approved, with a few minor cuts, by a meeting of Conservative ministers. Later that night, at 11.45 p.m., Attlee arrived to see Churchill for another discussion. 'I showed him the letter we had had composed. He did not at all demur to its general tenor but said he must consult his colleagues about it,' Churchill recorded.[63] Attlee, however, denied that he had seen the letter that night. In a later note, written to Churchill when the break-up of the Coalition became an explosive issue in the subsequent election campaign, he said with some grievance, 'I think your memory is at fault. At 11.45 on May 17th you did not show me the letter, but only gave me the general idea of your proposals.'[64]

Whatever the truth, the letter was delivered by hand to Attlee at 10 a.m. the next day, Friday 18 May, as the Labour ministers prepared to travel for their Annual Conference in Blackpool. As Attlee had promised, he consulted his senior colleagues about the proposal to extend the Coalition to the end of the Japanese war. Morrison was strongly opposed, warning that the conflict could drag on far into the future, but Attlee, Bevin and Dalton were more favourable, 'though we doubted whether the Conference would take it', wrote Dalton.[65] In an attempt to win over the Labour delegates to Churchill's proposal, Attlee put forward a compromise whereby Labour would stay in the Coalition if the Prime Minister would agree to make further progress on social reform. His idea was accepted by the other three Labour ministers. Interestingly, the innovative referendum scheme provoked little debate at their meeting. Attlee then went back to Downing Street at 3 p.m., armed with a single handwritten amendment to Churchill's letter. His note called for this new passage to be inserted after the reference to maintaining the Coalition until Japan's surrender: 'In the meanwhile, we would together do our utmost to implement the proposals for social security and full employment contained in the

White Papers which we have laid before Parliament.'[66] At the prospect of continuing the Coalition, Churchill immediately abandoned his longstanding antipathy to the implementation of social security policies in the current Parliament. 'I gladly agreed and inserted the exact words in the letter. He made no other suggestions […] I asked Mr Attlee whether Mr Bevin was in agreement with him, and he said this was so. The matter then seemed to be completed.'[67] The co-operative approach from Attlee also struck Jock Colville. 'Attlee came to see the PM at the Annexe and was favourably disposed to trying to persuade his party to continue at its Whitsun Blackpool Conference. He has Ernest Bevin with him on this.'[68] In the late afternoon of 18 May, Churchill sent the final version of the amended letter to Attlee. That evening he travelled down to Chartwell for the weekend in a buoyant mood, believing that his all-party Government had been secured. But it was a delusion.

There was a remarkable symmetry about the beginning of the Churchill Government and its end almost exactly five years later. In both cases, intensive discussions between the Conservatives and Attlee were followed by a Labour Conference, with whom the final decision rested. On each occasion the vital conference took place in a traditional English seaside resort: Bournemouth in May 1940 and Blackpool in May 1945. But the crucial difference was that in 1940, the Labour chiefs, the NEC and the delegates were united in favour of working alongside Churchill, whereas in 1945, Attlee's support of that approach was at variance with the mood of his party's activists. Co-operation with the Tories had been seen five years earlier as the path to national salvation. Now it was regarded as a barrier to socialism. Despite the new promise from Churchill of swift reform, the fierce opposition to the continuation of his Government was all too obvious from the moment the Labour ministers arrived in Blackpool. At meeting of the NEC, chaired by Ellen Wilkinson, Attlee read out Churchill's letter and, in his dry style, put the argument for maintaining the Coalition until Japan's surrender. But Morrison, whose own leadership ambitions meant that he had an ulterior motive in seeking to undermine Attlee, again strongly attacked this strategy. Morrison was backed up by Wilkinson, as well as Bevan, Shinwell and Labour Chief Whip Willie Whiteley, who said that 'the lads* will not stand for continuing the Coalition'.[69] Their view prevailed at the NEC, which decided to reject the deadline of the end of the Pacific war and instead push the Prime Minister to accept an October contest. Just three NEC members backed Attlee. At a highly charged session of the full Annual Conference on Monday 21 May, the delegates overwhelmingly agreed to the NEC's position. The anti-Churchill atmosphere was stoked by a rumbustious speech from Morrison, who described the Prime Minister's letter to Attlee as a form of 'election blackmail', a rather absurd charge given that Attlee was not only heavily consulted but had played a part in its drafting. But Morrison justified the accusation by claiming that Churchill had deliberately tried to engineer a snap summer poll by putting forward the unacceptable alternative of an indefinitely prolonged Coalition. An autumn election based on the new register, he said, would be much fairer to the electorate, particularly those in the services. What really caused anger in the Blackpool arena, however, was Churchill's proposal for a referendum on the future of the Coalition. 'The delegates were amazed and indignant at the idea that a referendum could be substituted for a General Election,' reported the *Daily Mirror*.

Attlee had been left badly isolated by the reversal. With his roots in East End campaigning for the socialist cause, he had always prided himself on his connection to the rank and file. But on the question of the election date, he had proved himself out of touch with the mainstream opinion in his party. The best way to restore his standing was to embrace the Conference's policy and go on the attack against Churchill. He did so in a sour letter to the Prime Minister, accusing him of opportunism, partisanship and even, in one egregious insult, of association with the methods of Nazism. Attlee opened the letter moderately with the well-rehearsed argument for an autumn election, followed by the case against going on until Japan were defeated. If the achievement of this victory were prolonged, party differences would

---

* Meaning the Parliamentary Labour Party.

become 'much more acute', he warned. His tone then became much more bitter as it turned to the subject of the proposed referendum, to which he had raised no previous objection. 'I could not consent to the introduction into our national life of a device so alien to all our traditions as the referendum, which has only too often been the instrument of Nazism and Fascism. Hitler's practices in the field of referenda and plebiscites can hardly have endeared these expedients to the British heart.' Attlee concluded with a personal attack: 'The reasons for rejecting an autumn election seem to me to be based not on national interests but on consideration of party expediency. It appears to me that you are departing from the position of a national leader by yielding to the pressure of the Conservative Party, which is anxious to exploit your own great service to the nation in its own interests.'[70]

That night Attlee read the text over the telephone from the Clifton Hotel in Blackpool to Churchill at Chequers, where he was dining with his son Randolph and Harold Macmillan. Having parted from Attlee on good terms the previous Friday, Churchill was perplexed by the Labour Leader's wholesale change. 'Winston was hurt at the unnecessarily waspish and even offensive tone of Attlee's reply,' recorded Macmillan in his diary.[71] Anthony Eden, who also called at Downing Street that evening, felt that Attlee's reserved character was partly to blame. Eden, who had 'never thought there was much chance' Labour would agree to the Japan deadline, noted: 'Winston had a strong impression from Attlee twice that he would recommend acceptance but I think this was only Attlee's timidity in interview.'[72] In his own account, written four weeks later, Churchill said that he did 'not blame Mr Attlee or Mr Bevin or other Socialist colleagues who agreed with them, for not having been able to carry their party with them. Obviously none of them was in a position to guarantee such a result. I must admit, however, that I was shocked and grieved by the harsh tone of the reply, coming from a man with whom I thought full agreement had been reached.'[73] Simmering with resentment, Churchill now set about his reply to Attlee. Several drafts were prepared, including versions by Macmillan and Randolph; advice was also proffered by

Beaverbrook, who insisted that no tribute should be paid to Attlee's war work. Randolph's draft had stated in its last paragraph his father's gratitude to Attlee and his Labour colleagues 'for the grand support they have given to the Island and its Empire in the struggle for life'.[74] This was removed on Beaverbrook's urging.

The finalised letter, sent on 22 May, expressed regret at Labour's decision not to 'work together until the defeat of Japan is achieved' but claimed that October was an impossibility because that would mean months of discord within Government, which would 'weaken the country before the world'. Then Churchill became more personal, attacking 'the aspersions' with which Attlee

> has darkened this correspondence. I have concerned myself solely with trying to create tolerable conditions under which we could work together. It is clear from the tone of your letter and the feelings of your party that these no longer exist and it is odd that you should accompany so many unjust allegations with an earnest request that we should go on bickering till the autumn. Such a process would not be a decent way of carrying on a British Government.[75]

Like Attlee's letter of 21 May, Churchill's reply was released to the press, worsening the friction and the controversy. Beaverbrook's *Daily Express*, privy to Churchill's inner thoughts, reported that the text

> caused a sensation among politicians. It is probably without precedent for two high-ranking ministers – the Premier and Deputy Premier – to engage in such strong attacks on each other. But Mr Churchill felt very strongly about what he regarded as a completely unfair distortion of the facts for the purpose of creating party propaganda for the Socialists in the coming election. In his view, Mr Attlee's whole attitude was unchivalrous and he therefore resolved, after careful thought, to deliver a smashing rebuke.[76]

The rift heralded the formal end of the war-winning Coalition. Later that day Churchill sent another, much shorter and less incendiary letter to Attlee, which explained that he proposed to tender his resignation to the King the next morning, Wednesday 23 May. That evening he wrote to George VI, setting out why the Coalition had to end. 'It would be no service to the nation to go forward with a pretence of a union which had in fact lapsed with the attainment of complete victory over Germany.'[77] At noon on 23 May, Churchill went to Buckingham Palace for his audience with the King, who accepted his resignation as Prime Minister. There was then a four-hour interval, designed to preserve the constitutional nicety of the royal prerogative, whereby the King could in theory have invited any senior politician to form a new Government. But in practice Churchill was the only possible choice, as the Leader of by far the largest party in the Commons. At four o'clock, he therefore returned to the Palace, where the King asked him to form a caretaker administration and agreed to the Dissolution of Parliament on 15 June, with the General Election to be held on 5 July, the slight delay in voting caused by the need to organise the ballot among the services personnel overseas.

The most successful coalition in British history was over. It had finished on an acrimonious note, partly because of Attlee's surprisingly shabby behaviour towards Churchill. During those fateful days, he initially misled Churchill in person about Labour's potential compliance, then later became aggressively dismissive on paper. 'Attlee was guilty of a great breach of taste (and tactics) in suggesting in his reply that Winston's suggestion of a referendum savoured of Hitlerite methods,' wrote Tommy Lascelles.[78] But the circumstances of its end could not diminish the scale of its achievement. It was an alliance that had saved Britain, and ultimately Europe from tyranny. Without Churchill's all-party Government, there would have been no VE Day, nor the survival British democracy. Churchill himself rose above the recent strife when he gave a farewell party in Downing Street for the departing ministers on 28 May, descending into lachrymose generosity, as Dalton described: 'He addressed us all, with tears visibly running down his cheeks. He said we had all come together and had stayed together as a united band of friends in a very trying time. History would recognise this. "The light will shine on every helmet."[79] In contrast to Churchill's effusive performance, said Lyttelton, Attlee adopted 'a correct but rather chilly attitude. He did not allow his humour off the chain that afternoon.'[80]

The General Election campaign turned to be one of the most contentious in the twentieth century, with the conflict between Churchill and Attlee at its heart. Its outcome was also highly unpredictable. The Leicester West MP Harold Nicolson articulated the views of many when he confessed, 'I do not think anybody of any party has any clear idea of how the Election will run. The Labour people seem to think that the Tories will come back with a majority of between 50 and 150. The Tories feel that the Forces will all vote for Labour and there may be a landslide to the left.'[81] But one unlikely figure had been certain of the outcome as early as March, months before the campaign began. On 19 March Josef Goebbels, the Nazi propaganda chief, had written: 'There is no doubt that shortly after the end of the war Churchill will be dispatched to the wilderness. It is, after all, the long-established British practice to tolerate men who amass an exaggerated plenitude of power in wartime but in peacetime to cast them off at once.'[82]

PART THREE

COMPETITORS

TWENTY-THREE

---◇---

CAMPAIGN

A S THE VICTOR in war, Churchill's position as Conservative Leader was unassailable immediately after the break-up of the Coalition, in contrast to his vulnerability within the party on taking office in May 1940. But he was never a straightforward Tory. He often looked back with nostalgia on his years as a Liberal, while his ideal type of government remained a coalition above the partisan fray. 'He had immense pride in being head of a Coalition that commanded nationwide support. I heard him say this very many times,' recalled the Cabinet Secretary Sir Edward Bridges.[1] That explained Churchill's regret over the end of his alliance with Labour. 'I was deeply distressed at the prospect of sinking from a national to a party leader. With all the news and grave issues pressing upon me, I earnestly desired that national comradeship and unity should be preserved,' he later wrote.[2] Even when Labour had left office, Churchill was determined to preserve some semblance of national government as he constructed his caretaker ministry. He therefore included a number of non-Conservative figures, such as the independent Sir John Anderson as Chancellor and the Liberal National Leader Ernest Brown as Minister for Aircraft Production, while Lloyd George's own son Gwilym, still nominally a Liberal MP, was made Minister of Fuel and Power. According to the Tory chief whip James Stuart, the task of forming the caretaker Government was carried out with typical Churchillian unorthodoxy over two days and nights. 'The Prime Minister seldom left his bed, eating his meals on a tray beside him. When he wished me to do so I joined him, eating at a small table near the bed. At the end of it all, I remember him saying to me, 'Well, that's it and all done by telephone from my bed. Think of poor old Mr Gladstone with all those letters he had to write.'[3]

Attlee's hold on the Labour leadership was not nearly so assured, his authority having been further dented by the internal row over the election date. 'Mr Attlee's position is not a happy one. Many socialists would like to displace him for someone with more dynamic qualities,' reported the *Sunday Times*.[4] At Labour's Conference, outgoing Chairman of the Labour Party and Jarrow MP Ellen Wilkinson briefed against Attlee to the *Daily Express*, which reported that Herbert Morrison was 'the idol of the delegates and undoubted leader of the party today'.[5] Her successor, Harold Laski, went even further by personally urging Attlee to resign because 'the continuance of your leadership in the party is a grave handicap to our hopes of victory in the coming General Election'. Drawing an analogy with Britain's wartime military command, Laski wrote: 'Just as Mr Churchill changed Auchinleck for Montgomery before El Alamein, so, I suggest, you owe it to the Party to give it the chance to make a comparable change on the eve of this greatest of our battles.'[6] Attlee waited a few days and then delivered a wonderfully brief reply, perhaps inspired by Churchill's short response to his own long rebuke of January:

> Dear Laski,
>   Thank you for your letter, the contents of which have been noted.
>   C. R. Attlee.[7]

Ironically, Churchill himself was to give the greatest boost to Attlee's troubled leadership at the start of the campaign, through his own aggressive but ill-judged style. Just as his pulse quickened at the thought of combat, so Churchill relished the boisterousness of the election trail. His early contests, at Oldham, Manchester, Dundee and Abbey, had all been turbulent affairs, filled with rollicking attacks and volatile rallies. That approach lingered on for him even in the post-war political world, where radio was becoming a much more important medium. In fact Attlee later said of Churchill's bullish tactics in the 1945 General Election, 'Well, he's very old fashioned in that way – kind of all's fair in politics.'[8] Churchill once told the National Labour MP Malcolm MacDonald 'with a gleam of reminiscent pleasure' that he 'very much enjoyed the mudslinging of such political battles'.[9] But in an election where the public yearned for an optimistic message about national reconstruction, those negative methods only succeeded in helping Labour and damaging his own cause.

That feeling of distaste among many voters was initially provoked by Churchill's first broadcast of the campaign, delivered live from Chequers on 4 June, when he launched a savage assault on Labour's belief in socialism, which he described as 'abhorrent to the British ideas of freedom'. In increasingly florid language, he spoke of the socialists' 'abject worship of the state' and 'hunger for controls of every kind'. And then came the vital passage, which caused widespread outrage and was to haunt Churchill for the rest of the campaign: 'No Socialist Government conducting the entire life and industry of the country could afford to allow free, sharp or violently worded expressions of public discontent. They would have to fall back on some form of Gestapo, no doubt very humanely directed in the first instance. And this would nip opinion in the bud.'[10]

The twenty-one-minute broadcast caused a political storm. The anti-socialist bombast was relished by some in his own party – like the former Chief Whip Viscount Margesson, who called the broadcast 'a beauty'.[11] Chips Channon visited the Commons the following afternoon and claimed to detect an atmosphere of fear among Labour MPs: 'Today the Labour boys seem very depressed and dejected by Winston's heavy pounding. I met Attlee in the lavatory and he seemed shrunken and terrified.'[12] But the more prevalent feeling among senior Tories was dismay. With its lurid charges of extremism against Labour, the broadcast was widely seen as a self-inflicted wound. In particular, Churchill's accusations of Nazi-like totalitarianism in Labour sounded outlandish, given that he had worked successfully with Attlee's party for the previous five years and had been keen for the alliance to continue. Harry Crookshank, the Postmaster General, noted in his diary that Winston's performance was 'very poor', full of 'very cheap anti-socialism'.[13] Quintin Hogg, the MP for Oxford, was at the Carlton Club when Churchill made his broadcast. 'In my opinion that broadcast will lose us between 250,000 and 500,000 votes,' he told his fellow listeners.[14]

The public certainly appeared to be hostile. According to a poll by Gallup, 69 per cent of voters disapproved of the broadcast. Similarly, the social-survey group Mass Observation reported that it was 'generally felt for a man of Churchill's prestige to be a very poor effort and a cheaply electioneering speech'.[15] The majority of Labour members were gleeful, sensing that Churchill had potentially handed them a huge political advantage. Geoffrey de Freitas, contesting Nottingham Central, wrote in his diary after hearing Churchill: 'I hope he makes more speeches like that because then we are certain to win.'[16] In the same vein, Ian Mikardo, standing for Labour in Reading, felt that Churchill had made 'a howling error' because the British people 'looked at Clem Attlee, the timid, correct, undemonstrative, ex-public schoolboy and couldn't see Adolf Hitler in him. They recalled how often Churchill had praised and thanked Labour leaders for the support and loyalty they had given him as members of the War Cabinet.'[17]

Churchill stood by the words in his broadcast, claiming two months later, 'the time would come when that particular speech would be recognised as one of the greatest he had delivered'.[18] He also said that his only regret was that he had referred to the Nazi secret police rather than the Soviet Union's NKVD. But this was misleading. The reality was that he had struggled badly with his text, unable to master the intimacy of radio or craft a persuasive theme. 'It was very unlike me,' he told Lord Moran. 'With an audience I can tell how things are and what they will take. But speaking into the microphone, I don't know what's there [...] I am worried about this damned election. I have no message for them now.'[19] Clementine witnessed how much trouble the performance had given her husband, as she wrote to their daughter Mary: 'Papa broadcasts tonight. He is very low, poor darling. He thinks he has lost his touch and grieves about it.'[20] With her sharp political antennae, Clementine recognised how incendiary his Gestapo analogy was. In a BBC interview, Mary remembered, 'He showed the speech to my mother before making it and she spotted it instantly. She said, "You cannot use this expression. It will be tremendously damaging. I think it will offend people." But he did not take her advice.'[21] Another of Churchill's daughters, Sarah, wrote to him soon after the broadcast that 'socialism as practised in the war did no one any harm and quite a lot of people good'.[22]

The apparent lapse in judgement was so great that there were suspicions as to who was really responsible for the words that Churchill delivered. Typical was the private opinion of Tommy Lascelles, who wrote of the broadcast: 'It gave me the impression of a tired man unwillingly reading something that had been written for him and that he didn't much like.'[23] Inevitably, the finger pointed at his two closest allies, Beaverbrook and Bracken. But neither man had much to do with the broadcast, which was Churchill's own composition. According to Beaverbrook's biographer A. J. P. Taylor, the only figures properly consulted were Randolph Churchill and the Chief Whip James Stuart. That point was confirmed by Colville, who saw Lascelles two days after the broadcast and told him that 'the PM had written every word of his speech on Monday'.[24] In his philippic against socialism, Churchill may have been influenced, not just by the Soviet threat, but also the writings of the Austrian academic Friedrich Hayek, now employed at the London School of Economics. The central theme of Hayek's recent work, most notably in *The Road to Serfdom* published in 1944, was that state control of economic life would ultimately destroy political and personal freedom. Hayek himself had given Churchill a copy of *The Road to Serfdom* and had 'little doubt' that the Gestapo broadcast was 'written under the influence' of the book.[25]

Yet it would be wrong to exaggerate the role of Hayek. After all, Churchill had been preaching the gospel of anti-socialism throughout most of his political career, right back to his days as an Edwardian Liberal. The very reason he switched parties in the early 1920s was because of his passionate opposition to the advance of this political creed, which he regarded as inimical to traditional British liberty. There was little in Hayek's theories that Churchill had not previously uttered. In a speech in 1920 Churchill said that Labour 'stood for a system of society where the whole business of the country would have to be run by Government officials, under the direction of political bosses'.[26] There was also a large element of hypocrisy in Labour's charge that Churchill's use of the term Gestapo was unprecedented or calumnious. As the historian Richard Toye has pointed out, associating opponents with Hitlerism and Fascism was a common element of politics at this time, with the experience of European conflict still so raw. Attlee himself had resorted to just such an accusation only days earlier when he rejected Churchill's proposal for a referendum on the future of the Coalition. In December 1944, Arthur Greenwood had complained in a Commons debate that British forces in Greece were in danger of acting 'as a sort of Gestapo' and in the same year Nye Bevan wrote that the 'the Tory is a potential Fascist element in the community'.[27]

But, shrewdly, Attlee avoided any of this kind of inflammatory rhetoric when, on the evening of 5 June, he gave his first radio broadcast of the campaign. Instead he shifted on to very different territory, presenting his party as the epitome of moderation with a practical scheme for peacetime renewal, the antithesis of Churchill's dark forebodings about Continental-style oppression. With a light but caustic touch, Attlee opened:

> When I listened to the Prime Minister's speech last night, in which he gave such a travesty of the policy of the Labour Party, I realised at once what was his object. He wanted the electors to understand at once how great was the difference between Winston Churchill, the great leader in war of a united nation, and Mr Churchill, the Party Leader of the Conservatives. He feared lest those who had accepted his leadership in war might

be tempted out of gratitude to follow him further. I thank him for having disillusioned them so thoroughly.

He then gave further credence to the theory that the Prime Minister had not written his own speech at all. 'The voice was that of Mr Churchill but the mind was that of Lord Beaverbrook.' Seeking to reinforce Labour's solid British credentials, he cleverly insinuated that Churchill had imported alien ideas from abroad, even worse, from the homeland of Hitler. 'I shall not waste time on this theoretical stuff which seems to me a second-hand version of the academic views of an Austrian professor – Friedrich August von Hayek – who is very popular just now with the Conservative Party.' The Tories, he said, were the sectional party representing 'the forces of property and privilege', whereas Labour was the party that 'most nearly reflects in its represen-tation and composition all the main streams which flow into the great river of our national life'.[28]

In defiance of all expectations, Attlee had emerged triumphant from his opening joust with Churchill. By common consent, he had sounded much more prime ministerial than the incumbent. The next day, when he attended the Commons, he was given 'quite a stirring ovation' by the PLP.[29] His mix of calmness and restraint were widely praised. 'Mr Attlee's broadcast was all that Mr Churchill's was not: moderate, sensible, constructive, fair,' said *The Economist*.[30] 'Attlee gave a good and dignified and reasoned and constructive reply to Winston. I believe Winston's broadcast may be a terrific liability to live down,' wrote Violet Bonham Carter.[31] The majority of the public and the press seemed to have felt the same way. Judy Haines, a young married woman from Chingford, said that 'after Churchill's outburst of last evening, I found it pleasant listening. He dealt with Churchill's accusation but didn't counter accuse.'[32] John Cole, then a young reporter in Northern Ireland, later renowned as the BBC's political correspondent, felt that Attlee's broadcast 'went for the jugular' through heavy irony. 'He was transformed into a formidable election warrior.'[33]

Before the descent into acrimony across the airwaves, Churchill had been keen to maintain civil relations with Attlee, for the sake of both the national interest and the smooth running of Government business, especially on foreign policy. In this spirit of co-operation, he wrote to the Labour Leader on 31 May with a generous proposal: 'I believe that we are in complete agreement on foreign and military policy at this time and I hope that we may so continue. Should you wish to share in our anxieties, though not in our responsibilities, in strict personal secrecy I should like to offer you facilities to see papers on the main developments in foreign affairs and strategy.' Churchill concluded that he would be 'very glad' if 'you wish to associate Mr Bevin with you in this arrangement'.[34] Attlee's reply the next day was warm but cautious: 'I see great public advantage in this but it has obvious implications which need careful consideration. Could I have your permission to discuss the matter in strict secrecy with some of my colleagues?'[35]

But then the issue of access to papers became embroiled in a much bigger foreign-policy question. For some time, Churchill had been pressing Truman and Stalin for a summit of the Allied powers to discuss the post-war settlement of Europe. After initial reluctance, the American and Soviet leaders agreed, though the conference could not be held before mid-July. This was after the General Election but before the results would be announced, for a three-week gap was necessary to allow the return of votes from serving personnel overseas. Given the possibility of a change of Government, Churchill decided that Attlee would have to attend. On 2 June he therefore extended an invitation:

> It now looks as if the Three Power meeting will open in Berlin on July 15. As the result of our polls will not be known until July 25, it would seem to me most necessary that you should be present in order that, however the election may go, the voice of Britain is united. I think this would make it necessary for you to study the telegrams before we go.[36]

Two days later, shortly before his Gestapo broadcast, Churchill wrote to President Truman to inform him of his plan to bring Attlee with him to the Conference. 'He is in full agreement at the present time with our foreign policy, but the United States and Soviet Union have a right to know that they are dealing with the whole of Britain whatever our immediate Party future may be.'[37] The idea of Attlee's participation in the summit did not impress Lieutenant General Sir Hugh Tudor, who had served alongside Churchill on the Western Front in the First World War and had remained a friend since then. 'The present Labour Leader as one of the Big Three seems to me rather like a mouse in a rat's job,' Tudor wrote to Churchill.[38]

Having consulted his colleagues, Attlee accepted the two offers from Churchill, on access to the files and attendance at the summit in Germany. 'I do not anticipate that we shall differ on the main lines which we have discussed together so often,' he wrote.[39] But the superficial cordiality of Attlee's letter was at variance with the growing bitterness of the campaign, of which the Gestapo controversy was typical. The ugly mood was again highlighted when Ernie Bevin, at his adoption meeting as Labour candidate in Wandsworth on 7 June, made a harsh personal attack on Churchill, accusing him of bad faith over the break-up of the Coalition and describing him as a 'Jekyll and Hyde' character, who had fallen from being 'a sort of national father' into 'a mere tool of the Tory Party'. In the *Daily Herald*'s report of his speech, Bevin claimed that Churchill had been manipulative about the election date and his correspondence with Attlee. 'I don't believe that political life needs to be conducted in the gutter,' he said.[40]

Churchill was appalled at this onslaught, not least because he was an admirer of Bevin's. A week earlier he had written personally to ask if he could submit his name for the Companionship of Honour, one of the Empire's highest awards, 'in view of your remarkable work at the Ministry of Labour'. It was the same honour that Churchill had just offered to Attlee, who, 'I am glad to say [...] is willing to have his name put forward.'[41] Bevin, who was never interested in social status despite his large ego, refused. 'The job I have undertaken, like thousands of others during the war, has been in the interests of the nation and I do not desire special honours,' he told Churchill.[42] But Churchill's bigger grievance was Bevin's claim that Labour ministers had been kept in the dark about the end of the Coalition, when, in reality, Attlee had been extensively consulted during 17 and 18 May. As a consequence, Churchill felt compelled to issue a public statement on 12 June with the schedule of his talks with Attlee over those crucial two days. 'Bevin's repeated charges of bad faith in regard to the circumstances of our unhappy separation force me to present to the public the actual facts of what took place,' Churchill wrote to Attlee, explaining his action.[43] In his press release, Churchill said that he 'could not face the difficulties of carrying on a Coalition Government in which the spirit of co-operation had vanished and many of my colleagues had their eyes fixed on an October or November election'.[44]

Attlee swiftly issued his own statement that disputed Churchill's version, claiming, 'I was anxious to do everything I could to preserve national unity', while the Conservatives pushed for a swift summer poll. For Attlee, 'the subsequent campaign of misrepresentation against Labour ministers and the sedulous attempt to make out that we have deserted the Government' confirmed that the Tories planned to 'force an election which they thought most suitable for exploiting the Prime Minister's great service to the country', though he conceded Churchill himself displayed a 'reluctance' to end the Coalition.[45] But this caveat could not prevent an inevitable frostiness between Labour and Churchill, even over access to the foreign policy documents. In the official Downing Street records, Jock Colville left a note on 15 June that explained how the Prime Minister had instructed him to place at Attlee's 'disposal' a room where 'he could see all the papers relevant to the imminent Conference'. But, crucially, 'Mr Bevin is not to be included in the arrangement.' Churchill had further told Colville that, though Attlee was feel 'free to communicate' any comments on the papers, 'he should not be encouraged to do so too frequently'.[46] A few days later, when Attlee still had not made any request to see the papers, Churchill told another of his aides, Leslie Rowan, 'to go slow' about chasing up the Labour Leader.[47]

But it was the build-up to the Conference itself that brought the relationship between Attlee and Churchill to a new level of friction. On 14 June, the Prime Minister wrote to Stalin to tell him that, because the summit would be under way 'before the British elections results are made known', he planned 'to bring Mr Attlee, the official Leader of the Opposition, in order that full continuity of British policy may be assured'.[48] Stalin agreed: 'The reasons which you gave for considering it necessary to include Mr Attlee in the British Delegation are fully understood.'[49] Also on 14 June, the penultimate day before dissolution, Churchill announced in the Commons that Attlee would accompany him to the Three Power talks in Berlin. 'Although Governments may change and parties may quarrel, yet on some of the main essentials of foreign affairs we stand together,' he told MPs.[50] Yet Professor Harold Laski, Chairman of Attlee's own Labour Party NEC, proved much less emollient than Marshall Stalin. That night, after Churchill's announcement in Parliament, Laski made an extraordinary intervention that was to reverberate until polling day. In a statement to the press, he said that while Attlee should attend the summit, he should do so 'in the role of observer only' for Labour could not be bound by its decisions. 'Labour has a foreign policy which in many respects will not be continuous with that of the Tory-dominated Coalition. It has, in fact, a far sounder foreign policy,' said Laski, adding that Attlee therefore 'should not accept responsibility for agreements which on the British side will have been concluded by Mr Churchill'.[51]

Churchill was affronted by this statement, which both smacked of spectacular presumption and undermined the united front between the parties on foreign policy. But, in purely electoral terms, Churchill also perceived that Laski's contribution could be a gift to the Tories since it opened an apparently potent new line of attack on Labour. Attlee could now be painted as the prisoner of a shadowy, unelected caucus, eager to impose its left-wing dogma on Britain. Furthermore, Laski's statement seemed to reinforce the message of Churchill's Gestapo broadcast, that Labour rule would enhance unaccountable political bureaucracy.

As an opening shot in his new drive to exploit Laski's chairmanship, Churchill wrote to Attlee the next day, 15 June:

> His Majesty's Government must of course bear the responsibility for all decisions. But my idea was that you should come as a friend and a counsellor, and help us on all the subjects on which we have been so long agreed [...] Merely to come as a mute observer would I think be derogatory to your position as the Leader of Your Party, and I should not have the right to throw this burden upon you in such circumstances.[52]

Attlee replied that day in a tone of reassurance, explaining to Churchill that there was 'never any suggestion that I should go as a mere observer'.[53]

Despite this response, Laski continued to elucidate publicly his view of the constitutional supremacy of Labour's NEC and the need for a separate socialist foreign policy. Just a day after Attlee had formally accepted the summit invitation, Laski declared that 'we cannot be saddled, when we win this Election, with any commitment that Mr Churchill may make that supports a body of decaying monarchism on one hand or a body of dubious privileges on the other'. Two days later, he stated that 'important as it is for Mr Attlee to be at the Three Power talks in Berlin, it was not less important there should be a clear understanding [...] that we Socialists are only committed to decisions which result in coherence with Socialism.'[54]

All this was more ammunition for Churchill in his effort to depict Labour as a dangerous menace to the British way of life. It suited his purposes to exaggerate Laski's importance, presenting him as the sinister puppet master pulling the strings of a future Attlee Government. In this task, he was noisily abetted by Beaverbrook, who used his newspapers and the platform to try to whip up a new red scare. 'I hereby declare that Laski is aiming at the destruction of the Parliamentary system of Great Britain,' Beaverbrook said at a meeting in Streatham on 20 June. Churchill had no inhibitions about targeting Laski, even though the professor trumpeted a personal attachment to him on the grounds that his own father Nathan, the leader of Manchester's Jewish community in the Edwardian age, had helped Churchill win his seat in the city as a Liberal in 1906. Laski even claimed that, in his youth, he had assisted Churchill's campaigning in Manchester, and had watched the MP rehearse his early speeches in the family home. But Laski was notorious for self-aggrandisement. A shameless attention-seeker and name-dropper, he was full of improbable stories, like the boast that he had played and beaten the American tennis star Maurice McLoughlin, twice winner of the US Open. Churchill himself told his office that he had 'no personal relations' with Laski,[55] and instructed his aide John Martin to dig into his background. 'You asked about Professor Laski's record in the last war. He appears to have spent the war years on the American continent,' Martin told Churchill on 18 June.[56] But Churchill, who was strongly pro-Jewish, warned against anything that smacked of prejudice. When his Conservative ally and fellow imperialist Henry Page Croft sarcastically described Laski as 'that fine old Englishman', Churchill wrote to him, 'Pray be careful, whatever the temptation, not to be drawn into any campaign that might be represented as anti-Semitism.'[57]

Churchill's focus on Laski was not wholly opportunistic. After all, the theory that the NEC could overthrow the will of the party leadership had recently been proved by Labour's Annual Conference in May, while Churchill's concern over disunity on foreign affairs was genuine. At the Cabinet on 20 June, he expressed his anxiety that if the Three Power summit proceeded before the election results were known, then 'he would not feel that the integrity of his position would be assured even though Mr Attlee were present with him at the meeting'. Churchill even wondered if the Berlin meeting should be postponed, and ordered the Foreign Office to prepare draft telegrams to Stalin and Truman suggesting a delay. But no further action was taken on this drastic step.[58] Instead, he returned to the fight against Laski with another explosive radio broadcast. The Conservative and Labour parties had each been allotted ten broadcasts for the campaign, with Churchill taking four of them. In contrast Attlee took just one of Labour's slots, showing the less dominant, more collegiate nature of his leadership. In his second broadcast, delivered on 13 June, Churchill had emphasised the Conservatives' embrace of social progress, as reflected in the Four Year Plan announced in March 1943, though he still had thrown in another barb at Labour. 'If our wealth and enterprise are not cracked and spoiled by the fetters of authoritarian socialism, there lie open vast possibilities of social endeavour in this vital sphere.'[59]

But in his third broadcast, on 21 June, he went back to the Laski theme with a vengeance. Referring to the forthcoming summit, he said,

> It was my conception that I should enjoy Mr Attlee's counsel at every stage of my discussions, and that what he said and agreed to he would naturally stand by. And from what I knew of him and his views over the last five years I did not expect there would be a single issue which could not be reconciled in an agreeable manner. In accepting my invitation, Mr Attlee showed that he shared this hopeful opinion. However a new figure has leaped into notoriety. The situation has been complicated and darkened by the repeated intervention of Professor Laski, chairman of the Socialist Party Executive. He has reminded all of us, including Mr Attlee, that the final determination on all questions of foreign policy rests, so far as the Socialist Party is concerned, with this dominating Socialist Executive.[60]

This speech gained little more public approval than the Gestapo one had. Vita Sackville-West wrote to her husband Harold Nicolson the following day: 'You know I have an admiration for Winston amounting to idolatry, so I am dreadfully distressed by the badness of his broadcast election speeches. What has gone wrong with him?'[61]

Far more important criticism came from Attlee, who gave a powerful response in a speech three days later to what he called Churchill's 'insinuations and misrepresentations'. No one, he said, 'really believes that the Labour Party, which is the most democratic in its structure of all political parties and throughout its history has steadfastly supported the cause of democracy all over the world, would ever betray the living principle of its being'. Attlee then claimed that Churchill's conduct showed he was badly out of touch with the electorate. 'When I heard of the Prime Minister's fantastic accusations against the Labour Party which put him in power and for five years supported him during the war, I was inclined to echo his question, "What kind of people does he think you are?" if he expects you to take this kind of talk seriously.'[62] But Churchill was undaunted. In his final broadcast of the campaign, on 30 June, he returned yet again to the Laski theme, warning that Labour's NEC had the power to demand 'the submission of Ministers to its will'. This meant, in effect, that party officials would be privy to state secrets, a development that represented 'one of the gravest changes in the constitutional history of England and Britain'.[63] Churchill's stint behind the BBC microphone was over. The great wartime orator had not distinguished himself. 'Better than the previous three, but not exciting,' was Jock Colville's verdict.[64] Londoner Jennifer McIntosh wrote to her sister in California, 'One of the most extraordinary things has been the terrific slump in the Churchill's prestige. I wish you could have heard his election broadcasts – they were deplorable, the last one pitifully cheap.'[65]

Attlee rose to new heights of dismissiveness after this broadcast. In a statement on Sunday 1 July, he labelled as 'disgraceful' Churchill's suggestion that Labour ministers might divulge official secrets to the NEC. 'He must indeed be badly rattled to stoop to making such charges against colleagues who served him so loyally.'[66] Attlee was even more scathing in a speech made the same day in Peckham. 'Mr Churchill complains of the breaking of comradeship in the election, yet it was he who deliberately lowered the whole tone of the contest in his first broadcast and his closest friend is the chief mudslinger, while Labour Ministers have striven to keep the discussion to principles and policy.' Attlee went on to say that the Prime Minister should 'not confuse recognition of him as the leader of the country in war and approval of him as the leader of the Conservative Party'.[67]

Yet Churchill still felt he was on to a winning strategy by invoking the Laski supremacy. On 2 July, just three days before polling, he wrote directly to Attlee in a letter designed for immediate publication. Despite some 'violent remarks', argued Churchill, the Labour Leader had still failed to answer the fundamental question about the powers of the NEC under the 'undisputed Chairman' Laski. 'It would appear that a Labour or Socialist Government would be subject to the directions of this committee and that matters of foreign affairs, and also, I presume, if they desired it, military affairs, would have to be submitted to them.'[68] Attlee replied from his home in Stanmore almost as soon as he received this latest missive. 'The new position with which you state we are confronted exists only in your own imagination,' he wrote, going on to set out the constitutional reality, complete with a pertinent example from the beginning of Churchill's own premiership. 'Naturally there are consultations between the Parliamentary Labour Party and the National Executive Committee [...] For instance when I decided to advise the Labour Party to support you in forming an All Party Government in 1940, I consulted the Executive Committee before bringing it before the Annual Conference of the Party then in session. You raised no objection then.'[69]

Indefatigable as ever, Churchill would not give up, despite Attlee's defence. He fired off another round, complaining again about the dominant role of Labour's Annual Conference and NEC. Even a future Labour Prime Minister, he argued, could be summoned before the NEC to explain 'his conduct of the Peace negotiations. How he could defend his actions without the disclosure of confidential information I fail to see.'[70] Now well acquainted with the rhythm of this relentless exchange, Attlee immediately replied from Heywood that night, sending copies of his letter to the press at the same time. Having accused Churchill of wilfully misinterpreting Labour's constitution, he concluded, 'I think you underestimate the intelligence of the public.'[71]

This perception was correct. Churchill's rhetorical barrage about Laski's powers left the public indifferent rather than scandalised. As *The Times* rightly predicted, 'the electorate will treat the whole affair as a distraction'.[72] In fact, Churchill's invective proved counter-productive because it made him look as if he had lost his sense of perspective, while Attlee came across as the sober, democratic statesman. Not prone to boasting, the Labour Leader told his brother Tom, 'Winston keeps slogging away at the silly Laski business but I don't think he gets the better of exchanges with me.'[73] The electorate was concerned, not with the minutiae of Labour's structure, but the more pressing issues of wartime reconstruction. As one Labour candidate put it, 'Sophisticated stories like the Attlee-Laski incident seem terribly far away in the streets and factories here. What people want to talk about is redundancy, housing, pensions and what will happen to ex-servicemen after the war.'[74]

In this context, Attlee's Labour Party was far more in tune with the electorate's outlook than Churchill's Conservatives. The war had not only reinforced the spirit of national solidarity but had also promoted a widespread faith in the central role of the state. In a sense, peacetime socialism was simply the extension of the wartime economy, with its emphasis on planning and controls. Scaremongering about left-wing economics carried little weight among a public that had experienced the conscription of labour, restrictions on profits and unprecedented levels of public expenditure. In 1938, state spending accounted for 28.87 per cent of Gross Domestic Product, a figure that soared to 65.7 per cent in 1944 and 70.34 per cent in 1945, by far the highest proportion in British history. The command economy had brought greater equality as well as Government debts. Post-tax incomes were distributed more evenly, full employment was reached and rationing meant better diets for low income families. All this was compared favourably in the public mind with the Tory-led 1930s, which had come to be associated with mass joblessness and lack of economic security. George Strauss, the Labour MP for Lambeth North, had this reflection on the widespread belief in progressivism.

Winston Churchill held a well-advertised open-air meeting on the borders of my constituency. He was warmly received but the mood of the crowd clearly reflected the advice proffered on the well-displayed, surrounding Labour posters: 'Cheer Churchill, Vote Labour.' That succinctly encapsulated the broad attitude of the electorate throughout the land. The election was not regarded as an opportunity to express gratitude to Churchill for his leadership during the war. At stake was the future, not the past, not personalities. To many people the choice was between a party that had been responsible for the unemployment, inequalities and hardships that had characterised pre-war society and one determined to bring about a fairer and happier one.[75]

Support for Labour was further heightened by Britain's alliance with the Soviet Union, whose fighting spirit and colossal industrial output appeared to be a compelling advertisement for socialism. That was recognised by BBC journalist Howard Marshall, who was embedded with an infantry brigade after D-Day. He wrote to Lord Woolton that the men 'see guns and tanks and equipment for war and say, "why can't we produce houses on that scale and just as fast?" And they add that Joe Stalin would do it quickly enough.'[76] But some felt that this anti-Conservative mood was deliberately stoked by the Army Bureau of Current Affairs (ABCA), which had been set up in 1941 ostensibly to provide citizenship education and raise morale. There were suspicions that the bureau fed the troops with left-wing propaganda about nationalisation, inequality and social justice, a charge based partly on the politics of its founder Bill Emrys Williams, who was once described as 'a skinny little radical from the valleys' imbued with 'vehement Welsh socialism'.[77] It was little wonder that Churchill was doubtful about the bureau, which he saw as an arena 'for the professional grouser and agitator with a glib tongue'.[78] His fears about the service's vote were well founded. During the campaign he could sense it slipping away, a feeling reinforced by his conversations with the military chiefs. Sir Arthur Harris, the head of Bomber Command, told him that about 80 per cent of the men in the RAF 'will vote Labour',[79] while Bill Slim, the victorious commander in Burma, said to him bluntly during a spell of leave, 'Well, Prime

Minister, if I know one thing, my army won't be voting for you.'[80]

Churchill's own daughter Mary, on duty with the Auxiliary Territorial Service in Europe, also forecast that 'the army votes will largely go to Labour'.[81]

The Tories' failure to match the political mood was worsened by their poor organisation. The Labour Party not only had more activists, but was also backed by the muscle of the trade-union movement, whose membership had increased during the war by more than 2 million to 7.5 million. More importantly, Labour had a clear, coherent plan, set out in its manifesto entitled *Let Us Face the Future*, which was largely the work of Herbert Morrison. One indicator of the enthusiasm for Labour was that the party actually sold 1.5 million copies. In contrast the Tory manifesto, called *Winston Churchill's Declaration of Policy to the Electors*, was a vague, uninspiring document, which even downplayed the Conservatives' existing proposals for reconstruction such as a universal, free healthcare system.

The Conservatives' reluctance to stress their domestic policies was primarily the result of a mistaken strategic decision to bank on the appeal of Churchill's character as an election winner. As with Lloyd George in the General Election of 1918, Churchill's record as the war victor was thought to be sufficient. 'The campaign was more efficiently conducted by the Labour Party than by the Conservatives who, of course, inevitably were relying on the tremendous prestige of Mr Churchill,' wrote Woolton.[82] In an attempt to reinforce his credentials as a national, rather than merely a Conservative, leader Churchill continued to portray his political support as a kind of grand coalition. Tellingly, in his notorious Gestapo broadcast, he barely mentioned his own party, spoke of the 'Conservative and National Government I have formed' and claimed that 'there is scarcely a Liberal sentiment' that 'we do not inherit and defend'.[83] In addition to forty-nine Liberal Nationals, effectively Tory allies, ten other pro-Churchill candidates stood on a purely National platform. But Attlee denounced Churchill's use of the National label as an act of deception. 'He knows perfectly well that the attempt to present the Conservatives, National Liberals and odds and ends as a National Party different from other parties is sheer humbug.'[84] Nor could Churchill's fluid party nomenclature counter the belief that he was unsuitable to be a peacetime premier, as the Labour candidate Geoffrey de Freitas put it: 'His greatness as a national leader for the European war was now quite outweighed by his inability to see modern, 20th century social changes except through the eyes of a great Elizabethan swashbuckler.'[85] The future Labour Foreign Secretary Michael Stewart, standing in Fulham, recalled that 'the Tories had a poster in the election that said simply, "Architect of Peace – Churchill or Attlee". The answer was self-evident to the electorate but not in the sense the Tories had expected.'[86] Attlee had his own experience of Churchill's despair at his inability to connect with the electorate. At one point during the contest, the two men ran into each other and, as Attlee later recounted, Churchill said: 'Well, I've tried them with pep and I've tried 'em with pap, but I don't know what it is they want.'[87]

Churchill's problems were further highlighted on the campaign trail. He embarked on a four-day grand tour of the country from 25 June, travelling by a special train that was equipped with telephones and a trailer with a Humber limousine, as well as a full complement of couriers and typists so he could conduct official business on the move. It was a frenetic trip, during which he covered over 1,000 miles and averaged ten speaking engagements a day. There was an air of a royal procession about his progress through the Midlands, the North and Scotland, as vast crowds gathered at every rally. At Coventry, the throng of people slowed his car down to walking pace as it tried to reach his venue. In Manchester, 50,000 people came to hear him, while Glasgow was said to have given him 'a tumultuous reception'.[88] The *Daily Express* exulted in the excitable atmosphere: 'It has been a victory tour, a roaring helter-skelter triumph for the man who won the war and is now at the head of a party seeking re-election.'[89] So regal did the tour appear that Labour's secretary Morgan Phillips complained to Long Maddox of the Newsreel Association about the alleged biased coverage of the Prime Minister, when Attlee was denied the same airtime. 'The Prime Minister's tour is considered to be of news interest, apart from any political interest and the newsreel companies are at liberty to film it,' replied Maddox.[90]

Huge crowds, however, did not translate into support for the Conservatives. Thousands wanted to salute him as Britain's war hero; others wanted to catch a glimpse of the country's biggest celebrity. But that did not stop them backing Labour. 'Just because we cheered the old bugger, doesn't mean we're going to vote for him,' said one elector.[91] Not all the spectators were supportive, either. When Churchill had finished his grand train tour, he carried out a series of rallies in London, where he encountered a much more hostile reception. He was loudly booed at meetings in Wandsworth, Battersea and Norwood. In Chelsea, as he made his famous V for Victory sign, 'nobody cheered and the silence was dire'.[92] In some places, there were even hints of violence. At Southwark, police had to intervene as a section of the crowd turned aggressive. During a rally in Tooting, a teenager threw a firework at Churchill which almost exploded in his face. The very last event, held on 3 July at the Walthamstow greyhound stadium, was described by *The Times* as 'one of the stormiest meetings he had addressed during the campaign'.[93] When he first rose to speak, some of the audience began to chant, 'We want Attlee! We want Attlee!' So loud and frequent were the interruptions that Churchill struggled to get through the remainder of his speech.[94]

Churchill's campaign across the country, combined with his official duties, meant that he could not devote much time to his own constituency in Essex. Because of population growth since 1935, the Epping seat was divided in two, with Churchill now the candidate for Woodford. In a tribute to his war leadership, both the Labour and the Liberal parties agreed not to run against him, but he still faced local opposition in the form of an eccentric farmer called Alexander Hancock, who stood as an independent. When asked by the press why he was challenging Churchill, he said, 'I'm as good a man as he is.' Questioned about his opinions, he replied, 'My views are bunk. I don't know anything about politics.'[95] In the fight against Hancock, Clementine had to serve as a substitute for her husband at the election meetings in Woodford, a task she performed with grace; although as a Liberal herself, she inevitably emphasised the progressive side of her husband's politics. 'It would make me very happy if, at the end of my husband's life, he were to be associated with the great reforms which he proposed in his Four Year plan issued two years ago,' she said at an eve-of-poll rally.[96]

Apart from the controversy it provoked, Churchill's grand tour also symbolised, in the public imagination, a crucial difference between the Prime Minister and his Labour opponent. While Churchill travelled in sumptuous style in his special train and Humber, Attlee was driven by his wife Violet across the country in their modest 1938 Hillman saloon. The publicity given to this contrast fed the narrative of Attlee as the austere, modern man of the people, compared to Churchill as the extravagant, anachronistic patrician. The imagery was all the more damning to Churchill because the bill for the train's use, which came to £372, was met by the taxpayer, though he paid some of the costs for food and service. The large payment from public funds was justified on the grounds that Churchill was not only Prime Minister but also acting Foreign Secretary, since Anthony Eden was ill with a duodenal ulcer, the beginning of stomach problems that were to blight the rest of his political career. Downing Street argued that, with conflict in the Pacific still raging, Churchill had to be 'in constant touch with London and to discharge his official business with the speed which wartime conditions required'. Furthermore, if the train had not been hired, 'It would have been necessary to take hotel rooms and install secure telephone apparatus on the route.'[97] Nevertheless, this was further self-inflicted damage in an already flawed campaign.

Attlee's choice of transport was politically acceptable yet physically unnerving. Violet was a confident but reckless driver, who, despite a qualification as an advanced motorist, was involved in a lengthy catalogue of serious accidents during her married life. 'It was curious, this taste for fast driving in a woman who otherwise had all the demure and retiring qualities required for a Prime Minister's wife,' wrote the *Daily Mail*'s political editor Walter Terry.[98] Fortunately Violet was not involved in any crashes in the 1945 campaign, during which her husband addressed no fewer than seventy meetings. Although he did not inspire the excitement generated by Churchill's fame and glamour, his events were all well attended, as Clement reported to his brother Tom in early July. 'I had a good four days in Northants last week. Vi drove me round to packed and enthusiastic meetings with large crowds, listening to the mike outside.'[99] To Dalton after the campaign, he wrote of 'the optimism of all our people' and 'the magnificent meetings' he had addressed in the Midlands and London.[100] After all the romance and melodrama of Churchill's wartime speeches, much of the electorate greeted Attlee's lack of colour with relief. Voters seemed to want the prose of solid, progressive governance, not the poetry of national defiance.

Even so, despite the strong Labour campaign, there was a widespread consensus among commentators and politicians of a Conservative victory, or at the very least a hung Parliament. Violet Bonham Carter noted in her diary, 'the general opinion is that the Tories will get in with a very small majority. Winston could have swept the board if he had behaved with dignity and ordinary common sense.'[101] Another Liberal backer, the *Manchester Guardian*, argued that 'this is not the Election to shake Tory England'.[102] Equally confident was Ralph Assheton, Chairman of the Tory Party, who predicated a majority of at least 100, while Beaverbrook wrote, 'I believe Winston will win, with at least a comfortable majority.'[103] His own paper, the *Daily Express*, even claimed that Labour had abandoned all hope. 'The Government's opponents have already decided that they have lost the election and that Mr Churchill is certain of a big working majority.'[104] The *Express*'s claim was not a mere fantasy. There were several senior Labour figures who felt defeat was inevitable. Hugh Dalton confided in his diary on the eve of poll that he believed Labour would gain eighty seats, but the Tories would still have a three-figure majority. Attlee himself told Jock Colville that 'with luck' the Conservative majority might be reduced to forty.[105] As for Churchill, his view was changeable, as Lord Moran noted, 'He is thinking a lot these days of the election. One moment he sees himself victorious, the next he pictures himself beaten.'[106]

Churchill was right to feel uncertain. The optimistic reports from Conservative Central Office were contradicted by opinion surveys, which gave a consistent lead to Labour throughout the campaign. The final Gallup survey showed Labour on 47 per cent, with the Tories on 41. Commenting on this poll, the *News Chronicle* said that the Conservatives' dependence on Churchill had been 'dangerous' because 'there is a deep-rooted distrust of the British people for personal Government'.[107] But to find out the accuracy of the Gallup forecast, Attlee and Churchill had to wait for three weeks until the count started, as the services vote came in from overseas. In the meantime, the pair were about to travel abroad themselves, to the Three Power summit in Germany.

TWENTY-FOUR

—◆—

POTSDAM AND PALACE

IN A DISCUSSION with his doctor Lord Moran shortly before leaving for Germany, Churchill referred to Attlee's presence at the forthcoming summit. 'His eyes twinkled; a smile hovered not far away. "We don't know whether we are on speaking terms until we meet at Berlin,"' recorded Moran.[1] As the doctor recognised, Churchill's words had been only in jest. Soon after the fierce election campaign, cordiality returned to the relationship between the two party leaders. In their long association, there was never the kind of personal animosity that infused other duels, like that between Benjamin Disraeli and William Gladstone. Attlee himself later recalled, 'I suppose that in most countries the idea that two leaders in a hotly contested Election should be able to meet again on easy terms and to co-operate, would seem strange, but we had so recently been colleagues that we experienced no difficulty.'[2] The affability was illustrated when Churchill wrote to Attlee on 11 July to offer 'a Government servant to look after your luggage and deal with your personal requirements during your mission'. In a delicious twist, the name of the servant that Churchill put forward could hardly have been more inapposite. 'If this is agreeable to you, I would therefore suggest that Chamberlain, whom you must know as one of the messengers at Number 10, should accompany you. He is thoroughly trustworthy and a very good valet.'[3] Attlee, socially conventional if politically radical, felt no guilt about accepting the offer.

The Three Power summit began on 15 July in the historic city of Potsdam, which lay on the edge of Berlin and had been the residence of the Prussian kings and the Kaiser. The goal of the conference was to finalise the post-war settlement of Germany and Eastern Europe, as well the terms for the surrender of Japan. Despite his experience of attending at the San Francisco event only a few months earlier, Attlee did not initially strike many of the British diplomats as an impressive figure when he arrived in Germany in advance of Churchill. On landing at Berlin airport by separate flights, both men had been given full military receptions, complete with music from a Royal Marine band. But the British interpreter George Leggett, an expert in the Russian and Polish languages, was taken by the difference in stature and charisma between the Prime Minister and the Labour Leader. According to Leggett's unpublished memoir of Potsdam, 'Winston Churchill stepped out of his plane and, clad in a Hussar Colonel's tropical uniform, paused on the steps to allow the throng of photographers to do their work while he beamed, fingering a cigar and waving greetings to old friends.' In contrast, 'Mr Attlee, an earlier arrival, had also been accorded a guard of honour, his small civilian figure appearing a little incongruous amidst this display of military splendour.'[4] Later that evening, Leggett accompanied Attlee to meet some British liaison officers and make a tour of Berlin. The interpreter warmed to him more over a glass of whisky that night. 'His voice has a peculiar quality of quiet, slightly high-pitched softness. He puffs at his pipe reflectively and takes it out to make some quietly humorous remark. He has a nice warm smile that savours of shyness.'[5]

The Foreign Office Permanent Secretary Sir Alexander Cadogan thought that the contrast between Churchill and Attlee was reflected in the accommodation provided for the British team at Potsdam. Cadogan wrote that Churchill had 'really a charming' villa but then 'several houses further on is a drab and dreary little building destined to house Attlee. Very suitable. It is just like Attlee himself.'[6] One US diplomat,

Chip Bohlen, was equally dismissive. Having witnessed Attlee's first appearance at the conference, he described the Labour Leader as 'a mechanical toy which, when wound up and placed on the table by Winston Churchill, would perform as predicted'.[7] But Churchill, still exhausted from the election on top of his five intensive years as premier, seemed to be struggling at the start. The Foreign Secretary Anthony Eden was horrified at Churchill's opening performance. 'Winston was very bad. He had read no brief and was confused and woolly and verbose.'[8]

As the conference went on, Churchill's performances improved, bolstered by the continual round of lunches and dinners. He was also galvanised by the sense of being at the heart of global politics in a land whose regime he had conquered. Neville Bullock, one of the marines who guarded him at Potsdam, later recalled that 'his health seemed remarkably good for his age. He was buoyant' and 'walked with a cheeky swing'. The only time Bullock saw Churchill depressed at Potsdam was on 23 July, after discussions which firmly established Soviet control over Poland. 'Even in my lowly rank, I had picked up the word: Polish freedom was being extinguished, and Mr Churchill was devastated and angry. Over Poland, he had only lukewarm support from Truman and he felt humiliated by Stalin.'[9] Yet there was nothing Churchill could have done. The fate of Poland had been decided long before Potsdam. It was fixed by the reality of Soviet might and the understandable refusal of the West to plunge immediately into another European conflict against its recent ally.

During the opening week, Truman revealed to Churchill that the first tests by the Americans on their atomic bomb, conducted in New Mexico on 16 July, had been a success. The USA now had a weapon of awesome destructive power. Under the terms of the Quebec Agreement of 1943, which stipulated Anglo-American co-operation on nuclear weaponry, Churchill had earlier given his formal approval to the potential use of the atomic bomb and according to Henry Stimson, the US War Secretary, he was 'intensely interested and cheered up' at the news.[10] For all Churchill's enthusiasm at the American breakthrough, the atomic issue was to cast a long shadow over his relationship with Attlee for another decade.

At Potsdam, there was a further shadow looming for the British delegation, for on 25 July the two party leaders had to return to Britain for the General Election result, now that the services vote had arrived. The night before he left, Churchill had a troubled dream about his own death, in which he could see his corpse laid out beneath a sheet in an empty room.[11] Yet, just as in England three weeks earlier, there was an expectation at Potsdam that Churchill would triumph. In a private conversation, Stalin suggested to Churchill that he would have a majority of about eighty, while on another occasion, referring to the Labour Leader's diffidence, Stalin said that 'Mr Attlee does not look to me like a man who is hungry for power'.[12] According to the British diplomat Sir Robert Bruce Lockhart, Churchill's large personality counted for more with Stalin than Attlee's left-wing politics. 'Uncle Joe, who now knows Winston pretty well, would prefer the devil he knows to the devil he doesn't.'[13] The rest of the Soviet team shared Stalin's belief in Churchill's impending triumph at the ballot box. 'No one in our conference delegation had the slightest doubt he would be re-elected,' said the Russian Admiral of the Fleet Nikolay Kuznetsov.[14] Attlee largely concurred with that forecast, as George Leggett recalled: 'He himself considered that the Conservatives were likely to obtain a majority of about 70 seats.'[15] Yet there were signs at Potsdam that Churchill's triumph was by no means guaranteed, for the British soldiers on duty in Germany seemed much more supportive of Attlee. Leggett recorded that at a victory parade on Saturday 21 July, when the two leaders mounted half-caterpillar lorries to carry out respective tours of inspection in front of a large number of British soldiers, 'the troops accorded to Mr Attlee a bigger cheer than to Mr Churchill'.[16] The disparity was also witnessed by the Chief of the Air Staff, Sir Charles Portal, who said Attlee's vehicle 'got the cheers'. But Portal, like so many others, simply refused to believe the evidence of his own eyes. 'Winston is said to be getting anxious about the election and Attlee was all smiles yesterday, but how can anyone know? I give the Conservatives a 70 to 80 majority.'[17]

By the afternoon of 25 July, Attlee and Churchill were back in London after flying in separate planes from Berlin to RAF Northolt. At the airport, Churchill had been met by a chauffeur with an official limousine, Attlee by Violet in the family Hillman. That evening Churchill had an audience with the King, met Beaverbrook at Downing Street, and then dined with his family, his daughter Mary recalling that he was 'full of confidence'.[18] Having worked until 1.15 a.m., he went to bed 'in the belief that the British people would wish me to continue my work'.[19] The same assessment was made on the eve of the count by Labour strategists at Transport House, who expected a Conservative majority of around thirty. Violet Attlee, though, had an inkling that there might be a different outcome – yet demonstrated remarkable electoral integrity, if not marital sympathy, by saying nothing about it. 'My wife, who always acts as a counting agent at Elections, had already seen the opening of the boxes of the Service voters, and had a good idea of how the land lay, but kept it to herself,' Attlee wrote later.[20]

While Attlee remained at Stanmore that night, Churchill slumbered in Downing Street. Just before dawn, the Prime Minister's sleep was interrupted by a strange sensation, as he later recounted in his war memoirs. 'I woke suddenly with a sharp stab of almost physical pain. A hitherto subconscious conviction that we were beaten broke forth and dominated my mind.'[21] Despondent, he returned to his sleep until nine o'clock. He worked in bed for an hour and then took a bath at ten. Below, in the Downing Street Map Room, which had been turned into a Government news centre, the first results were starting to arrive from the counts in the constituencies. They told a story of almost universal Labour advances. Captain Richard Pim, the trusted naval officer who was in charge of the Map Room throughout the war, had the unpleasant task of giving the news to Churchill. In a later BBC interview, Pim recalled the Prime Minister's reaction.

I took the first ten or twelve majorities and went to Churchill. He was in his bath. As soon as he heard the figures, he knew there had been a landslide and that his Government would be defeated. What he felt then, one can only guess, but he stuck out his chin and said, "We have no right to feel hurt. This is democracy. This is what we have been fighting for."[22]

By eleven o'clock 150 counts had been completed, with 60 of them gains for Labour. Even in the face of this rout, Churchill remained outwardly imperturbable, as his secretary Elizabeth Layton, also on duty that morning, recounted: 'I remember other members of the family coming to see him during the day, tearful and extremely worried how he would be feeling. But because his whole life had taught him that you can never be sure of anything, he stayed very calm. He seemed the strongest in that little group.'[23]

Two members of the family, Clementine and her daughter Mary, had gone in the morning to the count at Woodford, Essex, where the result confirmed the national trend against Churchill. In 1935, his majority had been over 20,000 but now, even though there was no Labour or Liberal candidate against him, his lead dropped to 17,000. Remarkably, the eccentric farmer Alexander Hancock polled over 10,000 votes. 'We must hurry back. Something is very much amiss,' said Clementine to Mary after the declaration.[24] On their return to Downing Street, Jock Colville reported that the picture was darkening all the time. 'It is a debacle,' he told them.[25] At one-thirty, the family sat down to lunch in 'Stygian gloom', to use Mary's phrase. Churchill kept up his studied impassivity, she recalled. 'Not for one moment in this awful day did Papa flinch or waver. "It is the will of the people," he said, robust, controlled.'[26] But he could not be cheered. When Clementine tried to lighten his spirits by saying that Labour's landslide might be 'a blessing in disguise', he replied, 'It seems quite effectively disguised.'[27]

In another part of London, Attlee was beginning to grasp the enormity of what had happened. With two of their daughters, he and Violet drove to the East End for the Limehouse count at Stepney Town Hall. In contrast to the experience of Churchill's family at Woodford, there was to be no disappointment for the Attlees at Stepney. On a huge swing of 17.3 per cent to Labour, he won over four-fifths of all votes in the Limehouse constituency, crushing his Tory opponent, Lieutenant Alfred Woodward, who only just held his deposit. After a brief acceptance speech, the Attlees travelled to Labour's headquarters at Transport House. 'There seemed to be much excitement outside and crowds of photographers. We were greeted with great enthusiasm and found that there was every indication of a landslide in our favour,' he recorded.[28]

Churchill had initially contemplated remaining in office, as was his constitutional right, until beaten by a vote in the new House of Commons. But the sheer scale of the defeat changed his mind that afternoon. Waiting for his eviction at the hands of Parliament risked humiliation. 'The verdict of the electors had been so overwhelmingly expressed that I did not wish to remain even for an hour responsible for their affairs,' he wrote.[29] At four o' clock, he therefore saw Tommy Lascelles to discuss the arrangements for the handover to Attlee. 'He did not look depressed, nor did he talk so,' recorded Lascelles.[30] Having decided that he would advise George VI to send at once for the Labour Leader, Churchill then wrote directly to Attlee: 'I propose to tender my resignation to the King at seven o'clock this evening on personal grounds. I wish you all success in the heavy burden you are about to assume.'[31]

Some in the Labour Party did not want Attlee to assume the burden, even in the hour of his triumph. He may have presided over by far Labour's greatest electoral victory, yet there were key figures in the movement who had never been reconciled to his leadership. They saw the landslide, not as the moment to accept his stewardship, but as an opportunity to ditch him. Foremost among his antagonists was his long-standing rival Herbert Morrison, whose eagerness to oust Attlee was backed by his devoted mistress Ellen Wilkinson. Others keen for a change at the top included Stafford Cripps, Nye Bevan and the Lambeth MP George Strauss, who wrote that 'many Labour MPs were unhappy' because Attlee 'appeared to lack completely the required charisma'.[32] The plotting went far beyond mere grumbles. Two days before the General Election results were declared, Morrison had sent Attlee a personal letter which urged that, when the Commons returned, the PLP should hold a leadership contest, thereby giving the new MPs a choice in their chief. 'If I am elected to the new Parliament, I should accept nomination for the leadership of the party,' he warned.[33]

At a meeting of the senior Labour politicians at Transport House on the afternoon of 26 July, Morrison pressed for the decision on the Leader to be placed in the hands of the PLP. But Ernie Bevin, who had long regarded Morrison as 'a scheming little bastard', was infuriated by this argument; 'we don't want any more personal leaderships like MacDonald's and Churchill's', he maintained.[34] When Morrison briefly left the meeting to take a phone call from Stafford Cripps, who had rung to pledge his support, Bevin urged Attlee to make his way to the Palace without further internal debate. In his own modest but resolute way, Attlee had already decided on just such a course. 'If the King invites you to form a Government, you don't say you can't give an answer for 48 hours,' he later argued.[35]

At seven o'clock, as arranged with the Palace, Churchill arrived for his audience with the King, who expressed his sympathy for the outgoing Prime Minister. George VI's own account ran: 'I told him I thought the people were very ungrateful after the way they had been led in the War. He was very calm and said that with the majority the Socialists had got over other parties and with careful management they could remain in power for years. He would be Leader of the Opposition.'[36] As a consolation, the King offered him the Garter, but Churchill declined. He later explained that the honour would hardly have been appropriate, given the electorate had just awarded him the 'Order of the Boot'.[37] Churchill left the Palace at 7.25, departing in his chauffeur-driven Humber, just as Violet drove into the royal courtyard in the Attlees' Hillman. She waited in the car as Attlee was ushered in to see the King. Tommy Lascelles felt he detected some hesitation in Attlee's demeanour. 'He was obviously in a state of some bewilderment – the poor little man had only a couple of hours before he was called upon immediately to fill Winston's place [...] Anyway, he kissed hands all right, so he is now committed to forming a Government – or trying to.'[38] Lascelles was also struck by Attlee's reticence throughout his trip to the Palace. 'I gather they call him Clem,' said the King after the audience. 'Clam would be more appropriate,' replied the private secretary.[39]

A Labour victory rally had been called that evening in the Methodist Central Hall, and Morrison, suffused with ever more desperate ambition, felt that this would be the ideal venue to lobby for Attlee's overthrow. Mingling with the jubilant crowd, he spoke to trade unionists and MPs, among them John Parker, just elected for Dagenham,* who recalled: 'He pushed me into the gents to talk to me privately. He said, "We cannot have that man as Prime Minister. The new Parliamentary Labour Party must have a chance to choose a new Leader." I said I sympathised with him but no-one would want to discard a leader who had led the Party to such a remarkable success.'[40] Morrison's efforts were to no avail. After his audience with the King, Attlee turned up at the Central Hall where, to wild cheering, he reported that he had just accepted the commission to form a Labour Government.

To Morrison's sorrow, Attlee's acceptance of the King's commission was approved at a meeting of the PLP the following morning, Friday 27 July. 'The Labour Party is fortunate in its Leader, and he merits our fullest confidence,' said Bevin in moving the resolution of support.[41] Referring to Attlee's 'fidelity to principle and unimpeachable integrity', Bevin also declared that 'the contrast between the two leaders during the election had enabled the country to realise who was Nature's Gentleman'.[42] When Attlee stood to thank the meeting, he was greeted by a three-minute ovation.

Morally and politically, the Parliamentary Party's decision was correct. Attlee had earned the right to the premiership through his conduct of the campaign and his adroit handling of Labour throughout the years of the wartime Coalition. Not only had his successful duel with Churchill been a key factor in the election victory but also his clear vision of post-war reconstruction had captured the mood of the country. Given that Labour had never won an overall majority before, Attlee's

---

* He was to hold the seat until 1983, becoming the Father of the House.

achievement was prodigious. Once all counts were completed, Labour had won 393 seats, compared to just 197 for Churchill's Conservatives and only 12 for the Liberals. In one very immediate respect, Churchill helped to make Attlee Prime Minister. By resigning at once and advising the King to send for Attlee, he ensured a swift change of office, with Morrison and his circle denied the chance to build any momentum behind their plot. But more importantly, there were two other, longer term ways in which Churchill paved Attlee's path to Downing Street. The first was his continual enhancement of Attlee's political credibility by giving him ever greater responsibilities during the Coalition, particularly after the row with Beaverbrook in February 1942. The second was Churchill's decision to pursue a policy of total war against Germany, which required most of the social and economic life of Britain to be brought under state control. As a result, Attlee's radicalism was seen by 1945 as mainstream, even patriotic. As the historian and former Labour MP David Marquand put it: 'war socialism transformed the public culture. Pre-war heresies came in from the cold; proposals that would have been ruled out of court in the age of Stanley Baldwin and Neville Chamberlain were absorbed into the conventional wisdom.'[43]

The new Prime Minister had no time to savour his landslide. Indeed, as soon as the scale of the victory became clear, Attlee had started to decide the composition of his Government. Morrison had agreed, with some reluctance, to become a kind of domestic supremo as Lord President and Leader of the Commons. In addition, Attlee had initially decided that two of the other most vital other jobs, the Treasury and the Foreign Office, should be filled by Bevin and Dalton respectively. But the King had had baulked at the idea of Dalton as Foreign Secretary, seeing him as untrustworthy and partisan. Similarly, the Foreign Office exerted pressure against Dalton, the outgoing Foreign Secretary Anthony Eden declaring that 'it should be Bevin'.[44]

The entreaties had their effect. Attlee changed his mind on 27 July, helped by Morrison's leadership manoeuvres. These so infuriated Bevin that Attlee grew convinced that the two men could not work together on domestic policy. But there has been a suggestion it was not just the

King, the Foreign Office and domestic concerns that changed Attlee's mind. According to one claim, Churchill himself had a crucial influence that day. Looking back some months later at this momentous time, Dalton wrote in his diary: 'It is thought by some that it was Churchill who intervened on the famous Friday following our election victory with Attlee in the luncheon interval to persuade him to change round Bevin and me.'[45] Years afterwards, the rumour was aired in public for the first time, through an article in the left-wing weekly newspaper *Tribune* by the Labour MP Sydney Silverman in November 1952. Referring to how Attlee 'changed his mind' on Friday, Silverman wrote, 'he lunched that day with Churchill, who inspired the change'.[46] The assertion drew a contemptuous response from Attlee in the next edition of the paper. He admitted that he had 'reconsidered' his first view about the Foreign Secretary appointment, but he categorically denied the tale about lunch with Churchill. 'There is no truth whatever in it. I am surprised that Silverman did not take the trouble to ascertain the facts before giving publicity to such a baseless statement,' he wrote.[47]

In fact, Attlee lunched with just Violet on Friday, while Churchill remained in Downing Street, going through the painful task of holding his final Cabinet, then saying his farewells, before heading down to Chequers in the evening. In his diary, Anthony Eden described the Cabinet meeting as 'a pretty grim affair', reflecting Churchill's own deepening gloom. 'He was pretty wretched, poor old boy. Said he didn't feel any more reconciled this morning; on the contrary, it hurt more, like a wound that becomes more painful after the first shock. He couldn't help feeling his treatment had been scurvy.'[48] Later, Churchill also saw Brooke, the Chief of the Imperial Staff, for an equally painful but dignified interview. 'It was a very sad and very moving little meeting at which I found myself unable to say much for fear of breaking down. He was standing the blow wonderfully well.'[49] Churchill's attempt to maintain his equanimity highlighted the absence of any personal bitterness towards Attlee. His dejection was focused on the loss of office, not on his political opponent. The future Tory minister Reginald Maudling, who worked as a party researcher in the 1940s, once said that

Churchill had 'a great and sincere respect for Attlee';[50] and that attitude certainly shone through his advice to staff on his departure in July. To his aide Paul Beards he said that 'Mr Attlee is a very nice man and you will be well to work with him'.[51] His private secretary Leslie Rowan was reduced to tears with Churchill's words, 'You must not think of me any more; your duty is to serve Attlee, if he wishes you to do so. You must therefore go to him, for you must think also of your future.'[52] The same generosity of spirit was exhibited as Churchill stayed in Chequers over the weekend. At dinner on Sunday evening, over large quantities of champagne, Churchill told his guests that 'the new Government would have the most difficult task of any government in modern times and that it was the duty of everybody to support them in matters of the national interest'.[53]

The grave questions of the British national interests arose that weekend as Attlee and Bevin flew back on Saturday 28 July to Berlin for the final round of the Potsdam Conference. Most of those at the summit had been astonished at the election result, having believed there would be an easy win for the Conservatives. The Soviet Union, in particular, was bewildered, both by the demonstration of raw democracy in action, so different to communist totalitarianism, and by the end of the unique relationship between Churchill and Stalin, which had been so vital to the Allied war effort. In a letter of commiseration on the result, the British Ambassador to Moscow Sir Archie Clark Kerr told Clementine, 'This evening I found myself with a bunch of gibbering and bewildered Russians. Molotov, grey in the face and clearly much upset, kept throwing up his fat hands and asking, "Why? Why?" Of course to the Russians it is inexplicable that a people should be allowed to put out of office a man who has led them through the darkest days in their history to a thumping victory.'[54] Soon after his arrival at Potsdam, Attlee was questioned by Stalin about the reason for Churchill's defeat. 'One should distinguish between Mr Churchill the Leader of the nation in war and Mr Churchill the Conservative Party Leader. Many people looked upon the Conservatives as a reactionary party which would not carry out a policy answering to peace requirements,' he replied.[55]

Attlee had made only a limited contribution to the conference proceedings before the announcement of the election result. But now, freed from the shadow of Churchill and equipped with the authority of the premiership, he became a more decisive figure, ably assisted by Bevin. With their ingrained hostility towards communism, the two men were robust in challenging the Soviet Union, especially over the independence of Greece and the maintenance of the German economy in face of heavy reparations, though they could do nothing about Russia's stranglehold on Eastern Europe, as epitomised by its insistence on the Western Neisse as the Polish border. But in general, Attlee was pleased with his first excursion as Prime Minister. In a letter to Churchill at the end of the conference, he reported that Stalin had been 'in good form' and Truman 'co-operative', while the 'results achieved are not unsatisfactory having regard to the way the course of the war dealt the cards'.[56] Churchill reciprocated this friendly spirit on 3 August. 'I am sorry about the Western Neisse and I fear the Russians have laid an undue toll even on Germany which is not in their zone. This was certainly not the fault of the British delegation [...] I shall look forward to talking things over with you when the House opens. We have an immense amount of work to do in common, in which we are both agreed and pledged.'[57]

Others felt that Attlee and Bevin showed a surprisingly assured touch during the negotiations. 'They are very businesslike and imperturbable, these new people and give confidence all around them,' wrote the diplomat Pierson Dixon.[58] President Truman, however, did not share this admiration and in a letter to his daughter, described Attlee and Bevin as 'sourpusses', compared to the 'likeable' Churchill.[59] What Cadogan, head of the Foreign Office, observed was the dominance of Bevin: 'He effaces Attlee, and at Big Three meetings he does all the talking, while Attlee nods his head convulsively and smokes his pipe.'[60]

The new Prime Minister and Foreign Secretary were back in London when Parliament briefly re-assembled on 1 August for the election of the Speaker and the swearing-in of MPs. Despite his heavy election defeat, Churchill was greeted by the chant of 'For He's a Jolly Fellow' from some on Conservative benches as he entered the Chamber. Joining in the acclamation was Ellen Wilkinson, the new Education Minister, and the sole Labour MP to give him a cheer. 'It is no use asking me about Winston. I am prejudiced in his favour,' she once said.[61] In contrast to Wilkinson's solitary cheer, most Labour MPs decided on a very different response, as Geoffrey de Freitas, Attlee's new parliamentary private secretary, noted in his diary, 'The Tories struck up an obviously rehearsed "For He's a Jolly Good Fellow". Poor Winston looked old and tired. Spontaneously and somewhat embarrassedly, Labour members joined in singing "the Red Flag". It was a demonstration that we believe in people as an organised body and not in individuals.'[62]

A few days after this scene in the Commons, the Americans brought the war to a dramatic and devastating climax by dropping atomic bombs on the Japanese cities of Hiroshima and Nagasaki. Attlee had been informed at Potsdam that the tests on his new weapon had been a success, but, in spite of the Quebec Agreement, he had no direct say or veto over its use. 'I was told by Harry Truman that they had this Bomb and he had already arranged with Churchill what was to be done and that it was their campaign, not ours,' he later recalled.[63] On 7 August, the day after the apocalyptic attack on Hiroshima, Attlee broadcast to the nation about the tremendous implications of the new weapon, though his transcript had actually been drafted by Churchill a fortnight earlier. Somewhat incongruously, the usually prosaic Labour Leader became the mouthpiece for Churchillian grandiloquence. 'The revelation of the secret's nature so long mercifully withheld from man should arouse the most solemn reflections in the mind and conscience of every human being,' ran one passage.[64]

Shortly before Emperor Hirohito formally capitulated on 15 August, Attlee sent a generous, handwritten letter to Churchill: 'I feel that the probability of the surrender of our last enemy is so great that I must at once, offer to you, our leader from the darkest hours through so many anxious days, my congratulations on this crowning result of your work.'[65] It was Attlee, however, who had the happy task of broadcasting to the nation the news of victory in the East. Churchill listened to the broadcast from his suite at Claridge's, where he had briefly taken up residence after his ejection from Downing Street. Among the Tory colleagues with him was Anthony Eden, who noted of the poignant moment, 'We adjourned to another large room where the wireless was turned on in a corner and we sat and listened in a circle. After a while, Mr Attlee barked out a few sentences, then gave the terms. The Japanese had surrendered. The war was over. There was silence. Mr Churchill had not been asked to say a word to the nation.'[66] His devoted friend Violet Bonham Carter instinctively empathised with him but felt him partly to blame for his predicament. 'Poor Winston! This should have been his triumph too and he handed it to Attlee. We could have finished the job altogether and had an autumn election if only Beaverbrook had not driven him on to the mad course he pursued. How bitter for him.'[67]

Churchill's sense of marginalisation was further illustrated in the wake of Japan's surrender, in response to an invitation from Attlee to attend a small reception with George VI after the broadcast, along with several members of his new Government. But Churchill refused the invitation as it stood, telling Attlee, 'Personally I should very much like to do so. I feel however that it might be misunderstood if I seemed to dissociate myself from my Conservative colleagues in the Coalition War Cabinet, namely Mr Eden, Sir John Anderson and Mr Lyttelton, and might be interpreted as a slur on them. Therefore I would venture to suggest that they should come too.'[68] Attlee replied in somewhat affronted terms:

> I am sorry that you feel the suggestion I made might be misunderstood and interpreted as a slur on your Conservative colleagues and the Coalition War Cabinet. I fear on the other hand if you were accompanied by them it might be misunderstood for other reasons. For example, it might suggest the idea of Coalition Government. I had hoped that you might feel that this was an unorthodox and personal tribute to yourself as the main architect of victory, quite apart from any political considerations.

Attlee concluded that if Churchill would not attend unless accompanied by his Tory colleagues, 'I am assured that the King will receive
you personally later in the day.'[69] As a result, Churchill went to the
Palace on his own, half an hour after Attlee's party had gone.

When Parliament reassembled for the beginning of the new session,
Attlee paid another, more public, tribute to Churchill: 'In the darkest
and most dangerous hour in her history, this nation found in my Right
Honourable Friend the man who expressed supremely the courage and
determination never to yield, which animated all the men and women
of this country.'[70] The political generosity that Attlee had shown in his
speech extended to his personal treatment of Churchill. Courteousness
and solicitude were the hallmarks of his private behaviour towards
his deposed rival. Immediately after the declaration of the results, he
offered the Churchills a decent interval to arrange their departure
from Downing Street, but Clementine wanted out 'quicker than
lightning', according to her daughter Sarah, because she now found
the place 'hateful'.[71] Nevertheless, according to Attlee's daughter
Janet, 'Clementine Churchill was very nice, very helpful, explained
everything to mother and helped her make the move.'[72] Having left
Number 10, the Churchills decamped, first to Claridge's and then to
the flat at Victoria owned by their daughter Diana and her husband
Duncan Sandys; though they also began to open up Chartwell again,
the house having been closed for the duration of the war. To clear up
his political affairs, Churchill asked that for a few days after his resignation 'he should have at his disposal the normal facilities as they exist
now'. Attlee told his aide Leslie Rowan that he 'entirely agreed', which
meant that Churchill was provided with a Government car and was
'able to use the Government machine for such telegrams as normally
pass through it'.[73] In addition, Attlee allowed the loyal Jock Colville to
be spared from some of his Downing Street duties to work part-time
for Churchill, an arrangement that had its amusing side when dealing
with some correspondence. 'It became my duty to go to Claridge's,
where Churchill had temporarily established his headquarters, and
help him draft a Joshua-like blast of the trumpet to Attlee. I delivered it

to Attlee and helped draft the withering reply.'[74] Attlee was also happy to allow Churchill to use official help for his regular travel abroad, as the Downing Street aide Leslie Rowan told Churchill's secretary Kathleen Hill in early August, 'The Prime Minister authorises me to say that, during the continuance of restrictions on air transport, the Government will be ready to allow Mr Churchill to use government aircraft for these purposes.'[75] Churchill had urgent reason to utilise this offer, because in September he planned to make a lengthy visit to Italy, where he hoped that the activity of painting in the sunshine by Lake Como might heal some of his wounds. Clementine, whose nerves were frayed by his post-election private despair, felt that he urgently needed a break, as she told her daughter Mary on 26 August: 'In our misery we seem, instead of clinging to each other, to be always having scenes. I'm sure it is all my fault, but I'm finding life more difficult than I can bear. He is so unhappy and that makes him very difficult.'[76]

As Attlee took the helm, all of the prime-ministerial staff noticed a great contrast in approach by the new chief. Much of the glamour, dynamism and excitement were now missing, but there were compensations in more normal hours and swifter decisions. Attlee once said that 'a sense of urgency, of dispatch,' was a central quality needed in a Prime Minister, and he lived up to that precept.[77] The change from Churchill's more colourful, discursive approach was noticed immediately by Downing Street secretary Marian Holmes, who wrote in her diary for 1 August: 'Working for the new PM is very different [...] No conversation or pleasantries, wit or capricious behaviour. Just staccato orders. Perfectly polite and I'm sure he is a good Christian gentleman. But it is the difference between champagne and water.'[78] Alternatively, Brooke experienced some relief at the arrival of a less frenetic regime, noting on 28 August that 'Attlee was infinitely easier to work with than Winston'. He further wrote that 'there was not the same touch of genius as with Winston, but there were more businesslike methods. We kept to the agenda, and he maintained order with a somewhat difficult crowd.'[79] It was the greater social conventionality of the Labour Leader and his wife that surprised

Colville when he was with them for a long weekend at Chequers in mid-August.

> I was greatly attracted by his simple charm and lack of osten-
> tation or ambition. The contrast with my previous weekends at
> Chequers was, however, notable. Mrs Churchill's superb cook
> had vanished and her ATS replacement, though she did her best,
> was not in the same class. The new Labour Prime Minister was
> more formal in his dress and behaviour than his Conservative
> predecessor. At dinner, a starched shirt and stiff butterfly collar
> were the order of the day.[80]

The change was too dramatic for a few. Private secretary John Peck at first found Attlee refreshing, as he explained to interpreter George Leggett during the Potsdam Conference: 'It was bewildering, after several years of continuous re-adjustment to Mr Churchill's habits, to have to work regular hours, to reserve the night for sleep, to send papers to the new Prime Minister and have them returned promptly, signed and settled. A lot of the work for Mr Churchill had been done in odd corners, at odd unearthly hours, sitting maybe on the lavatory seat while he dictated from the bath.'[81] Yet Peck could not adjust to the new regime, for all its more orderly nature. He later wrote that he left Downing Street because he 'never settled down with Attlee. The contrast with Churchill was too great.' Peck admitted that those who had long worked with Attlee 'spoke with affection about him. But to me he was grey and drab and utterly self-effacing.'[82]

Despite their differences, Attlee and Churchill did not clash much over politics in the months after the General Election. Their exchanges were largely administrative and often cordial. One highly sensitive matter related to Churchill's controversial friend the Duke of Windsor. Immediately after the end of the European war, a group of Allied historians, based in Marburg, had been commissioned to examine the surviving Nazi archives. There they found a number of incendiary documents about the Reich's conspiratorial designs on the Duke, including Operation Willi, the plot to kidnap him in the summer of 1940 while he was in Lisbon, with the aim of making him king in the event of a successful invasion of Britain.[83] Eager to suppress this material, as Bevin advised, Attlee sent Churchill a copy of the Windsor file on 25 August. 'Although clearly little or no credence can be placed in the statements, I feel sure that you will agree that publication of these documents might do the greatest possible harm,' he wrote.[84] Churchill concurred. 'I am in entire agreement with the course proposed by the Foreign Secretary and approved by you. I earnestly trust it will be possible to destroy all traces of these German intrigues.[85] The documents were not destroyed, largely because it would have been pointless to do so given that they had been microfilmed by the Americans, but they were kept from the public for the rest of Attlee and Churchill's lifetimes. With a less censorial attitude, they agreed at the end of August that the journals of the House of Commons during the war should now be published, since concerns about security no longer prevailed. There were also some lighter touches. Attlee asked Churchill for a signed photograph for the gallery of Prime Ministers at Downing Street. 'It ought to be a really good one; and I hope you make the selection yourself,' wrote Attlee.[86] When Churchill complied with the request, Attlee thanked him for 'the admirable portrait'.[87]

Before the end of August, there was a far more difficult issue for which Attlee asked Churchill's assistance, arising from the dire state of Britain's public finances because of war debts. Indeed, the great economist and Treasury adviser John Maynard Keynes said that the country was facing a 'financial Dunkirk'.[88] The situation was made all the worse by the decision of the Americans to close the Lend-Lease aid programme once the war against Japan ended. The Labour Government was therefore forced to consider requesting a new loan from the USA to stave off national bankruptcy, with the result that Keynes was sent to Washington on an urgent mission to begin negotiations with the American Treasury. But Attlee knew that the task would be highly controversial. Some Conservatives would object on the grounds that new borrowing was required to pay for Labour's extravagant social programme, others because they saw in the financial crisis the chance to move away from multilateralist economics towards a more protectionist, Empire-based policy. Churchill, however, still retained much of his old Liberal attachment to free trade, so he was co-operative when Attlee wrote to him and Anthony Eden on 23 August, expressing the hope that the Tories would not try to make political capital at the forthcoming announcement in the Commons of the plan to negotiate a new loan. 'There is the possibility of a ragged discussion in which things might be said by inexperienced Members which would defeat our purpose of creating a good atmosphere. I propose therefore to suggest to the House the inadvisability of any debate and it would be very helpful if you or Anthony could support me by stating your agreement.'[89] Churchill went along with this, confining himself in the Commons to criticism, not of the Labour Government, but of the Americans.

But Churchill's supportive attitude towards Attlee was to cause him serious trouble with his own party. Even as early as August, there were whispers against him, based on his alleged incapacity to lead the Opposition. Observing an appearance by Churchill at the backbench 1922 Committee on 21 August, Chips Channon wrote that 'he seemed totally unprepared, indifferent and deaf and failed to stir a crowded audience'.[90] There were also signs that Churchill found it difficult to adjust to his new, diminished situation. The new Dominions Under-Secretary John Parker recalled, perhaps with a degree of exaggeration: 'At the first reception Attlee gave to junior ministers and their wives at 10 Downing Street, after the election, he also invited the Churchills as a courtesy to their wartime collaboration. Churchill and his wife acted as though they were the hosts, both receiving guests and saying farewell. Mrs Attlee was most embarrassed and did not know where to look.'[91]

Churchill's post-election debility and dejection made it all the more urgent that he should take his Italian holiday. He left on 2 September from London in a Government-owned Douglas C-54 Skymaster, which Attlee had put at his disposal. His trip lasted five weeks, first at a villa by Lake Como used by Field Marshal Alexander as his divisional headquarters, then at various hotels on the French Riviera. Immediately, his immersion in art and break from British politics began to revive him, as he told Clementine: 'I am much better in myself, and am not worried about anything. We have had no newspapers since I left England and I no longer feel any keen desire to turn their pages.'[92]

But politics was not entirely absent. For all his claims to be happy ignoring Westminster, his thoughts occasionally strayed in that direction. One evening by Lake Como, when he was dining with his doctor Lord Moran, he became vexed by his recollection of the behaviour after the election of his long-standing ally Smuts, the South African statesman. 'I was offended by the telegram he sent Attlee about his "brilliant" victory. Brilliant indeed,' said Churchill. Moran's account continued, revealing how badly the result still rankled, 'His voice rose. "If he had just congratulated him on his victory it would have been different. Why brilliant?" The word stuck in his gorge. "It wasn't brilliant at all."'[93] Attlee intruded directly on Churchill's holiday over the question of the Labour Government's nuclear energy policy. Soon after the bombing of Hiroshima and Nagasaki, Attlee had set up two committees to deal with nuclear matters: one, called GEN 75, was made up entirely of Cabinet members; the other, entitled the Advisory Committee on Atomic Energy, was chaired by Sir John Anderson and included a number of scientists, among them the physicist and radical pro-Soviet socialist Patrick Blackett. When Attlee set out the Advisory Committee's composition, Churchill was disturbed by Blackett's inclusion, so much so that he even asked MI5 if there was any evidence of the scientist's subversion. He was 'entirely harmless', came the reply. Nevertheless, from the shores of Lake Como, Churchill wrote to Attlee to express his concern, 'not so much as to what Blackett will do as to what the Americans will do. I apprehend they will be increasingly shy of imparting further developments,' a reference to his cherished 1943 Quebec Agreement on Anglo-US nuclear co-operation.[94] Attlee stood firm on Blackett.

In the context of the Quebec Agreement, Attlee sought Churchill's advice on his desire to resume his dialogue with President Truman over the international oversight of the atomic bomb. Since his earliest involvement in politics, Attlee had believed in some kind of global governance to uphold peace. Now the nuclear issue gave him a further chance to pursue this dream. He therefore drafted a lengthy letter to President Truman, urging that they hold discussions about how this apocalyptic technology could be controlled through the structure of the United Nations. 'We must bend our utmost energies to secure that better ordering of man's affairs which so great a revolution at once renders necessary,' he wrote in his draft.[95] On 15 September, Attlee sent this document to Churchill with a covering note: 'I have been recently considering what we should now do about the future of the atomic bomb and its reactions on international relations and policy. It seems to me the first step would be to open the matter with the President of the United States, to give him our tentative views and to ascertain which way his mind is moving. This might be followed later by a personal discussion.'[96] Churchill did not like the draft at all, finding Attlee's internationalism both vague and a potential threat to the Quebec Agreement. 'The message does not seem to make clear what in fact you want the Americans to do,' he wrote, asking, 'Do you want them to tell the Russians? If so, I do not believe they will agree, and I personally should deem them right not to.' The Anglo-American understanding was the best hope of peace, he argued. 'I should greatly regret if we seemed not to value this and pressed them to melt our dual agreement into general international arrangement consisting, I fear, of pious empty phrases and undertakings which will not be carried out.'[97] Despite Churchill's advice, Attlee made only a couple of minor amendments to his letter before sending it to Truman on 25 September. The Americans were no keener on his ill-defined plan than Churchill was, though the White House tentatively agreed to a bilateral meeting in November.

In the meantime, Churchill came back from the Riviera in early October. 'I had a very pleasant holiday and painted a lot of daubs. I have returned to this country much refreshed,' he told Attlee.[98] Churchill's mood was further revived by greater financial and domestic stability.

While he was abroad, the Government confirmed that he would be paid his annual salary of £2,000 as Leader of the Opposition from the day of his resignation as Prime Minister, though this was a small sum compared to the vast earnings he could now make as a writer, his marketability having increased dramatically through his role as the victorious statesman. The growing security enabled him to buy an attractive London townhouse at 28 Hyde Park Gate for £24,696, which, after refurbishment, was ready for habitation in October. Churchill was also freed from the financial millstone of Chartwell, his beloved country home in Kent, which was purchased in November 1945 for the National Trust by a group of admirers headed by the newspaper proprietor Lord Camrose. In return for a rent of £350 per year, as well as the responsibility for the upkeep, Winston and Clementine were allowed to remain in Chartwell until their deaths, when the house would revert to the Trust. Coincidentally, Clement and Violet Attlee were also feeling less financially constrained after years of austerity, now that he enjoyed the prime-ministerial annual salary of £10,000, plus elegant accommodation in 10 Downing Street and Chequers. 'It is the first time in my life with Clem that I have ever known financial security,' Violet told Francis Williams, when he had become Attlee's press adviser.[99]

Despite his growing literary income and his wife's wishes, Churchill still had no plans for retirement from politics. He continued to see himself as an active statesman, able to offer leadership to the nation. Writing to the Duke of Windsor he emphasised his selflessness in continuing to lead the Opposition. 'It is only from a sense of duty and of not leaving my friends when they are in the lurch that I continue to persevere.'[100] But this was hardly the truth. Nursing his bruised ego, Churchill remained in office so he would have the chance to avenge the General Election humiliation of 1945. In the words of the civil servant Norman Brook, he wanted 'to erase this blot from his escutcheon'.[101] He could not contemplate departure from the political stage until he had regained the applause of the crowd, and the only way he could do that was by defeating Attlee in another contest. In this way, his leadership of the Opposition became a quest for political redemption.

Both Attlee and Churchill were looking vulnerable towards the end of the year. The Labour Government was beset with financial problems, as epitomised by the need for the American loan. The Prime Minister had flown to Washington on 9 November, partly to bolster US political support for a deal, and partly to hold his discussions with Truman about the future of nuclear weaponry. But on both fronts he achieved little. On the loan, the Americans were driving a hard bargain, particularly on the convertibility of sterling and the removal of trade controls on US imports. On the atom bomb, American sentiment was moving away from sharing information with Britain as outlined in the Quebec Agreement. To give some comfort to Attlee and provide the illusion of co-operation, the White House agreed in a joint communiqué to support the idea of establishing a United Nations Commission on Atomic Energy. But this measure had no real teeth. In practice, any further undertakings in line with Quebec would require the approval of Congress, a difficult obstacle to surmount in America's new mood of international supremacy. Attlee was further hindered on his US trip by unfavourable comparisons with Churchill, who had caused such a sensation when he had first addressed Congress in 1941. Speaking to the same assembly in November, Attlee received just three bursts of applause, and the most prolonged was a tribute to Churchill. Nor did he impress in a speech to the Canadian Parliament in Ottawa. Sir Ian Jacob, who had remained on the Downing Street staff and had accompanied Attlee on his North American visit, felt that 'the chamber was rather big for him. He has neither a commanding figure nor a resounding voice.' Jacob was also critical of Attlee's handling of the atomic issue with the Americans: 'I can't help feeling that if Winston had been doing the job, he would have arrived in Washington with a cut-and-dried idea and then he would have laid careful siege to the President so as to get his idea accepted and would have drafted the declaration in his incomparable language.'[102]

But the Conservative Leader was facing his own trouble. There was continued disgruntlement at his leadership, particularly after he missed a debate on Labour's nationalisation programme in November because of a visit to Paris and Belgium. Some backbenchers wanted him to show more vigour by challenging the Government through a vote of censure, instead of waiting patiently on events. Keen to reassert his authority and further weaken Attlee, Churchill agreed on 27 November to put down a confidence motion. It turned out to be a disastrous move, one that achieved the exact opposite of its intention.

TWENTY-FIVE

FULTON AND ZURICH

EXPECTATION MINGLED WITH tension at Westminster in the mid-afternoon of 6 December 1945, as MPs prepared to debate a Conservative motion of censure against the Labour Government. Many Tories anticipated that they were about to witness another of Churchill's parliamentary triumphs where his slashing rhetoric would inflict real damage on the Prime Minister. After long experience of watching Attlee in action, they believed that he would be no match for the Leader of the Opposition across the Dispatch Box.

At 3.20 Churchill rose to his feet, greeted by cheers from his own side. He opened with an expression of regret at how Labour had 'introduced acrimony into our proceedings', displaying a 'spirit of faction' and a determination 'to humiliate their defeated opponents'. With a sense of generosity, Churchill exempted Attlee from some of the blame for this growth in party antagonism. 'The Prime Minister has not sought in any way to embitter or inflame proceedings. Perhaps he will have to hurry up and toe the line this afternoon.' But Churchill was scathing about the Labour Government's 'confidence-killing, impulse sapping' policies and 'doctrinal trash'.[1]

As soon as Attlee began his reply, it became obvious that he was undaunted by Churchill's rhetorical assault. On the contrary, he was at his waspish best, using dry wit and cold reason to demolish his predecessor. It was absurd, he argued, for Churchill to adopt a tone of 'injured innocence' about partisanship, given his conduct during the election campaign. 'I have not forgotten the Right Honourable Gentleman's broadcast at the beginning of the Election, nor have the people of this country.' On a deeper level, he said the entire thrust of Churchill's complaint against the Government was illogical. 'The burden of the Right Honourable Gentleman's speech is this: why when you were elected to carry out a socialist programme, did you not carry out a Conservative programme?' To laughter from his MPs, Attlee said in his peroration that the mistake of Churchill in the election had been to present himself as the only alternative to the socialist programme. 'He had the spotlight. All those able and experienced frontbenchers, and those who have fallen by the wayside, were, after all, mere chorus girls. The prima donna held the stage [...] I am sure the Right Honourable Gentleman knows by now that it was not good tactics at the General Election, that this country does not like one-man shows.'[2]

There was no doubt that Attlee had emerged the winner of the duel. His was a resounding victory, made all the richer because it came as a surprise. James Callaghan, just elected for Cardiff South, recalled: 'Attlee was absolutely devastating. We really did roar our approval at him [...] This wasn't dutiful cheering. We really felt that Attlee had won the debate and that was something quite remarkable against Churchill's experience and his absolute control.'[3] Even the normally hostile *Daily Express* had to admit that Attlee had bettered the Opposition Leader and delighted his own Labour MPs in the process. 'He rallied them with a stream of jibes and jokes, mostly genial, some savage, against the same target, Churchill. Socialists rose and cheered for several minutes a speech which was regarded as the best fighting performance by Mr Attlee,' wrote the paper's political correspondent William Barkley.[4] Attlee himself felt the debate was a turning point in his career. In his papers at Cambridge is a note written in 1951 that briefly lists the most important achievements of his Labour leadership, one of which was: 'Speech in the House replying to Churchill which established my debating position vis a vis him.'[5]

Churchill's parliamentary fortunes took a further turn for the worse the following week, when the House debated the agreement on the US loan which Keynes and Lord Halifax, still the British Ambassador to Washington, had negotiated. The terms, settled at the beginning of December, were reasonable but not charitable. The Americans offered $3.75 billion at 2 per cent interest, to be repaid in fifty annual instalments from 1951. In return, Britain had to accept free trade and the end of imperial preference, as well as making sterling convertible for current transactions from July 1947, a stipulation which was likely to impose a huge strain on the country's reserves. As both an instinctive liberal free trader and, by heritage, an admirer of America, Churchill was inclined to support the agreement. But many in his party felt differently, some because they saw the deal as a result of socialist mismanagement; others because they preferred the alternative of imperial trade. After lengthy consultations in Westminster, the Conservatives reluctantly agreed to abstain on the agreement, a stance of 'impotence and futility', to use the words of Lord Halifax.[6]

Retreat never suited Churchill. When he wound up for the Opposition on 13 December, the second day of the debate, he made an unconvincing speech that tried to justify abstention on the feeble grounds of 'the indecent haste with which these most complex matters are thrust before us'.[7] According to the *Manchester Guardian*, Labour MPs greeted Churchill's performance 'with a mixture of incredulity and repressed anger, which occasionally broke out in loud indignant protests'.[8] In the subsequent division, the loan was approved by 345 votes to 98, with 71 Tories rebelling against the whip. Churchill's standing as Tory Leader had taken another heavy blow. 'Winston is very upset, talks of giving up, etc,' wrote Harry Crookshank in his diary, while Leo Amery recorded that the vote was 'a great shock to his leadership which now, in peace, is unnatural'.[9] The gloom enveloping Churchill at this moment was compounded by evidence of the overwhelming popularity of Attlee and Labour. One opinion poll conducted just after the censure vote showed that 59 per cent of the public were 'satisfied' with the Government. As Prime Minister, Attlee enjoyed an even higher approval rating at 67 per cent.

Churchill's spirits were lifted a little when he was awarded the Order of Merit in the New Year Honours List, a move welcomed by Attlee. As early as 5 October 1945, Tommy Lascelles had sounded out Attlee 'about Winston being given the OM for his literary achievements'[10] and the Prime Minister had 'cordially approved'. Attlee also proved co-operative on a much bigger question, one that was to transform Churchill's status as Opposition Leader, and reinforce his position as one of the world's most influential statesmen. The origins of this episode lay in a pair of enticing invitations he received in October 1945: the first from the wealthy Canadian industrialist Colonel Frank Clarke to stay at his house in Miami in January and February; the second from President Truman to make an address to Westminster College, Fulton, in his Midwest home state of Missouri. Churchill was attracted by the idea of spending almost three months on the other side of the Atlantic, but wanted the Labour Government's approval for the visit. Attlee therefore contacted Lord Halifax, who replied: 'I do not think an objection would arise to any part of the projected programme and if, as he doubtless would, Winston said the right sort of thing, I think it might have a very good effect, particularly if he went to the Middle West as suggested. As you know he is a very popular figure and Great Britain would draw a measure of reflected popularity.'[11]

Backed up by this advice from Halifax, Attlee and Bevin approved the visit. An additional factor for the Labour Government was the hope that Churchill might use his influence and contacts to buttress support for the American loan, the legislation for which was still to be passed by the Senate. With Labour's blessing, Churchill and his wife sailed from England on 9 January, reaching Miami on 15 January after disembarking in New York. For the next seven weeks, he enjoyed the tropical sunshine as he bathed in the sea and painted. But there was also some political work. As Attlee had hoped, Churchill lent heavyweight support to the political campaign for the American loan by lobbying press and politicians. 'If we're not given the opportunity to get back on our feet again, we may never be able to take our place among other nations,' he told journalists on his arrival in Miami.[12] The most important figure Churchill had to confront was his long-standing friend, the US financier and presidential adviser Bernard Baruch, who was an important voice behind the scenes in Washington. Like many Americans, Baruch was concerned that the loan might end up subsidising socialism, a worry that he expressed to Churchill when they met in Florida on 17 February 1946. After their conversation, Churchill sent a telegram to Attlee, explaining that Baruch felt that 'no case had been made out for so large an amount as four billion dollars'. Churchill admitted that he himself was 'not able to supply particulars of exactly what we wanted the loan for'; therefore he hoped that Attlee could 'let me have them in compendious form', so he could inform Baruch when they next met. But he assured Attlee that he had also warned Baruch 'that failure of the loan at this stage would bring about such distress and call for such privation in our island as to play into the hands of extremists of all kinds and lead to a campaign of extreme austerity'.[13] Attlee thanked Churchill and promised, having consulted Dalton, to send the information required. A detailed note from Dalton arrived three days later, explaining that the loan was needed partly for the purchase of the American goods and services, such as meat, steel, machinery and tobacco, and partly for the financing of Britain's colossal war debts. Churchill used this material to good effect. When he visited Washington on 10 March, he convinced an important group of senators, including the Speaker, to back the loan, mainly on the grounds that a trade war would result if it were rejected. Later, in New York, he managed to persuade Baruch not to denounce the loan in public, a step that helped to secure the agreement of Congress. With a sense of satisfaction, Churchill reported to Attlee on 19 March, 'I have had long talks with Mr Baruch and you can tell the Chancellor of the Exchequer that I do not think he will take any action against the loan. This does not mean his view has changed but he considers the Russian situation makes it essential that our countries stand together.'[14] Given the narrowness of the Senate's vote in favour of the loan, Churchill's patriotic intervention on behalf of the British Government was crucial. Indeed, Keynes wrote that American opposition was 'largely overcome by the firmness with which Mr Churchill at every opportunity, public and private, took the opposite line'.[15]

Churchill had held his final discussions on the loan after he had made his speech at Fulton on 5 March, travelling with Truman from Washington to Missouri by special train. The long journey left plenty of time for talks between Churchill and the President, as well as games of poker. It was during one of their onboard conversations that Churchill made perhaps his most famous remark about Attlee, as recorded by the White House aide Clark Clifford. Referring to the Prime Minister's recent visit to Washington to discuss the atom bomb, Truman said, 'Clement Attlee came to see me the other day. He struck me as a very modest man,' to which Churchill delivered his memorable reply: 'He has much to be modest about.'[16] In fact, Churchill's relations with Attlee at this moment were smoother than they had been for months, partly because the two leaders, along with Bevin, shared a similar view about the nature of the Soviet threat and the need for a strong strategic relationship with the USA. For all his belief in global governance and his past enthusiasm for disarmament during the early 1930s, Attlee had never been pro-Russian or pro-Communism, unlike some other figures on the left. The need to face the reality of Soviet power was to be a central theme of Churchill's forthcoming Fulton speech, as he told Attlee from Miami on 17 February. Planning to call for 'a special friendship' between Britain and America to provide 'mutual safety in case of danger', he reported that 'there is much fear of Russia here as a cause of future trouble'.[17] Attlee replied with typical succinctness, 'I am sure your Fulton speech will do good.'[18]

The excitement began to build even before the speech, a reflection of Churchill's global fame and the enduring fascination with his oratory. Churchill's typist Jo Sturdee, who accompanied him on the journey, wrote that in the small town of Fulton, there were 'crowds everywhere – all very well dressed, smiling, well-looking and very orderly'.[19] Delivered in front of 2,800 guests at Westminster College, the speech itself was a masterpiece of Churchillian eloquence, painting Anglo-American unity as the best assurance against Soviet totalitarianism. In its most famous passage, Churchill deployed the phrase he had used before in both the Commons and in correspondence with Truman: 'From Stettin in the Baltic, to Trieste in the Adriatic, an iron curtain has descended across the continent.'[20] The only defence against this oppression, he argued, was resolution in the west. With its uncompromising talk of division and confrontation, the Fulton speech caused a furore in Britain and across the world. To her parents, Jo Sturdee said, 'I feel it was – or will be proved in the future – to be quite a historic speech, although it hasn't half kicked up a shindig here.'[21]

She was right about the impact of the speech. In America, where there was a strong streak of post-war isolation, as well as hostility to British imperialism, Churchill's call for a new relationship was widely attacked. 'The United States wants no alliance, or anything that resembles an alliance, with any other nation,' said the *Wall Street Journal*, while the *Boston Globe* wrote that Churchill wanted the USA to become 'heir to the evils of a collapsing colonialism'.[22] Even more ferocious was the response in Russia. In a rare interview with the propaganda journal *Pravda*, Stalin accused Churchill of 'starting his process of unleashing war'. In one sense, Stalin's warning turned out to be true, for the Fulton speech prophetically signalled the beginning of the Cold War, the creation of NATO and the division of the developed world into two heavily armed, hostile camps.

Churchill's own political opponents in London, Attlee and Bevin, were far less exercised about the speech. Fulton was not only in line with their own increasingly Atlanticist thinking on defence policy, but Churchill's words also served as a counter to the Labour left's instinctive sympathy with the Soviet Union. Even when ninety-three Labour MPs, more than a quarter of the Parliamentary Party, put down a motion of censure in the Commons against Churchill, claiming his speech was 'inimical to the cause of world peace',[23] Attlee refused to utter a word of condemnation. 'Mr Churchill had spoken in an individual capacity on his own responsibility and there was no obligation on the Government either to approve or disapprove,' he told the press.[24] This echoed the words of Churchill in the lengthy telegraphed report he sent Attlee and Bevin two days after the speech, in which he wrote, 'Naturally I take complete and sole personal responsibility for what I said [...] I think you ought to know exactly what the position is and hope you will observe the very strong and precise terms in which I disclaim any official mission or status of any kind and that I spoke only for myself.'[25] The Downing Street press officer Francis Williams recorded that, in private, Churchill's 'frank and friendly' telegram 'pleased Attlee and Bevin greatly'.[26] Just as happy was King George VI, who told Attlee that the Fulton speech was 'the most courageous utterance I have ever heard from a public man'.[27]

Invigorated by the feeling of being at the centre of events again, Churchill refused to contemplate retirement, despite continued mutterings against him by some of his Tory colleagues. During the continuation of his American tour, he issued a statement that read, 'I have no intention whatsoever of ceasing to lead the Conservative Party until I am satisfied that they can see their way clear ahead and make better arrangements.'[28] Yet his desire to retain the Opposition leadership did not stop him being helpful towards the Labour Government. At the University Club in New York on 18 March, he gave a politically altru-istic speech, a report of which was sent to Attlee by Archie Mackenzie, an official at the British Embassy. In a section about the 'essential, underlying unity of the British people', Churchill made 'a very genuine and loyal expression of trust in the Government, notwithstanding his disagreement with aspects of policy. He spoke respectfully and admir-ingly of leaders skilled in Parliamentary practice, in Government and affairs, many of them close colleagues and friends in the Coalition.'[29] Normally so reserved, Attlee was touched by Churchill's attitude. After a report of another generous contribution, this one made at the National Press Club luncheon, Attlee wrote, 'I should like to send you my warm thanks and appreciation for the friendly line you took.'[30]

The cordiality was reinforced on Churchill's return from America on 26 March as he contemplated his biggest literary project: his Second

World War memoirs. When he was leaving for America in January, his literary agent Emery Reeves told him that he could make a fortune there over the next five years, including at least $2 million from his memoirs, $500,000 from radio broadcasts and $250,000 from newspaper articles. To reduce his tax liabilities, he would have to make complex financial arrangements, with payments channelled through a family trust or treated as capital receipts rather than income. But the most crucial necessity was for approval to use material from the wealth of official papers that he had produced during his wartime leadership. It was on this point that Attlee proved extremely helpful. The Prime Minister had already agreed, in October 1945, to end the ban on disclosing the secret sessions of the Commons during the war. Now, in 1946, his Cabinet went a stage further. Recognising that post-war years were bound to result in a flood of memoirs, the Government instituted a review, headed by the Cabinet Secretary Sir Edward Bridges, into the rules on the use of official documents. The review proposed keeping the tight regulations for civil servants, but suggested a degree of relaxation of the regime for ministerial memoirs, with a presumption in favour of publication except where the disclosure of information might be a threat to the national interest or be 'of value to a potential enemy'.[31] On Bridges' advice, Attlee sent the draft guidelines to Churchill on 27 May. In his covering note, Attlee wrote that 'the proposals represent, in the view of my colleagues and myself, at once a reasonable and workable basis on which to handle what is admittedly not an altogether easy question. As Prime Minister of the Coalition Government through more than five years of war, you have, of course, a very considerable concern in this matter,' a rather coy reference to Churchill's rumoured memoirs.[32] Churchill replied two days later, asking that in his own case, the guidelines be interpreted with the widest possible leeway. 'Permission ought not to be unreasonably withheld, especially as time goes by,' he told Attlee. Churchill went on to explain that 'an unusually large proportion of my work was done in writing, ie by shorthand dictation and there is therefore in existence an unbroken series of minutes, memoranda, telegrams, etc, covering the whole period of my Administration [...]

I certainly hope that, in accordance with the principles laid down, these, or many of them, may sometime see the light of day in their textual form.'[33] Attlee responded on 3 June, 'I am glad you are in general agreement.'[34]

The issue became a practical, immediate reality in the autumn of 1946 as Churchill began to negotiate the rights for his war memoirs. He wrote to Bridges in September to explain that he was being 'pressed from many quarters' to 'give my account of the British war story'; he therefore needed to know 'in principle' whether there would be any objection to the publication of official documents, though he stressed this would include nothing contrary to the public interest. Bridges, who strongly favoured Churchill's grand project because he saw it as a kind of popular official history that could boost Britain's prestige, wrote a paper for Attlee's Cabinet which advocated the acceptance of Churchill's terms. On 10 October, Bridges' paper was formally approved by ministers, with the one condition that Churchill's text would be 'submitted for final revision on behalf of His Majesty's Government'. After the meeting, Bridges gave Churchill the good news. 'As you will see, it is 100 per cent acceptance.' He then added, 'You know, I hope, that I and my colleagues in the Cabinet Office will always be ready to give you any help we can over these questions of documents and so forth.'[35] Bridges lived up to his word, giving Churchill's research team full access to official documents. Attlee himself also provided direct assistance occasionally, as in December 1946 when he sent Churchill a copy of a detailed Joint Intelligence Committee report, gathered from captured enemy archives, on 'Weaknesses in German Strategy and Organisation 1933 to 1945'. Churchill thanked Attlee fulsomely, while also expressing concern about the daunting burden of his memoirs. 'It is very interesting to me to check our own ideas and estimates at particular points – when all was unknown – by reference to the facts now available from enemy sources. I am worrying a good deal about this book. It is a colossal undertaking and I may well collapse before the end of the load is carried to the top of the hill.'[36]

As the manuscript of the first volume approached completion at the beginning of 1948, Bridges' successor as Cabinet Secretary, Sir Norman Brook, carried out the vetting in equally supportive style and allowed Churchill to quote at length from his own minutes and papers. Attlee was also co-operative, not least because Labour came out well from the story of the Coalition, but there was one point on which he raised an objection. In the chapter about the disastrous Norway campaign in 1940, Churchill had included a quotation from a paper by the Chiefs of Staff. 'I think we should stick to papers written by Churchill,' Attlee told Brook. In response, Brook argued that this should not be an absolute rule because it could lead to a one-sided version of events. 'Mr Churchill quotes so many of his own documents that there is a danger of his creating the impression that no one but he ever took the initiative.' Attlee agreed not to impose a complete ban, but warned that too open an approach might encourage any official criticised in the memoirs to demand redress by reference to other documents, a process that could become 'embarrassing'. This guidance prevailed throughout the production of all six volumes, prompting the historian David Reynolds to write, in his meticulous study of the war memoirs: 'Attlee's ruling ensured that relatively few replies were printed to Churchill's minutes, particularly in the form of official Cabinet papers.'[37] But such omissions detracted from neither the phenomenal appeal of the series nor Churchill's earnings. The worldwide sale of the rights in January 1947 brought in $2.5 million or £600,000. When the first volume, entitled *The Gathering Storm*, was published in the United States in the summer of 1948, it sold 565,000 copies within two months. Over the next five years, he published the remaining volumes to acclaim, though with the passage of time, there was growing criticism of his excessive reliance on official documents. The publishers found to their disappointment that when the first draft of Volume IV was delivered in early 1950, three-quarters of the text was made up of quotations from official papers. A major rewriting exercise was therefore required at a time of intense domestic political conflict. 'Volume IV is a worse tyrant than Attlee,' joked Churchill.[38]

Even with the help of his trusted assistants, Churchill's devotion to his literary endeavours raised more doubts about his continuing Opposition leadership. Throughout 1946 there was a sustained grumble about the need for him to retire. Smuts, one of Churchill's most loyal allies, was inclined in that direction, telling Harold Nicolson over dinner in June that the Conservative Party 'must rid itself of its older men, perhaps even some of its older leaders, perhaps even the greatest leader himself'.[39] Further growls were sparked by the sporadic nature of Churchill's attendance in the Commons. When he did appear, his conduct could sometimes provoke concern. On one occasion, in May 1946, he shocked MPs by sticking his tongue out at Ernie Bevin. Soon after this incident, the Liberal MP Clem Davies, who had helped to manoeuvre him into the premiership in May 1940, wrote to Archie Sinclair about Churchill's behaviour: 'He is a great man, a great figure and an outstanding personality, but something is going amiss. Sometimes he behaves like an ill-mannered gamin, making faces and putting out his tongue and so on. To me and a great number of us this is more than sad. It is a tragedy.'[40]

Churchill's lack of engagement was also seen as Attlee's Government embarked on its massive raft of domestic legislative changes, led by the twin flagship measures of the establishment of the NHS and the introduction of comprehensive social security, as set out in the Beveridge Report. In these two cases, however, Churchill's scope for direct opposition was restricted, given that both his Coalition Government and the Tory manifesto of 1945 had supported such plans. During 1946, Churchill largely confined his attacks about Labour's domestic policy to targets like the over-regulation of business and the extension of food rationing, both of which ran against his liberal spirit. His own Chief Whip James Stuart wrote of Churchill's early style in Opposition. 'Our leader did not often grace us with his presence but remained a law unto himself, taking part in such debates as he wished to.'[41]

Churchill was more invigorated by questions of empire, foreign affairs and defence, though even here his passion burned less brightly than in the past. One of the most difficult problems facing the Government

was the future of India, the question that had played such a large part
in the political careers of Churchill and Attlee in the inter-war years.
Labour came to power with a pledge to grant India self-governance
through dominion status, as envisaged by the Cripps mission in 1942.
But there were huge obstacles in the way of that goal, including the
strong anti-British feeling from nationalists of the Congress Party,
led by Jawaharlal Nehru, and the demand from Muslims, led by
Muhammad Ali Jinnah, for their own separate state. In an attempt
to overcome these difficulties, Attlee sent another mission headed by
Cripps to negotiate a settlement, but this again ended in failure, largely
because of the Muslim issue. The Government was now faced with
the grim prospect of imperial disorder, separatism and humiliation. For
Attlee the danger was epitomised by the strategy of the incumbent
Viceroy Lord Wavell, who came up with his own 'Breakdown Plan'.
This contingency scheme envisaged an immediate handover of power
to the Hindu provinces and principalities, followed by a swift evacuation by the British and their retreat to mainly Muslim areas. Rapidly
losing faith in Wavell, Attlee rejected his plan. 'I thought that was what
Winston would certainly quite properly describe as an ignoble and
sordid scuttle and I wouldn't look at it. I came to the conclusion that
Wavell had shot his bolt,' he later recalled.[42]

There were fears across the political spectrum that, given his past
record on India, Churchill might seek to capitalise on the Government's
problems by embarking on another crusade of imperial salvation. But
that was all in the past. The war had transformed the picture in Asia
and Churchill had no wish to relive his old battles. 'India must go.
It is lost. We have consistently been defeatist. We have lost sight of
our purpose in India,' he said privately.[43] But nor was he willing to
give unequivocal backing to the Government, as he explained in a
letter to Attlee of 14 May 1946 setting out his position on India. 'I
consider myself committed up to the Cripps Mission in 1942, though
you know what a grief this was to me.' But any settlement depends on
'an Agreement between the great forces composing Indian life. If that
Agreement is not forthcoming, I must resume my full freedom to point

out the dangers and evils of the abandonment by Great Britain of her mission in India.' He also pointed out that the constitution proposed by the 1942 Cripps Mission contemplated only dominion status. 'If at the present time you reach immediately a solution of independence, I should not be able to support this,' not least because of 'the dangers of civil war breaking out in India on our departure'.[44]

Attlee, frustrated by the continuing stalemate, was moving towards a dramatic new policy at the end of 1946. He decided that Wavell had to be replaced by the flamboyant naval commander Dickie Mountbatten, who was thought to possess the dynamic self-confidence to achieve a settlement. In addition, Attlee insisted that his Cabinet agree that Britain's withdrawal from India be fixed for June 1948, in order to heighten the pressure for an agreement. When the twin announcements of Wavell's replacement by Mountbatten and Britain's future exit were announced in Parliament on 20 February 1947, there was widespread surprise, and some anger from parts of the Conservative Party. Focusing on Wavell's departure, Churchill demanded from Attlee an explanation for the decision. When Attlee claimed that Wavell's had been a 'wartime appointment', Churchill repeated his question, pointing out that the war had been finished for eighteen months. According to the colourful account by the *Daily Mail*'s parliamentary correspondent,

> Mr Churchill jabbed his spectacles towards Mr Attlee and exclaimed, 'Surely the Prime Minister did not wake up one morning and say, "I'd like a new Viceroy." Laughter rippled through the Chamber and the galleries. Then began that barrage of 'Answer!' from the Conservative benches, which was to take up most of the remaining time. Mr Attlee lay back on the Treasury bench, impatiently rustling his papers up and down.

After Churchill put the question again, Attlee snapped at him: 'When you were Prime Minister you made a great many changes both in military and civil appointments, but I do not recall that there was any obligation on you to come to the House and state why those changes were made.'[45] Attlee was particularly annoyed because, before the debate, he had privately given Churchill an explanation of the reasons for Wavell's removal, based on the Government's rejection of the Viceroy's evacuation plan. 'I did not want him to cause difficulties for us through lack of knowledge,' Attlee later recalled of the confidential talks he held with Churchill. But, to Attlee's 'surprise and disappointment', Churchill – 'rather a mischief-maker' – proceeded to make his interventions 'quite at variance with the facts of which he had been told. This put me in perhaps the most embarrassing situation of my whole career since I could not divulge in detail all the facts of the matter and therefore could not give the lie to Winston. I find it very hard to forgive him for this. The extraordinary thing is that I can forgive him. Winston could get away with this. In any other man it would have been damnable and utterly unpardonable.'[46]

Churchill and Attlee renewed their bout on 6 March, in a Commons debate on the Government's bold new India policy. In his speech, Churchill again questioned the purpose of Mountbatten's appointment, before declaring in peroration that 'we must do our best in all these circumstances and not exclude any expedient that may help us mitigate the ruin and disaster that will follow the disappearance of Britain from the East. But at least let us not add – by shameful flight, by a premature, hurried scuttle – to the pangs of sorrow so many of us feel, the taint and smear of shame.'[47] The tone was more regret than anger, though he had been constrained by the fact that many in his own party, such as Lord Halifax, strongly backed the Government. 'A good speech, less violent than one might have expected,' wrote Cuthbert Headlam.[48] In his response Attlee hid behind one of his cherished cricket metaphors to avoid further discussion about Wavell's removal, 'If a change of bowling is desired, it is not always necessary that there should be an elaborate explanation.' Turning to Churchill's contribution, he told the House that the Conservative Leader's stance was anachronistic. 'I think his practical acquaintance with India ended some fifty years ago. He formed strong opinions – I might say prejudices – then. They have remained with him ever since.' Demands for a lengthy period of continued rule were unrealistic. 'We believe that the time has come when Indians must shoulder their responsibility. We must help them. We cannot take this burden on ourselves.' He concluded with an idealistic flourish as he told the House that Indian autonomy was not 'a betrayal' but the 'fulfilment of our mission'.[49] Attlee could rise to such unaccustomed eloquence because he had become so well versed in the subject of India over the previous two decades. Watching from the Public Gallery, Wing Commander Alan Campbell-Johnson, Mountbatten's press attaché, was impressed: 'The man burns with a hidden fire and is sustained by a certain spiritual integrity which enables him to scale the heights when the great occasion demands. Churchill was raked with delicate irony.'[50] Parliament approved Attlee's policy by 337 votes to 185.

Events moved with astonishing speed after that. Having set off on his mission, Mountbatten soon decided that the timetable for withdrawal was too long, given that the ethnic violence was escalating. He therefore planned to bring the date forward to August 1947. At the same time, through the force of his charismatic personality, he was able to secure agreement of the Indian leaders to a partition, with both India and the new state of Pakistan to become dominions. Mountbatten came back to London and quickly won all-party approval for his partition plan. Even Churchill was compliant, having recognised that Indian unity could not survive the end of British rule. In fact, at Mountbatten's request, he had urged the Muslim leader Jinnah to come into line on the partition deal. 'This is a matter of life and death for Pakistan if you do not accept this offer,' he said in a message to Jinnah.[51] On 21 May 1947, having consulted his colleagues, Churchill wrote to Attlee, 'I am in a position to assure you that if those terms are made good, so that there is an effective acceptance of Dominion status for several parts of a divided India, the Conservative Party will agree to facilitate the passage this session of the legislation necessary to confer Dominion status upon such several parts of India.'[52] The plan was presented by Attlee to the Commons on 3 June, a sweltering summer day on which the temperature reached 90 degrees Fahrenheit inside the chamber. But the stifling heat could not conceal the relief and jubilation at the deal, after so many years of futile negotiations. Among those congratulating Attlee was Churchill, for so long the enemy of Indian self-rule, now the magnanimous conciliator. 'If the hopes which are enshrined in this Declaration should be borne out, great credit will indeed be due, not only to the Viceroy, but to the Prime Minister who advised His Majesty to appoint him,' said Churchill.[53]

Indian freedom was formally declared on 15 August, after Attlee had guided the necessary legislation through the Commons. Along with the establishment of the NHS and the expansion of the welfare state, the end of the Indian Empire has been widely seen as one of Attlee's crowning achievements, made possible by his tenacity and knowledge of his subject. Indira Gandhi, Nehru's daughter and the first female Prime Minister of India, said that Attlee was 'more in tune with history than his distinguished predecessor who had ruled out the extinction of the Empire'.[54] As it turned out, the celebrations at independence were overshadowed by the subsequent descent into further conflict, which led to more than one million deaths and the displacement of 15 million people. Churchill's bleak warnings about blood-soaked chaos at the end of the Indian Empire turned out to be justified. Six years later, in conversation with President Eisenhower, he said that 'Britain's desertion of her duty in India was the most serious political blunder of the last decade.'[55] Yet, as even he had seen, there was no realistic alternative to independence. British rule was unsustainable.

At least, Attlee's Government had a clear goal on India. The same could not be said of its policy on Palestine, another imperial responsibility riven by ethnic strife. His Government had inherited the troubled mandate for the administration of Palestine, granted in 1922 by the League of Nations, along with the vague aspiration for the establishment of Jewish homeland there, as embodied in the Balfour declaration of 1917. At the end of the war, the pressure on Britain to fulfil the Balfour pledge dramatically intensified because of worldwide revulsion at the suffering of the Jewish people under the Nazi regime. The Zionist drive for a new state was heightened by waves of Jewish immigration to Palestine, which both defied British attempts to maintain strict limits on the numbers, and caused growing anger among the Muslim Arab population. The urgency for a new settlement was further heightened by the American Government of Harry Truman, who was a powerful supporter of the Zionist cause. In fact one of the first documents that Attlee found on his desk when entering 10 Downing Street in July 1945 was a letter from Truman to Churchill, sent two days before the General Election result was known. Having referred to Churchill's 'deep and sympathetic interest in Jewish settlement in Palestine', Truman expressed the hope that 'the British Government may find it possible without delay' to lift restrictions on immigration. Attlee replied blandly on 31 July that he could not give 'any statement of policy until we have had time to consider the matter'. Truman reiterated his demand for action in August, urging that 100,000 Jews be allowed immediately into Palestine. This irritated Attlee who replied in a lengthy telegram of 31 August 1945. He argued that other nationalities and groups had suffered grievously in the concentration camps, so the Jews should not be put 'in a special racial category at the head of the queue'. Moreover, the views of the Arabs had to be considered: a vast new influx could 'set aflame the whole Middle East'.[56]

Attlee's own Labour Party was broadly sympathetic to the Zionist cause, which was then seen on the left as a struggle for freedom against oppression. But neither Attlee nor his Foreign Secretary Bevin were so enthusiastic about the creation of Israel. They inclined towards the traditional Arabist view of the Foreign Office, which was more concerned about protecting Britain's imperial and commercial interests in the Middle East. Because of the mandate, they also had the heavy responsibility for security in Palestine, which was threatened not only by Arab unrest, but even more seriously by a deadly terrorist campaign waged by Zionist extremists, epitomised by the notorious bombing of the King David Hotel in Jerusalem in July 1946, an atrocity that left ninety-one people dead. But there have also been claims that an element of anti-Semitism inspired some of Attlee and Bevin's negativity towards Israel. According to Dalton, Attlee once explained that he excluded two Jewish backbenchers, Austen Albu and Ian Mikardo, from his

Government 'because they belonged to the Chosen People and he didn't think he wanted any more of them'.[57] Just as revealingly in a letter to his brother Tom in 1946 about American support for Jewish immigration, he described Zionism as 'a profitable racket. A Zionist is defined as a Jew who collects money from another Jew to send money to Palestine.'[58] Mikardo himself thought Attlee's alleged prejudice stemmed from 'his contacts with Jews during the many years he spent in the East End', as well as 'the fall-out from bitter conflict with Harold Laski'.[59]

Churchill could never be accused of anti-Semitism. With his romantic view of history, he was a profound believer in 'the genius' of the Jewish people, once describing them as 'the most formidable and remarkable race that has ever appeared in the world'.[60] This outlook was strengthened by his early experience as a Liberal MP in Manchester, where he worked closely with Jewish groups in the city. Through his Manchester connection, he became a friend of the Zionist leader and future President of Israel, Chaim Weizmann, who lived in the city for several decades. Under Weizmann's guidance, he became a supporter of the Zionist cause, a stance that was further galvanised by the horrors of the Nazi genocide. His own Coalition Government accepted in principle the future creation of a Jewish state through the partition of Palestine. Yet, even with this record, he did little to bring this policy to fruition after the war or challenge Labour's lukewarm approach. After years of warmth towards Zionism, he lost his sympathy for the cause at one of the most crucial moments in its history. The explanation for this change was simple. In November 1944, Lord Moyne, his close friend and Minister Resident in the Middle East, had been assassinated by the Stern Gang in Cairo. It was a crime that Churchill could not forget. For him, Zionism had become tainted by Moyne's blood. He even went so far as to describe the Stern group as 'a set of gangsters worthy of Nazi Germany'.[61] Consumed with anger at the terrorists, he avoided ever meeting Weizmann again. When the Zionist leader appealed to him in writing to lend his support in seeking a change of Labour Government policy, Churchill merely passed the message on to Attlee and told Weizmann, 'there is nothing personally I can do in the matter'.[62]

In March 1946, Churchill suggested to Attlee that Britain might have to hand the Palestinian mandate to the United Nations. 'I strongly favour putting all possible pressure upon the United States to share with us the responsibility and burden of bringing about a good solution,' he wrote. But if 'American assistance is not forthcoming' and Britain was 'plainly unable' to 'carry out our pledge to the Jews of building up a national Jewish home in Palestine', then 'we have an undoubted right to ask to be relieved of the mandate'.[63] Churchill's disillusion with hard-line Zionism was again illustrated in another letter he sent Attlee, in July 1946, in which he said that he still held himself 'bound by our national pledges', namely 'the establishment of a Jewish National Home in Palestine', but that 'terrorism is no solution for the Palestinian problem. Yielding to terrorism would be a disaster.'[64] In his reply, Attlee promised that 'we shall not accept any solution which represents abandonment of our pledges to the Jews or our obligations to the Arabs'.[65] But the Prime Minister could find no way to reconcile these twin objectives. In the absence of a settlement, Churchill's idea of passing responsibility to the UN had ever greater appeal. Scarred by the descent into violence, unable to stem the tide of illegal immigration, exasperated by the loss of British military lives, despairing of any solution that would satisfy both the Arabs and the Jews, the Government decided in September 1947 to return the mandate and leave Palestine by May 1948 without any settlement. Churchill accepted that this was 'the only possible policy in the disastrous conditions which had arisen'.[66]

The gradual withdrawal from Empire, combined with a determination to avoid another war, prompted a new debate about Britain's relationship with Europe. If the country was no longer to be a grand imperial power, perhaps its future lay in developing closer links with its Continental partners. Surprisingly, given his past belief in global government and an end to national sovereignty, this was an issue that left Attlee cold. He had once said that 'Europe must federate or perish'[67] but as Prime Minister he was not only focused on the implementation of Labour's socialist programme but had become more sceptical about integration. 'Can't trust the Europeans. They don't play cricket,' he said in old age.

In contrast Churchill was captivated for a moment as Opposition Leader by the idea of European unity. He had always been a politician for great causes – the Empire, social reform, naval power, free trade, anti-Nazism – and now his imagination was seized by the concept of achieving a permanent European peace through some kind of political integration, though he was always studiedly vague, even evasive, about its precise nature. His first foray on the quest for European unity took place in the northeastern French city of Metz, on Bastille Day in 1946, as he shared a platform with Robert Schuman, the French statesman and architect of the federal ideal. As with Fulton, Churchill went to considerable lengths to clear his visit with Attlee. Not only did Attlee approve the trip but, in this period of austerity, the Foreign Office agreed to fund it because of its importance. Churchill was grateful to the Labour Leader, as he wrote on 2 July. 'I was glad to hear that you have decided that my visit to Metz is of an exceptional and public character.'[68] In his speech, Churchill told his audience that 'without the aid of a United Europe', the 'great, new world organisation' of the United Nations 'may easily be rent asunder or evaporate in futility. Therefore the first word I give you here today is "Europe".'[69]

Churchill followed this up with an even more explicit call for unification when he spoke in the Swiss city of Zurich in September. The task of politicians, he said, was to 'recreate the European family, or as much of it as we can, and provide it with a structure under which it can dwell in peace, in safety and in freedom. We must build a kind of United States of Europe.' But he emphasised that Britain would play a separate role. 'We British have our own Commonwealth of nations.'[70] Inspired by the favourable reception of his Zurich speech, Churchill envisaged the creation of a new political movement to promote this concept of a united Europe. In October he issued a 'Statement of Aims' for the campaign, calling on 'the peoples of Europe' to 'come together in order to create an effective European Union'.[71] To organise this proposed movement, Churchill set up a small handling group, which he hoped would embrace all parties. But to his disappointment, Labour proved reluctant to take part. Lord Citrine, the former TUC chief, told

Churchill he was too busy with his duties at the new nationalised Coal Board, while the Labour MP George Hicks declined to participate after he took soundings from colleagues. After these rebuffs, Churchill wrote to Attlee, 'I cannot think it is contrary to Party interests of any kind that such an all-Party movement should be started. I certainly thought that was your feeling. I hope therefore that no general directions will be given preventing any Members of the Parliamentary Party from taking part in it.'[72] Attlee's reply confirmed his increasing scepticism about Churchill's project and his reluctance to lend it Labour support. 'It has been suggested that the objects aimed at by the organisation would be better achieved through the United Nations Association rather than through a separate society, the aims of which might be misunderstood and misrepresented.'[73] Despite this discouraging response, Churchill still pressed on with his campaign. In place of an all-party group, he established a non-political steering committee for the proposed movement at the end of 1946, in advance of taking a higher profile on Europe over the next three years.

Part of Churchill's rationale for a united Europe was his anxiety about the threat to peace from the Soviets in the East. It was a concern that also led to several exchanges with Downing Street over defence in 1946. The first, in March, was amicable enough, as Attlee consulted Churchill over Labour's plans to overhaul the machinery of defence administration by creating a Minister for the Armed Forces and establishing a new Cabinet committee. Churchill generally approved, though he felt that the new minister should 'certainly have the title and rank of Secretary of State'.[74] But in the autumn the mood became more strained, as Churchill developed the feeling that the Government was keeping vital information from him. This sense of exclusion was heightened by his fears that Russia was building up its strength in Eastern Europe, exacerbating the menace that he had outlined at Fulton. What worsened his grievance was the perceived contrast between this treatment and the generosity he had shown Attlee before Potsdam in 1945 over access to sensitive material on defence and foreign policy. When he saw the Cabinet Secretary Sir Edward Bridges on 24 September, he gave vent to his annoyance. As Sir Edward reported to Attlee after the meeting: 'His attitude seemed to be that he had quite understood that the Labour Party, on assuming office in August 1945, had not felt disposed to offer facilities in this matter to the Leader of the Opposition and any of his colleagues, but in his view the position had grown darker, and he thought that a situation had arisen in which granting of such facilities to Opposition leaders should be again considered.' Sir Edward added that 'it seemed clear to me that what was influencing Mr Churchill in this matter was a feeling of discomfort at the attitude of the Russian Government and of the relative military weakness of the Western Powers as compared with the Russians in Europe'.[75]

A fortnight later, on 6 October, Churchill wrote directly to Attlee in confidence: 'The European situation has deteriorated gravely. I am informed that the Soviet Government has over 225 divisions on a war footing beyond the Russian frontiers in the occupied territories of Europe. This compares to 25 British and American divisions, of which some are only Police divisions without artillery.' Churchill also referred to the obscurity that enshrouded the development of nuclear technology. 'We have no knowledge of what has happened about the atomic bomb.' On the basis of the Quebec Agreement, he argued, Britain was entitled not only to information but also 'to have a share of these bombs as they are produced'. Finally, he warned Attlee that he might go public with this complaint, perhaps by publishing their pre-Potsdam correspondence on access.[76] After consulting Bevin, Attlee replied three days later. He said he was 'quite willing' for the pre-Potsdam correspondence to be published, but those facilities had been offered 'in exceptional circumstances' because of the break-up of the Government, the impending Three Power summit and the imminence of the General Election. 'No one knew what the result would be,' Attlee wrote. Attlee emphasised, however, that he had 'repeatedly said that Bevin and I are always willing to see you or Eden or both of you if there were matters you wished to raise'. In a conciliatory conclusion, he wrote that 'like you, I am anxious that we should not have avoidable difference about matters of foreign affairs and defence'.[77]

True to his word, Attlee agreed to see a Conservative delegation led by Churchill on 5 November 1946, to discuss Soviet expansionism in Eastern Europe. But Churchill was right to feel that he was not being given the full picture of defence, for the Labour Government had secretly embarked on a programme to develop Britain's own nuclear weaponry. When Attlee told Churchill in his letter of 6 October that he 'should be glad' to provide 'information on the Atomic bomb', he was not being entirely straight. On coming to power in 1945, Labour had approved research into the uses of nuclear energy, building on the extensive knowledge that British scientists already possessed. By the summer of the following year the Chiefs of Staff had produced a paper which argued that Britain should produce its own bomb because of the Soviet threat. The pressure for Britain to acquire its own nuclear capability abruptly increased in August 1946 when the US Senate passed the McMahon Act,* which made it illegal for the American Government to share nuclear information with any other power. At a stroke, the legislation tore up Churchill's Quebec Agreement of 1943. In the new environment, Attlee acted quickly. On 25 October, at a meeting of the Gen 75 Cabinet sub-committee on nuclear policy, he put forward the proposal for Britain to build its own bomb. Cripps and Dalton had their doubts on grounds of funding, but the decisive voice was that of Bevin: 'We have got to have this thing over here whatever it costs. We've got to have the bloody Union Jack on top of it.'[78] The committee gave its provisional approval to the development programme, a decision that was confirmed by another, smaller Cabinet committee, Gen 163, in January 1947, which also decided to provide £100 million in financial support. But crucially, Attlee insisted that the new policy be kept secret, knowing that it would be unpopular with his own party. Not even Churchill or Attlee's own MPs knew about it. When the Government finally admitted to the project's existence in May 1948, the revelation was made in such an oblique, uninformative manner that it caused little controversy.

---

* Named after the Democratic Senator for Connecticut, Brien McMahon.

Away from the party political scene, there was little friction between him and Attlee in 1946. Churchill, often with Clementine, was invited to regular official dinners and receptions in Downing Street, like that in early June given in honour of the Canadian Prime Minister Mackenzie King and another in October for General Eisenhower. The two men lent their bipartisan backing to the initiative to build a memorial to President Roosevelt in Grosvenor Square, London. 'I consider it a privilege to support you on this occasion,' Churchill wrote to Attlee about the memorial.[79] They liaised smoothly on other subjects, such as Government hospitality, political broadcasts on the radio and the honours system. In a further sign of mutual goodwill, Churchill sent Attlee one of the special bronze medallions that he had struck for all the former ministers who had been in his wartime Coalition. In a generous letter of thanks, Attlee told Churchill, 'I value it very much as a tangible memorial of the five years in which I had the privilege of serving under you in a great administration when civilisation was saved by the British people.'[80] In response, Churchill downplayed its emotional significance. 'I am glad you liked the medallion. It will make an excellent paper-weight.'[81] The warmth was also highlighted at the beginning of January 1947, when Clementine and Winston sent the Attlees congratulations on their Silver Wedding anniversary. 'We wish you both joy upon your 25th wedding day and hope you will spend many more together.'[82] Clement Attlee reciprocated Clementine's kindness to him and Violet by advising the Palace in May 1946 that she should be appointed as a Dame Grand Cross of the Order of the British Empire. She deserved the recognition, Attlee told her, not only because of her work 'for the Aid to Russia Fund and for the promotion of Anglo-Russian relations, but also of those other many services which made so marked and brave a contribution during the years of war'. Clementine replied graciously to thank Attlee 'for the terms of the letter and it makes me happy that you feel I was able to help a little in these last terrific years when we all fought together in heart and mind'.[83]

But there was to be less amicability the following year, as both men were plunged into leadership crises.

TWENTY-SIX

◆

NEW JERUSALEM

A TTLEE'S FIRST EIGHTEEN months in office had been relatively successful. His Government's domestic agenda had both purpose and popularity, while he had grown in stature. Even his oratory appeared to have improved, perhaps as a result of taking on Churchill regularly. Listening to Attlee give 'quite a good reply' at a City dinner, Tommy Lascelles recorded in his diary: 'I noticed several obvious Winston inflections.'[1] Churchill himself agreed that his own example was responsible for the rise in the standard of Attlee's performance. After one waspish display by the Prime Minister in the Commons, Churchill was reputed to have said to a Tory colleague as he walked out of the chamber, 'feed a grub on Royal Jelly and it may turn out to be a Queen Bee'.[2]

Yet early in 1947 the storm clouds were gathering over Attlee's premiership, due to the deepening fuel crisis brought about by an exceptionally bitter winter. In the long weeks of freezing conditions, parts of the economy were almost paralysed, adding to the atmosphere of harsh austerity. State planning, the essence of Attlee's socialism, did not seem to be working. Much of the criticism of the Government focused on the Fuel Minister Manny Shinwell, whose noisy radicalism was not matched by his administrative competence, but Attlee also took a blow to his reputation.

Churchill had largely been quiescent on the domestic front since the General Election, but he now saw the chance to strike as the fuel crisis engulfed the Labour Government. Surveying the political landscape, he decided the time had come to mobilise the formidable resources of his rhetoric against what he regarded as socialist mismanagement. He opened this new, more energetic phase of his Opposition leadership with a pungent attack on Attlee's ministry during a Commons debate in March about the economic situation. 'Mouthing slogans of envy, hatred and malice, they have spread class warfare throughout the land and all sections of society, and they have divided this nation, in its hour of serious need, as it has never been divided.' But instead of meeting Churchill's barrage with his own bombardment, Attlee adopted a lighter, sardonic tone in his response. 'He likes this form of oratorical exercise. We all enjoy hearing him do his stuff, but I do not think he contributed very much to the serious side of the debate,' Attlee told the House, before continuing, 'His complaint is always this, "Why cannot you follow a Conservative Party policy and then we will support you?" He always seems to regard whatever views he holds as essentially above and beyond party – an amiable characteristic that has carried him through a long and varied career.'[3] *The Times* judged that Attlee once more had the better of the argument, reporting that he 'brought a daring liveliness, salted with wit, to his reply'.[4]

In his speech, Churchill had reserved some of his strongest invective for Labour's programme of industrial nationalisation, which had started with coal and was soon planned to embrace rail transport, steel, road haulage, electricity and gas. It was this hostility to public ownership that gave birth to a renowned but probably apocryphal story about an exchange with Attlee. On one occasion during the post-war Labour Government, Attlee was standing at a urinal in a gentlemen's cloakroom at the House of Commons. In walked Churchill and took up a position at the furthest urinal away from the Labour Prime Minister.

'Feeling standoffish today, are we, Winston?' asked Attlee.

'That's right, Clement. Whenever you see something that is big, private and works well, you want to nationalise it.'[5]

Churchill's dislike of state control and regulation did not extend to the armed forces. He therefore supported Labour's plans in early

1947 to introduce peacetime conscription through the National Service Bill, though in a swipe at the past record of Attlee and his colleagues, he told the Commons that in the 1930s 'the whole effort of their party was designed to make every preparation for the defence of the country and resistance to Hitler so unpopular that it was politically impossible'.[6] Churchill was even more disgruntled when a major Labour backbench rebellion on the Bill led the Government to cut the length of compulsory national service from eighteen to twelve months. The 'absurd' change, he argued, was the result of a surrender to '70 or 80 pacifists or "cryptos"' or that breed of degenerate intellectuals who have done so much harm'.[7] On the issue of national service, Attlee was not perturbed by the way Churchill had 'barged in' because, as he told Morrison, his effort 'properly handled, may consolidate our ranks'.[8] His prediction was correct. The legislation passed easily after the Labour rebellion evaporated, while many Tories did not share Churchill's insistence on eighteen months' service and felt he had failed to consult them on the Bill.

The political relationship between Churchill and Attlee had now returned to the friction of the 1945 General Election campaign. On 25 April the Labour Leader went on the attack when he addressed the Scottish TUC at the Younger Hall, St Andrews. There he unleashed uncharacteristically personal fire upon a wide range of targets, among them Churchill's lack of constructive policy, his 'obsolete imperialism' on India, his 'ridiculous' deceit about the purpose of nationalisation and his hypocrisy in criticising the Government for its reliance on the American loan, given his own wartime Coalition's dependence on Lend-Lease. 'It is incredible that he should stoop to such meanness,' said Attlee. But the Prime Minister's most withering contempt was reserved for Churchill's economic record, which, he said, rendered worthless his criticisms of the Labour Government. 'I remember very well when Mr Churchill was Chancellor of the Exchequer, the most disastrous Chancellor of the century. It was he that brought us back

---

* Crypto Communists.

to the gold standard, which led to the crisis in the coal industry from which we are suffering today. He inflicted untold misery on the people of this country.'[9]

Attlee's speech provoked fierce condemnation from his opponents. That very night, the Tory MP David Maxwell-Fyfe, later Home Secretary and Lord Chancellor, declared that it reminded him of 'nothing so much as the shrill, petulant shriek of a terrified mouse'.[10] Two days later, Churchill himself issued a detailed statement of rebuttal through Conservative Central Office. He strongly defended his record as Chancellor, pointing out that his five years at the Treasury had seen living costs, taxes and business rates all reduced, while pensions were increased. On the question of the Gold Standard, he said he acted 'on the advice of a committee appointed by Lord Snowden in the Socialist Government in 1924, of which Mr Attlee himself was a member'. But that was all in the past. 'Mr Attlee must feel himself very hard pressed to have to go back a quarter of a century to find excuses for the mismanagement and blunders of which he evidently feels his government guilty,' he concluded.[11]

Across much of the press, there was surprise that Attlee had descended into such unaccustomed, aggressive partisanship. A.J. Cummings, the political editor of the Liberal-inclined *News Chronicle*, stated that 'it was very nearly a case of Clem the Giantkiller. Few thought Mr Attlee capable of wielding the dialectical weapon so effectively. During the war, when he was Deputy Prime Minister, he developed a great and sincere admiration for Mr Churchill's personality, for his gay courage, for his resourcefulness of mind, for his superb oratory. Some of his friends said his hero worship went too far.' Now, Cummings went on, 'The members of his own party will enjoy the spectacle of Mr Attlee giving battle to Mr Churchill.' But Cummings felt that Attlee would 'command greater respect' if he concentrated on improving the economy.[12] In more forthright terms, the *Daily Dispatch* argued that Attlee 'should be above' making a 'soap box taunt' against Churchill,[13] while the *Daily Telegraph* felt that 'the Prime Minister must regret his curious impulse to scratch among the scrapheaps of the past for material with which to discredit his opponent'.[14] Attlee, however, had no such sentiment. As the controversy still raged, he wrote to his brother Tom: 'It was generally felt that Winston has asked for a correction. He is singularly inept as Opposition Leader and there is much discontent in Tory ranks.'[15]

Attlee wrote in the same vein to Morrison, who was recuperating on the French Riviera after he had suffered a thrombosis. In his letter Attlee pointed to Churchill's own health problems: 'Poor old Winston gets deafer every day. He intervened twice this afternoon, to ask why a motion had not been seconded – when the seconder had just sat down – and why the Government had not made a statement – when Greenwood had just made it. It is really embarrassing.'[16] But Churchill still had no intention of retiring. His determination to beat Attlee and finally win a General Election meant that he could not yet depart, much to the annoyance of some senior colleagues. In July 1947, the internal frustration with him reached such a level that a meeting of eight leading Tories was held at the home of Harry Crookshank in Pont Street, Knightsbridge. Among those attending were Lord Salisbury, Rab Butler, Lord Woolton, Oliver Stanley and the Tory Chief Whip James Stuart. The meeting decided Churchill had to be told that 'it was probably in the best interests of the party that he should seek peace in retirement'. The 'difficult and highly distasteful' task of conveying this message was entrusted to Stuart, who duly went to see Churchill in his room at the Commons, as he later recalled. 'He reacted violently, banging the floor with his stick and implying that I too had joined those who were plotting to displace him.' Churchill then told Stuart that he would 'soldier on to turn out the socialists'.[17]

At exactly the same time as Churchill was facing down the conspirators, pressure was mounting on Attlee. His virtues as Leader, such as his crisp chairmanship and military efficiency, now appeared to be outweighed by his weaknesses, including his lack of dynamism. Dalton regularly blazed in private with rage at 'the incompetent little Prime Minister';[18] while Stafford Cripps, the ascetic President of the Board of Trade, felt that Attlee had 'no initiative or drive'.[19] His struggles were relished by his political opponents too. Brendan Bracken wrote to Lord Beaverbrook in late April, 'I feel that if Attlee continues to lead the country nothing can stop a Tory revival.'[20] The crisis facing Attlee in the summer was made worse by a disastrous run on the pound, caused by the imposition of sterling's convertibility from 15 July, as stipulated by the terms of the Anglo-American loan. Within a week, there was a huge drain on capital, while gold reserves began to run out. Disparagement of the Government dramatically increased. The *News Chronicle* witheringly said that Attlee 'gives the impression that the situation is beyond his grasp'.[21] In the fraught atmosphere, a plot began to develop with the aim of replacing Attlee by Bevin. Inevitably Dalton, the arch-manipulator, was drawn into the intrigue, not least because the leader of plotters was his own parliamentary private secretary, George Brown, who openly gathered signatures in the tearoom to a resolution demanding Attlee's resignation. Remarkably, Dalton was also in touch with a few senior Tories, among them the anti-Churchill centrist Rab Butler, about the possibility of a national coalition under Bevin, in order to see the economy through the immediate upheaval. In his diary for 21 July, the diplomat Pierson Dixon described a lunch where Rab Butler's wife jeered that 'Winston would have a rude awakening when there was a Coalition and he was not the leader'.[22]

But this was fanciful talk. Few in the Labour Party wanted another peacetime coalition after the experience of 1931 under Ramsay MacDonald. The same was true of the Conservatives beyond the scheming Butler. Churchill won loud support at the backbench 1922 Committee on 22 July, when he had warned against any arrangement with Labour which would deprive the country of an alternative Government. Nor was Bevin remotely interested in deposing Attlee. On 28 July, Dalton wrote regretfully in his diary, 'George Brown tells me that the movement to make Bevin PM has petered out.'[23] But the sterling crisis certainly had not. The drain on the reserves was accelerating. Drastic action was needed. The Government finally took it by agreeing to Transitional – or Emergency – Powers legislation, as well as cuts in imports, particularly food and tobacco, longer hours in the coal industry, and the release of 80,000 men from the armed forces. These austerity measures prompted Churchill to make another of his assaults on Labour. 'The Socialist belief,' he told a Conservative rally at Blenheim Palace on 4 August, 'is that nothing matters much so long as the miseries are equally shared, and they have acted in accordance with their faith.'[24] Two days later Attlee introduced the Transitional Powers Bill at Westminster. In doing so, he resorted to a cricket metaphor in his attack on Churchill over the Blenheim speech: 'He hit around him very vigorously. Sometimes he hit at us, sometimes he hit at some of his friends opposite and sometimes the ball rebounded on to his own head.'[25] But this was a rare knockabout moment. In general, Attlee's speech was a solemn recital of the tough steps his Government planned to take. *The Economist* decided that Attlee was so arid that 'he touches nothing he cannot dehydrate'.[26] Churchill responded in the Chamber two days later with a denunciation of the proposed Transitional Powers, which he warned would be, if applied in their full force, 'the complete abrogation of Parliament and of all our dearly-bought rights and long-cherished liberties'. The House, he said, had been 'asked to give a blank cheque to totalitarian Government', but the Bill would do little for the 'recovery of the country'.[27] Given Labour's huge majority, the Bill easily passed the Commons, but not before Churchill's talk about the threat to British freedoms had caused alarm within the Palace. The King, usually anxious to avoid party controversy, felt compelled to challenge Attlee on the legislation. The Prime Minister assured George VI that the powers were designed for 'a real emergency' rather than a mere economic crisis, and added an expression of surprise that Churchill had 'whipped up fears that the Bill was designed for other hands'. In his own account, Attlee wrote that 'the King became quite happy again and realised that Churchill's fulminations were only an opportunistic stunt'.[28]

The financial crisis eased in the short-term when the Cabinet agreed on 20 August to suspend the convertibility of sterling, with the agreement of America. It was a humiliating but necessary step. Yet the longer term political problem of Attlee's leadership was still unresolved.

His Government had been tested and he had been found wanting. One opinion poll in August showed that, for the first time since the General Election, the Conservatives had overtaken Labour, leading by 44.5 per cent to 41 per cent. Intriguingly, Churchill had some private sympathy for Attlee's predicament, despite his public denunciations of his policies. He wrote to Clementine on 13 August, 'Everything is pretty grim and poor little Attlee is hard-pressed. I have no feelings of unfriendliness towards him. Bevan is making the running to gain power by extreme left-wing politics. If this proves true, we must certainly expect political crisis in addition to an economic collapse.'[29] But Churchill was wrong. It was not Nye Bevan who led a renewed plot to overthrow Attlee at this time, but another Cabinet colleague, Stafford Cripps, to whom Churchill could never warm. 'He has all the virtues I dislike and none of the vices I admire,' Churchill once said.[30] With his righteous, if naïve, zeal, Cripps now took up the baton for a change in leadership, believing the party and the country would be sunk without it. 'It was matter of life and death importance to get rid of Attlee. Bevin should take his place,' he told Jennie Lee, the Labour MP and wife of Nye Bevan.[31] In this mood, he approached Bevin in late August to ask him to seize the premiership, but once again the Foreign Secretary refused. 'What's Clem ever done to me?' he asked.[32]

Cripps was not deterred and still insisted on the need to replace Attlee with Bevin. On the night of 9 September, after dinner, he called alone on Attlee at 10 Downing Street. Attlee already had an inkling of the manoeuvre and listened with cool impassivity as Cripps set out the case for a change at the top of Government. Once Cripps had finished, Attlee picked up the telephone and asked to be put through to Bevin. As soon as the Foreign Secretary came on the line, Attlee said, 'Ernie, Stafford's here. He says you want my job.' Bevin strongly denied the claim. 'Thought not,' said Attlee, before replacing the receiver.[33] With equal self-possession and shrewd insight, Attlee then nullified Cripps's threat of resignation by offering him the new Cabinet post of Minister for Economic Affairs. Excited at the idea of becoming economic overlord, Cripps jumped at this new role. All thoughts of departure were banished. Attlee had shown tenacity, skill and an understanding of human psychology in outmanoeuvring the plotters. Indeed, his position as Labour Leader was not seriously threatened again.

Cripps did not last long in his new job. Within six weeks, Attlee had to move him as a result of one of the most bizarre Cabinet resignations in British political history, the fall-out from which involved Churchill. On the afternoon of 12 November 1947, the Chancellor Hugh Dalton was striding through the Members' Lobby of the Commons on his way to deliver his third Budget when he ran into John Carvel, the political correspondent of the *Star*, a London evening paper. Addicted to gossip and always eager to cultivate the press, Dalton gave the reporter an outline of the Budget's main features, a strict breach of protocol because of the need to protect market-sensitive information. In a reflection of both Carvel's journalism and the high-speed logistics of the *Star*, an edition with a brief Budget report was on the streets of the capital before Dalton had even sat down.

After the Cabinet the next day, Dalton offered his resignation, which Attlee did not accept. There was substantial support for him in the House that afternoon when he apologised for his 'grave error'.[34] Churchill, never censorious about human failings despite his personal dislike of Dalton, shared this mood of forgiveness. 'May I acknowledge on the part of the Opposition the very frank manner in which the Right Honourable Gentleman has expressed himself in the House and our sympathy with him on the misuse of his confidence which has occurred,' he said.[35] But after this intervention, he was forced to alter his attitude. One reason was that the Parliamentary Press Gallery told him that his attack on Carvel had been unfair, since the reporter was 'under no obligation of secrecy'.[36] More importantly, Tory backbenchers were eager for vengeance because Dalton, with his bombastic, self-satisfied partisanship, was the most despised Labour minister. In their eyes, with Attlee's Government in trouble, this was the moment for attack rather than chivalry. They therefore called for a Select Committee on the leak, a demand that Churchill put in writing to Attlee that day. The call for a Select Committee worked. When Dalton offered his resignation again later that day, Attlee accepted it. He had never been close to Dalton and was a stickler for personal integrity; he therefore thought the Chancellor's behaviour had been foolish at a time when the Government needed economic resolution. 'Perfect ass. He always liked to have a secret to confide to somebody else to please him,' said Attlee later.[37] But Churchill was embarrassed at the way the Chancellor had been compelled to quit. As he and Eden walked out of chamber on the day after Dalton's departure, Churchill was heard to remark, 'I would never have accepted a resignation in those circumstances.'[38] That was the view also held by one of Churchill's closet allies Brendan Bracken, now the MP for Bournemouth, who wrote, 'That petty Attlee has shown no consideration for what was only an aberration. One of the duties of a Prime Minster is to stand by erring colleagues. Attlee, who owes much to Dalton, hurled him to the wolves. He behaved like a Pontius Pilate in a panic.'[39]

Dalton's resignation meant the promotion of Cripps to head the Treasury, where his own lifestyle matched the austere policy of the times. It was precisely this spirit of self-sacrifice for which Churchill now attacked Labour exuberantly. Throughout the late summer and autumn he argued, sometimes in hyperbolic tones, that Attlee's Government had taken the drive for state planning and equality too far, crushing individual liberty, wealth creation and parliamentary democracy through its oppressive regime. Typical was a radio broadcast on 16 August which denounced the authoritarian impulse of Labour. 'I warn you solemnly that if you submit yourselves to the totalitarian compulsion and regimentation of our national life, there lies before you an almost measureless prospect of misery and tribulation.'[40] Despite all his political difficulties, Attlee still felt confident against such attacks. In September, he told the East Midlands regional branch of his party that Churchill 'has no policy. His tactics are to trust to the swing of the pendulum and to exploit for party ends every difficulty that faces the people [...] How different from the Churchill of the war, who exhorted the people to brave the inevitable hardships which the war entailed. He now exhorts them to whine and complain.'[41]

Another, related focus of Churchill's assault was Labour's plan to restrict further the powers of the House of Lords, so that the passage of socialist measures, especially on nationalisation, could not be thwarted. In October 1947, the Government proposed an update to the 1911 Parliament Act, whereby the time limit on the Upper House's capacity to delay legislation would be reduced from two years to just one. The new leaders clashed across the floor of the chamber when Attlee first announced the new Parliament Bill. The Prime Minister brought laughter to the House when he quoted some of Churchill's own words as a Liberal Cabinet member during the bitter struggle at Westminster over the 1911 Act. According to the report in the *Daily Express*, Churchill had been 'scowling at the Government benches' but 'could not forebear a grin' as Attlee reminded MPs that, thirty-six years earlier, Churchill had attacked the undemocratic nature of the Upper House. But the mood quickly became darker, as the *Express* reported, 'Mr Attlee, in his prim, dry style, said that this reform was only a precautionary measure and that Tory peers need not object if, in fact, they never meant to use their veto. Then Mr Churchill broke in with fierce emphasis, "It is a deliberate act of social aggression."'[42] This prompted Attlee to make one of his teasing retorts: 'The Right Honourable Gentleman must be in a reminiscent mood. He is thinking of the things said to him when he stood at this box in 1911.'[43]

Undaunted, Churchill stepped up his verbal assault a week later on 28 October in the debate on the King's Speech: 'I am sure this policy of equalising misery and organising scarcity will kill this island stone dead.'[44] The Government, however, easily won the vote on the Address by a majority of 147, and, as happened so often in the immediate post-war years, Attlee emerged on top from his duel in this debate with Churchill. At one point, after Churchill's fulminating attack on Government restrictions, Attlee directly asked him, 'Would you do away with food rationing now? We want to know!' In the *Daily Express*'s report:

At this there was a great outburst of Socialist cheers, and Mr Churchill got up and said, 'In my speech I was striking a note

(Socialist laughter) and that note was, "Set the people free."' A barrage of Socialist shouts stopped him. 'Answer the question,' they shouted. Mr Churchill stood his ground, and when he got the chance, completed his reply in emotional words, 'When you have loaded the people with chains, all the shackles cannot be stricken off in a day.' Mr Attlee, a mild figure in the storm, tut-tutted, 'This note which Mr Churchill has given to the nation is to wish them to be free. But not just now (laughter). It is an IOU on freedom.'[45]

Churchill's attack over the Address, however, went down well with many of his fellow Tories. 'His vitality and physical endurance are amazing. He spoke for nearly an hour and a half and never faltered in any way,' recorded Cuthbert Headlam.[46] Lord Woolton wrote to Churchill to say that he 'rejoiced in your speech' and that, over the Lords, 'we should reject the Government Bill and dare them to go to the country'.[47] Emboldened by this praise, Churchill launched another verbal fusillade when the Parliament Bill came before the Commons on 11 November 1947. Despite a heavy cold, he put little restraint on the robustness of his language as he warned against removing any legislative 'brake' on the Government. 'As a free-born Englishman, what I hate is the sense of being at anybody's mercy or in anybody's power, be he Hitler or Attlee. We are approaching very near to a dictatorship in this country, dictatorship that is to say – I will be quite candid with the House – without either its criminality or efficiency.'[48] But Churchill's invective could not prevent Labour pushing through the Bill.

Yet the Government's economic struggles throughout 1947 began to have an impact on the popularity of Labour and Attlee. A Gallup opinion poll in November put the Tories eleven points ahead, while in the local elections that month Labour lost no fewer than 687 seats – an outcome that Churchill described as 'a nationwide protest against socialist mismanagement'.[49] The Government's chief economic adviser Robert Hall saw the concern among Labour ministers. 'They are in a panic about their own very bad situation and about their own prospects.'⁵⁰ For all his acidity in the Commons against Churchill and his defeat of the Cabinet plotters, Attlee was a diminished figure towards the end of the year. After listening to the broadcast of Attlee's speech from the Mansion House in November, Harold Nicolson wrote, 'It is very thin and frail. Attlee is a charming and intelligent man but as a public speaker he is, compared to Winston, like a village fiddler after Paganini.'⁵¹

Away from the discord of party politics, the relationship between Churchill and Attlee remained amicable, if somewhat distant. The Labour Leader and his wife Violet were both guests at the wedding in February 1947 of the Churchills' youngest daughter, Mary, to Christopher Soames, the military attaché in Paris and aspiring Conservative MP. Churchill and Attlee co-operated on other, more public ceremonials, like the joint Address to the King in January 1947 on the royal family's departure for a tour of South Africa. A planned visit by Churchill to European royalty gave Attlee the chance to show his generosity towards his political rival. In July, Churchill had been invited to receive an honorary degree by the University of Oslo and King Haakon VII asked him to stay. After some negotiations behind the scenes with the Treasury and the Foreign Office, Attlee decided that the Government would officially support the trip 'in view of the fact that this is your first visit to this liberated country and that the King has asked you to stay with him during your visit'.⁵² The visit was postponed until May 1948, but the Government's backing remained in place. Attlee continued to be helpful towards Churchill over the research for his gargantuan war memoirs, while in June 1947, when Churchill was recovering from a hernia operation, Attlee sent him a copy of his own recently published book, a collection of speeches entitled *Purpose and Policy*, with a modest but friendly covering letter. 'When I was recovering from an operation in 1939, you kindly sent me a volume of your speeches which I read with much appreciation. As a very minor practitioner of an art of which you are an acknowledged master, I am sending you this volume, not for reading, but only as a tangible expression of my wishes for your speedy and complete restoration to health.'⁵³

The civility between the two men was also revealed in the regular expressions of congratulation on personal occasions. One typical note from Churchill to Violet and Clem, sent in early December 1947, ran: 'Thank you both so much for your good wishes on my birthday.'[54] While on holiday in Marrakesh that Christmas, Churchill was struck down by chicken pox, prompting him to send for Lord Moran, and the Attlees to send their sympathy and concern. 'Thank you for your message,' replied Churchill, adding that 'the cold persisted and the temperature developed. So in view of past experiences, which you perhaps remember, I asked Lord Moran and my wife to come out. But this does imply anything serious. I am normal again and hope to be about soon.'[55] The courtesy on a personal level continued throughout 1948. The Attlees sent a telegram of congratulations when Mary Soames had her first child Nicholas, the future Conservative MP. The Churchills reciprocated in August 1948 when the Attlees became grandparents for the first time, after their eldest daughter Janet had given birth to a girl. The previous November, shortly before the royal wedding, Janet had married electronic engineer Harold Shipton, with Clementine Churchill, along with Mary and Sarah but not Winston, attending the church ceremony followed by 'an austerity reception' at Chequers in Buckinghamshire.[56]

In another legacy of their bond forged in wartime, both Attlee and Churchill spoke at a special dinner on 12 April 1948 held at the Savoy in honour of Eleanor Roosevelt, after the unveiling of the statute of her late husband in Grosvenor Square earlier that day. The war also brought them together the following month, when both men spoke at the ceremony to lay the foundation stone of the new Commons chamber at the Palace of Westminster, the original having been destroyed by a Luftwaffe bombing raid in 1941. Attlee referred to the House, not as a building, but as 'a living fellowship, renewed through centuries'. Those sentiments were echoed by Churchill, who described the Commons as a 'deathless entity which survived unflinchingly the tests and hazards of war'.[57] The fall-out from the conflict was felt in another non-party issue. Churchill was aggrieved to learn in early May 1947 that the highly respected German commander Field Marshall Albert Kesselring had been sentenced to death by a British military tribunal for war crimes perpetrated in the Italian campaign. Churchill told his old wartime friend and colleague Field Marshal Alexander, now Governor General of Canada, that he planned to raise the issue in Parliament, but Attlee privately warned Churchill that he should leave the matter in abeyance for the moment because it was sub judice. Churchill agreed to do so and eventually Kesselring's death sentence was commuted to life imprisonment.*

The reverberations from the war could also be seen in Churchill's continuing drive for a united Europe, Along with his call for a stronger Anglo-American alliance, the quest for deeper European co-operation was one of his chief political priorities in Opposition, partly because he believed that greater unity was the best way to maintain peace, and partly because the cause gave him the kind of international platform of which he had been deprived by the election result. In January 1947, following the success of his Zurich speech, he had formed a new campaign group, the Movement for European Unity. By early 1948, Churchill was more drawn to the goal than ever. Central to his crusade was the forth-coming congress at The Hague in the Netherlands, where a huge cast of European politicians, intellectuals, and campaigners would gather in May to discuss plans for a formal supranational body. With his sense of the dramatic, Churchill saw this event as the chance to promote his vision of unification. In early February, talking to Violet Bonham Carter about his visit to The Hague, he said: 'My aim is to build a United Europe.'[58] Yet there was no unity within British politics. The Labour Government was lukewarm about the European movement, for a host of reasons. One was the suspicion of being too closely associated with an initiative of Churchill's. As Bevin's biographer Alan Bullock wrote, 'to the left, he was still the ogre of the Fulton speech now summoning Europe to unite in an anti-communist crusade led by the USA'.[59] There was also concern about the impact that European integration might

---

* Kesselring was actually released in 1952 on grounds of ill-health. He died in 1960.

have on Britain's relationship with the Commonwealth, which was responsible for more than 40 per cent of the country's trade, compared to Europe's share of 25 per cent.

Labour's coolness towards the project became clear when Churchill wrote to Attlee on 1 February to urge a 'wide measure of political support' for the Congress at The Hague: 'The cause of European unity is one which both have at heart.'[60] But Attlee, spurred on by Bevin, gave a negative response. 'It would be undesirable for the Government to take any official action in regard to this Conference. Any advice to members of the Labour Party as to their participation in the Conference is a matter for the Executive of the Labour Party.'[61] It was a measure of Churchill's determined pursuit of his European policy that he then approached Manny Shinwell, who was now Chair of the Labour Party. Shinwell, another Eurosceptic, was no more enthusiastic, telling Churchill on 10 February that the NEC had decided 'to reaffirm the decision to discourage members of the Labour Party from participating in the proposed Congress. It is felt that the subject of European Unity is too important to be entrusted to unrepresentative interests.'[62] Following this rebuff, Churchill wrote again, more insistently, to Attlee: 'I can only hope that this is not the last word that the British Labour Party and yourself, as its Leader and Prime Minister of Great Britain, have to say upon this issue. Whatever your decision, the International Organising Committee will, I am sure, go forward with the Conference.'[63] To this, Attlee delivered one of his laconically brief replies, merely thanking Churchill for his letter.

The Conference went ahead at The Hague and Churchill was the undoubted star. His speech, delivered on 7 May, was the highlight of the event, which Sir Philip Nichols, the British Ambassador to the Netherlands, described as 'a personal triumph' for Churchill.[64] In an unmistakable echo of his great 'Finest Hour' address on the eve of the Battle of Britain, he said that, if 'we firmly grasp the larger hopes of humanity, then it may be that we shall move the world into a happier, sunlit age'. But those high-minded words were not matched by detailed plans. To the disappointment of arch-federalists, it was not clear what

kind of overarching body he wanted. Even worse, he implied that
Britain might take a semi-detached approach. Cautioning against
'undue precipitancy', he argued that 'We in Britain must move in
harmony with our great partners in the Commonwealth.'[65] Opacity
like that later led the Labour minister Kenneth Younger to describe
Churchill's involvement with the European movement in the late 1940s
as 'one of the great frauds of history'.[66]

A key subject discussed at the Congress was the potential creation of
a European assembly, an idea that Churchill took up with alacrity. On
17 June, he led a delegation to Downing Street from his pressure group,
the Movement for European Unity, to present the case to Attlee and
Bevin. At the meeting, Churchill explained that 'the establishment of
some form of European Assembly' would 'serve to mobilise the forces of
public opinion in all countries of Europe in support of the conception
of European union', though he said he 'did not wish to dogmatise about
the constitution of this assembly'. In response, both Attlee and Bevin
raised a wide range of objections to the plan, using arguments that
were to dominate the debate about Britain's relationship with Europe
over the coming decades. Attlee said that he wanted to ensure that 'the
United Kingdom did not move away from the self-governing countries
of the Commonwealth'. Moreover, he 'would deprecate the creation
of unnecessarily elaborate machinery, or new machinery which would
tend to duplicate the work of existing organisations', while he was also
unsure about the role of 'the proposed Assembly. Would its members
represent the national Parliaments? And was it contemplated that its
resolutions would be binding on the Governments of participating
countries?' If anything, Bevin was even more antagonistic. Attacking
'any reference to the surrender of sovereign rights', he warned that 'such
an Assembly would doubtless advocate free movement between the
countries of Western Europe'.[67]

Despite the Government's scepticism, the idea of an assembly was
brought closer to fruition in July with a proposal from the French
Government for a Council of Europe which would be made up of
representatives of the national Parliaments. Once more Churchill was

enthusiastic. On 27 July he sent Attlee a copy of the French communiqué, along with his own 'tentative' outline for a purely consultative body, without legislative or executive powers. 'The creation of a European Assembly would represent an important, practical step in the advance towards a United Europe [...] In this the lead should be taken by Britain,' he told Attlee.[68] But the Prime Minister and Foreign Secretary remained sceptical. Reflecting his anti-Soviet credentials, Bevin now introduced a new argument. 'We cannot afford to overlook the danger that in the present circumstances communists and fellow-travellers would exploit a European Assembly.'[69] Attlee set out some of these points on 28 July at another Downing Street meeting with Churchill, following this up with a further letter on 30 July. 'This is not the right time for Governments to take this major initiative, when their hands are so full already with urgent and difficult problems,' he wrote.[70] Churchill was annoyed at this 'dusty answer' but delayed a reply because Attlee was on holiday in Ireland.[71] During the subsequent weeks, as the French Government pressed ahead with its scheme, Churchill grew more impatient. On 19 August, he rang Downing Street, while Attlee was still away, to warn that he might be compelled to publish the recent correspondence about the assembly if the Prime Minister remained hostile. Two days later he wrote to Attlee, now back in London, to say that he was 'naturally disappointed' at the 'negative character' of Attlee's last letter. 'I thought it wise to delay its publication until you had returned from your well-deserved holiday in the hopes that events in Europe might win a more favourable reply.' Referring to the France's 'practical form of action', Churchill ventured 'to hope that His Majesty's Government will find it possible to place themselves more in line with Western European opinion'.[72] When Bevin was shown Churchill's letter and phone message, he was defiant. 'I see no reason to yield to this somewhat bare-faced pressure,' he told Attlee. But with the cunning that had served him so well, Bevin suggested that Attlee should write a further letter to Churchill, which would emphasise the need to liaise fully with the Commonwealth before making any commitment. 'This is a line which will appeal to many Conservatives and may therefore embarrass Churchill's efforts to make trouble for us.'[73] That was exactly the position Attlee took when he wrote back to Churchill on 21 August, claiming that his Government would have to speak to the Commonwealth Prime Ministers 'before expressing any definite view'. He added that he had no objection to the release of their correspondence.[74] Sensing Attlee's indifference, Churchill decided not to publish. In private, however, he was scathing about Labour's European policy. 'Conceit, jealousy, and stupidity are all apparent in the behaviour of Bevin and other Socialist leaders concerned,' he wrote to Eden in early September.[75]

Labour maintained its unfavourable stance as the plans for the Council advanced during the autumn of 1948. In an attempt to resolve the deadlock over the issue of representation, the proponents of the assembly set up an international committee, but this only led to more wrangling. On 4 November Churchill wrote to Attlee, 'Since this body is in the nature of an independent commission, I presume it will be composed of persons drawn from public life, and that the main political parties will be represented. If this is the case, I should be glad to be consulted about the choice of suitable members of the Conservative Party.'[76] Once again, Attlee rebuffed him. Because the committee was 'to be responsible to Governments', he wrote to Churchill on 6 November, 'it is not our intention to ensure that the British members of the committee should represent the main political parties and the question raised in your letter does not therefore arise'.[77] Five days later, Churchill wrote back in a vexed tone, telling Attlee that his letter 'will exercise a depressing effect on the movement for European unity'. It would be 'a great pity' if the Government clung to a 'narrow and partisan view' that treated 'this great cause as a monopoly of the British Socialist Party'.[78] Attlee was dismissive of Churchill's argument, pointing out that the representatives were answerable to their national governments, not Parliament. But he also assured Churchill that his Government would send a British delegation which 'will be able to assist the Committee in making an effective and realistic study of this complex question'.[79] Through long negotiations during the winter, a compromise was finally reached at the end of January 1949 whereby the members of the new assembly would be appointed in accordance with their own Government's procedures. The way was now open for the formal creation of the Council of Europe, which was inaugurated in May 1949.

The debate about Europe's future took place against the backdrop of growing international tension because of the Soviet aggrandisement, epitomised by the Communist takeover of the Czechoslovakian Government in February 1948 and the Russian blockade of Western-occupied Berlin that began in June. Attlee, as a strong Atlanticist, had no doubts about the need for a strong Western response. That outlook was reflected not only in his backing for the creation of NATO and the organisation of the Berlin Airlift, but also in his determination to crack down on pro-Soviet subversion at home. In this spirit, he set up a Committee on Subversive Activities in 1947 and the following year introduced political vetting for civil servants. In a speech at Plymouth on May Day 1948 he set out his opposition to communism at home and abroad. 'Totalitarianism and the denial of freedom and human rights are no part of the socialist creed [...] Everywhere they are strong enough, the Communists have sought to destroy democracy.'[80] Churchill felt moved to write to Attlee, 'I cannot refrain from telling you how much I admired the courage of your May Day speech. I have a feeling that the next months are especially dangerous.'[81]

Churchill was not so pleased, however, with aspects of the Government's imperial policy in 1948. He bitterly attacked Attlee in the Commons over Labour's attitude towards unrest in the state of Hyderabad, where the Muslim princely ruler sought to maintain independence from India despite a Hindu majority and severe pressure from the New Delhi Government, exerted through economic sanctions. Churchill took up the cause of Hyderabad in July, arguing that Britain had a duty of protection, but Attlee, always disdainful of Churchill's views about the Indian subcontinent, reacted angrily. In the Commons, he pointed out that the Indian Government had asked Hyderabad to hold a plebiscite to ascertain the views of the population. He also argued that Churchill's rhetoric was only inflaming the problems: 'It is unfortunate that on the occasions when Mr Churchill speaks on this matter he does not seem to me to say anything at all to reconcile the conflicting parties in India.'[82] It was another duel on India won by the Prime Minister. 'What will the wits do now who have called Mr Attlee "a sheep in sheep's clothing"?' asked the *Manchester Guardian*.[83] To Anthony Eden, Churchill privately seethed that 'Attlee's contradictions are provably untrue' and that Hyderabad 'is now to be destroyed by the violent measures of the Government of India'.[84] He turned out to be correct. Hyderabad was forcibly annexed by India after a military invasion in September 1948.

Churchill also received short shrift from Attlee when he criticised Labour over another former part of the Empire, this one much closer to home. In the autumn of 1948 the Government of Eire declared its intention to leave the Commonwealth and become a fully-fledged republic, a development accepted by Attlee. Churchill, who had been one of the architects of the Irish Free State as a key negotiator of the Anglo-Irish Treaty in 1921, warned the House on 25 November that the Irish Republic would have 'the advantages of a new association with Britain but without obligations towards us'. He also predicted, with some prescience, that 'a ditch has been dug between Northern and Southern Ireland which invests partition with greater permanency and reality than it ever had before'.[85] All this provoked one of Attlee's schoolmastery rebukes; Churchill, he argued, should have shown 'better grace' or at least offered an alternative policy. To Labour cheers, Attlee said, 'I was rather sorry he seemed to condemn the Government's attitude without suggesting what he would have done.'[86]

Throughout 1948, Churchill kept up his attacks on socialist management at home. In addition to the usual targets such as nationalisation and excessive bureaucracy, he even criticised Labour's approach to healthcare under Nye Bevan. The handling of plans for the new NHS, he argued in a speech in April, 'had plunged health policy into its present confusion' where 'party and personal malignancy prevailed'.[87] Yet for all Churchill's bombast, Labour staged something of a recovery at this time, helped by the popularity of the NHS after its launch in July, as well as the economic impact of Cripps at the Treasury. The emphasis on the export drive began to produce results. The balance of payments deficit was wiped out in the second half of the year. Full employment was achieved, industry revived. On the political front, the party held on to every single seat at by-elections throughout 1948, including an easy win for Roy Jenkins, Attlee's first biographer, at Southwark Central in April. The Labour MP Ernest Thurtle, who had served as the junior Information Minister in Churchill's wartime Coalition, reflected on the wonder of Attlee's 'unchallenged' position at this time: 'He is still firmly in the saddle, with no rival even in sight. In the language of the Turf, never has an outsider landed long odds so effectively.'[88]

TWENTY-SEVEN

WOODFORD AND WALTHAMSTOW

THE AIR WAS thick with cigar smoke, the company distinguished. It was a summer evening in mid-July 1948 at a private room in Claridge's Hotel and, following an opulent dinner, the men had been left by the ladies to their port and political discussion. Among those present were the wealthy newspaper proprietor Gomer Kemsley[*] and the Tory MP Chips Channon. But it was another guest, Winston Churchill, who held the group in his thrall. In his diary, Channon recorded the impact of Churchill's scintillating conversation. 'The great man needed no prompting: he was gay, he was grave, he was witty, he was provocative and in the highest spirits, but he admitted, indeed insisted, that never before in our history had the position of England been so precarious. When asked by Gomer if he did not admire Attlee, he replied, "Anyone can respect him, certainly, but admire – no!"'[1]

Respect rather than admiration was always the hallmark of Churchill's attitude to his Labour rival. Yet, as Prime Minister, Attlee did attract wide praise for his leadership of the country through a period of extreme political difficulty. He had enacted a large part of Labour's radical programme, laying the foundations of a new progressive welfare

---

[*] Gomer Berry, 1st Viscount Kemsley. The *Sunday Times* and *Daily Sketch* were among the papers he owned.

settlement that were to last decades. He had held together a Cabinet of large but conflicting personalities. He had successfully guided Britain through international turbulence and the beginnings of the withdrawal from Empire. He had enhanced his party's prestige by his dignity in office. He had even regularly bested Churchill in the Commons, something that would have seemed unthinkable before 1945. Instead of being overwhelmed by the premiership, he had grown into it. Douglas Jay, who was one of Attlee's aides in 1945 and soon became a Labour minister after winning a by-election, later wrote that he had initially feared Attlee 'might not be able to do the job of PM'. But Jay left Downing Street in July 1946 convinced that Attlee 'was fully in command of the job and more likely than anyone else to steer the Government through four or five years of crises'.[2] The maverick Labour MP Woodrow Wyatt later judged that Attlee 'was a very good Prime Minister and for peacetime purposes greater than Churchill'.[3] Attlee's last private secretary, Sir David Hunt, gave the same verdict: 'What on earth would we have got into if we had had Churchill from 1945 onwards, I cannot bear to think. His talents were not suited to post-war reconstruction. Clement Attlee was exactly the man of the hour. He was conciliatory and sensible, but he gave great moral leadership. He was so transparently honest.'[4]

Attlee had little of Churchill's grandeur or magnetism. He could not captivate a gathering the way Churchill did. He was too reserved to generate or relish attention. Soon after he became Prime Minister in 1945, he told a group of his junior ministers, 'If I pass you in the corridor and don't acknowledge you, remember it is only because I am shy.'[5] Indeed, Arthur Moyle, his parliamentary private secretary between 1946 and 1955, once said that in his dislike of ostentation, 'he was the exact opposite of his great political colleague and opponent Winston Churchill'.[6] Jock Colville, who worked for both men, felt that Attlee was 'perhaps the first PM ever to have lacked either conceit or vanity. Churchill wasn't vain but he was certainly conceited.'[7]

Attlee brought other qualities to office, including the swiftness of his decision-making, and the orderliness of his methods. A very fast reader, he could regularly dispose of 90 per cent of his paperwork in a day. 'What struck me most I think – and what struck all of us – was the speed and crispness with which he did his job,' said Jay in a BBC interview, adding that, unlike Churchill, he 'wrote very little on paper'.[8] Sir David Hunt was equally impressed by Attlee's methods. 'He handled everything decisively and rather quickly. He was a great believer in the Duke of Wellington's dictum, "Do the day's work in the day."'[9] Arthur Moyle recalled that Attlee hated 'long-winded memoranda' and saw unpunctuality as 'an unforgiveable crime'; whereas Churchill was a notoriously poor time-keeper. As Colville put it, Churchill could sometimes be found 'in bed, correcting a speech, when he ought to have been on the Front Bench preparing to deliver it'.[10] But Moyle found that the Labour Leader, for all his self-discipline, was 'easy to work with, always ready to listen, co-operative and considerate. He showed himself to be a simple man, yet tough and resolute. He assimilated success and failure with equanimity. His own rise to fame was in his view purely fortuitous; there was always something of the fatalist about him.'[11]

Attlee's personal efficiency was also demonstrated by his confident, sharp chairmanship of meetings, where he usually tried to limit contributions, especially from himself. Loquacity for its own sake never impressed him, nor did ministers reading from their briefs. He could be harsh on any ministers or civil servants who had not mastered their subjects. Unlike Churchill, he regarded the Cabinet and most committees as forums for decision rather than arenas for debate. 'Democracy means government by discussion, but it is only effective if you can stop people talking,' Attlee said in retirement.[12] Tony Benn, one of the longest-serving MPs in post-war politics, thought Attlee was 'a brilliant chairman. I remember Dingle Foot* telling me that, when he went to the Cabinet during the war and Winston was there, he would have to listen to a half-hour historical account about the development of Western civilisation. And Dingle said, 'I'd leave the Cabinet without

---

* Brother of Michael Foot. He was a Liberal, then Labour MP, becoming Solicitor General in Harold Wilson's first Government. He also served in Churchill's wartime Coalition as a junior Minister for Economic Warfare.

knowing what the hell I had to do.' When Clem was in the chair, 'I'd come in and Clem would say, "Minister, what is your proposal? Right, everyone agreed." I left the room knowing exactly what I had to do. That was the difference between Attlee the chairman and Churchill the great world figure.'[13]

At times, Attlee's methods could appear to be infused with coldness. Although quick with his reprimands, he rarely dished out praise to his colleagues. Similarly, he was unsentimental about removing ministers who he thought were failing the Government, as he showed when he sacked John Wilmot as Minister of Supply in October 1947. 'Don't think you measure up to the job,' Attlee told him abruptly.[14] Harold Wilson thought he was 'the best butcher since the war'.[15] His Downing Street press officer Francis Williams wrote that Attlee's integrity was 'matched by his remarkable self-sufficiency'. His dislike of the trappings of power 'did not reflect any inner doubts about himself', wrote Williams.[16] The Labour Minister of State at the Foreign Office Kenneth Younger wrote in 1950 that 'Attlee certainly has an authority which would surprise outside observers. He is a very good co-ordinator and executive, and his detachment from personal relationships makes him formidable within his well-recognised limitations.'[17] Yet it would be wrong to exaggerate his effectiveness. Although he was far more orderly than Churchill, one of Attlee's serious failings was his excessive faith in the machinery of the state. Too often during his Government, the perceived answer to any problem was to set up a new committee, a new public body, which only gave the illusion of progress while introducing more bureaucratic paralysis. During his six years in office, there were no fewer than 148 standing committees and 313 ad hoc committees, lending some substance to Churchill's attacks about the dead hand of socialist planning. Indeed, the historian Corelli Barnett described this approach as 'a case of administrative elephantiasis never to be surpassed'.[18]

Furthermore, his self-containment did not make him easy company for anyone outside his family or inner circle. He was a notoriously awkward conversationalist, often creating long silences and giving an impression of aloofness. The Labour politician Wilfred Fienburgh once said that talking to Attlee was 'like throwing biscuits to a dog – all you could get out of him was yup, yup, yup'. [19] So stilted were his audiences with King George VI that both Downing Street and the Palace had to prepare speaking notes in advance for each of them. 'He was the most terse man I have ever met, sometimes embarrassingly so,' wrote the Labour MP George Strauss. Interestingly, despite all his gifts for stimulating table and political conversation when the mood took him, Churchill could also be poor at small talk, partly because his egocentricity and enfoldment in his work made it hard for him to feign empathy, partly because his declamatory style was more suited to an audience than a single person. 'He had no love of social dinner conversation,' recalled the Australian Prime Minister Sir Robert Menzies. [20] Even one of his closest friends, F. E. Smith, wrote that he could appear 'reserved or rude' because he 'contrives to give the impression to those who know him little that he does not desire to know them more'. [21]

Despite the absence of casual sociability, Attlee 'enjoyed being Prime Minister', according to his PPS Arthur Moyle. 'He never complained about his work and no matter how heavy his duties, he would not admit fatigue.' [22] Attlee's sense of perspective helped him cope with the pressures of office. He was rarely plagued by anxiety or stress. The post-war minister John Strachey had this telling illustration of that trait: 'Once in the Commons tea room, when the political situation was bleak, one MP remarked to Clem, "Well, Clem, you are looking particularly well today." Attlee replied, "Yes, I do feel extremely well. You see, I've got no worries." And he really meant it.' [23] The rising Labour star Hugh Gaitskell felt that Attlee's ability to relax was one of the keys to lightening his burden. 'The Prime Minister is perhaps so successful because he is content to let others do the work. I noticed that he was at Lords on Saturday morning and Wimbledon on Saturday afternoon, and went down to Chequers for the weekend,' recorded Gaitskell at the end of June 1949 during another financial crisis. [24] In fact Attlee admitted to Francis Williams that he found the premiership easier to handle than his previous senior jobs in politics because of his domestic arrangements: 'Great advantage of living on the job. Means you can see your family. And with luck you can get a bit of time off at the weekends.'[25]

Attlee's daily routine as Prime Minister could hardly have been more different from Churchill's. There was no lying in bed in the morning, no afternoon siestas, no alcohol-fuelled late nights. He was as methodical in his lifestyle as he was in his paperwork. He generally rose at 7.30 a.m. and then swiftly prepared for the day ahead. 'In all he did, he personified economy. He would bathe, shave, dress and present himself for breakfast in 20 minutes,' recalled Arthur Moyle.[26] Never much interested in the press, he glanced through the *Daily Herald* and *The Times*, looking at the latter mainly for the cricket or football scores, as well as the 'Births, Deaths and Marriages' column. If the weather was fine, he and Violet, accompanied by their black-and-tan Welsh terrier Ting and a personal detective, took a walk after breakfast in St James's Park, before Attlee settled down to work in the Cabinet room from 9.45 a.m. He had lunch at one o'clock, which could be a public engagement or a private meal with Violet in their flat at the top of Downing Street. After more work on his papers, an appearance in the House or more meetings, he had tea with Violet at 4.30 if possible, followed by another two-hour work session from 5 p.m.. After dinner, he would return to the Cabinet room at around 9.30 p.m. for a final hour. Unless there was a crisis, he retired to bed before midnight, rounding off the day with some light reading. 'Detective fiction, biography and travel tend to overwhelm the poets,' commented his contemporary biographer Vince Broome in 1949.[27] Helped by his restrained lifestyle, Attlee retained his lean figure throughout his premiership. At five feet five inches in height, Attlee was just an inch shorter than Churchill, but was much less heavy. Indeed, the Labour Leader's physique was in tune with his Government's austerity programme in the post-war era. 'He must be lightest man who has ever been Prime Minister. Yet he is extraordinarily strong and wiry. He plays golf well and he can keep his end up on the tennis court,' commented the Labour MP Evan Durbin.*[28]

At the centre of Attlee's domestic life was his devoted, but highly strung wife Violet, whose loyalty to her husband could sometimes translate into testiness towards Downing Street staff and Labour colleagues. Although she had no background in politics, she shared some of her husband's characteristics. 'She speaks in short sentences. Her whole approach to life is matter of fact. She is a little shy, particularly about public speaking, but entirely unaffected,' read an *Evening Standard* profile in July 1947.[29] Her dislike of the limelight meant that she was initially apprehensive about entering Downing Street. 'The last thing I wanted to be was the Prime Minister's wife,' she once said.[30] But she soon found that life at the top was much more comfortable than she had expected, aided by her husband's much bigger income and the support of staff at Downing Street and Chequers. Her contentment was revealed in a conversation with Violet Bonham Carter during a dinner at the French Embassy in 1946: 'When I asked her whether she wasn't very busy and hard-worked, she replied disarmingly, "Oh no, it's such a rest. I've put on a stone in weight. I've got so little to do. I have a secretary and a cook who does all the shopping."'[31] Violet was determined to transfer the homely atmosphere she had created in Heywood to Downing Street, and she did so by creating an eight-bedroom flat out of the top floor, whereas Winston and Clementine had used the great state rooms in the building. But Clementine seemed impressed with the redecoration, as Violet reported to her husband in 1946: 'Clemmie came to tea with me and I showed her the flat. She liked it very much.'[32] Violet's life was also made easier by the fact that most of her children had grown up by 1947. Alison, the youngest, was still at school, but Janet was now married and working as a psychologist in Bristol, Martin was in the Merchant Navy, and Felicity was a nursery-school teacher.

---

* Durbin, who was often tipped as a future Labour Prime Minister, tragically drowned off the Cornish coast in September 1948.

Violet once said, 'I know I'm no good to Clem as a PM's wife. I'm quite apolitical,'[33] but in reality she provided him with something far more valuable than political advice: the assurance of domestic security and unconditional love. In the words of Francis Williams, it was 'a great advantage' that she had 'no interest in politics. She surrounded him with affection and loyalty.'[34] Hugh Gaitskell also thought that she was a good consort for Attlee. Although he 'suspected her of being a bit of a snob', Gaitskell felt that 'she does her stuff as the PM's wife well and is an extremely pleasant, rather ordinary, middle-class woman'.[35] But her ferocious loyalty, combined with her health problems and her sometimes prickly, insecure nature, could make her difficult, especially for Downing Street staff. Sir David Hunt recalled that his predecessor, Laurie Pumphrey, was full of stories about 'how ghastly Mrs Attlee was' and she 'did not mind offending him a bit'. Hunt also found that she had 'a bad temper' which meant he had 'some terrible struggles' with her, especially over Hunt's demands on her husband. 'She felt I was not looking after him properly but she liked finding fault anyway.'[36]

Clementine, a Liberal by instinct all her life, was always much more political than Violet. With her mixture of charm and steeliness, she openly worked on his behalf during some of the crucial moments in his career, as in the aftermath of the Dardanelles, when he was in the trenches and she became his representative in London. 'She has made my life and work possible,' he once said.[37] Churchill's devotion to her was genuine, reflected in the long love letters he wrote to her whenever they were parted. Churchill's valet, Norman McGowan, recalled of their relationship: 'Sometimes I felt that it could be described as that between a mother and a small child, sometimes the almost telepathic understanding which one finds very occasionally between brother and sister. It was certainly more than the usual accepted companionship of a long married couple.'[38] Like Violet, Clementine could be fiercely loyal to her husband. On one occasion, Field Marshal Montgomery was playing croquet with her on the lawn at Chartwell when he casually observed that all politicians are dishonest. Clementine asked him to leave the house at once and only relented after he profusely apologised. Again, like Violet, Clementine did not relish public life. Although she became an accomplished speaker, she too could be nervy and quick-tempered, while she also suffered a severe bout of ill-health in the 1930s when she was gripped by depression. Some of her relatives thought she could be neurotic. 'Auntie Clementine was always going to bed instead of coming to lunch,' said her niece Clarissa, who married Anthony Eden.[39] In addition, her strong sense of morality and exacting standards made her a perfectionist, not easy to please. 'My mother always seemed calm and serene but she was a bomb waiting to go off,' said her daughter Mary.[40]

For all her loyalty, Clementine could find her husband exasperating at times. After the war, she continually yearned for him to retire so that she could have a more peaceful existence rather than remaining attached 'to the splendours and miseries of a meteor's train', in her daughter Mary's vivid phrase.[41] But there was no chance of that. All his adult life, politics had been his driving force; influence and office gave him his purpose. Since 1945 he had the additional incentive of seeking to reverse the humiliation of his defeat by Attlee. The quest for vindication explains why he wanted to press on with his war memoirs in the late 1940s, even though he was still Tory Leader. Because another General Election had to be held by July 1950 at the latest, he felt that he had to finish the bulk of them before that deadline, after which he hoped to be Prime Minister again.

But the mammoth task of completing the work meant that he was badly diverted from the party leadership. This distraction was compounded by his boredom with Opposition. What he wanted was to regain the premiership, not indulge in the details of policy-making or parliamentary management. As he focused on his literary endeavours, he left these duties largely to his colleagues, especially Anthony Eden, Rab Butler and Lord Woolton. Occasional grandiloquent Commons or platform speeches were the essence of his contribution in the late 1940s. Even Clementine became annoyed, thinking that if he was going to retain the job of Opposition Leader, he should do it properly. 'I have felt chilled and discouraged by the deepening knowledge that you only do just as much as will keep you in power,' she complained.[42] Clementine's words mirrored the feeling among many Tory backbenchers and activists, especially when opinion polls indicated that the party would perform better under Eden. In his diary for 7 March, Headlam wrote, 'It is not really surprising for Winston is a poor leader of a party – principally because he is so egotistical. A man cannot hope to be a successful leader (however great and grand an individual he may be) unless he concentrates entirely upon the job.'[43]

The disillusion reached such a level that the Shadow Cabinet made another attempt to persuade Churchill to leave, this time through Lord Halifax, who had returned to England in 1946 after retiring as British Ambassador to the USA. Halifax later gave Malcolm MacDonald an account of his mission, conducted over lunch. 'Halifax mentioned frankly some of Winston's growing faults as a chief, and commented with charming candour, "Winston, you are not doing yourself any good, you're not doing the party any good, and you're not doing the nation any good."' According to the tale that Halifax gave MacDonald, 'Churchill listened with kindly patience throughout this discourse. When he finished speaking the old man picked a cigar from his mouth, blew a quivering ring of smoke into the air and observed with a grin, "My dear Edward, you can tell our colleagues that one of the unalterable rules of my life is never to leave the pub until closing time."'[44]

If they could not change the Leader, many Conservatives felt they at least would have to change the party's strategy. Shaken by the 1945 landslide and continuing by-election defeats, they urged a new approach that would seize the imagination of the electorate and mark a break with the past. Churchill's acolyte Brendan Bracken was dismissive of this demand, as he told Beaverbrook in March 1949.

> Some of the more chicken-livered Tories are now in a state of great nervous excitement. They declare that we must have a policy to defeat the Socialists. It will be very difficult for the Tories to scratch up the sort of policy they want. Attlee and company have hit on a very good vote – getting policy which is

to bear gifts to the public. And as long as the Yanks continue to finance dollar socialism, I see no reason why Mr Attlee should not do quite well.[45]

Nevertheless, despite Bracken's cynicism and Churchill's semi-detachment, major internal reforms were undertaken during the post-war years of Opposition. Under the chairmanship of the dynamic Lord Woolton, the Conservative organisation was revitalised and modernised. Stronger management, media training, regional press operations and sophisticated polling were all introduced. Fundraising appeals and recruitment drives proved astonishingly successful, with membership rising by 1 million in 1948 alone. The inflow of cash meant that the party could expand its Central Office staff, as well as employ more agents.

Another important step taken towards widening the party's appeal was made through the development of a formal alliance with the Liberal Nationals, the influential group which had broken away from the Liberal Party in the 1930s. The pact was brokered in May 1947 by Woolton and the Liberal National Chairman Lord Teviot, who had been a pro-appeasement Scottish MP[*] and Government whip before his elevation to the peerage. The Woolton-Teviot accord was to play a useful part in the Tories' electoral revival, but it did not represent the broad, anti-socialist front after which Churchill still hankered. He therefore tried to reach an electoral deal with the mainstream Liberals, now led by Clement Davies, who had succeeded Sir Archibald Sinclair in 1945. Davies, however, was determined to protect the Liberals' independence and rejected these overtures as 'unworthy subterfuge', a stance that Churchill saw as 'vote-splitting on a fantastic scale'.[46]

Throughout the years of Opposition, Churchill came under pressure to revise his party's policies as well as its organisation. He was not enthusiastic about immersing himself in such an exercise, partly

---

[*] There is some evidence that in the 1930s he was involved with the notorious pro-fascist, anti-Semitic Right Club set up by the Tory MP Captain Archibald Ramsay, who lived in Teviot's constituency of Montrose Burghs.

because domestic affairs tended to fatigue him. In addition, as an anti-socialist, Churchill was wary of a slide to the left which would involve ever greater public ownership and taxation. Defending himself in front of the backbench 1922 Committee in March 1949, he argued that the Tories should 'not try to outbid the Labour Party by offering a programme of more extensive reform'.[47] But his caution did not prevent Rab Butler, who was in charge of policy development, from producing in the late 1940s a new, centrist programme that embraced key elements of Attlee's settlement, including the mixed economy, workers' rights, the drive towards equality and the welfare state.

The emphasis on policy was driven by the approach of the General Election, which added to the political, though not personal, distance between the two party leaders. That was highlighted in the long municipal saga over the decision by Leeds Council to offer the freedom of the city jointly to Churchill and Attlee. The award had first been made in March 1948, and Attlee had expressed his pleasure. 'I would be very glad and honoured to receive the freedom of Leeds together with Mr Churchill,' he told the press.[48] But throughout the year, Churchill delayed any commitment to the ceremony by pleading the weight of other engagements. By the beginning of 1949, the City Council grew so exasperated at Churchill's reluctance to fix a date that its leader, Alderman Charles Jenkinson, enlisted the help of Lord Swinton, the Yorkshire Tory grandee and wartime colleague of Churchill's. Jenkinson's letter to Swinton highlighted the widespread perception that Attlee, despite almost four years as Prime Minister, remained in Churchill's shadow. 'Mr Attlee has expressed his willingness to meet at Mr Churchill's convenience and, as none of us are under any illusion as to who – and rightly – will be the "lion" of the occasion, to get Mr Churchill to name a date is the only way to make progress,' the Alderman told Swinton, who duly wrote to Churchill urging him to come to Yorkshire.[49] In reply, Churchill still refused, now on the new grounds of political awkwardness in addition to his heavy diary. 'Although I am personally quite friendly with the Prime Minster, I do not think it would be very timely for me to appear on the same platform with him. It might well give rise to rumours of an impending Coalition.'[50] Ever more desperate, the City Council then suggested that the ceremony could be held in London, but this had no effect on Churchill's resistance. 'I have a high personal regard for Mr Attlee. He is a valued colleague of the late war and our personal friendship has been preserved. Nevertheless, I think it might give rise to all kinds of political speculation if we were both to attend a joint ceremony of this kind, either in Leeds or London and I do not think such a course advisable at the present time,' he told the Town Clerk at the end of February.[51]

Beyond the Leeds affair, Attlee and Churchill had several exchanges in the first half of 1949, most notably over defence. In February both made BBC broadcasts on behalf of the National Recruiting Campaign to stimulate applications to the regular armed forces. On 2 March Churchill led a Tory delegation to see Attlee at the Commons, where they discussed national service, the Soviet threat and the creation of NATO, which was to come into existence in April. Soon afterwards, Attlee sent Churchill a copy of the draft terms of the treaty, for which Churchill expressed his full support in the Commons. In early May, Churchill sent Attlee a lengthy memorandum about 'the state of our armed forces', in which he raised a wide range of concerns, including: the dissipation of 'an immense mass of munitions in rifles', possibly as many as three million; the disappearance of 'artillery of all kinds'; and 'disappointing figures' on the 'latest forms of jet fighters and fast bombers'.[52] At the end of the month, in another display of his anxiety, Churchill sent Attlee a second memorandum, which spoke of 'lack of "operational preparedness"'.[53] Displaying his co-operative spirit over defence once more, Attlee agreed to meet another senior Tory delegation. At the meeting, held on 13 July, Churchill once more raised his worries about Britain's defence capacity but was not entirely reassured by Attlee. He therefore sent the Prime Minister another missive afterwards, this one emphasising the weakness of Britain's air force and the misallocation of military expenditure. 'We are spending something like ten times as much on the air force as before the war, yet we have fewer fighting aircraft than in 1939,' he wrote.[54]

Apart from defence, Churchill contacted Attlee about a more sensitive issue in the spring of 1949. He was disturbed by a newspaper report that Princess Margaret, then eighteen, was to holiday in Italy for six weeks, but, under the Government's strict foreign exchange controls, would only be allowed a £30 currency allowance, the same as for an ordinary British tourist. 'I cannot think that it is desirable that the King's daughter should be forced, as would be inevitable in these circumstances, to be dependent upon private hospitality or favours from hotel-keepers and others,' Churchill protested to Attlee on 24 April, warning that he planned to raise the matter in the Commons.[55] Attlee passed this letter on to the King's private secretary Tommy Lascelles, who phoned up Churchill's office to say that 'a lot of money has been granted by the Treasury which has been absolutely ideal in these delicate negotiations'.[56] Following up this message two days later, Attlee took a slightly reproving tone with Churchill. 'I am a little surprised that you have relied on newspaper reports about this, but I can assure you the facts are not as you feared.'[57] Churchill replied that this response 'ends my anxieties on the subject'.[58]

In the same month, Attlee thanked Churchill for sending him the second volume of his war memoirs. 'I had some time at Chequers during the weekend to read a good deal of it,' he wrote on 19 April.[59] But this private cordiality contrasted with growing asperity in politics during the summer, fired by the pre-election atmosphere, Conservative policy-making and another financial crisis. The mood of friction was encapsulated by Churchill's long-standing foe Nye Bevan, who opened Labour's Annual Conference at Blackpool in June with a blood-curdling speech that predicted civil war if the Conservatives were returned to power. Describing this threat as 'naked and brutal', Churchill called on Attlee to repudiate Bevan.[60] The Labour Leader did nothing of the sort. Instead, in his Conference speech he paid a generous tribute to Bevan for his constructive work on housing and the NHS despite 'tremendous attacks'. In contrast, he said, Churchill's attempts to undermine Labour had ended only in 'complete fiasco'. Attlee was in a confident mood as he extolled Labour's achievements in office since 1945 and looked forward to the electoral battle ahead. 'A great movement inspired by ideals can make a new society,' he declared to loud applause.[61]

At its Conference, Attlee's party overwhelmingly agreed a new policy document *Labour Believes in Britain*, which outlined the next stages of public ownership, industrial intervention and welfare assistance. The Conservatives soon responded with their own major policy pamphlet called 'The Right Road for Britain', with the foreword written by Churchill. But his involvement brought a withering response from Attlee. In a speech at the Durham Miners' Gala on 23 July, Attlee said, 'The strength of Mr Churchill's language is in inverse ratio to his knowledge of the subject. The fact is that there was never so incoherent an opposition as the Conservative Party today. It is unfortunate that Churchill's words are taken at their face value in other countries. They don't realise it is just Winnie's way.'[62]

On the same day, Churchill spoke at a large rally in Wolverhampton, to where he had flown, with characteristic indifference to expenditure, from Biggin Hill airport near Chartwell. Stung by the Labour Party's boasts of its claim to be the unique champions of social progress, he passionately defended his own record. 'I participated in all the great reforms of the heyday of liberalism 40 years ago.' Interspersed with this personal history was savage criticism of 'socialist spendthrifts and muddlers' of the Labour Government, with their 'ignorant and obsolete party doctrines'.[63] Churchill's speech in the Midlands provoked one of the bitterest political attacks that Attlee ever made on him. At the beginning of August, he travelled with Violet to Poole in Dorset, where he spoke to a large demonstration held by the local Labour club. In contrast to Churchill's expensive private flight to Wolverhampton, the Attlees made the trip in their family saloon, picnicking on the way. But such modesty did not inhibit the Prime Minister's rhetoric. 'Mr Churchill let himself go on in abuse and misrepresentation of the grossest kind,' said Attlee in reference to the Wolverhampton address. Attlee then praised Churchill as a great war leader, which made the next passage all the more deadly.

During these last four years he has had a bad relapse into irresponsibility and party spite. But there is something more. He really knows very little of the facts. There are frequent opportunities in the House of Commons both at Question Time and in debates on the estimates when these vague accusations of squandering and waste can be examined and answered, but Mr Churchill is hardly ever in the House for more than a few minutes each week.

He concluded with the argument that the last General Election had a vital lesson for the forthcoming one. 'In 1945 Mr Churchill underrated the intelligence of the people. I remember telling him so in the course of a correspondence I had with him during that contest and I proved to. be right. He is still making the same mistake. I do not think that people will heed his violent abuse. I do not think that they will be taken in by the smooth words of his programme.'[64]

In fact, Attlee had a strong point about Churchill's reluctant appearances in the House and his regular, lengthy absences abroad, some of them justified by the need for peace to write his war memoirs. In political terms, the highlight of Churchill's sojourn on the Continent in the summer of 1949 was his visit to Strasbourg for the first meeting of the Council of Europe. On the evening of 12 August, he spoke in his underrated French to a vast crowd of 20,000 people gathered in the Place Kléber. Three days later he received the Freedom of the City, proving more co-operative about the acceptance of the award than he had been to Leeds City Council. Then, on 17 August at the European Assembly, he made another of his resounding appeals for unity, as well as calling for West Germany to be admitted to the Council. .

After a spell in the south of France, Churchill returned at the beginning of September to a country in the throes of economic trouble, caused by a renewed drain on reserves and a drop in dollar earnings sparked by a recession in the USA. Gripped by serious illness, Cripps wearily gave in to Cabinet pressure and agreed to a devaluation of 30 per cent, which would entail severe reductions in public expenditure.

As a courtesy, Cripps told Churchill of the decision on 18 September, before announcing it to the public the following day. Churchill now had another opportunity to attack Labour mismanagement. In the Commons debate on devaluation, beginning on 28 September, he launched a wide-ranging assault on the Government's economic policy, which he said 'oppresses every effort and transaction of public life' and had 'gobbled up' every capital reserve. He reserved his strongest criticism, however, for the 'integrity' of Cripps who had promised for months not to devalue but had now 'felt it right to turn completely round, like a squirrel in his cage, abandon his former convictions and do what he repeatedly said he would never do'.[65] Rather than wilting under this bombardment, Labour decided to go on the offensive against Churchill the next day. In his speech that closed the debate, Attlee condemned Churchill for questioning the integrity of Cripps. 'The Leader of the Opposition can be a very big man or a very small man. I am always sorry, as one who has seen him in great and generous mood, when he descends to that kind of pettiness and meanness which he displayed yesterday.'[66]

The policy of devaluation actually worked; the drain on the reserves stopped, the gold and dollar deficit shrank and exports increased. Once the crisis had passed, the biggest question facing Attlee was the date of the General Election, about which there had been intense specu-lation for months. Indeed Churchill, rather opportunistically, blamed some of the Government's economic problems on election uncer-tainties. Addressing a Conservative trade unionists' rally in October, he referred to 'the disturbance' of trade and industry. 'But whose fault is that?' he asked. 'It is the fault of one man, Mr Attlee, who could at any time in the last month have dispersed the rumours that he intended to spring a snap election.'[67] The Cabinet was divided in its opinion, but eventually agreed that the election would be in February, largely on the grounds that Labour badly needed a new mandate. In addition Cripps, always sensitive about his integrity, had insisted that it would be immoral to go to the country soon after a March Budget. On 10 January 1950, Attlee formally announced that polling would take place on 23 February, making it the first contest to be held in winter since the Liberal landslide of 1906.

When Attlee made his formal announcement, Churchill was on another of his foreign trips, painting and writing in Madeira. His mood was captured by one of his visitors, Brendan Bracken, who wrote to Beaverbrook, 'He was in high spirits and seemed to be in remarkable physical health. He ardently hopes to be back in Downing Street at the beginning of the spring. He says that if we lose the election he will promptly retire and spend the rest of his life enjoying himself.'[68] The Conservatives had an electoral mountain to climb, given the scale of Labour's triumph in 1945, since when the Government had not lost a single by-election. Yet there were some grounds for optimism. Labour may have recovered since devaluation, but one Gallup poll at the start of the campaign put the Tories three points ahead, while others showed the fight was finely balanced. Thanks to the work of Woolton and Butler, Churchill's party was much better organised than in 1945 and had a clear set of centrist policies set out in the manifesto, *This is the Road*. 'A cleverly crafted document', was the verdict of the Tory candidate in Dartford Margaret Roberts, who the following year was to marry Denis Thatcher.[69] The Conservatives were also helped by boundary changes which expanded the number of suburban constituencies at the expense of smaller, inner-city seats. The redistribution was potentially thought to cost Labour at least thirty seats, but Attlee, in a sign of his self-sacrificial preference for fairness over partisan interests, agreed to the overhaul because he felt that morally 'it would have been wrong to hold it up'.[70]

Labour was not as well prepared as in the last contest. Exhausted after almost five tumultuous years in office, the party exuded little of the boldness and idealism that had been on display in 1945. That was reflected in the bland manifesto *Let Us Win through Together*, which stressed Labour's plans for further nationalisation, including sugar, chemicals and insurance. Even so, many Labour figures were still confident of a comfortable victory, given the party's current parliamentary ascendancy. 'I am inclined to expect us to come back with a smaller, but still workable majority,' wrote Dalton in his diary for 2 January.[71] Hugh Gaitskell, a shrewder judge than Dalton, was more cautious, confiding in his diary, 'I fear that the Tories will get a lot of the Liberal vote and that this, together with redistribution, will make the contest very even.'[72]

The General Election of February 1950 was the first truly democratic election in British history. Under the 1948 Representation of the People Act, university seats and dual member constituencies were abolished, as were property qualifications which had allowed plural votes for some business owners. In addition, postal and proxy voting for civilians was introduced for the first time. But this progress was not matched by excitement on the campaign trail. The explosiveness that had characterised the 1945 election was largely absent. Churchill himself, in a speech at Wanstead in his own Essex constituency, called the contest 'one of the most well-conducted and demure' he had witnessed.[73] Tory MP Cuthbert Headlam at times found the campaign soporific. When Churchill made his first radio broadcast on 21 January, Headlam recorded that 'I fell asleep before it ended.'[74]

What might have partly accounted for the tameness of the 1950 contest was the reversal of roles between Attlee and Churchill. In 1945, Churchill had been the endlessly controversial, sometimes combustible, star of the Tory campaign. Indeed, the party's entire effort had been built around his personality, whereas Labour had stressed the reliability and strength of their team. But in February 1950, Attlee was the biggest figure in the Labour movement, a successful Prime Minister and a proven vote winner. Of his colleagues, Cripps and Bevin were seriously ill, Morrison's influence was on the wane, Dalton was tainted by his resignation, and Bevan was seen as divisive. The burden therefore fell on Attlee. In contrast, the Conservatives of February 1950 played up their collegiate approach, with Churchill adopting a quieter, less dominant role at the front. That was reflected in his limited campaign schedule, which, unlike his regal progress in 1945, involved just four visits to major cities, in addition to a trip to Plymouth Devonport, where his son Randolph was the Tory candidate, a number of appearances in his

Woodford constituency, and a couple of rallies in Kent near Chartwell. It was a different story with Attlee, who was driven almost 1,300 miles in a Humber Pullman by Violet to events all over the country. On 9 February, he spoke in no fewer than seven towns across the Midlands, including Wolverhampton, Stoke and Derby, while the following day he appeared at Stockport, Manchester, Liverpool, Bolton and Preston. Altogether he made thirty-four speeches on the trail. His and Violet's luggage comprised just one suitcase and a box containing a travel iron, although in another difference to 1945, Attlee's entourage was more extensive because of his role as Prime Minister. Two detectives travelled with him and Violet, and an accompanying official car carried a driver, a private secretary and two female typists, 'in order to enable him to transact essential Government business', as Downing Street put it to Labour's National Agent.[75]

For all its sedateness, the contest was not without its conflict between the two party leaders, both across the airwaves and on the platform. Churchill's opening radio broadcast lambasted 'socialist regimentation' that meant that 'the whole enterprise, contrivance and genius of the British nation is being increasingly paralysed'.[76] In a speech a week later in Woodford, he attacked Labour's pledge of further nationalisation. 'Having made a failure of everything they have so far touched, our socialist planners now feel it necessary to get hold of a few at present prospering industries so as to improve the general picture.'[77] Speaking at West Bromwich during his long tour, Attlee mocked the Tories' claims to liberalisation. 'The Conservative Party talked a great deal about controls and wanted some controls taken off. One thing they would like to keep is control over Mr Churchill. The party had put him on the leash in *The Right Road for Britain* but it was now clear that he had slipped the collar.'[78] The friction between the two leaders intensified after Churchill's most high-profile speech of the campaign. In Edinburgh on 14 February Churchill turned to the subject of the hydrogen bomb, a new American development whose existence had just been announced by Truman. To lessen the danger to mankind from this 'frightful weapon', he said that if he came back to power he would make a new attempt to establish talks with Russia. This was a very different approach to his post-Fulton outlook, full of bristling defiance against the Soviet Union, but Churchill explained that 'the idea appeals to me of a supreme effort to bridge the gulf between the two worlds, so that each can live their lives, if not in friendship, at least without the hatreds of the Cold War'.[79] The *Daily Express* hailed the speech as masterly: 'No other figure in any party is within measurable distance of his stature. The Socialists know it. That is why they have used and are using every cunning trick to discredit him.'[80] But Harold Nicolson, a fair observer, felt that Churchill's approach was wrong and demeaning. 'To suggest talks with Stalin on the highest level inevitably makes people think, "Winston could talk to Stalin on more or less the same level. But if Attlee goes it would be like a mouse addressing a tiger. Therefore vote Winston." No [...] it was a stunt and unworthy of him,' Nicolson told his wife Vita.[81] Attlee made the same criticism, as well as highlighting Churchill's sporadic record of attendance as Opposition Leader. In a speech at Nottingham two days later, Attlee declared that 'Mr Churchill is a great master of words. But it is a terrible thing when a master of words becomes a slave of words. There is nothing behind these words. They are just abuse.' Calls for a summit were actually a handicap to the conduct of British foreign policy, claimed Attlee, 'Mr Churchill is like a cock that crows and thinks that it produced the dawn.'[82]

Churchill gave his second and final radio broadcast of the campaign on 17 February, with a warning that more socialism would leave Britain 'absolutely alone in the civilised world', whereas by 'one more heave of her shoulders' the country 'can shake herself free'.[83] His doctor Lord Moran felt that Churchill's grandiloquence was sounding outdated, and had futilely urged him to pay more attention to the skill of broadcasting. 'I saw he is hardly listening. He isn't going to learn any new techniques.'[84] The following evening, 18 February, Attlee made Churchill one his central themes in his last broadcast of the campaign. Claiming that the Conservative Leader had fallen 'far below the standards which one would expect from a statesman of his distinction', he then dismissed

Churchill's portrait of a miserable Britain held captive by the bonds of socialism. 'Mr Churchill has described this country as "a bureaucracy brooding over a dispirited and broken people". This odd and fanciful picture of our people seems to be confined to disgruntled politicians.'[85] Hugh Gaitskell felt that this powerful address, like the rest of the campaign, showed how Attlee had grown in authority as Prime Minister. 'He certainly displayed his remarkable political instinct and gifts at their very best. He always found the exact words to counter Churchill and it is generally considered that his broadcast was outstanding.'[86]

By one of those coincidences that regularly appear in the saga of Attlee's relationship with Churchill, the Labour Leader now hoped to become the MP for an Essex constituency close to Woodford. Ever since his first involvement in politics, his democratic base had been in the East End of London. But as a result of the redistribution he had agreed in 1948, his Limehouse constituency, with its shrinking population, had been abolished. He was therefore adopted as the Labour candidate in the relatively safe seat of Walthamstow West, which had been held by the party since 1922 and whose boundaries were near Epping Forest. It was to Walthamstow Town Hall, one of the most impressive municipal edifices in Britain, that he and his family went on 24 February to witness the local count. He emerged as the overwhelming victor, with a majority 12,107 against the second-placed Conservative candidate. Nearby, in Woodford, Churchill had an equally convincing win after the setback in 1945 against the idiosyncratic farmer Alexander Hancock. His personal vote went up by over 10,000 and his majority against Labour was a massive 18,499.

During the national campaign, Labour's confidence had increased, partly because of Attlee's growing stature and reports of enthusiastic receptions for his rallies. The final Gallup poll put Labour on 45 per cent, the Conservatives on 43.5 per cent. One prime-ministerial aide, Philip Jordan, said ten days before polling that 'Attlee expects to get back with a majority of 60'.[87] The initial results appeared to be heading in that direction, with Labour piling up the votes in the cities and its industrial heartlands. Herbert Morrison went to bed convinced that

Labour would have a significant majority. But the next day showed a very different pattern, as Conservatives swept through the suburbs and the south of England. 'Our vigil the other night was a case of evening red, morning blue,' Churchill wrote to Lord Salisbury.[88] When all the counts had been completed, Labour has suffered 78 losses, down to 315 MPs, while the Tories had made 90 gains, up to 298 seats. Parliament was now on the verge of hung Parliament territory, with Attlee's party having a majority of just six over all other parties. Despite the narrowness of the victory, there were some grounds for satisfaction among Labour supporters. On a turnout of 84 per cent, the largest in British political history, Labour had secured 13.3 million votes and 46.1 per cent of the popular vote, three points ahead of the Conservatives. The result could be interpreted as a public endorsement of the Attlee Government and a continued mandate for socialism. On the other hand, Labour had been placed in a precarious position, vulnerable to internal rebellions and Opposition ambushes. Various reasons were advanced for the heavy losses: a rebellion against rationing, especially by middle-class, suburban households; the regular economic crises; the doctrinaire focus on nationalisation; and the winter poll. 'If we had waited until May, there would have been a bigger majority,' said Douglas Jay.[89] Attlee himself blamed the redistribution of seats, especially from inner London and several of the big industrial centres. 'We suffered for being too moral on that,' Attlee said wistfully years later.[90]

Despite the recovery that the Tory Party had made since 1945, Churchill's celebrations had to be muted. He had still lost a second consecutive General Election, trailing significantly behind Attlee in terms of votes and seats. But for all his disappointment, there was no chance that he was about to resign as Leader. The margin of defeat had been too small; Labour's hold on power was too weak. As he put it to Tommy Lascelles, 'I think that another General Election in the next few months is inevitable.'[91] The prize of a return to Downing Street was still tantalisingly within his grasp.

TWENTY-EIGHT

EUROPE AND KOREA

D ESPITE HIS PARTY'S heavy election losses, Attlee had no plans to quit soon. His willingness to fight was immediately demonstrated when the new Parliament convened for the debate on the Address. In keeping with his recent contributions on the campaign trail, Churchill made a powerful speech as he highlighted the 'ideological differences' between the ruling socialists who believe in 'controlling all the means of production, distribution and exchange', and their opponents who 'exalt the individual and allow freedom of enterprise'.[1] In response Attlee adopted that satirical tone that had served him so well against Churchill since 1945, teasing the Conservative Leader about his awkward relations with independent Liberals. 'He has been a very ardent lover of this elderly spinster, the Liberal Party. The elder sister, the National Liberals, was married long ago; she is now deceased. This is the younger sister, but she is getting on. I can never make out whether the Right Honourable Member for Woodford is going to play Petruchio or Romeo. He gives a slap in the face, then offers her a bunch of flowers.'[2] Turning to Labour's position, he pledged resolution: 'The duty of the Government is clear. The King's Government must be carried on. Clearly, the functioning of Government in these conditions is not easy, but it should be carried on in the common interest of all.'[3]

The Tories had put down an amendment to the King's Speech, whereby the nationalisation of the steel industry would be delayed until nine months after a further General Election. This amounted to a vote of confidence in the Government, and Attlee warned that, if Labour were defeated in the division, 'his proper course would be to advise the King to send for Mr Churchill'.[4] In the event, the Government won by 310 votes to 296, with Clement Davies's nine-strong band of Liberals refusing to side with the Opposition. But when, at the end of the month, the Government was beaten by 26 votes after an Opposition Adjournment debate about the mishandling of the coal industry, Attlee did not consider resignation. The scene in the Commons following the vote was described by the *Daily Mail*'s political correspondent. 'The Conservatives did not restrain their jubilation. They shouted and waved their order papers in a furious storm. There was an overwhelming demonstration of joy as Mr Churchill stood, before leaving the House.'[5] The euphoria was short-lived. Attlee treated the defeat as a minor matter that had no wider implications. 'It was a vote on an Adjournment, and in those conditions I do not intend to regard that as a Vote of Censure,' he told Churchill across the Dispatch Box.[6]

At the beginning of May, there was a tie on an Opposition motion to reduce the salary of the Minister of Transport, again illustrating the weakness of the Government. The next day at a Spanish Embassy luncheon, Chips Channon saw Churchill, who was shortly to hold a meeting with Attlee about parliamentary business. 'He had obviously enjoyed last night's frolic,' noted Channon. 'As he left, and apologised for leaving, he added, "The Prime Minister wants to see me. I suppose he will suggest a Coalition." There was scorn in his voice as he suggested the words Prime Minister.'[7] It amused Churchill at this time to play up the idea of an accord. Harold Nicolson was talking to him at a French Embassy reception in March when Attlee walked past. 'Well, Attlee, if we have any more parties like this we shall be in a Coalition together without noticing at all,' said Churchill.[8] But the jokes about working together were baseless. Immediately after the election, according to George VI's official biographer John Wheeler Bennett,

> There was some talk of an all-party conference to consider the question of carrying on the King's Government, but the idea

was rejected by both the Prime Minister, who was determined to meet the new House of Commons, and by Mr Churchill, who expressed the view that 'the new House of Commons has a right to live if it can and should not be destroyed until some fresh issue or situation has arisen to place before the electors'.[9]

No new issue had arisen. There was no desperate crisis facing the nation. Labour still had an overall majority and a determined leader. 'The Prime Minister seems to have more sense than almost anybody else. Undoubtedly his position in the Government is stronger than it has ever been,' noted Hugh Gaitskell in his diary.[10] Sir David Hunt, his private secretary in 1950, believed that one of the reasons Attlee remained effective despite Labour's setback was his ability as a parliamentary manager and speaker. 'That is one of the ways in which Attlee has been underestimated as against Churchill. When it comes to rhetoric, to oratory, we all know that there was simply no comparison between Churchill and Attlee. It is often said that Attlee had a reedy voice and he maundered on a bit. But if there was something really important on, he could rise to the heights.' Hunt drew another contrast in the two men's performances in the Commons. 'Winston was at his best in his opening speech, where his brilliant stuff rolled out. But he was nothing like so good at winding up, whereas Attlee was very good. It was half extempore. It was always in a vigorous, you could say ranting style. It heartened the party in that Parliament and sent them cheering into the lobbies.'[11] Attlee himself detected little drop in Labour morale after the election, writing to his brother Tom, 'Our folk are in very good heart.'[12]

Confirmed in office, Attlee's regime remained as methodical and spartan as ever. He and Violet embodied the austerity that they proclaimed as the right policy for the country. A glimpse into their spirit of self-sacrifice can be seen in a note from Downing Street to the Treasury in July 1950 about a prime-ministerial trip that the Attlees made to Dunoon. 'Mrs Attlee is driving and they have dispensed with the official car and driver.'[13] With the same puritanism, they insisted on leaving the windows open in the dining room at Chequers, even on cold days in the spring and autumn, prompting some guests to keep on their coats. A few visitors were also disturbed that pre-prandial drinks at Chequers would often consist of nothing more than half a glass of sherry. Self-discipline meant Violet Attlee started the day with a cold bath, and refused to make any fuss over meals. Her husband 'takes what he is given', she once told an interviewer briskly.[14] Restrained practicality also led to the Attlees' decision in 1949 to sell their large suburban house in Stanmore and buy a modest property called Cherry Cottage for £9,500 in Great Missenden, Buckinghamshire. Given that the Attlees were staying in Downing Street after February 1950, they initially did not use the house themselves but rented it out to a retired colonel.

By the time of the election, all Churchill's worries about money and homes were long in the past. His enormous post-war literary success had made him a wealthy man, with a fortune too large to be significantly dented by his extravagance. In the financial year 1949–50 alone, he earned £80,000, of which he managed to shield all but £5,000 from tax through the use of trusts and capital allocations. One great advantage of losing the election was that he still had the time to complete the final two volumes of his Second World War saga. His income enabled him to keep two well-staffed households at Chartwell and Hyde Park Gate, as well as the finest drink and dishes, such as his cherished 1928 Pol Roger champagne, of which Madame Pol Roger guaranteed him a unique supply. His vast earnings also allowed him to enjoy the ownership of a number of thoroughbred racehorses and to extend the estate at Chartwell; it had 80 acres when he bought it in 1922, but after the Second World War, he added over 400 acres.

As usual with the two men, the intensity of electoral politics had not lessened their mutual civility. Attlee continued to invite Churchill and his wife to attend functions at Downing Street, while both men exchanged telegrams of congratulations on their birthdays. In late April 1950, Churchill sent Attlee a paper about the genealogy of the brotherhood of Trinity House, the venerable body in charge of lighthouses and pilotage in British waters. Churchill had become a Trinity House Elder Brother on his elevation to the Admiralty and was fond of wearing its uniform on any naval-related occasions. Always attracted to traditionalist institutions, Attlee had joined him in the Brotherhood on his entry to the premiership. 'It is an interesting and distinguished list. I see that you have only a year to go to beat the record tenure,' wrote Attlee. In the same letter, he told Churchill that he had just been to an exhibition of his paintings. 'I greatly enjoyed seeing your pictures last night. I particularly admired the snow scene.'[15] On another creative front, Churchill in June sent Attlee a copy of *The Grand Alliance*, the third volume of his war memoirs, which had just been published to favourable reviews. 'I look forward to reading it with much pleasure and it will take its place with its fellows on my shelf dedicated to your works,' replied Attlee.[16] Another literary endeavour brought Churchill and Attlee together in 1950, when the Government was asked to provide an annual sum of £15,000 for twenty years to cover the costs of a major research project into the history of Parliament, an initiative first conceived in the 1930s by the maverick Labour politician Josiah Wedgwood, who had died in 1943. 'I should very much like to know whether you consider this a worthy scheme and that you would be in favour of a Government grant,' asked Attlee.[17] Despite his love of history, Churchill at first opposed the suggestion after Anthony Eden informed him that a large fund had previously been raised by Wedgwood through private subscriptions, yet nothing had happened. But he eventually relented after pressure from leading Tories, including Rab Butler. 'In view of the considerable support that I find exists for the scheme, I think it should be allowed to go forward,' he told Attlee in October.[18]

Churchill's favourability towards the project had been enhanced by the imminent reopening of the Commons chamber that month, following extensive restoration after major bomb damage from the Luftwaffe in May 1941. On 24 October, just before moving into the renovated accommodation, the Commons met for the last time in the House of Lords, where sittings had been held since the destruction. In his address hailing the return of MPs to their rightful place, Attlee declared that 'we now have a House of great beauty, a monument of British architecture and craftsmanship', which was worthy 'of the greatest democratic assembly in the world'. The old chamber had been 'the scene of the memorable speeches of the Right Honourable Gentleman the Leader of the Opposition in our darkest and finest hour'. Now Attlee told MPs that the chamber's main entrance, rebuilt faithfully with stones salvaged from the rubble, would be called 'the Churchill Arch' as 'a symbol of the continuity of our institutions'.[19] Churchill was touched by the gesture. 'I must thank the Prime Minister for his personal references to me. I am a child of the Commons and I have been here, I believe, longer than anyone. I was much upset when I was violently thrown out of my collective cradle. I certainly wanted to get back to it as soon as possible.'[20] That evening, when he saw his friend Lord Camrose, Churchill said that 'Attlee had been very nice' in naming the arch after him.[21] Not everyone was so impressed. The Conservative MP Somerset de Chair complained that architect Giles Gilbert Scott, 'has contrived to make the doors of the Churchill Arch look like the entrance to some Midland bank'.[22] That was a minority opinion. There was huge public excitement, demonstrated in long queues at Westminster, when the King and Queen performed the official opening ceremony on 26 October, followed by the first session led by Attlee and Churchill, as their wives Violet and Clementine sat beside each other in the new Ladies' Gallery overlooking the chamber. It was, said Attlee, 'a great event' which would 'dwell in all our memories'.[23]

Yet all this celebration of Britain's parliamentary tradition could not detract from the intensity of party politics. Since the General Election, Labour had undergone an apparent recovery, helped by a pragmatic Budget from Cripps that combined tough expenditure limits with the removal of some economic controls. Attlee's own popularity had increased significantly in the months since the election. A Gallup survey in May put his public approval rating on 50 per cent, up from 40 per cent in January. 'It is hardly too much to say that he is the party's greatest asset in the popular mind,' said the *Manchester Guardian*. At the time those words were written, however, the skies were already darkening over his premiership because of foreign and defence policy.

The first controversy arose over moves towards European unity, the issue on which Churchill and Attlee had clashed in the previous Parliament. The two men had liaised amicably enough over the composition of the eighteen-strong British delegation to the next meeting of the Council of Europe, to be held in Strasbourg in August. Attlee suggested to Churchill on 18 April that the group, reflecting the make-up of the Commons, should comprise nine Labour representatives, eight Conservatives and one Liberal. 'I accept the composition proposed,' wrote Churchill.[24] But the weight that each party attached to the European cause was apparent when the nominations were unveiled. The Labour band was both Eurosceptic and unimpressive, headed by the anti-German Hugh Dalton, now in the twilight of his career. The Tory element, in contrast, was to be led by none other than Churchill himself, backed up by Harold Macmillan and the brilliant lawyer David Maxwell-Fyfe, a prosecutor at Nuremburg and the architect of the European Convention on Human Rights.

Labour's Euroscepticism was even more graphically revealed in the wake of the announcement in May by the French Foreign Minister Robert Schuman of a proposed new supranational body to oversee coal and steel production in Western Europe. The Schuman plan appeared to herald not only a new era in Franco-German co-operation, but also the path to European integration. Britain was invited to join the discussions for the new organisation, but Labour remained profoundly suspicious, an attitude that was reflected in a briefing on European policy drafted for the NEC by Dalton and the party's international officer Denis Healey, later a rumbustious Cabinet minister. Called *European Unity*, it stated that 'no socialist party could accept a system by which important fields of national policy were surrendered to a European representative authority'.[25] Sir David Hunt put Attlee's own view more demotically, 'He felt that Britain ought not to be bossed about by a lot of frogs.'[26]

On 2 June, the Cabinet decided to reject the invitation to join the Schuman plan, fearing 'the surrender of sovereignty in a European system which the French are asking us to accept in principle'.[27] The problem for Attlee was that, diplomatically, he did not want to make too categorical and swift a dismissal of British involvement. For the sake of official relations with other European powers and the USA, he planned to maintain the illusion of a possible participation in the distant future. But that equivocation was blown apart in an embarrassing scene in the Commons on the afternoon of 13 June, when Attlee made a defensive statement on the Schuman plan. Unfortunately for him, the NEC's negative briefing document had been published as a pamphlet the very morning he spoke, contradicting all his evasive words. Churchill immediately leaped on the inconsistency. 'We have two versions presented to us of the policy of the party opposite,' he said, prompting Attlee to argue that 'the Labour Party document is not, of course, a statement of Government policy in this matter'. After demanding a full debate on Schuman, Churchill then ironically offered his sympathy to Attlee, 'the only Socialist Prime Minister, outside the Iron Curtain and Scandinavia, in the whole of Europe, the whole of the British Commonwealth of Nations or the whole of the English-speaking world'. Attlee snapped back, 'I would remind him that during the war he was the only Conservative Prime Minister among the Allies and in the British Commonwealth and he was indebted to strong support from the Labour Governments in the Commonwealth.' Churchill continued the exchange: 'I would assure the Right Honourable Gentleman that I was only expressing my sympathy with his loneliness'; to this Attlee replied, 'I shall fortify myself by the example of the way the Right Honourable Gentleman stood up to it during the war.'[28]

The row rumbled on for several days. On 15 June, the normally emollient Eden told Attlee that the 'extraordinarily timed' pamphlet from Labour's NEC had caused 'very considerable consternation as to where we stand among our friends in all parts of the world'. Attlee claimed that the publication, driven by the printer's deadline, was simultaneously both 'unfortunate' and 'routine', a response that led Eden to accuse him of evading his 'responsibility'.[29] Yet Attlee soon recovered his equilibrium, sensing that the Schuman plan had gained little traction with his party or the British public. His imperturbability was further helped by the fact that the issue had not been pressed hard in the Commons the previous week by Churchill himself, whose ardour for the European cause was beginning to fade, despite the pleas of several leading Tories for him to challenge Labour more vigorously. Harold Macmillan said that this was 'a golden opportunity' for the Conservatives 'to secure the peace of Europe',[30] a line also taken by Bob Boothby, who told Churchill on 20 June, 'that, at a critical moment of history, the Western democratic world is looking to you for the leadership it has not had since 1945'.[31] Eventually, Churchill galvanised himself into putting down a motion to demand that the Government join the forthcoming Schuman negotiations in Paris. The *Daily Mail* predicted that if only 'three or four socialist MPs' voted with the Opposition 'Mr Attlee will be in danger of defeat'.[32]

But when the Commons came to debate the motion on 27 June, there was no sign of a Labour split. Churchill again tried to fly the flag for the idea of a united Europe, attacking the Government for its 'hostile' and 'squalid attitude', as epitomised by the NEC's statement. He turned his fire personally on Attlee as he drew a comparison between the Prime Minister's current anti-federalism and his past dismissal of national sovereignty. 'His own political creed and record are, if I may say so, in a sad plight. We all remember how before the war he said that national patriotism and national armaments were wrong.' But now, said Churchill, the Prime Minister 'comes forward' as 'the champion of the extreme insular view, which is inconsistent with the trend of what is going on, and also inconsistent with much that he himself has done. He seeks to win for himself and his party popular applause by strutting around as a Palmerstonian jingo.'[33] It was audacious of Churchill to accuse Attlee of both political inconsistency and excessive national pride, but the Prime Minister did not rise to the bait. He merely condemned Churchill for trying 'to make ill blood' between Britain and France, while, on the substance of Schuman, he warned of giving away too much power to 'an irresponsible body appointed by no-one and responsible to no-one'.[34] Labour won the subsequent division comfortably. Attlee told his brother that Churchill had 'made a fool of himself' and that his own party 'generally had the better of the debate'.[35]

The Paris talks led to the creation of the European Coal and Steel Community in 1951, with France, Germany, Italy and the three Benelux countries making up the initial membership. As its supporters predicted and its critics feared, the body ultimately paved the way for political integration and the establishment of the European Union. But Britain was to play no part in these early developments. Dean Acheson, Harry Truman's Secretary of State, felt that the refusal to participate in the Schuman plan was the country's greatest mistake in the immediate post-war era. 'It was not the last chance for Britain to enter Europe, but it was the first wrong choice,' he wrote.[36] Yet such a verdict underestimated the strength of sceptical feeling within the Labour Government. For most ministers, federalism represented a potential threat to working-class solidarity, industrial planning and the Government's capacity to implement a socialist programme. That attitude was summed up by Morrison's initial reaction to the Schuman plan, 'It is no good. We cannot do it. The Durham miners won't wear it.'[37] Attlee himself put it this way at the end of June, 'I have never regarded the United Kingdom as a purely European state. We are the centre of a Commonwealth and Empire extending over wide areas in other continents. Our position is therefore widely different from that of continental countries.'[38]

Even as Parliament debated the Schuman plan, a greater and more immediate foreign crisis had arisen. At dawn on 25 June 1950, the combined military forces of North Korea crossed the border into the territory of their southern neighbour in a bid, backed by China, to unite the two countries under Communist rule. The much smaller army of South Korea was soon overwhelmed and in headlong retreat. The capital Seoul, in the north of the country, fell within three days of the start of the invasion. But help was at hand for the embattled Republic, as Truman's administration decided that North Korean aggression had to be resisted. In the heightened Cold War atmosphere, the US President feared that the collapse of South Korea to communism might spark a chain reaction across the world, threatening the very existence of Western democracy in Europe and Asia. Under American pressure, the United Nations Security Council unanimously passed a resolution which condemned the invasion, though Russia did not take part in the vote because it had been boycotting the Council since January 1950 in a dispute over Taiwan. Two days later, the UN agreed to send military forces to the peninsula. Attlee decided that the United Kingdom, as a member of the Security Council and America's closest ally, had to give military support to the campaign. Royal Navy ships in Japanese waters were put at the disposal of the US 7th Fleet, while preparations began to deploy British and Commonwealth troops to the region. At the end of July, Attlee broadcast to the nation, setting out the case for Britain's involvement. 'If the aggressor gets away with it, aggressors all over the world will be encouraged.'[39] The Communist *Daily Worker*, which later became the *Morning Star*, felt that Attlee had given a poor imitation of his illustrious predecessor: 'The colourless, prim voice of the Right Honourable Clement Attlee came over the air from Chequers last night in his most viperish, anti-Communist utterance yet. It was a Churchill-and-water version of the blood, toil, tears and sweat oration of 1940.'[40]

In the Commons on 5 July Churchill gave his public backing to Attlee, arguing that there was nothing else 'the Government could have done in the circumstances'.[41] In private, Churchill expressed relief that he did not have to deal with the crisis, since any decision by him to deploy British troops would have inevitably led to the familiar accusations of bellicosity. 'I could not have managed this situation had I been in Attlee's place. I should have been called a warmonger,' he told the Shadow Cabinet.[42] But after discussing the British contribution directly with the Prime Minister, Churchill told Violet Bonham Carter that Attlee was struggling with the burden of the conflict. 'Winston arrived hot from Attlee (if one can be such a thing), looking pink and well and without the bulging, lowering look of doom about his forehead which I thought the world situation warranted. I asked him whether he thought Attlee was feeling the Atlas weight of his responsibility. "Yes," he said, "his hand shook as

I was talking to him. My hand doesn't shake – look at it – it's quite steady.'"[43]

Churchill's biggest concern was the state of Britain's military preparedness. Since the election, he had kept up his drumbeat of concern about potential weaknesses in the armed forces. On 24 May, for instance, he had written to Attlee a lengthy letter about inadequacy of Western defences in Europe: 'In my long experience I have never seen a situation so perilous and strange.' Therefore, to put the position before the Commons, he asked that Attlee agree to a secret session as had happened during the war.[44] After consulting his Cabinet colleagues, Attlee refused this request. 'I believe that the holding of a Secret Session would give rise to serious public alarm, and a crop of irresponsible rumours.' Attlee admitted that, like Churchill, he found that 'there are many features in the present situation which are disquieting' but he felt the way forward was through 'further confidential meetings in Downing Street'.[45]

The Korean crisis brought a new urgency to the discussions about defence. In the immediate aftermath of Communist invasion, Churchill told Attlee on 29 June that he still believed 'a Secret Session is desirable and necessary' but he could not press the point 'while the present tension lasts. I also feel that the renewal of inter-party conversations such as we had last year had better wait developments.'[46] A fortnight later, however, he was once more pressing for a Commons debate on defence, preferably in secret, though Attlee again refused. Among the Prime Minister's arguments was the inevitability of provoking 'a good deal of criticism' against Western governments 'at this critical time in which the authority of the United Nations is being challenged'. Furthermore, Attlee thought that 'the general public might be disturbed by the fact of a secret session', while the Americans would demand to know what occurred in such proceedings. 'We could not tell them without a breach of privilege.'[47] Churchill told Attlee that the Labour Government's position was absurd, given both the scale of the Korean crisis and the imminence of the summer parliamentary recess. 'According to the views expressed in your letter, the House ought to have no information on the subject of Defence, either in Secret or in Public Session, before it separates for its prolonged holiday. I will consult my colleagues upon the situation thus created, but I cannot doubt that they will share my view that we must warn Parliament of the dangers which are gathering.'[48]

The Government soon gave way after the Defence Minister Manny Shinwell, keen to announce a further £100 million for rearmament, pressed for the very parliamentary debate that Attlee had rejected. It was to open on 26 July. That day Churchill wrote with an air of triumph to Attlee: 'The fact that he (Shinwell) has asked for this shows how necessary was the public debate which you have deprecated in your correspondence with me.' But he also warned Attlee that the Conservatives would still demand a 'secret or private session' due to the 'increasing gravity' of the Korean situation.[49] Again Attlee repeated his antipathy to any idea of any secret session, telling Churchill that such a step 'will tend to cause the greatest amount of suspicion and uneasiness at home and abroad'.[50] When the debate continued the following day, 27 July, Churchill used the time-honoured parliamentary device for demanding a secret session. 'I spy strangers,' he said from the Dispatch Box. The Speaker called for a division, and Churchill's resolution was defeated by a single vote, 295 to 296. In his subsequent, public, speech, he again warned that Britain's armed forces 'fall a long way short of requirements even on the most conservative basis', particularly in view of the Soviet strength in tanks, submarines and aircraft. Britain was now over-reliant on the American atomic bomb, he argued. 'Without it, we are more defenceless than we have ever been.'[51]

Churchill was not assured when Attlee saw him privately on 2 August, after the House had risen. 'Winston was very gloomy about the defence situation,' recorded Harold Macmillan, who dined with him a few days later. 'He was much depressed about his interview the other day with Attlee. It seems that to scrape together 3,000 men and their equipment for Korea will take two months.'[52] Nor did Churchill find much sign of inspiring leadership. Despite his courteousness, Attlee was, he said, 'uncertain and baffled by the difficulties and dangers'.[53] In a letter to Attlee thanking him for the interview, Churchill assured the

Prime Minister that the Conservatives would 'give our support to all measures proposed by the Government for national defence', but this pledge would not 'in any way' inhibit the right of his party to criticise 'the existing state of our defences'.[54] In a memorandum to Attlee that he enclosed with this letter, Churchill further spelled out a number of his anxieties. One was that the establishment of the US bomber fleet's bases in East Anglia put the area 'in the bull's eye of any Soviet target should they decide to make war'. It was therefore vital 'to bring over with the utmost speed the largest number of fighter aircraft from the United States to guard the air base'. Churchill's belief in European unity led him to another conclusion. He maintained that the need to counter the Soviet threat on land required the creation of a European army 'as quickly as possible', made up of thirty-five divisions, including fifteen from France, six from Britain, six from the USA and three from the Benelux countries. The other five divisions, he boldly suggested, should come from Germany, though they would draw their 'equipment from a European pool and not from separate German sources'.[55]

Churchill vigorously took up the theme of a European army in public that week, as he led the Conservative delegation to Strasbourg for the Council of Europe meeting. In an address to Assembly on 11 August, he made an impassioned appeal for the nations of Western Europe, including the German Federal Republic to create 'a real defensive front' in the face of Soviet aggression.[56] To his pleasure, the Assembly approved his proposal. 'This is of course the fruition of what I have laboured for ever since my speech at Zurich four years ago,' he wrote exultantly to President Truman.[57]

Soon after Strasbourg, Churchill turned back his gaze to Britain's own defences and the Korean War. His effort was now focused on his demand for an early recall of Parliament to debate the reported slowness in the dispatch of British forces. The Government suggested a return on 12 September, but Churchill thought this reeked of complacency. He wrote to Attlee on 13 August that 'the date you propose is altogether too remote and bears no relation to the crisis and the new facts which are before us. I therefore have to ask you on behalf of the

Conservative Party to be so kind as to consider the recall of Parliament in a week or ten days at the latest.'[58] In response, Attlee complained that Churchill had not disclosed 'any particular reason why an earlier date should be chosen', but he was willing to see the Opposition Leader at Downing Street to discuss the matter.[59] Churchill took up the offer and on the evening of 16 August, accompanied by Eden and the Liberal Leader Clem Davies, he had an interview with Attlee. At the meeting, Churchill again pressed for a swift recall, as well as urging the deployment of British troops from Hong Kong. Attlee saw neither justification for the first nor imperative for the second. The next day Attlee reported to King George VI:

> Mr Churchill talked at considerable length on the dangers of the present situation, mostly on the lines of his last speech in the Defence debate in the House. I was unable to find any substantive reason for an earlier recall as it did not seem to me that another debate without definite action to be taken by the House would be useful. Mr Churchill showed considerable annoyance and suggested that in not accepting his date the Government were acting dictatorially. I was unable to accept this view as it would seem that Mr Churchill's demand might be considered as an attempt to dictate to the Government.[60]

The King was sympathetic to Attlee's decision to stick to 12 September, largely on personal grounds. 'I hope very much that it will be possible for you to get some rest between now and then as, so far, you cannot have had a real holiday,' he wrote from Balmoral.[61]

Churchill's annoyance with Attlee was real, as the journalist Malcolm Muggeridge discovered when he visited Chartwell on 23 August. During a lengthy talk about his memoirs, European history, German rearmament and the wildlife on the estate, Churchill 'broke off to speak about his conversation with Attlee concerning the advancement of the summoning of Parliament. Attlee, he said, now takes in at most 50 per cent of what is said to him. He referred scornfully to the fact that Attlee had insisted to him (Churchill) that there was no possibility of taking troops from Hong Kong to Korea.'[62] Churchill's irritation was further made clear when he made a broadcast to the nation about defence policy on 26 August. As *The Times* put it, he ran through 'a rich vocabulary of reproach to make his indictment', with Attlee's Government variously accused of: 'improvidence and want of foresight'; 'disconnection of thought and action'; 'lack of grip, conception and design'; and 'feebleness of purpose'.[63]

Attlee replied in his own broadcast on 2 September with another of those mocking attacks on Churchill that had become his speciality since 1945. Referring to Churchill's demand for a recall of Parliament, Attlee said, 'I should describe his attitude as dictatorial. For the last 20 years, Mr Churchill seems to me to have regarded Parliament mainly as a place where he makes speeches. He comes down like a prima donna, delivers his oration, and then, except for an occasional appearance at Question Time, is seen no more.' On the question of the deployment of troops from Hong Kong, Attlee claimed that the Americans had not initially asked Britain to send reinforcements. 'We were told that a balanced force, such as we offered, even though it would necessarily arrive later, would be more useful. It was only later that we had a request for the immediate dispatch of infantry. Mr Churchill knows this but apparently it's not much good giving him information.'[64] In 1945, Attlee had scored a triumph with his radio broadcast in reply to Churchill's infamous 'Gestapo' assault. But this effort was greeted much more negatively; it was widely seen as both peevish and inappropriate for the moment. The *Daily Mail* wrote of 'the contrast between the two men. One is a politician. The other is a statesman who may err in the small things but who makes no mistakes in the measures necessary to save his country.'[65] Even the normally sympathetic *Manchester Guardian* stated: 'One cannot help feeling that the tone of the broadcast was at this moment a mistake.'[66]

The long-awaited defence debate went ahead in the Commons on 12 September. By then, the arguments had been well rehearsed on both sides. When Churchill raised the question of delays in sending

British troops to Korea, Attlee said that, as someone who has 'more experience of conducting military affairs than anyone in the House', Churchill should recognise that 'the campaign in Korea is being run by the Americans. We respond to their requests, and if the request changes from what it was before, it is not the fault of His Majesty's Government.' On a more substantial note, Attlee reported that the rearmament programme would now be expanded to £3,600 million over the next three years, a huge sum that was bound to have a heavy impact on Labour's commitment to social services and welfare. But Attlee was in an optimistic mood after the debate. He told his brother Tom, 'I don't think the Tory attack on us was very effective. I doubt that it will divert people from the strongly held fear that, if Winston got in, he would lead us into war.'[67] Throughout all their friction in these months, there was still little venom in their relations. The mutual decency was revealed in an incident during Churchill's speech in the Defence debate, when he suddenly developed a bad cough. According to the *Daily Mail*'s parliamentary correspondent, 'Mr Attlee was slumped in his seat opposite, doodling on a piece of paper. Suddenly, to the surprise of his colleagues, the Prime Minister jumped from his seat, seized a glass of water which had been placed by the Dispatch Box, and offered it to Mr Churchill.'[68]

A few days after the Defence debate, Churchill was on the attack again, this time over Attlee's announcement that the Government would press ahead with the steel nationalisation at the beginning of October. Churchill called it 'a reckless, wanton and partisan measure'[69]; Attlee replied that if Churchill really wanted national unity, as he claimed, then he would support the policy. Attlee was also on combative form when he addressed Labour's Annual Conference in Margate at the beginning of October. In his speech, he extolled the 'unparalleled achievements' of the Labour Government, but also warned that, in a time of international crisis, his ministry would not be 'afraid of taking unpopular steps where those steps are right'.[70] Attlee's grip on Labour was highlighted by the *Evening Standard*, which commented that 'For all his deficiencies, he completely dominates the Party. His position is impregnable.'[71] Soon after Margate, Churchill argued in the Commons that if Attlee were really so confident then he should go to the country instead of allowing uncertainty to hang over the economy and the political scene. 'All I can say is that the Right Honourable Gentleman is indulging his personal power in these matters in a manner most costly to the community,' he told MPs.[72]

By October, the worst of the Korean crisis seemed to be over, as General MacArthur led a successful counter-offensive against the Communist forces, recapturing Seoul and driving them back beyond the 38th parallel. MacArthur was so bullish about his advance that he issued North Korea with an ultimatum for surrender. But far from feeling beaten, America's enemy stepped up the war in dramatic fashion. On 24 November, a vast army of 250,000 Chinese soldiers swept across the Yalu River and pushed back MacArthur, who declared that, with this intervention, 'We now face a new war.'[73] He demanded from the White House the right to bomb Chinese territory. Truman seemed willing to accede to his commander's request. At a press conference on 30 November, the President said that MacArthur was free to use whatever weapons he felt were needed, which implied the possible use of the atomic bomb. When the news of this statement reached London, there was alarm, despite a subsequent clarification from the White House that only the President could authorise a nuclear attack. After consternation was expressed on all sides of the Commons at the prospect of nuclear conflict, the Cabinet agreed that Attlee should fly to Washington for an urgent summit with the President. The Prime Minister would have to travel on his own, for Bevin was plagued by illness and was now functioning only sporadically as Foreign Secretary.

Before he left on 2 December, Attlee received a phone call from Churchill, who gave him his best wishes for the trip and stressed the continued importance of Anglo-American nuclear co-operation, as enshrined in the Quebec Agreement signed with Roosevelt in 1943. But on this point, Churchill was in for a disappointment. Attlee had to tell him that, because of the McMahon Act passed by Congress in 1946, the clause in the agreement concerning mutual approval for the use of the atomic bomb had been allowed to lapse. In a subsequent letter to Churchill written after their phone conversation, Attlee further explained the rationale for the abandonment of the Quebec accord. For the American Government, he wrote, the existence of the agreement 'put them in a very embarrassing position with Congress', which had 'not been told' about it. Because a formal treaty would be impracticable, 'the best solution for them therefore was that it should be allowed to lapse' with the exception of technical provisions about the exchange of information and raw materials. Attlee assured Churchill that his own Government had been working since 1945 'to restore the war-time co-operation with the Americans which they had broken off', though he felt that personal friendship and understanding was more likely to promote 'harmony of action' than any 'written agreement'. Recognising that Churchill would be aggrieved at this failure to maintain one of his wartime legacies, Attlee concluded on an emollient note.

> I do not of course for a moment wish to detract from the very great importance to us of the Quebec Agreement during the war. You will remember very well the difficulty you had in getting the Americans to conclude it, and it was a great achievement. But I think you may also agree that, in the quite different circumstances of peace, the secret war-time agreement no longer had the same character as a binding understanding between the two countries.[74]

For all Attlee's talk about working on close co-operation with the USA, this was actually his first visit to Washington since 1945, a graphic contrast with Churchill's enthusiasm for international summitry. His conference with the President turned out to be more successful than the critics had suggested, not least because Truman and Attlee established an effective relationship built on mutual respect. Truman's Secretary of State Dean Acheson later said that Attlee was 'adroit, extremely adroit, his grasp of the situation was masterly'.[75] Kenneth Younger, who was present at some of the talks, was equally impressed. 'The PM was very good, as he always is on Asian questions.'[76] Attlee was able to secure promises from the Americans about exercising greater control over the adventurism of MacArthur and avoiding a deliberate escalation of the war with China, though his suggestion of a ceasefire in Korea was firmly rejected. Nor was America any nearer to recognising the regime of Communist China, as Attlee urged. There were two other serious drawbacks from Attlee's point of view. The first was America's insistence that the British Government embark on a much more extensive programme of rearmament over the next three years, a demand that was soon to provoke a major crisis in the Labour Party. The second was the failure to secure any concrete deal from America about the approval to use the atom bomb. Truman was full of warm words to Attlee on this issue but refused to accept any practical restrictions on his powers.

The Prime Minister returned to Britain on 11 December to widespread approval. 'There is no doubt that this week's close contact between the two men has been of great value to Washington as well as London,' reported *The Times*.[77] Yet the acclaim was not universal. In the Commons, Churchill said that Attlee's trip had done 'nothing but good' but he expressed his concern about the absence of any tangible agreement on the bomb. When Attlee said in his own report to the House that 'I received assurances which I consider to be perfectly satisfactory', Churchill interrupted to say that 'We do not know what the assurances are' – a point that Attlee just ignored.[78] There were also ominous signs of trouble within the Labour Party. As Jim Callaghan told Dalton, many of his members were 'very unhappy' with the Government's international policy. They had 'been upset by Truman on the Atom Bomb, thought Attlee hadn't been strong or outspoken enough at Washington, and generally feared that we had become a satellite of the USA'. Dalton had heard similar stories from other MPs. 'It is clear that dissatisfaction and concern are growing rather fast in the party.'[79]

TWENTY-NINE

⬦

ABADAN

IN THE YEARS since the war, Churchill had often struggled politically. But by the end of 1950 there was a sense that the tide was
turning, as the crises facing the Government deepened. On every front,
from the economy to foreign affairs, Labour was in trouble. Fixated
by the need for vindication at the ballot box, Churchill now saw the
chance to heighten the pressure for another election. The dream of a
return to Downing Street, which had sustained him throughout his
frustrating period in Opposition, began to look closer to reality. One
opinion poll in January 1951 put the Tories on 44 per cent and Labour
on just 33, an eleven-point lead that would bring a resounding victory.
Furthermore, by 1951, Churchill felt that Attlee's sting at the Dispatch
Box was having less impact than in the recent past. After one attack
by Attlee, Churchill reportedly said to a colleague, 'It was rather like
being savaged by one's pet lamb, don't you think?'[1] Sensing new hope
amid Attlee's decline, Brendan Bracken wrote to Beaverbrook that
'the Tories, smelling the blood of office, are now 100 per cent behind
Churchill. It would be a great thing for you and me if Winston were
back in Downing Street.'[2]

The political conflict magnified in the New Year over steel nationalisation, which was about to come into effect, with the vesting day
for the new board set for 15 February. Unlike the previous measures
of public ownership, this had only limited popular support and led to
Tory claims about the triumph of socialist dogma over tough economic

realities. On the eve of the steel debate, Chips Channon was fascinated by the excitable atmosphere that had gripped the House.

> Much election chatter. I am inclined to think that Attlee will be forced to resign this week, which would make an Election almost but not quite inevitable because there is always the possibility that Winston might agree to head a provisional government for a few months: this is what many Labour Members would prefer. Prefer certainly to an Election which would result in their certain defeat and loss of many seats.[3]

During the actual debate on 7 February, Churchill accused Attlee of pursuing a doctrinaire policy against the troubled economic and international backdrop to appease the Labour left. 'This unpatriotic step is being taken by the Prime Minister to placate his unhappy tail,' he said, before launching into a highly personal passage about his own reputation and that of Attlee.

> I would rather be banished from public life forever than be responsible for the action which the Prime Minister is taking, in asking the House to vote for the 15th vesting date tonight. I earnestly trust that Parliament will restrain him. So tremendous a situation, such awful hazards, such an unworthy contribution – I can hardly believe that the Attlee who worked at my side for more than five years of a life and death struggle is willing to have his reputation injured in his way.[4]

According to the *Daily Express*, Churchill was in 'his most vigorous and varied mood' as he made his speech, while Attlee 'sat low in the seat of power, doodling as usual, taking everything in but putting little out'. The paper noted that Churchill's use of Attlee's name was highly unusual in any parliamentary exchange, where references to a member's office or constituency were meant to be used. 'There would have been howls of protest if he had said "Mr Attlee" but after 50 or more years in Parliament, the shrewd old parliamentarian conferred either a historic or derisive title which just got by the rules in the phrase – "The Attlee".' For all Churchill's fulminations, Labour still managed to pass the resolution, by ten votes. Churchill, who, like other Tories, had harboured hopes of victory, was disappointed at the margin of the Government's win, as Dalton recorded. 'After the division, Winston was heard saying to Lyttelton, "It looks as though these bastards can stay in as long as they like."'[5]

Despite this setback, Churchill decided to crank up the pressure on Labour by putting down a motion of no confidence over the Government's defence policy. The debate was set for 15 February and once more there was feverish speculation about Attlee's potential demise. In his speech, Churchill attacked Labour's record of 'vacillation and delay'. Even though the Government had announced an increase in the defence budget to £4.7 billion over three years, up from the previous estimate of £3.6 billion, Churchill was concerned that the new funds would be squandered because of the 'ineptitude and incompetence of the Government'. One prime example he cited of Labour's ineptitude was the supposed failure to develop Britain's own atomic bomb, particularly as Russia had now built its own nuclear weapons. Once again, Churchill demonstrated with this utterance how far Attlee had kept Parliament, the Opposition and most of his own party in the dark about Britain's nuclear programme. The Prime Minister was not about to make any revelation now. When he rose to contradict Churchill, he did so only in vague terms. 'The Right Honourable Gentleman really ought not to mislead the country on a matter like this,' he said, 'it is utterly untrue to suggest that there has been a failure to develop it here.' Churchill at once came back, stating that 'in the five and a half years' since the end of the war, 'no success has rewarded our efforts in making it'. Once more Attlee told Churchill that he was 'quite wrong. There has been successful development. He is not producing any evidence whatever to show that given the resources and possibilities over here as compared with the resources they have in the United States of America, we could have done more than we have done now.' Churchill, still unaware of the facts, was more dismissive than ever, 'What is the meaning of that interruption? I say we have not succeeded in making the atomic bomb completely in this country in the five and a half years since the war,' he declared.[6]

The Government won by twenty-one votes, with most of the Liberals backing Labour. In the tense climate of party conflict at Westminster, Channon felt that there was for once some personal animosity between Churchill and Attlee, as he noted an incident that occurred in a corridor outside the Commons Smoking Room five days after the Defence debate:

> I saw Winston, immaculately dressed, pleased with himself and puffing a cigar, approach. Immediately in front of us walked Attlee and Arthur Moyle, his PPS. There was almost a collision; Winston did not make way (Attlee did, slightly) but made them one of his courtly little half-bows which he reserves for people he does not like. I was fascinated; as he passed me a second later, he smiled, winked and passed on.[7]

The feeling was perhaps mutual. Tony Benn saw Attlee with a group of Labour MPs socially at Downing Street on the afternoon of 27 February: 'Tea was not exciting and Clem's conversation never rose above the ordinary except in his digs at Churchill. I think he has an inferiority complex.'[8]

One of Churchill's central concerns at this time, as he showed in the defence debate, was the abandonment of the 1943 Quebec Agreement, an issue which he felt symbolised Attlee's inadequate leadership. Churchill's new demand in early 1951 was that the Quebec Agreement should be published, partly on the grounds that the Americans now had an air base in East Anglia which could be used for the atomic bomb. His argument was that if the agreement were made public, then the Americans would be under moral pressure to uphold the principle that the consent of Britain was needed before the deployment of the bomb against Russia in Europe. Inevitably, there was also a political motive, in that publication could help the Conservatives to portray Labour as weak on the protection of Britain's national interests.

At Prime Minister's Questions on 30 January, Churchill asked Attlee that now the agreement had been 'revoked' was there 'any reason why its terms should not be stated in public'? Attlee replied that he would prefer 'to have a word with the Right Honourable Gentleman on this matter. It is, as he knows, rather complicated and rather delicate.'[9] Supported by the senior diplomat Sir Roger Makins, Attlee duly met Churchill the following day at Downing Street. At Attlee's request, Sir Roger ran through the difficult history of Britain's relationship with America on the bomb since the war, including the vital milestone of the McMahon Act, but he told Churchill that 'the prospects of a more comprehensive agreement in the atomic energy field' were 'once more reasonably promising'. In his note of the meeting, Sir Roger recorded how Churchill 'maintained his view that the publication of the Quebec Agreement, which had now been superseded, would do no harm and might indeed strengthen the United Kingdom's negotiating position. The Prime Minister made it clear that he did not share this opinion, but said he was quite willing to obtain the views of the United States Government on the publication of the Agreement.'[10]

Increasingly impatient, Churchill then took the bold step of writing directly to President Truman on 12 February. The letter stated that he had 'lately learned' how the Quebec Agreement 'had been superseded by other agreements made by you with Mr Attlee's Government in 1945. Nothing was said to the British Parliament at the time about this very important change and I feel it my duty to press for the disclosure of the original document.' This request had 'new and practical significance' because of the air base in East Anglia. 'I have little doubt that Parliament would consider that this base should not be used for the atomic bomb without the consent of His Majesty's Government,' he wrote, adding that 'the publication of the original document would place us in a position where this guarantee would be willingly conceded by the United States'.[11] To Attlee on the same day, Churchill explained the reason for his unorthodox diplomatic approach to the White

House. 'As a co-signatory of the original Agreement, I have thought it right to communicate myself with the President of the United States, and I trust he will at least agree that the atomic weapon shall not be used from British bases without our prior consent.'[12]

Denis Rickett, the Prime Minister's principal private secretary, was shocked at Churchill's presumption and said so to Attlee. 'The suggestion in the last paragraph that because Mr Churchill signed an Agreement with President Roosevelt in 1943 this gives him a right to deal direct with the President on these matters at the present time is very extraordinary.'[13] This was the line that Attlee took with Churchill on 14 February, ticking him off for his constitutional impropriety: 'While the Quebec Agreement was made between Roosevelt and yourself, it was of course in your capacities as President and Prime Minister. I do not see that personal communication of the kind which you have made will advance a matter which is at present under discussion between Governments.'[14] Soon afterwards, Truman sent a handwritten note to Churchill, telling him that he could not accede to the request: 'I hope you won't press me in this matter. It will cause unfortunate repercussions both here and in your country, as well embarrassment to me and to your government. The reopening of this discussion may ruin my whole defense program both here at home and abroad. Your country's welfare and mine are at stake in that program.'[15] Churchill had to let the issue drop.

Despite winning the skirmish with Churchill over Quebec, the burdens on Attlee were mounting. Policy crises like defence, Korea and public finances were exacerbated by the breakdown in health of key ministers. Cripps had been forced to resign in October 1950, having developed cancer of the spine. His place as Chancellor was taken by Hugh Gaitskell, an appointment that disturbed the Bevanite left because of his fiscal and Atlanticist hawkishness. In a later reshuffle in January 1951, Bevan, with some misgivings, became Minister of Labour, a position which Attlee felt would force the Welsh radical to accept the discipline of economic restraint. More changes were needed in the Cabinet when Ernie Bevin's physical decline made it impossible for

Attlee to keep him as Foreign Secretary. On 9 March 1951, Attlee moved him to the largely honorific post of Lord Privy Seal, much to Bevin's chagrin. 'I am neither a Lord, nor Privy, nor a Seal,' he was reported to have told Attlee.[16] Florence Bevin was crestfallen on her husband's behalf, calling the decision 'a dreadful thing to do' and admitting that she 'could have murdered Attlee and all of them'.[17] Bevin did not last long as Lord Privy Seal. He died on 14 April 1951, holding in his hand the key to his red box. Soon afterwards Attlee wrote to Churchill to suggest that he be granted 'the dignity of a burial' in Westminster Abbey in view of his 'conspicuous services rendered to this country'.[18] A profound admirer of Bevin's, Churchill agreed: 'I certainly feel that your proposal is most fitting and I shall be glad to support you.'[19]

Bevin's replacement as Foreign Secretary was Morrison, a man in whom Attlee had far less trust. Soon after Morrison took over at the Foreign Office, Attlee was struck down with his own ailment, as he developed severe intestinal trouble. Diagnosed with a duodenal ulcer, he was taken into St Mary's, Paddington on 21 March. As so often before, Churchill and his wife were personally sympathetic to Attlee in his plight, sending him a bouquet soon after his admission to St Mary's. 'Thank you so very much for the lovely flowers which arrived just when Vi was with me. I have to stay in for two or three weeks but expect to be all right after that,' he wrote to the couple on 22 March.[20] But such courtesies did not inhibit the party battle between the two leaders. Two days before Attlee had gone into hospital, Churchill had made a political broadcast in which he said that the Conservatives would 'do their utmost to bring about an appeal to the nation at the earliest moment' to end 'this hateful uncertainty'. What Britain needed was a Government 'unhampered by narrow doctrinal party dogma or by the interests of a particular class'.[21]

Attlee felt sufficiently provoked by Churchill's broadcast to leave his sick bed, travel to the BBC radio studio and make his reply across the airwaves. As had become his habit, he focused on Churchill's record in Opposition. 'A year ago he kept telling me, as he does now, that we needed a united nation and the way to get it was in a general election.

Well, we had one. He failed to win it. However much he tries to juggle with the figures in order to make out that Labour did not win, one thing is certain: he lost. But he is not satisfied. He lost the cup tie but demands a replay on his own ground.' Attlee continued in this personal vein.

> The unity of 1940 was due to the Labour Party that put him in office and sustained him loyally through five long and difficult years. He has always done his utmost to belittle the achievements of the Labour Government. I do not complain of this, but I cannot see why he should pose as being a superior non-political superman, concerned only with national unity. He is out to get back into power by hook or by crook.[22]

Almost six years on from the 1945 campaign, Attlee's condemnation of Churchill now seemed more peevish than pointed. Harold Macmillan, who was no tribal partisan, privately thought that Attlee's broadcast was 'pretty feeble. There was an attack on Churchill and the rest was an apology in the Baldwin manner. What a long way from the enthusiasm and fire of socialism in 1945.'[23]

The hospitalisation of Attlee could not have come at a worse time for the Government, just as a huge row exploded in the Cabinet over the fiscal consequences of the rearmament programme and the rising costs of the National Health Service. When the tough-minded Chancellor Hugh Gaitskell insisted on the introduction of NHS charges in his April Budget, Bevan threatened to resign. The breach widened during a series of tense Cabinet meetings, chaired by Morrison in the absence of Attlee, who could only relay his views from his hospital bedside. After Gaitskell refused to make any concessions, Bevan felt he had no option but to depart. He was followed out of the Government by Trade Secretary Harold Wilson and the junior Supply Minister John Freeman.

In the immediate term, the Cabinet turmoil inflicted serious damage on Labour. With some justification, Gaitskell thought that Attlee had to bear some responsibility for the crisis: 'Part of the trouble at the moment is that we are not getting enough leadership within the party.'[24] Staying at Chequers for further recuperation after his release from hospital, Attlee admitted to his brother Tom that 'this Bevan business is a nuisance. The real wonder is that we kept him reasonably straight for so long. But with this and Ernie's death I did not have as restful a time as I should have liked.'[25] Inevitably, Churchill welcomed Labour's internal warfare since it advanced his own political cause, though he had little time for Bevan, whose speeches had regularly needled him over the years. 'I could wish for a revival of manners of ancient times. I would challenge him to a duel,' Churchill once said.[26] On 27 April, in a speech at the Albert Hall to the Primrose League, he declared,

> We are all glad that the Prime Minister has left hospital and can turn from the jigsaw puzzles of Cabinet shuffling to the urgent tasks which confront him. It is hard on any country when no one is looking after it. Mr Attlee combines a limited outlook with strong qualities of resistance. He now resumes the direction of that cluster of lion-hearted limpets [...] who are united by their desire to hold on to office at all costs to their reputations and their country's fortunes.[27]

Churchill had originally intended to describe Attlee alone as 'this lion-hearted limpet'; but Harold Macmillan, having seen the draft during a visit to Chartwell, suggested that the singular be changed to plural because of sensitivities over Attlee's recent illness.

Within the Commons, the Conservatives ruthlessly exploited Labour's vulnerability through procedural manoeuvres that led to long sittings and obstructions to Government business. Then, in the summer of 1951, a new source of trouble blew up for Labour overseas. Its cause, like in so many post-war flashpoints, was the collision between Britain's fading empire and the insurgent spirit of nationalism. In May the new Prime Minister of Persia Mohammad Mosaddegh, whose National Party had recently won the country's General Election, announced the nationalisation of all foreign oil assets there. These included the highly lucrative refineries and wells of the huge Anglo-Iranian Oil Company (AIOC, later to become British Petroleum or BP) in Abadan, which had made an astonishing profit of £170 million in 1950. Beyond commercial concerns, there was widespread alarm in Britain that Mosaddegh's policy represented a blow to national prestige, a threat to strategic global interests and a vehicle for further anti-colonial Sovietisation in the Middle East. But the Labour Government slid into a muddled response, mainly because of the insecurity and inexperience of the new Foreign Secretary Herbert Morrison. On one hand, in a conciliatory vein, he organised negotiations between Iran and the AIOC, whom he encouraged to compromise. On the other, he sometimes resorted to a stance of strident bellicosity, even ordering a parachute brigade and a naval force to the eastern Mediterranean when the talks broke down. The Foreign Office Minister Kenneth Younger was appalled at his chief's approach. 'Herbert makes bold, fierce noises which have no substance behind them. He is ignorant, amateurish, cheap and reactionary.'[28]

Much of Churchill's career, stretching back to his days as a cavalry officer in the Sudan and India, had been built on the defence of the Empire. He was not about to abandon those instincts now, especially when there was a chance to attack the ruling socialists over imperial retreat and neglect of the Soviet risk. In addition, he had a historic stake in this matter, since he had negotiated the majority British holding in the Abadan oilfields in 1914 when he was First Lord of the Admiralty. On 29 June, he made another of his unconventional forays into transatlantic diplomacy with a further letter to President Truman. 'I cannot think of any Soviet aggression more dangerous to our common cause than for the region between the Caspian Sea and the Persian Gulf to fall under Russian-stimulated Tudeh[*] Communist control,' wrote Churchill, only to receive another bland reply from the

---

[*] The Iranian Communist Party, founded in 1941, which played a key role in Mosaddegh's drive for nationalisation.

White House, which expressed the hope that the 'counsels of moderation will yet prevail and that a satisfactory solution can be found'.[29] In the Foreign Office there was a suspicion that the Americans were only too willing to support nationalisation because the departure of the AIOC would open up new opportunities for US enterprises like the Arabian American Oil Company. That was also the view of Randolph, now a full-time international journalist, who told his father that 'American industrial diplomacy and free enterprise, aided by intelligent government, has naturally scored over Socialist sloth and Socialistic monopolistic greed'.[30]

Churchill held several discussions with Attlee in his attempt to shore up the defence of British power in the region. After the third of these conversations, he wrote on 9 July to the Prime Minister to set out his thinking. Among the points he made was that 'the Anglo-Iranian personnel should be encouraged to remain at their posts in Abadan'; it would be 'a disaster' if they were 'hustled and bullied out'. In addition, he urged 'the strongest representations should be made to the United States to take positive action in supporting the common interests of the Atlantic Powers'. Most importantly, 'if the worst came to the worst, the Government should not exclude the possibility of the forcible occupation of Abadan. We have made it clear that should such regrettable measures be forced upon you, you could count on our support.'[31] Attlee gave Churchill a non-committal reply, promising him that pressure was being exerted on the USA to provide support. Dissatisfied, Churchill attacked the Government's equivocal approach to Abadan at a speech in his constituency on 21 July: 'Mr Attlee doodles, Mr Morrison gapes.'[32] In the Commons a week later, he spoke in more unrestrained terms. 'If they use their precarious and divided majority to cast away one of the major interests of the nation,' he told the House, 'then I say the responsibility will lie upon them for this shameful disaster, diminution and impoverishment of our world position.'[33] Alongside Churchill on the Opposition front bench, Harold Macmillan was impressed. 'He was on tremendous form and established a complete ascendancy over the party and indeed the House.'

But Macmillan was also taken with Attlee's measured response. 'He really took the best line in answering Winston that he could do and is expert at lowering the temperature and generally reducing the whole thing to a pleasant Sunday afternoon at the boys' club.'[34]

But, for all his highly charged rhetoric, Churchill did not press the Government as hard as he might have done. As over Ireland, Palestine and India, he showed a willingness to accept the limits of British power and the realities of the new post-war world. After one of his meetings with Attlee, he said that the Government were being 'moderate and cautious', and it 'would be foolish for the Tory Party to stick its neck out'.[35] The two strands of Attlee's outlook on Abadan were, first, that Morrison had proved his incompetence with his inconsistency, and, second, that British military intervention was never a starter except in an emergency to save the lives of oil workers. The consequence of the former was that, from July, he increasingly took over the handling of Abadan from the Foreign Secretary. The result of the latter was that in September, he secured the agreement of the Cabinet to pass the problem over to the United Nations, against Morrison's advice. It was another retreat from empire, but Attlee had no doubt that it was the right course, as he later explained, 'I think if we had used force we would have raised the whole of Asia against us and a great deal of public opinion in the rest of the world too. And it would have been quite wrong morally and politically. It was impossible for us as a Labour Government to say that you couldn't nationalise the oil industry.'[36] Lacking any support from the Government, the British oilmen had to evacuate Abadan on 3 October.

At that point the General Election, so long anticipated, was finally under way. The decision to call it in the autumn of 1951 had been driven in part by political factors such the need for a bigger majority and the risks of carrying on into the darkness of winter. But Attlee was also influenced by his desire to accommodate George VI who was due to undertake a lengthy Commonwealth tour in early 1952 and wanted political uncertainty to be eliminated before he left. 'I do not think it would be fair to the King to let him go away with the possibility of a political crisis hanging over him. He takes things hard and is apt to worry when he is away,' Attlee told Morrison.[37] The King himself gently increased the pressure at the beginning of September, warning Attlee that 'it would be disastrous' if his Commonwealth visit 'had to be postponed, or even interrupted, on account of upheavals at home'.[38] To the King's relief, Attlee was able to reassure him: 'I have come to the conclusion that the right course would be to have a dissolution of Parliament in the first week of October.'[39]

It was not until he had privately acceded to the King's request that Attlee formally told his Cabinet of the decision. As it turned out, the question of the King's Commonwealth tour soon became redundant. Long in poor health aggravated by his heavy smoking, George VI was told by his doctor that he would have to undergo a major operation to remove part of his cancerous left lung. The surgery, the deadly seriousness of which was kept from the public and the King himself, precluded any visit overseas, though plans were made to send Princess Elizabeth in her father's place. Now aged twenty-five, the princess was already undertaking more royal duties and, at the moment of the King's operation, was preparing to embark on a tour of North America. As an ardent monarchist, Churchill welcomed her growing prestige but worried about her transport arrangements for this visit, as he wrote to Attlee on 23 September. 'I ought to let you know that it would be, in my opinion, wrong for The Princess Elizabeth to fly the Atlantic. This seems to me more important than any of the inconveniences which may be caused by changing plans in Canada.' He also added a postscript about the King's health. 'Thank God the operation this morning has so far been successful, but a period of grave anxiety lies before us.'[40] In his handwritten reply, Attlee tried to allay Churchill's concerns about the Princess's travel. 'Nowadays the risk in flying the Atlantic does not seem too greater than that flying over own land.' He also offered Churchill a cautiously optimistic report on the King: 'It is an immense relief that the operation has been successful, but the anxiety will remain for some time.'[41]

Despite the King's aborted tour, Attlee would not be swayed from his decision. The election was fixed for 25 October. On 20 September, he sent Churchill a typically brief note, 'I have decided to have a General Election in October. I am announcing it tonight after the nine o'clock news.'[42] Attlee may have been socially conservative, but in this case he was a political pioneer, becoming the first Prime Minister to make such an announcement on the radio. The *New Statesman* was struck by the unvarnished brevity with which he performed the task: 'The Prime Minister's capacity for making everything sound sensible and important was seldom heard to better advantage. If Winston had been speaking, his voice would have conjured up visions of rich robes and pageants; the majestic procession of history would once more have culminated in the great arbitrament of the nation.'[43] The poll was the step that Churchill had been demanding for months, and he was in an optimistic mood as he prepared for battle. 'I think our prospects are very favourable so long as we do not indulge in over-confidence,' he said to his friend Lord Kemsley, while he told Macmillan that he hoped for a majority of fifty.[44] To his doctor Lord Moran, he was even more bullish after a conversation with Beaverbrook. 'Max is talking of a majority of a hundred and fifty, or at any rate a hundred.'[45]

Churchill's early belief in a comfortable Tory victory was shared by many on the Labour side, who believed that the party had lost its way and needed to renew itself in Opposition. Dalton felt that Labour would lose at least fifty seats, a view in line with a Gallup poll that gave the Tories a lead of 7.5 per cent. Peter Shore, a senior official at Labour headquarters and later a Cabinet minister, despaired of both his party's prospects and its leadership. 'My forecast – a Tory majority of at least 70,' he wrote in his diary the night that Attlee broadcast the news of the election. Complaining that 'our support has ebbed away', Shore felt that 'the economic consequences of rearmament are slowly eliminating the main achievements of our six years in office'. Little more than a week later, his disillusion had deepened: 'The party is intellectually bankrupt and has no leadership.'[46]

That point appeared to be reinforced at the end of September, when Attlee made a prosaic speech to the Annual Conference in Scarborough, the very opposite of a rallying cry to the troops. To be fair to him, the

Conference took place at a difficult moment for the Government, as Mosaddegh had proclaimed that British personnel had just a week to leave Abadan, a declaration that reinforced the Opposition charges of surrender. Yet there was an ominous sign for the Conservatives in how the pressure of the election seemed to bring Labour together. After all the viciousness of the Bevanite split months earlier, the party left Scarborough in better heart than when it had arrived. That was partly due to Bevan himself who made an uplifting, reconciliatory speech in praise of Attlee and in condemnation of Churchill: 'Those difficult, complicated economic operations require economic and mental discipline and not merely perorations. That is why the quiet, moderate, balanced approach of Clem Attlee is more adjusted to the international situation than the romanticism of Churchill.'[47]

On 3 October, the Conservatives published their manifesto, *Britain Strong and Free*, a distinctly Butlerite, centrist document that emphasised the party's commitment to social reform and state intervention, as shown in the promise to build no fewer than 300,000 new homes a year. But the Labour Party and its supporters were determined to trounce Churchill's attempt to present himself as the restrained elder statesman. Instead, by exploiting the public's anxieties about the turbulent international climate, they aimed to portray him as a reactionary warmonger, still infused with his dreams of imperial adventure and class conflict. This ruthless approach was encapsulated early in the contest by a notorious *Daily Mirror* headline which asked the pointed question 'Whose finger on the trigger? Churchill's or Attlee's?' With its implication that Churchill could plunge Britain into nuclear Armageddon, the article was dreamed up by the *Mirror* editor Silvester Bolam, an enthusiast for sensational journalism, who had been jailed in 1949 for publishing legally sensitive material that could have prejudiced the trial of acid-bath serial killer John Haigh. When the *Mirror* article appeared, Churchill was appalled. His valet Norman McGowan later recalled that, when he saw the headline, he was overtaken by 'mystified horror', then 'stumbled out of bed and rushed to Clemmie, calling for her as he went'.[48] Soon afterwards, he addressed the charge directly in

Left: Churchill at the Walthamstow Greyhound Stadium, 26 June 1945, making the final speech of his doomed General Election campaign. 'I have no message for them now,' he privately confessed.

Below: Attlee talking to his Limehouse constituents in July 1945. His election campaign struck a chord with the British public yearning for renewal after six years of war.

Above: Attlee and his wife Violet at Labour's headquarters, Transport House, after the announcement of his party's historic landslide victory, 26 July 1945. 'I wish you all success in the heavy burden you are about to assume,' wrote Churchill to Attlee that night.

Left: Churchill delivers his renowned 'Iron Curtain' speech in March 1946 at Fulton, Missouri. 'The most courageous utterance I have ever heard from a public man,' King George VI told Attlee.

Left: 'A modest man.' Attlee mows the lawn at Heywood, his home in Stanmore, 1945.

Below: With his wife Violet behind the wheel, Attlee embarks from Downing Street on his nationwide tour in the 1950 General Election.

Left: Churchill the artist at work in his studio at Chartwell, his country home in Kent, 1946. Painting was a solace to him after his General Election defeat.

Below: Churchill arrives at the Gloucester Road polling station to cast his vote in the General Election of October 1951. His victory over Attlee meant a return to Downing Street at the age of 76.

Right: At Heathrow airport, Attlee and Churchill greet the new Queen, Elizabeth II, on her flight back to Britain from Kenya, following the death of her father. 'She is showing great poise and dignity,' wrote Attlee to his brother soon after she began her reign.

Below: Attlee travelling by bus to the Labour Conference in Morecambe, September 1952. Alongside him are his wife Violet and Barbara Castle, the Labour MP for Blackburn East.

Above: With a powerful speech at the close of the 1953 Tory Conference in Margate, Churchill showed that he had made a dramatic recovery from the stroke that threatened his premiership. His wife Clementine looks on in happy relief.

Left: At the ceremony in Westminster Hall to mark Churchill's eightieth birthday, Attlee presented him with a portrait by the artist Graham Sutherland. Churchill hated it and after his death, his wife had it burnt.

Churchill and Attlee deep in conversation at a dinner in the Dorchester Hotel, June 1959. Despite their political clashes, their personal relations were almost always civil.

Attlee is assisted down the steps of St Paul's Cathedral after Churchill's funeral, 30 January 1965. Earlier, Attlee's frailty had almost caused a catastrophe at the start of the service.

Above: The statue of Winston Churchill in his Woodford constituency, by David McFall. It was unveiled in 1959, with Churchill himself present at the ceremony.

Left: The unveiling at the House of Commons in 1979 of the statue to Clement Attlee, by Ivor Roberts-Jones. James Callaghan, Edward Heath, Harold Wilson and Margaret Thatcher pay tribute to the longest-serving British party leader of the twentieth century.

a speech at his Woodford constituency on 6 October. 'I am sure we do not want any fingers upon any trigger, least of all a fumbling finger [...] In any case, it will not be a British finger that will pull the trigger of a Third World War. It may be a Russian finger, or an American finger, or a United Nations Organisation finger, but it cannot be a British finger.'[49] Despite his rebuttal, the accusation against Churchill and his party was frequently made during the rest of the contest. All this was much to the disgust of Conservative Party chairman Lord Woolton, who wrote that 'the Labour campaign was pretty disgraceful and a black mark against Attlee'.[50]

Attlee and Churchill kept up their personal duel for the next fortnight of the campaign. Launching his campaign in his Walthamstow constituency on 5 October, Attlee condemned Churchill for his misrepresentations over Abadan and his appetite for political discord. 'Mr Churchill said when victory was won in 1945 that we had no less need of unity and comradeship than in the struggle. Who broke that unity and comradeship? You remember Mr Churchill's broadcast in 1945 – that was not much good for keeping unity and comradeship, was it? The Conservative Party, as always, is a party of class. It does not prevent Mr Churchill from fermenting a class war.'[51] On 8 October, Churchill made the first Conservative broadcast of the campaign, exuding the kind of reasonableness that defied Labour's caricature of his outlook. 'Why not make a change in this harassed island and get a steady, stable government sure of its strength, fostering the expansion of our society, making sure of our defences, being faithful to our allies?' he asked.[52] With more experience of the microphone, Churchill had vastly improved his radio technique, as well as dropping the platform bombast. His performance was a far cry from the Gestapo disaster of 1945. The Oxford psephologist David Butler later wrote that 'in his moderation and vigour, in his clarity and technical adroitness in delivery, Mr Churchill gave the best Conservative broadcast of the election, perhaps the best broadcast for any party. It was thought by many to have been his finest personal effort since the war.'[53] Labour official Peter Shore was not so sure about its impact, noting in his diary, 'I heard ten minutes of Winston last night in a pub. The radio was in a public bar and everyone was listening. They adore him but they were not convinced.'[54] In response to the broadcast, Attlee took on Churchill during a speech in Lowestoft on 9 October: 'It is quite untrue that the country is declining. Ever since we came in Mr Churchill has been prophesying ruin. The trouble is that our prima donna wants a black background so that the spotlight can show him up more brightly.'[55]

The two-way bombardment did not slacken, as Attlee denounced Churchill for partisan denigration of Britain and Churchill accused Attlee of presiding over failure. At one point, referring to trouble brewing for the Government south of Egypt, Churchill said that Attlee was suffering from a 'trio of misfortune – Abadan, Sudan and Bevan', a phrase that captured the imagination of the press.[56] Churchill also used humour. Speaking in his own constituency on 12 October, he mocked a speech made in Leicester by Attlee in which the Prime Minister had said that, after six years in office, there was still much more work to be done to 'clear up the mess of centuries'. In a vein of rich irony, Churchill said, 'We can leave out the great achievements of the past', such as Magna Carta, the establishment of Parliament democracy and the creation of the British Empire; 'Gladstone and Disraeli must have been pygmies'; John Stuart Mill and Adam Smith 'were small fry'; 'But at last a giant and a Titan appeared to clear up the mess of centuries. Alas! He has had only six years to do it. Naturally he has not been able to accomplish his mission.'[57] In Labour's final broadcast of the campaign, Attlee had harsh words for Churchill on the theme of Britain's alleged decline as he compared the Tory Leader unfavourably to his own deputy Anthony Eden.

> Mr Eden is honourably distinguished from some others by the responsible manner in which he deals with international affairs. He has been Foreign Secretary. I wonder how, in that capacity, he would have appreciated having a man of worldwide reputation like Mr Churchill constantly telling the world that

Britain was paralysed, ruined, and in a far worse case than other countries, in fact doing everything to weaken British influence.[58]

One listener, Elizabeth Hogarth of Fordingbridge in Hampshire, was infuriated by Attlee's broadcast. 'If English men and women of all classes don't vote Mr Attlee out of Government after his attack on our beloved war leader, I for one shall be ashamed of my countrymen.'[59]

Attlee's own experience of the public was inevitably very different. Of his lengthy election tour from 8 to 17 October, which started in the east of England, swept through the Midlands and the North, then covered the West Country before a return to London, he said: 'Everywhere we had packed and enthusiastic meetings, the audience sometimes reaching five figures. I recall, especially, one at Nottingham where the police said there were 30,000 people in the square.'[60] The *Manchester Guardian* thought that Attlee's 'dull and respectable' method fitted the mood of the nation 'perfectly'. He had 'never cheapened himself or his argument to gain applause. He has just been his quiet, assured self [...] It is an admirable exhibition of one of the supreme arts of politics, the enhancement of personal respect.'[61] As always, he was driven round the country by Violet, complete with his detective, his private secretary Sir David Hunt, and a portable electric iron, all in the Humber Pullman. It was a tough schedule, during which he made seventy-eight speeches. Churchill had a less energetic campaign, spending much of the time in his Woodford constituency, but still, at the age of almost seventy-seven, he undertook an impressive number of engagements across the country, including a trip through Yorkshire to Glasgow between 15 and 18 October. Like Attlee, he encountered tremendous enthusiasm at his rallies. On a visit to St James's Hall in Newcastle, he addressed an audience of 4,000, with another 16,000 gathered in a nearby park. As *The Times* reported, 'crowds of people wishing to see Mr Churchill as he drove through Newcastle brought the traffic to a standstill'.[62]

Both men made personal visits in support of relatives and friends during the campaign. On 13 October, Attlee went to speak for his nephew Christopher, the Labour candidate in Eastbourne, a commitment which involved a trip by car of 400 miles from Lancashire. 'The agent here is doing a magnificent job of organisation and I am sure I shall get any results I am capable of. I hope Winston keeps it up on Abadan,' wrote Christopher to his uncle shortly before the visit.[63] Just before polling day, Churchill travelled to Plymouth Devonport to speak for his son Randolph, who was up against Michael Foot, the future Labour Leader. But a more important, less conventional journey by Churchill took place the week before to the constituency of Colne Valley in Yorkshire to support his close friend and Liberal candidate Violet Bonham Carter. In a reflection of his affection for her, his nostalgic devotion to the Liberal cause, and his continuing attachment to the idea of an anti-socialist pact, he had persuaded the local Conservative Association to stand down in her favour. 'He has been consistent throughout as a Whig Coalitionist,' complained Leo Amery of this move.[64] Despite some local Tory and Liberal hostility, Churchill received a rapturous welcome in the Colne Valley constituency, with more than 7,000 assembling in front of Huddersfield town hall to hear him. Lady Violet found him 'in wonderful looks and form, very calm and Pickwickian'.[65] Attlee had been sufficiently disturbed by this development, which threatened the incumbency of Labour veteran Glenvil Hall, to make his own visit to Colne Valley before Churchill's. In his speech at the neighbouring town of Slaithwaite, he argued that all Liberals who co-operated with the Conservatives were doomed, as had happened with the National Liberals. 'Never have I seen the slightest independence on their part. I described them once as dead flies caught in the Tory web. Lady Violet if returned would be just another of them.' As to Churchill's claims to support the welfare state, Attlee pointed out: 'Mr Churchill once said in an unguarded moment that the machine requires an engine and a brake. The Tory Party is the brake. You may be sure that if the Tories are returned the brake will be put on and then the engine will be put into reverse.'[66]

On Churchill's visit to Huddersfield, he was accompanied by his doctor Lord Moran, who recorded some frank private thoughts on his oratory: 'When he spoke to his text, his voice was strong, and he spoke with vigour and conviction. But he kept introducing asides, and this he did in a very uncertain and hesitant manner which was anything but impressive. Winston, of course, is a born writer, but in speaking it is only by blood and sweat that he has become as effective as he is.'[67] An insight into Attlee's speaking style and demeanour at the end of the campaign were provided by the *Daily Herald*'s editor Percy Cudlipp, who saw the Prime Minister three days before polling.

> He was as I have always found him – quick-thinking but calm, confident yet modest; surely the least dramatic man who has ever held a great position. At the beginning of the campaign, a friend said to me, 'One of the jobs the *Daily Herald* must do is to build up Attlee. He is an enormous electoral asset.' I replied that the *Daily Herald* would report Attlee but would certainly not attempt to 'build him up' for three reasons: 1. He won't be built up. 2. He can't be built up. 3. He doesn't need building up. And it is precisely for those reasons that he is so powerful an electoral asset. He hates showmanship. When he speaks, he is intent only on expressing his thoughts, not on how he is looking or how he is sounding. His sincerity grips an audience much more than any tricks of oratory. It is the secret of that quiet magic which the Prime Minister exercises on his audiences.

In his talk with Cudlipp, Attlee was dismissive of the idea that if 'Churchill came to power he would be able to talk to Stalin on much more level terms than other statesmen and with a better chance of good results'. For Attlee, 'these suggestions that the whole of the destiny of mankind could be settled by a few big fellows sitting around a table smack too much of the Führer principle'.[68]

As the campaign drew to a close, the stakes could not have been higher for Churchill. The only possible outcomes for him were victory or retirement. After two previous defeats to Attlee, his party would not have allowed him to carry on after a third, especially not at his age. His prospects still looked reasonable, as *The Times* reported two days before polling: 'The Conservatives are now completely certain about the swing to the right in progress in most parts of the country. They expect to have a comfortable working majority in the House of Commons. Some of the independent forecasts put the possible majority of the Conservatives and their associates from 70 to 100.'[69] Yet there were some indicators that this confidence was misplaced. When Churchill saw the psephologist David Butler on 20 October he asked him frankly if he was a liability to his party. Somewhat diffidently, Butler replied, 'I don't think you are the asset you once were.'[70] Even after six years in Government, Labour remained a formidably powerful electoral force, buttressed by class solidarity and a strong trade-union organisation. For those who had benefited from the NHS, expanded welfare, or full employment, there was little appeal in Churchill's language about enterprise and freedom. Morgan Phillips, Labour's General Secretary, publicly stated that his party could win as many as 14 million votes, by far the largest total ever garnered. As he campaigned across the country, Kenneth Younger 'never got any sense of a swing against Labour'. As he noted in his diary, the Labour candidates 'were working hard and seemed optimistic; everywhere crowded, attentive meetings and limited opposition'.[71] Another factor in Labour's favour was that the personal attacks on Churchill had undoubtedly had an impact, as Wilson Broadbent of the *Daily Mail* reported on 23 October after speaking to Tory strategists: 'It was admitted last night that the Socialist warmongering campaign against Mr Churchill has done the Conservative cause a lot of damage, especially among women.'[72]

On polling day the *Daily Mirror*, which had pursued a near vendetta against Churchill during the contest, repeated its controversial headline, 'Whose Finger on the Trigger?' on its front page, accompanied by a photograph of a man with a cigar in half-profile. Churchill was so infuriated that he sued the paper for libel and ultimately won his case, the *Mirror* issuing an apology for calling him a warmonger. The paper's vitriol had no effect in Churchill's own Woodford seat, where he had a huge majority of 18,579, with his vote rising by over 3,500 since 1950. In nearby Walthamstow West, Attlee also enjoyed a big majority of

11,574 against his youthful opponent Edward du Cann, later to be a Conservative MP, party chairman and leadership contender before his political career was destroyed by his dubious financial dealings. Taking his first plunge in electoral politics, du Cann was struck by Attlee's modesty. 'He treated his young and impertinent opponent with a courtesy and generosity I can never forget. It was a surprise to be regarded as an equal by a man who was the Leader of the Labour Party and Prime Minister.'[73]

The national result was far closer than in either of these two constituencies. On a nail-biting day, the outcome long remained in doubt. Finally, once all the ballots papers had been tallied, it emerged that Labour had the biggest total, with 13,948,883, not far short of Morgan Phillips's prediction of 14 million. The Tories and National Liberals were behind, with 13,717,850. The problem for Attlee was the distribution of his party's support, which piled up in their safe seats, but marginally fell in the suburbs and rural areas. The Tories' distribution was more efficient, thanks in part to Lord Woolton's well-organised electoral machine, which saw them win 321 seats to Labour's 295. Inadvertently, Clement Davies's party turned out to be as vital a prop for Churchill. Desperately short of funds, the Liberals fielded just 109 candidates, almost 400 fewer than in 1950. In practice, therefore, Churchill had the co-operative pact that he craved, if only by omission. Attlee himself noted that, in areas where their party was not standing, the Liberals tended to give three votes to the Conservatives for every two they gave to Labour.[74] In this Liberal collapse, only six of their candidates were elected, but Violet Bonham Carter was not one of them. Nor did Christopher Attlee and Randolph Churchill succeed.

Churchill was at Conservative Central Office in Abbey House, Victoria Street on 26 October when the pivotal result came through from Basingstoke, where victory finally took the Tories and National Liberals past the threshold of an overall majority. There were tears streaming down his face as the news was reported. After six years, he had fulfilled his mission. That evening, Attlee went to the Palace to tender his resignation. Soon afterwards, Churchill arrived to accept the commission to form a new Government. That night a large, cheering crowd gathered outside his home in Hyde Park Gate. Despite his tiredness, Churchill eventually acceded to their noisy requests to make an appearance, as his valet Norman McGowan described. 'The shouts became louder and more insistent. Then, with Mrs Churchill beside him and Rufus* in his arms, he went to the window. In his dressing gown, he grinned to the people and gave the V sign.' Churchill let the curtains fall, bade Clementine goodnight, and then made his way to bed, but not before ordering a whisky and soda. McGowan's account continues:

> I brought him one, and as he sipped it, he said, as if speaking to himself: 'We've won, Norman. I have the reins of the country in my hands again. But we're in a bloody mess.'
>
> He paused and took another slow slip.
>
> 'I have so little time left,' he finished in almost a whisper.[75]

He was the oldest Prime Minister since William Gladstone, and the only one in the history of British democracy to have made a comeback after two successive General Election defeats. 'I do hope Winston will be able to help the country. It will be uphill work, but he has a willing, eager heart,' wrote Clementine.[76]

---

* His dog.

THIRTY

❖

SUMMIT

UNTIL THE GENERAL Election of 1951, the last they were to contest as opposing leaders, the long duel between Churchill and Attlee had been about the fight for supremacy. For both men, the next few years were about the fight for survival. The battle was waged, not so much against each other, but against their own party opponents who were yearning for their respective retirements. In a sense the two great rivals were engaged in the same struggle against the dying of the light, clinging on to office when many of their colleagues thought that their departures were long overdue. In a narrative of mutual decline, Churchill, seventy-seven at the start of his third premiership,* and Attlee, sixty-nine at the end of his second, were both widely seen as too elderly and fatigued for leadership. 'He is getting very, very old, tragically old,' said Bob Boothby of Churchill just after the election.[1] 'Attlee has shown signs of ageing and weakening lately,' wrote Dalton a few months later.[2]

Both their wives longed for some peace after years in the public spotlight. Churchill's secretary of the 1950s, Anthony Montague Browne, wrote that Clementine was 'very against' Winston taking the premiership again, having been 'strongly influenced by the formidable stresses she had endured over the years'.[3] Dalton believed that Violet had been 'frightened by the deaths of Ernie and Stafford and wanted

---

* Including his brief Caretaker Ministry in 1945.

Clem for a few years to herself'.[4] But the two men soldiered on. This was partly out of a genuine sense of public duty. Churchill believed that, at home, he could save the country from what he saw as the excesses of socialist dogma, while abroad, his influence as a global statesman could help to achieve a lasting peace. Attlee stayed because he felt that he was the only figure who could prevent the Labour Party tearing itself apart in the ideological battle between left and right, of which the Bevan-Gaitskell split over the NHS had been a grim precursor. But there were also less edifying reasons. In his majestic belief in his own destiny, Churchill could not imagine his life without political power. There also lurked within him the suspicion that his anointed successor, Anthony Eden, was not up to the job. The same determination to keep out his obvious heir, Herbert Morrison, was a key factor for Attlee. 'In no circumstances' should Morrison succeed him 'as leader of the party', he told the journalist Leslie Hunter.[5]

Churchill and Attlee therefore remained at their posts from 1951. Inevitably, through their lingering slide into the sunset, much of the animation behind their long-standing rivalry had evaporated. But there was another reason that the fires of their competition had been doused. This lay in Churchill's embrace of much of Attlee's post-war programme. Throughout his years in Opposition, he had raged against socialism and promised to 'set the people free'. But after his arrival in office, there was little attempt to reverse the major features of Labour's settlement. Churchill may have presided over the nation's salvation in war, but it was Attlee who shaped the structure of post-war Britain for decades to come. This was exactly what the perceptive Kenneth Younger had privately predicted just after the announcement of Attlee's defeat in October 1951: 'I don't think the Tories will be able to throw over the really important things we have done. Labour has performed the essential task in a democracy by shifting the whole political thinking of the country out of its 19th century groove so that there can be no going back.'[6] In that spirit, the Conservatives kept the NHS and the social security system intact, and vastly expanded the drive for house building. The only denationalisations were of the road haulage sector and the steel industry, but even those measures did not happen until 1953 and 1954. Similarly meat rationing, for Churchill one of the oppressive symbols of bureaucratic state control, remained in place until 1954. In power, Churchill actually turned out to be less hawkish than Attlee on defence spending, largely because he recognised the short-term economic distortions that resulted from the demands of massive rearmament. Painting himself as the benevolent healer of the nation, he was also determined to avoid any confrontation with the trade unions. He 'wanted industrial peace at all cost', recalled his Minister for Labour, Walter Monckton.[7]

It was the same story with Churchill's much-vaunted belief in European unity. Since 1946, he had presented himself as the champion of the European cause, priding himself on his role as the architect of the European Assembly. Yet this conviction appears to have been shallow. On his arrival in Downing Street, he donned Attlee's mantle of patriotic scepticism as he stressed Britain's global position and links to the Commonwealth. In an early memorandum to his new Cabinet, in October 1951, he wrote that federalism was a matter only for the Continent, exactly as Attlee had argued after the Schuman declaration. 'I am not opposed to a European Federation including (eventually) the countries behind the Iron Curtain, provided that this comes about naturally and gradually. But I never thought that Britain or the British Commonwealth should either individually or collectively become an integral part of a European Federation and have never given the slightest support to the idea.'[8] In the face of the realities of power, Churchill's pro-Europeanism, always rather vague, turned out to be ephemeral, though, as Crossman remarked after one Commons exchange about European policy in December 1951, Labour could not criticise him on that score: 'Attlee was not able to berate him for going back on the leadership of the European Movement for the simple reason that Labour has been wholly isolationist itself.'[9]

Most of Churchill's Cabinet choices were obvious for reasons of weight and experience. Eden, who once more went to the Foreign Office, insisted that Churchill give him the position of Deputy Prime Minister on the grounds that 'Attlee had this title during the war and

Morrison in the recent Government'.[10] Despite misgivings from the
Palace, which feared that the role was an infringement of the royal
prerogative, Churchill quickly agreed. Butler became Chancellor, and
Maxwell-Fyfe Home Secretary. In a nostalgic throwback to the war,
Churchill took the Defence portfolio himself, though he handed it
over four months later to his favourite wartime general Lord Alexander
of Tunis, who turned out to be a poor appointment, unable to adjust
to Cabinet politics. In a further attempt to rekindle the glories of
his wartime administration, he made Lord Cherwell his Paymaster-
General and Hastings 'Pug' Ismay, who had been ennobled in 1947, his
Secretary for Commonwealth Relations. Appointments like this gave
rise to accusations not just of cronyism but also excessive reliance on
unaccountable peers. As usual, Churchill wanted to give his administration a national, coalitionist flavour beyond party labels, so he
invited the Liberal Leader Clement Davies to serve as Education
Minister and Asquith's son Cyril as Lord Chancellor. Both rejected
the offers, although Churchill did manage to persuade Lloyd George's
son Gwilym to become Minister for Food. The Bevanite backbencher
Richard Crossman, an often shrewd observer of the political scene, felt
that the composition of the new Government highlighted Churchill's
determination to pursue a moderate course: 'The general make-up of
the Churchill Cabinet means that it will be only very slightly to the
right of the recent Attlee Cabinet. Just as Attlee was running what was
virtually a coalition policy on a party basis, so is Churchill.'[11]

Churchill always felt more comfortable with old, familiar faces and
initially seemed suspicious of the Downing Street machine he inherited
from Attlee. Jock Colville, a reassuring figure who was brought back
by Churchill to Number Ten from the Foreign Office, recalled the
Prime Minister's reaction when he was introduced by the Cabinet
Secretary Sir Norman Brook to some of his staff. 'He flung open the
door connecting the Cabinet room to the Private Secretaries' offices
[...] He gazed at them, closed the door without saying a word, shook
his head and proclaimed to Norman Brook, "Drenched in Socialism."'[12]
The remark was made in jest, as Churchill did not purge any of these

officials. But he was more serious about trying to dismantle another administrative legacy of Attlee's: the elaborate committee structure at the heart of Whitehall, which again he thought smacked of socialist mismanagement and an addiction to bureaucracy. One of his first acts was to instruct Brook to oversee 'the slaughter of a great number of second and third grade committees which now, I am assured, cumber the ground'.[13] After some hesitation, Brook came up with names of a few sub-committees for the axe, but essentially, in time-honoured Whitehall fashion, he stonewalled and was backed up by other top rank civil servants who feared that the pruning of Attlee's system would mean a loss of co-ordination across government. Churchill's proposed shake-up made little impact.

The Prime Minister failed to make progress on this front largely because he was nothing like the dynamic leader he had been at the peak of the Second World War. More than a decade after he had presided over Britain's Finest Hour, he no longer possessed the volcanic energy or the searching impatience to galvanise the Government machine. His ineffectiveness should not be exaggerated. He remained a figure of enormous imagination and stature. His own Minister for Aviation John Boyd-Carpenter recalled that he 'conducted the affairs of Government with great energy and complete authority'.[14] The historian Peter Hennessy pointed out that in one respect Churchill could be regarded as even more productive than Attlee. In the first full year of his premiership, 1952, his office produced 315 files of official correspondence, up 46 per cent on Attlee's tally of 215 files in 1948. In April 1953 he boasted to his doctor Lord Moran that he had held 110 Cabinets in the previous 12 months, compared to 85 held by Attlee in his last year in office.[15]

Yet all this cannot disguise the fact that Churchill's faculties for leadership had badly diminished by 1951. Attlee felt that 'his post-war premiership was a mistake' and 'it was a pity Winston could not have retired after he had won the war'.[16] Churchill no longer had his former phenomenal capacity for work, nor his ferocious powers of concentration. 'A sense of urgency was no longer his constant companion,' recalled Brook.[17] One graphic symbol of the change was that, according to Jock Colville, he left untouched the set of red labels with the slogan 'Action This Day' which had been attached to his stream of directives and minutes during the Second World War.[18] Churchill's style of governance in his third term was well captured by Sir David Hunt:

> Plenty of people in those early days came up to me and said, 'You must see a great change between the two Prime Ministers you have been serving.' Oh yes, a tremendous change, you simply can't imagine the difference between them. On the one hand, there is a man who is decisive, quick, looks at a question and says yes or no before passing on to the next question. On the other hand there is a man who says, 'Oh, I am not going to decide. It is an important question. It must come to Cabinet.' Or, 'I won't look at that now, bring it down to Chartwell at the weekend.' When I said Chartwell, there was always a double-take.

In the same interview, Hunt said that Churchill's approach slowed down the Cabinet.

> The nuisance of him was that he would not read his papers. That was Attlee's great strength. Attlee always read all the Cabinet papers so he was the best informed man in the Cabinet. But Winston wouldn't and he would pick up things halfway through and something would suddenly catch his eye. He would go off on that. Everyone would groan because they thought they had done that.[19]

That is also the memory of some of those who served in his Cabinet. His method, wrote Lord Woolton, was 'all very irritating to busy Ministers' and was 'completely disruptive of good committee work'.[20] Even more exasperated was the Lord Privy Seal Harry Crookshank, who wrote in his diary after Cabinet on 22 April 1952 that 'Winston was intolerable.

We went line by line through the White Paper on transport until after 1.30 and did nothing else.' Almost a month later, Crookshank recorded after another meeting, 'Winston too woolly for words.'[21]

When Winston and Clementine moved into Downing Street in October 1951, they rented out Hyde Park Gate to the Cuban Ambassador and initially used the self-contained flat on the top floor of Number Ten that the Attlees had occupied. But Churchill did not like this modest arrangement and soon moved below to the grander state rooms, which he had refurbished. Meanwhile, the Attlees took up residence in their rural home of Cherry Tree Cottage in Great Missenden, Buckinghamshire, where Violet looked after the house and garden. 'This is a lovely place. I know we are going to be very happy here,' she said on moving day in early November 1951.[22] Attlee, who never shared Churchill's craving for office, was relaxed about his departure from Downing Street. 'It seems quite odd to be free of heavy responsibility and to look forward to a whole day with nothing particular to do,' he told his brother Tom just after the move into the cottage.[23] Remarkably for a politician who was the Leader of his party and still aspired to become Prime Minister, Attlee had no base in London. He tended to travel on the 9.06 train from Great Missenden, driven to the station by Violet, and if he was detained overnight by business at Westminster, he stayed at his club, the Oxford and Cambridge. Attlee's logistical modesty was in contrast to the social elevation he had achieved. On 6 November, the King appointed him to the Order of Merit, a distinction that Churchill had gained in 1946.

The new Parliament opened that day with the traditional debate on the King's Speech. In a mildly satirical contribution, very different to the 'trigger' abuse that Churchill had endured in the election, Attlee mocked the Prime Minister for the ermine-heavy composition of his Cabinet. 'It seems to me a return to the 19th century or possibly even 18th century practice.' He also teased Churchill about the narrowness of his electoral victory. 'In the last Parliament the Right Honourable Gentleman stressed the point that we should be careful how we acted because we had only so many hundred thousand votes more than the

Conservative Party. Of course, we can now stress the fact that the Government have fewer votes than the Labour Party. I am sure the Right Honourable Gentleman will willingly take his own medicine.'[24] In his response, Churchill was initially generous to Attlee about the Order of Merit. 'I should like to congratulate him on the honour he has received from the Crown. The news was especially gratifying to those who served so many years with him in the hard days of the war.' Then Churchill became more serious in a reference to the recent election. 'We think on this side that the "Warmonger" campaign did us great harm and is probably answerable for the slender majority upon which His Majesty's Government must rest.' Revealing his bitterness, Churchill called it 'this cruel and ungrateful charge'; he promised that his ministry would prove it wrong 'not merely by words but by deeds'.[25] A month later, in a debate on defence, Churchill again struck a moderate tone by saying that, on his arrival in office, he had found that Labour had kept the armed forces in better shape than he expected. But he also warned that his Government would not be able to meet Attlee's expenditure target of £4.7 billion over the next three years. Cleverly sowing division in the Opposition's ranks, something that was to be a feature of the parliamentary side of his third premiership, he praised Bevan 'for having, it appears by accident, perhaps not from the best of motives, happened to be right'.[26]

Defence was the area where Churchill and Attlee clashed most bitterly in the final phase of their rivalry, as both men struggled with the great questions of the Soviet relations, NATO, and, above all, the further development of nuclear weaponry. Having complained so vociferously about the failure of the Labour Government to exploit Britain's technological expertise, Churchill was astonished to learn how advanced the domestic atomic programme really was. Sir David Hunt recalled that Churchill 'was very excited in the first couple of months when he discovered we were making an atomic bomb. "I would never have dared. Not a word in the estimates. £100 million, hidden away, no accountability to Parliament. It is an extraordinary thing. Mr Attlee is a very brave man,"' he said.[27] In Lord Moran's account, Churchill

expressed his anger to Anthony Eden at how Labour had so extrava-
gantly attacked him in the election while harbouring this secret. 'The
Labour Government spent £100 million on atomic research without
telling anyone, without any Parliamentary sanction whatever. Their
party knew nothing about it. I could not have done it. How was it done?
Oh, they just divided the money between seven or eight departments.
And they called me a warmonger.'[28] Despite his annoyance at Attlee's
deceit, he agreed to Lord Cherwell's demand that he approve the next
stage of the atomic programme, the testing of Britain's bomb at Monte
Bello off the Australian coast sometime in the autumn of 1952.

The question of nuclear weaponry was inevitably raised when
Churchill travelled to the USA in January 1952 to meet Truman and
to address Congress. Although his speech on Capitol Hill, in which
he asked for American help in raw materials for the rearmament
programme, was another resounding success, his talks with Truman
were less fruitful. The President refused to consider Churchill's idea
of an international peace summit with the Russians, one of the Prime
Minister's favourite themes during his last years in office. Truman was
also at times curt with Churchill and frustrated by his deafness, though
the British diplomat Evelyn Shuckburgh admitted that the Prime
Minister could be difficult at times; on one occasion, 'he appeared
under the impression he was addressing the British Cabinet'.[29] The
Government's economic adviser Robert Hall was even more dismissive:
'The Prime Minister was very bad indeed' and 'he was on most things
not very clear in his thoughts'.[30] There was, however, one vital piece of
information that Churchill gained from his trip. In Washington, he
had lunch with Senator McMahon, who told him that he had been
ignorant of the 1943 Quebec Agreement before pushing through the
legislation that banned US nuclear co-operation. 'If I had known this,
the Act would never have been passed. But Attlee never said a word,'
exclaimed McMahon. Churchill now felt fully vindicated in his belief
that his Labour predecessor had been responsible for the breakdown in
British-American relations over the bomb. Churchill later complained
to Cherwell that Attlee's policy had exacted a heavy financial and

technological cost on Britain, 'We have probably been forced to spend £100 million in Attlee's day, and are now spending more through being unfairly treated because the Americans were not told the fact and because Attlee was feeble and incompetent. It is true that he to some extent redeemed himself by the secret manufacture which he achieved but we are still left a great loser by the bargain he made,' Churchill wrote in 1953.[31]

Unaware of Churchill's conversation with McMahon, the Labour Party sought to make political capital out of his American visit by implying that he had reached a secret deal with the White House to support wider US military action in the Far East if China broke the fragile truce in Korea. But Labour were playing a dangerous game, for Churchill had discovered – through a search of Foreign Office telegrams – that the reports of Labour's supposed restraint on America had been exaggerated. On the contrary, the documents revealed that, in the event of heavy air attacks by China on UN forces, Morrison and Attlee had been willing to back US military retaliation, even beyond the boundaries of Korea. Along with the news about Attlee's secret atomic programme, this built a deadly arsenal of ammunition that Churchill planned to deploy with devastating effect against the Opposition.

But before he could do so, civic life in Britain was brought to a halt by the death of George VI on 6 February. Both Churchill and Attlee, having worked so closely with the King for more than a decade, were deeply affected. Indeed, for one of the few times in his career, Attlee showed real emotion in public when he was given the news by Sir David Hunt while he attended a meeting of the PLP. 'Attlee was an outstanding example of the stiff upper lip, but he wiped away his tears then,' recalled Hunt.[32] Churchill was similarly crestfallen, as Jock Colville, who had actually worked for Princess Elizabeth in the late 1940s, described in his diary. 'When I went to the Prime Minister's bedroom, he was sitting with tears in his eyes, looking straight in front of him and reading neither his official papers nor the newspapers. I had not realised how much the king meant to him.'[33] The end of one reign and the beginning of another led to a spirit of unity on the political scene. Churchill and Attlee, along with several other Privy Councillors, went to London Airport, now Heathrow, to greet the new Queen Elizabeth, who had been in Africa at the beginning of her Commonwealth tour. That night, Churchill made a solemn broadcast to the nation in which he praised the fortitude of the late king, especially during the war and in his final illness. After the proclamation of the new monarch, the House of Commons gathered on 11 February to send messages of loyalty and sympathy to the royal family. In his speech, Churchill said of the Queen: 'A fair and youthful figure – Princess, wife and mother – is the heir of all our traditions and glories even greater than in her father's day, and to all our perplexities and dangers.'[34] In his tribute, Attlee described George VI as 'a great King and a very good man. We now turn our loyal service to our young Queen. She comes to the Throne with the goodwill and affection of all her subjects. She takes up a heavy burden, but I am confident that she will sustain it.'[35] For once, the normally pithy Attlee spoke at much greater length than Churchill. 'I think the fact is that Clem has been more moved by the King's death than by anything in the last four years,' wrote Crossman.[36] Attlee said as much to his brother Tom: 'I was much attached to the King and knew him very well, seeing him week after week,' though he was also impressed by the new Queen who 'is showing great poise and dignity'.[37]

Churchill, too, was delighted at how quickly she adjusted to her new role, bringing a sense of rejuvenation to Britain. His innate romanticism was captivated both by her regal elegance and the way in which she embodied the excitement of a new Elizabethan age. One morning in early 1953, Lord Moran found Churchill gazing at a photograph of the Queen in a long white dress. 'Lovely, inspiring. All the film people in the world, if they had scoured the globe, could not have found anyone so suited to the part,' said Churchill.[38] Sir David Hunt later said of Churchill's feelings: 'He was a violently convinced monarchist and the young Queen touched every chord in his heart.'[39] From a personal and political viewpoint, the arrival of the new monarch also had the great advantage of giving him another excuse to remain longer in office, in that he could now claim that he could not leave before her Coronation, due to be held in June 1953.

Yet the idea of a long continuation of Churchill's premiership caused despair among some senior figures in his circle. Eden, increasingly frustrated in his ambition to inherit the leadership, claimed that his fellow Tories 'are more and more concerned about the conduct of Government, especially Winston's lack of grip'.[40] Even the loyal Colville lamented that the 'PM is not doing his work'.[41]

Churchill's vulnerability served as a stimulus to the Labour Party, which thought that his Government might be brought down at any moment. Following the resumption of normal politics after a period of national mourning for the late king, Labour sought to exploit the Prime Minister's apparent weakness by tabling a motion of censure against him over his policy towards Korea. With the debate to be held on 26 February, Attlee and his front bench were confident that Churchill could be seriously damaged by the charge of potential collusion in US aggression. But the move backfired disastrously. Opening for the Opposition, Morrison accused Churchill of being 'woolly and evasive' about what he had secretly agreed with America during talks at the White House on Korea.[42] But Churchill comprehensively demolished the Opposition by explaining that, in Government, Morrison and Attlee had agreed to the very step for which they now attacked him. Based on his reading of the official documents, Churchill told the House that the Labour Government had decided 'they would associate themselves with action not confined to Korea' if there were Chinese air attacks on UN forces. His own policy on Korea was therefore no different to Labour's. The Prime Minister further piled the agony on Labour by revealing the extent of Attlee's secret atomic programme. 'The Leader of the Opposition is one who did good by stealth and blushed to find it shame. He will have to do a good deal of blushing in the explanations which he will have to make to some of his followers.'[43]

Churchill's performance caused uproar in the chamber and dismay among Labour MPs. 'A wall of astonishment broke from the Opposition benches. Mr Attlee glowered. Mr Morrison's lips tightened,' reported the *Daily Mail*.[44] Nigel Nicholson, who had just been elected the Tory MP for Bournemouth East, described the drama to his father Harold. 'There was pandemonium. I was sitting directly opposite Attlee. He was sitting hunched like an elf just out of its chrysalis and stared at Winston, turning slowly white. The Labour benches howled – anything to make a noise to cover up the moment of shock. Winston sat back beaming.'[45] From the Labour side, Crossman recorded that 'Churchill's bomb had worked its effect of creating the impression that Attlee and Morrison had been sheerly disingenuous in staging the debate'.[46] The Government won the subsequent division by thirty-three votes, prompting Churchill to tell Moran gleefully, 'we put them on their backs'.[47] Attlee's humiliation was made all the greater when he put out a statement effectively admitting the truth of what Churchill had told the House. In the view of the last Labour Government, he explained, it would have been 'unreasonable' to preclude retaliatory action against airfields 'on the far side of the Yalu river' if the UN came under heavy air attack.[48] His admission did nothing to quell the discontent in the Labour Party. What was so destructive about the episode is that it further opened up the fissure between the Bevanite left and the leadership, which had been briefly healed by the election.

The disunion worsened even further in early March during a debate on the Government's Defence White Paper, which put a new emphasis on deterrence, particularly through creation of a nuclear-armed V-bomber force. The Bevanites, now in a rebellious mood, wanted outright rejection. In contrast, Attlee put an amendment which expressed support for the strategy but declared a lack of confidence 'in the capacity of His Majesty's present Ministers to carry it out'.[49] Although the PLP agreed to support the amendment, the Bevanite group thought this was a meaningless compromise. During the debate itself, Crossman so seethed with anger that, as he noted in his diary, 'I was tempted to get up on a Point of Order and ask whether Attlee was moving a vote of censure or supporting Mr Churchill. There was no censure at all, and the longer he spoke, the more it was clear the Amendment was mere tactics.'[50] In an indicator of the worsening discord in Attlee's party, fifty-seven Labour MPs refused to back his amendment, thereby giving Churchill a majority of ninety-five.

Through his shrewd parliamentary tactics and continuing grasp of foreign and defence policy, Churchill had played his part in fomenting Labour's internal strife. Lord Beaverbrook felt that this was a powerful example of Churchill's underrated skill as a political operator. 'He separated the Opposition Front Bench from those sitting behind, left-wing from right [...] It was a model of political generalship, which has been too little remarked upon and admired by connoisseurs. Churchill had a gift for carrying the Opposition along into impotence, just as he also had an uncanny skill in detecting the motives of other men.'[51] Emboldened by this Commons success, Churchill seemed only too keen to remain in power despite all the Tory concerns about his fitness for the premiership. During a radio broadcast before the municipal elections in May 1952, Churchill declared: 'We have the will, and I believe we have the power to continue for another three or four years of steady, calm and resolute government at home and abroad.'[52] At a rally in Glasgow in front of 10,000 Attlee was caustic about Churchill's political prospects.

> Mr Churchill is asking for three or four more years of rule. I think it is going to be a short interlude. Mr Churchill is a man of infinite variability. When we were returned to the House of Commons with a small majority we had hardly got in before he was asking for another election. Now he is in with a minority of votes and a small majority, he wants to stay for three or four years. Everything is quite different if Mr Churchill is at the head of affairs.[53]

The local elections in May 1952 superficially went well for Labour. But this image of Opposition success was illusory. In reality, Labour was sinking in the mire of division and feuds. It was the paradox of Attlee's position in these years that he was simultaneously viewed as the only possible Leader who could hold the party together and the pedestrian compromiser who could give no real sense of direction. In effect, he was the glue for unity and the barrier to revival. Attlee himself was aware of this contradiction and, on occasions, appeared willing to contemplate retirement. At a dinner in June 1952 with Patrick Gordon-Walker and several other moderate MPs, he discussed the Bevanite conflict, then 'suddenly said that no-one ought to be Prime Minister after 70. Had it not been for the split in the party, he would certainly have made up his mind to go. We should give our mind to finding another leader.'[54]

But Attlee had no genuine intention of quitting. At a lunch given in London to Labour agents in July, Attlee contradicted press rumours about an illness and said he was 'in excellent health', unlike Churchill's Government which was 'suffering from extremely low blood pressure'. Turning to his own future and the General Election, he said, 'It is my hope that I shall lead the Labour Party when the next time comes along.'[55] That quelled the speculation but not the disunity. In the coming weeks, there were yet more internal disputes over defence, foreign affairs, and economic policies, as the Bevanites campaigned for a more vigorous brand of socialism. The drive to refashion the party that year culminated in a fractious Annual Conference at the Lancashire seaside resort of Morecambe, where the appalling weather matched the stormy mood of proceedings. 'The worst for bad temper and general hatred since 1926,' wrote Dalton.[56] At the Conference, the Bevanites predominated through their strength among constituency delegates. Both Dalton and Morrison were voted off the NEC, while Attlee was widely criticised by moderates for doodling and puffing on his pipe rather than providing leadership. 'His speech must have been the flattest ever delivered by a leader,' wrote Crossman.[57] Soon after Morecambe, Bevan reinforced his dominance by gaining re-election to the Shadow Cabinet, much to the anger of the Labour right.

The tortuous developments in the Labour Party were followed with deep interest by Churchill. 'The row between Attlee and Bevan is flaring up very nicely and it is a pleasure to see newspapers full of Socialist splits instead of only our own shortcomings,' wrote Churchill to his wife in August.[58] Lord Moran recorded that Churchill was intrigued by coverage of Labour's turmoil, not least because he fantasised that, like the Liberal division after the First World War, it could revive the concept of a centrist, intra-party alliance. 'The split might deepen and lead to a Coalition. I should not be against it,' said Churchill.[59] That was wishful thinking, given Attlee's experience of 1931 and the depths of Labour's tribal hostility to the Tories. More realistically, according to Moran, Churchill was also annoyed by what he saw as the rash conduct of Labour, increasingly driven to the left by Bevanite pressures: 'It is a perplexing time, much worse than the war: all talk and no co-operation. Attlee and his people are behaving badly, currying popularity by attacking America.'[60]

Yet, as they had done throughout their careers, Attlee and Churchill managed to keep their personal relations civil. They continued their long-established tradition of sending each other telegrams on their respective birthdays. 'Many thanks for your birthday greetings, which I greatly appreciate,' Attlee cabled Churchill, during the Prime Minister's visit to Washington in January 1952.[61] Clementine Churchill was among the 300 guests at the Anglican Church in Great Missenden when Alison, Attlee's youngest daughter, married Captain Richard Davis in March, though Winston 'could not attend because of pressure of work'.[62] In September, Churchill sent Attlee a copy of the fifth volume of his Second World War memoirs, *Closing the Ring*. 'I hope you will accept it with my good wishes,' he wrote.[63] Just as Attlee had done during his premiership, Churchill extended invitations to Downing Street and Chequers. Anthony Montague Browne, a former diplomat who began working for Churchill from 1952, recalled a happy afternoon at Chequers that highlighted the virtue of British democracy. 'He and Clementine had taken on Attlee and his wife at post-lunch croquet. I reflected that the spectacle of the Leader of the Opposition playing croquet with the Prime Minister was unlikely to be found elsewhere.'[64]

Even in the political arena, their exchanges could be light-hearted. During the debate on the Address in November 1952, Attlee had noted the sceptical tone of the passage about the priority attached to Commonwealth and American relations above involvement with

European integration. 'There was a time when the Prime Minister looked as if he was going to be, so to speak, stroke of the European boat, but he is now only offering a few helpful suggestions from the towpath.'[65] In response, Churchill made a gibe at Attlee's troubles with the Bevanites. 'I can only hope that the moderation and sobriety of his statement will not expose him to any undue risk among his own friends. I am sure I may offer him my congratulation on his being able to address us from those benches as stroke and not, to quote the term he has just used, from the tow-path.'[66] When Churchill accepted a knighthood from the Queen in April 1953, having turned one down from her father in 1945, Attlee expressed the Opposition's congratulations. Richard Crossman, a formidable critic, was taken with Churchill's humour when he heard him offer the toast at a Commonwealth parliamentary banquet in May 1953, just before the Coronation. 'I have never heard him speak better. Despite the solemnity of the occasion, he made a light-hearted Parliamentary oration.' Referring to some current difficulties with America over treaty rights, he said he had to tread carefully. 'I will therefore content myself with the observation that no constitution was written in better English.' Crossman continued, 'Everyone was convulsed with laughter and though it is sheer imagination, one could have thought one heard the Queen laughing through the microphone. Attlee, I am told, was first appalled and then delighted by this chivalrous support in the middle of a speech which was supposed to be thanking the Queen.'[67]

On the party-political stage, Attlee was still fighting on two fronts from late 1952: against the Conservatives and the Bevanite left. He was falling back on both. In the Commons in early December, he tried to galvanise Labour with a technical motion criticising the Government for its mismanaged conduct of business in the House, though this was really a cover for an attack on the Tory pledge to denationalise the road haulage and steel industries. Once again, just as in February, Attlee's move turned out to be counter-productive, due to a swashbuckling speech by Churchill that demolished Labour. 'Rarely has the Premier shown such dash and pep,' reported the *Daily Mail*.[68] Answering Attlee's charges of incompetence, Churchill described the censure motion as 'a yelp of anger from men who have been fairly beaten in all their manoeuvres, however disreputable. We have been the victors in over 250 divisions with majorities almost double what our majority is on paper.' Churchill then proceeded to read out the roll-call of his parliamentary victories since the election, concluding with the triumphant question: 'Is that incompetence?' Turning to Attlee's own position, he expressed the hope that his 'denunciation of the Government will be considered sufficient and that he will not be "left at the post" when the Right Honourable Member for Ebbw Vale* resumes the role of virtuous indignation, reinforced with abuse, for which he is celebrated.'[69] The Government won by twenty-four votes. That night, Macmillan wrote in his diary that 'Churchill just crushed Attlee'.[70]

Defeated in the Commons, Attlee was unable to stamp his authority on Labour. He had been a largely successful Prime Minister because of his gifts as an administrator, but the party now needed inspiration, something he was ill-equipped to provide. The burden led him to complain towards the end of 1952 that 'the last year has been the unhappiest I have had in my 17 years of leadership'.[71] Appalled at Attlee's failure to take on the Bevanite rebels, moderates like Dalton and Gaitskell felt that their Leader was guilty of worsening vacillation. 'I said Nye was getting more ego-soaked and impossible. He said Attlee was weaker and weaker,' Dalton noted of a conversation with Gaitskell.[72] The Labour MP Richard Stokes wrote directly to Attlee, asking him to 'move over and give Herbert a chance', to which Attlee replied that he had to stay to prevent turmoil in the party.[73] From the left, Dick Crossman described him as 'a little man' of 'imperturbable unimaginativeness which is breathtaking'.[74]

That lack of imagination was again highlighted when Churchill, in early February 1953, invited Attlee to all-party talks on the reform of the House of Lords, a cause that Churchill had once championed and now wished to revive. He thought the Upper House was ripe for

---

*   Bevan.

change; according to the Marquess of Salisbury, he regarded the place as 'a rather disreputable collection of old gentlemen'.[75] In his letter of 3 February to Attlee, Churchill wrote that reform 'is urgently required' and the invitation was 'sent in a sincere desire to achieve an agreed and enduring solution of this long-standing and difficult problem to the advantage of Parliament and the Nation'. But Attlee was uninterested in the initiative, fearing that co-operation with the Tories would further undermine him with the left. 'We have come to the conclusion that no useful purpose would be served by our entering such a discussion,' he wrote.[76]

In contrast to Attlee, Churchill seemed to be reinvigorated after more than a year in Downing Street. Now he was fully in charge, the premiership acted like an elixir. 'I am really wonderfully well,' he said to Moran one morning in early 1953. He enjoyed the sense of presiding over a benign, centrist government that was gradually spreading prosperity without political upheaval. Churchill was strengthened by the performance of the economy. Dalton admitted in his diary that Tory rule 'was not so bad as we had prophesised. Unemployment, prices, wages, social services (especially housing), foreign affairs all better than we expected.'[77] The economic recovery brought political dividends. In May the Conservatives sensationally won the Sunderland South by-election, the first time a sitting Government had taken a seat off the official Opposition since 1924. 'It will certainly upset the socialists and they will begin to quarrel still more,' wrote Macmillan gleefully.[78]

Churchill's vigour was further restored when he took over the Foreign Affairs portfolio in April, after Anthony Eden had to undergo a gallbladder operation. The procedure was almost fatally botched and Eden had to go to Boston in the USA for remedial surgery, which put him out of action for months just at the time when he might have expected to take over from Churchill after the Coronation. Eden's medically induced withdrawal gave Churchill a new lease of life, not only because he far preferred foreign to domestic policy, but also because the role brought him a new sense of purpose. In direct contra-diction of Labour's propaganda about his warmongering, he started to see himself as an international catalyst for peace. He conceived that this could be achieved by a revival of the kind of high-powered summitry that had served him so well in the Second World War. As a result of this conviction, he began to push for a peace conference with Russia, with the death of Stalin in March 1953 serving as an opportunity to foster new relations with Moscow. In the House, during a debate on foreign affairs in May, Attlee praised Churchill's constructive approach. 'The Prime Minister made a very remarkable speech and he will have realised that its general tone and approach were warmly welcomed on this side of the House [...] We are all united in this House and in this country in our earnest desire for peace, and we all welcome the signs of change in the attitude on the part of Soviet Russia.'[79] The White House, now under Eisenhower, was far less receptive to the international summit idea, though the President did eventually agree to a meeting of Western powers to be held in Bermuda later in the summer. But Churchill was not dissuaded from his mission of a new peace deal. He told Attlee in the House that he hoped Bermuda could be 'the definite step to a meeting of greater import'.[80]

But before Churchill could make another move, he was struck a blow that looked certain to bring a swift end to his premiership.

THIRTY-ONE

❖

COMMONS

O N 23 JUNE 1953, after a dinner at Downing Street for the Italian
Prime Minister Alcide de Gasperi, Churchill experienced a
massive stroke. Initially the impact of this episode did not seem too
destructive, and Churchill even talked of making an appearance in
the Commons, a course from which he was dissuaded by Colville
and Moran. But Churchill's condition drastically deteriorated and on
Friday 26 June he had to be taken down to Chartwell. The situation
was so grave that Colville telephoned the Palace and discussed with
Tommy Lascelles the possibility of asking Lord Salisbury, the Lord
President, 'to form a caretaker Government on the express understanding that he would retire when Eden was well enough to form a
new Government'.[1]

Yet Churchill was not completely incapacitated. He could still
communicate with his family, Colville and Moran, and was sufficiently
alert to compose a telegram for President Eisenhower, explaining that
he could not now come to the talks in Bermuda, for which he had
been due to sail the following week. The sudden cancellation of the
visit was bound to lead to press speculation so a bland press release was
issued from Chartwell on Moran's advice, with the support of Butler
and Salisbury. It read, 'The Prime Minister has had no respite for a long
time from his very arduous duties and is in need of a complete rest. We
have therefore advised him to abandon his journey to Bermuda and to
lighten his duties for at least a month.'[2]

On that final weekend in June, it seemed that a permanent end to his duties was imminent. The severity of the stroke would have killed many a lesser man. The idea that a seventy-eight-year-old could continue to run the country after such a traumatic experience sounded fanciful. Indeed, Churchill would almost certainly have been compelled to resign immediately if Eden had not been in America undergoing more surgery. But the knowledge that he could not quickly be supplanted by his heir gave Churchill an additional determination to fight on. His astonishing recovery, almost in defiance of medical science, began that weekend. As early as Sunday 28 June, he demonstrated that his sparkle had not deserted him, as he read through front page newspaper reports of the lightening in his duties. 'Today, I have knocked Christie off the headlines,' he said proudly, a reference to the grisly serial killer Reginald Christie of 10 Rillington Place,* whose trial had just started at the Old Bailey. At dinner on 4 July he gave an indication that he now felt he could carry on as Prime Minister. 'I shall do what is best for my country,' he said, before adding with a whimsical smile: 'Circumstances may convince of my indispensability.'[3]

While Churchill continued his recovery, Lord Salisbury flew to Washington for talks with the US Secretary of State Foster Dulles. But this was nothing like the precursor to the high-powered Bermuda summit that Churchill had planned before his illness. Devoid of any enthusiasm for engagement with the new Soviet regime under Stalin's successor Georgy Malenkov, the Americans barely went through the formality of discussions, from which nothing concrete emerged. When Butler, standing in for Churchill and Eden during a foreign affairs debate in the Commons on 21 July, announced the paltry outcome of the Salisbury visit, Labour were indignant. In fact, Butler's poor performance prompted the incongruous sound of Labour MPs rushing to the aid of the absent Churchill in defence of his call for negotiations with Russia. In his response to Butler, Attlee said Churchill in May had

---

* The renowned 1971 British film *10 Rillington Place* starred Richard Attenborough as Christie. The following year Attenborough directed the movie *Young Winston*, based on Churchill's book *My Early Life*.

'raised great hopes' but that Butler's statement on the recent Washington Conference did 'not seem to be forward looking enough or to be really in tune with the Prime Minister's speech'. At the end of July, Attlee again praised Churchill's push for a summit and also criticised Dulles for pursuing a unilateral policy on Korean unity without consulting his UN partners. Unless the UN was upheld in 'a broad and statesmanlike way, it will not be the beginning of a new era of peace', Attlee warned.[4] According to Crossman, Attlee got 'an enormous ovation for his strong denunciation of the smothering of the Churchill peace initiative'.[5] Even the *Sunday Express*, normally hostile to Attlee, said that the Labour Leader had 'seized the chance offered by Mr Churchill's illness to give the country a lead, and roll the Tory Second Eleven in the mud'.[6]

The wish to reignite his global initiative gave Churchill another reason to fight for the retention of his premiership. After seeing Jock Colville on 22 July, the diplomat and Eden ally Evelyn Shuckburgh recorded that 'it seems the Old Man has made a miraculous recovery from his stroke and is far from thinking of throwing in the sponge'.[7] During the next few weeks, Churchill's rehabilitation and his ambition intensified. Violet Bonham Carter visited him on 6 August, little more than six weeks after the stroke. When she came away, she reflected: 'The light is still burning – flashing – in its battered framework – the indomitable desire to live still militant and intact.'[8] Churchill was so determined to prove his capacity that he chaired a Cabinet meeting on 18 August, his first since June. 'He was in tremendous form,' recorded Macmillan, who was struck by the size of the crowd which had gathered in Downing Street to cheer him.[9]

The crucial test for Churchill was whether he could effectively deliver his speech to the Conservative Conference at Margate in early October. In front of a large audience, there would be no hiding place. By coincidence, Labour's Annual Conference was also held that autumn in Margate. The atmosphere in the Kent resort could not have been more different to the one in Morecambe the year before. Over the previous months, Attlee's low-key approach had brought about a mood of reconciliation between both wings of his party. 'We had a very good

Conference at Margate, an excellent spirit and an absence of personal jars,' he wrote to his brother.[10] Privately, Bevan was not so happy at the spirit of compromise. 'Margate was indeed a flop,' he wrote.[11]

Margate was anything but a flop for Churchill. In the build-up to the speech, to be made on 10 October, he felt under intense pressure, unsure whether he would be able to deliver or even remain upright for the forty minutes of its duration. 'I don't know if I can stand that time. I haven't been on my feet for more than a few minutes at a time since it happened,' he told Moran, who noted: 'The PM has put his shirt on this speech. If he could hold the meeting, all would be well. If he failed in that, life for him was over.'[12] The Conservative representatives at the Winter Gardens in Margate shared his anxiety as he rose on the platform, an electric sense of nervous anticipation hanging in the seaside air. When he reached his peroration, it was cleared that he had pulled off another triumph. It was fitting that, once more, he should end with a passage about his quest for 'a sure and lasting peace', which he declared was now the final goal of his career.[13] He sat down to resounding, relieved applause. He had secured his survival.

Throughout the last phase of Churchill's faltering premiership, illness and the passage of the years did nothing to diminish the mutual respect, at times even affection, between him and Attlee. On 6 September 1953, while he was recovering, he had Attlee to lunch at Chequers. They also sent each other birthday, Christmas and New Year greetings. At the end of December 1953, Churchill dispatched the sixth and final volume of his Second World War memoirs. 'It completes a remarkable series and I look forward with pleasure to reading it,' Attlee replied. July 1954 saw Attlee sending a more incongruous note of gratitude.[14] 'Thank you for sending me the cheese. It was most kind of you.'[15] More publicly, on 20 November 1953, Churchill gave the main speech in the Mansion House at the ceremony to mark Attlee's award of the Freedom of London. 'I do not pretend that he does not, from time to time, say things both in the country and in the House of Commons, which do not command my whole-hearted accord,' Churchill said before turning to the landmarks of Attlee's record which 'entitle him to respectful tributes of all', including his military service in the First World War, his 'philanthropic work' for the poor in east London, and his long premiership. Then, in the most generous passage he ever used about Attlee, Churchill said, 'My bond with him is the fact that he was my colleague and comrade for more than five years through the grim and awful ordeal of the war and that he acted as my Deputy with very high loyalty and efficiency throughout the whole period when I bore the chief responsibility.' After more words about cross-party unity in the war, he concluded, 'It is with sincere affection that I propose this afternoon to this distinguished company the health of a statesman for whom it is no mere term of art for me to describe as my Right Honourable Friend.'[16]

In his reply Attlee said that the honour the City had done him was 'enhanced by having his health proposed by the Prime Minister. That is a thing that would happen in hardly any other country. There are many countries in which the leader of one party not only wishes ill-health to his opposite number but ensures it.' Recalling his work in Churchill's wartime Coalition, Attlee said, 'There are times when the emphasis is on the things that unite us and not on the things that divide us. It is always well to keep that in memory.'[17] Contrasting Attlee's socialism with the City's raw capitalism, the William Hickey column in the *Daily Express* called the event 'a staggering, wonderful, mysterious action which only an Englishman can understand'. The column also delighted in the social and fashionable side of the ceremony. 'Lady Churchill, in black with a red scarf, got a great reception, which she enjoyed,' while Violet Attlee was 'pretty and smart in a pink and red coat'. But the writer could not resist a political barb at Attlee: 'that unimpressive man whose slant eyes and smile mask the iron will that carried through a revolution'.[18]

The occasional display of platform brilliance was not enough for many of Churchill's Tory colleagues, who continued to feel the time had come for him to depart. The Leader of the Commons Harry Crookshank complained that Churchill was 'unable to perform his functions properly' and displayed 'maddening hesitations and incapacity or unwillingness to transact ordinary routine business'.[19] Salisbury considered resigning on the grounds of age to try to set an example to

Churchill, while Rab Butler urged Eden to quit the Foreign Office to force Churchill's hand. Exasperation with Churchill deepened when in December he attended the Bermuda conference, which had been postponed from the summer. Once more, he had hoped that this could be the beginning of a process to negotiations with the Russians, but Eisenhower, truculent at Churchill's infirmity and violently opposed to Communism, refused to give his blessing to Anglo-Soviet talks. 'I have been humiliated by my own decay,' Churchill told Moran as the conference ended in failure.[20] Even his own office was shaken at his decline. Jane Portal, one of Churchill's devoted secretaries, told Shuckburgh: 'He half kills himself with work, cannot take in the papers he is given to read and can hardly get upstairs to bed.' Portal added, tragically, that 'it is impossible for him to resign, because he can no longer write, dreads solitude and oblivion and fears rest'.[21]

The concern about Churchill's fitness escalated to a new level in April 1954, due to one of his most explosive parliamentary clashes with Attlee. The confrontation was sparked by reports that the USA had experimented with a new, far more powerful, version of the hydrogen bomb. Tests in the Pacific on this deadly new device, the first lithium-deuteride-fuelled thermonuclear weapon, showed that the fall-out was far greater than had been predicted. The concern of the British public at these findings was reflected at Westminster, where there was now renewed pressure for an international peace initiative of the sort that Churchill had advocated. This seemed a golden moment for him to renew his mission about talks. But, because of advancing debilitation, mixed with a thirst for partisanship, his touch dramatically deserted him. The first sign of trouble came on 30 March, when he made an inept statement to the House about the hydrogen bomb tests, simultaneously extolling the mighty power of the USA and then admitting he could provide MPs with little information because the Americans had not consulted his Government. There was dissatisfaction on all sides with his performance. The *Daily Mirror* reported that, 'old and tired, he mouthed comfortless words in the twilight of his career'.[22] But this was just a prelude to a much more incendiary row during a full debate on the hydrogen bomb, called by Labour, on Monday 5 April.

As always before a major Commons event, Churchill put a great deal of preparation into his speech. On this occasion, he decided that his central theme would be, not the search for global peace but rather the imprudence of the last Attlee Government in allowing the rupture in Anglo-American nuclear co-operation. He had long nursed his resentment at the abandonment of his Quebec Agreement with Roosevelt and the debate seemed the perfect opportunity to hurt the Opposition with his accusation of transatlantic neglect. He was further whipped up to this position by Lord Cherwell, who shared his disdain for Attlee's failure to uphold the Agreement. In one letter to Churchill, Lord Cherwell admitted that the Agreement had been superseded by the Senate's passage of the 1946 McMahon Act but said 'Attlee's error was in not taking more vigorous action when they did this. Apparently he did protest but his protest was unanswered and he left it at that.'[23] According to Lord Moran's diary, Cherwell 'carefully coached' Churchill over his H-bomb speech, encouraging the Prime Minister to believe that he 'was going to knock Mr Attlee through the ropes'. But Moran refused to put much of the blame on Cherwell. 'If he led Winston astray, it was because Winston wanted to go that way [...] He loved a fight. He is still at heart the red-haired urchin, cocking a snook at anybody who gets in the way.' There were doubts in Churchill's circle that this was the right tactic, wrote Moran, with some Tories 'hoping he would leave Attlee alone'.[24] But Churchill would not be dissuaded. At the Cabinet a few days before the debate, he revealed that 'he planned to make public the private agreement that had been made between him and Roosevelt as to the use of the atomic bomb'. This, he thought, 'would lay Attlee flat'.[25] Having heard Churchill's plan to reveal the story of Quebec, Macmillan, unlike some Conservatives, was enthusiastic. 'If he does, it will be devastating for Attlee.'[26] The gentlemanly Eden, however, seemed anxious. In his diary, Lord Woolton recorded: 'Eden insisted that Churchill should tell Attlee what he prepared to do and this he did on Saturday morning.'[27]

Even though he may have been aware of Churchill's intentions, Attlee was hoping to steer the debate in a very different direction. In place of an internecine quarrel, he wanted to concentrate on the call for a global summit in this dangerous new era. This approach, he estimated, would not only cement Labour unity but would reassure the country. The sense of a moral imperative seemed to galvanise Attlee when he addressed the PLP before the debate. Often a fierce critic, Crossman recorded, 'Attlee made the best speech of his life. I was sitting just below him and saw how his hands shook with emotion. But his voice was collected and he swept the whole Party off its feet.'[28] He was just as authoritative when he opened the debate in the Commons as he emphasised the need to rise above narrow political considerations in the quest for a new accommodation between East and West. Lord Woolton, who watched Attlee's performance from the Peers' Gallery, recorded that 'he paid Churchill compliments indicating the tremendous power he had because of his personal position – and he left the way open for a great speech such as probably only Churchill could give and it would have gone round the world'. Woolton also noted that, despite the apparent warning on Saturday, Attlee said nothing about the Quebec disclosure, perhaps hoping that Churchill would not press the point. Indeed, based on a conversation he had with Morrison, Woolton was informed that Attlee had not told 'any of his followers that he had had a note from Churchill'.[29] What followed therefore came as all the greater a surprise to Labour's ranks, exacerbating their anger.

Churchill rose to the Dispatch Box, as the House waited for one of his noble, historic orations. Attlee himself later wrote to his brother, 'I had given him the opportunity to make a great speech on a high level – to give a lead to the world, so to speak.'[30] Churchill started quietly, but within minutes he had launched his prepared attack on Attlee over Quebec. Attlee immediately leaped to his feet and tartly pointed out that the abandonment was not of his making but that of the US Senate. Churchill ploughed on with his charge, prompting further angry interjections from Attlee. 'Every time he intervened, he scored,' wrote Woolton.[31] The diplomat Evelyn Shuckburgh was also a spectator, and saw Attlee grow 'red in the face, quivering with rage' as he responded to Churchill, who would not drop the issue, despite the growing uproar in the House and the fury from the Labour MPs. For Shuckburgh, tragedy was mixed with entertainment in the chaos that erupted:

> the backbenchers shouting and booing, the Tories glum and silent. (Mrs Braddock,* like a London fishwife, shouting over and over again, 'Look behind yer, look behind yer'); all the tough guys putting on their expressions and yelling 'disgraceful', 'shocking', 'another red letter day', 'resign', and the Old Man looking utterly dumbfounded, plunging further and further where he had not intended to go, and making it seem as if he blamed Attlee for the fact that McMahon had not known of the existence of the Quebec Agreement.[32]

While most of the Tories sat in appalled silence, Churchill's former ally Bob Boothby stood up and, to Labour cheers, walked out of the chamber – 'a characteristic act of disloyalty', commented Macmillan.[33] 'I have the right to be heard,' said Churchill at one point in desperation, which only heightened the abuse. Richard Crossman, a noisy participant, even felt a sense of self-disgust at the mood of the House. 'The scene worked up to a fever, with all of us shouting, "Guttersnipe! Swine! Resign!" with Churchill standing there swaying slightly and trying to plough through his script [...] How nauseating we were, howling for the old bull's blood. I really think we would have lynched him if we could.'[34] Churchill struggled on, determined to finish. 'His voice was that of a very old man; he had somehow to get through a set piece before he sat down as if his only purpose was to get to the end,' noted Moran, another spectator.[35] 'I thought it was the most distressing thing I had ever seen in the House [...] The extraordinary thing was

---

* Bessie Braddock, the outspoken Liverpool MP.

that Churchill had done nothing else except that speech for three days, which shows completely he is out of touch with what this country and indeed the world wants from him', wrote Woolton.[36]

Churchill comprehensive misjudgement of the House's mood was emphasised when Eden wound up in powerful but assured style. Unlike the Prime Minister, he managed diplomatically to challenge Attlee's version of the Quebec saga without incurring the wrath of Labour. The debate reinforced Eden's claims to succeed, while obliterating Churchill's credibility. Most of the press coverage of his performance was hostile. The *Manchester Guardian* said that he had 'blundered', while *The Times* felt that his sense of occasion had 'deserted him sadly yesterday'.[37] In addition to his failure to read the mood of the Commons after the H-bomb test, another problem for Churchill was his lifelong fear of speaking extempore, so he felt he had to stick to his manuscript, no matter how flawed it was. Rather absurdly, he even used his notes, wrote Woolton, 'to the extent of thanking the House for the consideration they had given him. It is extraordinary that so practical a politician should not have realised that his notes were all wrong for the occasion after Attlee's speech.'[38] Macmillan regarded the episode as Churchill's 'greatest failure' since the 1936 abdication and shrewdly made that point in his diary that night: 'He has never been very mobile and his method of speaking (with every word prepared) had this inherent danger.'[39] Churchill himself admitted to Moran soon after the debate, 'I have been too tethered to my notes.'[40] Later in life, he was at a dinner where one guest described him as 'a great orator'. Churchill replied, 'Afraid it's balls. I was never an orator.' He went on to explain that the true orators never knew in advance what they would say. 'Their phrases were dictated by some inner god. But I carefully wrote out every speech I had ever given.'[41]

The irony of the debacle was that Churchill shared Attlee's view about the need for a new diplomatic initiative with the Russians. Indeed, even in the wake of his catastrophe, he felt that such a demand gave him a further justification to stay in office, claiming he had been handed a mandate by the Commons to secure a summit meeting with the Soviets. But few

Conservatives could accept such a rationale. The bombshell he had tried to explode under Attlee had shattered his own authority. As Anthony Montague Browne, his loyal secretary, wrote, 'It was the beginning of the end for him as Prime Minister.'[42] Shuckburgh recorded that, in the wake of the fiasco, Eden and his top colleagues had decided that 'in no circumstances' could Churchill attend a top-level conference, while the Chief Whip, Patrick Buchan-Hepburn, and Sir Norman Brook, the Cabinet Secretary, 'both think the Prime Minister must resign'.[43]

The Labour Party was understandably jubilant at Churchill's collapse. There was suddenly a new sense of unity in the Parliamentary Party and a renewed admiration for the veteran Leader. Just as Churchill's stock had taken a plunge, so Attlee's had risen. Crossman felt that Attlee 'has behaved like an impeccable patriotic leader, putting the country before party'. After the debate, Crossman went to celebrate at the Press Club, where he ran into the *Mirror*'s editorial director Hugh Cudlipp, who was thrilled at the role his paper had played in undermining Churchill. 'Hugh was as elated as I was. If we are the gutter press, we had provoked Churchill to enter the gutter with us and thereby probably ruin himself,' recorded Crossman.[44] But the harmony could not last, and the catalyst for another outbreak of disunity was, inevitably, Bevan. Attlee once said that 'Nye seemed to kick through his own goal only when his side was winning'.[45] Soon after Labour's H-bomb triumph, Bevan did so in extravagant style by implicitly challenging Attlee on the floor of the House over the Leader's support for the Government on the development of a security pact in Southeast Asia, a kind of NATO for the region. In contradiction of Labour policy, Bevan described the potential alliance as a surrender to American pressure. Attlee was irate and at a meeting of the Shadow Cabinet the next morning rebuked Bevan, later repeating the criticism at a meeting of the PLP. Bevan subsequently resigned from the front bench. Gaitskell was glad to see him go, describing him as 'an evil genius'.[46]

Despite sniping from Bevan, Attlee generally remained supportive of the Government's foreign policy, especially the need for a global summit. But he and Churchill still clashed in the House occasionally, though with nothing like the stupendous impact of the H-bomb debate. Attlee gained the upper hand in a debate in July 1954 about troop withdrawals from Egypt, a policy that had been initiated by his Government and continued by Churchill's, much to the fury of the Tory right. Moran was a witness to the confrontation at the Dispatch Box and left this account: 'Mr Attlee recalled that when the plan to withdraw our troops was announced by the head of the Labour Government, Mr Churchill said it was "a most painful blow". "He must have been in acute pain yesterday," said Mr Attlee, thrusting forward his hatchet face as if he was about to cleave the Prime Minister's skull.' Moran recorded that 'it had been a savage and damaging attack, so effective that I found my heart thumping. I hated every minute of it. Winston's face was grey and expressionless as if he no longer knew what was happening.'[47] The next month, still clinging to his dreams of a global summit, Churchill was privately envious when Attlee led a Labour delegation to Moscow as part of a lengthy global tour. 'I had the initiative. Now we have lost it. I might have pushed on and done something. As it is, people will say it is very sensible on Attlee's part,' he complained to Moran, adding that he had hoped for a grand international conference in September. Now Attlee's visit, 'had taken the bloom off the peach'.[48]

Since the H-bomb debacle, Churchill had fought a magnificent but self-serving rearguard action, ruthlessly exploiting the chivalry of Eden, the reluctance of his Cabinet to move against him and the fading lustre of his name. He may have been in decline, but he displayed titanic willpower in clinging on to his position. Every time a date for his departure appeared to have been fixed, he found a new excuse to stay, usually involving a new political crisis or a hint from Washington or Moscow about the distant possibility of a summit. 'No one is going to push me out,' he declared to his family.[49] He even told Macmillan that he was now 'in far better health', could ride out any threats of resignation from Cabinet ministers, would 'form another and more powerful administration' and planned to lead the party 'into the next General Election'.[50] Now beginning to despise Churchill, Eden complained that 'the old man is really a crook!'[51]

As immovable as his Cabinet was irresolute in forcing his departure, Churchill therefore remained in post through the autumn of 1954, though his popularity was on the wane. On the eve of the Tory Conference in Blackpool, a poll in the *News Chronicle* revealed that half of the public wanted him to go and the Tory vote would rise by 13 per cent if he did so. But Churchill was in a determined mood as he made his way to the Lancashire resort. 'I can harangue the bastards for 50 minutes,' he told Moran.[52] Unlike his appearance at Margate the year before, his Blackpool performance was not so successful. Both Jane Portal and Jock Colville felt his delivery was poor. In the opinion of Christopher Soames, even worse was the content of his address, dominated by foreign policy and tributes to Labour. This was not what the party wanted to hear with a General Election possibly less than a year away. As Soames put it to Moran, 'here was a leader of the party singling out Mr Attlee and Mr Morrison, praising them because they were consistent in foreign policy. That, of course, was magnanimous and all that, but it was not going to help the Conservatives on the hustings.'[53]

Political magnanimity continued when Attlee led the address by both Houses of Parliament in the unprecedented ceremony at Westminster Hall to mark Churchill's eightieth birthday. 'Dignified, restrained, noble', was Harold Macmillan's verdict. In addition to speeches by Attlee and Churchill, the Father of the House Dai Grenfell, who had been the Labour MP for Gower since 1922, gave his tribute. 'He has been our greatest leader in our greatest national trial,' said Grenfell in words that showed how Churchill, at his best, rose above the strife of party.[54] After the Westminster ceremony, Churchill had an audience at Buckingham Palace with the Queen, who presented him with a gift of four silver wine stands for decanters, embossed with royal ciphers. On his return to Downing Street, Churchill took part in a television broadcast that opened with birthday greetings from friends and colleagues, before he expressed his gratitude for this outpouring of affection. That night, a crowd gathered in Downing Street to cheer him as he stood at a first floor window and gave his unique V-sign. The only jarring note in the day was the portrait by Graham Sutherland. Although Churchill was diplomatic about it at the ceremony in Westminster Hall, he privately loathed it from the first moment he saw it: 'It makes me look half-witted, which I ain't.'⁵⁵ Many shared his view. On leaving Westminster Hall, Lord Hailsham* was just as acerbic, 'It's a filthy colour. Churchill has not had so much ink on his face since he left Harrow.'⁵⁶

There was more magnanimity from Attlee following a clumsy political indiscretion in the wake of his birthday celebrations. In a speech in his Woodford constituency, accepting a gift from his local Conservative Association, he blurted out that in May 1945 he had ordered Field Marshal Montgomery by telegram to stockpile surrendered German arms 'so that they could easily be issued again to the German soldiers whom we should have to work with if the Russian advance continued'.⁵⁷ A major controversy ensued, made all the more incendiary because Churchill's telegram in 1945 to Montgomery appeared to undermine his current pursuit of Soviet rapprochement. Churchill himself privately admitted that he had made a mistake, and in public tried to backtrack by questioning whether he had actually sent the telegram. That ruse was quickly undermined by Montgomery, who declared unequivocally, 'Yes I received that order. A Churchill statement does not need confirmation. I carried out the order. I am a good soldier.'⁵⁸ But Churchill was fortunate. The row quickly fizzled out because Attlee, anxious to maintain cross-party unity on Soviet diplomacy, did not take up the issue in the Commons, despite pressure from some of his own MPs. In a discussion about disarmament during the debate on the Address, Attlee complained that the Government had shown insufficient 'urgency' over potential talks with Russia, but he made no mention of the Montgomery telegram.⁵⁹ 'Socialist backbenchers waited in the Commons last night for Mr Attlee to give leadership to the "Churchill must go" campaign. But they waited in vain [...] Mr Attlee shocked and mystified many of his supporters by his failure to refer to the "stack German arms" order,' reported the *Daily Mail*.⁶⁰

* The former MP Quintin Hogg, who was elevated to the peerage on the death of his father in 1950.

Attlee's refusal to hound Churchill showed a streak of compassionate mellowness. That warmth also shone through their personal exchanges. On 3 January 1955 Winston and Clemmie telegraphed Cherry Tree Cottage to tell Attlee, 'We do hope you are having a Happy Birthday. We wish you many more.'[61] Attlee replied with a handwritten note to both of them, 'Thank you very much for your kind good wishes. I hope that you and all the family had a good Christmas. It is bitter cold and sleeting down. I've just read Frank Owen's *Lloyd George* – slick and inaccurate journalism but not really good.'[62] Churchill and Attlee continued to meet at civic and royal functions, with the Labour Leader also showing signs of advancing age. Clarissa Eden noted in her diary 'an interminable lunch' at the Mansion House in October 1954: 'Winston gets rather fidgety and very impatient. Attlee goes to sleep and his lighted cigar falls on the table cloth.'[63] After another Palace function in February, Churchill was delighted to tell Moran of an episode that appeared to show that Attlee's frailty was greater than his own. 'Some of the others are not lasting as well as I am; they are feeling the strain and show it. Last night Attlee came up to me at the Palace. I could see he was quivering, and then he fainted in my arms. I'm not very strong, but I managed to get him to a couch. Poor Attlee, he is getting old; he is 72.'[64]

Churchill's own eightieth birthday might have seemed the obvious time to depart, but he still rejected the idea of retirement. Four years earlier, he had called the Labour front bench 'lion-hearted limpets'. That was an exact description of his own behaviour now. Far from resigning, he attempted to renew his leadership through a Cabinet reshuffle in October, in which he elevated the Home Secretary Maxwell-Fyffe to the Woolsack as Lord Kilmuir, replaced him with Gwilym Lloyd George, and moved Harold Macmillan from Housing to Defence. In the weeks after the Westminster Hall ceremony, he remained adamant about his retention of office. According to the record made by Woolton, he was as obstinate as ever at a meeting of Cabinet on 22 December. 'I know you are trying to get rid of me and it is up to me to go to the Queen and hand her my resignation and yours – but I won't do it. But if you feel strongly about it you can force my hand by a sufficiently large number of Ministers handing in their resignations, in which case an Election is inevitable. But if this happens, I shall not be in favour of it and I shall tell the country so.'[65]

While still in Downing Street, Churchill continued to focus on the great questions of defence, nuclear weapons and the lingering hope of a Soviet summit, which remained a chimera. On 12 January 1955 he wrote to Eisenhower, stressing the need for international talks before Russian nuclear strength reached 'saturation point'. He also reported that Britain's own nuclear programme, including the development of a hydrogen bomb, was going well. 'We are making atomic bombs on a steadily increasing scale, and we and our experts are confident that we have the secret, perhaps even with some improvements, of the hydrogen bomb.' Mention of the nuclear technology enabled Churchill to give some qualified praise to Attlee.

> If the agreement signed between me and FDR had not been shelved we should probably have been able to add a substantial reinforcement to your vast and formidable deterrent power. We have, however, through Attlee's somewhat unconstitutional exertions in making vast sums available for nuclear development without disclosing the fact to Parliament, mastered the problems both of the atomic and the hydrogen weapons by our own science independently.[66]

There was one domestic issue which increasingly troubled him at this time, and that was Commonwealth immigration to Britain. Compared to Britain in the twenty-first century, the numbers were minuscule. Migration from the New Commonwealth stood at just 3,000 arrivals in 1953 and 11,000 in 1954.[67] But that was enough to disturb Churchill, who had retained from his Victorian youth many of his strong views and prejudices on race, an outlook that had led to his opposition to Indian self-government. When told of the proposal to set up a fund from public subscriptions for his eightieth birthday, Churchill said, 'I don't want them to raise a sum for charity just to bring home some coloured gentleman from Jamaica to complete his education.'[68] On immigration to Britain, he complained that, if it continued unabated, it would create a 'magpie society' and 'that would never do'.[69]

Far less enthusiastic about imperialism, Attlee had little of this mentality. As Prime Minister, he had presided over the British Nationality Act of 1948, which had given British citizenship to all subjects within the Empire, a move that, along with the expansion of global transit, encouraged the initial waves of Commonwealth immigration after the war. In June 1948, two days after the ship *Empire Windrush* had docked at Tilbury with a group of almost 500 Jamaican migrants, Attlee received a letter from eleven Labour MPs who warned that the 'influx of coloured people' might undermine 'the harmony, strength and cohesion' of British life. [70] Attlee was dismissive of this anxiety: 'It is traditional that British subjects, whether of Dominion or Colonial origin (and of whatever race or colour) should be freely admissible to the United Kingdom. That tradition is not, in my view, to be lightly discarded.' It was wrong, he warned, to 'regard these people as undesirables or unemployables. The majority of them are honest workers, who can make a genuine contribution to our labour difficulties.'[71] But Attlee was no dogmatist on the subject. As the numbers grew, in early 1950 he set up a Cabinet committee to see whether checks on 'the immigration of coloured people into this country' should be instituted. Chaired by Chuter Ede, the committee reported that in February 1951 that 'restrictions were unnecessary for the time being'.[72] Sir Alec Atkinson, the civil servant who helped to draft the committee report, recalled later that, in the 'liberal-minded' mood prevailing in Whitehall, 'there was a strong deposition among some people to hope that any problems were temporary ones'.[73]

On coming to office, Churchill was dissatisfied with this and set up his own enquiry under the Home Secretary Maxwell-Fyfe. Reporting to the Cabinet on 3 February 1954, Maxwell-Fyfe outlined some of the worrying trends that his study had uncovered, such as the number of migrants living on welfare. But he argued that the scale of immigration 'had not yet assumed sufficient proportions to justify legislation'. In the Cabinet discussion that followed, as recorded in the notes of Sir Norman Brook, Churchill told his colleagues that 'problems will arise if many coloured people settle here. Are we to saddle ourselves with colour problems in the UK?'[74] He even suggested the introduction of an annual migration quota, but in the end, the Cabinet decided to take no action, partly because any controls would significantly alter relations with the Commonwealth. 'We should be reversing the age-long tradition that British subjects have the right of entry to the Mother Country of Empire. We should offend liberals, also sentimentalists,' said Maxwell-Fyfe.[75] Churchill reluctantly accepted this, arguing that it would be 'wise to wait' so as 'to allow public feeling to develop more'.[76] But he continued to worry about the issue and in October 1954 he told Maxwell-Fyfe that further inaction would not be acceptable. The predicable official response, however, was to set up yet another committee; this time under the new Home Secretary Lloyd George. As Churchill recognised, the administrative manoeuvre was just a delaying tactic to avoid any decision on immigration. 'It is the most important issue facing the country, but I cannot get my Ministers to take any notice,' he grumbled to the *Spectator* editor Ian Gilmour in January 1955.[77] In starker terms, during a Cabinet discussion on race relations towards the end of that month, he said that '"Keep Britain White" would be a good slogan'.[78]

By then, Churchill's resistance had finally begun to crumble. The battle against retirement could be waged no longer, especially as he now faced up to the reality that there was little chance of a summit. On 17 January 1955, after a visit to the Prime Minister, Brendan Bracken reported to Beaverbrook: 'Our friend, now under pressure from Clemmie, Eden or other Ministers, intends to depart before July. Naturally, the news is in our bond of secrecy. He says, without a sign of regret, that it is time he gave up. His only wish now is to find a small villa in the South of France where he can spend the winter months in the years which remain in him.'[79] The date he privately fixed for his departure was 6 April, the beginning of the parliamentary Easter recess. Inevitably, he soon wobbled in his resolution to stick to his decision, using the excuse of a possible financial crisis. After a meeting with Churchill on 25 February, an alarmed Rab Butler told Macmillan, 'He is now trying to run out of his engagement with Anthony.' Macmillan reflected in his diary: 'He can be the nicest, noblest, kindest of men. He can be unscrupulous, with a child's lack of any sense of wrong-doing.'[80] But the storm passed almost as quickly as it had arrived, and Churchill was soon preparing for his departure once more.

Churchill's last major speech in the Commons was at the beginning of March. As in his disaster the previous spring, the subject was the hydrogen bomb, with Churchill revealing to the Commons that Britain had begun its manufacture. But this time, his performance was a triumph, while all the problems were Attlee's. In keeping with his general, bi-partisan support for the Government's defence policy and his strong belief in Britain's independent deterrent, Attlee did not want to censure the decision to build the H-bomb; he therefore put down an amendment which merely questioned the lack of the Government's frankness about defence spending. This was a red rag to the Bevanites, who opposed the entire H-bomb project. Bevan himself called Attlee's amendment 'a monstrous evasion of a cataclysmic issue', and during the debate openly flouted the leadership's authority. In the ensuing row in the chamber, while Churchill was praised for his commanding performance, Attlee was humiliated by the left's rebellion. But Bevan did not just criticise Attlee. He also claimed that Churchill had avoided the Bermuda talks the previous year on the instructions of the White House, because of America's hostility to a peace summit. For the first time, Churchill admitted the extent of his stroke. 'I was struck down by a very sudden illness which paralysed me completely, physically. That is why I had to put it all off.'[81] As usual, Churchill followed the Labour feud with relish, though he could not conceal either his personal respect for Attlee or his continued belief in a cross-party alliance, as he explained to Moran after the debate. 'Attlee has been very upset but he has come out of it with no discredit. He has shown great courage. Bevan is eructating bitterness. There will be a split. Some of them may come over to us. There might be a coalition. If I had been a younger man, I might have led it.'[82]

Bevan's attack on Attlee was far more serious than his mistaken insinuations about Churchill. In the division, sixty-two Labour MPs refused to support Attlee's amendment. Soon after the debate, the Shadow Cabinet voted overwhelmingly to recommend the withdrawal of the whip from Bevan. The motion was then referred to the full PLP, which only narrowly voted in favour of it by 141 to 112 at a packed meeting on 15 March. Despite the narrowness of the Parliamentary Party's vote, the Labour right-wingers, led by Gaitskell and Arthur Deakin, the head of the huge Transport and General Workers' Union, were still out for Bevan's blood. In advance of a crucial meeting of the NEC on 24 March, they put forward a resolution to have him expelled from the Labour Party. But Attlee, who now saw his role as a conciliator for the sake of unity, was firmly against such a step. He came up with a compromise proposal at the NEC, whereby Bevan would just have to make an apology and give reassurances about his future conduct. Much to the outrage of the right, Attlee's scheme was passed by a single vote after a long, stormy discussion.

Attlee had achieved his unity at a high personal price in his own reduced authority. But there may have been a crucial external factor that forced Attlee to compromise against the wishes of a large section of his party. On 20 March, just four days before the vital NEC meeting, the *Sunday Express* carried a report, orchestrated by Beaverbrook, that Churchill would resign shortly, the first time that the Cabinet's secret had been revealed to the public. It was obvious that, having taken over, Eden would swiftly call a General Election to win a renewed mandate. In such circumstances, Labour could hardly fight the campaign as a divided party, with one of its best-known figures in the wilderness. Churchill's imminent resignation had inadvertently been a balm to Labour's wounds. But the path to the *Sunday Express* revelation had hardly been a straightforward one. Much to Eden's fury, Churchill had seized on another excuse to stay in office when he had misinterpreted a telegram from the British Embassy in Washington, which he read to mean that Eisenhower might be willing to consider a European summit as a prelude to high-powered talks with the Soviets. Churchill's over-excitement at the Embassy telegram led to a painful Cabinet where Eden asked Churchill if he was suggesting that no one else but he was capable of conducting international diplomacy. Amid all this tension, the issue was left unresolved by the Cabinet meeting, but a day later, Churchill's argument was shot down by a telegram from the White House which showed, as he put it to Clementine, 'Ike was not willing to participate in a meeting with Russia.'[83] There was no justification for changing his retirement plans, though Churchill still felt bitterly towards Eden. To Selwyn Lloyd, the Minister of Supply, Churchill described Eden as 'the most selfish man he had ever known, he thought only of himself, was a prima donna and quite impossible to work with'.[84]

Churchill's farewell in April led to an extended series of valedictions, which his unique service had so richly merited. The first event in this poignant but esteemed procession was a seventieth-birthday party for Clementine in Downing Street, with Violet Bonham Carter among the guests. Churchill told her that 'he would have been happy to stay until next spring' but 'I've had my turn – a good turn. I can't keep others waiting forever.'[85] Also invited to this social gathering were the Attlees, something that pleased Lord Moran in its political catholicity: 'It is pleasant to see the Attlees at the most intimate family parties at Number Ten and Clemmie kissing Mrs Attlee. I find it comforting after Bevan and Dalton.'[86] There was a much grander occasion on 4 April, when the Churchills held a dinner for the Queen and the Duke of Edinburgh at Downing Street. It was another mark of Churchill's respect that the Attlees were again invited. After the meal Churchill made his very last speech as Prime Minister, a toast to the Queen, whom he called the country's 'young and gleaming champion'.[87] Macmillan struggled to hold back his tears. 'Now that he has really decided to go, we are all miserable.'[88]

The next day, Churchill held his final Cabinet. It was another emotional occasion, in which Anthony Eden paid him a fulsome tribute, all the more heartfelt because it came after their recent thorny relations. Only the night before, after the dinner for the Queen, Churchill had confessed to Colville, 'I don't think Anthony can do it.'[89] Now Eden, on the verge of power at last, was in a generous mood towards Churchill. 'They would remember him always – for his magnanimity, for his courage at all times and for his unfailing humour, founded in his unrivalled mastery of the English language. They would always be grateful for his leadership and friendship.'[90] Harry Crookshank, who had fallen out badly with Churchill in recent months, was more cynical about all this praise. 'You might think he was dead,' he wrote in his diary.[91] After the Cabinet, there was a farewell meeting for junior ministers, among them John Boyd-Carpenter who recalled, 'Tears appeared in surprising eyes.'[92]

The tributes continued in the House the next day, 6 April, led by Attlee and Eden. In his address, Attlee said that Churchill 'gave leadership to this country when it needed it most, and in history, as one of the greatest of all Prime Ministers, his place is assured'. Attlee went on, 'I do not know whether there will be occasions on which the Right Honourable Gentleman will address this House again, but he is now leaving the front-line. He is to have a well-earned rest. Instead of continuing to make history we hope that he will be continuing to write it. But he carries the warm good wishes of us all.'[93] Clarissa Eden, watching from the Ladies' Gallery, later wrote to Clementine, 'Everybody in the House today was moved. Attlee made an excellent speech about Uncle Winston.'[94] In a private letter to Churchill written the same day, just before his Commons appearance, Attlee said, 'While I shall be saying a few words in the House this afternoon, I cannot refrain from writing to thank you and Clemmie for the many kindnesses which Vi and I have received from you both during these years. I hope that you will have an enjoyable holiday in Syracuse* and thereafter, though ceasing to make history, have many years to write it.'[95]

The long duel was over. Churchill and Attlee were never again to face each other across the Dispatch Box. Amazingly Attlee, elected as his party's chief five years earlier than Churchill, had outlasted him in the leadership. But his own political end was fast approaching.

---

* The Churchills were about to go on a trip to Sicily.

THIRTY-TWO

ST PAUL'S AND TEMPLE

WITHIN LESS THAN a month of taking office, Anthony Eden had, as predicted, called the General Election. It was the first contest for two decades in which Churchill and Attlee were not the respective leaders of the main parties, another illustration of their astonishing political longevity. It was also Attlee's fifth campaign in charge of his party, a record equalled only by Harold Wilson and Stanley Baldwin in the twentieth century. Despite all the recent divisions in Labour, hopes were high in the party, particularly after a Gallup poll at the start put the Conservatives just one point ahead.

Even at seventy-two and after twenty years at the top, Attlee still showed energy and determination on the campaign trail. Between 12 and 20 May, he addressed no fewer than forty meetings and travelled 1,200 miles, driven as usual by Violet. Yet there was little of the overt enthusiasm for Labour that had characterised recent elections. Rallies were often poorly attended, crowds a disappointment. 'Empty seats faced Mr Attlee everywhere he spoke today. In some towns meeting halls were only half full. There were rows of vacant chairs,' reported the *Liverpool Echo* of the Lancashire stage of his tour.[1] In an address at St Andrew's Hall, Glasgow, the venue was only two-thirds full, whereas when Eden spoke there a day later, three overflow meetings were required to accommodate the throng. In some of his utterances, Attlee admitted that Labour's campaign was failing to grip the public. 'Wake up this election! The Tories hope to keep it quiet and sneak back in,' he said in Scotland.[2] 'Apathy is as big a danger as the H-bomb,' he cried unconvincingly at each stop on the campaign.[3]

Attlee was also in danger of looking anachronistic in the new media age. Television was becoming an increasingly important force in politics, as shown by the fact that Eden was the first Prime Minister to make a party television broadcast. He gave a suave, polished performance, helped by his experience of appearing on American TV. Attlee was the opposite. Interviewed by the journalist Percy Cudlipp, he made little attempt to engage with the public and his answers were so short that his host was left struggling to fill the airtime. 'Mr Cudlipp is an experienced broadcaster. He must have been in agony,' wrote the *Manchester Guardian* in its review, which also described the Labour Leader as 'a bit tedious'.[4] That was the verdict of many viewers. 'Uninspiring, colourless, dull,' said one member of a representative panel. 'If I had not known who Mr Attlee was, I should not have known what he was talking about,' said another.[5]

During the campaign, Attlee was not helped by a flaccid manifesto, *Forward with Labour*, which smacked of an awkward compromise between left and right. Bevan described it as 'cold porridge strained through a blanket'.[6] In addition, the party's organisation was poor, reflecting years of internal battles and lack of inspiration at the top. As the journalist Leslie Hunter put it, 'Under the tired and vacillating leadership of Attlee, the Labour Party had been split by devastating quarrels which left ordinary voters bewildered and uninterested.'[7] But all the blame for Labour's lacklustre campaign could not be put on Attlee or the party machine. Over the previous four years, the Conservatives had run a far more successful Government than Labour had ever expected. Industrial discontent was low; living standards were rising. As one local councillor put it in Oldham when asked to explain the poor attendance for Attlee's visit, 'We have full employment. Everyone is at work.'

In his diary, Hugh Dalton described the 1955 General Election as the dullest he had ever fought: 'There were no live issues and there was great apathy all over the country.' But one charismatic figure did his best to enliven the contest. Despite his retirement from Downing Street, Churchill had no intention of quitting politics. He might not have a national role in the election, for Eden had made it clear that he 'didn't want to be regarded as Winston's nominee for the Premiership'.[8] But he was still standing in Woodford, enabling him to fire off repeated denunciations of Labour. In this his nineteenth campaign, Attlee was a favourite target, especially over defence and renationalisation. Speaking in his constituency on 16 May to a crowd of over 1,000 people, he claimed that Attlee's policies were contradictory because of the failed attempt to square the national interest with Bevanite radicalism.

> Mr Attlee, who was my wartime Deputy Prime Minister, is certainly tough or he would not have kept the lead of his party so long. I have no doubt that he wishes to do the right thing. He has bluntly and boldly declared himself in favour of our making the hydrogen bomb. He could hardly do otherwise, considering that he made the atomic bomb secretly for four years without even telling Parliament. But all the time he has to keep on side with his party. His real struggle is less with the Tories than his own left-wing. His choice is therefore a hard and delicate one. On the whole the best he can do is to be a piebald.[9]

Attlee seemed amused at Churchill's organic reference. In Edinburgh the next day, he said, 'I really don't mind but the charge comes rather oddly from Sir Winston, who has always been a bit of a chameleon himself […] I can remember when Sir Winston was a Conservative and when for eighteen years he was a Liberal again. I don't know whether that has made him piebald or skewbald.'[10]

The *Daily Mail* welcomed the exchange for its entertainment value. 'They say this is a dull election. It was until Sir Winston Churchill entered the fray. He even caused Mr Attlee to emit a small spark, and that takes some doing.'[11] The two men kept up their verbal jousts on the campaign. Attlee boasted that industrial output had been higher under the last Labour Government than under the Conservatives, an assertion challenged by Churchill, who also attacked Labour's plan to reduce the length of national service. Churchill claimed to perceive a similar weakness, because of the left's influence over Labour, in Attlee's attachment to a British independent nuclear deterrent. Speaking on 19 May in support of the Tory candidate John Harvey in Walthamstow East, next to Attlee's own constituency, he said: 'I am astonished that Mr Attlee would allow his name and authority in the country to be used in Bevanite propaganda against the H-bomb. Last week, *Tribune* quoted him prominently on the front page as saying that the idea of the H-bomb as a deterrent was a profound delusion.'[12] This was a reheated version of the Laski charge, that the Labour front bench was really controlled by a sinister left-wing caucus. Attlee was categorical in dismissing Churchill's accusation of duplicity. In another speech on his tour, he quoted from his March statement in the Commons, in which he had expressed full support for the British manufacture of the H-bomb. 'What more he wants I do not know,' said Attlee, before rounding on the Labour campaigners who opposed Britain's first use of nuclear weapons. 'It would be like facing a heavyweight boxer with a revolver and telling him you were not going to be the first to fire [...] I have never found that a generous gesture brought any response from the Russian side. They are tough people. It is no use going to the Kremlin thinking you can read them the sermon on the mount.'[13]

Voting was set for 26 May and, after a measured but confident campaign by the Tories, Churchill was optimistic about his party's prospects. 'I think we have a very good chance of a working majority,' Churchill wrote to Sir Norman Brook forty-eight hours before the polling stations opened.[14] He turned out to be right. Attlee easily retained his West Walthamstow seat, but both his majority and overall vote were marginally down on 1951. That reflected the trend across the country. The results, beamed across the nation in the first-ever televised coverage of election night, showed a narrow but decisive swing away from Labour. Attlee's party lost twenty-three seats, giving the Conservatives a safe majority of fifty-nine in the new House of Commons. In his own constituency of Woodford, where this time he was up against only a Labour candidate, Churchill's vote share increased from 63 to 73 per cent. Lord Beaverbrook told him that he deserved much of the credit for the national victory. 'The result is due to your wise and far seeing foreign policy and your sound administration at home,' he told Churchill on 27 May.[15]

On 8 June, when the new Commons met to be sworn in, Churchill was given a rapturous welcome by his own MPs, as Walter Terry of the *Daily Mail* reported. 'He hesitated, as though deafened by the wild, excited cheering. Then he strode to his corner, backbench seat below the gangway.' There soon followed a chivalrous gesture by Attlee, as MPs lined up to sign themselves in. Precedence went to frontbenchers, so Sir Winston, now in his less-elevated status, 'looked due for a long wait', wrote Terry. 'But as the last junior Minister passed by, Mr Attlee darted across to Sir Winston. Warmly they shook hands. A startled Sir Winston was guided from his seat into the queue by the Opposition leader. Generous in defeat, genuine in kindness, the Socialist leader had given up his place to the Tory warrior.'[16] The cruel eye of Dalton, returned again for Bishop Auckland, observed Churchill had aged badly since his resignation. 'Winston has suddenly gone very old. Like the fish who live at a great depth, subject to tremendous pressure and, when they are brought to the surface and the pressures relax, burst and die.'[17]

Yet the most immediate struggle had to be faced be Attlee. In view of his age and length of service, as well as his two successive election defeats, his departure from the leadership was inevitable. But he did not go immediately. In fact, at the first Shadow Cabinet meeting after the election, he was asked to stay until the end of the current Commons session, a decision that was endorsed by the Parliamentary Party and subsequently accepted by Attlee. It later turned out the end of the session could be as distant as early 1956 but, unlike the agonising saga of Churchill's departure from the premiership, Attlee was not acting purely out of vanity. There was still the wish to keep the party together so the wound of the split might heal. Moreover, factional interests worked against his immediate retirement. Part of the left thought that every passing day would weaken Morrison, seen by many of them as the chief rival to Bevan. Alternatively, the group around Gaitskell believed that he needed more time to be built up, given his relative lack of experience. As for Morrison, he was unwilling to make an open bid for the leadership, having been rejected by the party in the past. His respect for Attlee, however, had been further lowered by the Bevanite imbroglio: 'I am no closer to him today after working with him all these years that I was when we first became acquainted. He trusts nobody. He confides in no-one. I do not understand the man. He is peculiarly middle-class. He has no real contact with the working-class. He wants the middle of the road all the while – the best of both worlds – but sometimes you have to come off the fence and fight. He won't do that.'[18]

Attlee himself thought that one of his prime duties was to keep out Morrison. 'I'd go at once if I thought Morrison could hold the party together but I don't think he can. He's too heavy handed, you know, and he might wreck the whole show. I may have to hang on a bit and see,' he had said privately during the previous Parliament.[19] That was still his thinking. When the journalist Leslie Hunter had a long talk with Violet and Clement in October, he was amazed at the strength of their feelings towards Morrison. 'He and his wife together now demonstrated a savage animosity little short of hatred,' Hunter wrote. Justifying this attitude, Attlee said that 'Herbert makes a complete mess of things. He makes a mess of everything he touches.'[20] In preference to Morrison, Attlee had once thought Bevan, with all his passionate idealism, might make a good Leader but had been disillusioned by his destructive rebelliousness. 'He's so unstable, all over the place, you never know where you are with him. Anyway, he's cooked his goose for the time being and the party would never stand for him.'[21] In contrast, he though Gaitskell 'had a first-class brain and a great chance'.[22]

Trying to ensure the right successor, Attlee limped on after the 1955 election, his purpose largely negative and his health becoming worse. In August he suffered a stroke, which, though only minor compared to Churchill's, still left him listless and lacking in energy at Labour's

Annual Conference in Margate. Speculation in the press began to mount about retirement. In private Violet was urging him to go. 'I just can't keep driving Clem about all over the place in this mad rush, and, as you know, he can't drive himself,' she complained.[23] By November, there was less justification for his remaining in post, since Morrison's star had badly faded and Gaitskell's now shone brightly, helped by growing support in the Parliamentary Party. 'Hugh has the leadership in the bag,' wrote Dalton on 3 November.[24] Little more than a week later, the *Daily Herald* gave a heavy hint, based on an off-the-record interview with Attlee, that he was about to retire, though on the publication of this story Morrison commented bitterly, 'I'll believe he's going when he's gone and not before.'[25] But Attlee had made up his mind, as he wrote to his brother on 6 December. 'I am tomorrow going to give up the leadership of the Party. As you know, I wanted to go after the last Election, but stayed on to oblige. There is, however, so much speculation as to the next leader going on that I think it best to retire now. The party is in good heart.'[26] The following day, 7 December 1955, Attlee announced in his usual clipped manner his resignation to the Shadow Cabinet, having given no advance warning to his colleagues. Later in the morning, he made same announcement to a meeting of the full PLP in just a few short sentences. Crossman was amazed at his brevity. 'Who's going to believe that the man who was leader for 20 years would finish his speech in under a minute?'[27] Barbara Castle was dismayed at the likely political outcome. 'His resignation made my heart sink to my boots since it was clear that Gaitskell would romp home.'[28]

Once Attlee had moved out the chair, Morrison took his place and moved a vote of thanks. This was followed by a number of tributes from MPs, though the meeting of the PLP was only half full because of the lack of any notice about the historic decision. At the end, there was a spirited rendition of 'For He's a Jolly Good Fellow'. 'Mr Attlee sat sucking on his pipe, but his eyes were moist,' reported the *Daily Herald*.[29] On his retirement from the premiership in April, Churchill had been offered by the Queen the title of Duke of London, but he turned it down, not only because he wanted to remain in the Commons but also because he did not want to restrict the political ambitions of Randolph, who still harboured hopes of re-entering Parliament. Attlee had no such qualms when he was offered an Earldom, the usual recognition for former Prime Ministers. He had joked in October that he had 'always been attracted to the title of Lord Loveaduck of Limehouse, ever since I went to the East End'.[30] But he now accepted the simpler, more dignified title of Earl Attlee, though several prominent socialists regretted his decision to move to the Lords. On the TV panel show *Free Speech*, broadcast less than a week after his resignation, the left-wing MP Michael Foot described his acceptance of a peerage as 'deplorable', while the historian A. J. P. Taylor said: 'We who built the Labour Party and the Socialist movement are not proud today.'[31]

There was no such language in the Commons on 8 December when MPs gathered to hear tributes from Eden, Morrison and Clement Davies. Now an increasingly silent backbencher, Churchill came to the Commons to show his respect. Although he did not speak, his presence added some grandeur to the occasion, as well as moving Violet, now Lady Attlee, who watched from the gallery. The *Daily Mail's* account ran:

> Sir Winston Churchill came to sit in silence on a day of memories in the House of Commons. For the first time since the summer recess, the former Prime Minister strode into the chamber, pink-cheeked, clear-eyed, to be greeted by a sudden burst of affectionate applause [...] Sir Winston had made the special journey for one reason. He had come to pay tribute to Clement Attlee, his political adversary and old personal friend [...] Above Sir Winston, looking down, pale and rather near to tears, was Mrs Attlee. She had come to hear the Commons say farewell to her husband. As Sir Winston entered the Chamber, Mrs Attlee smiled in pleasure at this tribute.[32]

Attlee, having just been elevated to the Lords, was not present, but that same day he gave a press conference at Transport House, the headquarters of the Labour Party, in which he said, with typical understatement, that leaving the Commons after thirty-three years was 'rather a break' but he hoped not to be 'very far off and would be able to keep contact'. Interestingly, he revealed that 'the most dramatic moment' of his Commons career had been the division after the Norway Debate, which heralded Churchill's Coalition. But *The Times* said he was 'characteristically undramatic' during the press conference. 'His gait was as self-effacing as ever and his smile as deprecatory', yet 'in the quiet cheerfulness, one could discern signs of relief from the long burden of responsibility'.[33] Other papers carried their own tributes. An editorial in the *Daily Herald* extolled how he had shaped the fabric of post-war British society: 'There is national recognition that this remarkably modest and undramatic man, Mr Attlee, is also one of the very greatest statesman our country has produced. He will be more than a name in history.'[34] In the *Daily Mail*, the Labour MP Desmond Donnelly highlighted Attlee's parliamentary clashes with his Conservative rival. 'As the opponent of Sir Winston Churchill he has been the perfect foil – and on most occasions, amazing as it seems, the decisive victor in Parliamentary debate. Indeed he has always taken a delight in pricking the bubbles of great reputations.'[35]

Churchill and Attlee were never to be parliamentary opponents again. Two new men were in charge of their parties. Gaitskell easily won the Labour leadership contest in December, pulling in 157 votes in the Parliamentary Party, compared to just 70 for Bevan and a dismal 40 for Morrison. In humiliation, Morrison resigned as Deputy Leader and left all his senior positions in the party. Badly bruised by the outcome, he cut off all contact with Attlee, whom he partly blamed for his downfall. Gaitskell, however, soon proved himself a brave and articulate Leader, his attacks on Eden in 1956 over the Suez crisis resonating with the public. After his election triumph Eden, still on heavy medication as a consequence of his botched stomach surgery, had lived down Churchill's worst fears with his erratic, impulsive management. Attlee, as ever resorting to a cricket metaphor, gave his own explanation of the reason for Eden's failure after Churchill's long reign, as Gaitskell recounted of a conversation in January 1956 with his former Leader. 'I was saying how extraordinary it was that the Government had gone down so much in the last nine months and added, "After all, the only important change is the disappearance of Winston. Who would have thought it would make so much difference?" Clem said, "Yep, it's the heavy roller, you know. Doesn't let grass grow under it."'[36]

Churchill's vitality fluctuated in the wake of his retirement from the premiership. At times he could seem as lively as ever. The author Rupert Hart-Davis saw him at a literary awards ceremony in December 1956, at which Churchill made a brief speech: 'Winston, like an old hunter wanting more than a sniff of the chance, got up and said another sentence or two. It was all very moving and exactly right. Champagne flowed freely and the old warrior drank some as he beamed round at his friends. Even in the grip of withering old age, he makes the present rulers look like pygmies.'[37] At other times, his decline was all too obvious. Rather pathetically, he told Sir Walter Monckton that same month that: 'I still have ideas but you know I cannot find the words to clothe them.' He also informed Monckton that he would 'never speak in the Commons again' because he 'just couldn't stand to make a speech'.[38] Clement Attlee noticed the degeneration, as he told his brother in December 1957. 'We lunched with the Churchills last week. Winston is very deaf and won't use his instrument which made conversation difficult. He recalled with satisfaction that he and I either as Allies or as Government and Opposition leaders covered 15 years between us.'[39] Although their political relationship was at an end, they maintained their social contact, marked as usual by warm good wishes for personal landmarks. After his seventy-fifth birthday in 1958, Attlee wrote: 'My Dear Winston and Clemmie, Thank you so much for your kind greetings. Seventy-five is rather a milestone, but your example, Winston, shows that it not the end of the road for all [...] Vi joins me in wishing all happiness in 1958.'[40]

Both men were still public figures, elder statesmen and parliamentarians. Churchill continued to sit in the Commons, attending debates in silence. Intrigued by these mute vigils, the Labour MP Arthur

Bottomley commented to Attlee one day that he thought Sir Winston 'wanted to die in the chamber'. According to Bottomley's account, 'Attlee said I was probably right, but I should remember that Winston had never been a good listener. He had a lot of time to make up.'[41] Attlee himself regularly took part in debates in the Lords. In December 1955, on his move to the Upper House, he had told Oliver Baldwin, the former Labour MP and son of the long-serving Tory Prime Minister, 'It is rather a wrench leaving the House of Commons after all these years. I wonder if I shall like the other place. If not I will call upon you to help me paint the place red.'[42] Yet Attlee, who grew attached to almost every institution with which he was involved, soon came to enjoy the Lords and his trips to London from Great Missenden, usually travelling second class on his commuter train. 'I see no point in first-class compartments,' he said.[43] In the Lords, he said that he got through 'a lot of work' on legislation, but admitted he had 'a tendency to have a siesta after lunch'.[44] There was a strange paradox at work in the late 1950s between Churchill and Attlee. The former, once renowned for his volubility, became increasingly taciturn; while the latter, famous for his reserve, became more garrulous. Indeed, Michael Foot told Francis Beckett, one of Attlee's biographers, that 'there was something self-satisfied and unkind about this new found talkativeness'.[45] One outlet for this openness was writing. Remarkably for the author of a notoriously dry autobiography, Attlee developed a new career as a commentator and book reviewer with a sardonic touch. 'Lord Attlee's pen is a force in journalism,' declared the *Evening Standard* in 1958. Some of his most waspish comments were for old colleagues. When Churchill's *History of the English People's Peoples* was published, Attlee observed, 'It might have been better called "things in history which have interested me".'[46] Years later, Attlee's daughter-in-law Anne was going through Clement's copy of Churchill's wartime memoirs, and was amused to find frequent handwritten 'notes in the margin where Pa reckoned Churchill was blethering'.[47] In December 1959, Herbert Morrison gave a lengthy television interview, in advance of the publication of his memoirs, during which he stated that Attlee was 'distant', 'a follower not a leader' and had 'deliberately hung on' to the leadership in 1955 to prevent his succession.[48] 'Lord Attlee, were you cold and distant?' asked a journalist in the wake of the controversy over Morrison's interview. 'Well, I have never been a gusher,' he replied with some self-awareness.[49]

Morrison had left the House of Commons by late 1959, retiring at the October General Election. But Churchill, indefatigably, had stood again in Woodford, his eighth defence of the constituency and his twentieth parliamentary campaign. At the age of almost eighty-five, he had gone ahead despite pleas from Clementine and family, as well as severe doubts from his local Conservative Association about his capacity to represent the constituency. But he allayed some of those concerns at his formal adoption meeting in April 1959, when he made a punchy, full-blooded speech. 'I know of no other candidate who can command or deserves such loyalty and affection,' said his agent Colonel Hugh Barlow-Wheeler.[50] During the contest, the Labour candidate Arthur Latham tried to exploit doubts about Churchill's fitness and constituency work. To this Churchill issued a press release pointing out that: he had only been abroad for seventeen days in the last year; though he had a pairing arrangement, he was a regular attendee at the Commons; and that all constituency matters were dealt with promptly by his office. His final speech of the campaign, delivered on 29 September and written by Montague-Browne, was a warning about socialist antipathy to free enterprise, the subject of his very first clash with Attlee in the Commons thirty-four years earlier. The speech went well. As his Association Chairman John Harvey put it, 'the mere act of rising to his feet on a political platform seemed somehow to rejuvenate him'.[51] In a landslide national victory for the Conservatives, now led by Macmillan, Churchill retained his seat with an ever greater share of the Woodford vote, though with a marginally reduced majority. As the longest-serving MP, he was now the Father of the House.

But Churchill went into further decline after this, suffering a series of falls and serious infections. 'Very old and stiff and deaf,' Violet Bonham Carter wrote in February 1960 after lunch with him, at which he had told her bleakly, 'During the last five years I have had no appetite for life. No, when it comes to dying, I shall not complain, I shall not miaow.'[52] Her diaries at this time formed a tragic commentary on the slide towards the end. 'It is so difficult to find anything that will reach or engage his mind. The past is blurred as well as the present,' she wrote in February 1962. In November that year she recorded, 'He knows nothing of what is going on in the world and even the distant past is gradually fading.'[53] Churchill still occasionally went to public events, though to other guests such appearances often emphasised his infirmity, as Harold Nicolson recorded of a dinner at the Royal Academy. On leaving, 'Winston had almost to be carried down the steps. He is frightfully old. His eyes are bleary and immobile. I watched his huge bald head descending the staircase and I blessed it as it disappeared. "We may never see that again," said a voice behind me. It was Attlee.'[54] As the list of ailments and illnesses lengthened, Attlee publicly expressed faith in Churchill's resilience. In an interview with the *Daily Mail* in July 1962, after Churchill had undergone an operation for a broken hip sustained in a fall during a stay in Monte Carlo, Attlee said, 'He is a genius. He has immense strength.'[55] Attlee tried to be as supportive in private. After Clementine had written in January 1963 to congratulate him reaching the age of eighty, he wrote back, 'My dear Winston and Clemmie, thank you so much for your kind congratulations on my eightieth birthday. I am a mere stripling compared to you, Winston. I have rejoiced to hear of the constant improvement in your health. I suspect that you will see me out. We celebrated the occasion with a dinner in the Lords with a large company, though a few octogenarians and residents in Surrey which seems to be hard hit by snow had to be dug out.'[56]

Churchill's advancing old age rendered his position as an MP untenable, even for his loyal local Conservative Association. As early as April 1960, Donald Forbes, his friend and leading Woodford activist, summoned the courage to broach the subject of his retirement, only for Churchill to brush the question aside. The issue became more urgent as his decline accelerated, yet in a grisly reprise of the battle to force him out of the premiership, he again refused to give any indication he would stand down before the next election, even though he would be almost ninety by then. Finally he accepted reality. In April 1963, he wrote to the Chairman saying that his hip accident the previous year had 'greatly decreased my mobility and it has become difficult for me to attend the House of Commons as often as I would wish'.[57] Private relief was mingled with public expressions of regret at the news, which a few months later led to a sentimental public call for Churchill to be made an MP for the remainder of his life. Attlee denounced the very idea as an affront to parliamentary democracy. 'I have never heard a more preposterous proposal. I would yield to no one in supporting any reasonable proposition for doing honour to a great man, but as an old House of Commons man, I should bitterly resent any proposal for diluting its membership by adding to it a person not elected by the electors of a real constituency,' he told the *Daily Sketch*. He concluded, 'I cannot believe that Sir Winston, a good House of Commons man, would approve of a proposal to dilute the elected basis of the House, even though it is done merely to do him honour.'[58]

Attlee's own health was beginning to fail. On his eightieth birthday, his former PPS Arthur Moyle asked what it felt like to have reached the milestone. 'Better than the alternative,' he replied morbidly.[59] Like Churchill, he had decreased mobility, as a result of which he and Vi moved in 1963 from Cherry Cottage to a nearby bungalow called Westcott. 'We're getting old,' she said to explain the move.[60] Although she was actually nearly thirteen years younger than him, it was Violet who died first, when, in June 1964, she suffered a fatal brain haemorrhage. Superficially, he took the loss of his beloved companion with characteristic but astonishing stoicism. On the day of her death, he phoned the Indian High Commission, where he was due to attend an event that evening: 'I am sorry. I can't come to the reception tonight. My wife's just died and there's no one to drive me.' But her loss was devastating. 'It has been a sudden and shattering blow. I always hoped that I would go first,' he told Francis Williams, his former press officer.[61] Inwardly, he was so distraught that he burned all his correspondence with Violet, while he also decided to sell Westcott because it so heavily bore her imprint. As a widower now, he moved to a flat at King's Bench Walk in the Temple District of London, where he was looked after by his manservant, Alfred Laker, who developed a strong bond with him.

Another bond with the past was about to break. Churchill had left the Commons at the General Election of July 1964, a campaign in which Attlee had spoken at several rallies to support Labour Leader Harold Wilson, the man he had made the youngest Cabinet minister of the twentieth century. Of one of Attlee's speeches, at St Pancras Town Hall, the *Guardian* wrote that 'he did sharp, rather than rough justice. He chipped away with his long, accurate memory as if it had been a chisel, carving a swift and decisive memorial to Conservative selfishness.'[62] The advent of Wilson's Labour Government saw Churchill sinking fast. He quietly celebrated his ninetieth birthday at home in November, then on 12 January 1965, he suffered his most serious stroke. He slid into a coma and remained in that state for twelve days, while crowds of anxious well-wishers gathered outside Hyde Park Gate and personal visitors, including Wilson, came to honour the national hero whose life was ebbing away. Attlee watched from a distance anxiously. 'We are all waiting here for the death of old Winston but he hangs on amazingly. I am very sorry for poor Clemmie; it must be an awful strain,' Attlee wrote to Moyle.[63] The end came on the morning of 24 January, exactly the same day as his father Lord Randolph had died.

Britain had lost one its greatest statesmen and Attlee an esteemed colleague. His death now heightened in the public consciousness the admiration for the scale of his achievements, above all his central role in winning the war. As his Deputy during that pivotal moment in Britain's story, Attlee was inevitably the focus of intense media attention. In a statement on the day after Churchill's death, *The Times* reported Attlee's description of him as 'the last of the great Victorians' who in 1940 had been 'able to symbolise for the people their determination to resist and win. He was a man of wide outlook. He lived in the eye of history. He saw himself as playing his part in the wide stage of history.'[64] The same day, in the House of Lords, Attlee told his fellow peers: 'We have lost the greatest Englishman of our time – I think the greatest citizen of the world of our time.'[65] The *Daily Mail* captured some of Attlee's intense feelings behind his passive exterior. 'Emotion choked Earl Attlee's voice to near inaudibility as he described tears rolling down Sir Winston's cheeks when he spoke of Nazi atrocities.'[66]

In fitting with Churchill's stature as one of British history's greatest leaders, he was accorded a state funeral, the first such tribute to a commoner since Gladstone's funeral at Westminster Abbey in 1898.

On this occasion, the event was to be held at St Paul's on Saturday 30 January. Planning had been under way since 1958, and the ceremony was to be conducted with all the magnificent pageantry, military pomp and meticulous precision that matched the grandeur of the departed giant. Yet, for all the preparation, the ceremony had a near-catastrophe at its heart, and Attlee was to be the inadvertent cause of this alarming moment. At Churchill's own request, Attlee was to be one of the pallbearers at St Paul's, accompanying the coffin as it was carried by a party of Guardsmen into the cathedral. The fact that Attlee been chosen for this mournful but important duty, along with figures like Lord Alexander of Tunis, Harold Macmillan and Lord Mountbatten of Burma, was another mark of the esteem in which Churchill held his former Deputy. Unfortunately, at the rehearsal he had to stand in the biting cold of a winter's day, and badly felt the effects when he returned to his Temple flat. Laker his manservant told Janet that Attlee came back 'in a condition bordering on collapse. I warmed his slippers on him and wrapped a blanket around him by the fire, then tried to get him to take a sip of brandy.'[67] Attlee himself confessed to Janet that, after the rehearsal, he suffered 'violent shivering followed by vomiting'.[68] Attlee was still feeling poorly on the morning of the funeral, but, with his tremendous sense of honour, it was not an occasion he would miss, as Laker recalled. 'He had great admiration and affection for Lady Churchill and told me how very kind and helpful she had been to him and his wife when they had to move into Number Ten.'[69]

But Attlee's heroic determination was to have almost disastrous consequences for the eight Guardsmen, who had the onerous task of carrying the lead-lined coffin from the gun carriage up the steps of St Paul's, where 3,000 people, including the Queen and a host of global heads of state, were waiting inside the cathedral. The first problem was that the soldiers had not practised with a coffin of the same weight, so on the day its heaviness came as a shock. The second problem was that Attlee, making his way into the cathedral in front of the bearer party, was also struggling with the steps. Lance Sergeant Lincoln Perkins later recalled what happened: 'Halfway up the second flight, Lord Attlee stumbled going into St Paul's and we had to come to a stop and the coffin did actually slide off the two front shoulders of the two bearers. It was very lucky that we had the two gentlemen at the back who were what we call "pushers", who pushed us up.' Perkins further remembered, 'I was telling Sir Winston, "don't worry, we'll look after you", and of course I was really talking to myself because you could actually feel him sliding off the shoulders. If we had dropped him, I don't know what it would have been – very embarrassing. But we didn't.'[70] Even after the slide had been halted, the soldiers needed a moment to recover their composure before moving back up the steps. The rest of the funeral passed off in dignity and without incident. The return journey to the gun carriage was much easier for the bearer party, helped by the downward force of gravity, though Attlee, now exhausted, had to be assisted down the steps of St Paul's and provided with a chair as he watched the cortege leave the cathedral.

Yet for the public, Attlee's dedication to his task on another freezing day was a further example of the heroism that Churchill could inspire. Part of the *Daily Mail*'s vivid account read:

There was only a jingle of harness in the still air. The waiting pall-bearers, Churchill's contemporaries in power, his advisers, his captains of war, turned on each flank to escort their old friend. And none in all that brave scene showed more courage than the deathly frail, deathly pale old man to whom the coffin came first. Earl Attlee won the sympathy of countless thousands because it seemed he, at any rate, would go through the funeral of his old chief even though it put his own life in hazard. But he saw it through.[71]

Many viewers who saw his stumble and need for a chair were so concerned that Attlee's daughter-in-law Anne, Viscountess Prestwood, had to issue a statement of reassurance about his health. 'He was quite all right […] He was determined to go. He had the greatest admiration for Sir Winston. After the ceremony, he was very tired, but went home to rest.'[72] The Attlee family were touched by the demonstration of solicitude, as his son Martin told his sister Janet who now lived in the USA. 'Since Winston's funeral, Pa has been getting a wonderful press. The whole nation was impressed with his guts. Many thought he would never make it, he looked so fragile.'[73]

After the service at St Paul's, Churchill's coffin was transported by boat along the Thames to Waterloo Station, where it was transferred to a special train and taken for burial at the churchyard in Bladon, Oxfordshire, beside the grave of Sir Winston's parents. Nine months later a green marble slab was installed at Westminster Abbey with the legend, 'Remember Winston Churchill', to mark the twenty-fifth anniversary of the Battle of Britain. During his life, Churchill had not feared death; nor had he a devout belief in God. As he once said, he was more of a 'flying buttress' than 'a pillar' of the Church.[74] Lord Moran recorded that 'he did not believe in another world, only in eternal sleep',[75] while he also told Violet Bonham Carter that 'eternal life seemed a nightmare possibility'.[76] That largely matched Attlee's own religious outlook. He told his biographer Kenneth Harris that when it came to Christianity, he believed 'in the ethics' but not in the 'mumbo-jumbo'. In classic Attlee style, when asked if he was an agnostic, he just said, 'I don't know'; to the question as to whether there is an afterlife, he replied, 'possibly'.[77]

Attlee's health continued to deteriorate after the St Paul's service, though he displayed a Churchillian determination to fight. After a stay by Attlee in the Chelsea hospital for stomach trouble in February 1967, his son Martin wrote to his sister Janet, 'If I had to make a forecast now, I would say, "Anything from six months to five years." He's such a tough old bird, you never can tell.'[78] The former prediction proved the more accurate. In early September, he was admitted to the Westminster Hospital with an infection that was compounded by a stroke; and by the twenty-fourth, Anne was telling her sister-in-law Janet that Attlee was 'gravely ill'.[79] As his condition worsened, Martin reported on 2 October that 'the doctors are amazed at his strength and determination',[80] but once he developed pneumonia, there was no hope. Clement Attlee passed away on the night of 8 October 1967. His son Martin was at his bedside. The funeral service, arranged by Attlee with his usual foresighted organisation, took place at the Temple Church in London.

The obituaries were rightly full of praise for his moral integrity, his political adroitness, his mastery of Government business and his drive for social progress. 'He is identified with such profound political and economic changes as will give him a place in history,' declared the *Guardian*.[81] *The Times* said that 'for most of his political career he was underrated by his contemporaries. He was a shrewder politician and a harder man than they took him for.' *The Times* also referred to his impact of his Government's social settlement. 'The most lasting domestic achievement of the Attlee administration was its further instalment of the welfare state. So acceptable has this proved to the people that all later governments have been frightened to do any more than running repairs.'[82] More unconventionally, *Newsweek* drew a favourable comparison with his wartime chief. 'Unlike the uninhibited rogue elephant Churchill belonging to no time or place, Attlee had all the virtues and defects of the Victorian middle-class from which he had sprung. Behind the diffidence, he was resolute, courageous and above all humane.'[83]

A memorial service was held for Attlee at Westminster Abbey on 7 November, at which the Prime Minister Harold Wilson read the lesson from Ecclesiastes, a call for deeper faith. The hymns, chosen by Attlee, were strong reflections of his character. Combining an innate British patriotism with a belief in building a better society, they were Cecil Spring Rice's 'I vow To Thee My Country'; William Blake's

'Jerusalem' and John Bunyan's 'To be a Pilgrim'.[84] His ashes were buried in the abbey, just a few yards from the Battle of Britain stone inscribed 'Remember Winston Churchill'.

ENDNOTES

Introduction: Westminster Hall

1   Moran, C., *Churchill: The Struggle for Survival, 1945–1965, Taken from the Diaries of Lord Moran*.
2   Churchill, W., 1954–1955, Papers, CHUR 2/422, Churchill Archives, Churchill College, Cambridge.
3   Morgan, J. (ed.), *The Backbench Diaries of Richard Crossman*.
4   Jenkins, R., *Churchill*.
5   Montague Browne, A., *Long Sunset: Memoirs of Winston Churchill's Last Private Secretary*.
6   Hudson, R. (ed.), *The Lyttelton–Hart-Davis Letters*.
7   Gilbert, M., *Winston S. Churchill: Never Despair, 1945–1965*.
8   Beaton, C., *The Strenuous Years: 1948–55*.
9   Harris, K., *Attlee*.
10 Soames, M., *Clementine Churchill*.
11 *Times*, 1 December 1954.
12 Moran, *Churchill, op. cit.*
13 *The Times*, 1 December 1954.
14 Attlee, C. R., *As It Happened*.
15 Hart, L., Interview with Bonham Carter, V., 17 August 1967, Liddell Hart Papers, LH 1/25, King's College London.
16 Jago, M., *Clement Attlee: The Inevitable Prime Minister*.
17 Boyd-Carpenter, J., *Way of Life: The Memoirs of John Boyd-Carpenter*.
18 Williams, F., *Nothing So Strange: An Autobiography*.
19 King, C., *With Malice Toward None*.
20 Crookshank, H., Diary, 11 June 1940, Crookshank Papers, MS Eng. d. 360, Bodleian Library, Oxford.
21 Self, R. (ed.), *The Neville Chamberlain Diaries and Letters (Volume 1)*.
22 Paterson, M., *Winston Churchill: His Military Life 1895–1945*.
23 Burridge, T., *Clement Attlee: A Political Biography*.
24 Chandos, O. L., *The Memoirs of Lord Chandos*.
25 Citrine, W., *Men and Work: An Autobiography*.
26 Chandos, *op. cit.*
27 Jackson, A., *Churchill*.
28 Mikardo, I., *Backbencher*.
29 Williams, P. (ed.), *The Diary of Hugh Gaitskell, 1945–1956*.
30 Shipton, J., Interview, 2001, 22578, IWM Archives.
31 Purnell, S., *First Lady: The Life and Wars of Clementine Churchill*.
32 *New Statesman*, 24 April 1954.
33 Nel (nee Layton), E., Interview, 1994, 15119, IWM Archives.

34   Schneer, J., *Ministers at War: Churchill and His War Cabinet.*
35   Thomas-Symonds, N., *Attlee: A Life in Politics.*
36   Brooke, A. to Brookeborough, C., 27 August 1945, 71/47/1, IWM Archives.
37   Colville, J., Profile of Churchill, Colville Papers, CLVL 2/13, Churchill Archives, Churchill College, Cambridge.
38   Menzies, Sir R., *Afternoon Light.*
39   Colville, J., *The Fringes of Power: Downing Street Diaries, 1939–1955, Volume II.*
40   Hunt, Sir D., Interview, 1994, 15261, IWM Archives.
41   Jay, D., Lecture, February 1983, Shore 19/175, LSE Archives.
42   Samuel, Sir A., Report of Carlton Club meeting, 18 October 1922, 60391A, British Library.
43   Harris, *op. cit.*
44   Pottle, M. (ed.), *Daring to Hope: The Diaries and Letters of Violet Bonham Carter, 1947–1969.*
45   Churchill, W., to Cherwell, Lord, Letter, 3 December 1953, EG 1/36, National Archives.
46   Interview, *Sunday Times*, 27 November 1960.
47   Pitts, D., The Granada Historical Records Interviews, 1967.
48   Dellar, G. (ed.), *Attlee As I Knew Him.*
49   Roberts, A., *Churchill: Walking with Destiny.*
50   *Observer*, 31 January 1965.

One: Blenheim and Putney

1   Manchester, W. and Reid, P., *The Last Lion: Winston Churchill, Defender of the Realm, 1940–1965.*
2   Attlee, *As It Happened, op. cit.*
3   Attlee, C. R., *The Churchill Digest.*
4   *Daily Mail*, 21 June 1948.
5   Graham, J., to Churchill, W., Letter, 31 November 1927, CHAR 1/194/94, Churchill Archives, Churchill College, Cambridge.
6   Graham, J., to Churchill, W., Letter, 19 December 1927, CHAR 1/194/109, Churchill Archives, Churchill College, Cambridge.
7   Churchill, W., to his mother, Letter, 2 September 1885, CHAR 28/13/176, Churchill Archives, Churchill College, Cambridge.
8   *Evening Standard*, 20 July 1939.
9   Churchill, W., *My Early Life.*
10   Pelling, H., *Winston Churchill.*
11   Cowles, V., *Winston Churchill: The Era and the Man.*
12   Harris, *op. cit.*
13   Churchill, *My Early Life, op. cit.*
14   Jay, D., *Change and Fortune: A Political Record.*
15   Lee, C. and Lee, J., *The Churchills: A Family Portrait.*
16   Haigh, G., *Silent Revolutions: Writings on Cricket History.*
17   Attlee, *As It Happened, op. cit.*
18   Thomas-Symonds, *op. cit.*
19   Harris, *op. cit.*
20   Attlee, *As It Happened, op. cit.*
21   Harris, *op. cit.*

22 Paterson, *op. cit.*
23 Clemens, C., *The Man from Limehouse: Clement Richard Attlee.*
24 Churchill, W., Speech at Westminster Hall, 1954, Papers, CHUR 2/422, Churchill Archives, Churchill College, Cambridge.
25 Pearson, J., *The Private Lives of Winston Churchill.*
26 *The Times*, 7 April 1898.
27 *Spectator*, 14 April 1898.
28 *Observer*, 31 January 1965.
29 Attlee, *The Churchill Digest, op. cit.*

Two: Lancashire and Stepney

1 Harris, *op. cit.*
2 Bew, J., *Citizen Clem: A Biography of Attlee.*
3 Attlee, *As It Happened, op. cit.*
4 Churchill, W., Speech, 1897, CHAR 2/21/1, Churchill Archives, Churchill College, Cambridge.
5 Toye, R., *Churchill's Empire: The World that Made Him and the World He Made.*
6 Blumenfeld, R. D., *Across the Pond: An American Gentleman in Victorian London.*
7 Attlee, *The Churchill Digest, op. cit.*
8 Jenkins, *op. cit.*
9 Shelden, M., *Young Titan: The Making of Winston Churchill.*
10 Churchill, W., Correspondence with Samuel Smethurst, autumn 1902, WCHL 1/24, Churchill Archives, Churchill College, Cambridge.
11 Pelling, *Winston Churchill, op. cit.*
12 Black, J., *The Tory World: Deep History and the Tory Theme in British Foreign Policy, 1679–2014.*
13 Bonham Carter, V., *Winston Churchill: As I Knew Him.*
14 Attlee, *As It Happened, op. cit.*
15 Beckett, F., *Clem Attlee: Labour's Great Reformer.*
16 Attlee, *As It Happened, op. cit.*
17 Harris, *op. cit.*
18 Shipton, J., Interview, 2001, 22578, IWM Archives.
19 *Daily Mail*, 12 January 1906.
20 Churchill, W., to Dilke, Sir C., 21 January 1906, Dilke Papers, Add Ms 43,877, British Library.
21 Shelden, *op. cit.*
22 Colville, J., *Winston Churchill and His Inner Circle.*
23 Addison, P., *Churchill on the Home Front, 1900–1955.*
24 McMenamin, M. and Zoller, C., *Becoming Winston Churchill: The Untold Story of Young Winston and His American Mentor.*
25 Pelling, *Winston Churchill, op. cit.*
26 Attlee, *op. cit.*
27 Account of lecture by Dr Richard Toye, *Independent*, 27 November 1906.
28 Attlee, *As It Happened, op. cit.*
29 Attlee, *As It Happened, op. cit.*
30 Wells, H. G., to the electors of North West Manchester, April 1908, WCHL 1/16, Churchill Archives, Churchill College, Cambridge.
31 Jenkins, *op. cit.*
32 Attlee, *The Churchill Digest, op. cit.*

Three: Sidney Street

1 McMenamin and Zoller, *op. cit.*
2 Soames, *Clementine Churchill*, *op. cit.*
3 McMenamin and Zoller, *op. cit.*
4 Soames, *Clementine Churchill*, *op. cit.*
5 Jenkins, *op. cit.*
6 Shelden, *op. cit.*
7 Purnell, *op. cit.*
8 Soames, *Clementine Churchill*, *op. cit.*
9 'Smoothing the Path of Genius', *Observer*, 31 March 1963.
10 Jenkins, *op. cit.*
11 Briggs, A. and Macartney, A., *Toynbee Hall: The First Hundred Years*.
12 Attlee, *As It Happened*, *op. cit.*
13 Webb, B., Diary, 22 June 1909, LSE Archives.
14 Shelden, *op. cit.*
15 Attlee, *As It Happened*, *op. cit.*
16 Harris, *op. cit.*
17 Attlee, *As It Happened*, *op. cit.*
18 Attlee, *As It Happened*, *op. cit.*
19 Harris, *op. cit.*
20 *Toynbee Record*, June 2010.
21 *Toynbee Record*, January 2010.
22 Addison, *Churchill on the Home Front*, *op. cit.*
23 Churchill, W., Memorandum on Tonypandy, CHUR 2/86A, Churchill Archives, Churchill College, Cambridge.
24 *The Times*, 9 November 1910.
25 Shelden, *op. cit.*
26 Parker, J., Paper on Attlee and Churchill, 1 April 1980, Parker Papers, Parker 1/9, LSE Archives.
27 Manchester and Reid, *op. cit.*
28 Churchill, W., *Thoughts and Adventures: Churchill Reflects on Spies, Cartoons, Flying and the Future*.
29 *The Times*, 4 January 1911.
30 *Daily Chronicle*, 4 January 1911.
31 Attlee, *As It Happened*, *op. cit.*
32 *Daily Sketch*, 25 January 1965.
33 *Daily Mirror*, 4 January 1911.
34 Churchill, *Thoughts and Adventures*, *op. cit.*
35 Rose, J., *The Literary Churchill: Author, Reader, Actor*.
36 Morgan, K. (ed.), *Lloyd George Family Letters, 1885–1936*.
37 Rogers, C., *The Battle of Stepney – The Sydney Street Siege*, *op. cit.*
38 Pottle, *Daring to Hope*, *op. cit.*
39 Harris, *op. cit.*
40 Harris, *op. cit.*
41 Attlee, *As It Happened*, *op. cit.*
42 Attlee, *As It Happened*, *op. cit.*
43 David, E. (ed.), *Inside Asquith's Cabinet: From the Diaries of Charles Hobhouse*.
44 Thorne, A. (ed.), *The Diaries of Cecil Harmsworth 1909–1922*.

Four: Gallipoli

1   Soames, M., *Speaking for Themselves: The Personal Letters of Winston and Clementine Churchill*.
2   Marquand, D., *Ramsay MacDonald*.
3   D'Este, C., *Warlord: A Life of Winston Churchill at War, 1874–1945*.
4   Burkin, H., Memoir, undated, 2–118, Burdett Archive.
5   Attlee, C. R., Unpublished war memoirs, 1934, Lancashire Infantry Museum.
6   Attlee, War Memoirs, *op. cit.*
7   Jenkins, *op. cit.*
8   Churchill, *Thoughts and Adventures*, *op. cit.*
9   Freeman, R., *'Unsinkable': Churchill and the First World War*.
10 Pelling, *Winston Churchill*, *op. cit.*
11 Brock, M. and E. (eds), *H. H. Asquith's Letters to Venetia Stanley*.
12 Rose, J., *op. cit.*
13 Brock, *H. H. Asquith's Letters to Venetia Stanley*, *op. cit.*
14 Bell, C. M., *Churchill and the Dardanelles*.
15 Bell, *op. cit.*
16 Curran, T. and Bonnell, A., *The Grand Deception: Churchill and the Dardanelles*.
17 Curran and Bonnell, *op. cit.*
18 Churchill, W. to Balfour, A., Letter, 8 April 1915, Balfour Papers, Add Ms 49464.
19 Pelling, *Winston Churchill*, *op. cit.*
20 Shelden, *op. cit.*
21 Taylor, A. J. P. (ed.), *Lloyd George: A Diary by Frances Stevenson*.
22 Strawson, J., *Churchill and Hitler: In Victory and Defeat*.
23 Jenkins, *op. cit.*
24 Freeman, *op. cit.*
25 Jenkins, *op. cit.*
26 Lady Cynthia Asquith, *Diaries 1915–1918*.
27 Attlee, War Memoirs, *op. cit.*
28 Attlee, War Memoirs, *op. cit.*
29 Attlee, War Memoirs, *op. cit.*
30 Attlee, War Memoirs, *op. cit.*
31 Attlee, War Memoirs, *op. cit.*
32 Attlee, War Memoirs, *op. cit.*
33 Attlee, War Memoirs, *op. cit.*
34 Lieutenant H. Lechler, Diary, IWM 4744, IWM Archives.
35 Attlee, War Memoirs, *op. cit.*
36 Attlee, War Memoirs, *op. cit.*
37 Roberts, *Churchill*, *op. cit.*
38 Attlee, *As It Happened*, *op. cit.*
39 *Spectator*, 27 April 1956.
40 *Sunday Times*, 11 November 1957.
41 Soames, *Speaking for Themselves*, *op. cit.*
42 Strawson, *op. cit.*

Five: Plugstreet and Kut

1   Jenkins, *op. cit.*
2   Soames, *Speaking for Themselves, op. cit.*
3   Scott, C. P. and Wilson, T. (ed.), *The Political Diaries of C. P. Scott 1911–1928.*
4   Soames, *Speaking for Themselves, op. cit.*
5   Williamson, P. (ed.), *Modernization of Conservative Politics: William Bridgeman's Diaries and Letters 1904–35.*
6   Pelling, *Winston Churchill, op. cit.*
7   Lechler, Lt H., Diary, 29 January 1916, 4744, IWM Archives.
8   Harris, *op. cit.*
9   Paterson, *op. cit.*
10   Paterson, *op. cit.*
11   Downes, B., Private memoir, undated, 4871, IWM Archives.
12   Williamson, *op. cit.*
13   Brock, M. and E. (eds), *Margot Asquith's Great War Diary 1914–1916: The View from Downing Street.*
14   Jenkins, *op. cit.*
15   Tudor, Sir H., Diary, May 1916, 2658, IWM Archives.
16   Attlee, War Memoirs, *op. cit.*
17   Attlee, War Memoirs, *op. cit.*
18   Attlee, C. R. to Attlee, T., 19 April 1916, Attlee Papers, MS Eng. c. 4792, Bodleian Library, Oxford.
19   Churchill, W., *The Gathering Storm: The Second World War, Volume 1.*
20   Attlee, C. R. to Jenkins, R., 22 October 1947, Roy Jenkins Papers, Ms Jenkins 350, Bodleian Library, Oxford.
21   Wilson, J. K., 12007, IWM Archives.
22   Churchill, W., *The World Crisis 1911–1918* (Volume II).
23   Attlee, *As It Happened, op. cit.*
24   Wilson J. K., Private memoir, 1970, 12007, IWM Archives.
25   Attlee, C. R., to Attlee, T., 20 March 1917, Attlee Papers, MS Eng. c. 4792, Bodleian Library, Oxford.
26   Attlee, C. R., Note on England, written at Walney Island, early 1918, Attlee Papers, 1/6, Churchill Archives, Churchill College, Cambridge.
27   Churchill, W. to Spears, E., 27 October 1916, SPRS 1/18, Churchill Archives, Churchill College, Cambridge.
28   Sheffield, G. (ed.), *Douglas Haig: War Diaries and Letters 1914–1918.*
29   Attlee, War Memoirs, *op. cit.*
30   Attlee, War Memoirs, *op. cit.*
31   Churchill, *The World Crisis, op. cit.*
32   Shipton, J., Interview, 2001, 22578, IWM Archives.

Six: Limehouse and Dundee

1   Paterson, *op. cit.*
2   *Observer*, 31 January 1965.
3   *Daily Herald*, 10 April 1922.
4   Norwich, Lord J. J. (ed.), *The Duff Cooper Diaries: 1915–1951.*
5   Young, K., *Churchill and Beaverbrook.*
6   Addison, *Churchill on the Home Front, op. cit.*

7   Cowling, M., *The Impact of Labour*.
8   Harris, *op. cit.*
9   Bew, *op. cit.*
10 Dellar, *op. cit.*
11 Bew, *op. cit.*
12 Harris, *op. cit.*
13 Shipton, J., Interview, 2001, 22578, IWM Archives.
14 Churchill, W. to Northcliffe, Lord, Letter, 1 July 1921, Northcliffe Papers, Add Ms 62156, British Library.
15 Purnell, *op. cit.*
16 Lough, D., *No More Champagne: Churchill and His Money*.
17 Norwich, *op. cit.*
18 Bew, *op. cit.*
19 *Limehouse Election News*, 4 November 1922, Working Class Movement Library.
20 *Edinburgh News*, 18 November 1922.
21 Churchill, *Thoughts and Adventures*, *op. cit.*
22 Pelling, *Winston Churchill*, *op. cit.*
23 *Daily Herald*, 18 November 1922.
24 Harris, *op. cit.*
25 Attlee, *As It Happened*, *op. cit.*
26 Bew, *op. cit.*
27 Williamson, P. and Baldwin, E. (eds), *The Baldwin Papers, 1908–1947*.
28 Gilbert, *Never Despair*, *op. cit.*
29 Gilbert, *Never Despair*, *op. cit.*
30 Norwich, *op. cit.*
31 Addison, *Churchill on the Home Front*, *op. cit.*
32 Burridge, *Clement Attlee*, *op. cit.*
33 Harris, *op. cit.*
34 Harris, *op. cit.*
35 Gilbert, *Never Despair*, *op. cit.*

Seven: Treasury

1   Gilbert, M., *Winston S. Churchill: The Prophet of Truth, 1922–1939*.
2   Soames, *Speaking for Themselves*, *op. cit.*
3   *Morning Post*, 20 February 1924.
4   *People*, 27 February 1924.
5   Churchill, *Thoughts and Adventures*, *op. cit.*
6   Churchill, *Thoughts and Adventures*, *op. cit.*
7   Gardner, B., *Churchill in Power: As Seen by His Contemporaries*.
8   *Daily Mail*, 12 March 1924.
9   *Manchester Guardian*, 12 March 1924.
10 *Observer*, 16 March 1924.
11 *Daily Express*, 21 March 1924.
12 Williams, *Nothing So Strange*, *op. cit.*
13 Gilbert, *The Prophet of Truth*, *op. cit.*
14 Pelling, *Winston Churchill*, *op. cit.*
15 *Observer*, 16 November 1924.
16 Williamson and Baldwin, *op. cit.*

17 Gilbert, *The Prophet of Truth*, *op. cit.*
18 Langworth, R. (ed.), *Churchill by Himself: The Definitive Collection of Quotations.*
19 *Observer*, 31 January 1965.
20 Best, G., *Churchill: A Study in Greatness.*
21 Reynolds, D., *In Command of History: Churchill Fighting and Writing the Second World War.*
22 Attlee, *As It Happened*, *op. cit.*
23 Self, *The Neville Chamberlain Diaries and Letters (Volume 2)*, *op. cit.*
24 Bew, *op. cit.*
25 *The Times*, 16 June 1925.
26 Hansard, 13 April 1926.
27 Churchill, W. to Grigg, J., 11 April 1926, PJGG 2/12/10, Churchill Archives, Churchill College, Cambridge.
28 Rhodes James, R., *Memoirs of a Conservative: J. C. C. Davidson's Memoirs and Papers 1910–37.*
29 Self, *The Neville Chamberlain Diaries and Letters (Volume 2)*, *op. cit.*
30 Williamson, *op. cit.*
31 McMenamin and Zoller, *op. cit.*
32 Norwich, *op. cit.*
33 Thomas-Symonds, *op. cit.*
34 Thomas-Symonds, *op. cit.*
35 Bew, *op. cit.*
36 Bew, *op. cit.*
37 *Daily Express*, 1 May 1929.
38 Pelling, *Winston Churchill*, *op. cit.*

Eight: India

1   *Daily Telegraph*, 29 April 1964.
2   Attlee, *As It Happened*, *op. cit.*
3   Pelling, *Winston Churchill*, *op. cit.*
4   Rose, J., *op. cit.*
5   Nicolson, N. (ed.), *Harold Nicolson – Diaries and Letters 1930–1939.*
6   Rhodes James, R., *Victor Cazalet: A Portrait.*
7   Jackson, *op. cit.*
8   Hansard, 11 July 1932.
9   Gilbert, *The Prophet of Truth*, *op. cit.*
10 Gilbert, *The Prophet of Truth*, *op. cit.*
11 Self, *The Neville Chamberlain Diaries and Letters (Volume 3)*, *op. cit.*
12 Hansard, 2 February 1931.
13 Jenkins, *op. cit.*
14 Jenkins, *op. cit.*
15 Gilbert, *The Prophet of Truth*, *op. cit.*
16 Attlee, *As It Happened*, *op. cit.*
17 MacDonald, R., Diary, 24 August 1931, PRO 3O/69/1753, British Library.
18 Stewart, G., *Burying Caesar: Churchill, Chamberlain and the Battle for the Tory Party.*
19 Churchill, W., *The River War: An Account of the Reconquest of the Sudan.*
20 Attlee, *As It Happened*, *op. cit.*

21 Bew, *op. cit.*
22 Attlee, *As It Happened, op. cit.*
23 Williams, *Nothing So Strange, op. cit.*
24 Attlee, C. R. to Attlee, T., Letter, 16 November 1931, Attlee Papers, MS Eng. c. 4792, Bodleian Library, Oxford.
25 Clemens, *op. cit.*
26 Personal record of parliamentary speeches, Attlee Papers, 1/3, Churchill Archives, Churchill College, Cambridge.
27 Hansard, 11 December 1931.
28 Hansard, 20 April 1932.
29 Attlee, C. R. to Attlee, T., 15 July 1932, Attlee Papers, MS Eng. c. 4792, Bodleian Library, Oxford.
30 Self, R. (ed.), *The Austen Chamberlain Diary Letters.*
31 Attlee, C. R. to Attlee, T., 3 April 1933, Attlee Papers, MS Eng. c. 4792, Bodleian Library, Oxford.
32 Attlee, C. R. to Attlee, T., 3 April 1933, Attlee Papers, MS Eng. c. 4792, Bodleian Library, Oxford.
33 Beckett, *op. cit.*
34 Dupree, M. (ed.), *Lancashire and Whitehall: The Diary of Sir Raymond Streat 1932–1957.*
35 Swift, J., *Labour in Crisis: Clement Attlee and the Labour Party in Opposition, 1931–1940.*
36 *Daily Express*, 17 April 1934.
37 Attlee, C. R. to Attlee, T., 18 June 1934, Attlee Papers, MS Eng. c. 4792, Bodleian Library, Oxford.
38 Self, *The Austen Chamberlain Diary Letters, op. cit.*
39 Gilbert, *The Prophet of Truth, op. cit.*
40 Pelling, *Winston Churchill, op. cit.*
41 Hansard, 13 June 1934.
42 *Daily Express*, 7 February 1935.
43 Hansard, 5 March 1935.
44 Hansard, 5 March 1935.
45 Rhodes James, *Memoirs of a Conservative, op. cit.*
46 Young, *Churchill and Beaverbrook, op. cit.*

Nine: Germany

1 *Oxford Dictionary of National Biography.*
2 Stewart, G., *op. cit.*
3 Manchester, W., *The Caged Lion: Winston Spencer Churchill, 1932–1940.*
4 Attlee, C. R. to Attlee, T., 1 January 1933, Attlee Papers, MS Eng. c. 4792, Bodleian Library, Oxford.
5 Hansard, 13 July 1934.
6 Note of lunch at the Oesterreichischer Hof, Bad Hofgastein, Salzburg, June 1932, Marsh Papers, Box 6, Churchill Archives, Churchill College, Cambridge.
7 Gilbert, *The Prophet of Truth, op. cit.*
8 Hansard, 13 April 1933.
9 Gilbert, *The Prophet of Truth, op. cit.*
10 Hansard, 7 November 1933.

11 Hansard, 7 November 1933.
12 *The Times*, 17 January 1934.
13 Hansard, 6 February 1934.
14 Hansard, 8 March 1934.
15 Hansard, 8 March 1934.
16 Gilbert, M. *Winston S. Churchill: The Wilderness Years*.
17 Hansard, 30 July 1934.
18 Hansard, 30 July 1934.
19 Note on Southport speech, 1934, Churchill Papers, CHUR 5/35B, Churchill Archives, Churchill College, Cambridge.
20 Gilbert, *The Prophet of Truth*, *op. cit.*
21 Gilbert, *The Prophet of Truth*, *op. cit.*
22 Hansard, 11 March 1935.
23 Hansard, 11 March 1935.
24 Churchill, W. to Churchill, C., 5 April 1935, CHAR 1/273/116–122, Churchill Archives, Churchill College, Cambridge.
25 Hansard, 8 May 1935.
26 Pimlott, B. (ed.), *The Political Diary of Hugh Dalton, 1918–40, 1945–60*.
27 Langworth, R. (ed.), *Churchill in His Own Words*.
28 Hansard, 17 April 1935.
29 Gilbert, *The Prophet of Truth*, *op. cit.*
30 Williamson and Baldwin, *op. cit.*
31 Cannadine, D. and Quinault, R., *Winston Churchill in the Twenty-First Century*.
32 Hansard, 7 June 1935.
33 Hansard, 11 July 1935.
34 Eden, A., *Full Circle: The Memoirs of Sir Anthony Eden*.
35 Parker, R. A. C., *Churchill and Appeasement*.
36 Pugh, M., *Speak for Britain! A New History of the Labour Party*.
37 Bew, *op. cit.*
38 Bew, *op. cit.*
39 Attlee, C. R., to Spears, E., 12 October 1935, Spears Papers, SPRS 1/18, Churchill Archives, Churchill College, Cambridge.
40 Stewart, G., *op. cit.*
41 Swift, *op. cit.*
42 *The Times*, 12 November 1935.
43 Donoughue, B. and Jones, G. W., *Herbert Morrison: Portrait of a Politician*.
44 Jones, T., *A Diary with Letters, 1931–1950*.
45 Peter Shore Papers, 19/175, LSE Archives.
46 Swift, *op. cit.*
47 Pimlott, *The Political Diary of Hugh Dalton*, *op. cit.*
48 Donoughue and Jones, *op. cit.*
49 Donoughue and Jones, *op. cit.*

Ten: Fort Belvedere

1 Rhodes James, R. (ed.), *'Chips': The Diaries of Sir Henry Channon*.
2 Hansard, 26 March 1936.
3 Hansard, 26 March 1936.
4 Pimlott, *The Political Diary of Hugh Dalton*, *op. cit.*

5   Gilbert, *The Prophet of Truth, op. cit.*

6   Attlee, C. R. to Churchill, W., 21 July 1936, Churchill Papers, CHAR 2/270, Churchill Archives, Churchill College, Cambridge.

7   Attlee, C. R. to Attlee, T., 26 October 1936, Attlee Papers, MS Eng. 4792, Bodleian Library, Oxford.

8   Swift, *op. cit.*

9   Webb, B., Diary, 31 October 1936, LSE Archives.

10   Stewart, G., *op. cit.*

11   Guest to Churchill, 25 November 1936, Churchill Papers, CHAR 2/260, Churchill Archives, Churchill College, Cambridge.

12   Churchill to Guest, 27 November 1936, Churchill Papers, CHAR 2/260, Churchill Archives, Churchill College, Cambridge.

13   Thompson, N., *The Anti-Appeasers: Conservative Opposition to Appeasement in the 1930s.*

14   Churchill to Cecil, 21 October 1936, Cecil Papers, Add MS 51073, British Library.

15   Cecil to Churchill, 23 November 1936, Cecil Papers, Add MS 51073, British Library.

16   Churchill to Cecil, 26 November 1936, Cecil Papers, Add MS 51073, British Library.

17   Churchill to Cecil, 2 December 1936, Cecil Papers, Add MS 51073, British Library.

18   Cecil to Churchill, 5 December 1936, Cecil Papers, Add MS 51073, British Library.

19   *The Times*, 4 December 1936.

20   Jenkins, *op. cit.*

21   Colville, J., Note on Churchill, 16 May 1971, Colville Papers, CLVL 2/7, Churchill Archives, Churchill College, Cambridge.

22   Attlee, *As It Happened, op. cit.*

23   Kramnick, I., and Sheerman, B., *Harold Laski: A Life on the Left.*

24   Attlee, *As It Happened, op. cit.*

25   Note on Attlee and Churchill, 1 April 1980, Parker Papers, Parker 1/9, LSE Archives.

26   Williamson and Baldwin, *op. cit.*

27   Harris, *op. cit.*

28   Williams, *Nothing So Strange, op. cit.*

29   Jago, *op. cit.*

30   Middlemass, K. and Barnes, J., *Baldwin.*

31   MacDonald, R., Diary, 2 December 1936, PRO 30/69/1753.

32   Headlam, C., *Parliament and Politics in the Age of Churchill and Attlee: The Headlam Diaries, 1935–1951.*

33   Williamson and Baldwin, *op. cit.*

34   *Daily Express*, 4 December 1936.

35   Gilbert, *The Prophet of Truth, op. cit.*

36   Gilbert, *The Prophet of Truth, op. cit.*

37   Citrine, *op. cit.*

38   Citrine, *op. cit.*

39   Gilbert, *The Prophet of Truth, op. cit.*

40   Gilbert, *The Prophet of Truth, op. cit.*

41 *The Times*, 7 December 1936.
42 *The Times*, 7 December 1936.
43 *Daily Express*, 7 December 1936.
44 Bloch, M., *The Reign and Abdication of Edward VIII*.
45 Bloch, *op. cit.*
46 *Daily Express*, 8 December 1936.
47 *Daily Express*, 8 December 1936.
48 *Daily Express*, 8 December 1936.
49 Stewart, G., *op. cit.*
50 Manchester, *The Caged Lion*, *op. cit.*
51 MacDonald, R., Diary, 7 December 1936, PRO 30/69/1753, British Library.
52 Nicolson, *op. cit.*
53 Hansard, 10 December 1936.
54 Hansard, 10 December 1936.
55 Hansard, 10 December 1936.
56 Hore-Belisha, L., Diary, 11 April 1939, HOBE 1/5, Churchill Archives, Churchill College, Cambridge.
57 NEC Minutes, 7 December 1936, People's Museum of Labour History.
58 Morgan, K., *Lloyd George Family Letters*, *op. cit.*
59 Rhodes James, *Memoirs of a Conservative*, *op. cit.*
60 Pitts, D., The Granada Historical Records Interviews, *op. cit.*
61 Attlee, *As It Happened*, *op. cit.*
62 MacDonald, M., *Titans and Others*.
63 Reynolds, *op. cit.*
64 *Observer*, 31 January 1965.
65 Hansard, 10 December 1936.
66 Young, *Churchill and Beaverbrook*, *op. cit.*

Eleven: Munich

1 Pelling, *Winston Churchill*, *op. cit.*
2 Self, *The Neville Chamberlain Diaries and Letters (Volume 4)*, *op. cit.*
3 Pitts, D., The Granada Historical Records Interviews, *op. cit.*
4 Langworth, *Churchill in His Own Words*, *op. cit.*
5 Attlee, *As It Happened*, *op. cit.*
6 Hansard, 16 December 1937.
7 Webb, B., Diary, 25 May 1937, LSE Archives.
8 Bew, *op. cit.*
9 *Star*, 18 April 1937.
10 Shipton, J., Interview, 2001, 22578, IWM Archives.
11 *The Times*, 21 November 2018.
12 Soames, *Clementine Churchill*, *op. cit.*
13 Purnell, *op. cit.*
14 Citrine, *op. cit.*
15 Hansard, 28 February 1938.
16 *Daily Express*, 28 February 1938
17 Hansard, 28 February 1938.
18 Harris, *op. cit.*
19 Gilbert, *The Prophet of Truth*, *op. cit.*

20   Pimlott, *The Political Diary of Hugh Dalton*, *op. cit.*
21   Pimlott, *The Political Diary of Hugh Dalton*, *op. cit.*
22   Harvey, J. (ed.), *The Diplomatic Diaries of Oliver Harvey, 1937–1940*.
23   Nicolson, *op. cit.*
24   Nicolson, *op. cit.*
25   Pimlott, *The Political Diary of Hugh Dalton*, *op. cit.*
26   Charmley, J., Churchill: *The End of Glory, A Political Biography*.
27   Churchill, W. to Attlee, C. R., Letter, 17 March 1938, Churchill Papers, CHAR 2/238, Churchill Archives, Churchill College, Cambridge.
28   Attlee, C. R. to Churchill, W., Letter, 17 March 1938, Churchill Papers, CHAR 2/238, Churchill Archives, Churchill College, Cambridge.
29   Churchill, W. to Lloyd George, D., 13 August 1938, Lloyd George Papers, LG/G/4/5/19, Parliamentary Archives, House of Lords.
30   Harris, *op. cit.*
31   Gilbert, *The Prophet of Truth*, *op. cit.*
32   Harris, *op. cit.*
33   Harvey, *The Diplomatic Diaries of Oliver Harvey*, *op. cit.*
34   Inskip, G., Diary, 17 September 1938, Caldecote Papers, INKP 1, Churchill Archives, Churchill College, Cambridge.
35   Bew, *op. cit.*
36   Pimlott, *The Political Diary of Hugh Dalton*, *op. cit.*
37   Pimlott, *The Political Diary of Hugh Dalton*, *op. cit.*
38   Burridge, *Clement Attlee*, *op. cit.*
39   Gilbert, *The Prophet of Truth*, *op. cit.*
40   Nicolson, *op. cit.*
41   Harris, *op. cit.*
42   Nicolson, *op. cit.*
43   *Daily Mirror*, 24 September 1938.
44   Gilbert, *The Prophet of Truth*, *op. cit.*
45   Gilbert, *The Prophet of Truth*, *op. cit.*
46   Cooper, D., *Old Men Forget*.
47   Hart, Liddell, *op. cit.*
48   Charmley, *op. cit.*
49   Norwich, *op. cit.*
50   Bew, *op. cit.*
51   Jenkins, *op. cit.*
52   Both quotations from Addison, P., *The Road to 1945: British Politics and the Second World War*.
53   Burridge, *Clement Attlee*, *op. cit.*
54   Boyd-Carpenter, *op. cit.*

Twelve: Admiralty

1   Harris, *op. cit.*
2   Webb, B., Diary, 26 March 1939, LSE Archives.
3   Nicolson, *op. cit.*
4   Thomas, D., Churchill: *The Member for Woodford*.
5   Thomas, *op. cit.*
6   Gilbert, *The Prophet of Truth*, *op. cit.*

7   *Daily Mirror*, 17 March 1939.
8   Hore-Belisha, L., Diary, 11 April 1939, HOBE 1/5, Churchill Archives, Churchill College, Cambridge.
9   Self, *The Neville Chamberlain Diaries and Letters (Volume 4)*, *op. cit.*
10 Self, *The Neville Chamberlain Diaries and Letters (Volume 4)*, *op. cit.*
11 Self, *The Neville Chamberlain Diaries and Letters (Volume 4)*, *op. cit.*
12 *Observer*, 2 July 1939.
13 Attlee, C. R. to Churchill, W., Letter, 1 July 1939, Churchill Papers, CHAR 8/628, Churchill Archives, Churchill College, Cambridge.
14 Manchester, *The Caged Lion*, *op. cit.*
15 Manchester, *The Caged Lion*, *op. cit.*
16 Manchester, *The Caged Lion*, *op. cit.*
17 Hansard, 27 April 1939.
18 Hansard, 27 April 1939.
19 Rhodes James, *'Chips'*, *op. cit.*
20 *Daily Mirror*, 29 April 1939.
21 Pimlott, *The Political Diary of Hugh Dalton*, *op. cit.*
22 Rhodes James, *Victor Cazalet*, *op. cit.*
23 Pimlott, *The Political Diary of Hugh Dalton*, *op. cit.*
24 Gilbert, *The Prophet of Truth*, *op. cit.*
25 Hansard, 2 August 1939.
26 Self, *The Neville Chamberlain Diaries and Letters (Volume 4)*, *op. cit.*
27 Attlee, *As It Happened*, *op. cit.*
28 Gilbert, *The Prophet of Truth*, *op. cit.*
29 Pelling, *Winston Churchill*, *op. cit.*
30 Hansard, 3 September 1939.
31 Gilbert, *The Prophet of Truth*, *op. cit.*
32 Gilbert, *The Prophet of Truth*, *op. cit.*
33 Pelling, *Winston Churchill*, *op. cit.*
34 Stewart, G., *op. cit.*
35 D'Este, *Warlord*, *op. cit.*
36 Sylvester, A. to Lloyd George, D., 15 September 1939, Lloyd George Papers, LG/G/24/1, Parliamentary Archives, House of Lords.
37 Hansard, 26 September 1939.
38 Nicolson, *op. cit.*
39 Inskip, G., Diary, 9 October 1939, Caldecote Papers, INKP 1, Churchill Archives, Churchill College, Cambridge.
40 Gilbert, M., *Winston S. Churchill: Finest Hour, 1939–1941*.
41 Sylvester, A. to Lloyd George, D., 10 October 1939, Lloyd George Papers, LG/G/24/1, Parliamentary Archives, House of Lords.
42 Gilbert, *Finest Hour*, *op. cit.*
43 Dellar, *op. cit.*
44 Dalton, H., Note on Labour Leadership, 1939, Dalton Papers, DALTON 2/9/28, LSE Archives.
45 *Daily Herald*, 9 November 1939.
46 *The Times*, 10 November 1939.
47 *Daily Mail*, 7 December 1939.
48 Harvey, *The Diplomatic Diaries of Oliver Harvey*, *op. cit.*
49 King, *op. cit.*

50 Webb, B., Diary, 1 March 1940, LSE Archives.
51 *Sunday Express*, 25 February 1940.
52 Sylvester, A. to Lloyd George, D., 21 September 1939, Lloyd George Papers, LG/G/24/1, Parliamentary Archives, House of Lords.
53 Gorodetsky, G., *The Maisky Diaries: Red Ambassador to the Court of St James's, 1932–1943*.

Thirteen: Norway

1   Pelling, *Winston Churchill, op. cit.*
2   Cabinet minutes, Feb 12 1940, CAB 65/3/39, National Archives.
3   Gilbert, *Finest Hour, op. cit.*
4   Harvey, *The Diplomatic Diaries of Oliver Harvey, op. cit.*
5   Sylvester, A. to Lloyd George, D., 26 March 1940, Lloyd George Papers, LG/G/24/1, Parliamentary Archives, House of Lords.
6   Sylvester, A. to Lloyd George, D., 21 March 1940, Lloyd George Papers, LG/G/24/1, Parliamentary Archives, House of Lords.
7   Gilbert, *Finest Hour, op. cit.*
8   *Daily Herald*, 22 April 1940.
9   Self, *The Neville Chamberlain Diaries and Letters (Volume 4), op. cit.*
10 Shakespeare, N., *Six Minutes in May: How Churchill Unexpectedly Became Prime Minister*.
11 Keyes, Sir R., to Churchill, W., 29 April 1940, Keyes Papers, British Library.
12 Pelling, *Winston Churchill, op. cit.*
13 Spears, Sir E., *Prelude to Dunkirk*.
14 Rhodes James, *'Chips', op. cit.*
15 Emrys-Evans, P., to Thompson, L., Letter, 3 June 1965, Emrys-Evans Papers, MS Add 58,268, British Library.
16 Witherell, L., 'Lord Salisbury's "Watching Committee" and the Fall of Neville Chamberlain, May 1940', *English Historical Review*, November 2001.
17 Pimlott, *The Political Diary of Hugh Dalton, op. cit.*
18 Nicolson, *op. cit.*
19 Schneer, *op. cit.*
20 Clarke, P., *The Cripps Version: The Life of Sir Stafford Cripps, 1889–1952*.
21 Gorodetsky , *op. cit.*
22 Self, *The Neville Chamberlain Diary Letters (Volume 4), op. cit.*
23 Hansard, 7 May 1940.
24 Stuart, C. (ed.), *The Reith Diaries*.
25 Hansard, 7 May 1940.
26 Hansard, 7 May 1940.
27 Roberts, A., *Eminent Churchillians*.
28 Nicolson, *op. cit.*
29 *Observer*, 31 January 1965.
30 *Sunday Express*, 25 July 1965.
31 Wyburn-Powell, A., *Clement Davies: A Biography*.
32 Amery, L., *My Political Life*.
33 Harris, *op. cit.*
34 Blake, 'How Churchill Became Prime Minister', in Blake, R. and Louis, W. R. (eds), *Churchill*.

35 Donoughue and Jones, *op. cit.*
36 Donoughue and Jones, *op. cit.*
37 Donoughue and Jones, *op. cit.*
38 Pimlott, *The Political Diary of Hugh Dalton, op. cit.*
39 Swift, *op. cit.*
40 Emrys-Evans, P. to Addison, P., Letter, 14 April 1965, Emrys-Evans Papers, MS Add 58,268, British Library.
41 Pimlott, *The Political Diary of Hugh Dalton, op. cit.*
42 Hansard, 8 May 1940.
43 Hansard, 8 May 1940.
44 Schneer, *op. cit.*
45 Boothby, R., Interview, 1972, 2720, IWM Archives.
46 Paterson, *op. cit.*
47 Manchester, *op. cit.*
48 Roberts, *Churchill, op. cit.*
49 Hansard, 8 May 1940.
50 Pimlott, *The Political Diary of Hugh Dalton, op. cit.*
51 Crookshank, H., Diary, 8 May 1940, Crookshank Papers, MS Eng. d. 360, Bodleian Library, Oxford.
52 Schneer, *op. cit.*
53 Pimlott, *The Political Diary of Hugh Dalton, op. cit.*
54 Colville, *The Fringes of Power, op. cit.*
55 Cranborne, Viscount to Emrys-Evans, P., 7 May 1940, Emrys-Evans Papers, MS Add 58,268, British Library.
56 Dilks, D. (ed.), *The Diaries of Sir Alexander Cadogan 1938–1945.*
57 Shakespeare, *op. cit.*
58 Birkenhead, Lord, *The Life of Lord Halifax.*
59 Addison, *The Road to 1945, op. cit.*
60 Amery, L., Diary, 9 May 1940, Amery Papers, AMEL 7, Churchill Archives Centre, Churchill College, Cambridge.
61 Witherell, *op. cit.*
62 Eden, A., *The Reckoning: The Eden Memoirs.*
63 Pimlott, *The Political Diary of Hugh Dalton, op. cit.*
64 Donoughue and Jones, *op. cit.*
65 Shinwell, E., Interview, 1972, 2733, IWM Archives.
66 Note on Attlee and Churchill, 1 April 1980, Parker Papers, Parker 1/9, LSE Archives.
67 Emrys-Evans, P. to Attlee, C. R., Letter, 30 November 1960, Emrys-Evans Papers, MS Add 58,268, British Library.
68 Pimlott, *The Political Diary of Hugh Dalton, op. cit.*
69 Boyle, A., *Poor Dear Brendan: The Quest for Brendan Bracken.*
70 Moran, *Churchill, op. cit.*
71 Eden, *The Reckoning, op. cit.*
72 Wyburn-Powell, *op. cit.*
73 Attlee, C. R. to Emrys-Evans, P., 31 December 1960, Emrys-Evans Papers, MS Add 58,268, British Library.
74 Manchester, *The Caged Lion, op. cit.*
75 Gilbert, *Finest Hour, op. cit.*
76 Note by Lord Camrose in Schneer, *op. cit.*

77 Williams, F., *A Prime Minister Remembers: The War and Post-War Memoirs of the Rt. Hon. Earl Attlee.*

78 Amery, L., Diary, Amery Papers, AMEL 7, Churchill Archives Centre, Churchill College, Cambridge.

79 Gilbert, *Finest Hour, op. cit.*

80 Jenkins, *op. cit.*

81 Gilbert, *Finest Hour, op. cit.*

82 Manchester, *The Caged Lion, op. cit.*

83 Gilbert, *Finest Hour, op. cit.*

84 Rose, J., *op. cit.*

85 Jenkins, *op. cit.*

86 Shakespeare, *op. cit.*

87 Roberts, A., *The Holy Fox: The Life of Lord Halifax.*

88 Stewart, G., *op. cit.*

89 Manchester, *The Caged Lion, op. cit.*

90 Gilbert, *Finest Hour, op. cit.*

91 Manchester, *The Caged Lion, op. cit.*

92 *Daily Mirror*, 10 May 1940.

93 Templewood, Viscount, *Nine Troubled Years.*

94 Churchill, W., *The Gathering Storm, op cit.*

95 Nicolson, *op. cit.*

96 Barnes, J. and Nicholson, D., *The Empire at Bay: The Leo Amery Diaries, 1929–1945.*

97 Pimlott, *The Political Diary of Hugh Dalton, op. cit.*

98 *The Times*, 11 May 1940.

99 Eden, *The Reckoning, op. cit.*

100 Schneer, *op. cit.*

101 Harris, *op. cit.*

102 Gilbert, *Finest Hour, op. cit.*

103 Wheeler Bennett, J., *King George VI: His Life and Reign.*

104 Sylvester, A. to Lloyd George, D., 10 April 1942, Lloyd George Papers, LG/G/24/1, Parliamentary Archives, House of Lords.

105 Churchill, *The Gathering Storm, op cit.*

106 Thompson, W., *Sixty Minutes with Winston Churchill.*

107 Churchill, *The Gathering Storm, op cit.*

108 Both quotations from Kelly, J., *Never Surrender: Winston Churchill and Britain's Decision to Fight Nazi Germany in the Fateful Summer of 1940.*

109 Headlam, *op. cit.*

110 Both quotations from Hermiston, R., *All Behind You, Winston: Churchill's Great Coalition 1940–45.*

111 King, *op. cit.*

112 *News Chronicle*, 27 April 1959.

113 *Observer*, 31 January 1965.

114 *Observer*, 31 January 1965.

115 Jackson, *op. cit.*

Fourteen: Dunkirk

1 Wheeler Bennett, J., *Action This Day: Working with Churchill.*

2 Thomas-Symonds, *op. cit.*

3   *Observer*, 31 January 1965.
4   Churchill, W., *Their Finest Hour*, *op. cit.*
5   Churchill, *Their Finest Hour*, *op. cit.*
6   Hermiston, *op. cit.*
7   Williams, *A Prime Minister Remembers*, *op. cit.*
8   Williams, *A Prime Minister Remembers*, *op. cit.*
9   Self, *The Neville Chamberlain Diaries and Letters (Volume 4)*, *op. cit.*
10 Self, *The Neville Chamberlain Diaries and Letters (Volume 4)*, *op. cit.*
11 Pimlott, *The Political Diary of Hugh Dalton*, *op. cit.*
12 Pimlott, *The Political Diary of Hugh Dalton*, *op. cit.*
13 Bartley, P., *Ellen Wilkinson: From Red Suffragist to Government Minister*.
14 Pimlott, B. (ed.), *The Second World War Diary of Hugh Dalton: 1940–45*.
15 Nicolson, *op. cit.*
16 Pottle, M. (ed.), *Champion Redoubtable: The Diaries and Letters of Violet Bonham Carter, 1914–1945*.
17 Gorodetsky , *op. cit.*
18 Pimlott, *The Second World War Diary of Hugh Dalton*, *op. cit.*
19 Pimlott, *The Second World War Diary of Hugh Dalton*, *op. cit.*
20 Schneer, *op. cit.*
21 *Daily Express*, 13 May 1940.
22 Harris, *op. cit.*
23 Swift, *op. cit.*
24 Amery, L., Diary, 14 May 1940, Amery Papers, AMEL 7, Churchill Archives Centre, Churchill College, Cambridge.
25 Jackson, *op. cit.*
26 *Observer*, 31 January 1965.
27 Crookshank, H., Diary, 13 May 1940, Crookshank Papers, MS Eng. d. 360, Bodleian Library, Oxford.
28 Rhodes James, *'Chips'*, *op. cit.*
29 Hansard, 13 May 1940.
30 Minutes of the War Cabinet, 13 May 1940, CAB 65/13, National Archives.
31 Minutes of the War Cabinet, 15 May 1940, CAB 65/13, National Archives.
32 McLeod, R. and Kelly, D. (eds), *The Ironside Diaries 1937–1940*.
33 Lawlor, S., *Churchill and the Politics of War, 1940–1941*.
34 Bridges, Sir E., Reminiscence, 1967, Normanbrook Papers, NRBK 1/3, Bodleian Library, Oxford.
35 Hollis, Sir L., Private memoir, 1952, 2773, IWM Archives.
36 Holmes, M., Interview, 1999, 19835, IWM Archives.
37 Jenkins, *op. cit.*
38 Williams, *A Prime Minister Remembers*, *op. cit.*
39 Clemens, *op. cit.*
40 *The Times*, 23 May 1940.
41 Pitts, D., The Granada Historical Records Interviews, *op. cit.*
42 Kelly, *op. cit.*
43 Minutes of the War Cabinet, 26 May 1940, CAB 65/13, National Archives.
44 Minutes of the War Cabinet, 26 May 1940, CAB 65/13, National Archives.
45 Minutes of the War Cabinet, 26 May 1940, CAB 65/13, National Archives.
46 Kelly, *op. cit.*
47 Ismay, H., The *Memoirs of General Lord Ismay*.

48 Minutes of the War Cabinet, 27 May 1940, CAB 65/13, National Archives.
49 Pimlott, *The Second World War Diary of Hugh Dalton*, *op. cit.*
50 Minutes of the War Cabinet, 27 May 1940, CAB 65/13, National Archives.
51 Birkenhead, *op. cit.*
52 Colville, *The Fringes of Power*, *op. cit.*
53 Kelly, *op. cit.*
54 Hansard, 28 May 1940.
55 Minutes of the War Cabinet, 28 May 1940, CAB 65/13, National Archives.
56 Minutes of the War Cabinet, 28 May 1940, CAB 65/13, National Archives.
57 Reynolds, *op. cit.*
58 Barnes and Nicholson, *op. cit.*
59 Hugh Dalton, *The Fateful Years*
60 Minutes of the War Cabinet, 28 May 1940, CAB 65/13, National Archives.
61 Churchill, W. to Reynaud, P., 28 May 1940, CAB 65/13, National Archives.
62 Spears, *op. cit.*
63 Spears, *op. cit.*
64 Williams, *A Prime Minister Remembers*, *op. cit.*
65 Ismay, *op. cit.*
66 Harvey, *The Diplomatic Diaries of Oliver Harvey*, *op. cit.*
67 Minutes of the War Cabinet, 2 June 1940, CAB 65/13, National Archives.
68 Minutes of the War Cabinet, 3 June 1940, CAB 65/13, National Archives.
69 Hansard, 4 June 1940.
70 Best, G., *Churchill and War*.
71 Nicolson, *op. cit.*
72 Rhodes James, *Victor Cazalet*, *op. cit.*

Fifteen: Empire and Commonwealth

1 Self, *The Neville Chamberlain Diaries and Letters (Volume 4)*, *op. cit.*
2 King, *op. cit.*
3 Roberts, *The Holy Fox*, *op. cit.*
4 Webb, B., Diary, 9 June 1940, LSE Archives.
5 Kramnick and Sheerman, *op. cit.*
6 Headlam, *op. cit.*
7 Headlam, *op. cit.*
8 Gilbert, *Finest Hour*, *op. cit.*
9 Minutes of the War Cabinet, 13 June 1940, CAB 65/13, National Archives.
10 Minutes of the War Cabinet, 13 June 1940, CAB 65/13, National Archives.
11 Gilbert, *Finest Hour*, *op. cit.*
12 Tombs, R. and I., *That Sweet Enemy: The French and the British from the Sun King to the Present*.
13 Churchill, *Their Finest Hour*, *op. cit.*
14 McLeod and Kelly, *op. cit.*
15 *Observer*, 31 January 1965.
16 Jenkins, *op. cit.*
17 Nicolson, *op. cit.*
18 Rose, J., *op. cit.*
19 Pimlott, *The Second World War Diary of Hugh Dalton*, *op. cit.*
20 King, *op. cit.*

21 Addison, *The Road to 1945*, *op. cit.*
22 Jones, *op. cit.*
23 Sylvester, A. to Lloyd George, D., 28 June and 9 July 1940, Lloyd George Papers, LG/G/24/1, Parliamentary Archives, House of Lords.
24 Williams, *op. cit.*
25 *Observer*, 31 January 1965.
26 Wheeler Bennett, *Action This Day*, *op. cit.*
27 Minutes of the War Cabinet, 24 June 1940, CAB 65/13, National Archives.
28 Clayton, T. and Craig, P., *Finest Hour: The Battle of Britain*.
29 Churchill, *Their Finest Hour*, *op. cit.*
30 Ansel, W., *Hitler Confronts England*.
31 Colville, *The Fringes of Power*, *op. cit.*
32 Danchev, A. and Todman, D. (eds), *Alanbrooke War Diaries 1939 1945: Field Marshall Lord Alanbrooke*.
33 Gilbert, *Finest Hour*, *op. cit.*
34 Colville, *The Fringes of Power*, *op. cit.*
35 Ismay, *op. cit.*
36 Keane, T., *Cloak of Enemies: Churchill's SOE, Enemies at Home and the Cockleshell Heroes*.
37 Pimlott, *The Second World War Diary of Hugh Dalton*, *op. cit.*
38 Bew, *op. cit.*
39 Taylor, A. J. P., *Beaverbrook*.
40 Pimlott, *The Second World War Diary of Hugh Dalton*, *op. cit.*
41 Taylor, *Beaverbrook*, *op. cit.*
42 Rhodes James, *'Chips'*, *op. cit.*
43 Schneer, *op. cit.*
44 Martin, Sir J., *Downing Street: The War Years – Diaries, Letters and a Memoir*.
45 Attlee, C. R. to Attlee, T., 15 October 1940, Attlee Papers, MS Eng. c. 4791, Bodleian Library, Oxford.
46 Colville, *The Fringes of Power*, *op. cit.*
47 Topham, A. M. R. to Colville, J., Letter, undated, CHAR 20/3, Churchill Archives, Churchill College, Cambridge.
48 Colville, J. to Topham, A. M. R., Letter, 19 October 1940, CHAR 20/3, Churchill Archives, Churchill College, Cambridge.
49 Young, K. (ed.), *The Diaries of Sir Bruce Lockhart*.
50 Pawle, G., *The War and Colonel Warden*.
51 Eden, *The Reckoning*, *op. cit.*
52 Pitts, D., The Granada Historical Records Interviews, *op. cit.*
53 Gilbert, M., *The Churchill Documents: Never Surrender*.
54 Ismay, *op. cit.*
55 Ismay, H., Speech, 30 June 1949, Ismay Papers, ISMAY 1/7, King's College London.
56 Bew, *op. cit.*
57 Attlee, *As It Happened*, *op. cit.*
58 Winterbotham, F., Interview, 1984, 7462, IWM Archives.
59 Hansard, 5 November 1940.
60 Boothby, R., Interview, 1972, 2720, IWM Archives.
61 Danchev and Todman, *op. cit.*
62 Stelzer, C., *Dinner with Churchill: Policy-Making at the Dinner Table*.

63 Burridge, T., *British Labour and Hitler's War*.
64 Burridge, *Clement Attlee*, op. cit.
65 Addison, *The Road to 1945*, op. cit.
66 Clarke, *The Cripps Version*, op. cit.
67 Terms of Reference, War Cabinet Business, 23 August 1940, PREM 4/6/9, National Archives.
68 *Daily Mirror*, 28 August 1940.
69 Soames, *Clementine Churchill*, op. cit.
70 Harvie-Watt, G. S., *Most of My Life*.
71 Hansard, 12 November 1940.
72 Rhodes James, *'Chips'*, op. cit.
73 Pimlott, *The Second World War Diary of Hugh Dalton*, op. cit.
74 Colville, *The Fringes of Power*, op. cit.
75 Pimlott, *The Second World War Diary of Hugh Dalton*, op. cit.
76 Woolton, Lord, Diary, 24 December 1940, Bodleian Library, Oxford.
77 Sylvester, A. to Lloyd George, D., 13 December 1940, Lloyd George Papers, LG/6/25/1, Parliamentary Archives, House of Lords.

Sixteen: Atlantic

1   Lukacs, J., *The Duel: The Eighty-Day Struggle Between Churchill and Hitler*.
2   Gilbert, M., *Churchill and America*.
3   Hastings, M., *Finest Years: Churchill as Warlord 1940–45*.
4   Churchill, *Their Finest Hour*, op. cit.
5   Colville, *The Fringes of Power*, op. cit.
6   Rhodes James, *'Chips'*, op. cit.
7   King, op. cit.
8   Sylvester, A. to Lloyd George, D., 23 April 1941, Lloyd George Papers, LG/G/24/2, Parliamentary Archives, House of Lords.
9   Sylvester, A. to Lloyd George, D., 8 May 1941, Lloyd George Papers, LG/G/24/2, Parliamentary Archives, House of Lords.
10 King, op. cit.
11 King, op. cit.
12 Pimlott, *The Second World War Diary of Hugh Dalton*, op. cit.
13 Hansard, 6 May 1940.
14 Pimlott, *The Second World War Diary of Hugh Dalton*, op. cit.
15 Bridges, E., Report, 10 March 1941, PREM 4/6/9, National Archives.
16 Woolton, Lord, Diary, 12 and 21 March 1941, Woolton papers, Bodleian Library, Oxford.
17 Pimlott, *The Second World War Diary of Hugh Dalton*, op. cit.
18 Pimlott, *The Second World War Diary of Hugh Dalton*, op. cit.
19 Chisholm, A. and Davie, M., *Beaverbrook: A Life*.
20 Chisholm and Davie, op. cit.
21 Pimlott, *The Second World War Diary of Hugh Dalton*, op. cit.
22 Brodsky, V. to Beaverbrook, Lord, 13 June 1941, Churchill Papers, CHAR 20/24, Churchill Archives, Churchill College, Cambridge.
23 Kramnick and Sheerman, op. cit.
24 Harris, op. cit.
25 Crowcroft, R., *Attlee's War: World War II and the Making of a Labour Leader*.

26   Addison, *Churchill on the Home Front, op. cit.*
27   Churchill, W. to Greenwood, A., 4 January 1941, PREM 4/88/1, National Archives.
28   Attlee, C. R. to Churchill, W., April 1941, Attlee Papers, ATLE 2/2, Churchill Archives, Churchill College, Cambridge.
29   Attlee, C. R. to Churchill, W., July 1941, Churchill Papers, CHAR 20/20, Churchill Archives, Churchill College, Cambridge.
30   Churchill, W. to Wood, K., 27 July 1941, Churchill Papers, CHAR 20/20, Churchill Archives, Churchill College, Cambridge.
31   Wood, K. to Churchill, W., 27 July 1941, Churchill Papers, CHAR 20/20, Churchill Archives, Churchill College, Cambridge.
32   Attlee, C. R. to Churchill, W., 16 July 1941, Churchill Papers, CHAR 20/34, Churchill Archives, Churchill College, Cambridge.
33   Gilbert, *Finest Hour, op. cit.*
34   Minutes of the War Cabinet, 23 June 1941, CAB 65/18, National Archives.
35   Ede, C., Diary, 5 July 1941, Add Ms 59,690, British Library.
36   Jablonsky, D., *Churchill: The Great Game and Total War.*
37   Colville, *The Fringes of Power, op. cit.*
38   Churchill, W. to George VI, 27 July 1941, Churchill Papers, CHAR 20/20, Churchill Archives, Churchill College, Cambridge.
39   Colville, *The Fringes of Power, op. cit.*
40   Jacob, Sir I., Diary, August 1941, Jacob Papers, JACB 1/10, Churchill Archives, Churchill College, Cambridge.
41   Churchill, W. to Attlee, C. R., 3 August 1941. Attlee Papers, MS ATTLEE DEP 3, Bodleian Library, Oxford.
42   Hansard, 6 August 1941.
43   Ede, C., Diary, 6 August 1941, Add Ms 59,690, British Library.
44   Attlee, C. R. to Churchill, W., 8 August 1941, Churchill Papers, CHAR 20/23, Churchill Archives, Churchill College, Cambridge
45   Jago, *op. cit.*
46   Clarke, P., *Mr Churchill's Profession: Statesman, Orator, Writer.*
47   Gilbert, *Finest Hour, op. cit.*
48   Gilbert, *Finest Hour, op. cit.*
49   Hastings, *op. cit.*
50   Churchill, W. to Attlee, C. R., 11 August 1941, Churchill Papers, CHAR 20/48, Churchill Archives, Churchill College, Cambridge.
51   Churchill, W. to Attlee, C. R., 12 August 1941, Churchill Papers, CHAR 20/48, Churchill Archives, Churchill College, Cambridge.
52   Dobson, L. V., 'International Diplomacy at the Atlantic Conference', *Review of International Studies*, April 1984.
53   Pressnell, L. S. and Hopkins, S. V., 'A Canard of Time? Churchill, the War Cabinet and the Atlantic Charter', *Review of International Studies*, July 1988.
54   Pressnell and Hopkins, *op. cit.*
55   Churchill, W. to Attlee, C. R., 11 August 1941, Churchill Papers, CHAR 20/48, Churchill Archives, Churchill College, Cambridge.
56   Attlee, C. R. to Churchill, W., 12 August 1941, Churchill Papers, CHAR 20/48, Churchill Archives, Churchill College, Cambridge.
57   Jacob, Sir I., Diary, August 1941, Jacob Papers, JACB 1/10, Churchill Archives, Churchill College, Cambridge.

58 Dilks, *The Diaries of Sir Alexander Cadogan, op. cit.*
59 *Daily Mirror*, 20 August 1941.
60 Churchill, W. to Attlee, C. R., 12 August 1941, Churchill Papers, CHAR 20/48, Churchill Archives, Churchill College, Cambridge.
61 Harvie-Watt, *op. cit.*
62 Attlee, C. R. to Attlee, T., 15 August 1941, Attlee Papers, MS Eng. c. 4792, Bodleian Library, Oxford.
63 Ede, C., Diary, 15 August 1941, Add Ms 59,690, British Library.
64 Barnes and Nicholson, *op. cit.*
65 Toye, *Churchill's Empire, op. cit.*
66 Toye, *Churchill's Empire, op. cit.*
67 Toye, *Churchill's Empire, op. cit.*
68 Toye, *Churchill's Empire, op. cit.*
69 Sylvester, A. to Lloyd George, D., 4 September 1941, Lloyd George Papers, LG/G/24/2, Parliamentary Archives, House of Lords.
70 Sylvester, A. to Lloyd George, D., 25 September, Lloyd George Papers, LG/G/24/2, Parliamentary Archives, House of Lords.
71 Gilbert, *Finest Hour, op. cit.*
72 Churchill, W. to Auchinleck, C., 18 October 1941, Churchill Papers, CHAR 20/44, Churchill Archives, Churchill College, Cambridge.
73 Pimlott, *The Second World War Diary of Hugh Dalton, op. cit.*
74 Attlee, *As It Happened, op. cit.*
75 Kimball, W. F., *Churchill and Roosevelt: The Complete Correspondence.*
76 Attlee, C. R. to Attlee, T., 21 November 1941, Attlee Papers, MS Eng. c. 4793, Bodleian Library, Oxford.

Seventeen: Washington and Singapore

1 Pimlott, *The Second World War Diary of Hugh Dalton, op. cit.*
2 Pimlott, *The Second World War Diary of Hugh Dalton, op. cit.*
3 Pimlott, *The Second World War Diary of Hugh Dalton, op. cit.*
4 King, *op. cit.*
5 King, *op. cit.*
6 Sylvester, A. to Lloyd George, D., 31 October 1941, Lloyd George Papers, LG/G/24/2, Parliamentary Archives, House of Lords.
7 Bullock, A., *Ernest Bevin: A Biography* (Volume 2).
8 Bullock, *op. cit.*
9 Ede, C., Diary, 16 December 1941, ADD MS 59,690, British Library
10 Crowcroft, *op. cit.*
11 Crowcroft, *op. cit.*
12 Attlee, C. R. to Churchill, W., 24 September 1941, Attlee Papers, ATTLEE DEP 3, Bodleian Library, Oxford.
13 Ede, C., Diary, 1 October 1941, ADD MS 59,690, British Library
14 Ede, C., Diary, 14 October 1941, ADD MS 59,690, British Library
15 Ede, C., Diary, 3 December 1941, ADD MS 59,690, British Library
16 Ede, C., Diary, 4 December 1941, ADD MS 59,690, British Library
17 Rhodes James, *Victor Cazalet, op. cit.*
18 Schneer, *op. cit.*
19 King, *op. cit.*

20 Harris, *op. cit.*
21 Webb, B., Diary, 15 September 1941, LSE Archives.
22 Danchev and Todman, *op. cit.*
23 Gilbert, M., *Winston S. Churchill: Road to Victory, 1941–1945.*
24 Dilks, *The Diaries of Sir Alexander Cadogan, op. cit.*
25 Harvey, J. (ed.), *The War Diaries of Oliver Harvey, 1941–1945.*
26 Dilks, *The Diaries of Sir Alexander Cadogan, op. cit.*
27 Gilbert, *Finest Hour, op. cit.*
28 Churchill, *The Grand Alliance, op. cit.*
29 Stelzer, *op. cit.*
30 Farmelo, G., *Churchill's Bomb: A Hidden History of Science, War and Politics.*
31 Farmelo, *op. cit.*
32 Pelling, *Winston Churchill, op. cit.*
33 Ede, C., Diary, 26 December 1941, ADD MS 59,690, British Library
34 Moran, *Churchill, op. cit.*
35 Moran, *Churchill, op. cit.*
36 Danchev and Todman, *op. cit.*
37 Kennedy, Sir J., *The Business of War: The War Narrative of Major-General Sir John Kennedy.*
38 Harvie-Watt, G. to Churchill, W., 20 December 1941, Harvie-Watt Papers, HARV 1/1, Churchill Archives, Churchill College, Cambridge.
39 Attlee, C. R. to Churchill, W., 20 December 1941, Churchill Papers, CHAR 20/23, Churchill Archives, Churchill College, Cambridge.
40 Kennedy, *op. cit.*
41 Harvie-Watt, G. to Churchill, W., 8 January 1942, Harvie-Watt Papers, HARV 1/1, Churchill Archives, Churchill College, Cambridge.
42 Sylvester, A. to Lloyd George, D., 8 January 1942, Lloyd George Papers, LG/G/24/2, Parliamentary Archives, House of Lords.
43 *Daily Mirror*, 19 February 1942.
44 Nicolson, *op. cit.*
45 Sylvester, A. to Lloyd George, D., 13 January 1942, Lloyd George Papers, LG/G/24/2, Parliamentary Archives, House of Lords.
46 Gilbert, *Road to Victory, op. cit.*
47 Ede, C., Diary, 27 and 28 January 1942, ADD MS 59,691, British Library
48 Hansard, 28 January 1942.
49 Crookshank, H., Diary, 28 January 1942, Crookshank Papers, MS Eng. d. 360, Bodleian Library, Oxford.
50 Ede, C., Diary, 29 January 1942, ADD MS 59,691, British Library
51 Jenkins, *op. cit.*
52 Gilbert, *Road to Victory, op. cit.*
53 Hastings, *op. cit.*
54 Soames, *Clementine Churchill, op. cit.*
55 Rhodes James, *'Chips', op. cit.*
56 Woolton, Lord, Diary, 13 and 18 February 1942, Woolton Papers, Bodleian Library, Oxford.
57 Headlam, *op. cit.*
58 Ede, C., Diary, 2 February 1942, ADD MS 59,691, British Library
59 Taylor, *Beaverbrook, op. cit.*
60 Eade, C., Diary, 30 September 1942, Eade Papers, EADE 2/1, Churchill Archives, Churchill College, Cambridge.

61   Cripps, S. to Churchill, W., 30 January 1942, Cripps Papers, SC36/2, Bodleian Library, Oxford.
62   Churchill, W. to Cripps, S., 31 January 1942, Cripps Papers, SC36/2, Bodleian Library, Oxford.
63   Pottle, *Champion Redoubtable*, *op. cit.*
64   Crowcroft, *op. cit.*
65   Clarke, *The Cripps Version*, *op. cit.*
66   Pimlott, *The Second World War Diary of Hugh Dalton*, *op. cit.*
67   Harvey, *The War Diaries of Oliver Harvey*, *op. cit.*
68   Bryant, C., *Stafford Cripps: The First Modern Chancellor.*
69   Harvey, *The War Diaries of Oliver Harvey*, *op. cit.*
70   Schneer, *op. cit.*
71   Taylor, *Beaverbrook*, *op. cit.*
72   Churchill, *The Hinge of Fate*, *op. cit.*
73   Hermiston, *op. cit.*
74   Taylor, *Beaverbrook*, *op. cit.*
75   Woolton, Lord, Diary, 19 February 1942, Woolton Papers, Bodleian Library, Oxford.
76   Taylor, *Beaverbrook*, *op. cit.*
77   Attlee, C. R. to John, W., 3 April 1942, Attlee Papers, ATTLEE DEP 5, Bodleian Library, Oxford.
78   Pimlott, *The Second World War Diary of Hugh Dalton*, *op. cit.*
79   Sylvester, A. to Lloyd George, D., 25 February 1942, Lloyd George Papers, LG/G/24/2, Parliamentary Archives, House of Lords.
80   Attlee, C. R. to Churchill, W., 27 February 1942, PREM 4/88/1, National Archives.
81   Attlee, C. R. to Churchill, W., 26 February 1942, PREM 4/88/1, National Archives.
82   Attlee, C. R. to Attlee, T., 25 February 1942, Attlee Papers, MS Eng. c.4793, Bodleian Library, Oxford.
83   Ede, C., Diary, 25 February 1942, ADD MS 59,691, British Library
84   Woolton, Lord, Diary, 19 February 1942, Woolton Papers, Bodleian Library, Oxford.
85   Crookshank, H., Diary, 20 February 1942, Crookshank Papers, MS Eng. d. 360, Bodleian Library, Oxford.
86   Crowcroft, *op. cit.*
87   Ede, C., Diary, 25 and 27 January 1942, ADD MS 59,691, British Library
88   Rhodes James, *Victor Cazalet*, *op. cit.*
89   *Daily Mirror*, 12 March 1942.
90   Harvey, *The War Diaries of Oliver Harvey*, *op. cit.*
91   Pimlott, *The Second World War Diary of Hugh Dalton*, *op. cit.*
92   King, *op. cit.*

Eighteen: Russia and Egypt

1   Toye, *Churchill's Empire*, *op. cit.*
2   Harris, *op. cit.*
3   Bryant, *op. cit.*
4   French, P., *Liberty or Death: India's Journey to Independence and Division.*

5   Hermiston, *op. cit.*
6   Toye, *Churchill's Empire, op. cit.*
7   Schneer, *op. cit.*
8   Nicolson, *op. cit.*
9   Clarke, *The Cripps Version, op. cit.*
10   Brookshire, J., *Clement Attlee.*
11   Windsor, Duke of to Churchill, W., 18 April 1942, Churchill Papers, CHAR 20/63, Churchill Archives, Churchill College, Cambridge.
12   Attlee, C. R. to Churchill, W., May 1942, Churchill Papers, CHAR 20/63, Churchill Archives, Churchill College, Cambridge.
13   Churchill, W., Note on telegram from Smuts, J. C., 30 May 1942, Churchill Papers, CHAR 20/63, Churchill Archives, Churchill College, Cambridge.
14   Churchill, W. to Auchinleck, C., 1 March 1942, DO 121/10B, National Archives.
15   Attlee, C. R. to Churchill, W., 1 March 1942, DO 121/10B, National Archives.
16   Hastings, *op. cit.*
17   Attlee, C. R. to Churchill, W., 16 April 1942, DO 121/10B, National Archives.
18   Churchill, W. to Attlee, C. R., 16 April 1942, 1942, DO 121/10B, National Archives.
19   Crowcroft, *op. cit.*
20   Crowcroft, *op. cit.*
21   Burridge, *Clement Attlee, op. cit.*
22   Donoughue and Jones, *op. cit.*
23   Hansard, 19 May 1942.
24   Harvie-Watt, G. to Churchill, W., 21 May 1942, HARV 1/1, Churchill Archives, Churchill College, Cambridge.
25   Nicolson, *op. cit.*
26   Pimlott, *The Second World War Diary of Hugh Dalton, op. cit.*
27   Pimlott, *The Second World War Diary of Hugh Dalton, op. cit.*
28   Pimlott, *The Second World War Diary of Hugh Dalton, op. cit.*
29   Nicolson, *op. cit.*
30   Moran, *Churchill at War, op. cit.*
31   Harvey, *The War Diaries of Oliver Harvey, op. cit.*
32   Moran, *Churchill at War, op. cit.*
33   Rhodes James, *Victor Cazalet, op. cit.*
34   Rhodes James, *'Chips', op. cit.*
35   Ede, C., Diary, 30 June 1942, ADD MS 59,691, British Library
36   Ede, C., Diary, 25 June 1942, ADD MS 59,691, British Library
37   Harvey, *The War Diaries of Oliver Harvey, op. cit.*
38   Boothby, R., Interview, 1972, 2720, IWM Archives.
39   Driberg, T., Interview, 1972, 2767, IWM Archives.
40   Rhodes James, *'Chips', op. cit.*
41   Hansard, 2 July 1942.
42   Hansard, 2 July 1942.
43   Eden, *The Reckoning, op. cit.*
44   Farmelo, *op. cit.*
45   MacDonald, *op. cit.*
46   Woolton, Lord, Diary, 12 July Woolton Papers, Bodleian Library, Oxford.
47   Young, *Churchill and Beaverbrook, op. cit.*

48 Harvey, *The War Diaries of Oliver Harvey, op. cit.*
49 13 July 1942, Lloyd George Papers, LG/G//24/2, Parliamentary Archives, House of Lords.
50 Schneer, *op. cit.*
51 *Daily Express*, 13 July 1942.
52 Attlee, C. R. to Churchill, W., 10 July 1942, PREM 3/499/9, National Archives.
53 Churchill, W. to Attlee, C. R., 29 July 1942, PREM 3/499/9, National Archives.
54 Eden, *The Reckoning, op. cit.*
55 Auchinleck to Brooke, 31 July 1942, CAB 65/31 National Archives.
56 Minutes of the War Cabinet, 1 August 1942, CAB 65/31, National Archives.
57 Moran, *Churchill at War, op. cit.*
58 Churchill, W. to Attlee, C. R., 6 August 1942, CAB 65/31, National Archives.
59 Attlee, C. R. to Churchill, W., 7 August 1942, CAB 65/31, National Archives.
60 Churchill, W. to Attlee, C. R., 7 August 1942, CAB 65/31, National Archives.
61 Attlee, C. R. to Churchill, W., 8 August 1942, CAB 65/31, National Archives.
62 Harvey, *The War Diaries of Oliver Harvey, op. cit.*
63 Churchill, W. to Attlee, C. R., 13 August 1942, Churchill Papers, CHAR 20/87, Churchill Archives, Churchill College, Cambridge.
64 Churchill, W. to Attlee, C. R., 15 August 1942, Churchill Papers, CHAR 20/87, Churchill Archives, Churchill College, Cambridge.
65 Moran, *Churchill, op. cit.*
66 Danchev and Todman, *op. cit.*
67 Churchill, W. to Attlee, C. R., 15 August 1942, Churchill Papers, CHAR 20/87, Churchill Archives, Churchill College, Cambridge.
68 Woolton, Lord, Diary, 7 September 1942, Woolton Papers, Bodleian Library, Oxford.
69 Woolton, Lord, Diary, 8 September 1942, Woolton Papers, Bodleian Library, Oxford.
70 Ede, C., Diary, 9 September 1942, ADD MS 59,691, British Library
71 Harris, *op. cit.*
72 Bryant, *op. cit.*
73 Pearce, R. (ed.), *Patrick Gordon Walker: Political Diaries 1932–1971.*
74 Pearce, *op. cit.*
75 Eden, *The Reckoning, op. cit.*
76 Bryant, *op. cit.*
77 Bryant, *op. cit.*
78 Eden, *The Reckoning, op. cit.*
79 Eden, *The Reckoning, op. cit.*
80 Sylvester, A. to Lloyd George, D., 20 October 1942, Lloyd George Papers, LG/G//24/2, Parliamentary Archives, House of Lords.
81 Jeffreys, K., *The Churchill Coalition and Wartime Politics, 1940–1945.*
82 Pelling, *Winston Churchill, op. cit.*
83 Ede, C., Diary, 10 November 1942, ADD MS 59,691, British Library

Nineteen: Downing Street

1 Shipton, J., Interview, 2001, 22578, IWM Archives.
2 Longford, F., contribution in Dellar, *op. cit.*
3 Holmes, M., Interview, 1999, 19835, IWM Archives.

4   D'Este, *Warlord*, *op. cit.*
5   Jacob, Sir I., Interview, 1982, 6191, IWM Archives.
6   Normanbrook, Lord, Reminiscence, 1967, Normanbrook Papers, NBRK 1//1, Bodleian Library, Oxford.
7   Wheeler Bennett, *Action This Day*, *op. cit.*
8   Wheeler Bennett, *Action This Day*, *op. cit.*
9   Citrine, *op. cit.*
10 Holmes, M., Interview, 1999, 19835, IWM Archives.
11 Clemens, *op. cit.*
12 Dilks, D., *Churchill and Company: Allies in War and Peace.*
13 Nel (nee Layton), E., Interview, 1994, 15119, IWM Archives.
14 *Sunday Times*, 26 April 1980.
15 Broome, V., *Clement Attlee.*
16 Williams, *Nothing So Strange*, *op. cit.*
17 Montague Browne, *op. cit.*
18 Stelzer, *op. cit.*
19 Stelzer, *op. cit.*
20 Holmes, M., Interview, 1999, 19835, IWM Archives.
21 Shipton, J., Interview, 2001, 22578, IWM Archives.
22 Burridge, *Clement Attlee*, *op. cit.*
23 Hunter, L., *The Road to Brighton Pier.*
24 Cripps, H., Interview, 1998, 18337, IWM Archives.
25 *Star*, 31 January 1941.
26 Broome, *op. cit.*
27 Rose, N., *Churchill: An Unruly Life.*
28 Stuart, J., *Within the Fringe.*
29 Colville, J., Interview, 1982, 6380, IWM Archives.
30 *Observer*, 31 January 1965.
31 Stuart, J., *op. cit.*
32 Lord Brabazon of Tara, *The Brabazon Story.*
33 Soames, *Clementine Churchill*, *op. cit.*
34 *Sunday Times*, 26 April 1980.
35 Cairncross, A. (ed.), *The Robert Hall Diaries: 1954–1961.*
36 Holmes, M., Interview, 1999, 19835, IWM Archives.
37 Nel (nee Layton), E., Interview, 1994, 15119, IWM Archives.
38 Addison, P., *Churchill: The Unexpected Hero.*
39 Thompson, R. W., *Churchill and Morton: Correspondence Between Major Sir Desmond Morton and R. W. Thompson.*
40 Boothby, R., Interview, 1972, 2720, IWM Archives.
41 Healey, D., *The Time of My Life.*
42 Eden, *Full Circle*, *op. cit.*
43 Williams, *Nothing So Strange*, *op. cit.*
44 Nel (nee Layton), E., Interview, 1994, 15119, IWM Archives.
45 Colville, J., Interview, 1982, 6380, IWM Archives.
46 Thompson, R. W., *op. cit.*
47 Williams, *Nothing So Strange*, *op. cit.*
48 Menzies, *op. cit.*
49 Best, *Churchill and War*, *op. cit.*
50 Lyttelton, O., Interview, 1972, 2739, IWM Archives.

51 Holmes, M., Interview, 1999, 19835, IWM Archives.
52 Blackburn, R., *I Am an Alcoholic.*
53 Harvie-Watt, *op. cit.*
54 Moran, *Churchill at War, op. cit.*
55 *Observer*, mid-1944.
56 Stuart, J., *op. cit.*
57 Jay, D., Interview, 1994, 15260, IWM Archives.
58 Martin, K., Article on Attlee, *Sunday Times*, 15 October 1967.
59 Dalton, H., Note on Attlee, 6 January 1957, Dalton Papers, 2/12/12, LSE Archives.
60 Danchev and Todman, *op. cit.*
61 Chandos, *op. cit.*
62 Lawford, V., Diary, 23 February 1943, Lawford Papers, LWFD 2/6, Churchill Archives, Churchill College, Cambridge.
63 *Observer*, 1 January 1965.
64 McGowan, N., *My Years with Churchill.*
65 Headlam, *op. cit.*
66 Safire, W., *Safire's Political Dictionary.*
67 Bew, *op. cit.*
68 Harris, *op. cit.*
69 Colville, J., Interview, 1982, 6380, IWM Archives.
70 Beckett, *op. cit.*
71 Churchill, M. to Attlee, J., 12 June 1942, Shipton Papers, University of Iowa.
72 Shipton, J., Interview, 2001, 22578, IWM Archives.

Twenty: Conference and Cabinet

1   Bullock, *Ernest Bevin* (Volume 2), *op. cit.*
2   Jones, *op. cit.*
3   Beckett, *op. cit.*
4   Ede, C., Diary, 12 November 1942, Add Ms 59,691, British Library
5   Schneer, *op. cit.*
6   Barnett, C., *The Audit of War: The Illusion and Reality of Britain as a Great Nation.*
7   Addison, *The Road to 1945, op. cit.*
8   Minutes of the War Cabinet, 26 November 1942, CAB 192/2, National Archives.
9   Gilbert, *Road to Victory, op. cit.*
10 *Observer*, 31 January 1965.
11 Hermiston, *op. cit.*
12 Attlee, C. R. to Churchill, W., 15 February 1943, Attlee Papers, ATLE 2/2, Churchill Archives, Churchill College, Cambridge.
13 Hermiston, *op. cit.*
14 Minutes of the War Cabinet, 15 February 1943, CAB 192/2, National Archives.
15 Minutes of the War Cabinet, 16 February 1943, CAB 65/31, National Archives.
16 Crowcroft, *op. cit.*
17 Hermiston, *op. cit.*
18 Attlee, C. R. to Attlee, T., 22 February 1942, Attlee Papers, MS Eng. d. 4792, Bodleian Library, Oxford.
19 Middleton, J. (Secretary of the Labour Party) to Attlee, C. R., 25 February 1943, Attlee Papers, DEP 7, Bodleian Library, Oxford.

20 Crowcroft, *op. cit.*
21 Middleton, J. to Attlee, C. R., 25 February 1943, Attlee Papers, DEP 7, Bodleian Library, Oxford.
22 *Observer*, 19 February 1943.
23 Addison, *The Road to 1945*, *op. cit.*
24 Sylvester, A. to Lloyd George, D., 22 March 1943, Lloyd George Papers, LG/G/24/2, Parliamentary Archives, House of Lords.
25 Durbin, E. to Attlee, C. R., 22 March 1943, Piercy Papers, 8/2, LSE Archives.
26 *Daily Express*, 25 March 1943.
27 Churchill, W. to Attlee, C. R., 18 January 1943, Churchill Papers, CHAR 20/127, Churchill Archives, Churchill College, Cambridge.
28 Attlee, C. R. to Churchill, W., 20 January 1943, CAB 65/37, National Archives.
29 Churchill, W. to Attlee, C. R., 24 January 1943, CAB 65/37, National Archives.
30 Churchill, W. to Attlee, C. R. and Eden, A., 26 January 1943, Churchill Papers, CHAR 20/127, Churchill Archives, Churchill College, Cambridge.
31 Churchill, W. to Attlee, C. R. and Eden, A., 26 January 1943, Churchill Papers, CHAR 20/127, Churchill Archives, Churchill College, Cambridge.
32 Churchill, W. to Attlee, C. R., 31 January 1943, Churchill Papers, CHAR 20/127, Churchill Archives, Churchill College, Cambridge.
33 Headlam, *op. cit.*
34 Churchill, W. to Attlee, C. R., 10 May 1943, Churchill Papers, CHAR 20/128, Churchill Archives, Churchill College, Cambridge.
35 Harvie-Watt, G. to Churchill, W., 14 May 1943, Harvie-Watt Papers, HARV 3/1, Churchill Archives, Churchill College, Cambridge.
36 Nicolson, *op. cit.*
37 Churchill, W. to Attlee, C. R., 16 May 1943, Churchill Papers, CHAR 20/128, Churchill Archives, Churchill College, Cambridge.
38 Gilbert, *Churchill and America*, *op. cit.*
39 Churchill, W. to Attlee, C. R., 21 May 1943, Churchill Papers, CHAR 20/128, Churchill Archives, Churchill College, Cambridge.
40 Attlee, C. R. and Eden, A. to Churchill, W., 23 May 1943, CAB 65/40, National Archives.
41 Harvey, *The War Diaries of Oliver Harvey*, *op. cit.*
42 Churchill, W. to Attlee, C. R., 30 May 1943, Churchill Papers, CHAR 20/128, Churchill Archives, Churchill College, Cambridge.
43 Churchill, W. to Attlee, C. R., 30 May 1943, Churchill Papers, CHAR 20/128, Churchill Archives, Churchill College, Cambridge.
44 *Daily Express*, 15 June 1943.
45 *News Chronicle*, 15 June 1943.
46 Amery, L. to Churchill, W., 13 November 1942, PREM 5/532, National Archives.
47 Amery, L. to Churchill, W., 18 April 1943, PREM 5/532, National Archives.
48 Churchill, W. to George VI, 24 April 1943, PREM 5/532, National Archives.
49 Eden, *The Reckoning*, *op. cit.*
50 Gilbert, *Road to Victory*, *op. cit.*
51 Churchill, W. to Attlee, C. R., 2 September 1943, Churchill Papers, CHAR 20/129, Churchill Archives, Churchill College, Cambridge.
52 Danchev and Todman, *op. cit.*

53 Churchill, W. to Attlee, C. R., 11 August 1943, Churchill Papers, CHAR 20/129, Churchill Archives, Churchill College, Cambridge.
54 Farmelo, *op. cit.*
55 Gowing, M., *Britain and Atomic Energy 1939–1945.*
56 Sylvester, A. to Lloyd George, D., 27 September 1943, Lloyd George.
57 King, *op. cit.*
58 Dilks, *The Diaries of Sir Alexander Cadogan*, *op. cit.*
59 Minutes of the Cabinet, 14 October 1943, CAB 65/40, National Archives.
60 Minutes of the Cabinet, 14 October 1943, CAB 65/40, National Archives.
61 Radice, G., *Odd Couples: The Great Political Pairings of Modern Britain.*
62 Minutes of the Cabinet, 21 October 1943, CAB 65/36, National Archives.
63 Pimlott, *The Second World War Diary of Hugh Dalton*, *op. cit.*
64 Pimlott, *The Second World War Diary of Hugh Dalton*, *op. cit.*
65 Pimlott, *The Second World War Diary of Hugh Dalton*, *op. cit.*
66 Woolton, Lord, Diary, 2 November 1943, Woolton Papers, Bodleian Library, Oxford.
67 Churchill, W. to Attlee, C. R., 24 November 1943, Churchill Papers, CHAR 20/130, Churchill Archives, Churchill College, Cambridge.
68 Danchev and Todman, *op. cit.*
69 Jenkins, *op. cit.*
70 Churchill, W. to Attlee, C. R., 1 December 1943, Churchill Papers, CHAR 20/130, Churchill Archives, Churchill College, Cambridge.
71 Gardner, *Churchill in Power*, *op. cit.*
72 Churchill, W. to Attlee, C. R., 14 December 1943, Churchill Papers, CHAR 20/130, Churchill Archives, Churchill College, Cambridge.
73 Churchill, W. to Eden, A., 14 December 1943, Churchill Papers, CHAR 20/130, Churchill Archives, Churchill College, Cambridge.
74 Attlee, C. R. to Churchill, W., 23 November 1943, PREM 4/39/5, National Archives.
75 Churchill, W. to Attlee, C. R. and Morrison, H., 25 November 1943, PREM 4/39/5, National Archives.
76 Morrison, H. to Churchill, 26 November 1943, PREM 4/39/5, National Archives.
77 Churchill, C. to Churchill, W., 28 November 1943, PREM 4/39/5, National Archives.
78 Minutes of the Cabinet, 29 November 1943, CAB 65/36, National Archives.
79 Attlee, C. R. to Churchill, W., 29 November 1943, CAB 65/40, National Archives.
80 Churchill, W. to Attlee, C. R., 1 December 1943, PREM 4/39/5, National Archives.
81 Churchill, W. to Bevin, E., Draft telegram, 1 December 1943, PREM 4/39/5, National Archives.
82 Churchill, W. to Attlee, C. R., Draft telegram, 1 December 1943, PREM 4/39/5, National Archives.
83 Moran, *Churchill at War*, *op. cit.*
84 Hermiston, *op. cit.*
85 Hart-Davis, D. (ed.), *King's Counsellor: Abdication and War – The Diaries of Sir Alan Lascelles.*

Twenty-One: Normandy and Italy

1   Gardner, B., *Churchill in His Time: A Study in a Reputation, 1939–1945.*
2   Mitchell, J., *Churchill's Navigator.*
3   Soames, *Speaking for Themselves, op. cit.*
4   Churchill, S., *A Thread in the Tapestry.*
5   Churchill, W. to Attlee, C. R., 8 January 1944, Churchill Papers, CHAR 20/179, Churchill Archives, Churchill College, Cambridge.
6   Transcript of broadcast, 31 December 1943, Attlee Papers, DEP 11, Bodleian Library, Oxford.
7   Letters to Attlee, C. R., 1 and 3 January 1944, Attlee Papers, DEP 12, Bodleian Library, Oxford.
8   Nicolson, *op. cit.*
9   Pimlott, *The Second World War Diary of Hugh Dalton, op. cit.*
10 French, *op. cit.*
11 Moran, *Churchill at War, op. cit.*
12 Minutes of the War Cabinet, 1 February 1944, CAB 65/35, National Archives.
13 King, *op. cit.*
14 Attlee, C. R. to Bevin, E., 1 March 1944, Attlee Papers, DEP 12, Bodleian Library, Oxford.
15 Addison, *The Road to 1945, op. cit.*
16 Nicolson, *op. cit.*
17 Jeffreys, *The Churchill Coalition and Wartime Politics, op. cit.*
18 Attlee, C. R. to Bevin, E., 1 March 1944, Attlee Papers, DEP 12, Bodleian Library, Oxford.
19 *Daily Express*, 28 February 1944.
20 Attlee, C. R., Speech to Labour's Midlands Regional Council, 13 May 1944, Attlee Papers, DEP 12, Bodleian Library, Oxford.
21 Pimlott, *The Second World War Diary of Hugh Dalton, op. cit.*
22 Churchill, W. to Attlee, C. R., 27 May 1944, Churchill Papers, CHAR 20/137, Churchill Archives, Churchill College, Cambridge.
23 Harris, *op. cit.*
24 Nicolson, *op. cit.*
25 Ede, C., Diary, 29 March 1944, MS Eng. 59,693, British Library
26 Ede, C., Diary, 29 March 1944, MS Eng. 59,693, British Library
27 *Daily Mirror*, 2 April 1944.
28 Hailsham, Lord, A Sparrow's Flight: The *Memoirs of Lord Hailsham of St Marylebone.*
29 Pimlott, *The Second World War Diary of Hugh Dalton, op. cit.*
30 Churchill, *The Hinge of Fate, op. cit.*
31 Gilbert, *Road to Victory, op. cit.*
32 Colville, J., Speech on Churchill, 1975, Colville Papers, 2/14, Churchill Archives, Churchill College, Cambridge.
33 Danchev and Todman, *op. cit.*
34 Pimlott, *The Second World War Diary of Hugh Dalton, op. cit.*
35 Kennedy, *op. cit.*
36 Jenkins, *op. cit.*
37 Bew, *op. cit.*
38 Hart-Davis, *King's Counsellor, op. cit.*
39 Bew, *op. cit.*

40 Danchev and Todman, *op. cit.*
41 Churchill, W. to Attlee, C. R., 16 August 1944, Churchill Papers, CHAR 20/180, Churchill Archives, Churchill College, Cambridge.
42 Danchev and Todman, *op. cit.*
43 Pimlott, *The Second World War Diary of Hugh Dalton, op. cit.*
44 Pimlott, *The Second World War Diary of Hugh Dalton, op. cit.*
45 Attlee, *As It Happened, op. cit.*
46 Churchill, W. to Attlee, C. R., 17 August 1944, Churchill Papers, CHAR 20/180, Churchill Archives, Churchill College, Cambridge.
47 Pimlott, *The Second World War Diary of Hugh Dalton, op. cit.*
48 Colville, *The Fringes of Power, op. cit.*
49 Churchill, W. to Attlee, C. R. and Eden, A., 10 September 1944, Churchill Papers, CHAR 20/257, Churchill Archives, Churchill College, Cambridge.
50 Hastings, *op. cit.*
51 Churchill, W. to Attlee, C. R., 15 September 1944, Churchill Papers, CHAR 20/257, Churchill Archives, Churchill College, Cambridge.
52 Churchill, W. to Attlee, C. R. and Anderson, J., 15 September 1944, Churchill Papers, CHAR 20/257, Churchill Archives, Churchill College, Cambridge.
53 Moran, *Churchill at War, op. cit.*
54 Crowcroft, *op. cit.*
55 Harris, *op. cit.*
56 King, *op. cit.*
57 Churchill, W. to Attlee, C. R., 20 November 1944, PREM 4/88/1, National Archives.
58 Headlam, *op. cit.*
59 Jenkins, *op. cit.*
60 Churchill, W. to Attlee, C. R. and the War Cabinet, 17 October 1944, Churchill Papers, CHAR 20/181, Churchill Archives, Churchill College, Cambridge.
61 Nicolson, *op. cit.*
62 Addison, *Churchill on the Home Front, op. cit.*
63 Ede, C., Diary, 28 November 1944, MS Eng. 59,693, British Library.

Twenty-Two: Britannia

1 Addison, *The Road to 1945, op. cit.*
2 Gilbert, *Road to Victory, op. cit.*
3 Hastings, *op. cit.*
4 Hansard, 8 December 1944.
5 Jenkins, *op. cit.*
6 Ede, C., Diary, 13 December 1944, Ede Papers, ADD MS 59,700, British Library.
7 Ede, C., Diary, 13 December 1944, Ede Papers, ADD MS 59,700, British Library.
8 Labour resolution on Greece, 14 December 1944, PREM 4/81/4, National Archives.
9 Burridge, *Clement Attlee, op. cit.*
10 Hastings, *op. cit.*
11 Danchev and Todman, *op. cit.*
12 Attlee, C. R., Note, 17 January 1945, PREM 4/6/9, National Archives.

13 Hermiston, *op. cit.*

14 Attlee, C. R. to Churchill, W., Draft letter, 19 January 1945, Attlee Papers, ATLE 2/2, Churchill Archives, Churchill College, Cambridge.

15 Attlee, C. R. to Churchill, W., Finalised letter, 19 January 1945, Churchill Papers, CHUR 2/4, Churchill Archives, Churchill College, Cambridge.

16 Jenkins, *op. cit.*

17 Attlee, C. R. to Churchill, W., Finalised letter, 19 January 1945 Churchill Papers, CHUR 2/4, Churchill Archives, Churchill College, Cambridge.

18 Transcript of BBC broadcast, 2 January 1983.

19 Churchill, W. to Attlee, C. R., First draft of letter, 20 January 1945, Churchill Papers, CHUR 2/4, Churchill Archives, Churchill College, Cambridge.

20 Churchill, W. to Attlee, C. R., Second draft of letter, 20 January 1945, Churchill Papers, CHUR 2/4, Churchill Archives, Churchill College, Cambridge.

21 Transcript of BBC broadcast, 2 January 1983.

22 Transcript of BBC broadcast, 2 January 1983.

23 Churchill, W. to Attlee, C. R., 22 January 1945, Churchill Papers, CHAR 20/193A, Churchill Archives, Churchill College, Cambridge.

24 Colville, *The Fringes of Power, op. cit.*

25 Gilbert, *Road to Victory, op. cit.*

26 Gilbert, *Road to Victory, op. cit.*

27 Dilks, *The Diaries of Sir Alexander Cadogan, op. cit.*

28 Churchill, W. to Attlee, C. R., 14 February 1945, Churchill Papers, CHAR 20/233, Churchill Archives, Churchill College, Cambridge.

29 Jenkins, *op. cit.*

30 Langworth, R., *Churchill, Myth and Reality: What He Actually Did and Said.*

31 Williams, *A Prime Minister Remembers, op. cit.*

32 Gilbert, M., 'Churchill and Bombing Policy', Fifth Churchill Centre Lecture, 18 October 2005.

33 Gilbert, 'Churchill and Bombing Policy', *op. cit.*

34 Beckett, *op. cit.*

35 *Daily Express*, 23 March 1945.

36 Harvie-Watt, G. to Churchill, W., 20 April 1945, Harvie-Watt Papers, HARV 5/1, Churchill Archives, Churchill College, Cambridge.

37 Colville, *The Fringes of Power, op. cit.*

38 Churchill, *The Triumph and the Tragedy, op. cit.*

39 Gilbert, *Road to Victory, op. cit.*

40 Gilbert, *Road to Victory, op. cit.*

41 Durbin to Attlee, 10 May 1945, Piercy Papers, 8/2, LSE Archives.

42 Meade, J., *The Collected Papers: Cabinet Office Diary of James Meade, 1944–46.*

43 Gilbert, *Road to Victory, op. cit.*

44 Tate, E., Letter, 10 May 1945, Tate Papers, 95/4/1, IWM Archives.

45 Paterson, *op. cit.*

46 Headlam, *op. cit.*

47 Bishop, A. and Bennett, Y., (eds), *Wartime Chronicle: Vera Brittain's Diary 1939–1945.*

48 Packwood, A. *How Churchill Waged War.*

49 Jeffreys, *The Churchill Coalition and Wartime Politics, op. cit.*

50 Pimlott, *The Second World War Diary of Hugh Dalton, op. cit.*

51 Both quotations from Schneer, *op. cit.*

52   Blackburn, *op. cit.*

53   Churchill, W. to Eden, A., 9 May 1945, PREM 4/65/4, National Archives.

54   Eden, A. to Churchill, W., 9 May 1945, Churchill Papers, CHAR 20/218, Churchill Archives, Churchill College, Cambridge.

55   Attlee, C. R. to Churchill, W., 11 May 1945, PREM 4/65/4, National Archives.

56   Pimlott, *The Second World War Diary of Hugh Dalton, op. cit.*

57   Churchill, W. to Eden, A., 11 May 1945, PREM 4/65/4, National Archives.

58   Eden, A. to Churchill, W., 12 May 1945, PREM 4/65/4, National Archives.

59   Churchill, W. to Eden, A., 12 May 1945, PREM 4/65/4, National Archives.

60   Churchill, W. to Eden, A., 14 May 1945, PREM 4/65/4, National Archives.

61   Churchill, W., Draft statement to the press, 8 June 1945, Churchill Papers, CHAR 2/550, Churchill Archives, Churchill College, Cambridge.

62   Churchill, W. to Attlee, C. R., First draft of letter, 17 May 1945, Churchill Papers, CHAR 2/550, Churchill Archives, Churchill College, Cambridge.

63   Churchill, W., Draft statement to the press, 8 June 1945, Churchill Papers, CHAR 2/550, Churchill Archives, Churchill College, Cambridge.

64   Attlee, C. R. to Churchill, W., 12 June 1945, Churchill Papers, CHAR 2/550, Churchill Archives, Churchill College, Cambridge.

65   Pimlott, *The Second World War Diary of Hugh Dalton, op. cit.*

66   Attlee, C. R., Note, 18 May 1945, PREM 4/65/4, National Archives.

67   Churchill, W., Draft statement to the press, 8 June 1945, Churchill Papers, CHAR 2/550, Churchill Archives, Churchill College, Cambridge.

68   Colville, *The Fringes of Power, op. cit.*

69   Wigg, Lord, *George Wigg.*

70   Attlee, C. R. to Churchill, W., 21 May 1945, PREM 4/65/4, National Archives.

71   Macmillan, H., *The Tides of Fortune 1945–1955.*

72   Eden, *The Reckoning, op. cit.*

73   Churchill, W., Draft statement to the press, 8 June 1945, Churchill Papers, CHAR 2/550, Churchill Archives, Churchill College, Cambridge.

74   Churchill, R., Draft, Churchill Papers, CHAR 2/550, Churchill Archives, Churchill College, Cambridge.

75   Churchill, W. to Attlee, C. R., 22 May 1945, PREM 4/65/4, National Archives.

76   *Daily Express*, 23 May 1945.

77   Gilbert, *Never Despair, op. cit.*

78   Hart-Davis, *King's Counsellor, op. cit.*

79   Pimlott, *The Second World War Diary of Hugh Dalton, op. cit.*

80   Harris, *op. cit.*

81   Nicolson, *op. cit.*

82   Hugh Trevor-Roper (ed.), *The Goebbels Diaries: The Last Days*

Twenty-Three: Campaign

1   Bridges, Sir E., Reminiscence, 1967, Normanbrook Papers, NRBK 1/3, Bodleian Library, Oxford.

2   Jeffreys, K., *War and Reform: British Politics During the Second World War.*

3   Stuart, J., *op. cit.*

4   *Sunday Times*, 10 June 1945.

5   Bartley, *op. cit.*

6   Kramnick and Sheerman, *op. cit.*

7   Harris, *op. cit.*
8   Interview, *News Chronicle*, 20 April 1959.
9   MacDonald, *op. cit.*
10   Toye, R., 'Winston Churchill's "Crazy Broadcast": Party, Nation and the 1945 Gestapo Speech', *Journal of British Studies*, Volume 49, Issue 3, July 2010.
11   Gilbert, *Never Despair, op. cit.*
12   Rhodes James, *'Chips', op. cit.*
13   Crookshank, H., Diary, 4 June 1945, Crookshank Papers, MS Eng. d. 360, Bodleian Library, Oxford.
14   Hailsham, *op. cit.*
15   Pugh, *op. cit.*
16   De Freitas, G., Diary, 4 June 1945, De Freitas Papers, Bodleian Library, Oxford.
17   Mikardo, *op. cit.*
18   Toye, 'Winston Churchill's "Crazy Broadcast"', *op. cit.*
19   Moran, *Churchill at War, op. cit.*
20   Soames, *Clementine Churchill, op. cit.*
21   Programme on 1945 General Election, BBC Radio 4, July 2005.
22   Packwood, A. *How Churchill Waged War, op. cit.*
23   Hart-Davis, *King's Counsellor, op. cit.*
24   Hart-Davis, *King's Counsellor, op. cit.*
25   Addison, *Churchill on the Home Front, op. cit.*
26   Toye, 'Winston Churchill's "Crazy Broadcast"', *op. cit.*
27   Toye, 'Winston Churchill's "Crazy Broadcast"', *op. cit.*
28   Harris, *op. cit.*
29   Pelling, H., 'The 1945 General Election Reconsidered', *The Historical Journal*, Volume 23, Issue 2.
30   Clemens, *op. cit.*
31   Pottle, *Champion Redoubtable, op. cit.*
32   Kynaston, D., *Austerity Britain: 1945–51.*
33   Programme on 1945 General Election, BBC Radio 4, July 2005.
34   Churchill, W. to Attlee, C. R., 31 May 1945, PREM 4/7/7, National Archives.
35   Attlee, C. R. to Churchill, W., 1 June 1945, PREM 4/7/7, National Archives.
36   Churchill, W. to Attlee, C. R., 2 June 1945, PREM 4/7/7, National Archives.
37   Churchill, W. to Truman, H., 4 June 1945, PREM 4/7/7, National Archives.
38   Tudor, H. to Churchill, W., 28 May 1945, Churchill Papers, CHAR 20/201, Churchill Archives, Churchill College, Cambridge.
39   Attlee, C. R. to Churchill, W., 8 June 1945, PREM 4/7/7, National Archives.
40   *Daily Herald*, 8 June 1945.
41   Churchill, W. to Bevin, E., 29 May 1945, Bevin Papers, BEV 3/1, Churchill Archives, Churchill College, Cambridge.
42   Bevin, E. to Churchill, W., 30 May 1945, Bevin Papers, BEV 3/1, Churchill Archives, Churchill College, Cambridge.
43   Churchill, W. to Attlee, C. R., 12 June 1945, Churchill Papers, CHAR 20/194, Churchill Archives, Churchill College, Cambridge.
44   Churchill, W., Press statement, 12 June 1945, Churchill Papers, CHAR 2/550, Churchill Archives, Churchill College, Cambridge.
45   *The Times*, 13 June 1945.
46   Colville, J., Note on instructions, 15 June 1945, PREM 4/7/7, National Archives.
47   Rowan, L., Note, 22 June 1945, PREM 4/7/7, National Archives.

48 Churchill, W. to Stalin, J., 14 June 1945, Churchill Papers, CHAR 20/221, Churchill Archives, Churchill College, Cambridge.
49 Stalin, J. to Churchill, W., 19 June 1945, Churchill Papers, CHAR 20/221, Churchill Archives, Churchill College, Cambridge.
50 Hansard, 14 June 1945.
51 *Daily Herald*, 15 June 1945.
52 Churchill, W. to Attlee, C. R., 15 June 1945, PREM 4/65/4, National Archives.
53 Attlee, C. R. to Churchill, W., 15 June 1945, PREM 4/65/4, National Archives.
54 Rowan, L. to Churchill, W., Note with quotations, 2 July 1945, Churchill Papers, CHAR 2/552, Churchill Archives, Churchill College, Cambridge.
55 Schneer, *op. cit.*
56 Martin, J. to Churchill, W., 18 June 1945, Churchill Papers, CHAR 2/552, Churchill Archives, Churchill College, Cambridge.
57 Addison, *The Road to 1945, op. cit.*
58 Burridge, T., 'Postscript to Potsdam: The Churchill-Laski Electoral Clash, June 1945', *Journal of Contemporary History*, Volume 12, No. 4, October 1977.
59 Gilbert, *Never Despair, op. cit.*
60 Gilbert, *Never Despair, op. cit.*
61 Nicolson, *op. cit.*
62 *The Times*, 25 June 1945.
63 Gilbert, *Never Despair, op. cit.*
64 Colville, *The Fringes of Power, op. cit.*
65 Hastings, *op. cit.*
66 Harris, *op. cit.*
67 *The Times*, 2 July 1945.
68 Churchill, W. to Attlee, C. R. 2 July 1945, Churchill Papers, CHAR 2/552, Churchill Archives, Churchill College, Cambridge.
69 Attlee, C. R. to Churchill, W., 2 July 1945, Churchill Papers, CHAR 2/552, Churchill Archives, Churchill College, Cambridge.
70 Churchill, W. to Attlee, C. R., 3 July 1945, Churchill Papers, CHAR 2/552, Churchill Archives, Churchill College, Cambridge.
71 Attlee, C. R. to Churchill, W., 3 July 1945, Churchill Papers, CHAR 2/552, Churchill Archives, Churchill College, Cambridge.
72 Kramnick and Sheerman, *op. cit.*
73 Attlee, C. R. to Attlee, T., 3 July 1945, Attlee Papers, MS Eng. c. 4793, Bodleian Library, Oxford.
74 Adelman, P., 'The British General Election, 1945', *History Review*, Issue 40, September 2001.
75 Strauss, G., Draft of unpublished autobiography, Strauss Papers, STRS 1/1, Churchill Archives, Churchill College, Cambridge.
76 Marquis, F., *The Memoirs of the Rt Hon the Earl of Woolton.*
77 Inglis, F., *Richard Hoggart: Virtue and Reward.*
78 Pugh, *op. cit.*
79 Pugh, *op. cit.*
80 Hastings, *op. cit.*
81 Packwood, *op. cit.*
82 Marquis, *op. cit.*
83 Toye, R., *The Roar of the Lion: The Untold Story of Churchill's World War II Speeches.*
84 *The Times*, 2 July 1945.

85   De Freitas, G., Diary, 30 June 1945, De Freitas Papers, Bodleian Library, Oxford.
86   Stewart, M., *Life and Labour*.
87   *Observer*, 31 January 1965.
88   Pawle, *op. cit.*
89   *Daily Express*, 26 June 1945.
90   Pugh, *op. cit.*
91   Schneer, *op. cit.*
92   Kynaston, *op. cit.*
93   *The Times*, 4 July 1945.
94   *The Times*, 4 July 1945.
95   Clemens, *op. cit.*
96   Thomas, *op. cit.*
97   Rowan, L., Paper, 12 December 1945, PREM 4/654, National Archives.
98   *Daily Mail*, 8 June 1964.
99   Attlee, C. R. to Attlee, T., 3 July 1945, Attlee Papers, MS Eng. c. 4793, Bodleian Library, Oxford.
100 Attlee, C. R. to Dalton, H., 13 July 1945, Dalton Papers, 2/8/1, LSE Archives.
101 Pottle, *Champion Redoubtable*, *op. cit.*
102 Kynaston, *op. cit.*
103 Taylor, *Beaverbrook*, *op. cit.*
104 *Daily Express*, 2 July 1945.
105 Schneer, *op. cit.*
106 Moran, *Churchill*, *op. cit.*
107 Pawle, *op. cit.*

Twenty-Four: Potsdam and Palace

1   Moran, *Churchill at War*, *op. cit.*
2   Attlee, *As It Happened*, *op. cit.*
3   Churchill, W. to Attlee, C. R., 11 July 1945, Churchill Papers, CHAR 20/194B, Churchill Archives, Churchill College, Cambridge.
4   Leggett, G., Potsdam Diary, Leggett Papers, Churchill Archives, Churchill College, Cambridge.
5   Leggett, G., Potsdam Diary, Leggett Papers, Churchill Archives, Churchill College, Cambridge.
6   Dilks, *The Diaries of Sir Alexander Cadogan*, *op. cit.*
7   Jago, *op. cit.*
8   Jenkins, *op. cit.*
9   Bullock, N., 'Eye-Witness to Potsdam', *Finest Hour*, No. 145, Winter 2009–10.
10   Farmelo, *op. cit.*
11   Leeming, B., *Churchill Defiant*.
12   Dilks, *The Diaries of Sir Alexander Cadogan*, *op. cit.*
13   Young, *The Diaries of Sir Robert Bruce Lockhart*, *op. cit.*
14   Hastings, *op. cit.*
15   Leggett, G., Potsdam Diary, Leggett Papers, Churchill Archives, Churchill College, Cambridge.
16   Leggett, G., Potsdam Diary, Leggett Papers, Churchill Archives, Churchill College, Cambridge.

17   Richards, D., *Portal of Hungerford: The Life of Marshal of the Royal Air Force Viscount Portal of Hungerford*.
18   Soames, *Clementine Churchill*, *op. cit.*
19   Gilbert, *Never Despair*, *op. cit.*
20   Attlee, *As It Happened*, *op. cit.*
21   Churchill, *The Second World War*, *op. cit.*
22   Programme on the 1945 General Election, BBC Radio 4, July 2005.
23   Nel (nee Layton), E., Interview, 1994, 15119, IWM Archives.
24   Programme on the 1945 General Election, BBC Radio 4, July 2005.
25   Programme on the 1945 General Election, BBC Radio 4, July 2005.
26   Soames, *Clementine Churchill*, *op. cit.*
27   Gilbert, *Never Despair*, *op. cit.*
28   Attlee, *As It Happened*, *op. cit.*
29   Hough, R., *Winston and Clementine: The Triumph of the Churchills*.
30   Hart-Davis, *King's Counsellor*, *op. cit.*
31   Gilbert, *Never Despair*, *op. cit.*
32   Strauss, G., Unpublished autobiography, Strauss Papers, 1/1.
33   Morrison, H. to Attlee, C. R., 24 July 1945, Attlee Papers, DEP 18, Bodleian Library, Oxford.
34   Thomas-Symonds, *op. cit.*
35   Williams, *Nothing So Strange*, *op. cit.*
36   Wheeler Bennett, *King George VI*, *op. cit.*
37   Charmley, *op. cit.*
38   Hart-Davis, *King's Counsellor*, *op. cit.*
39   Beckett, *op. cit.*
40   Parker, J., Paper on Attlee and Churchill, 1 July 1980, Parker Papers, 1/9, LSE Archives.
41   Pelling, 'The 1945 General Election Reconsidered', *op. cit.*
42   Bew, *op. cit.*
43   Marquand, D., 'Clement Attlee: Labour's Own Captain Mainwaring', *New Statesman*, 8 September 2016.
44   Eden, *The Reckoning*, *op. cit.*
45   Pimlott, *The Political Diary of Hugh Dalton*, *op. cit.*
46   *Tribune*, 14 November 1952.
47   *Tribune*, 21 November 1952.
48   Eden, *The Reckoning*, *op. cit.*
49   Danchev and Todman, *op. cit.*
50   Reginald Maudling, *Memoirs*.
51   Gilbert, *Never Despair*, *op. cit.*
52   Hastings, *op. cit.*
53   Colville, *The Fringes of Power*, *op. cit.*
54   Kerr, C. to Churchill, C., 27 July 1945, Clementine Churchill Papers, CSCT 3/56, Churchill Archives, Churchill College, Cambridge.
55   Kynaston, *op. cit.*
56   Attlee, C. R. to Churchill, W., 1 August 1945, Churchill Papers, CHUR 2/3, Churchill Archives, Churchill College, Cambridge.
57   Churchill, W. to Attlee, C. R., 3 August 1945, Churchill Papers, CHUR 2/3, Churchill Archives, Churchill College, Cambridge.
58   Burridge, *British Labour and Hitler's War*, *op. cit.*

59   Gilbert, *Never Despair, op. cit.*
60   Dilks, *The Diaries of Sir Alexander Cadogan, op. cit.*
61   Bartley, *op. cit.*
62   De Freitas, G., Diary, 1 August 1945, De Freitas Papers, Bodleian Library, Oxford.
63   *Observer*, 12 November 1967.
64   Attlee, C. R., Statement, 6 August 1945, Churchill Papers, CHUR 2/3, Churchill Archives, Churchill College, Cambridge.
65   Attlee, C. R. to Churchill, W., 10 August 1945, Churchill Papers, CHUR 2/140, Churchill Archives, Churchill College, Cambridge.
66   Eden, *The Reckoning, op. cit.*
67   Pottle, *Champion Redoubtable, op. cit.*
68   Churchill, W. to Attlee, C. R., 14 August 1945, Churchill Papers, CHUR 2/140, Churchill Archives, Churchill College, Cambridge.
69   Attlee, C. R. to Churchill, W., 14 August 1945, Churchill Papers, CHUR 2/140, Churchill Archives, Churchill College, Cambridge.
70   Hansard, 16 August 1945.
71   Purnell, *op. cit.*
72   Shipton, J., Interview, 2001, 22578, IWM Archives.
73   Rowan, L. to Bridges, Sir E., 27 July 1945, Churchill Papers, CHAR 2/4, Churchill Archives, Churchill College, Cambridge.
74   Colville, J., *Footprints in Time.*
75   Rowan, L. to Hill, K., 8 August 1945, Attlee Papers, DEP 18, Bodleian Library, Oxford.
76   Soames, *Clementine Churchill, op. cit.*
77   Williams, *A Prime Minister Remembers, op. cit.*
78   Gilbert, *Never Despair, op. cit.*
79   Danchev and Todman, *op. cit.*
80   Colville, *The Fringes of Power, op. cit.*
81   Leggett, G., Potsdam Diary, Leggett Papers, Churchill Archives, Churchill College, Cambridge.
82   Peck, J., *Dublin from Downing Street.*
83   Petropoulos, J., *Royals and the Reich: The Princes von Hessen in Nazi Germany.*
84   Attlee, C. R. to Churchill, W., 25 August 1945, Churchill Papers, CHUR 2/140, Churchill Archives, Churchill College, Cambridge.
85   Churchill, W. to Attlee, C. R., 26 August 1945, Churchill Papers, CHUR 2/140, Churchill Archives, Churchill College, Cambridge.
86   Attlee, C. R. to Churchill, W., 16 October 1945, Churchill Papers, CHUR 2/140, Churchill Archives, Churchill College, Cambridge.
87   Attlee, C. R. to Churchill, W., 25 November 1945, Churchill Papers, CHUR 2/140, Churchill Archives, Churchill College, Cambridge.
88   Johnson, E. and Moggridge, D. (eds), *The Collected Writings of John Maynard Keynes.*
89   Attlee, C. R. to Churchill, W., 23 August 1945, Churchill Papers, CHUR 2/3, Churchill Archives, Churchill College, Cambridge.
90   Rhodes James, *'Chips', op. cit.*
91   Parker, J., Paper on Attlee and Churchill, 1 July 1980, Parker Papers, 1/9, LSE Archives.
92   Soames, *Speaking for Themselves, op. cit.*
93   Moran, *Churchill, op. cit.*

94   Farmelo, *op. cit.*
95   Attlee, C. R., Draft letter to President Truman, 15 September 1945, Churchill Papers, CHUR 2/3, Churchill Archives, Churchill College, Cambridge.
96   Attlee, C. R. to Churchill, W., 15 September 1945, Churchill Papers, CHUR 2/3, Churchill Archives, Churchill College, Cambridge.
97   Churchill, W. to Attlee, C. R., September 1945, Churchill Papers, CHUR 2/3, Churchill Archives, Churchill College, Cambridge.
98   Churchill, W. to Attlee, C. R., 6 October 1945, Churchill Papers, CHUR 2/3, Churchill Archives, Churchill College, Cambridge.
99   Williams, *Nothing So Strange, op. cit.*
100 Gilbert, *Never Despair, op. cit.*
101 Normanbrook, Lord, Reminiscence, 1967, Normanbrook Papers, NBRK 1/1, Bodleian Library, Oxford.
102 Both quotations from Jacob, Sir I., Diary, 19 November 1945, JACB 1/23, Churchill Archives, Churchill College, Cambridge.

Twenty-Five: Fulton and Zurich

1   Hansard, 6 December 1945.
2   Hansard, 6 December 1945.
3   'Everybody's Politician', BBC Radio 4, 2 January 1983.
4   *Daily Express*, 7 December 1945.
5   Attlee, C. R., Note, 1951, Attlee Papers, ATLE 1/5, Churchill Archives, Churchill College, Cambridge.
6   Toye, R., 'Britain's Financial Dunkirk', Exeter University Research Paper.
7   Hansard, 13 December 1945.
8   *Manchester Guardian*, 14 December 1945.
9   Toye, 'Britain's Financial Dunkirk', *op. cit.*
10   Hart-Davis, *King's Counsellor, op. cit.*
11   Halifax, Lord to Attlee, C. R., 1 November 1943, Attlee Papers, DEP 25, Bodleian Library, Oxford.
12   Toye, 'Britain's Financial Dunkirk', *op. cit.*
13   Gilbert, *Never Despair, op. cit.*
14   Toye, 'Britain's Financial Dunkirk', *op. cit.*
15   Johnson and Moggridge, *op. cit.*
16   Langworth, *Churchill by Himself, op. cit.*
17   Gilbert, *Never Despair, op. cit.*
18   Reynolds, *op. cit.*
19   Sturdee, J., Letter, 8 March 1945, Onslow Papers, ONSL 2, Churchill Archives, Churchill College, Cambridge.
20   Pelling, *Winston Churchill, op. cit.*
21   Sturdee, J., Letter, 8 March 1945, Onslow Papers, ONSL 2, Churchill Archives, Churchill College, Cambridge.
22   Wright, P., *Iron Curtain: From Stage to Cold War.*
23   Bullock, *Ernest Bevin* (Volume 3), *op. cit.*
24   Jenkins, R., Kemper Lecture, National Churchill Museum, Fulton, 17 March 2002.
25   Churchill, W. to Attlee, C. R. and Bevin, E., 7 March 1945, Churchill Papers, CHUR 2/4, Churchill Archives, Churchill College, Cambridge.

26 Williams, *Nothing So Strange, op. cit.*
27 Muller, J. (ed.), *Churchill's 'Iron Curtain' Speech Fifty Years Later.*
28 Reynolds, *op. cit.*
29 Mackenzie, A., Report, 18 March 1946, Attlee Papers, DEP 34, Bodleian Library, Oxford.
30 Attlee, C. R. to Churchill, W., 14 March, Churchill Papers, CHUR 2/4, Churchill Archives, Churchill College, Cambridge.
31 Cabinet paper, 10 May 1946, CAB 129/29, National Archives.
32 Attlee, C. R. to Churchill, W., 27 May 1945, Churchill Papers, CHUR 2/4, Churchill Archives, Churchill College, Cambridge.
33 Churchill, W. to Attlee, C. R., 29 May 1945, Churchill Papers, CHUR 2/4, Churchill Archives, Churchill College, Cambridge.
34 Attlee, C. R. to Churchill, W., 3 June 1945, Churchill Papers, CHUR 2/4, Churchill Archives, Churchill College, Cambridge.
35 Reynolds, *op. cit.*
36 Churchill, W. to Attlee, C. R., 28 December 1946, PREM 8/217, National Archives.
37 Reynolds, *op. cit.*
38 Lough, *op. cit.*
39 Nicolson, *op. cit.*
40 Toye, R., *Lloyd George and Churchill: Rivals for Greatness.*
41 Stuart, J., *op. cit.*
42 Williams, *A Prime Minister Remembers, op. cit.*
43 Gilbert, *Never Despair, op. cit.*
44 Churchill, W. to Attlee, C. R., 14 May 1946, Churchill Papers, CHUR 2/42A, Churchill Archives, Churchill College, Cambridge.
45 *Daily Mail*, 21 February 1947.
46 *Observer*, 31 January 1965.
47 Hansard, 6 March 1945.
48 Headlam, *op. cit.*
49 Hansard, 6 March 1945.
50 Harris, *op. cit.*
51 Gopal, S., 'Churchill and India', in Blake and Louis, *op. cit.*
52 Churchill, W. to Attlee, C. R., 21 May 1947, PEM 8/565, National Archives.
53 Hansard, 3 June 1947.
54 Dellar, *op. cit.*
55 Gopal, *op. cit.*
56 Williams, *A Prime Minister Remembers, op. cit.*
57 Pimlott, *The Political Diary of Hugh Dalton, op. cit.*
58 Thomas-Symonds, *op. cit.*
59 Mikardo, *op. cit.*
60 Rose, N., 'Churchill and Zionism', in Blake and Louis, *op. cit.*
61 Rose, N., 'Churchill and Zionism', *op. cit.*
62 Rose, N., 'Churchill and Zionism', *op. cit.*
63 Churchill, W. to Attlee, C. R., 1 May 1946, Churchill Papers, CHUR 2/4, Churchill Archives, Churchill College, Cambridge.
64 Churchill, W. to Attlee, C. R., 2 July 1946, Attlee Papers, DEP 39, Bodleian Library, Oxford.
65 Gilbert, *Never Despair, op. cit.*

66 Churchill, W., Draft statement, 5 April 1947, Churchill Papers, CHUR 2/46A, Churchill Archives, Churchill College, Cambridge.
67 Attlee, *As It Happened*, *op. cit.*
68 Churchill, W. to Attlee, C. R., 2 July 1946, Attlee Papers, DEP 39, Bodleian Library, Oxford.
69 Churchill, W., 'The Sinews of Peace' (Iron Curtain Speech).
70 Watson, A., *Churchill's Legacy: Two Speeches to Save the World*.
71 Gilbert, *Never Despair*, *op. cit.*
72 Churchill, W. to Attlee, C. R., 27 November 1946, Churchill Papers, CHUR 2/18, Churchill Archives, Churchill College, Cambridge.
73 Attlee, C. R. to Churchill, W., 4 December 1946, Churchill Papers, CHUR 2/18, Churchill Archives, Churchill College, Cambridge.
74 Churchill, W. to Attlee, C. R., 31 March 1946, Churchill Papers, CHUR 2/29, Churchill Archives, Churchill College, Cambridge.
75 Bridges, Sir E. to Attlee, C. R., 24 September 1946, PREM 8/309, National Archives.
76 Churchill, W. to Attlee, C. R., 6 October 1946, PREM 8/309, National Archives.
77 Attlee, C. R. to Churchill, W., 9 October 1946, PREM 8/309, National Archives.
78 Hennessy, P., *Cabinets and the Bomb*.
79 Churchill, W. to Attlee, C. R., 22 June 1946, Attlee Papers, DEP 38, Bodleian Library, Oxford.
80 Attlee, C. R. to Churchill, W., 20 June 1946, Churchill Papers, CHUR 2/495, Churchill Archives, Churchill College, Cambridge.
81 Churchill, W. to Attlee, C. R., 25 June 1946, Attlee Papers, DEP 38, Bodleian Library, Oxford.
82 Churchill, C. and W. to Attlee, C. R. and V., 10 January 1957, Churchill Papers, CHUR 2/4, Churchill Archives, Churchill College, Cambridge.
83 Soames, *Clementine Churchill*, *op. cit.*

Twenty-Six: New Jerusalem

1   Hart-Davis, *King's Counsellor*, *op. cit.*
2   Hailsham, *op. cit.*
3   Hansard, 12 March 1947.
4   *The Times*, 13 March 1947.
5   Gilbert, M., *Churchill: A Life*.
6   Hansard, 31 March 1947.
7   Hansard, 7 May 1947.
8   Attlee, C. R. to Morrison, H., 8 April 1947, Morrison Papers, 8/3, LSE Archives.
9   Attlee, C. R., Text of speech to TUC, 25 April 1947, Attlee Papers, DEP 52, Bodleian Library, Oxford.
10 *The Times*, 26 April 1947.
11 Churchill, W., Statement, 27 April 1947, Churchill Papers, CHUR 2/4, Churchill Archives, Churchill College, Cambridge.
12 *News Chronicle*, 29 April 1947.
13 *Daily Dispatch*, 28 April 1947.
14 *Daily Telegraph*, 28 April 1947.
15 Attlee, C. R. to Attlee, T., 2 May 1947, Attlee Papers, MS Eng. c. 4793, Bodleian Library, Oxford.

16 Attlee, C. R. to Morrison, H., 16 April 1947, Morrison Papers, 8/3, LSE Archives.

17 Stuart, J., *op. cit.*

18 Brown, G., *In My Way: George Brown Memoirs.*

19 Bryant, *op. cit.*

20 Cockett, R. (ed.), *My Dear Max: The Letters of Brendan Bracken to Lord Beaverbrook, 1925–1958.*

21 Morgan, K., *Labour in Power, 1945–51.*

22 Gilbert, *Never Despair, op. cit.*

23 Pimlott, *The Political Diary of Hugh Dalton, op. cit.*

24 Green, D., *The Churchills of Blenheim.*

25 Hansard, 6 August 1947.

26 Bew, *op. cit.*

27 Hansard, 8 December 1947.

28 Burridge, *Clement Attlee, op. cit.*

29 Soames, *Speaking for Themselves, op. cit.*

30 Ramsden, J., *The Man of the Century: Winston Churchill and His Legend Since 1945.*

31 Bryant, *op. cit.*

32 Harris, *op. cit.*

33 Harris, *op. cit.*

34 Harris, *op. cit.*

35 Hansard, 13 November 1947.

36 Pimlott, B., *Hugh Dalton: A Life.*

37 Pitts, D., The Granada Historical Records Interviews, 1967.

38 Pimlott, *Hugh Dalton, op. cit.*

39 Lysaght, C. E., *Brendan Bracken.*

40 Churchill, W., Text of broadcast, 16 August 1947, Attlee Papers, DEP 57, Bodleian Library, Oxford.

41 Attlee, C. R., Speech to East Midlands Labour Party, 27 September 1947, Attlee Papers, DEP 61, Bodleian Library, Oxford.

42 *Daily Express*, 22 October 1947.

43 Hansard, 21 October 1947.

44 *Daily Express*, 29 October 1947.

45 *Daily Express*, 30 October 1947.

46 Headlam, *op. cit.*

47 Woolton, Lord to Churchill, W., 28 October 1947, Churchill Papers, CHUR 2/66, Churchill Archives, Churchill College, Cambridge.

48 Hansard, 11 November 1947.

49 Harris, *op. cit.*

50 Cairncross, *op. cit.*

51 Nicolson, *op. cit.*

52 Attlee, C. R. to Churchill, W., 18 July 1947, Attlee Papers, DEP 57, Bodleian Library, Oxford.

53 Attlee, C. R. to Churchill, W., 27 June 1947, Churchill Papers, CHUR 2/145B, Churchill Archives, Churchill College, Cambridge.

54 Churchill, W. to Attlee, C. R. and V., Telegram, 5 December 1947, Attlee Papers, DEP 65, Bodleian Library, Oxford.

55 Churchill, W. to Attlee, C. R., 4 January 1948, Attlee Papers, DEP 66, Bodleian Library, Oxford.

56 British Pathé newsreel, 11 November 1947.
57 *New York Times*, 27 May 1948.
58 Pottle, *Daring to Hope, op. cit.*
59 Bullock, *Ernest Bevin* (Volume 3), *op. cit.*
60 Churchill, W. to Attlee, C. R., 1 February 1948, Churchill Papers, CHUR 2/21B, Churchill Archives, Churchill College, Cambridge.
61 Attlee, C. R. to Churchill, W., 4 February 1948, Churchill Papers, CHUR 2/21B, Churchill Archives, Churchill College, Cambridge.
62 Shinwell, E. to Churchill, W., 10 February 1948, Churchill Papers, CHUR 2/21B, Churchill Archives, Churchill College, Cambridge.
63 Churchill, W. to Attlee, C. R., 12 February 1948, Churchill Papers, CHUR 2/21B, Churchill Archives, Churchill College, Cambridge.
64 Morgan, K., *Labour in Power, op. cit.*
65 Speech at The Hague, 7 May 1948, Winston Churchill Society.
66 Morgan, K., *Labour in Power, op. cit.*
67 Report of Deputation to Downing Street, 17 June 1948, PREM 8/875, National Archives.
68 Churchill, W. to Attlee, C. R., 27 July 1948, PREM 8/875, National Archives.
69 Foreign Office note on Bevin's views to 10 Downing Street, 28 July 1948, PREM 8/875, National Archives.
70 Attlee, C. R. to Churchill, W., 30 July 1948, PREM 8/875, National Archives.
71 Graham-Harrison, F., Note, 19 August 1948, PREM 8/875, National Archives.
72 Churchill, W. to Attlee, C. R., 21 August 1948, PREM 8/875, National Archives.
73 Bevin, E. to Attlee, C. R., 21 August 1948, PREM 8/875, National Archives.
74 Attlee, C. R. to Churchill, W., 21 August 1948, PREM 8/875, National Archives.
75 Churchill, W. to Eden, A., 12 September 1948, Churchill Papers, CHUR 2/68, Churchill Archives, Churchill College, Cambridge.
76 Churchill, W. to Attlee, C. R., 4 November 1948, Churchill Papers, CHUR 2/75A, Churchill Archives, Churchill College, Cambridge.
77 Attlee, C. R. to Churchill, W., 6 November 1948, Churchill Papers, CHUR 2/75A, Churchill Archives, Churchill College, Cambridge.
78 Churchill, W. to Attlee, C. R., 11 November 1948, Churchill Papers, CHUR 2/75A, Churchill Archives, Churchill College, Cambridge.
79 Attlee, C. R. to Churchill, W., 12 November 1948, Churchill Papers, CHUR 2/75A, Churchill Archives, Churchill College, Cambridge.
80 Attlee, C. R., Text of speech in Plymouth, 1 May 1948, Attlee Papers, DEP 70, Bodleian Library, Oxford.
81 Churchill, W. to Attlee, C. R., 5 May 1948, Attlee Papers, DEP 70, Bodleian Library, Oxford.
82 Hansard, 31 July 1948.
83 Bew, *op. cit.*
84 Churchill, W. to Eden, A., 12 September 1948, Churchill Papers, CHUR 2/68, Churchill Archives, Churchill College, Cambridge.
85 Hansard, 25 November 1948.
86 *Daily Express*, 26 November 1948.
87 Addison, *Churchill on the Home Front, op. cit.*
88 *Daily Express*, 23 May 1948.

Twenty-Seven: Woodford and Walthamstow

1   Rhodes James, *'Chips'*, *op. cit.*
2   *The Times*, 26 April 19.
3   Dellar, *op. cit.*
4   Hunt, *op. cit.*
5   Harris, *op. cit.*
6   Dellar, *op. cit.*
7   'Everybody's Politician', BBC Radio 4, 2 January 1983.
8   Jay, D., Interview, 15260, IWM Archives.
9   Hunt, *op. cit.*
10   Colville, *Footprints in Time*, *op. cit.*
11   *Sunday Times*, 30 December 1962.
12   Hennessy, P., *The Prime Minister: The Office and its Holders Since 1945*.
13   Programme about the 1945 General Election, BBC Radio 4, July 2005.
14   Williams, *Nothing So Strange*, *op. cit.*
15   Hennessy, *The Prime Minister*, *op. cit.*
16   Williams, *Nothing So Strange*, *op. cit.*
17   Warner, G. (ed.), *In the Midst of Events: The Foreign Office Diaries and Papers of Kenneth Younger, February 1950–October 1951*.
18   Barnett, C., *The Lost Victory: British Dreams, British Realities, 1945–1950*.
19   Hennessy, *The Prime Minister*, *op. cit.*
20   Menzies, *Afternoon Light*, *op. cit.*
21   The Earl of Birkenhead, *Contemporary Personalities*.
22   *Sunday Times*, 30 December 1962.
23   *Forward*, 17 December 1955.
24   Williams, *The Diary of Hugh Gaitskell*, *op. cit.*
25   Williams, *Nothing So Strange*, *op. cit.*
26   Thomas-Symonds, *op. cit.*
27   Broome, *op. cit.*
28   Thomas-Symonds, *op. cit.*
29   *Evening Standard*, 1 July 1947.
30   *Daily Mail*, 9 February 1950.
31   Pottle, *Daring to Hope*, *op. cit.*
32   Beckett, *op. cit.*
33   Pottle, *Daring to Hope*, *op. cit.*
34   Williams, *Nothing So Strange*, *op. cit.*
35   Williams, *The Diary of Hugh Gaitskell*, *op. cit.*
36   Hunt, *op. cit.*
37   Purnell, *op. cit.*
38   McGowan, *op. cit.*
39   Purnell, *op. cit.*
40   Lovell, M., *The Churchills: A Family at the Heart of History – from the Duke of Marlborough to Winston Churchill*.
41   Soames, *Clementine Churchill*, *op. cit.*
42   Farmelo, *op. cit.*
43   Headlam, *op. cit.*
44   MacDonald, *op. cit.*
45   Cockett, *op. cit.*
46   Pottle, *Daring to Hope*, *op. cit.*

47 Pelling, *Winston Churchill, op. cit.*
48 *Yorkshire Evening Post*, 8 April 1948.
49 Jenkinson, C. to Swinton, Lord, 17 January 1949, Churchill Papers, CHUR 2/339, Churchill Archives, Churchill College, Cambridge.
50 Churchill, W. to Swinton, Lord, 7 February 1949 Churchill Papers, CHUR 2/339, Churchill Archives, Churchill College, Cambridge.
51 Churchill, W. to Radley, O. A., 28 February 1949, Churchill Papers, CHUR 2/339, Churchill Archives, Churchill College, Cambridge.
52 Churchill, W., Memorandum, 9 May 1949, Churchill Papers, CHUR 2/29A, Churchill Archives, Churchill College, Cambridge.
53 Churchill, W. to Attlee, C. R., 27 May 1949, Churchill Papers, CHUR 2/29A, Churchill Archives, Churchill College, Cambridge.
54 Churchill, W. to Attlee, C. R., 24 July 1949, Churchill Papers, CHUR 2/29A, Churchill Archives, Churchill College, Cambridge.
55 Churchill, W. to Attlee, C. R., 24 April 1949, Churchill Papers, CHUR 2/84A, Churchill Archives, Churchill College, Cambridge.
56 Lascelles, A., Message to Churchill's office, Churchill Papers, CHUR 2/84A, Churchill Archives, Churchill College, Cambridge.
57 Attlee, C. R. to Churchill, W., 28 April 1949, Churchill Papers, CHUR 2/84A, Churchill Archives, Churchill College, Cambridge.
58 Churchill, W. to Attlee, C. R., 28 April 1949, Churchill Papers, CHUR 2/84A, Churchill Archives, Churchill College, Cambridge.
59 Attlee, C. R. to Churchill, W., 19 April 1949, Churchill Papers, CHUR 4/51, Churchill Archives, Churchill College, Cambridge.
60 *Recorder*, 8 June 1949.
61 Attlee, C. R., Speech to Labour Conference, 10 June 1949, British Political Speech Archive.
62 Attlee, C. R., Speech to Durham Miners' Gala, 23 July 1949, Attlee Papers, DEP 86, Bodleian Library, Oxford.
63 Churchill, W., Speech to Wolverhampton rally, 23 July 1949, Attlee Papers, DEP 86, Bodleian Library, Oxford.
64 Attlee, C. R., Speech to Poole Labour Club, 1 August 1949, Attlee Papers, DEP 86, Bodleian Library, Oxford.
65 Hansard, 28 September 1949.
66 Hansard, 29 September 1949.
67 *Daily Mail*, 16 October 1949.
68 Boyle, *op. cit.*
69 Ball, S. and Seldon, A. (eds), *Recovering Power: The Conservatives in Opposition Since 1967.*
70 Williams, *Nothing So Strange, op. cit.*
71 Pimlott, *The Political Diary of Hugh Dalton, op. cit.*
72 Williams, *The Diary of Hugh Gaitskell, op. cit.*
73 *Daily Mail*, 17 February 1950.
74 Headlam, *op. cit.*
75 Pumphrey, L. to Windle, R., 11 January 1950, Attlee Papers, DEP 94, Bodleian Library, Oxford.
76 *The Times*, 23 January 1950.
77 *The Times*, 29 January 1950.
78 *The Times*, 10 February 1950.

79 Gilbert, *Never Despair*, op. cit.
80 *Daily Express*, 15 February 1950.
81 Nicolson, *op. cit.*
82 *Daily Mail*, 16 February 1950.
83 Gilbert, *Never Despair*, op. cit.
84 Moran, *The Struggle For Survival*, op. cit.
85 Attlee, C. R., Text of broadcast, 18 February 1950, Attlee Papers, DEP 98, Bodleian Library, Oxford.
86 Williams, *The Diary of Hugh Gaitskell*, op. cit.
87 Nicolson, *op. cit.*
88 Gilbert, *Never Despair*, op. cit.
89 Jay, D., Interview, 15260, IWM Archives.
90 Williams, *A Prime Minister Remembers*, op. cit.
91 Gilbert, *Never Despair*, op. cit.

Twenty-Eight: Europe and Korea

1   Hansard, 7 March 1950.
2   Hansard, 7 March 1950.
3   Attlee, C. R., Text for speech, 7 March 1950, Attlee Papers, DEP 99, Bodleian Library, Oxford.
4   Gilbert, *Never Despair*, op. cit.
5   *Daily Mail*, 30 March 1950.
6   Hansard, 31 March 1950.
7   Rhodes James, *'Chips'*, op. cit.
8   Nicolson, *op. cit.*
9   Wheeler Bennett, *King George VI*, op. cit.
10 Williams, *The Diary of Hugh Gaitskell*, op. cit.
11 Hunt, *op. cit.*
12 Attlee, C. R. to Attlee, T., 2 March 1950, Attlee Papers, MS Eng. c. 4794, Bodleian Library, Oxford.
13 Downing Street to Treasury, 17 July 1950, Attlee Papers, DEP 143, Bodleian Library, Oxford.
14 *Evening News*, 29 September 1952.
15 Attlee, C. R. to Churchill, W., 28 April 1950, Churchill Papers, 2/166, Churchill Archives, Churchill College, Cambridge.
16 Attlee, C. R. to Churchill, W., 28 June 1950, Churchill Papers, 4/55, Churchill Archives, Churchill College, Cambridge.
17 Attlee, C. R. to Churchill, W., 16 January 1950, Churchill Papers, 2/98, Churchill Archives, Churchill College, Cambridge.
18 Churchill, W. to Attlee, C. R., 9 October 1940, Churchill Papers, 2/98, Churchill Archives, Churchill College, Cambridge.
19 *The Times*, 25 October 1950.
20 *The Times*, 25 October 1950.
21 Gilbert, *Never Despair*, op. cit.
22 Letter to *The Times*, 27 October 1950.
23 Hansard, 26 October 1950.
24 Churchill, W. to Attlee, C. R., 20 April 1950, Churchill Papers, CHUR 2/76A, Churchill Archives, Churchill College, Cambridge.

25 Ionescu, G. (ed.), *The New Politics of European Integration.*
26 Hunt, *op. cit.*
27 Hennessy, P., *Never Again: Britain 1945–1951.*
28 Hansard, 13 June 1950.
29 Hansard, 15 June 1950.
30 Williams, *Harold Macmillan, op. cit.*
31 Boothby, R. to Churchill, W., 20 June 1950, Churchill Papers, CHUR 2/101A, Churchill Archives, Churchill College, Cambridge.
32 *Daily Mail*, 21 June 1950.
33 Hansard, 27 June 1950.
34 Hansard, 27 June 1950.
35 Attlee, C. R. to Attlee, T., 30 June 1950, Attlee Papers, MS Eng. c. 4794, Bodleian Library, Oxford.
36 Radice, *op. cit.*
37 Griffiths, R. T., *Socialist Parties and the Question of Europe in the 1950s.*
38 Statement by Attlee, C. R., Statement, 31 June 1950, Attlee Papers, DEP 102, Bodleian Library, Oxford.
39 Harris, *op. cit.*
40 Harris, *op. cit.*
41 Hansard, 5 July 1950.
42 Roberts, *Churchill, op. cit.*
43 Pottle, *Daring to Hope, op. cit.*
44 Churchill, W. to Attlee, C. R., 24 May 1950, PREM 8/1160, National Archives.
45 Attlee, C. R. to Churchill, W., 13 June 1950, Churchill Papers, CHUR 2/29B, Churchill Archives, Churchill College, Cambridge.
46 Churchill, W. to Attlee, C. R., 29 June 1950, Churchill Papers, CHUR 2/29B, Churchill Archives, Churchill College, Cambridge.
47 Attlee, C. R. to Churchill, W., 14 July 1950, Churchill Papers, CHUR 2/29B, Churchill Archives, Churchill College, Cambridge.
48 Churchill, W. to Attlee, C. R., 15 July 1950, Churchill Papers, CHUR 2/29B, Churchill Archives, Churchill College, Cambridge.
49 Churchill, W. to Attlee, C. R., 26 July 1950, Churchill Papers, CHUR 2/29B, Churchill Archives, Churchill College, Cambridge.
50 Attlee, C. R. to Churchill, W., 26 July 1950, Churchill Papers, CHUR 2/29B, Churchill Archives, Churchill College, Cambridge.
51 Hansard, 27 July 1950.
52 Catterall, P., (ed.), *The Macmillan Diaries: The Cabinet Years, 1950–57.*
53 Macmillan, *op. cit.*
54 Churchill, W. to Attlee, C. R., 6 August 1950, Churchill Papers, 2/28, Churchill Archives, Churchill College, Cambridge.
55 Memorandum by Churchill, 6 August 1950, Churchill Papers, 2/28, Churchill Archives, Churchill College, Cambridge.
56 Gilbert, *Never Despair, op. cit.*
57 Gilbert, *Never Despair, op. cit.*
58 Churchill, W. to Attlee, C. R., 13 August 1950, PREM 8/1258, National Archives.
59 Attlee, C. R. to Churchill, W., 13 August 1950, PREM 8/1258, National Archives.
60 Attlee, C. R. to George VI, 17 August 1950, PREM 8/1258, National Archives.

61 George VI to Attlee, C. R., 21 August 1950, PREM 8/1258, National Archives.
62 Muggeridge, M., *Like It Was: The Diaries of Malcolm Muggeridge*.
63 *The Times*, 28 August 1950.
64 *Daily Mail*, 4 September 1940.
65 *Daily Mail*, 4 September 1940.
66 Harris, *op. cit.*
67 Attlee, C. R. to Attlee, T., 25 September 1950, Attlee Papers, Oxford MS Eng. c. 4794, Bodleian Library, Oxford.
68 *Daily Mail*, 13 September 1940.
69 *Daily Mail*, 15 September 1940.
70 *The Times*, 6 October 1950.
71 Harris, *op. cit.*
72 Hansard, 31 October 1950.
73 Warner, *op. cit.*
74 Attlee, C. R. to Churchill, W., 3 December 1950, PREM 8/1559, National Archives.
75 Harris, *op. cit.*
76 Warner, *op. cit.*
77 *The Times*, 9 December 1950.
78 Hansard, 14 December 1950.
79 Pimlott, *The Political Diary of Hugh Dalton*, *op. cit.*

Twenty-Nine: Abadan

1   Wilson Broadbent in profile of Attlee, *Daily Mail*, 21 September 1951.
2   Cockett, *op. cit.*
3   Rhodes James, *'Chips'*, *op. cit.*
4   Hansard, 7 February 1951.
5   Pimlott, *The Political Diary of Hugh Dalton*, *op. cit.*
6   Hansard, 15 February 1951.
7   Rhodes James, *'Chips'*, *op. cit.*
8   Benn, T., *Years of Hope: Diaries, Letters and Papers, 1940–62*.
9   Hansard, 30 January 1951.
10 Makins, Sir, R., Note, 31 January 1951, PREM 8/1559, National Archives.
11 Churchill, W. to Truman, H., 12 February 1951, Churchill Papers, CHUR 2/28, Churchill Archives, Churchill College, Cambridge.
12 Churchill, W. to Attlee, C. R., 12 February 1951, PREM 8/1559, National Archives.
13 Rickett, D. to Attlee, C. R., 13 February 1951, PREM 8/1559, National Archives.
14 Attlee, C. R. to Churchill, W., 14 February 1951, PREM 8/1559, National Archives.
15 Gilbert, *Never Despair*, *op. cit.*
16 Beckett, *op. cit.*
17 BBC Radio Profile of Bevin, 24 April 1957, Citrine Papers, 10/3, LSE Archives.
18 Attlee, C. R. to Churchill, W., 17 May 1951, Churchill Papers, CHUR 2/167, Churchill Archives, Churchill College, Cambridge.
19 Churchill, W. to Attlee, C. R., 24 May 1951, Churchill Papers, CHUR 2/167, Churchill Archives, Churchill College, Cambridge.

20 Attlee, C. R. to Churchill, W. and C., 22 March 1951, Churchill Papers, CHUR 2/166, Churchill Archives, Churchill College, Cambridge.
21 *The Times*, 19 March 1951.
22 *The Times*, 2 April 1951.
23 Catterall, *op. cit.*
24 Williams, *The Diary of Hugh Gaitskell, op. cit.*
25 Attlee, C. R. to Attlee, T, 30 April 1951, Attlee Papers, MS Eng. 4794, Bodleian Library, Oxford.
26 Blackburn, *op. cit.*
27 Gilbert, *Never Despair, op. cit.*
28 Warner, *op. cit.*
29 Gilbert, *Never Despair, op. cit.*
30 Churchill, R. to Churchill, W., 22 July 1951, Churchill Papers, CHUR 2/126, Churchill Archives, Churchill College, Cambridge.
31 Churchill, W. to Attlee, C. R., 9 July 1951, Churchill Papers, CHUR 2/126, Churchill Archives, Churchill College, Cambridge.
32 Thomas, *op. cit.*
33 Hansard, 30 July 1951.
34 Catterall, *op. cit.*
35 Catterall, *op. cit.*
36 Williams, *A Prime Minister Remembers, op. cit.*
37 Attlee, C. R. to Morrison, H., 27 May 1951, Morrison Papers, 8/3.
38 *Daily Telegraph*, 9 March 1999.
39 Harris, *op. cit.*
40 Churchill, W. to Attlee, C. R., 23 September 1951, Churchill Papers, CHUR 2/114A, Churchill Archives, Churchill College, Cambridge.
41 Attlee, C. R. to Churchill, W., 23 September 1951, Churchill Papers, CHUR 2/114A, Churchill Archives, Churchill College, Cambridge.
42 Attlee, C. R. to Churchill, W., 20 September 1951, Churchill Papers, CHUR 2/128, Churchill Archives, Churchill College, Cambridge.
43 Harris, *op. cit.*
44 Gilbert, *Never Despair, op. cit.*
45 Moran, *The Struggle For Survival, op. cit.*
46 Shore, P., Diary, 20 September, 4 and 6 October 1951, Shore Papers, 3/36, LSE Archives.
47 Harris, *op. cit.*
48 McGowan, *op. cit.*
49 Gilbert, *Never Despair, op. cit.*
50 Marquis, *op. cit.*
51 *Daily Mail*, 6 October 1951.
52 Gilbert, *Never Despair, op. cit.*
53 Butler, D., *The British General Election of 1951.*
54 Shore, P., Diary, 10 October 1951, Shore Papers, 3/36.
55 *Daily Mail*, 10 October 1951.
56 Churchill, R., *Stemming the Tide: Speeches 1951 and 1952 by Winston S. Churchill.*
57 *Daily Mail*, 1 October 1951.
58 Attlee, C. R., Text of broadcast, 20 October 1951, Attlee Papers, DEP 128, Bodleian Library, Oxford.

59 Letter to *The Times*, 22 October 1951.
60 Attlee, *As It Happened, op. cit.*
61 *Manchester Guardian*, 8 October 1951.
62 *The Times*, 17 October 1951.
63 Attlee, C. to Attlee, C. R., 9 October 1951, Attlee Papers, DEP 127, Bodleian Library, Oxford.
64 Amery, L., Diary, 4 October 1951, Amery Papers, AMEL 7, Churchill Archives, Churchill College, Cambridge.
65 Pottle, *Daring to Hope, op. cit.*
66 Attlee, C. R., Transcript of speech in Slaithwaite, 29 September 1951, Attlee Papers, DEP 126, Bodleian Library, Oxford.
67 Moran, *Churchill, op. cit.*
68 *Daily Herald*, 22 October 1951.
69 *The Times*, 23 October 1951.
70 Thorpe, D. R., *Eden: The Life and Times of Anthony Eden.* The story is also in Benn, *op. cit.*
71 Warner, *op. cit.*
72 *Daily Mail*, 23 October 1951.
73 Dellar, *op. cit.*
74 Morgan, K., *Labour in Power, op. cit.*
75 McGowan, *op. cit.*
76 Gilbert, *Never Despair, op. cit.*

Thirty: Summit

1   Nicolson, *op. cit.*
2   Pimlott, *The Political Diary of Hugh Dalton, op. cit.*
3   Montague Browne, *op. cit.*
4   Pimlott, *The Political Diary of Hugh Dalton, op. cit.*
5   Hunter, *op. cit.*
6   Warner, *op. cit.*
7   Benn, *op. cit.*
8   Bullock, *Ernest Bevin* (Volume 3), *op. cit.*
9   Morgan, J., *op. cit.*
10 Shuckburgh, E., *Descent to Suez: Diaries, 1951–56.*
11 Morgan, J., *op. cit.*
12 Hennessy, *The Prime Minister, op. cit.*
13 Finlayson, J. M., *The Cabinet Committee System and the Development of British Colonial Policy.*
14 Boyd-Carpenter, *op. cit.*
15 Seldon, A., *Churchill's Indian Summer: The Conservative Government, 1951–55.*
16 *Observer*, 31 January 1965.
17 Wheeler Bennett, *Action This Day, op. cit.*
18 Wheeler Bennett, *Action This Day, op. cit.*
19 Hunt, *op. cit.*
20 Marquis, *op. cit.*
21 Crookshank, H., Diary, 22 April and 17 May 1952, Crookshank Papers, MS Eng. d. 360, Bodleian Library, Oxford.
22 *Daily Mail*, 2 November 1951.

23 Attlee, C. R. to Attlee, T., 14 November 1951, Attlee Papers, MS Eng. 4794, Bodleian Library, Oxford.
24 *Hansard*, 6 November 1951.
25 *Hansard*, 6 November 1951.
26 *Hansard*, 6 December 1951.
27 Hunt, *op. cit.*
28 Moran, *The Struggle For Survival*, *op. cit.*
29 Shuckburgh, *op. cit.*
30 Cairncross, *op. cit.*
31 Churchill, W., to Cherwell, Lord, *op. cit.*
32 Hunt, *op. cit.*
33 Colville, *The Fringes of Power*, *op. cit.*
34 *Daily Telegraph*, 12 February 1952.
35 Attlee, *As It Happened*, *op. cit.*
36 Morgan, J., *op. cit.*
37 Attlee, C. R. to Attlee, T., 18 February 1952, Attlee Papers, MS Eng. 4794, Bodleian Library, Oxford.
38 Moran, *Churchill*, *op. cit.*
39 Hunt, *op. cit.*
40 Shuckburgh, *op. cit.*
41 Moran, *Churchill*, *op. cit.*
42 *Daily Telegraph*, 27 February 1952.
43 *Daily Telegraph*, 27 February 1952.
44 *Daily Mail*, 27 February 1952.
45 Nicolson, *op. cit.*
46 Morgan, J., *op. cit.*
47 Moran, *Churchill*, *op. cit.*
48 *Daily Mail*, 29 February 1952.
49 Harris, *op. cit.*
50 Morgan, J., *op. cit.*
51 Young, *Churchill and Beaverbrook*, *op. cit.*
52 *Daily Mail*, 5 May 1952.
53 *Daily Mail*, 5 May 1952.
54 Pearce, *op. cit.*
55 Harris, *op. cit.*
56 Pimlott, *The Political Diary of Hugh Dalton*, *op. cit.*
57 Moran, *The Struggle For Survival*, *op. cit.*
58 Soames, *Speaking for Themselves*, *op. cit.*
59 Moran, *The Struggle For Survival*, *op. cit.*
60 Moran, *The Struggle For Survival*, *op. cit.*
61 Attlee, C. R. to Churchill, W., 8 January 1952, Churchill Papers, CHUR 2/179, Churchill Archives, Churchill College, Cambridge.
62 *Daily Mail*, 8 March 1952.
63 Churchill, W. to Attlee, C. R., 7 September 1952, Churchill Papers, CHUR 2/179, Churchill Archives, Churchill College, Cambridge.
64 Montague Browne, *op. cit.*
65 *Hansard*, 4 November 1952.
66 *Hansard*, 4 November 1952.
67 Morgan, J., *op. cit.*

68 *Daily Mail*, 5 December 1952.
69 Hansard, 4 December 1952.
70 Catterall, *op. cit.*
71 Morgan, J., *op. cit.*
72 Pimlott, *The Political Diary of Hugh Dalton, op. cit.*
73 Donoughue and Jones, *op. cit.*
74 Morgan, J., *op. cit.*
75 Moran, *The Struggle For Survival, op. cit.*
76 Correspondence quoted by Viscount Swinton, House of Lords Debate, 24 February 1953.
77 Pimlott, *The Political Diary of Hugh Dalton, op. cit.*
78 Catterall, *op. cit.*
79 Harris, *op. cit.*
80 Leeming, *op. cit.*

Thirty-One: Commons

1 Gilbert, *Never Despair, op. cit.*
2 Gilbert, *Never Despair, op. cit.*
3 Moran, *The Struggle For Survival, op. cit.*
4 Hansard, 30 July 1953.
5 Morgan, J., *op. cit.*
6 *Sunday Express*, 9 August 1953.
7 Shuckburgh, *op. cit.*
8 Pottle, *Daring to Hope, op. cit.*
9 Catterall, *op. cit.*
10 Attlee, C. R. to Attlee, T., 13 October 1953, Attlee Papers, MS Eng. c. 4794, Bodleian Library, Oxford.
11 Harris, *op. cit.*
12 Moran, *The Struggle For Survival, op. cit.*
13 Gilbert, *Never Despair, op. cit.*
14 Attlee, C. R. to Churchill, W., 30 December 1953, Churchill Papers, CHUR 2/179, Churchill Archives, Churchill College, Cambridge.
15 Attlee, C. R. to Churchill, W., 15 July 1954 Churchill Papers, CHUR 2/179, Churchill Archives, Churchill College, Cambridge.
16 Churchill, W., Text of speech, 20 November 1953, Churchill Papers, CHUR 5/52C, Churchill Archives, Churchill College, Cambridge.
17 *Daily Telegraph*, 21 November 1953.
18 William Hickey column, *Daily Express* 21 November 1953.
19 Catterall, *op. cit.*
20 Moran, *The Struggle For Survival, op. cit.*
21 Shuckburgh, *op. cit.*
22 *Daily Mirror*, 1 April 1954.
23 Cherwell to Churchill, 1 December 1953, EG 1/36, National Archives.
24 Moran, *The Struggle For Survival, op. cit.*
25 Woolton, Lord, Diary, 6 April 1954, Woolton Papers, Bodleian Library, Oxford.
26 Catterall, *op. cit.*
27 Woolton, Lord, Diary, 6 April 1954, Woolton Papers, Bodleian Library, Oxford.
28 Morgan, J., *op. cit.*

29 Woolton, Lord, Diary, 6 April 1954, Woolton Papers, Bodleian Library, Oxford.
30 Attlee, C. R. to Attlee, T., 8 April 1954, Attlee Papers, MS Eng. c. 4794, Bodleian Library, Oxford.
31 Woolton, Lord, Diary, 6 April 1954, Woolton Papers, Bodleian Library, Oxford.
32 Shuckburgh, *op. cit.*
33 Catterall, *op. cit.*
34 Morgan, J., *op. cit.*
35 Moran, *The Struggle For Survival, op. cit.*
36 Woolton, Lord, Diary, 6 April 1954, Woolton Papers, Bodleian Library, Oxford.
37 Gilbert, *Never Despair, op. cit.*
38 Woolton, Lord, Diary, 6 April 1954, Woolton Papers, Bodleian Library, Oxford.
39 Catterall, *op. cit.*
40 Catterall, *op. cit.*
41 Schneer, *op. cit.*
42 Montague Browne, *op. cit.*
43 Moran, *The Struggle For Survival, op. cit.*
44 Morgan, J., *op. cit.*
45 Harris, *op. cit.*
46 Williams, *The Diary of Hugh Gaitskell, op. cit.*
47 Moran, *The Struggle For Survival, op. cit.*
48 Moran, *The Struggle For Survival, op. cit.*
49 Haste, C. (ed.), *Clarissa Eden: A Memoir – from Churchill to Eden.*
50 Catterall, *op. cit.*
51 Seldon, *op. cit.*
52 Moran, *The Struggle For Survival, op. cit.*
53 Moran, *The Struggle For Survival, op. cit.*
54 *Daily Express*, 1 December 1954.
55 *Daily Express*, 1 December 1954.
56 *Daily Express*, 1 December 1954.
57 Pelling, *Winston Churchill, op. cit.*
58 *Daily Express*, 2 December 1954.
59 Hansard, 6 December 1954.
60 *Daily Mail*, 7 December 1954.
61 Churchill, W. and C. to Attlee, C. R., 3 January 1955, Churchill Papers, CHUR 2/179, Churchill Archives, Churchill College, Cambridge.
62 Attlee, C. R. to Churchill, W. and C., 3 January 1955, Churchill Papers, CHUR 2/179, Churchill Archives, Churchill College, Cambridge.
63 Haste, *op. cit.*
64 Moran, *The Struggle For Survival, op. cit.*
65 Woolton, Lord, Diary, 22 December 1954, Woolton Papers, Bodleian Library, Oxford.
66 Churchill, W. to Eisenhower, D., 12 January 1955, Churchill Papers, CHUR 6//3A, Churchill Archives, Churchill College, Cambridge.
67 Roberts, *Eminent Churchillians, op. cit.*
68 Lough, *op. cit.*
69 Roberts, *Eminent Churchillians, op. cit.*
70 Roberts, *Eminent Churchillians, op. cit.*

71   Attlee, C. R., Speech to delegation of Labour MPs, 5 July 1948, HO 213/715, National Archives.
72   *The Times*, 2 January 1982.
73   *The Times*, 2 January 1982.
74   In a report on the release of Sir Norman's Cabinet notebooks, *Daily Telegraph*, 5 August 2007.
75   *Guardian*, 6 August 2007.
76   *Daily Telegraph*, 5 August 2007.
77   Gilmour, I., *Inside Right: A Study of Conservatism*.
78   Catterall, *op. cit.*
79   Young, *Churchill and Beaverbrook, op. cit.*
80   Catterall, *op. cit.*
81   Hansard, 2 March 1955.
82   Moran, *The Struggle For Survival, op. cit.*
83   Gilbert, *Never Despair, op. cit.*
84   Lloyd, S., Memory in diary, August 1961, Selwyn Lloyd Papers, SELO 4/22, Churchill Archives, Churchill College, Cambridge.
85   Pottle, *Daring to Hope, op. cit.*
86   Moran, *Churchill, op. cit.*
87   Gilbert, *Never Despair, op. cit.*
88   Catterall, *op. cit.*
89   Colville, *The Fringes of Power, op. cit.*
90   Gilbert, *Never Despair, op. cit.*
91   Crookshank, H., Diary, 5 April 1955, Crookshank Papers, MS Eng. d. 360, Bodleian Library, Oxford.
92   Boyd-Carpenter, *op. cit.*
93   Hansard, 6 April 1955.
94   Eden, C. to Churchill, C., 6 April 1955, Clementine Churchill Papers, CSCT 3/56, Churchill Archives, Churchill College, Cambridge.
95   Attlee, C. R. to Churchill, W., 6 April 1955, Churchill Papers, CHUR 2/481E, Churchill Archives, Churchill College, Cambridge.

Thirty-Two: St Paul's and Temple

1   *Liverpool Echo*, 19 May 1955.
2   Harris, *op. cit.*
3   *Liverpool Echo*, 19 May 1955.
4   *Manchester Guardian*, 12 May 1955.
5   *Daily Express*, 12 May 1955.
6   Hunter, *op. cit.*
7   Hunter, *op. cit.*
8   Moran, *Churchill, op. cit.*
9   *Daily Mail*, 17 May 1955.
10   Harris, *op. cit.*
11   *Daily Mail*, 17 May 1955.
12   *Daily Mail*, 19 May 1955.
13   Harris, *op. cit.*
14   Gilbert, *Never Despair, op. cit.*
15   Gilbert, *Never Despair, op. cit.*

16   *Daily Mail*, 9 June 1955.
17   Pimlott, *The Political Diary of Hugh Dalton*, *op. cit.*
18   Donoughue and Jones, *op. cit.*
19   Hunter, *op. cit.*
20   Hunter, *op. cit.*
21   Harris, *op. cit.*
22   Hunter, *op. cit.*
23   Hunter, *op. cit.*
24   Pimlott, *The Political Diary of Hugh Dalton*, *op. cit.*
25   Hunter, *op. cit.*
26   Attlee, C. R. to Attlee, T., 6 December 1955, Attlee Papers, MS Eng. 4794, Bodleian Library, Oxford.
27   Morgan, J., *op. cit.*
28   Castle, B., *Fighting All the Way*.
29   *Daily Herald*, 8 December 1955.
30   Hunter, *op. cit.*
31   *Daily Telegraph*, 12 December 1955.
32   *Daily Mail*, 9 December 1955.
33   *The Times*, 9 December 1955.
34   *Daily Herald*, 8 December 1955.
35   *Daily Mail*, 9 December 1955.
36   Williams, *The Diary of Hugh Gaitskell*, *op. cit.*
37   Hudson, *op. cit.*
38   Benn, *op. cit.*
39   Attlee, C. R. to Attlee, T., 26 December 1956, Attlee Papers, MS Eng. 4794, Bodleian Library, Oxford.
40   Attlee, C. R. to Churchill, W. and C., 5 January 1958, Churchill Papers, CHUR 2/179, Churchill Archives, Churchill College, Cambridge.
41   Dellar, *op. cit.*
42   Attlee, C. R. to Baldwin, O., 18 December 1955, Baldwin Papers, HL/PO/RO/1/89, Parliamentary Archives, House of Lords.
43   *Sunday Times*, 15 September 1963.
44   *Sunday Times*, 15 September 1963.
45   Beckett, *op. cit.*
46   Roberts, *Churchill*, *op. cit.*
47   Attlee, A. to Shipton, J., 3 November 1974, Shipton Papers, University of Iowa.
48   *Daily Telegraph*, 19 December 1959.
49   *Daily Express*, 19 December 1959.
50   Thomas, *op. cit.*
51   Thomas, *op. cit.*
52   Pottle, *Daring to Hope*, *op. cit.*
53   Pottle, *Daring to Hope*, *op. cit.*
54   Nicolson, *op. cit.*
55   *Daily Mail*, 4 July 1962.
56   Attlee, C. R. to the Churchills, 5 January 1963, Churchill Papers, 2/179, Churchill Archives, Churchill College, Cambridge.
57   Thomas, *op. cit.*
58   *Daily Sketch*, 16 September 1963.
59   Harris, *op. cit.*

60 *Daily Express*, 23 January 1961.
61 Attlee, C. R. to Williams, F., 14 June 1964, Williams Papers, 8/1, Churchill Archives, Churchill College, Cambridge.
62 Harris, *op. cit.*
63 Harris, *op. cit.*
64 *The Times*, 25 January 1965.
65 Lords Hansard, 25 January 1965.
66 *Daily Mail*, 25 January 1965.
67 Dellar, *op. cit.*
68 Beckett, *op. cit.*
69 Beckett, *op. cit.*
70 BBC News Magazine, 28 January 2015.
71 *Daily Mail*, 1 February 1962.
72 *Daily Mail*, 1 February 1962.
73 Attlee, M. to Shipton, J., 1 March 1965, Shipton Papers, University of Iowa.
74 Roberts, A., *Hitler and Churchill: Secrets of Leadership*.
75 Moran, *The Struggle For Survival, op. cit.*
76 Pottle, *Daring to Hope, op. cit.*
77 Harris, *op. cit.*
78 Attlee, M. to Shipton, J., 4 February 1967, Shipton Papers, University of Iowa.
79 Attlee, A. to Shipton, J., 24 September 1967, Shipton Papers, University of Iowa.
80 Attlee, M. to Shipton, J., 2 October 1967, Shipton Papers, University of Iowa.
81 *Guardian*, 9 October 1967.
82 *The Times*, 9 October 1967.
83 *Newsweek*, 16 October 1967.
84 Bew, *op. cit.*

BIBLIOGRAPHY

PRIMARY SOURCES

Alanbrooke, Lord, Papers, Imperial War Museum Archives

Alexander, C., Papers, Imperial War Museum Archives

Allen, G., Interview, Churchill Archives, Churchill College, Cambridge

Attlee, C. R., First World War memoir, Lancashire Infantry Museum

Attlee, C. R., Papers, Bodleian Library, Oxford

Attlee, C. R., Papers, Churchill Archives, Churchill College, Cambridge

Baldwin, O., Papers, Parliamentary Archives, House of Lords

Balfour, A., Papers, British Library

Baxter, C. W., Papers, Imperial War Museum Archives

Bevin, E., Papers, Churchill Archives, Churchill College, Cambridge

Boothby, R., Interview, Imperial War Museum Archives

Bracken, B., Papers, Churchill Archives, Churchill College, Cambridge

Brockman, R., Interview, Imperial War Museum Archives

Burkin, H., Memoir, Burdett Archive, Brunel University

Campbell–Bannerman, Sir H., Papers, British Library

Carron, W. J., Diaries, Churchill Archives, Churchill College, Cambridge

Churchill, Lady C., Papers, Churchill Archives, Churchill College, Cambridge

Churchill, Lady R., Papers, Churchill Archives, Churchill College, Cambridge

Churchill, W., Churchill Archives, Churchill College, Cambridge

Colville, Sir J., Interview, Imperial War Museum Archives

Colville, Sir J., Papers, Churchill Archives, Churchill College, Cambridge

Cook, T. L., Papers, Imperial War Museum Archives

Cripps, H., Interview, Imperial War Museum Archives

Cripps, S., Papers, Bodleian Library, Oxford

Crookshank, H., Papers, Bodleian Library, Oxford

Dalton, H., Papers, London School of Economics Archives

Davies, C., Papers, National Library of Wales

Dawson, G., Papers, Bodleian Library, Oxford

Dilke, Sir C., Papers, British Library

Dorell, H., Memoir, Burdett Archive, Brunel University

Downes, B., Papers, Imperial War Museum Archives

Driberg, T., Interview, Imperial War Museum Archives
Durbin, E., Papers, London School of Economics Archives
Ede, C., Diary, British Library
Edmonds, J. E., Papers, Imperial War Museum Archives
Election Addresses, Working Class Movement Library, Salford
Emrys–Evans, P., Papers, British Library
Fagan, H., Memoir, Burdett Archive, Brunel University
Gladstone, H., Papers, British Library
Gorrell Barnes, Sir W., Papers, Churchill Archives, Churchill College, Cambridge
Griggs, Sir J., Papers, Churchill Archives, Churchill College, Cambridge
Hankey, Lord, Papers, Churchill Archives, Churchill College, Cambridge
Hollis, Sir L., Papers, Imperial War Museum Archives
Hore-Belisha, L., Papers, Churchill Archives, Churchill College, Cambridge
Hunt, Sir D., Interview, Imperial War Museum Archives
Inskip, Sir T., Papers, Churchill Archives, Churchill College, Cambridge
Ironside, Lord, Papers, Imperial War Museum Archives
Jacob, Sir I., Papers, Churchill Archives, Churchill College, Cambridge
Jay, D., Interview, Imperial War Museum Archives
Jenkins, R., Papers, Bodleian Library, Oxford
Jones, J., Interview, Imperial War Museum Archives
Keyes, Sir R., Papers, British Library
King, C., Interview, Imperial War Museum Archives
Labour General Secretary's Papers, People's Museum of Labour History
Labour National Executive Minutes, People's Museum of Labour History
Lawford, V., Diaries, Churchill Archives, Churchill College, Cambridge
Lechler, H., Papers, Imperial War Museum Archives
Lee, D., Papers, Imperial War Museum Archives
Leggett, G., Potsdam Diary, Churchill Archives, Churchill College, Cambridge
Lewis, W., Memoir, Imperial War Museum Archives
Liddell-Hart, B., Papers, King's College London
Lloyd George, D., Papers, Parliamentary Archives, House of Lords
Lord Cecil of Chelwood, Papers, British Library
Lord Chandos, Interview, Imperial War Museum Archives
Lord Citrine, Papers, London School of Economics Archives
MacDonald, R., Diaries, British Library
Marsh, E., Papers, Churchill Archives, Churchill College, Cambridge
Martin, Sir J., Papers, Imperial War Museum Archives
Morrison, H., Papers, London School of Economics Archives
Nel (nee Layton), E., Interview, Imperial War Museum Archives
Normanbrook, Lord, Papers, Bodleian Library, Oxford
Northcliffe, Lord, Papers, British Library

Onslow (nee Sturdee), J., Papers, Churchill Archives, Churchill College, Cambridge
Parker, J., Papers, London School of Economics Archives
Piercy, W., Papers, London School of Economics Archives
Prime Minister's Papers, National Archives
Rhodes-James, R., Papers, Churchill Archives, Churchill College, Cambridge
Selwyn-Lloyd, Lord, Diaries, Churchill Archives, Churchill College, Cambridge
Shinwell, E., Interview, Imperial War Museum Archives
Shipton, J., Interview, Imperial War Museum Archives
Shipton, J., Papers, Iowa State University
Shore, P., Papers, London School of Economics Archives
Smethurst, S., Papers, Churchill Archives, Churchill College, Cambridge
Spears, Sir E., Papers, Churchill Archives, Churchill College, Cambridge
Spicer, nee Holmes, M., Interview, Imperial War Museum Archives
Strauss, G., Papers, Churchill Archives, Churchill College, Cambridge
Swinton, Lord, Papers, Churchill Archives, Churchill College, Cambridge
Tate, E., Letters, Imperial War Museum Archives
Tudor, Sir H., Papers, Imperial War Museum Archives
War Cabinet Papers, National Archives
Webb, B., Papers, London School of Economics Archives
Wigg, G., Papers, London School of Economics Archives
Williams, F., Papers, Churchill Archives, Churchill College, Cambridge
Willink, Sir H., Papers, Churchill Archives, Churchill College, Cambridge
Wilson, J. K., Papers, Imperial War Museum Archives
Winnifrith, Sir J., Interview, Imperial War Museum Archives
Woolton, Lord, Diaries, Bodleian Library, Oxford

PUBLISHED PRIMARY SOURCES

Asquith, Lady C., *Diaries 1915–18* (1968)
Ball, S. (ed.), *The Headlam Diaries 1935–1951* (1999)
Beaton, C., *The Strenuous Years: Diaries 1948–55* (1973)
Benn, T., *Years of Hope: Diaries, Letters and Papers, 1940–62.*
Best, G., *Churchill: A Study in Greatness* (2000)
Bishop, A. and Bennett, Y. (eds), *Wartime Chronicle: Vera Brittain's Diary 1939–1945.*
Blumenfeld, R. D., *Across the Pond* (1930)
Bonham Carter, V., *Lantern Slides: Diaries and Letters 1904–1914* (1996)
Brock, M. and E., *H. H. Asquith: Letters to Venetia Stanley* (1982)
Cairncross, A. (ed.), *The Robert Hall Diaries 1947–1953* (1989)
Cassell, A. (ed.), *The Wartime Diaries of Flight Lieutenant Henry Chessell* (2009)
Catterall, P. (ed.), *The Macmillan Diaries 1950–57* (2003)
— *Champion Redoubtable: Diaries and Letters 1914–1945* (1998)
Cockett, R. (ed.), *The Letters of Brendan Bracken to Lord Beaverbrook* (1990)

Colville, J., *The Fringes of Power* (Two volumes, 1985–87)

Danchev, A. and Todman, D., *Field Marshal Lord Alanbrooke War Diaries* (2001)

— *Daring to Hope: Diaries and Letters 1946–1969* (2000)

David, E. (ed.), *Inside Asquith's Cabinet: From the Diaries of Charles Hobhouse* (1977)

David, S. (ed.), *The War Diaries and Letters of Captain N.A.C. Weir* (2013)

DeWolfe Howe, M. (ed.), *The Laski–Holmes Correspondence* (1953)

Dilks, D. (ed.), *The Diaries of Sir Alexander Cadogan 1938–1945* (2010)

Dupree, M. (ed.), *The Diary of Sir Raymond Streat* (1987)

Eden, Sir A., *Full Circle* (1960)

— *Facing the Dictators* (1962)

Gorodestky, G., *The Maisky Diaries* (2015)

Hart-Davis, D. (ed.), *The Diaries of Sir Alan Lascelles*

Harvey, J. (ed.), *The Diaries of Oliver Harvey: 1937–1940* (1970)

— *The War Diaries of Oliver Harvey 1941–1945* (1978)

Hudson, R. (ed.), *The Lyttelton Hart–Davis Letters* (2003)

Jebb, M. (ed.), *The Diaries of Cynthia Gladwyn* (1995)

Jeffrey, K. (ed.), *The Military Correspondence of Field Marshal Sir Henry Wilson* (1985)

Jones, T., *A Diary with Letters: 1931–1950* (1954)

Kennedy, J. F., *European Diary, Summer 1945* (1995)

Mackenzie, N., *The Letters of Sidney and Beatrice Webb* (1978)

Macleod, R. and Kelly, D. (ed.), *The Ironside Diaries 1937–1940* (1962)

Macmillan, H., *Tides of Fortune 1945–55* (1969)

— *Margot Asquith's Great War Diary 1914–1916* (2014)

Meade, J., *The Cabinet Office Diary 1944–46* (1990)

Moody, J., *From Churchill's War Rooms* (2007)

Moran, Lord, *Churchill at War 1940–45* (1966)

— *The Struggle For Survival 1945–1960* (2009)

Morgan, J. (ed.) *The Backbench Diaries of Richard Crossman* (1981)

Morgan, K. (ed.), *The Lloyd George Family Letters* (1973)

Muggeridge, M., *Like It Was: Diaries* (1982)

Nicholson, J. and Barnes, D., *The Leo Amery Diaries* (Two volumes, 1980–88)

Nicolson, N., *Harold Nicolson: Diaries and Letters* (Three volumes, 1966–1968)

Norwich, J. J., *The Duff Cooper Diaries* (2005)

Pearce, R. (ed.), *Patrick Gordon Walker: Political Diaries 1932–1971* (1991)

Pimlott, B. (ed.), *The Political Diary of Hugh Dalton* (1986)

— *The Second World War Diary of Hugh Dalton* (1986)

Pitts, D., *Clem Attlee: The Granada Historical Records Interview* (1967)

Ramsden, J. (ed.), *The Political Diaries of Sir Robert Sanders* (1984)

Rhodes James, R. (ed.), *The Diaries of Sir Henry Channon* (1967)

— *The Memoirs and Papers of J.C.C. Davidson* (1969)

Self, R. (ed.), *The Austen Chamberlain Diary Letters* (1995)

— *The Neville Chamberlain Diary Letters* (Four volumes, 2000)

Sheffield, G. and Bourne, J. (ed.), *Douglas Haig War Diaries and Letters* (2005)

Shuckburgh, E., *Descent to Suez: Diaries 1951–56* (1986)

Soames, M. (ed.), *The Personal Letters of Winston and Clementine Churchill* (1998)

Stevenson, F., *Lloyd George: A Diary* (1971)

Stuart, C. (ed.), *The Reith Diaries* (1975)

The Countess of Ranfurly, *Wartime Diaries 1939–5* (1995)

Thorpe, A. (ed.), *Kenneth Younger: Foreign Office Diaries* (2006)

Thorpe, A. and Toye, R. (eds), *The Diaries of Cecil Harmsworth 1909–1922* (2016)

Trevor-Roper, H. (ed.), *The Goebbels Diaries* (1977)

— *War Diaries: The Mediterranean 1943–45* (1984)

Warner, G. (ed.), *In the Midst of Events: The Foreign Office Diaries and Papers of Kenneth Younger, February 1950–October 1951* (2004).

Williams, P. (ed.), *The Diary of Hugh Gaitskell 1945–56* (1983)

Williamson, P. (ed.), *Modernisation of Conservative Politics: the Diaries and Letter of William Bridgeman 1904–1935* (1988)

Williamson, P. and Baldwin, E. (eds), *The Baldwin Papers* (2009)

Wilson, T. (ed.), *The Political Diaries of C.P.Scott 1911–1928* (1970)

Young, K. (ed.), *The Diaries of Sir Robert Bruce-Lockhart* (Volume 2, 1981)

Ziegler, P. (ed.), *Personal Diary of Admiral Lord Louis Mountbatten 1943–1946* (1988)

SECONDARY SOURCES

Adams, R. J. Q., *Bonar Law* (1999)

Addison, P., *The Road to 1945* (1975)

— *Churchill on the Home Front* (1992)

— *Churchill: The Unexpected Hero* (2005)

Aldrich, R. J. and Cormac, R., *The Black Door* (2016)

Earl Alexander of Tunis, *The Alexander 1940–1945* (1961)

Amery, L., *My Political Life* (Three volumes: 1953–1955)

Andrew, C., *The Defence of the Realm* (2009)

Ansel, W., *Hitler Confronts England* (1960)

Attlee, C. R., *The Social Worker* (1920)

— *As It Happened* (1954)

— *The Churchill Digest* (1965)

Bardens, D., *Churchill in Parliament* (1967)

Barnett, C., *The Audit of War* (1986)

— *The Lost Victory* (1995)

Bartley, P., *Ellen Wilkinson* (2014)

Beasley, W., *Churchill: The Supreme Survivor* (2013)

Beckett, F., *Clem Attlee* (1997)

— *The Rebel Who Lost His Cause* (1999)

Beevor, A., *The Second World War* (2012)

Bell, C. M., *Churchill and the Dardanelles* (2017)

Bernstein, G. L., *Liberalism and Liberal Politics in Edwardian England* (1986)

Best, G., *Churchill: A Study in Greatness* (2000)
— *Churchill and War (2005)*

Bew, J., *Citizen Clem* (2016)

Bird, S. L., *Stepney* (2012)
— *Bloody British History: East End* (2015)

1st Earl of Birkenhead, *Contemporary Personalities* (1924)

2nd Earl of Birkenhead, *The Life of Lord Halifax* (1965)

Bishop, P., *Battle of Britain* (2009)

Black, J., *The Tory World* (2015)

Blackburn, R., *I Am An Alcoholic* (1959)

Blake, R., *The Conservative Party from Peel to Churchill* (1970)

Blake R. and Louis, W. R., (eds), *Churchill: A Major New Assessment* (1993)

Bloch, M., *The Reign and Abdication of Edward VIII* (1990)

Bonham Carter, V., *Winston Churchill As I Knew Him* (1965)

Bowyer, M. J. F., *The Battle of Britain* (1990)

Boyd-Carpenter, J., *Way of Life* (1980)

Boyle, A., *Poor Dear Brendan* (1974)

Lord Brabazon of Tara, *The Brabazon Story* (1956)

Briggs, A. and Macartney, A., *Toynbee Hall* (1986)

Brivati, B., *Hugh Gaitskell* (1960)

Broad, L., *The Path to Power* (1964)

Brookshire, J. H., *Clement Attlee* (1995)

Broome, V., *Clement Attlee* (1949)

Brown, G., *In My Way* (1970)

Bryant, C., *Stafford Cripps* (1997)

Bullock, A., *Ernest Bevin: Trade Union Leader* (1960)
— *Ernest Bevin: Minister of Labour* (1967)
— *Ernest Bevin: Foreign Secretary* (1983)

Burgess, S., *Stafford Cripps* (1999)

Burridge, T., *British Labour and Hitler's War* (1976)
— *Clement Attlee* (1985)

Butler, D., *The British General Election of 1951* (1952)

Butler, R., *The Art of the Possible* (1971)

Callaghan, J., *Time and Chance* (1987)

Calvocoressi, P., Wint, G. and Pritchard, J., *The Second World War* (1989)

Campbell, J., *F. E. Smith* (1983)
— *Nye Bevan* (1987)

Cannadine, D. and Quinault, R., *Winston Churchill in the 21st Century* (2004)

Carlyon, L. A., *Gallipoli* (2002)

Casey, Lord., *Personal Experience 1939–1946* (1962)

Casey, S., *Cautious Crusade* (2001)

Castle, B., *Fighting All The Way* (1993)

Chandos, Lord., *Memoirs* (1962)

Charmley, J., *Chamberlain and the Lost Peace* (1991)
— *The End of Glory* (1993)

Chisholm, A. and Davie, M., *Beaverbrook* (1992)

Churchill, R., *Winston S. Churchill* (First two volumes of the official biography, 1966–1968)

Churchill, S., *A Thread in the Tapestry* (1967)

Churchill, W., *The River War* (1899)
— *Savrola* (1899)
— *Lord Randolph Churchill* (1906)
— *The World Crisis* (Six volumes, 1923–31)
— *My Early Life* (1930)
— *Thoughts and Adventures* (1932)
— *The Second World War* (Six volumes, 1948–1953)

Citrine, Lord., *Men and Work* (1964)

Clarke, P., *A Question of Leadership* (1991)
— *The Cripps Version* (2002)
— *Mr Churchill's Profession* (2012)

Clayton, T. and Craig, P., *Finest Hour* (1999)

Clemens, C., *The Man from Limehouse* (1946)

Clifford, C., *The Asquiths* (2002)

Cohen, D., *Churchill and Attlee* (2018)

Colville, J., *Footprints in Time* (1976)
— *Winston Churchill and his Inner Circle* (1981)

Cooper, D., *Old Men Forget* (1953)

Corrigan, G., *Blood, Sweat and Arrogance* (2006)

Costello, J., *Ten Days That Saved the West* (1991)

Cowles, V., *Churchill: The Era and the Man* (1953)

Cowling, M., *The Impact of Labour* (1971)
— *The Impact of Hitler* (1975)

Crowcroft, R., *Attlee's War* (2011)

Curran, T., *The Grand Deception: Churchill and the Dardanelles* (2015)

Dalton, H., *Call Back Yesterday* (1953)
— *The Fateful Years* (1957)
— *High Tide and After* (1962)

Davies, A. J., *To Build a New Jerusalem* (1992)

Deighton, L., *Blood, Tears and Folly* (1993)

Dell, E., *A Strange Eventful History* (2000)

Dellar, G., (ed.), *Attlee As I Knew Him* (1983)

D'Este, C., *Warlord* (2008)

Dilks, D., *Churchill and Company* (2015)

Dix, A., *The Norway Campaign and the Rise of Churchill 1940* (2014)

Dixon, Sir P., *Double Diploma* (1968)

Donoughue, B. and Jones, G. W., *Herbert Morrison* (1973)

Downing, T., *Churchill's War Lab* (2010)

Driberg, T., *Ruling Passions* (1977)

Dudley, J., *Winston Churchill & Me* (2017)

Dutton, D., *The Liberals in Schism* (2008)

Ede, C., *Churchill by his Contemporaries* (1953)

Eden, C., *From Churchill to Eden* (2007)

Emy, H.V., *Liberals, Radicals and Social Politics 1892–1914* (1973)

Ensor, R.C. K., *English History 1870–1914* (1936)

Evans, R., *The Third Reich at War* (2008)

Farmelo, G., *Churchill's Bomb* (2015)

Farr-Hockley, A., *The British Part in the Korean War* (1995)

Feiling, K., *The Life of Neville Chamberlain* (1946)

Feis, H., *Between War and Peace: The Potsdam Conference* (1960)

Florey, R. A., *The General Strike of 1926* (1980)

Freeman, R., *Unsinkable: Churchill and the First World War* (2013)

French, D., *Raising Churchill's Army* (2000)

French, P., *Liberty or Death* (1997)

Freudenberg, G., *Churchill and Australia* (2008)

Frewen, O., *Sailor's Soliloquy* (1961)

Gardner, B., *Churchill in Power* (1970)

Garfield, S., *We are at War* (2009)

Gilbert, M., *Winston S. Churchill* (Six volumes of the official biography, 1971–1988)
    — *Churchill: The Wilderness Years* (1981)
    — *Churchill: A Photographic Portrait* (1988)
    — *Churchill's War Leadership* (200)
    — *Churchill and America* (2005)

Gilmour, I., *Inside Right: A Study of Conservatism* (1978)

Gowing, M., *Britain and Atomic Energy* (1964)

Bronte Green, D., *The Churchills of Blenheim* (1984)

Griffiths, R. T., *Socialist Parties and the Question of Europe* (1993)

Groves, P., *Behind the Smoke Screen* (1934)

Gunther, J., *Inside Europe* (1936)

Haigh, G., *Silent Revolutions* (2006)

Hailsham, Lord., *A Sparrow's Flight* (1990)

Hamilton, N., *The Full Monty* (2001)

Harris, F., *My Life and Loves* (1922)

Harris, K., *Attlee* (1982)

Hart, P., *The Great War 1914–1918* (2013)

Harvie-Watt, G. S., *Most of My Life* (1980)

Hastings, M., *Finest Years: Churchill as Warlord 1940–45* (2009)

Healey, D., *The Time of My Life* (1989)

Heffer, S., *Great British Speeches* (2010)

— *The Age of Decadence* (2017)

Hennessy, P., *Never Again* (1992)

— *The Prime Minister* (2000)

— *Cabinets and the Bomb* (2007)

Heppell, T., *Leaders of the Opposition from Churchill to Cameron* (2012)

Hermiston, R., *All Behind You Winston* (2016)

Hickman, T., *Churchill's Bodyguard* (2005)

Higham, C., *Dark Lady* (2006)

Hill, M., *Churchill: The Radical Decade* (1999)

Inglis, F., *Richard Hoggart: Virtue and Reward* (2013)

Holland, J., *The Battle of Britain* (2010)

— *The War in the West* (2015)

Holmes, R., *In the Footsteps of Churchill* (2005)

— *Churchill's Bunker* (2009)

— *The World at War* (2007)

Hough, R., *Winston and Clementine* (1990)

Hunter, L., *The Road to Brighton Pier* (1959)

Hurd, D., *Choose Your Weapons* (2010)

Ismay, H., *Memoirs* (1960)

Inglis, F., *Richard Hoggart: Virtue and Reward* (2013)

Ionescu, G., *The New Politics of European Integration* (1972)

Jablonsky, D., *Churchill, the Great Game and Total War* (1991)

Jackson, A., *Churchill* (2011)

Jago, M., *Clement Attlee* (2014)

— *Rab Butler* (2015)

Jay, D., *Change and Fortune* (1980)

Jefferys, K., *The Churchill Coalition and Wartime Politics* (1991)

Jenkins, R., *Mr Attlee: an Interim Biography* (1948)

— *A Life at the Centre* (1992)

— *Churchill* (2001)

Johnson, B., *The Churchill Factor* (2014)

Johnson, P., *Churchill* (2009)

Judd, D., *George VI* (1982)

— *Empire* (1997)

Keegan, J., *The Second World War* (1989)

— *Churchill's Generals* (1991)

Keene, T., *Cloak of Enemies* (2012)

Kelly, J., *Never Surrender* (2015)

Kennedy, Sir J., *The Business of War* (1957)

Kersaudy, F., *Norway 1940* (1990)

Kershaw, I., *Making Friends with Hitler* (2004)

— *Hitler* (1998)

Kimball, W., *The Complete Roosevelt–Churchill Correspondence* (1987)

King, C., *With Malice Towards None* (1970)

King, G., *Wallis* (2000)

Klos, F., *Churchill's Last Stand: The Struggle to Unite Europe* (2017)

Kramnick, I. and Sheerman, B., *Harold Laski* (1993)

Kynaston, D., *Austerity Britain 1945–51* (2007)

Langworth, R., *Churchill by Himself* (2008)

Lawlor, S., *Churchill and the Politics of War* (1994)

Lee, C. and Lee, J., *The Churchills* (2010)

Leeming, B., *Churchill Defiant* (2010)

Leslie, A., *Jennie* (1969)

Longford, F., *Eleven at No.10* (1984)

Lough, D., *No More Champagne* (2015)

Lowe, K., *How the War Changed Us* (2017)

Lovell, M., *The Churchills: A Family at the Heart of History* (2011)

Lovell, R., *Churchill's Doctor* (1992)

Lukacs, J., *The Duel* (1990)
   — *Five Days in London: May 1940* (1999)
   — *Blood, Toil, Tears and Sweat* (2008)

Lysaght, C., *Brendan Bracken* (1979)

McCallum, R. B., *The Liberal Party from Earl Grey to Asquith* (1963)

McGowan, N., *My Years with Churchill* (1958)

Macksey, K., *Invasion* (1980)

McArthur, B., *The Penguin Book of Modern Speeches* (2015)

MacDonald, M., *Titans and Others* (1972)

McMenamin, M. and Zoller, C., *Becoming Winston Churchill* (2009)

McPherson, N., *American Intelligence in Wartime* (2004)

Macrae, S., *Winston Churchill's Toyshop* (2008)

Maiolo, J., *Cry Havoc* (2010)

Mallison, A., *Fight the Good Fight* (2013)

Manchester, W., *The Caged Lion: Winston Churchill 1932–1940* (1988)

Manchester, W. and Reid, P., *The Last Lion: Winston Churchill. Defender of the Realm* (2012)

Marquand, D., *Ramsay MacDonald* (1977)

Martin, H., *Battle: The Life Story of Winston Churchill* (1940)

Martin, Sir J., *The Downing Street War Years* (1991)

Martin, R., *Lady Randolph Churchill* (1969)

Maudling, R., *Memoirs* (1978)

Menzies, Sir R., *Afternoon Light* (1967)

Merlin, S. G., *General Smuts* (1936)

Middlemas, K. and Barnes, J., *Baldwin* (1969)

Mikardo, I., *Backbencher* (1988)

Mitchell, J., *Churchill's Navigator* (2010)

Montague Browne, A., *Long Sunset* (1995)

Montgomery, Field-Marshal, *Memoirs* (1958)

Morgan, K., *Labour in Power 1945–1951* (1984)
— *Labour People* (1987)

Morgan, Sir F., *Peace and War* (1961)

Mosley, L., *Backs to the Wall* (1971)

Muller, J., *Churchill's Iron Curtain Speech 50 Years Later* (1999)

Olson, L., *Troublesome Young Men: The Churchill Conspiracy of 1940* (2007)

Owen, F., *Lloyd George: His Life and Times* (1954)

Packwood, A., *How Churchill Waged War* (2018)

Pankhurst, S., *The Suffragette Movement* (1931)

Parker, R. A. C., *The Second World War* (1989)
— *Churchill and Appeasement* (2000)

Paterson, M., *Winston Churchill* (2005)

Pawle, G., *The War and Colonel Warden* (1963)

Pearson, J., *The Private Lives of Mr Churchill* (1991)

Peck, J., *Dublin from Downing Street* (1978)

Pelling, H., *Winston Churchill* (1974)

Perkins, A., *The General Strike* (2006)

Petropoulos, J., *The Royals and the Reich* (2006)

Phillips, A., *The King Who Had to Go* (2017)

Pimlott, B., *Hugh Dalton* (1985)

Pugh, M., *Speak for Britain* (2011)

Purnell, S., *First Lady* (2015)

Radice, G., *The Tortoise and the Hares* (2008)
— *The Odd Couples* (2015)

Ramsden, J., *The Man of Century* (2002)

Reynolds, D., *In Command of History* (2004)

Rhodes James, R., *Gallipoli* (1965)
— *Victor Cazalet* (1976)

Rhodes, R., *The Making of the Atomic Bomb* (1986)

Richards, D., *Portal of Hungerford* (1975)

Roberts, A., *The Holy Fox* (1991)
— *Eminent Churchillians* (1995)
— *Churchill: Walking with Destiny* (2018)

Rogers, C., *The Battle of Stepney* (1981)

Rose, J., *The Literary Churchill* (2014)

Rose, N., *Churchill: An Unruly Life (1994)*

Roskill, S., *The Navy at War* (1960)
— *Churchill and the Admirals* (1977)
— *Hankey: Man of Secrets* (1977)

Ruane, K., *Churchill and the Bomb* (2016)

Rumbelow, D., *The Houndsditch Murders and the Siege of Sidney Street* (1973)

Samuel, Viscount, *Memoirs* (1945)

Schneer, J., *Ministers at War* (2015)

Searle, G. R., *The Quest for National Efficiency* (1971)

Sebag-Montefiore, H., *Dunkirk* (2006)

Seldon, A., *Churchill's Indian Summer* (1981)

Seldon, A, and Ball, S. (ed.), *Recovering Power* (2005)

Seymour-Jones, C., *Beatrice Webb* (1992)

Shakespeare, N., *Six Minutes in May* (2017)

Shelden, M., *Young Titan* (2013)

Sheridan, C., *The Naked Truth* (1928)

Skidelsky, R., *Oswald Mosley* (1975)

Smith, C., *England's Last War against France* (2009)

Smith, J. E., *FDR* (2007)

Soames, M., *A Daughter's Tale* (2011)

Spears, Sir E., *Prelude to Dunkirk* (1954)

Stafford, D., *Roosevelt & Churchill* (1999)

Steel, D. and Hart, P., *Defeat at Gallipoli* (1994)

Stelzer, C., *Dinner with Churchill* (2011)

Stern, J. (ed.), *The Essential Wisden* (2013)

Stewart, A., *February 1942* (2015)

Stewart, M., *Life and Labour* (1980)

Stewart, G., *Burying Caesar* (1999)

Strawson, J., *Churchill and Hitler* (1997)

Stuart, J., *Within the Fringe* (1967)

Swift, J., *Labour in Crisis* (2001)

Symons, J., *The General Strike* (1957)

Taylor, A. J. P., *English History 1914–1945* (1965)
   — *Beaverbrook* (1972)

Templewood, Viscount, *Nine Troubled Years* (1954)

Thomas, D. A., *The Member for Woodford* (1995)

Thomas-Symonds, N., *Attlee* (2010)
   — *Nye* (2015)

Thompson, N., *The Anti–Appeasers* (1971)

Thompson, R.W., *Churchill and Morton* (1976)

Thompson, W., *Beside the Bulldog* (2003)

Thomson, M., *Churchill: His Life and Times* (1965)

Thorpe, A., *Parties at War* (2009)

Thorpe, D. R., *Eden* (2004)
   — *Supermac* (2010)

Tiratsoo, N. (ed.), *The Attlee Years* (1991)

Tombs, I. and R., *That Sweet Enemy* (2006)

Toye, R., *Lloyd George and Churchill* (2007)
   — *Churchill's Empire* (2010)
   — *The Roar of the Lion* (2013)

Trevor-Roper, H., *Hitler's Table Talk* (1953)

Warner, P., *Auchinleck* (1981)

Weisbrode, K., *Churchill and the King* (2013)

Wells, H, G., *Tono Bungay* (1909)

Wheeler-Bennett, Sir J., (ed.), *King George VI* (1958)

— *Sir John Anderson* (1962)

— *Action This Day: Working with Churchill* (1968)

Williams, C., *Harold Macmillan* (2009)

Williams, F., *A Prime Minister Remembers* (1961)
   — *Nothing So Strange* (1970)

Williams, Sir H., *Politics Grave and Gay* (1949)

Williams, P. M., *Hugh Gaitskell* (1979)

Wilson, Sir A., *Thoughts and Talks* (1938)

Winter, P., *Defeating Hitler* (2012)

Winterton, Earl, *Fifty Tumultuous Years* (1955)

Woods, F., (ed.), *Young Winston's Wars* (1972)

Earl of Woolton, *Memoirs* (1959)

Worley, M., *Labour Inside the Gate* (2005)

Wright, P., *Iron Curtain* (2007)

Wright, R., *Dowding and the Battle of Britain* (1969)

Wrigley, C., *A. J. P. Taylor* (2006)

Wynburn-Powell, A., *Clement Davies* (2003)

Young, K., *Churchill and Beaverbrook* (1966)

Ziegler, P., *King Edward VIII* (1990)

ARTICLES, BROADCASTS AND LECTURES

Adelman, P., 'The British General Election 1945' (*History Today*, September 2001)

Attlee, C. R., 'The Labour Exchange in Relation to Boy and Girl Labour' (*Toynbee Record*, June 1910)

Bullock, N., 'Eye Witness to Potsdam' (*Finest Hour*, Winter 2009–10)

Burridge, T. D., 'The Churchill–Laski Electoral Clash' (*Journal of Contemporary History*, October 1977)

Cole, J., *The 1945 General Election* (BBC Radio 4, July 2005)

Cynewulf Robbins, R., 'Sixty Years On: The Atlantic Charter 1941' (*Finest Hour*, Autumn 2011)

Dilks, D., 'The Queen and Mr Churchill' (*Finest Hour*, summer 2007)

Dobson, A., 'Economic Diplomacy at the Atlantic Conference' (*Review of International Studies*, April 1984)

Farr, M., 'The Labour Party and Strategic Bombing in the Second World War' (*Labour History Review*, September 2009)

Fletcher, G., 'Spencer Churchill at Harrow School' (*Finest Hour*, Spring 2007)

Gilbert, M., 'Churchill and Bombing Policy' (Churchill Centre, October 2005)

Finlayson, J. M., *The Cabinet Committee System and the Development of British Colonial Policy* (Leeds University thesis, 2002)

Freeman, D., 'Who Really Put Churchill in Office' (*Finest Hour*, Spring 2002)

Golant, W., 'Mr Attlee' (*History Today*, August 1983)

Golding, R., 'Guarding Greatness' (*Finest Hour*, Autumn 2009)

Hamill, J. and Prescott, A., 'The Mason's Candidate' (*Labour History Review*, April 2006)

Hunger, C., 'Of Overlords and the General Strike' (*Finest Hour*, Summer 2000)

Langworth, R., 'Churchill and India' (*Finest Hour*, Autumn 2007)

Mather, J., 'Lord Randolph Churchill: Maladies et Mort' (*Finest Hour*, Winter 1996–97)

Patterson, D., 'Churchill, Zionism and the Holocaust' (*Finest Hour*, Autumn 2015)

Pelling, H., 'The 1945 General Election Reconsidered' (*Historical Journal*, 1980)

Pressnell, L. S. and Hopkins, S. V., 'A Canard of Time? Churchill, the War Cabinet and the Atlantic Charter' (*Review of International Studies*, July 1988)

Reardon, T., 'The Reluctant Retiree' (*Finest Hour*, Spring 2011)

Roberts, A., 'The English Speaking Peoples – The Role of the State' (*Finest Hour*, Summer 2012)

Ruane, K., 'Churchill, God and the Bomb' (*History Today*, August 2016)

Simonds, G. W., 'Churchill and Hayek' (*Finest Hour*, Spring 2002)

Toye, R., *Churchill and Britain's Financial Dunkirk* (Exeter University research paper, 2004)

— 'Winston Churchill's Crazy Broadcast' (*Journal of British Studies*, July 2010)

Ward, P., 'Preparing for the People's War' (*Labour History Review*, August 2002)

INDEX

Barrow-in-Furness, Cumbria, 77
Barrymore, Ethel, 41
Baruch, Bernard, 462
Bastianini, Giuseppe, 221
Bath, Somerset, 29, 38
Battle of Arras (1917), 126
Battle of Britain (1940), 234, 244–5, 248, 253, 311, 336, 498, 630
Battle of El Alamein (1942), 319, 338, 345, 410
Battle of France (1940), 203, 216, 220, 222, 224, 225, 227–30
Battle of Hanna (1916), 7, 74
Battle of Omdurman (1898), 27
Battle of Stalingrad (1942–3), 338
Battle of the North Cape (1943), 363
Beards, Paul, 444
Beatty, David, 57
Beaverbrook, Lord, see Aitken, William
Beckett, Francis, 623
Beckett, John, 86
Belfrage, Bruce, 270
Belgium, 57, 71–3, 74, 203, 225
Benghazi, Libya, 286
Benn, Anthony 'Tony', 506, 551
Benn, William Wedgwood, 1st Viscount Stansgate, 368
Berchtesgaden, Bavaria, 159
Berkhamsted School, Hertfordshire, 42
Berlin Blockade (1948), 502
Berlin, Isaiah, 330
Bermuda Conference (1953), 590–93, 596
Berry, Gomer, 1st Viscount Kemsley, 505, 561
Berry, William Ewart, 1st Viscount Camrose, 170, 199, 202, 455, 533
Betts, Barbara, 350
Bevan, Aneurin 'Nye'
  and Attlee's leadership, 260, 279, 304, 339, 341, 490, 618
  Bevanites, 553, 562, 574, 583, 585–8, 616, 618
  Blackpool Conference speech (1949), 518
  Budget (1951), 555, 572
  and Chamberlain's leadership, 192
  and Churchill's leadership, 276, 286, 307–9, 317–18, 339, 382
  Churchill's praise of, 578
  Defence White Paper debate (1952), 583
  Edward VIII abdication crisis (1936), 142
  on Fascism, 414
  and Gandhi, internment of (1942), 317–18

General Election (1945), 402, 439
General Election (1950), 523
General Election (1952), 562, 564
  H-bomb, opposition to, 609–10, 616
  Margate Conference (1953), 594
  Minister of Labour (1951–9), 553
  and nationalisation, 279
  NHS established (1948), 503–4, 518
  and North African campaign inquiry (1942), 307
  Popular Front, support for, 166–7
  Southeast Asia security debate (1954), 601
Bevanites, 553, 562, 574, 583, 585–8, 616, 618
Beveridge Report (1942), 339–45, 396, 469
Beveridge, William, 339
Bevin, Ernest, 16, 171, 232, 242, 396
  and Attlee's leadership, 488, 490
  Atlantic Charter (1941), 269
  Beaverbrook, relationship with, 259, 277, 310
  Cabinet reshuffle (1942), 297
  Cabinet reshuffle plan (1944), 367–8
  Churchill's opinion of, 376, 469
  Churchill's US tour (1946), 461
  Czech crisis (1938), 164
  death (1951), 554, 556, 571
  Edward VIII abdication crisis (1936), 142, 149
  European unity, views on, 498, 499, 500, 501
  Foreign Secretary (1945–51), 442–3, 490
  General Election (1945), 398, 400, 401, 416, 417–18, 440, 441
  General Election (1950), 523
  Greek crisis (1944), 384
  Greenwood's leadership (1939), 171
  illness, 523, 545, 553
  Import Executive, 251
  Israel, views on, 475
  and Lansbury's leadership, 131, 134
  Lindemann, dispute with (1940), 241
  Lord Privy Seal (1951), 554
  Minister of Labour (1940–45), 212, 289
  Mosley release crisis (1943), 359–61
  Need for Decisions, The (1943), 354
  Popular Front proposal (1938), 166
  Potsdam Conference (1945), 445
  Production Executive, 251
  rearmament policy, 137, 152
  Soviet Union, views on, 445, 463

A NOTE ABOUT
THE AUTHOR

Leo McKinstry is a first-class historian and author of the acclaimed Second World War trilogy *Spitfire*, *Hurricane* and *Lancaster*. His biography of the nineteenth-century Liberal Prime Minister Lord Rosebery won the Channel Four Political Book of the Year in 2006. He has a column in the *Daily Express* and also writes regularly for the *Daily Mail*, *Daily Telegraph*, *The Sun* and the *Spectator*. Born in Belfast, he was educated in Ireland and at Cambridge University.